Rotterdam
NETHERLANDS
Knokke-Heist
Zeebrugge
Oostende
Antwerpen
Gent
Roeselare
Mechelen
Dunkerque
St-Omer
Kortrijk
page 157
Roubaix
Lille
Nord-Pas-de-Calais
Béthune
Lens
Tournai
Bruxelles
BELGIUM
Charleroi
Maastricht
Liège
Aachen
Verviers
Namur
Köln
Bergisch Gladbach
Bonn
Siegen
GERMANY
Koblenz
Rhein
Douai
Valenciennes
Arras
Cambrai
Dinant
Abbeville
page 162
Amiens
Somme
Bastogne
Wittlich
Bingen am Rhein
Mainz
LUXEMBOURG
page 176
Mosel
Hirson
St-Quentin
Roye
Laon
Charleville-Mézières
Picardie
Beauvais
Compiègne
page 136
page 187
Luxembourg
Merzig
Kaiserslautern
Mannheim
Longwy
Neunkirchen
Ludwigshafen am Rhein
Saarbrücken
Thionville
Meuse
Vouziers
Reims
Oise
Château-Thierry
Verdun
Landau
Metz
Marne
Châlons-en-Champagne
PARIS
Meaux
Karlsruhe
Bar-le-Duc
Toul
page 190
Sarrebourg
page 196
Créteil
page 104-5
Île-de-France
Nancy
Strasbourg
Vitry-le-François
St-Dizier
Provins
Lorraine
Lunéville
Champagne-Ardenne
Alsace
Offenburg
Étampes
Neufchâteau
Troyes
St-Dié
Sélestat
Seine
Nemours
Freiburg im Breisgau
Chaumont
Colmar
Sens
Épinal
Vosges
Grand Ballon 1424
Orléans
Montargis
Châtillon-sur-Seine
Langres
Plateau de Haute-Saône
Mulhouse
Auxerre
Loire
Gien
Lure
Belfort
Bourgogne
Cosne-Cours-sur-Loire
Selongey
Saône
Vesoul
Basel
Rhein
Avallon
Mont Tasselot
434
Dijon
Delémont
Vierzon
Doubs
Besançon
Biel
Bourges
Haut-Folin 901
Autun
Beaune
page 221
Dole
Franche-Comté
Pontarlier
Bern
Nevers
Luzern
St-Amand-Montrond
FRANCE
Côte d'Or
Chalon-sur-Saône
Lons-le-Saunier
Yverdon
Fribourg
Interlaken
Jura
Moulins
Tournus
Lausanne
SWITZERLAND
Plaine de la Loire
Digoin
Lac Léman
Montreux
Mâcon
Brig
Montluçon
Lapalisse
Genève
Sion
Le Buet 3099
page 214
Allier
Bourg-en-Bresse
Aubusson
Roanne
Martigny
Clermont-Ferrand
Thiers
Sallanches
Annecy
Puy de Dôme 1464
Balbigny
Villeurbanne
Mt Blanc 4808
Aosta
Lyon
Albertville
Ussel
Auvergne
Rhône-Alpes
Puy de Sancy 1885
Issoire
St Étienne
Vienne
Chambéry
Moûtiers
Alpi Graie
ITALY
Monts d'Auvergne
Bort-les-Orgues
Grande Casse 3852
Voiron
Massif Central
Le-Puy-en-Velay
Rhône
Grenoble
Modane
Torino
St-Flour
Aurillac
Valence
Massif du Pelvoux
Briançon
Asti
Pradelles
Clelles
Carmagnola
Signal de Randon 1551
Aubenas
Mende
Montélimar
Gap
A16
A26
A25
A1
A4
A5
A6
A26
N4
A31
N57
A35
N71
A10
A6
N7
A71
N145
N83
A40
A89
A41
A72
A75
N88
A7
A49
A41
A89

D1761079

INSIGHT GUIDES

NORTHERN FRANCE

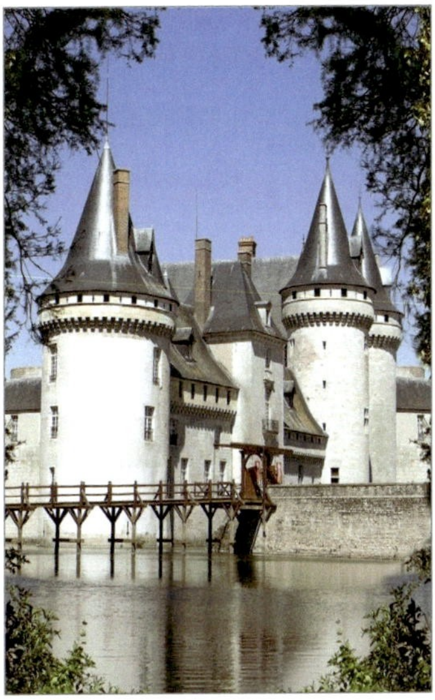

APA PUBLICATIONS

Part of the Langenscheidt Publishing Group

INSIGHT GUIDE
NORTHERN FRANCE

Editorial

Project Editors
Tom Le Bas, Carine Tracanelli
Art Director
Steven Lawrence
Picture Manager
Tom Smyth
Series Manager
Rachel Lawrence

Distribution

UK & Ireland
GeoCenter International Ltd
Meridian House, Churchill Way West
Basingstoke, Hampshire RG21 6YR
sales@geocenter.co.uk

United States
Ingram Publisher Services
1 Ingram Blvd, PO Box 3006
La Vergne, TN 37086-1986
customer.service@ingrampublisher services.com

Australia
Universal Publishers
PO Box 307
St. Leonards NSW 1590
Ph: (02) 9857 3700
Email: sales@universalpublishers.com.au

New Zealand
Hema Maps New Zealand Ltd (HNZ)
Unit 2, 10 Cryers Road
East Tamaki, Auckland 2013
sales.hema@clear.net.nz

Worldwide
Apa Publications GmbH & Co. Verlag KG (Singapore branch)
7030 Ang Mo Kio Avenue 5
08-65 Northstar @ AMK
Singapore 569880
apasin@singnet.com.sg

Printing

CTPS-China

©2011 Apa Publications GmbH & Co. Verlag KG (Singapore branch)
All Rights Reserved

First Edition 2011

CONTACTING THE EDITORS
We would appreciate it if readers would alert us to errors or outdated information by writing to:
Insight Guides, PO Box 7910, London SE1 1WE, England.
insight@apaguide.co.uk

NO part of this book may be reproduced, stored in a retrieval system or transmitted in any form or means electronic, mechanical, photocopying, recording or otherwise, without prior written permission of *Apa Publications*. Brief text quotations with use of photographs are exempted for book review purposes only. Information has been obtained from sources believed to be reliable, but its accuracy and completeness, and the opinions based thereon, are not guaranteed.

www.insightguides.com

ABOUT THIS BOOK

The first Insight Guide pioneered the use of creative full-colour photography in travel guides in 1970. Since then, we have expanded our range to cater for our readers' need not only for reliable information about their chosen destination but also for a real understanding of the culture and workings of that destination. Now, when the internet can supply inexhaustible (but not always reliable) facts, our books marry text and pictures to provide those much more elusive qualities: knowledge and discernment. To achieve this, they rely heavily on the authority of locally based writers and photographers.

Insight Guide: Northern France is structured to convey an understanding of the region and its people as well as to guide readers through its attractions:

◆ The **Features** section, indicated by a pink bar at the top of each page, is a series of illuminating essays that cover the natural and cultural history of the region, as well as daily life, architecture and the arts.

◆ The main **Places** section, indicated by a blue bar, is a complete guide to all the sights and areas worth visiting, divided up into five regions. Places of special interest are coordinated by number with the maps.

◆ The **Travel Tips** listings section, with a yellow bar, provides full information on transport, hotels, activities from culture to shopping to sports, an A–Z section of essential practical information, and a handy phrasebook. An easy-to-find contents list for Travel Tips is printed on the back flap, which also serves as a bookmark.

Left: Place du Tertre, Montmartre, Paris.

The contributors

This first edition of Insight Guide Northern France was commissioned and project-managed by **Carine Tracanelli** and **Tom Le Bas** at Insight Guides' London office, with additional copyediting by **Cathy Muscat**.

Nick Inman, who wrote the chapters on People, Landscape and Wildlife, Architecture, The English Channel, Paris and Around, The East and The Centre, plus all the listings for those areas, is a freelance travel writer and photographer who specialises in France and Spain. He lives in an old bigourdane farmhouse near the Pyrenees in southwest France with his wife and their two children. A self-confessed Francophile, he is particularly passionate about the country's vernacular and medieval architecture, and its wildlife. He has contributed to over 60 travel guides including numerous titles for Insight and Berlitz. His non-travel books include *Politipedia* and *The Optimist's Handbook*.

The first experience **Nick Rider** remembers of France is of a crêpe stand in Brittany when he was six years old. Since then he has explored a great many parts of the country, following interests from art and battlefields to Norman cider farms, and among other things has written a guide made up of selected itineraries around northern France each one focussed around a fine lunch. Nick provided the chapters on Food and Drink, Art and Artists, Traces of War, The North, The West and the listings for those areas.

The book was indexed by **Helen Peters** and proofread by **Jan McCann**. The principal photographer was Britanny-based **Sylvaine Poitau**.

Map Legend

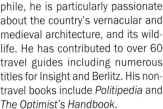

- International Boundary
- Regional Boundary
- Département Boundary
- Border Crossing
- National Park/Reserve
- Ferry Route
- Metro
- Airport: International/ Regional
- Bus Station
- Tourist Information
- Post Office
- Church/Ruins
- Monastery
- Mosque
- Synagogue
- Castle/Ruins
- Archaeological Site
- Cave
- Statue/Monument
- Place of Interest

The main places of interest in the Places section are coordinated by number with a full-colour map (eg ❶), and a symbol at the top of every right-hand page tells you where to find the map.

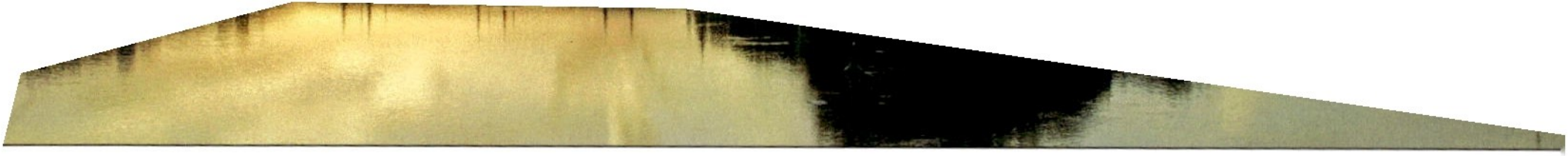

Contents

LEFT: sunset over the Ile de la Cité and the Seine. **RIGHT:** beauty in everyday objects: a classic tin of fish soup from Brittany, ornate Parisian Metro sign.

Travel Tips

Maps

The Best of Northern France: Top Attractions

From the city of light to the glorious châteaux of the Loire, the hills of Alsace to Mont-St-Michel, here is a rundown of Northern France's most spectacular attractions

△ Louis XIV's palace of **Versailles** within easy reach of a day trip from Paris takes regal excess to a new limit. Its splendid interiors are matched by its formal gardens. *See page 137*

◁ Gothic architecture reaches its pinnacle in northern France, and nowhere more than in **Chartres Cathedral**, with its magnificent stained glass. *See page 234*

◁ Celebrations all over the world are incomplete without a bottle of **champagne**, which can only come from France's most northern vineyards. See how it is made in the region named after it. *See page 182*

△ **Paris** is filled with enough legendary sights to fill a lengthy stay. Top of the list are the Eiffel Tower, the Louvre, the Champs-Élysées, Notre Dame and Montmartre. *See page 107*

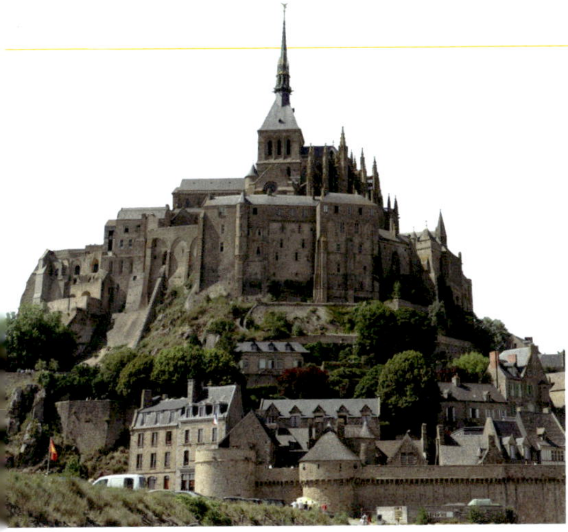

△ The medieval abbey of **Mont-St-Michel** stands on an isolated rock rising out of a vast tidal bay. It is reached by a causeway from the mainland.
See page 279

△ Impressionist painter Claude Monet found inspiration in his later years from the exquisite garden of his house at **Giverny**, with its lily pond spanned by a Japanese-style bridge.
See page 267

△ Museums and memorials along the **D-Day landing beaches** of the north Normandy coast are a sobering reminder of the battle fought for the liberation of France in 1944. *See pages 275*

△ A splendid multicoloured roof shelters the charity hospital of **Hôtel Dieu** in **Beaune**, Burgundy, which has a collection of art inside.
See pages 222

▷ **Alsace**, on the German border between the Vosges mountains and the Rhine, has picture-perfect villages and waterfront city quarters.
See page 193

◁ The lower valley of the River Loire is home to a string of elegant Renaissance **châteaux**. Highlights include Azay-le-Rideau, Chambord (pictured) and Chenonceau – which is built on piers over the water.
See page 229

THE BEST OF NORTHERN FRANCE: EDITOR'S CHOICE

Our selection of the top cultural and historical sights, the most beautiful urban and rural spots, memorable food and drink, highlights for children and handy pointers to help you get the most out of your euros

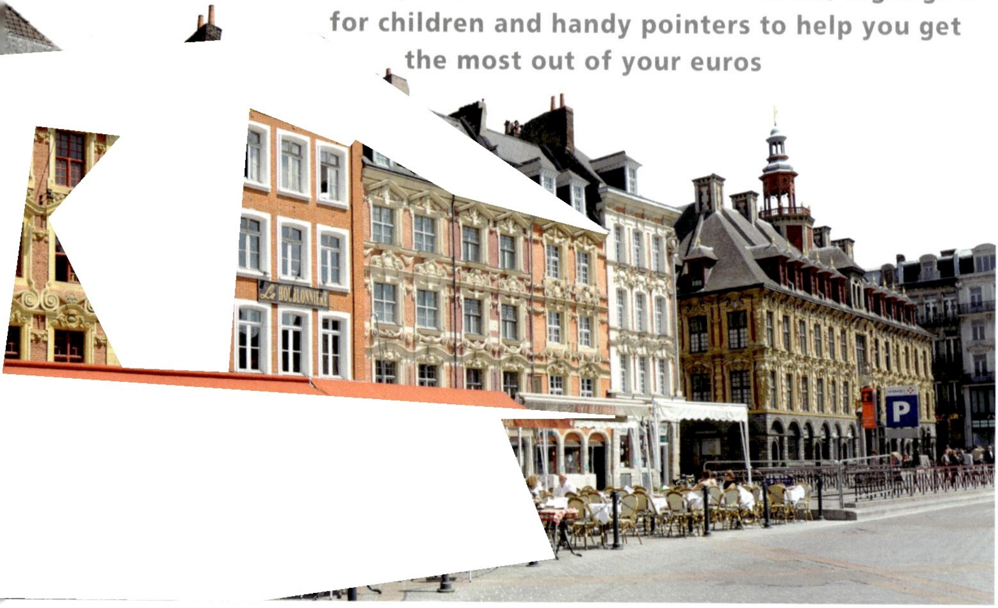

BEAUTIFUL TOWNS AND VILLAGES

- **Riquewihr (Alsace)** The region's prettiest town with decorative details everywhere you look. *See page 203*
- **Vézelay (Burgundy)** Hilltop town dominated by its exquisite abbey church, a masterpiece of Romanesque art. *See page 218*
- **St-Thégonnec and Lampaul-Guimiliau (Brittany)** The two prettiest examples of Brittany's "parish closes", harmonious sacred enclosures around a church. *See page 295*
- **Honfleur (Normandy)** This picturesque fishing port was favoured by the Impressionists for its luminous, ever-changing light. *See page 269*
- **Arras (Pas de Calais)** A handsome northern provincial town of 17th- and 18th-century Flemish houses arranged around two beautiful cobbled squares. *See page 158*

MOST INTERESTING CITIES

- **Rouen (Normandy)** The capital of Normandy and birthplace of novelist Gustave Flaubert has many preserved half-timbered houses in the streets around its Great Clock. *See page 259*
- **Lille (Pas de Calais)** This Flemish city on the Belgian border has delightful architecture and a plethora of quality shops and restaurants. *See page 156*
- **Nancy (Lorraine)** Lorraine's main city is 18th-century architecture and town planning at its most elegant, along with some works of Art Nouveau. *See page 189*
- **Strasbourg (Alsace)** At the heart of this picturesque city is Petite France, a pretty cluster of immaculately maintained houses built on an island in the Rhine. *See page 196*
- **St-Malo (Brittany)** Handsome – and once extremely prosperous – seaport at the mouth of the Rance River which features a complete set of ramparts. *See page 283*

LEFT: Honfleur harbour. **ABOVE:** café-lined Grand'Place, Vieux Lille.

CASTLES

- **Fougères (Brittany)** One of the most impressive fortresses in France, with ramparts and towers to explore. *See page 288*
- **Haut Koenigsbourg (Alsace)** Restored by the German Kaiser in the early 20th century and looking as every castle is meant to. *See page 201*
- **Château-Gaillard (Normandy)** The majestic ruins of Richard the Lionheart's castle overlooking a bend of the Seine at Les Andelys. *See page 267*
- **Angers (Loire Valley)** A 13th-century castle in the lower Loire Valley which now contains a series of medieval tapestries. *See page 248*

ABOVE: the formidable Château d'Angers.

BEST HISTORICAL SITES

- **Carnac (Brittany)** Over 3,000 upright stones placed in parallel lines, the best known of Brittany's many prehistoric monuments. *See page 302*
- **Bayeux (Normandy)** The famous tapestry tells the story of William the Conqueror's invasion of England in 1066. *See page 275*
- **Somme Battlefields (Picardy)** The horrors of World War I are remembered in memorials and cemeteries in towns and villages across now-peaceful Picardy. *See page 165*
- **D-Day Beaches (Normandy)** The north coast of Normandy has several museums recalling the events of 6 June 1944. Begin at the Mémorial de Caen. *See pages 274–5*
- **Verdun (Lorraine)** A town in northern Lorraine held sacred in France because of its resistance to attack in 1916. *See page 185*
- **Alise Ste-Reine (Burgundy)** Site of the hilltop last stand of the Gauls against the invading Roman armies under Julius Caesar. *See page 218*

ABOVE: Bayeux tapestry. **RIGHT:** Parc Astérix.

BEST ATTRACTIONS FOR KIDS

- **Disneyland (Ile-de-France)** Divided into five zones, Disneyland needs time and planning to explore. *See page 143*
- **Parc Astérix (Picardy)** A theme park on a more Gallic theme, built around the exploits of the famous comic-book hero and his companions. *See page 169*
- **Cité des Sciences (La Villette, Paris)** The capital's popular science museum includes a planetarium, space station, hothouses, interactive exhibits and an IMAX/3D entertainment dome, La Géode. *See page 132*
- **Cité de la Mer (Cherbourg)** A voyage to the bottom of the world's oceans, by means of an aquarium, museum and walk-aboard nuclear submarine. *See page 278*
- **Machines de Nantes (Nantes)** A weird and wonderful collection of machines including a 50-tonne lumbering, hydraulically powered elephant. *See page 250*
- **Puy de Fou (Vendée)** History is brought to life in spectacular re-enactments including a Roman chariot race, a Viking raid and the storming of a medieval castle. *See page 253*

Events to Look Out For

- **Lille Braderie** (first weekend of Sept)
Europe's biggest flea market is a bargain hunter's paradise visited by 1–2 million people. *See page 158*
- **Strasbourg Christmas market** (late Nov to end Dec)
Held in the city centre since 1570. Crafts goods and *bredle* – little advent cakes. *See page 197*
- **Hospice de Beaune wine auction** (third weekend in Nov)
A public sale of *grand* and *premier cru* Burgundy wines for charity, accompanied by a street festival and wine tasting. *See page 222*
- **Embroiderers Festival (Pont l'Abbé)**
Dance, music, song, street parades, competitions, in celebration of the culture of Brittany. There is a "village" market of crafts and traditional food and drink. *See page 298*
- **Tour de France (July)**
The famous round-France bicycle tour, taking a different route each year but always ending on Champs-Élysées in Paris. *See pages 253, 344–5*

Celebrated Food and Drink

- **Cheeses**
Many pastoral regions in the north, especially in Normandy, are renowned for their cheeses. Premier examples are Camembert, Brie, Comté, Pont l'Evêque, Livarot and Neufchatel. *See page 70*

- **Wine**
Burgundy, Champagne, Alsace and the Loire Valley all produce highly renowned wines. Less well known are those of the Jura mountains, Brittany and Lorraine. *See page 68*
- **Beer**
Alsace, unusually, makes both good beers and wines. The city of Lille is also known for its beer. *See page 69*
- **Crêpes**
Brittany is the origin of France's teatime snack of choice, also available in savoury versions. *See page 67*
- **Cider**
Normandy's speciality derives from its extensive apple orchards. Also good is Calvados – apple brandy. *See page 69*

Top: last stage of the Tour de France. **Left:** Strasbourg Christmas market. **Above:** Normandy specialities.

BEST BEAUTY SPOTS

- **Forêt de Fontainebleau (Ile-de-France)**
Beautiful forest of oak, beech, birch and pine around the royal château of the same name, within easy reach of Paris. *See page 144*
- **Etretat (Normandy)**
Footpaths north and south from the town lead to the top of dramatic cliffs of chalk towering above the Côte d'Albâtre. *See page 264*
- **Cascades du Hérisson (Franche-Comté)**
Classic there-and-back walk to see a string of waterfalls in the Hérrison River. *See page 226*
- **Pays d'Auge (Normandy)**
The quintessence of bucolic French countryside: beautiful scenery to drive through and pretty villages to stop and visit. *See page 272*
- **Côte de Granit Rose (Brittany)**
The "pink granite coast" named for the reddish tinge to its cliffs is at its best between Perros-Guirec and Ploumanac'h. *See page 292*

ABOVE: above the clouds in the Hautes-Vosges.
ABOVE RIGHT: the dramatic cliffs of Etretat.

GREAT VIEWPOINTS

- **Grand Ballon (Alsace)**
The highest summit in the Vosges, easy to climb. Views across the Rhine Valley and over it towards the Black Forest and the Alps. *See page 194*
- **Eiffel Tower (Paris)**
The iconic monument still provides the best view of the capital. *See page 119*
- **Pointe de Penhir (Brittany)**
The most spectacular of the four main headlands of the Crozon Peninsula, looking down on the rocky Atlantic coast from a height of 70m (230ft). *See page 297*
- **Le Lieu Unique (Nantes)**
An unusual moving platform in the tower of an old biscuit factory giving a splendid view over the city. *See page 250*

MONEY SAVING TIPS

- **Menu du jour**
Almost all restaurants serve a *menu du jour* at midday on weekdays which is cheaper than ordering à la carte. It will include a limited number of choices or none at all, and may or may not have wine included. Some restaurants offer a *plat de jour* (dish of the day) with either starter or dessert.
- **Roadside hotels**
If you just want an overnight stop, France has lots of cheap prefab hotels on the outskirts of its cities such as the rudimentary Formule 1. Rooms are functional and there are no public spaces but formalities are minimal: you can book online.
- **Motorways**
Tolls can add up if you use a lot of motorways, but some sections around cities are free. With a good map and a little planning you can make use of smaller cross-country roads which can be just as quick.
- **Half-Board and other deals**
Many hotels do special deals for dinner, bed and breakfast – it's always worth asking if they will do you a special price. City hotels that cater for business customers often offer cheaper rooms at weekends.
- **What's On**
Ask in the tourist information office or check the local paper for places and events with free admission. Most monuments and museums have free visiting days and wine producers often offer free tastings in the autumn after the grape harvest. Such events are often called *portes ouvertes* (open days).

JOIE

DE VIVRE

THE GLORIES OF THE NORTH

Great sights, great places to stay, great food and wine: you will be spoilt for choice for all these in the north of France

There are good reasons why France is the most visited country in the world, attracting over 77 million visitors a year. The country offers an unparalleled variety of things to see and do. And many of its greatest sights are packed into the north. Whether your taste is for the monumental or the modest, urban or rural, sedate or active, you are likely to find it here. Historic towns and cities, fascinating museums, attractive and accessible countryside, outdoor activities and things to entertain the kids: it's all here.

All this makes the region a great place to spend a holiday. For a start, it's easy to get around. The motorway and high-speed rail networks are superb; but if you want to take the slow way you'll find backroads country par excellence with any number of meandering, but well-signposted, scenic routes to explore by car or – even better – on a bicycle. Alternatively, you can travel even more slowly by boat, and navigate through the landscape on the extensive network of interlinked canals and rivers. If you prefer to take off on foot, there are many long-distance walking routes from the easiest strolls to challenging hikes.

And it's a hospitable place with long experience of catering to visitors. The choice of where to stay and eat is legendary, ranging from the cheap and rudimentary to the posh, pretentious and pricey. Hoteliers and restaurateurs generally strive to keep standards high, not least because their fellow countrymen are keen tourists themselves and proverbially demanding.

Which points to the most powerful but least tangible allure of France: its way of life as epitomised by the national attitude to food and wine. This is the home of Champagne and the exalted red and white wines of Burgundy. Everywhere you go there are fine cheeses and tasty local dishes to try. Meals are to be savoured at length and at leisure. A long lunch of carefully prepared courses and delicious wine on a shady restaurant terrace overlooking some slow-flowing green river or picturesque medieval village – what more could life offer? ❑

PRECEDING PAGES: Place des Vosges, Paris; Le Touquet beach resort; Cathédrale Notre-Dame, Laon. **LEFT:** vineyards of Hautvilliers, homeland of Dom Pérignon champagne. **TOP:** Le Coq Gallois, a national emblem. **ABOVE LEFT:** mouthwatering patisserie from Alsace. **ABOVE RIGHT:** beach huts at Yport on the Normandy coast.

PEOPLE OF THE PAYS D'OÏL

France is a country of extraordinary diversity unified by a distinctive way of life which is the envy of the world

France is a highly centralised nation in which regional differences are cherished and celebrated – but only as long as they are kept in check and never threaten the unifying culture. To understand how the people of the country think and live it's necessary to grapple with this paradox: to appreciate the variety of the parts and how they fit into the harmonising whole of French politics and culture.

North-South

The country can be subdivided in many ways, but one clear distinction is that which exists between north and south. The north differs from the south in obvious and subtle ways.

To begin with, the north is where political power is concentrated. Historically, it could be argued, northern France conquered and colonised the south. One visible sign of this is linguistic. The north gave the south its language: the *langue d'oïl* became the basis of standard French at the expense of Occitan, the *langue d'oc*.

There are fundamental geographical differences: southern France is predominantly mountainous, the north is largely flat. This and significant differences in climate and natural resources have conspired to give the north of the country the economic muscle: the northeastern coalfields made the region the crucible of France's industrial revolution in the 19th century. It is more densely populated than the south and with much better communications, not only with Paris but also with the other countries of Western Europe. The frontiers of the north are quite different to those of the south. Whereas the Alps and the Pyrenees allow traffic in and out of France only with bloody-minded geographical reluctance – you have to go round, over or through the mountains to get anywhere – between the North Sea and Switzerland there is no serious obstacle to the free movement of cross-border traffic.

The eastern frontiers are sometimes imperceptible; just an arbitrary a line on a map to distinguish France from non-France. Many people live within walking distance or a bus ride of another country: some commute over the border to work. As a result, northeastern France is at the heart of a uniting Europe: it is close to Brussels, and Strasbourg is the home of international institutions.

LEFT: street performer in Strasbourg. **RIGHT:** in common with other western nations, France has an ageing population.

From here, things tend to get more subtle. The people of northern France are not in any sense "Latin": Roman civilisation left less of a mark here and its neighbours are Belgium and Germany rather than Spain and Italy. Their character is different and this might have as much to do with the climate as anything else. The weather in the north is generally cool and wet rather than hot and dry, reducing the number of months in which life can be lived out of doors and, more importantly, shortening the growing season and limiting the crops which can be grown. *Joie de vivre* and a relaxed attitude to time are not northern concepts. The people of the north are therefore – by reputation at least and often in practice – less extrovert, warm, spontaneous and friendly than their fellow countrymen in southern regions; conversely, they are more organised, prudent, business-like and industrious.

All these qualities are stereotypes, of course, but there is some truth in them and they give at least a basis for understanding the mentality of the north.

> *I believe only in French culture, and regard everything else in Europe which calls itself 'culture' as a misunderstanding.* Nietzsche Ecce Homo, 1888

The divided north

The divide between north and south, however, shouldn't be pushed too far, certainly not without simultaneously considering the divisions that exist within the north itself. Brittany, in particular, is an exception – both for its geographical characteristics as a rugged Atlantic-storm-lashed peninsula, and for its inhabitants who are sometimes classed as an ethnic group, one of the six Celtic nations on the western fringes of Europe. At the other extreme is Alsace, whose language and culture are Germanic in origin. Normans living on the Atlantic coast lead different lives to the landlocked peoples of Lorraine and Burgundy. And it is possible to go on subdividing the regions almost ad infinitum: one commune in Champagne may have only superficial similarities with another a few kilometres away.

Demographic differences

Across northern France, as across the whole country, there are differences between people which have nothing to do with regions. One fundamental split is between the growing urban areas and the increasingly marginalised countryside. The inhabitants of any provincial *grand ville* do not see life quite in the same way as people living in isolated houses or market towns. The picture of settlement pattern is complicated by the *banlieues* – out-of-town ghettoes of socially and economically disadvantaged people who do not feel as if they have the same stake in society as their fellow man – and by *rurbanisation*, the morphing of rural-urban fringes into dormitory estates.

The French tend to think of themselves as a classless society. The 19th century was a staccato process of finishing off the monarchy and aristocracy in favour of a society in which birth did not guarantee privilege – and, in theory at least, anyone in France can succeed whatever their background. As in any country, there are always rich and poor people; and certainly wealthy and powerful families – including some with residual aristocratic titles – who know how to look after their own. But these people do not constitute a definable caste and there is no discernible pecking order of deference.

There is, though, an educated elite that keeps the country functioning. France deliberately nurtures this elite and refreshes it with new talent through the system of *grandes écoles* (universities which take only the highest flyers).

Immigration

The differences are compounded by immigration which is apparently making France a multicultural society. Officially, though, there are no ethnic minorities in France, just French people and foreign residents who are entitled to their own private notions of self-identity. In 1872 it was decided that the state had no right to keep data about the faith or racial origin of its citizens. This policy was reinforced at the birth of the Fifth Republic in 1958, which preached the virtues of inclusivity and assimilation for good reason. Between 1940 and 1944 all Frenchmen and women had not been equal, and the stigma of what happened to Jews – who in all other respects were as French as their neighbours – has hung heavy over society ever since.

Religion

And then there is religion. France is still, de facto, an overwhelmingly Catholic country. While 25 percent of people tell pollsters that they don't practise any religion and only 13 percent say they

> *The English view of law is [that it is] a sacrosanct thing in itself, to be obeyed to the letter, and the French point of view [is] that it is an instrument designed to prevent one's neighbour from enjoying one iota more of any benefit than one's self...*
> Eugene Fodor, 1960

FAR LEFT: couple at the window of their half-timbered house in Alsace. **LEFT:** locals relaxing in Belleville Park, eastern Paris. **RIGHT:** enjoying beer and a pizza at the Strasbourg Fête de la Musique.

POLITE PEOPLE

Wherever two French people meet, they begin with a formal salutation. To fail to greet someone, even a supermarket check-out assistant, is considered rude. The average French person is capable of kissing, or shaking hands with, a whole room of friends, family or acquaintances before starting a conversation or getting down to urgent business. The number of kisses varies from two to four, depending on the region.

Everyone scrupulously respects the distinction between *vous* (polite and distant) and *tu* (intimate) and is careful not to ask intrusive personal questions of a new acquaintance by way of chitchat – certainly not his name or what he does for a living.

do, an average of 65 percent of the population claims to be at least nominally Catholic. Protestantism accounts for just 2 percent, although historically it has formed important pockets in northern cities such as Strasbourg. For most people, Catholicism is part of the background fuzz of French culture. It caters for most funerals, but otherwise there is no need to go to church and many people avoid it. For every three marriages celebrated there are now two civil partnership agreements (*pacte civil de solidarité*, or *PACS*).

The second religion of France is Islam, at 6 percent – higher than anywhere else in western Europe. France also has Europe's largest populations of Buddhists and Jews.

There is not much that 21st-century France can agree on about religion except that it must be kept away from anything to do with the state, including public schools. This explains the furore over Muslim girls wearing headscarfs to school, which prompted the government to reiterate the rules requiring all things religious to be kept in the private domain.

It is because of all these differences that most people welcome the rigidly unifying force of the French state. This is seen as common property with the important task of upholding the culture of the nation, without which France would cease to be a place worth living in and an important presence in the world.

A proud language

The national tongue is a source of pride to its owners, who are often pedantic about its correct use. It is a mistake, however, to assume you have to speak perfect French or else keep your mouth shut. Parisian waiters may have a reputation for being brusque with customers who get their genders wrong or fail to annunciate their vowels correctly, but almost every other French person tends to be grateful to any foreigner who takes the trouble to speak to them in appalling French.

> “*It is more fun for an intelligent person to live in an intelligent country. France has the only two things toward which we drift as we grow older – intelligence and good manners.* F Scott Fitzgerald, New York World, April 1927”

The rules of French are rigidly defined by the venerable Académie Française, which often steps in to provide a “proper” French word in place of some creeping American import. The Anglophone world often finds this puritanical linguistic policy incomprehensible and amusing, but it offers an insight into the fundamental premise of French culture. “No foreigner should ever mock the French language,” warns Theodore Zeldin in his classic 1982 study, *The French*: “first because he does not understand it properly, and secondly because it has divine status in France… If one forced the French to strip-tease, discarding one by one all the outward disguises that give them their national identity, the last thing one would be left with would be their language.”

Yet French is by no means the only language spoken across the northern half of the country. More than 20 highly localised tongues are still in common usage. Most of these are Romance languages and, like French, derivatives of the *langue d'oïl*. Examples include Picard, spoken in the northeastern corner of France; and Cauchois, a variant of Norman, of the Pays de Caux in northern Normandy. A few, however, are dialects of the *langue d'oc* – Occitan, the dialect of the south, such as Jurassien, a form of Fran-

Left: France is still a predominantly Catholic country. **Right:** young Parisian gendarmes.

co-provencale which is spoken in the southern Franche-Comté. A handful of French-German hybrid languages survive in Alsace.

Precisely what is a language and what is a dialect is debatable and politically contentious. To reduce French from *the* language to *a* language is to surrender cultural control to minorities and therefore to weaken the power of Paris. But northern France does have one "alternative" language that is acknowledged as such and given official status: Breton, the Celtic language of Brittany. All other regional tongues were recognised in an amendment to the constitution in 2004 as being part of French heritage rather than serious tools of everyday life.

Changing times

The vast majority of the French and the millions of tourists who visit their country share one aspiration in common. They would like France to stay the way it is, that is, how they imagine it at its best – with its legendary, privileged way of life and its rich legacy of tradition.

But the truth is that France is evolving. For some it is in a long, slow decline from a peak reached sometime in the 1970s. For others, it is merely in transition towards a different kind of country, one which will be able to retain the best of its qualities while shedding those that can't be sustained in the modern world.

The pace of transformation is being set by forces from outside France, in particular the Anglo-Saxon concept of *liberalisme* – "working more to earn more," as Nicolas Sarkozy put it in his election campaign. This militates against some strongly ingrained French notions, such as expecting the state to provide for its citizens' needs while working fewer hours and retaining the fundamental right to strike.

In many ways, the people of northern France have embraced the proliferation of market forces better than those in the south. The prime example of this is Lille, once a centre of manufacturing, which has exploited its transport links to become a city of shops and services. With the decline of its traditional industrial base, the north has broadly come to terms with the inevitability of finding a new role for itself – just as France is having to find a new role for itself in a rapidly changing world. ❑

FOOD, GLORIOUS FOOD

If anything constitutes a line in the sand between French and Anglo-Saxon culture it is the attitude to food. As chef Raymond Blanc puts it, "to eat well in France is a universal right – the realistic expectation of the majority, not the privilege of the few."

More than any other nation in Europe, France looks with adoration on its countryside and on farmers as the providers of edible wealth. The French word for peasant, *paysan*, has none of the belittling connotations it has in English. "Tilling and grazing are the two breasts by which France is fed" wrote the Duc de Sully in 1638, and the French would like to think that their agricultural produce is as good as it ever was.

Food is considered too important to be left to the whims of economic theory, but, in truth, the French know that liberalism is hard to resist. Modern farming practices have done away with many of the labour-intensive forms of cultivation and preparation that French cuisine holds inviolable. Shoppers may eulogise about the small farmer and his old-fashioned way of growing vegetables, but in reality they are happy to buy imported tomatoes out of season from hypermarkets. They drink ever smaller quantities of their own wines however much they praise them over New World upstart vintages. And they are aware that all the while McDonald's is doing brisk business in every part of France.

E. L. BOLTON
EDMON T. LITTLE

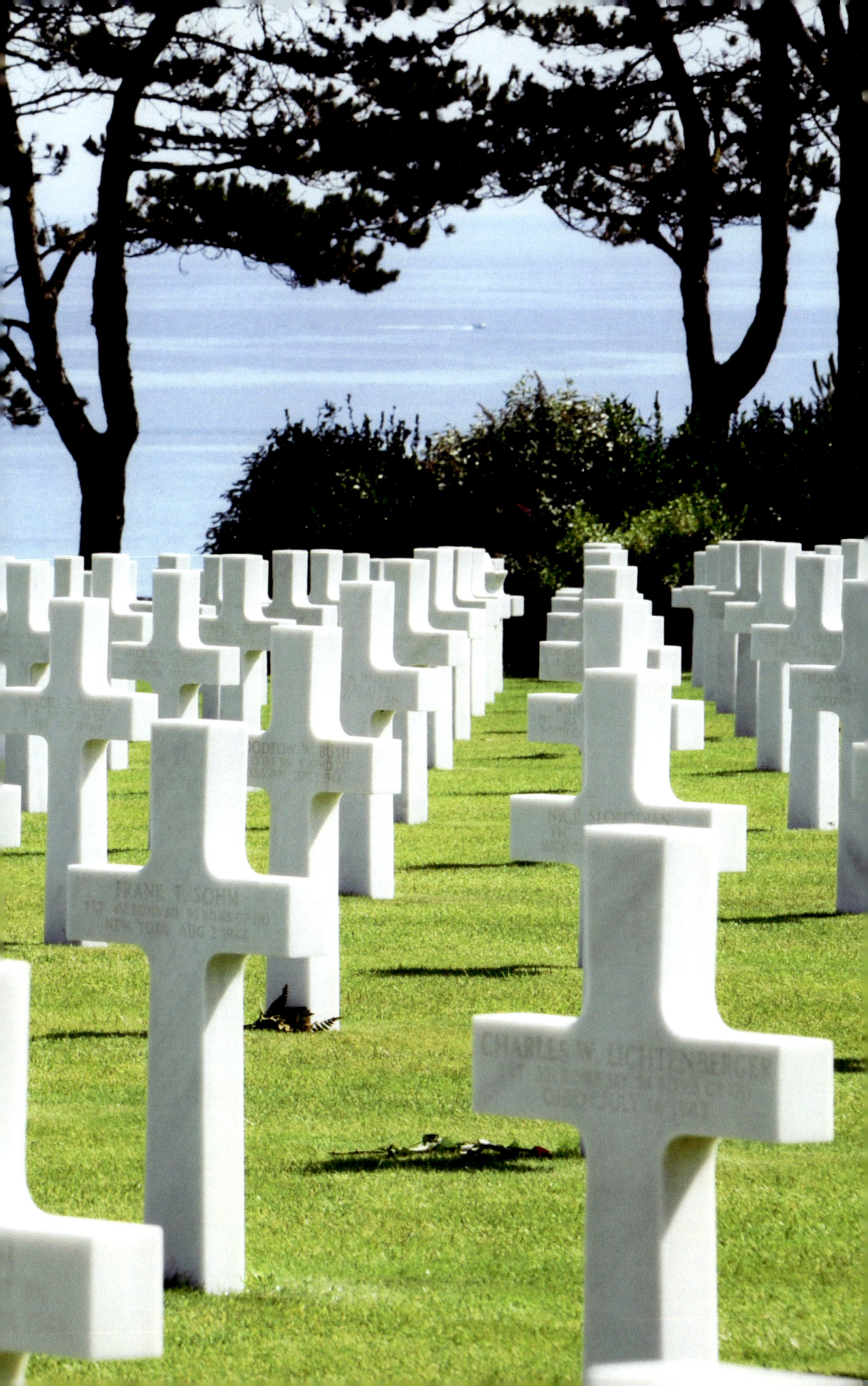
FRANK T. SOHM
CHARLES W. LICHTENBERGER

Decisive Dates

Gauls and Romans

52 BC
Romans defeat Gauls at Alésia and conquer northern Gaul.

c.AD 250
St Denis martyred in Paris.

c.400
Northern Gaul invaded by Franks and other Germanic tribes.

Franks and Others

c.400–600
Migrations of Celts from Wales and Cornwall to Brittany.

c.496
Clovis, King of the Franks, becomes a Christian.

732
Charles Martel defeats Moorish army at Tours.

800
Charlemagne crowned Holy Roman Emperor.

851
Frankish king acknowledges effective independence of Brittany.

911
Duchy of Normandy established.

The Middle Ages

987
Hugues Capet becomes first King of France.

1066
William, Duke of Normandy, conquers England.

1095
First Crusade initiated.

1154
Henry II of England and Normandy succeeds to the "Angevin Empire".

1204
Philippe Auguste seizes Normandy.

1337
Hundred Years War begins.

1348–50
Black Death kills millions.

1428–9
Joan of Arc ends English siege of Orléans.

1477
King Louis XI seizes the main Duchy of Burgundy for France.

Renaissance and Religious Wars

1532
Edict of Union incorporates Brittany into France.

1539
Decree makes Parisian French the official language of government.

1562–93
Wars of Religion.

1598
Edict of Nantes grants toleration to Protestants.

The *Grand Siècle*

1639
Alsace occupied by France.

1648–53
Fronde rebellion.

1640–78
Artois, Hainaut, and French Flanders taken by France.

1685
Louis XIV revokes Edict of Nantes.

Ancien Régime and Revolution

1751
First volume of Diderot's *Encyclopédie* published.

1789
Louis XIV calls the Estates-General to discuss financial

crisis; Third Estate becomes National Assembly. Storming of the Bastille.

1792
Republic declared.

1793–4
The Terror: royal family and many others executed.

1793–96
Royalist revolts in Brittany and the Loire valley.

1799
Napoleon takes power.

1804
Napoleon declares himself Emperor.

1814
Napoleon defeated. Bourbon monarchy restored under Louis XVIII.

1815
Napoleon returns but is defeated at Waterloo.

PRECEDING PAGES: US war cemetery above Omaha Beach. FAR LEFT TOP: stained glass window depicting Charlemagne as Holy Emperor. LEFT: the Battle of Crécy, 1346. ABOVE: demolition of the Bastille prison, 1789. RIGHT: President Nicolas Sarkozy on election day, 2007.

RESTORATION AND SECOND EMPIRE

1830
July Revolution: Charles X replaced by Louis-Philippe.

1848
Revolution establishes Second Republic.

1849–52
Louis Napoleon Bonaparte elected President, and later declares himself Emperor Napoleon III.

1870–1
Defeat in Franco-Prussian War leads to fall of Napoleon III. Alsace-Lorraine taken by Germany.

1871
Revolutionary Commune in Paris is bloodily suppressed.

THIRD REPUBLIC

1881–2
Jules Ferry laws establish free, non-religious public education.

1914–18
World War I leaves over 1,300,000 French dead, and devastates the northeast.

1919
Alsace-Lorraine returned to France.

1936–7
Popular Front government.

1940
Fall of France leads to German occupation of northern France; General de Gaulle calls for continued resistance from London.

1944
France liberated after devastating fighting in Normandy and many other areas.

MODERN TIMES

1945
Fourth Republic gives votes to women.

1957
Common Market, precursor of European Union, established.

1958–9
Algerian uprising leads to return of De Gaulle, and establishment of Fifth Republic.

1968
Student revolt and strikes in Paris and across France. De Gaulle retires the following year.

1982
Mitterand government revives regional administrations for the first time since 1789.

1994
Channel Tunnel opens.

2002
Euro comes into everyday use.

2007
Nicolas Sarkozy elected President of France.

2010
French Assembly approves ban on women wearing a full veil or *burqa* in public.

FIRST FORMATION

Celts, Romans, Franks and Norsemen all played their part in creating the historical map of northern France

France, with Paris as its unquestioned hub, has such a strong identity in most people's minds that it can appear to be as natural an entity as the landscape. However, it has only come together over centuries, and out of many very disparate elements.

Human habitation in this part of Western Europe can be traced back at least as far as the late Palaeolithic era, from around 35,000 to 10,000 BC. France's most famous prehistoric relics are all in the south, in the caves of the Dordogne and the Ardèche, but by the Neolithic era, from about 4500 BC, areas across the north were settled by peoples who grew crops and made pottery. The great river valleys of the Seine, Loire and Rhône were highways for the movement of peoples, as they have been ever since. The most significant Neolithic monuments, however, are in the far northwest, at sites such as Carnac in Brittany, testimony to the existence of quite sophisticated, large communities there at that time. From around 1800 BC their descendants began to work metals.

Gauls and Romans

The Celts first entered what is now France a little after 1000 BC, from the northeast. They were never united; the Romans vaguely called the whole area *Gallia* or Gaul, and Julius Caesar said the Gauls were divided into three groups, the *Aquitani* in the southwest, the *Belgae* roughly northeast of the Seine and the *Celtae* in the middle, but this did not mean any of them had a single ruler. Nevertheless, they were skilled metal workers, and traded with each other and with Rome and the Mediterranean.

The Romans had the southern reaches of Gaul under firm control by 120 BC as the province of *Gallia Narbonensis*. They took little interest in the north until 58 BC, when Julius Caesar arrived as governor of southern Gaul, eager for victories to boost his prestige. Skilfully exploiting inter-Gaulish conflicts, he conquered one tribe after another. His chief opponent emerged as Vercingetorix, chief of the Arverni tribe in what is now the Auvergne, who built up a powerful anti-Roman alliance. It didn't last: at Alesia near Dijon in 52 BC the Gauls were crushed, and Caesar carried Vercingetorix off to Rome to be humiliated. Roman control was

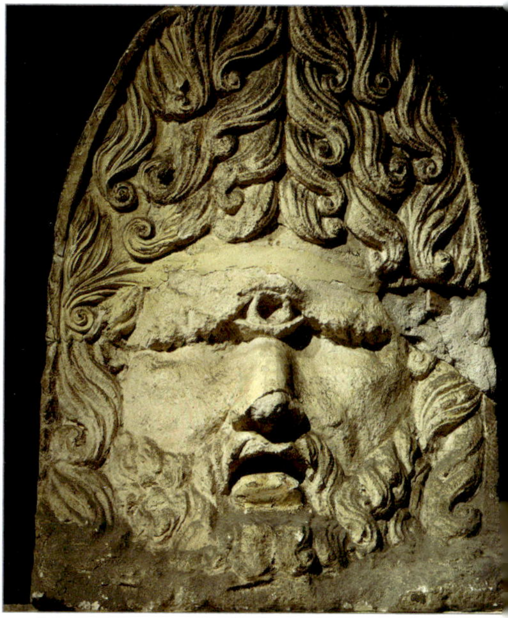

LEFT: Leader of the Gauls, Vercingetorix (72–46 BC).
RIGHT: Gallo-Roman funerary mask.

complete, and subsequent revolts were ruthlessly suppressed.

The Romans divided their conquest into three provinces: *Gallia Aquitania* in the southwest, *Gallia Lugdunensis* and *Gallia Belgica* in the centre and north They also began to build cities – the largest being *Lugdunum* (Lyon), capital of the central province. Caesar's men had also captured the settlement of a people called the *Parisii*, on an island in the Seine that is now Paris' Ile de la Cité, and founded Roman *Lutetia*, ancient ancestor of modern Paris, on the south bank where the Latin Quarter is today. Other cities were also founded at river crossings, such as *Rotomagus* (Rouen), *Caesarodunum* (Tours), *Durocortum* (Reims) and *Samarobriva* (Amiens).

The Gauls – especially the aristocracy – accepted Romanisation, and while this was never as complete in the north as in Mediterranean France, over most of the country a "Gallo-Roman" culture was established, the Roman-ness of which often varied with proximity to towns. Roman gods were mixed with Celtic ones, and variants of Latin became the principal language.

New religion

Christianity began to spread across Roman Gaul during the 3rd century. Ecclesiastical tradi-

Parisian Preachers

The future prominence of Paris, once only one of many Gallo-Roman cities, was greatly helped by its association with two legendary figures of early Christianity. First was St Denis, the missionary and first Bishop of Paris in around 250. He was martyred on Montmartre (the "Mount of Martyrs"), the spot becoming a sacred shrine. He became France's patron saint, and from the time of Clovis, St Denis would be a sacred church for Frankish and French kings.

Paris' own patron saint, St Genevieve, rose to prominence when Attila the Hun and his ferocious army were approaching the city in 451. The citizens duly panicked, but Genevieve, a saintly mystic living on the hill now called the Montagne Ste-Geneviève, told them that God would spare them if they showed their faith with prayer and fasting. Women and the poor, especially, joined her to pray on the hilltop. Attila miraculously turned away from Paris and sacked Orléans instead, which does not say much for the piety of that city. Clovis, the first Christian Frankish king, was a great devotee of the aged Genevieve and built a church for her on her hill, where he and his queen St Clotilde were buried.

tion celebrates the efforts of seven missionaries sent from Rome around the year 250, of which two went to the north – the martyr St Denis, in Lutetia (Paris), and St Gatien, first Bishop of Tours. They met a great deal of resistance, but from 313, when Emperor Constantine made Christianity Rome's official religion, the missionaries had official support. By 400 the church had bishops established across the country.

There were still interruptions to the advance of Christianity, notably in 360, when troops in Lutetia proclaimed their commander, the Roman prince Julian, as Emperor. Damned by the church as "Julian the Apostate", in his short reign before he died in battle he tried to return Rome to paganism, blaming Christianity for weakening the Empire. And by this time, the Roman empire was indeed crumbling. The legionaries could no longer hold back the wave after wave of invasions by the Germanic tribes – the Visigoths, Vandals, Franks and others. In 451 the Huns, led by Attila, poured south and west, sacking towns across the country. They were only driven away from Paris, the legend goes, by the piety of St Genevieve *(see panel, opposite)*.

LEFT: Roman Gaul colony, 1st century BC.
ABOVE: 16th-century painting of St Genevieve watching her flock.

Franks, Burgundians, Bretons

Out of the chaos that followed the Roman collapse in 410, a pattern eventually emerged. Most of northern Gaul was occupied by the Germanic Franks, many of whom were unified under a leader called Merovech, whose power base was in Flanders and Picardy. Another Germanic tribe, the Burgundians, controlled the Upper Rhône valley. In Brittany, the 5th and 6th centuries saw migrations of Celts from Wales and Cornwall, escaping Anglo-Saxon and Irish invaders in their homelands, so that Celtic culture in Brittany grew much stronger rather than weakening after the fall of Rome. The collapse of Gallo-Roman culture and urban life was never as overwhelming in Mediterranean Gaul as in the north.

Over time, all the communities of old Gaul would speak languages that were a mixture of Gallo-Roman Latin and the speech of the recent invaders, but a major linguistic difference would persist between the more Frankish-influenced *langues d'oïl* (so-named because they all used variants of *oïl* for yes) of the north and the southern *langues d'oc*, the origin of Occitan and Provençal. The linguistic divide, which has only weakened in modern times, ran from southern Burgundy across the north of the Massif Central and to the Gironde near Bordeaux.

As Roman authority collapsed, the Church – the only solid institution in society – looked around for protection. In 493 Merovech's grandson Clovis – who ironically had destroyed the last vestiges of Roman power in the north by defeating the Gallo-Roman King Syagrius at Soissons in 486 – married a Christian Burgundian princess, Clotilde, and was baptised. To the Church he became a semi-saintly figure, and his queen Clotilde was actually made a saint. Clovis then went on to conquer most of northern and western Gaul, and he and his dynasty, the Merovingians (descendants of Merovech), created the first true Frankish kingdom, absorbing the Burgundians. He was also the first ruler to make Paris his capital.

The Merovingian kingdom was still a chaotic entity, with little to bind it together. Traditional Frankish customs on inheritance meant that the kingdom was divided between all of a king's sons on his death, as happened between the four sons of Clovis in 511. Hence Merovingian princes continually plotted against each other. Later Merovingian kings became weaker and weaker, and known (though this may be legend) for various kinds of decadence and gluttony.

The Carolingians

By the early 8th century the most powerful figure in the kingdom was Charles Martel, "the Hammer", one of the Merovingians' chief servants. In 732 he defeated an Arab army at Tours, turning back Muslim expansion in Europe. He subsequently triumphed in other campaigns, particularly against the pagan Saxons in Germany.

In 751 Charles' son, Pepin the Short, deposed the last Merovingian and had himself proclaimed King of the Franks at Soissons, ushering in the Carolingian dynasty. In 754 he offered sanctuary to Pope Stephen II, driven north by the Lombard invasion of Italy, and the pope himself anointed Pepin in St-Denis outside Paris. Accepting the role of the Church's right arm, Pepin accordingly drove the Lombards back in Italy. No other king in Europe had such a direct papal seal of approval, and it gave the Frankish kings and their successors a special aura that they would be very careful to cultivate.

Frankish power reached its peak under Pepin's son, Charlemagne, or Charles the Great (r. 768–814). With prodigious energy and ambition, he overwhelmed the Saxons and created an empire that included virtually the whole of old Gaul, the Netherlands, much of Germany and northern Italy, with a new capital at Aachen (Aix-la-Chapelle). Himself illiterate, he brought scholars to his court from across Europe, and encouraged an artistic and cultural renaissance. The Church saw this as a potential return to the stability lost with the fall of Rome, and on Christmas Day 800 the pope crowned Charlemagne Holy Roman Emperor.

The system eventually known as feudalism developed out of Frankish customs, as refined by Charlemagne. Essentially it was a means of governing large territories when the only effective instruments of power were armed force and personal loyalty, based on mutual obligation. A local lord, count or duke received authority over land from the king, to whom he made a sacred oath of loyalty as their vassal, to come to their aid in time of need; in return, the king had an obligation to aid his vassals against third parties. Similar obligations were repeated down the social pyramid, although at the bottom, peasant serfs had many obligations and few effective rights. It became established that lords could pass on their fiefdoms to their sons, which further encouraged their independence and sense of their own importance. The system was inherently unstable, since lesser lords were natural rivals, loyalty was open to endless interpretation, and an effective local baron could easily become more powerful than a weak king.

Nonetheless, only kings were anointed by the Church, and this – combined with the papal sanction – gave the French monarchy a rare symbolic power.

Newcomers and a new king

Charlemagne's son Louis the Pious more or less held the empire together, but the Franks still had a problem with inheritance. On his death his three sons fought each other, and at Verdun in 843 they divided the empire into three, an eastern portion in Germany, a central section that ran from the Netherlands south through Lorraine down to Provence and Italy, and the remaining "West Francia", which would develop into France. However, none of these kingdoms gained any stability.

Royal authority was especially undermined by the kings' inability to respond to external threats. In Brittany, a Celtic lord called Nominoë attacked Frankish towns in the Loire valley and established an effectively independent Duchy of Brittany that the Frankish king was forced to recognise. A more significant threat was the Vikings, sailing up the Seine valley, whose attacks became ever more intense from around 840. In 911 King Charles the Simple bought off one of the Viking leaders, Rollo (or Rolf, or *Rollon* in French), by accepting his control over the lands north of the River Epte in return for Rollo's becoming a Christian and pledging a very theoretical allegiance as his feudal vassal. The lands of the Norsemen thus became Normandy.

> *When he became Charles the Simple's vassal, Rollo refused to kiss his foot, as was the Frankish custom, but told a henchman to do it. He did so, but in the process tipped the king out of his throne.*

Towards the end of the first millennium the Carolingian dynasty had dwindled away, and in 987 an assembly of nobles and bishops at Senlis chose a new king in Hugues Capet, Count of Paris. He is considered the first King of the French state that has continued into the modern era, although his successors were numbered to retrospectively include the Carolingians; this was thought to add legitimacy and to evoke Pepin's papal coronation (thus Louis the Pious was the first of France's 18 King Louis). For a long time, this would be virtually all the authority they had. ❑

LEFT: stained glass window depicting the baptism of King Clovis, founder of the first Frankish kingdom.
ABOVE: Charlemagne crowned by Pope Leo III in 800.

The Rise and Fall of the Monarchy

France's monarchs built up their power over eight centuries, only to see it come crashing down in the explosive revolution of 1789

As ruling monarchs, the effective authority of Hugues Capet and his descendants (the Capetians) extended little beyond the Ile de France. The effort to impose royal authority on a large, diverse, disorderly country, and extend Parisian power, would be a theme of the next 800 years.

Robber barons and saintly monks

Around the year 1000, few inhabitants of France were aware of the existence of a king at all. Real power was fragmented between local lords, some of them great regional magnates. In the northeast, the Counts of Flanders were the strongest power. In the Loire Valley, Fulk Nerra, Count of Anjou, a "plunderer, murderer, robber and swearer of false oaths", according to one chronicler, carved out a powerful domain from his castle in Loches. Strongest of all were the Normans. Settling into their new lands and intermarrying with locals, the Norsemen became the most significant military power of the time.

The Normans also became great builders, and great patrons of another movement that humanised the brutality of the age: monasticism. In the year 910, the Benedictine Order founded a new abbey at Cluny in southern Burgundy that would strictly observe the Benedictine rule. Immensely influential, Cluny inspired a new wave of monastery building.

For all its apparent brutality, this was a superstitious and curiously legalistic age, in which symbolic acts such as oaths and the anointing of a king were of great importance. The early Capetian kings might appear to have been powerless and irrelevant, but their coronation gave them a status that few feudal lords were ready to disregard completely. For William the Conqueror, Duke of Normandy, the idea of becoming a king in his own right was a primary incentive for his invasion of England in 1066.

In Normandy, however, William remained a French vassal despite his English conquest, a situation that put new strains on the disordered system. In the early 12th century the imbalance between local and royal Capetian power grew further when King Henry II of England and Normandy became the Count of Anjou, before acquiring much of southwest France through his marriage to Eleanor of Aquitaine. The

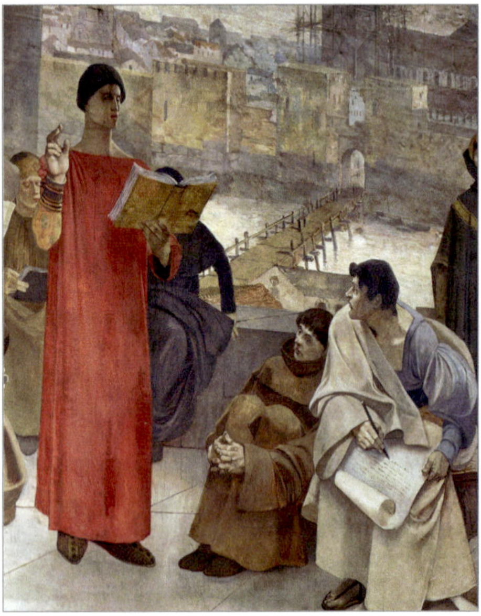

Above: medieval philosopher and theologian Pierre Abelard lecturing on the Montagne Ste Genevieve. **Right:** the coronation of Philippe Auguste in Reims.

so-called "Angevin Empire" thus created covered the whole of western France down to the Pyrenees, dwarfing the lands under the control of his supposed overlords the Capetians, whom Henry treated with contempt.

France emerges

Nevertheless, other elements were appearing that would finally increase royal power. By the 1150s the focus of wealth was beginning to move away from land and the power of men on horseback, and towards the growing trade in textiles, metalwork and other goods, particularly in the towns of Picardy, Flanders, Champagne and Burgundy. Merchant towns were more favourable to royal authority than to armed barons. Paris itself grew in wealth and prominence. Suger, Abbot of St-Denis, began to improve royal administration, and revolutionised architecture, rebuilding St-Denis as the first large Gothic building. Paris also acquired the first university in northern Europe *(see panel, below)*.

These new developments proceeded apace during the reign of King Philippe Auguste (1180–1223), the Capetian who could be called the creator of the French state. He was a great builder, particularly in Paris, and skilfully expanded his power, taking control of

BIRTH OF THE INTELLIGENTSIA

In fulfilment of several clichés, Paris' university – the oldest in northern Europe – was born with doses of rebelliousness and romance. Around 1110, a scholar at the Cathedral School of Notre-Dame, Peter Abelard, began (like some other scholars) to lecture on philosophy in the open air on Montagne Ste-Geneviève, south of the Seine. It was said that students from all over Europe came to hear him. He also impressed Fulbert, the Cathedral Canon, who asked Abelard to teach his unusually educated niece, Héloïse. Fulbert had not expected the passionate affair that developed, which was impossible to deny when Héloïse became pregnant. Fulbert demanded they separate, but they didn't obey, and he had Abelard castrated. Héloïse was sent off to a nunnery, but she and Abelard continued to exchange love letters, which, preserved and later published, have become classics of romantic literature.

Abelard retired to the Abbey of St-Denis, and became still more famous as an original thinker in an age of orthodoxy. Finding the monastery uncongenial, he lived for a while as a hermit in a hut at Nogent-sur-Seine south of Paris, where students sought him out. Later, he returned to Montagne Ste-Geneviève. Around 1140 he was challenged by the Cistercian Bernard of Clairvaux, who regarded Abelard's rationalism as heresy. Abelard died before the pope could decide on the matter. Paris University grew out of the Ste-Geneviève schools, together with the school of Notre-Dame, and was functioning by 1150.

Normandy and so bringing the Anglo-Norman dual monarchy to an end.

The great building boom was continued by Philippe's grandson Louis IX (1226–70). This was the first great age of Gothic, when the style pioneered at St-Denis and Laon was expressed in masterpieces such as Paris' Ste-Chapelle and Amiens Cathedral. Louis was known for his piety, and died on his second Crusade, for which he was made St Louis; having a saint among their numbers would become another part of the grand self-image of French monarchy.

Philip IV "the Fair" (1285–1314) gave the state more visible institutions. In 1302 he called the first meeting of the Estates-General *(Etats Généraux)*, with assemblies of the "Three Estates" (the nobility, clergy and commoners, initially representatives of merchant towns) as an early, limited form of parliament. This had the role of passing on opinion in the different social sectors to the king and, especially, helping in raising taxes.

War and plague

In 1328 the direct Capetian male line came to an end when Charles IV died leaving only daughters. Under the Salic Law inherited from the Franks, only men could inherit the crown, and Philip of Valois, Charles' cousin, became King Philip VI. However, Edward III of England argued he had a stronger claim through his mother, Charles' sister – sparking the Hundred Years War. This was partly an internal conflict, for Edward found many allies among French lords who saw a chance to resist the encroachment of central authority.

Edward III defeated the French at Crécy in Picardy in 1346, and besieged Calais. Two years later the Black Death swept across France, killing up to half of the population – but not halting the war. These twin evils led to a breakdown in feudal order, and the situation was made worse in 1356 when the Dauphin Charles (later Charles V) attempted to raise taxes, as more funds were needed to pay for the ruinous war. Parisian crowds led by Etienne Marcel revolted and briefly took over the city. In the countryside, meanwhile, the collapse in population aggravated resentments at the demands of feudal lords, and there were frequent peasant revolts.

At the famous Battle of Agincourt in 1415 Henry V of England appeared to win total victory, and obliged King Charles VI to disinherit his own son, the Dauphin Charles, to marry his daughter to Henry and accept that their descendants would be kings of France and England. Nevertheless, resistance continued around the Dauphin, later Charles VII.

The war's latter stages were marked by a more nationalistic tone, epitomised by the figure of Joan of Arc. Her sudden intervention at Orléans in 1428 raised morale enough to enable the French to end the English siege of the city and regain control of most of the Loire valley *(see opposite)*, and Charles VII was able to build further on the popular support thus created. Following French victories in Normandy in the 1450s, the interminable conflict finally drew to an end.

The challenge from Burgundy

The French monarchy still faced challenges, however – above all from Burgundy. Its dukes were a branch of the same Valois clan as the ruling house, and through astute marriages had acquired territories inside and outside France that included Picardy, Artois, Flanders and the modern Netherlands, an untidy entity containing the richest cities in northern Europe.

This powerful force had supported the English in the war, and it was only after they changed sides again in 1435 that the French made decisive advances. Duke Philip "the Good" (1419–67) created a magnificent court in his capitals of Dijon, Lille, Bruges and Brussels.

The balance of power shifted after Philip's son, Charles the Bold, died without leaving a male heir. Louis XI of France took advantage of Salic Law to seize the feudal fief of Burgundy for the crown. Nevertheless, the remaining territories – including Flanders and Artois – were retained by Charles' daughter Marie de Bourgogne, who married the Habsburg Emperor Maximilian.

Renaissance

With France entering a period of calm after years of war and plague, the northern towns enjoyed a surge of prosperity. By the end of the 15th century, the Loire valley began to develop royal connections, with Louis XII indicating his suspicion of unruly Paris by periodically taking his court to Blois, a "second capital". He built one of the first Loire châteaux here, clearly intended as a palace rather than a fortress.

King François I (1515–47) is traditionally credited with bringing the Renaissance to France. Fascinated by all the new ideas and styles coming from Italy, he was a patron of artists and above all Leonardo da Vinci, to whom he gave shelter at Amboise. His vast palace-châteaux at Fontainebleau and Chambord were both in the new Renaissance style.

> *French replaced Latin as the official language of government in 1539. However, the language was not defined, but rather assumed to be the language of Paris and its area – even though less than half the population understood it.*

It was François I who resolved the long-running issue of Brittany. Anne de Bretagne, heiress to the Duchy of Brittany *(see page 35)*, was virtually a French prisoner, and was forcibly married in succession to both kings Charles VIII and Louis XII. Between marriages she struggled to maintain Brittany's independence, for which *Duchesse Anne* has become a Breton heroine. After her death, however, François I married her daughter by Louis XII (she produced no male heir), and in 1532 Brittany finally came under crown authority.

European affairs were less satisfactory. Philip, son of Marie de Bourgogne and Emperor Maximilian, had married Juana, daughter of Ferdinand and Isabella of Spain. This meant that their son, Emperor Charles V, became ruler of the old Burgundian Netherlands, the Habsburg lands in Germany and Italy, and Spain. This vast inheritance surrounded France, and it would be an aim of French rulers for the next century to break this ring. In the opening rounds, France was the loser. After defeat at Pavia in Italy in 1525 François I was held prisoner in Madrid, and following another defeat at St-Quentin, his son Henri II had to agree to an unsatisfactory peace, in 1559.

LEFT: Joan of Arc, the Maid of Orléans. **RIGHT:** St Bartholomew's Day Massacre, the slaughter of thousands of protestants by royal troops.

Huguenots and Bourbons

As elsewhere in Europe, France was plunged into a period of unrest by the emergence of Protestantism, and the resulting backlash from the Catholic authorities. French Protestants, the Huguenots, won converts particularly in port towns such as Dieppe and La Rochelle. By the time significant Protestant communities emerged in France in the 1550s, the Catholic Counter-Reformation had also gathered speed. France's Wars of Religion were exceptionally savage, with massacre followed by counter-massacre. In 1572, a slaughter of Protestants in Paris left over 5,000 dead, the "St Bartholomew's Day Massacre".

Aristocratic rivalries also played a part, with the Catholic League led by the Duke of Guise.

King Henri III attempted a conciliatory policy towards the Huguenots, against League opposition, and in 1588 he had Guise assassinated in Blois. The following year Henri was murdered by a member of the League.

The heir to the throne was Henri of Navarre, of the house of Bourbon – a Huguenot, and a pragmatist. He agreed to become Catholic to be accepted as King Henri IV, supposedly remarking "Paris is well worth a Mass". In 1598 he issued the Edict of Nantes, granting toleration to Protestants. He set about rebuilding prosperity, and has gone down in history as the best of French kings. He sponsored agricultural projects, and in Paris, which had hated him, he built much-loved features such as the Pont-Neuf and place des Vosges. He and his minister Sully extended the practice of relying on the *noblesse de la robe*, lawyers and middle-class bureaucrats who bought their positions, rather than traditional aristocrats to fill state posts. For a while, it seemed to work.

In the north, Flanders and Artois had a separate experience. With the rest of the Catholic Southern Netherlands they remained loyal to the Spanish crown in its bitter war with the Protestant Dutch. Douai and St-Omer sheltered English Catholics. These conflicts were, however, no barrier to trade, and in the early 17th

Grandes Dames

Kings all over Europe had their infidelities, but France stood out for the prominence given to its royal mistresses. One of the first to attract attention was Agnès Sorel, who gained such influence over Charles VII in the 1440s it was said she was poisoned by his son, the future Louis XI. Most celebrated in the 16th century was Diane de Poitiers. Her style and refinement attracted attention at the court, and in 1531, when she was 32, François I asked her to educate his son Henri, then 12, in good manners. They became lovers while he was still a teenager. He adored her and, after he became King Henri II, consulted her on state business, let her run the royal household and gave her Chenonceau château on the Loire. His wife Catherine de Medici naturally detested her, but even the pope, when sending a gift to the queen, also sent one to Diane. When Henri died suddenly in 1559, Catherine seized Chenonceau for herself.

Under Henri IV, the title *maitresse-en-titre* became semi-official for the chief mistress, with rights and privileges. Madame de Montespan, most prominent of Louis XIV's many mistresses, revelled in the role, though it did not stop her being downgraded when the king's attention moved on; Madame de Pompadour lived cosily at times with Louis XV, and was friendly with his Polish queen Marie Leszczynska. Their out-of-wedlock children were acknowledged, and given titles and lands.

century towns such as Lille and Arras experienced something of a golden age.

Great century

Despite his popularity, Henri IV was assassinated by a Catholic fanatic in 1610. His son, Louis XIII, was only eight, and his mother Marie de Medici

Nowhere was feudalism more complex, or more well rooted, than in its northern French homeland; feudal law intertwined with brute force in a kind of bizarre dance, but never vanished entirely.

acted as regent. A former bishop, Cardinal Richelieu, emerged as the king's chief minister.

Richelieu was a byword in his own lifetime for political cunning and cynicism, the first great modern practitioner of *raison d'état*, reasons of state. His aim was simple: to increase the power of the French state. Internally, this meant expanding the powers of the state machine, and clamping down on aristocratic and Protestant revolts. Externally, he sought to end the Habsburg encirclement of France, which principally involved toppling Spain from its position as principal power in Europe. To achieve this, he was prepared to make alliances with Protestant powers. The Spanish were slowly driven back and French power was extended to areas that had never before been considered French: Richelieu decided France's frontier should be on the Rhine, and so in the 1640s it acquired Lorraine and Alsace, previously held by the Habsburgs or their allies.

These successes initiated France's "great century", *le grand siècle*. Not only was it a great military power, it was the most populous country in Europe, with 20 million people. In the 1630s the first *hôtels particuliers* – classical town mansions – appeared in Paris, while François Mansart developed the Mansard roof, visual keystones of Frenchness to this day.

The Sun King

Richelieu and Louis XIII died within a year of each other, in 1642–3, leaving as king the five-year-old Louis XIV, with government in the hands of Richelieu's protégé Cardinal Mazarin. The wars continued, and by the time Mazarin died in 1661, Spain had effectively been broken as a military power in central Europe. The Spanish-Habsburg encirclement of France, established in the early 1500s, had ended, a development that left France as by far the most powerful state on the continent, and its new king was not slow to exercise its strength.

After Mazarin's death Louis XIV took up personal rule. His experience of rebellion had convinced him of the need for absolute authority. His instrument – without the independence of the great Cardinal-Ministers Richelieu and Mazarin – was Jean-Baptiste Colbert. The system of tax collection was refined, and the supervision of local government by officials called *intendants*, initiated by Richelieu, was institutionalised. The Fronde rebellion (1648–53), in which aristocrats and local *Parlements* attempted to reclaim traditional rights, was the last of France's revolts in defence of feudal privileges. The aristocracy were offered access to huge wealth, so long as they behaved. And the army was made the most professional in Europe.

Colbert promoted economic development, with the aim of making France self-sufficient. State support was given, for example, to lace-

LEFT: Cardinal Richelieu on the sea wall of La Rochelle, during the siege of 1628. **RIGHT:** Louis XIV receives his brother, the Duc d'Anjou.

Vauban and France's Frontier Walls

As Louis XIV established the borders of France, they were marked out with an unmistakeable architectural style

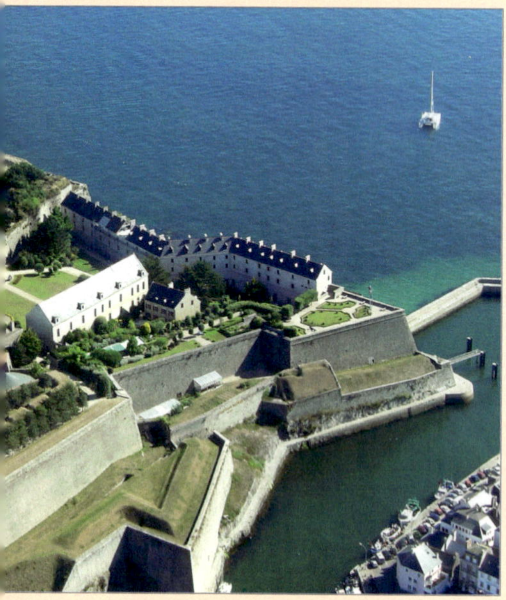

Sébastien Le Prestre de Vauban, Marshal Vauban (1633–1707), is one of the most visible of French architects, if not the most famous – although perhaps the term military engineer is more accurate than architect. He was one of the first of his kind to benefit from a modern technical and scientific training. As *Commissaire Général des Fortifications* for Louis XIV, Vauban built or rebuilt more than 300 fortifications around the edges of France, and though some have been demolished they are still a ubiquitous presence, especially along the northeast and eastern borders and around the coast, from the giant citadels of Lille or Neuf-Brisach in Alsace to isolated coastal *Tours Vauban* such as Ambleteuse near Boulogne or Camaret-sur-Mer near the westernmost point of Brittany.

Vauban began his career not as a builder of fortifications but as an expert in breaking into them, a specialist in sieges. From this he developed his ideas on fortress-building. His services were required because of a peculiarly French dilemma. In the south and southeast, the Pyrenees and the Alps provided clear and easily defended borders. But France was acquiring large territories in the north and east, and a lack of natural frontiers left them wide open to attack. Louis XIV gave Vauban huge resources to ensure they would stay French forever. Later, as the threat of English or Dutch attack from the sea increased, he turned his attention to the coast, including entire ports such as St-Malo.

A Vauban fortress is a far more scientific construction than old-style castles. Many are star-shaped pentagons, with angled bastions to ensure that any attacker would be caught in a crossfire. Among his greatest works is his "queen of citadels" in Lille, part of his *pré carré* or "squared field" of 28 fortresses on the Flanders border, from Dunkerque down to Charleville, built with the idea that any attacker would be trapped between them. He established an entire school of French military engineers, such as Siméon Garangeau, chief architect of St-Malo.

Glowering Vauban fortresses were not the only architectural means by which frontier territories were secured. A clear example is Lille. Before 1667 it had been a Flemish city oriented to the northeast, to the Porte de Gand or Ghent gate. Louis XIV's planners redesigned it to point it southwards, to the Porte de Paris, with a Baroque triumphal arch with an image of the Sun King to celebrate the city's conquest. Everywhere, restrained *ancien régime* Baroque was the prescribed style for new public buildings; together with the Mansard roof, it became an indispensable mark of Frenchness.

Near the end of his life some of Vauban's fortresses were overrun, and some suggested they were a waste of money. Nevertheless, fortress building, and the idea of building solid defences around France, remained – as is seen most vividly in the attempt to seal the German border with the Maginot Line in the 1930s. ❑

LEFT: the Vauban Citadel of Belle-Ile.

ABOVE: architects with a model of a Vauban fortress.

making in Alençon, so France would no longer have to import Italian lace. Overseas expansion was encouraged, and the Quebec colony in distant Canada, founded in 1613, was put on a solid footing. When Colbert discovered that Quebec was overwhelmingly male, a thousand women of child-bearing age, the *filles du roi*, were given royal sponsorship to emigrate. Many French-Canadians living in eastern Canada today are descendants of these "King's daughters".

The wealth created by all this managed to exalt Louis' image as the greatest monarch Europe had ever seen: the "Sun King". Colbert built one of the first Baroque squares in Paris, the place des Victoires, around a statue of the king. Louis XIV, however, disliked Paris since he had fled *Fronde* mobs as a child, and in 1682 he moved his court to his new palace of Versailles, a dazzling theatre of royal power.

War and conquest were also integral to Louis' idea of his own glory. For twenty years his armies seemed invincible, and the French frontiers in the north and east were driven outwards more or less to their current point, to Flanders and the Franche Comté on the Swiss border. The scale of French power, however, both generated and united opposition, from the Dutch, Habsburg Austria and a resurgent England. In later wars from the 1690s to 1713, Louis' armies suffered major defeats.

The extravagance and constant war were ruinously expensive, and the treasury plunged deep into debt. Heavy taxes provoked a widespread peasants' revolt in Brittany in 1675. To make matters worse, after Colbert died in 1683 Louis' decisions were often self-destructive. In 1685 he revoked Henri IV's Edict of Nantes granting toleration to Protestants, which he regarded as an intolerable challenge to royal authority. Many Huguenots – among the economically valuable groups fostered by Colbert – left to settle in Holland and England. By the time Louis XIV died in 1715, France was exhausted.

Ancien régime

Louis XIV outlived his son and grandson, and was succeeded by another five-year-old child, Louis XV. If no longer able to dominate, France's Bourbon monarchs still cut a grand figure in the 18th century. With slightly fewer wars, the economy revived. The court continued to live in extreme luxury: the wealth of the nobility can be seen in the number of Louis XV-style châteaux that dot the French countryside.

This was also, famously, one of France's great eras of intellectual ferment. Enlightenment *philosophes* such as Montesquieu, Voltaire, Diderot and Rousseau examined the institutions of society in the light of reason, and found them wanting. On estates in Normandy, enlightened aristocrats pondered how to improve relations with their peasants.

And yet, the Bourbon state was creaking at

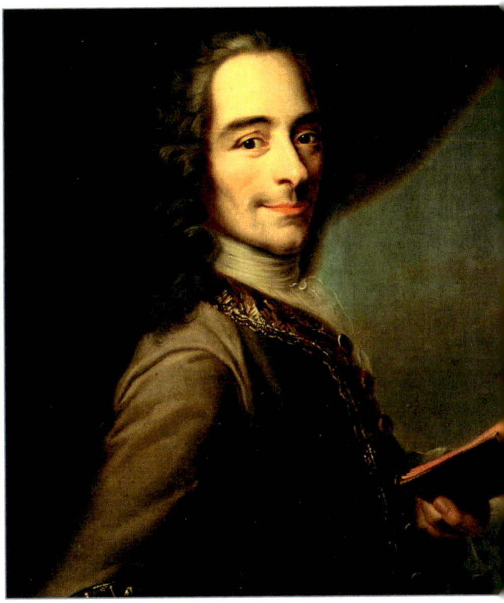

RIGHT: Voltaire, the great Enlightenment writer and philosopher, known for his razor sharp wit.

the seams. The administrative expansion of Richelieu and Colbert had often consisted of refining a feudal system. The main taxes were still the *gabelle* (salt tax) and a tax on peasant land, which bore down disproportionately on the poor. The aristocracy and Church had given up all political power to the Crown, but retained immense privileges, including exemption from taxation. To raise money quickly, "tax farming" was relied on, whereby individuals "bought" the right to collect taxes, keeping back some of the proceeds for themselves. Understandably, this generated intense resentment, while creating so many powerful vested interests that ministers lacked the will, or the nerve, to push through reform.

Internationally, France came into increasing rivalry with Britain in its attempts to gain profitable colonies and extend its global trade. In the 1660s, the ever-active Colbert had founded a new port of Lorient (from "The Orient") in Brittany as a centre for trade with Asia, and several French trading outposts were established in India; ports such as Lorient, Nantes and St-Malo grew richer still by taking full part in the slave trade with France's new Caribbean colonies, bringing back immensely valuable sugar and tobacco. Colonial rivalry culminated in the Seven Years' War (1756–63), which effectively "launched" Britain as a global empire, although its consequences for France were more ambiguous: French expansion in India was halted, France lost its major foothold in North America in Quebec and suffered humiliating defeats, but it retained its Caribbean territories of Guadeloupe, Martinique and St-Domingue (later Haiti). For French ministers these immensely profitable colonies were far more important than Quebec, which, in contrast to the British American colonies, had been regarded as an expensive liability for years.

France under Louis XVI, king from 1774, was not backward: new industries were created, ports were expanded, more people could read. The middle classes and townspeople were also newly patriotic, especially in Paris and the main towns, and increasingly saw royal and aristocratic privilege as holding the country back. The court had become a symbol of decadence.

In the 1780s France had a successful war, supporting the American colonists against Britain (sweet revenge for the defeats of 1756–63), and for a while this enhanced the monarchy's prestige. However, it also reduced its finances to chaos. Financial scandals and agricultural crises followed. In 1789 Louis XVI, desperate, called the Estates-General, which had not met since 1615, to discuss new taxation. When it met, the Third Estate refused to sit in the medieval style (with the aristocracy and church having their own separate assemblies), and called for a single National Assembly. Louis reluctantly agreed. However, Paris was full of rumours of royal plots to crush the Assembly, and on 14 July a mob stormed the Bastille prison.

ROAD BUILDERS

One of the most hated impositions of the *ancien régime* was the *corvée royale*, the obligation on peasants to spend time each year building roads, unpaid. It was established in 1738 by Philibert Orry, Louis XV's finance minister, to give France a network of *routes royales*, many of which are now modern roads. Aristocrats (of course), priests, townspeople and several others were exempt. The *corvée* was administered by parish, and the time demanded varied; six days in some villages, a whole month in others. It was notoriously inefficient, since one village might complete its stretch of road before another had started. It was abolished early in the Revolution, in August 1789.

Revolution and response

The attack on the Bastille unleashed pent-up violence. The end of July saw the "Great Fear", when hungry peasants sacked châteaux in response to rumours of aristocrat conspiracies to confiscate the remaining grain. Paranoia was just as rife in Paris. In October, Parisian women protesting at the price of bread marched on Versailles and forced the royal family to return with them to Paris.

The National Assembly, meanwhile, set about remaking France on an egalitarian, rational and patriotic model, initially as some kind of constitutional monarchy. The Rights of Man were declared. France's historic provinces were divided into purely administrative *Départements*, since in future there was to be only one focus of loyalty, the nation. The church lost virtually all its lands and in 1790 monasteries were closed, their historic buildings often sold off as building stone.

The Assembly's debates on a final constitution dragged on, and were overwhelmed by the atmosphere of violence. In June 1791 Louis XVI and his family tried to flee Paris, and were brought back as prisoners. The belief spread that they were in league with Queen Marie Antoinette's Austrian relatives to crush the Revolution. The following May, France declared war on Austria and Prussia. Foreign invasion brought a new wave of revolutionary fervour, and a part-volunteer army yelling *Vive la Nation!* threw back Prussian regular troops at Valmy in Champagne.

> *The French Revolution discovered an unprecedented weapon,* levée en masse *– the mass conscription of a citizen army, which overwhelmed the smaller mercenary armies of European monarchies.*

The proclamation of a Republic in September 1792 was the natural background to the rise to power of the most radical sector of the Revolution, the Jacobins. Influenced by Arras lawyer Maximilien Robespierre, they denounced moderates as traitors. In the terror of 1793–4, thousands were executed by guillotine and other means, including Revolutionary leaders as well as Louis XVI and Marie Antoinette. Religion was abolished completely, and churches turned into "Temples of Reason".

In Brittany and the Vendée, south of the Loire, Catholic peasants rejected the suppression of the church and conscription into Revolutionary armies, and saw the Republic's representatives as Parisian dictators. They joined local aristocrats in royalists revolts, and Breton guerrillas, the *Chouans*, fought on for years. Fierce Revolutionary repression left around 200,000 dead. One consequence of this still-sensitive episode was a persistent suspicion of all Breton nationalism.

The Great Egoist

In 1794 the Jacobins were finally overthrown. However, the Republic was still at war, and the regime chronically unstable. In 1799 power was seized by its most successful general, Napoleon Bonaparte, as First Consul.

Napoleon artfully combined elements of the Revolution – notably the zealous and patriotic energy of the citizen army, and a cult of science, progress and modernity – with a desire for authority, order and effective government. This was combined with all-new monarchical paraphernalia after he made himself Emperor in 1804. In the interests of order he came to an agreement with the church. With incredible energy he set about reforming every institution he could find, from the legal system (the *Code Napoléon*) to the implantation of metric measurements. In France he was initially popular, in part because his grand-scale building schemes – for example the the *quais* along the Seine in Paris, and the completion of the port of Cherbourg – provided a great deal of employment.

He was, above all, a great general. From 1796 to 1808 Napoleon was virtually unbeatable on land, even though his navy was beaten by Britain. Then he over-extended himself in Spain and Russia. France too was exhausted, and by 1813 peasants across France took to the woods to avoid conscription. Many were happy to see his final departure in 1815, but the Napoleonic dream has haunted France ever since. ❑

LEFT: the execution by guillotine of Louis XVI, 1793.
RIGHT: *Napoleon in his Study,* by Jacques Louis David, 1812.

DE
LA
PEINE
DU

MODERN TIMES

After the upheavals of the revolution, France found its way into modernity, while striving doggedly to stay true to itself and its ideals

With the fall of Napoleon, and at the behest of the victorious European powers which had defeated him at Waterloo, the Bourbon monarchy returned to rule France. But nothing could be the same again. The new king, Louis XVIII (Louis XVI's brother), issued a limited constitution that was supposed to bring national reconciliation, but the question of the extent of democracy would be a source of political instability for decades.

Despite the royalists' return, post-Revolution Paris was the political laboratory of Europe, its foremost generator of radical ideas, with an effervescent, unruly working population. French fashions and art had been hugely influential since the time of Louis XIV. The Revolution and Romanticism added the idea that new art should be ground-breaking, and Paris quickly became a magnet for anyone interested in artistic innovation.

Away from Paris there were different worlds. The capital dwarfed every other town in France, with 800,000 people in 1831, when Rouen, next-largest city in the north, had only 88,000. One feature of 19th-century France was its slowness in joining the industrial revolution, the consequences of which can be seen in the prevalence of small towns rather than cities in most of the country. Industrialisation only took root on a large scale in the northeast, where Lille and its surrounding towns built on long-standing textile traditions to become centres of cotton, wool and linen industries. A major coalfield was discovered to the south, from Valenciennes to Lens, and another industrial hub developed in Lorraine, with coal mines and steel works.

LEFT: Lamartine proclaims the founding of the Second Republic, 1848. **RIGHT:** Sunday at the Tuileries, depicted in a 19th-century print.

Other areas, especially in Normandy, the Loire and Brittany, remained deeply rural, separated from the restless capital by long, bumpy roads. Country people were grateful for the Revolution's removal of feudal impositions and other hard-won gains, such as the beloved right to hunt and rights to their land, but once this was achieved many settled back into a conservative way of life, suspicious of Parisian novelties. In many places aristocratic life re-established itself, when families returned from exile in 1815 to buy back their châteaux, or sometimes, notably in Brittany, to find the local commune waiting respectfully to return the keys.

Revolution, again...

Politically, the Bourbon Restoration tried to come to terms with the passions unleashed by the Revolution, but only in a very restricted form; the "Charter" or Constitution established a Chamber of Deputies that was elected only by men aged over 30 owning large amounts of property. Charles X, youngest brother of Louis XVI and king from 1824, tried to rein in elements of the restoration constitution, and was toppled by a fresh revolution in July 1830. His replacement, King Louis-Philippe of the Bourbons' Orléans branch, set out to be a constitutional monarch, but still with an electorate restricted to only about 500,000 male voters out of a total population of around 33 million. In the 1840s his governments encouraged France's first burst of railway-building. However, acute economic crisis led to demands for radical change, and crowds and barricades appeared again in Paris streets. Louis-Philippe abdicated in February 1848, and a Second Republic was declared.

The leaders of the 1848 Revolution, Romantic idealists such as the poet Lamartine, had little idea of the gulf between Paris and the provinces. They introduced universal male suffrage, and outside Paris the new electorate voted for an Assembly of conservatives, calling for a restoration of order.

Liberty, Equality, Fraternity (Men only)

One peculiarity of French Republics (First, Second and Third) was their long-standing reluctance to give voting rights to women. In 1791 the early feminist Olympe de Gouges had answered the *Declaration of the Rights of Man* with her *Declaration of the Rights of Women* and the Female Citizen, but she was sent to the guillotine by the Jacobins. When the Second Republic proclaimed universal male suffrage in 1848, a campaign to extend it to women did not amount to much.

Resistance hardened further during the Third Republic, when Republicans saw Catholicism as the great enemy of progress and democracy. Far more women than men, it was known, went to church, to be filled with reactionary propaganda. This could be personal, as there were many stories of Republican politicians whose wives still went to Mass. Women, the stereotype went, were "under the thumb of the priests" – especially in the countryside – and could not be trusted to make rational decisions.

A law giving votes to women was proposed, as in many countries, after World War I, but was blocked by the Senate, where Senator Alexandre Bérard declared that it would "seal the tombstone of the Republic". The polarisation of French politics did not help either: the right were equally opposed, and the Communist left treated it as a side issue. In the end it took the cataclysm of World War II to bring about the change, with French women voting for the first time in 1945.

The Republic was to have a single president, and in December voters elected Louis Napoleon Bonaparte, nephew of the great Napoleon. In Bonapartist style he made himself president for life in 1851, and a year later Emperor Napoleon III (Napoleon I's son having been, for Bonapartists, Napoleon II for a few weeks in 1814).

...and empire

Trading, naturally, on the family name, Napoleon III deployed the Bonapartist combination of inclusive patriotism with authority, meritocracy and monarchy. He could satisfy the respectable classes' desire for order while offering benefits to working people, notably the emerging labour unions.

His greatest success was in promoting modernisation, his foremost legacy the transformation of Paris carried out by Baron Haussmann from 1853. Broad boulevards were cut through medieval *quartiers*, parks opened, and the capital given the characteristic appearance so familiar today.

Yet Napoleon III lacked his uncle's energy, and was more obviously pleasure-loving. His own neo-Gothic château at Pierrefonds and the voluptuous Paris Opera ideally represent the Second Empire's extravagant style. For years, France didn't seem to care, since it also appeared to be doing well. Railways allowed the burgeoning middle classes of Paris and cities like Rouen and Le Havre to enjoy new pleasures, such as the newly discovered seaside at Trouville.

In the interests of national – and Napoleon's own – esteem, the Second Empire demanded an active foreign policy. This, however, brought problems. The stategy appeared successful in the wars that united Italy, but the bizarre attempt to make the Austrian Archduke Maximilian Emperor of Mexico was an expensive fiasco. Then in 1870, Napoleon was outfoxed by the wily Prussian Chancellor Bismarck, who manipulated a minor dispute in such a way that France was compelled to declare war (Bismarck knew that anti-French feeling would then get other German states to agree to his goal of German unification in the face of the French threat).

Contrary to all Napoleonic expectations, the French were crushed, and Napoleon III himself taken prisoner at Sedan. A "Government of National Defence" declared a Third Republic and continued resistance. Paris was besieged through the winter of 1870–71, while its people ate anything they could find, including the animals in the zoo. Eventually the new government accepted the inevitable and sued for peace. In a premonition of later events, France lost Alsace and eastern Lorraine to the new Germany.

The defeat also brought civil war, with the last 19th-century Parisian revolution and the culmination of the animosity between radical Paris and the conservative provinces. Hurried elections produced a conservative National Assembly that, fearing the atmosphere in Paris, moved to Versailles. The National Guard (or citizens' militia) of Paris rejected the peace terms and refused to disarm, taking over the city in March 1871 and forming the revolutionary Paris Commune. After two months *Versaillais* troops, many of peasant origin, fought their way in and took savage reprisals on the *Communards*, killing around 20,000 people.

> *Even in the 1880s, when artists such as Sérusier and Gauguin wanted to find a simple world away from modernity, they had to go no further than Pont Aven in Brittany, with its women in traditional dress.*

LEFT: the Duchess of Orleans' claims for regency rejected in the French parliament, February 1848. **RIGHT:** massacre of *communards*, 1871.

Beautiful hindsight

France was humiliated and in shock. The loss of Alsace-Lorraine was a deep wound, added to which were the deep resentments left by the bloody ending of the Commune.

The Third Republic was not expected to last long. Most of the Assembly wanted another monarchy, but having two candidates (Bourbon and the heirs of Louis-Philippe) made agreement difficult, and in the end the Republic struggled on until 1940. Its politics were polarised and embittered. Governments were unstable coalitions of small parties. A French peculiarity was that divisions between right and left were rarely based on any notion of socialism, but between a right obsessed with Catholicism as a pillar of an orderly society and a left devoted to the sacred principles of 1789. Socialist movements did gather strength, particularly in the northern factories and coalfields, but had to cooperate with Republicans.

Republicans believed in education for all citizens, and in 1881–2 the minister Jules Ferry introduced the laws that carry his name, establishing free, secular, public education. The ferocious argument over the role of the Catholic Church in public education culminated in the 1900s with a Republican, secular victory, a position still reflected in the recent ban on Muslim girls wearing headscarves (as "religious symbols") in French schools. Republicans were also concerned over language as a source of division, ever since it had been discovered at the time of the Revolution that under half of French people actually spoke French. The Third Republic's schools stamped down rigidly on regional languages such as Breton and Flemish, and set out to teach everyone correct French.

> *The buildings of the Belle Epoque, from lavish Art Nouveau Parisian brasseries to local train stations and mairies, still form the essential landscape of many parts of France today.*

The divisiveness of French politics reached a peak with the Dreyfus case. The Catholic right was increasingly anti-Semitic, and in 1894 Captain Alfred Dreyfus, a Jewish army officer, was accused of spying for Germany and imprisoned on Devil's Island. It soon emerged there was only the flimsiest evidence against him; right and left lined up over whether the case should be reopened, in an *affaire* that obsessed France until the captain was pardoned in 1906.

And yet, these years would be remembered as an era of great well being. The economy expanded rapidly. France became a major imperial power, with vast territories in Africa and a significant presence in Southeast Asia. The middle classes had money to spare, and expansive villas proliferated around coastal resorts. The image of Paris as the *Ville Lumière*, the City of Light, the international benchmark for fashion, fine food, art, pleasure, novelty and all the finer things in life, has never shone brighter than between the 1889 Paris exhibition, which produced the Eiffel Tower, and 1914. In the 1920s, after the catastrophe of World War I, the term Belle Epoque would be coined for this "beautiful era", a lost time of *joie de vivre* and innocent confidence.

The catastrophe of war

France had been a full contributor to the antagonisms that led to World War I, with the many calls for *revanche* (revenge) for 1870 and the recovery of Alsace-Lorraine. The conflict, however, left 1,300,000 French dead, and another 3,000,000 wounded. France emerged as a victor, but with the sensation it had done so by the skin of its teeth.

Alsace-Lorraine returned to France after

being German for 47 years. French was reintroduced, with an intensive campaign to remove German and Alsatian dialect from schools and the press. France demanded Germany pay for its reconstruction in the Versailles peace treaty, but Germany had problems of its own, and the French eventually had to accept lower payments, especially when the Great Depression struck after 1929. Industrial unemployment rose rapidly from 1932.

The war's psychological legacy was more diffuse. In the 1920s Paris released its tension in the hedonism of the Jazz Age, while art movements like Dada explored the newly disjointed world. Elsewhere, collective depression was more patent. Social and political conflicts revealed deep mutual antagonisms. Extreme right-wing groups grew, and were even more anti-Semitic than in the Dreyfus era. On the left, Communists led large-scale strikes. In 1936 France elected a Popular Front government of Socialists and Republicans, with Communist support, led by the Socialist Léon Blum. It introduced social reforms such as paid holidays and the right to strike that have become national institutions, but fell apart after a year.

The army, baying for blood in 1914, was now one of the most pessimistic sectors of all.

All these divisions contributed to the fall of France to Hitler's Germany in 1940. Once it had surrendered, the extreme right were the closest supporters of the regime set up by Marshal Pétain, and true to their traditions began persecuting Jews even before the Nazis asked them to. Though based at Vichy in the unoccupied south, the Pétain regime was also responsible for civil administration in the north, which was occupied by German troops. For some time the regime also had at least the acquiescence of many who saw little alternative, for few saw much hope in the call for continued resistance issued by an obscure general, Charles De Gaulle, from London in June 1940.

The experience of the occupation was painful and complex, and collaboration could take many different forms. Resistance involved huge risks and began sporadically, gaining pace particularly after the Communists became involved when Hitler invaded the Soviet Union in 1941. De Gaulle's belligerently independent attitude, which infuriated his allies, was part of a deliberate attempt to create a new mythology, of a resistant, patriotic France that took charge to a large extent of its own liberation. In this he was remarkably successful, backed by the sacrifices made by *résistants* and ordinary French people.

LEFT: Jewish army officer, Alfred Dreyfus, protagonist in the Dreyfus Affair that gripped France for a decade. **ABOVE:** fighting in the trenches near Arras, 1918.

A new France: 1945 to 1968

Following the end of the war, French cities were in ruins, and political reconstruction was also needed. De Gaulle withdrew from politics in 1946. The Fourth Republic was actually similar to the Third, with weak, revolving-door governments, but was far more successful in its economic management. France's planning commission, led by Jean Monnet, showed great imagination, laying the basis for reconstruction and proposing that future progress should be on the basis of European integration, the germ of the future European Union. A welfare state was created. Middle-class living standards began to rise

rapidly, and culture was vibrant, from writers such as Sartre and Camus to the first New Wave cinema or the international cult of Brigitte Bardot.

The Fourth Republic's downfall was its indecision on France's decaying empire. It tried to hold onto Indochina, but ignominiously failed. When a nationalist revolt began in Algeria, government's attempts to negotiate were flatly rejected by French Algerian settlers and their sympathisers in the army command. A military coup seemed possible. The only solution was to ask De Gaulle to return and take control, in 1958. He arrived as the settlers' friend, but once he realised holding on to Algeria was impossible he outmanoeuvred them and their army supporters and gave Algeria independence.

In October 1958 De Gaulle introduced the constitution of the Fifth Republic. It had a Bonapartist feel; a directly elected president would be the centre of government, with extensive powers to overrule the National Assembly. His great aim was to restore the "grandeur" of France, underlying his ever-independent anti-American foreign policy. Internally, education and other institutions maintained a traditionally authoritarian style.

In May 1968, a series of strikes in Paris universities led – after the police reacted with excessive violence – to an anarchistic student uprising, and then to 10 million workers coming out on strike in sympathy and making their own demands. De Gaulle was caught out. He appealed to the nation for support, and large counter-demonstrations were held, a replay of the many occasions when provincial France had shown its dislike of unrest by Parisian sophisticates. The revolt died out, but in 1969 De Gaulle lost a referendum on constitutional reforms and retired, dying a year later.

From the mid-1950s, France's middle classes got a first taste of the move to affluence that would spread across Europe in the next 20 years, with holidays, cars, villas by the sea and other essentials.

Modernity, maybe

Although conservative governments continued to be elected through the 1970s, May 1968 did mark a watershed, a French equivalent of what elsewhere was just called the '60s. France became a more open society. Elitism at the top levels didn't change that much, but other areas – social care, authority within institutions, sexuality – were open to discussion and change. One major change was the opening up of opportunities to women. Over the years formerly taboo subjects in national life, such as the fate of French Jews under occupation, have also been opened up.

France's first Socialist president, François Mitterrand, elected in 1981, established regional governments, anathema to Republicans since 1789, a loosening of centralism that has proved effective in stimulating local economies. This in part responded to a revival in local cultures and

LEFT: General Charles de Gaulle addressing the crowds at Strasbourg, 1947. **RIGHT:** France's first lady, Carla Bruni, with President Sarkozy.

languages, especially in Brittany, that had been growing since the 1960s. Mitterrand was also famed for his *grands projets*, giant infrastructure schemes with added grandeur. Most famous are his *projets* in Paris, such as the Louvre renovation, but his government also collaborated in a transformation of the Lille area, in deep depression since the decline of its old textile and coal industries in the 1970s, into a modern services hub and fashion centre. In the Mitterrand era France felt itself at the forefront of modernity, with ground-breaking schemes such as the first TGV high-speed rail lines.

One of the most visible changes in France since 1945 is immigration, particularly from North Africa and former French African colonies like Senegal. The social impact of immigration has been significantly moulded by the tendency for non-white communities to be isolated in *banlieue* suburbs. French attitudes to immigrants (and their second- or third-generation descendants), especially Muslims, head in different directions. North African music is an integral part of French youth culture, and statistics show a high rate of inter-marriage between indigenous French people and Algerians in particular, but non-whites complain of persistent racism, and groups like the National Front have a limited but solid basis of support.

Part of France feels deep disquiet at the supposed threat of "Islamisation", as reflected in recent measures taken against the wearing of Muslim headscarves or full veils by women. At the same time, France's Jewish community complains of high levels of anti-Semitism, coming mainly from Muslims.

For some time France as a whole – at least, as expressed in media comment – has been defensive about the future. Modernity seems to offer threats as much as possibilities, and there are strong concerns about the watering down of French values and identity by the European Union. Labour unions are particularly keen on state protection for hard-won benefits. Since 2000, civil servants and those working for large companies have enjoyed a 35-hour week, intended to reduce unemployment. Those who work for themselves – restaurant owners, shopkeepers, farmers, essential elements of *la vie française* – find that this simply increases their costs, and feel disheartened about the prospects of carrying on in the face of supermarket conglomerates and other modern globalised giants.

President Nicolas Sarkozy, elected in 2007, is typically contradictory, promising to liberalise the economy, but praising the protection offered by traditional French ways when the global economic crisis blew up. Someone once said that the French like to be intellectually radical and socially conservative, a classic French paradox. ❑

THE LANDSCAPES AND WILDLIFE OF NORTHERN FRANCE

An enormous breadth of countryside, from plain to peak, is inhabited by a prodigious variety of wildlife, sometimes closer to you than you think

If France is a hexagon, as it is often described, then northern France can be neatly defined by a line drawn across it obliquely from lower left to upper right across the top of the Massif Central. Below the line, southern France is conspicuously mountainous; above it the north consists predominantly of plains and gentle river valleys.

The lie of the land

In the northwest, Normandy and Brittany have ranges of inland hills but nowhere does the altitude exceed 400m (1,300ft), while along the Belgian and Luxembourg borders in the northeast the wooded Ardennes rise to 504m (1,654ft). The pattern of lowland is only broken by the Vosges in Alsace (1,424m/4,672ft) and the Jura on the Swiss borders of Franche-Comté (1,720m/5,643ft).

This marked absence of serious relief makes travelling easy. Northern France is crisscrossed by a dense grid of roads, motorways and high-speed rail lines. These, of course, are recent additions to the landscape. Historically, the simplest way to get around was to go with the flow of the many rivers which were connected up between the 16th and 19th centuries by an ingenious system of canals. France's two longest rivers, the Loire and the Seine and their respective tributaries, give distinctive shape to the topography. Other major rivers, generally wide and slow-moving, are the Meuse, Moselle, Marne, Saone, Doubs and the Rhine, which skirts past Alsace.

The coasts, with their beaches, headlands, cliffs, islands and seaports large and small historically dependent on fishing and Atlantic seafaring, are almost a world unto themselves, particularly along the peninsula of Brittany.

Inland, the north is a busy interconnected landscape. The ease of communications, coupled with the proximity of other countries – Belgium, Holland, Germany, Switzerland – has always made northern France a place of trade and this has encouraged a greater density of population than in the mountainous south.

Geology has reinforced man's presence: the coal and iron ore deposits of Nord and Lorraine ensured that these regions became the country's industrial heartlands in the 19th century – only to be dismantled in recent decades.

PRECEDING PAGES: the Vosges mountains.
LEFT: Brittany sunset. **RIGHT:** Loire Valley sunflowers.

Urban and rural

Paris is by far the largest city, with Nantes, Strasbourg and Lille the only other conurbations. Other sizeable cities – Amiens, Angers, Besançon, Brest, Caen, Dijon, Le Havre, Le Mans, Metz, Orléans, Reims, Rennes, Rouen and Tours – are all small by European standards. Although more populous than the south of the country, the average density of population in northern France is rather low: just over 100 people per square kilometre (260 per square mile), which attests to a land largely organised around towns and villages.

Although the urban area is eating the countryside at a voracious rate, it is still easy to find some corner where silence lingers and there are no street lights to disturb a perfect view of the stars. There is also a seemingly endless choice of backroads to cycle down and footpaths suitable for a short walk or a marathon hike.

Agriculture in northern France

It is this vision of "perfect countryside" that attracts many people to France, and farming is a perennially important part of the picture. Although agriculture has declined since World War II and now only employs only about 3 percent of the country's workforce, some 35 percent of the land surface of France is divided into 545,000 farms. French cereals, wine, sugar beet, maize and sunflowers ensure that this is still Europe's leading agricultural producer and exporter.

There are essentially three distinct types of farmed landscape. On the plains and in the wide valleys, farms are large and fields open with few features to relieve the eye, although often broken up by large patches of woodland. Villages are functional: compactly arranged around a church or in a line, hugging a main road.

> *Nantes (city population 280,000) is the second-largest city in northern France but, oddly enough, only ranks sixth in the country as a whole – with the southern centres of Marseille, Lyon, Toulouse and Nice comfortably ahead. (If the entire urban area is included, Lille is much larger.)*

A more varied landscape is *bocage*, most in evidence across Normandy, in which a patchwork of small fields is divided up by hedges and small woods. Villages in *bocage* country are small clusters of dispersed houses, sometimes with thatched roofs. In the wetter western regions, many of the fields are used for grazing cows to produce some of France's most famous cheeses, including camembert.

The third type of agricultural landscape is the vineyard. The cultivation of the vine has an almost mystical significance to the French and great energy is expended in discussing and studying the value of this or that *terroir*: a particular combination of soil, microclimate and local grape variety that together produce a great wine. There are vineyards in every region of northern France except Brittany and Normandy (which has cider apple orchards instead) – albeit just a few in Picardy, Flanders and Nord. In the famous vineyards of Champagne, the vine reaches its most northerly extent.

French farmers are famously believed to live easy lives, financed by generous subsidies under the Common Agricultural Policy. But in truth, many of them struggle to make a living from land of marginal profitability. For many, farming is almost an ancestral duty which they undertake in order not to part with a family

LEFT: Normandy's climate and landscape is ideal for dairy farming. **RIGHT:** harvesting potatoes in Flanders. **FAR RIGHT:** vineyards in Burgundy.

plot. Part-time farming is an increasingly common phenomenon and many farmers supplement their variable incomes with some other form of employment, or by taking in paying guests for bed and breakfast.

Preserving tradition

The "survival" of the countryside of France – and hence the survival of the traditional rural crafts that contribute to the uniqueness of French cuisine – is always a hot political topic, but one way it is kept alive is by the peculiar organisation of local government. France is divided into 36,500 communes, varying in size from Paris (population over 2 million) to seven villages of the Meuse *département* which have been left uninhabited since World War I. Each commune has a mayor, a team of local councillors and a budget. While there are many valid criticisms of the commune system, one advantage is that it upholds a sense of local pride, which ensures that villages and their monuments are maintained.

French forests

Where there isn't either habitation or farm, there are trees, almost always planted rather than ancient and wild, although there are a few

REGIONS, DÉPARTEMENTS, PROVINCES, PAYS AND TERROIRS

Northern France is composed of 13 of France's 22 mainland regions: Nord-Pas-de-Calais, Picardy (Picardie), Champagne-Ardenne, Lorraine, Alsace, Lower and Upper Normandy (Haute and Basse Normandie), Ile de France (which includes Paris), Burgundy (Bourgogne), Franche-Comté, Brittany (Bretagne), Pays de la Loire and Centre. Each region is subdivided into *départments*, usually named after a geographical feature such as a river and identified by a number, further divided into thousands of communes. To make things more confusing, the map is superimposed on a pre-existing geography of duchies, provinces, *pays* and *terroirs* such at the Artois, Flanders, Anjou, Berry and Touraine: territorial units without precise boundaries which hark back to pre-Revolutionary days.

A *pays* is a swathe of country in which the food, architecture and traditions form part of a shared heritage as perceived by the inhabitants. The word *terroir*, meanwhile, is often used in association with foods and wines to denote an area of common agricultural production. It emphasises the locality and unique identity of dishes and their ingredients.

The result of all this overlapping geography can be confusing. The name "Loire Valley", for example, can be used to refer to at least three areas of differing definition: a geographical feature of greater or lesser extent depending on the context; a wine region composed of a myriad of scattered vineyards; and a tourist destination which crosses two official regions and several *départements*.

venerable old specimens here and there by the wayside. France is a thickly wooded country and the north has its fair share of sizeable forests – some of them old royal hunting grounds. Two-thirds of the trees are deciduous, with oak, chestnut and beech much in evidence. Plane trees, meanwhile, line the roads or else cast shade over village squares. The forests are not only attractive; in the past they provided the vital material for the north's characteristic vernacular building, the half-timbered house. Until recent times, logging and woodworking were particularly important to the economy of the Vosges. And many serve as sources of firewood: trees that need to be felled (for example after storm damage) go to providing timber for sawmills, or are chopped into logs and sold as firewood to the local inhabitants. And these stretches of woodland also harbour wildlife.

Wildlife

Although the landscape is largely managed by people, there is an abundance of wildlife to be seen in the north of France. The region is full of pockets of very deep, old countryside, comparable ecologically with southern England but less spoilt, and there are always interesting plants, animals and habitats if you know where to look.

There are no national parks in the north of France (there are 6 in the south) but there are nature reserves of other kinds, some run by local councils, others private. Most in evidence are the 21 *parcs naturels regionaux* (PNR, regional nature parks) which cover particular areas of the countryside with the aim of protecting not just the wildlife within their boundaries, but also traditional forms of human life by applying a policy of sustainable development. These *parcs* usually have visitor centres providing information about the local flora and fauna, marked footpaths and a programme of organised nature trips. In addition, there are numerous smaller-scale *reserves naturelles nationaux* and *reserves naturelles regionaux* across the region.

Parcs naturels regionaux vary in level of interest for the nature-lover but some have exceptional character. The PNR d'Amorique in Finisterre, at the extreme western tip of Brittany, is visited by the storm petrel, and dolphins and grey seals can be seen off its shores. PNR Caps Marais d'Opale in Nord Pas de Calais is also good for seabird spotting as well as maritime flora. The PNR de la Brenne (south of Loches) is an extensive wetland area sheltering the rare European terrapin plus black terns, purple herons and agile tree frogs. The PNR de la Forêt d'Orient in Champagne has at its heart three reservoirs, a stopover for ospreys and black storks. Common cranes are another visitor here. In spring and autumn they can be seen flying overhead in

V-formations noisily calling to each other. Fire salamanders and palmate newts can be seen in the numerous streams. The PNR Somme Estuary is notable for wintering birds. The PNR Ballons des Vosges protects France's limestone grasslands and woods of PNR Haut-Jura are a

Northern France is a windy place and 2,000 MW-worth of windfarms are installed on its blustery coasts and hilltops. There are plans to install more turbines offshore to meet the government's ambitious targets for renewable energy.

sanctuary for one of France's "superpredator" species, the lynx.

But you don't have to seek out nature reserves to see wildlife. Anywhere in northern France will yield rewards if you keep your eyes open and preferably go armed with a pair of binoculars and a field guide or two. On the other hand, a deer may break cover right in front of you out of a field of maize and dart across the footpath you are following. On quiet country roads near woodland at dawn and dusk, you have to be alert to the possibility of colliding with a wild boar. It's the chance of such impromptu encounters that makes a trip into the countryside of northern France such a delight.

With their extreme tides, the varied coasts of Brittany, Normandy and the Vendée, together with their offshore islands, are good places to watch seabirds and peer into rock pools. Sit by a river and you'll see dragonflies and maybe a kingfisher too. Chalk hills are often dotted with orchids. The eastern mountains are good for subalpine plants, while in open country birds of prey, especially buzzards, are relatively common. Almost everywhere, even in city gardens, there is a variety of beetles, butterflies and other insects crawling on the ground or on the wing in the warmer months.

Walking in northern France

With a well-marked network of footpaths threading their way across the expansive countryside, northern France is well suited to exploration on foot. Any local tourist office will provide ideas for short or long walks of varying degrees of interest and difficulty.

There are three kinds of marked footpath:

1) **Grande Randonnée** (GR). Classic, long-distance paths marked with red and white blazes painted on rocks, trees and other wayside landmarks. Even the shortest take several days to walk. They link up villages providing food and accommodation. Classic routes include the GR3 which follows the Loire River; the GR5 running down eastern France from Luxembourg to Provence; the GR11 circling Paris around the Ile de France and the GR34 which skirts the coast of Brittany.

2) **Grande Randonnée de Pays** (GRP). Long-distance footpaths confined to a region and designed to be walked in stages. Marked by yellow and red blazes.

3) **Shorter Footpaths.** Marked in yellow, these are often classified as **Promenade et Randonnée** (PR). Some paths lead around historic towns or their outskirts, or around nature reserves.

Whether you go for a short stroll or a lengthy ramble, it's wise to take common-sense precautions. Wear sensible footwear, plan your route, let someone know where you are going and go equipped with a good map – the best all-round ones are IGN TOP 100s (1:100 000), but even better are the 1: 50 000 and 1: 25 000 series. ❑

LEFT: wild boar in the Fôret de Rambouillet.
RIGHT: long-distance trails, or *Grandes Randonnées*, indicated by red-and-white striped signs, are well maintained and easy to follow.

Cerises
2,50 €
barq. 500
AISACE.

THE FOOD AND DRINK OF NORTHERN FRANCE

France's dedication to its food has produced an extraordinary, wonderfully enjoyable variety

It is stating the obvious to say that the French care about their food, and that exploring its cuisine is one of the great pleasures of any visit to France. The very word *restaurant* is French, invented in Paris in the 1760s. Eating is still generally given far more time and attention than in most English-speaking countries, and one of the core elements of French life has been the depth of its *culture gastronomique*, the interest in, knowledge of and concern for good food across the country. When French people themselves visit other parts of their country, trying out the local specialities is always a priority.

Among the great strengths of good French cooking are its enormous variety, and that, without losing sight of basic essentials, like the need for fresh ingredients, it places a high premium on individual creativity and inventiveness, so that traditional dishes are reinvented, personalised and subtly altered. Tradition combines with flexibility, and dishes can run from earthily simple to highly refined even in apparently out-of-the-way places. The charge is now laid that restaurant cooking is in something of a crisis, due to the economic pressures on small businesses – most local restaurants are family-run – and the spread of industrialised and fast food *(see page 65)*. This is a complex issue, and often crudely simplified, but if there is now more production-line food in France, this means the skills and approach of restaurants that keep up their standards are to be treasured even more.

The basis of quality in traditional French cooking is an immense sense of craft, a willingness to take trouble, and the paramount importance given to fresh, seasonal ingredients.

LEFT: Alsace cherries make top-quality kirsch brandy.
RIGHT: a brasserie in Burgundy.

If the French largely invented the restaurant, they also set out the way a proper one is run. For decades French *haute cuisine*, invented in the grand restaurants and hotels of Paris, was considered the only respectable cuisine in most of the Western world. In provincial France it was emulated by *restaurants bourgeois* with plush curtaining, similarly formal service and elaborate dishes on the Parisian model. However, a hallmark of French cuisine, as well as the blend of classic dishes and creativity, has been the interplay between highly professionalised restaurant cooking and traditional country dishes.

Added to this is the concern for *terroir*, an obsession in modern French cooking. *Terroir* means earth, or rather that of a particular place or region, with the implication that each *terroir* has its special characteristics and is best suited to producing particular foods. Associated with attention to *terroir* is a focus on using only the finest quality, freshest ingredients, following the seasons and using only those that are locally sourced. Another aspect of *terroir* is the re-evaluation of local dishes, which displace old cui-

sine classics on many menus. With the freshness suggested by the *terroir* there is often a more relaxed style than in the *bourgeois* archetype.

France has also shown itself particularly open to international cuisines. North African food – couscous, tagines, merguez sausages – is almost as French as any other, and in any medium-sized town there are Chinese, Vietnamese and other non-French options.

Places to eat

Eating places in France, as everywhere, come in several different kinds. Some of their labels are quite vague, but others, thanks to the French habit of classification, are precise. One point to be clear on, to avoid disappointment, is **when** to eat. Keeping proper times is part of traditional French dining culture. In rural areas and small towns, especially, anywhere called a restaurant will probably expect to take orders for lunch on weekdays around 12.30–1.30pm, and for dinner from 8–9pm, with a bit more flexibility for Sunday lunch. This does not mean you have to rush your meal, for once you've ordered you can stay as long as you like. Many restaurants are also closed on Sunday evenings and all day Monday. In cities and coastal resorts restaurant hours are more flexible, but don't expect good French restaurants to be open much before 7.30pm in the evenings.

It's a good idea to book restaurants at weekends, and upscale restaurants at any time. Nearly all French restaurants offer a range of set-price menus, which provide the most economical (and usual) way to order; ordering *à la carte* will be much more expensive. Bargain menus are often called a *formule*, while finer restaurants generally offer an expensive *menu gourmand* or *dégustation*, where they show what they can do.

The traditional flexible alternative to restaurants is the **brasserie**, originated by Alsatians

ABOVE: city bistros and brasseries stay open until the small hours. **RIGHT:** the neighbourhood café is still an intrinsic part of French life. **FAR RIGHT:** summer festivals often involve alfresco feasts.

who moved to Paris rather than stay under German rule in the 1870s. With a less formal style, and often doubling as cafés, a proper city brasserie offers a huge menu with everything from snacks and single dishes to a four-course feast, specialities being steaks and *frites*, salads and a big choice of fish and seafood. Brasseries in cities and seaside resorts in season also offer service *à toute heure*, at all hours, or at least all day and late at night.

A **bistro** is not really a specific type of restaurant but just suggests a more relaxed, neighbourhood place, often with more variable hours.

Now fashionable in towns are **salons de thé**, which as well as tea (and usually alcohol) serve light lunch menus with such things as quiches and mixed salads. Other options for a lighter meal (loved by children) are **crêperies**, offering savoury *galettes* and sweet *crêpes*. They are everywhere in Brittany, and there is at least one in most French towns. Neither *salons de thé* nor *crêperies* tend to be open much after 7pm.

In the countryside, **auberges du terroir** are country inns that serve only local dishes made with local produce; **ferme-auberges** are farms that serve home-cooked meals made entirely with their own produce. It is essential to book

TERRE DU MCDO

It may challenge every stereotype, but the fact is undeniable: France is the second-most profitable territory in the world for McDonald's hamburgers (or *McDo*, in French slang), after the USA. In a country that has made appreciation of good food and taking time for a proper meal correctly served anchors of national identity, data like this produces a kind of vertigo among some commentators in France's slightly schizophrenic meditations over where it stands between traditional habits and globalisation, often taken to mean Americanisation.

There are other fast-food outlets too, like the Quick chain (part-owned by the French state) and places selling kebabs, falafel, merguez and so on. They are part of a modern France of highways and hypermarkets, cheap and less staid for a younger public than conventional restaurants. At the same time, many traditional restaurants complain of how hard it is to keep going nowadays in the face of regulations and taxes, part of the ongoing problems of all France's small family businesses. Some writers pick up on the discovery of run-down local restaurants as evidence that French culinary culture is definitively on the slide. Reports of its demise, though, are exaggerated. Even many *McDo*'s regulars eat out "properly" a few times a month, and French restaurants can adapt to change, too, and become less formal. The dedication to quality and craft that is the basis of good French dining is deep-rooted, and still not too hard to find.

at both. The pub-like **estaminets** are specific to Flanders, while Alsace has its timber-lined **winstubs** for sampling local wines with stout Germanic fare.

Terroirs: North and East

In Paris one can find food from all over the world, and every kind of French cuisine, from the most traditional to the most experimental. Elsewhere, *terroir* reasserts itself. Traditionalist French gourmets have tended to see a hierarchy in French regional cuisines, with Paris and Lyon at the top. One region they have often unjustly disregarded is the Nord-Pas-de-Calais.

The food of the **Pas-de-Calais** and **Artois** is distinctly northern, with fine use of vegetables such as leeks and shallots, but also often subtle, taking advantage of excellent local fish and seafood. The region makes punchily strong cheeses such as Maroilles and Rollot, and a local standard is the *tarte flamiche*, rather like a quiche of cheese and leeks, but without a pastry rim.

Flanders has distinctive, enjoyable fare that is scarcely French at all, typically served in cosy Flemish *estaminet* pubs; single dishes like *tartines* (open sandwiches) and *potjevleesch* (platters of cold meats), with chips and excellent local beer.

Picardy's cuisine similarly makes much of northern green vegetables, especially from the *hortillonages* marsh gardens of Amiens, and the Baie de la Somme is famed for its sole, *lieu* (pollack) and *pré-salé* lamb, raised on salt marshes to give the meat a special flavour. The region's signature dish is the *ficelle picarde*, a thick savoury *crêpe* filled with ham, mushrooms, onions and other fillings and baked in a cheese sauce.

> *Despite its fame, Burgundy's cuisine has clear country roots and an earthy, full-on quality, based on the high quality of its produce and a generous use of wine.*

One special product is the natural focus of attention in **Champagne**, but the Ardennes forest in the north and the Chaumont area to the south are also prime hunting territory, and game – venison, boar, pheasant – appears on many menus, especially in winter. Also a local classic is *potée champenoise*, a stew of sausage, smoked ham and cabbage often eaten around the time of the autumn grape harvest.

Lorraine has conquered the world with one dish, the *quiche lorraine*. Naturally, it should be best of all in its *terroir*, where there are many variations on the basic ham and cheese tart. The region is said to produce France's finest potatoes, and other specialities include rich pork pâtés and salads of *pissenlits* ("bedwetters", or dandelions) and bacon.

In eastern Lorraine food blends into that of **Alsace**, which stands out from all others in France by being completely Germanic. The classic dish is *choucroute*, a gallicisation of *sauerkraut*, carried all across France as a standard on brasserie menus. A proper *choucroute* is a hefty platter, with shredded and fermented cabbage plus, normally, boiled potatoes and several varieties of pork (smoked pork, frankfurter-style sausages, bacon and more). Also on the Alsatian menu is *flammekeuche* or *tarte flambée*, or Alsatian pizza, a dough base topped with crème fraîche, onions and bacon. Alsace's wines and beers both go equally well with local food.

Terroirs: Burgundy and the Loire

Unlike that of the north, the cuisine of **Burgundy** is one of the most esteemed in France, and for well over a century its classic dishes have formed part of the general repertory of "French cuisine", such as *boeuf bourguignon* (beef braised in red wine with mushrooms, onions, garlic, herbs and often *lardons*, chopped bacon) and *coq au vin* (chicken in white wine with similar ingredients). Other specialities include *oeufs en meurette* (poached eggs with a red wine, shallot and *lardons* sauce) and *jambon persillé* (ham and parsley terrine). The region is also known for its *escargots* and gourmets consider wild Burgundy snails to be among the finest. Dijon, as well as being the hub of the winelands, is of course famous for its AOC mustard, and southern Burgundy is home to France's most renowned breed of chicken, the *poulet de Bresse*. The region also produces a superb range of cheeses, highlights being the pungent Époisses, Chaource and several goat's milk cheeses.

The **Loire Valley** is a land of abundance, and another area with a long-celebrated traditional cuisine. Particular specialities are freshwater fish from the Loire and its many tributaries, especially salmon and *sandre* (pike-perch or zander), often served in a simple *beurre-blanc* sauce, or small fish served deep-fried as a *friture*. As well as fine wines the Loire produces superb fruit, notably pears and greengage *(reine claude)* plums, and asparagus, and prized mushrooms are grown in caves near Saumur. Excellent *rillettes* (potted pork) and other preserved meats are found all around the region, and a treasured speciality of Chartres is *pâté de Chartres*, a rich concoction of duck or partridge with foie gras and truffles, in a pastry crust. The Loire is also famous for its goat's cheeses, such as *crottin de chavignol*.

Terroirs: Brittany and Normandy

When it comes to food, the greatest attraction of **Brittany** is its fine fish and seafood, especially oysters, mussels, *coquilles st-jacques* scallops, sardines and lobster. Ask most French people to name a Breton dish, though, and they'll probably just say *crêpes*. The staple Breton diet for centuries, they come in two kinds, thicker *galettes de sarrazin*, or buckwheat pancakes, served with savoury toppings, and thinner wheatflour *crêpes* with sweet things. They're a great alternative to more elaborate French meals for kids.

Normandy has one of the most distinctive culinary traditions, based in a repertoire from the lush Norman *terroir*: cream, butter, cider and apples. This can sound excessively rich and heavy, but handled properly it is not at all. Norman classics include *jambon au cidre* (ham braised in cider) and the *vallée d'auge* sauce, of *crème fraîche*, onions, sautéed apples, mushrooms and a dash of calvados, served with chicken, pork or other meats. Around Rouen and in the Seine

LEFT: the classic Alsatian dish of *choucroute*, boiled potatoes, sausages and smoked bacon is a standard item on brasserie menus. **ABOVE:** Cancale oysters.

Maritime, duck is the basis of many dishes. Any fish or seafood with *normande* or *à la crème normande* tagged on will be with cream and cider. Superb fish and seafood can be found all around the coast, and Normandy is a major producer of mussels. The Bay of Mont-St-Michel produces salt marsh or *pré salé* lamb, and, since so much of Normandy is deeply rural, it still prizes earthy foods like *andouillette* gut sausages and *boudin noir*, black pudding or blood sausage, the best of which comes from the Perche in southern Normandy. Plus, Normandy is home to some of France's most famous cheeses – Camembert, Livarot, Pont l'Evêque and Neufchâtel.

Winelands

Burgundy has more *appellations contrôlées (see below)* than any other region in France. It is also one of the regions that sticks most rigidly to a hierarchy in its AOCs and vineyards, from *Grand Cru* down to *Régional*. Nevertheless the wine region and its southern offshoot Beaujolais are remarkably compact, a narrow strip down the west side of the Rhône from Dijon to Lyon. All the *Grand Cru* vineyards producing the finest Burgundy reds are in the Côte d'Or near Dijon (or Côte de Nuits in wine terms), such as Gevrey-Chambertin or Nuits-Saint-Georges. The Côte de Beaune a little further

Know your Appellations

Habitually systematic, the French have a system to point you towards the best foods and wines, the *Appellation d'Origine Contrôlée* or AOC. Essentially, it means only goods produced within a precisely defined geographical area and to tightly policed quality standards can use a particular name. It is based in a very French idea that something made in the place it originated will always be the best.

Curiously, legal protection for wine regions originated in Italy, in the 18th century. The first French wine recognised by international agreement was Champagne, in 1891, and its status was actually reaffirmed in the Treaty of Versailles. Official regulation of table wines began in the 1930s, when most major AOCs – Côtes du Rhone, varieties of Burgundy and Bordeaux – were registered, and there are now over 300 French wine AOCs. *Appellations* for other foods appeared after World War II, regulating sometimes-medieval local customary laws. Proper *crème fraîche* (and fine butter) come from AOC Isigny-sur-Mer in Calvados, and there is an AOC for Bresse chickens. All the best cheeses naturally have AOCs, and the "Camembert de Normandie" *appellation* was introduced after the Camembert name alone had become so widespread it had been devalued.

Critics (mostly non-French) say the AOC with its emphasis on place of origin is out of date, and encourages complacency. However, as tasters experience, in general, and especially for foods and smaller wine regions, it works.

south is equally esteemed for its superb reds and Chardonnay whites, and has some of the most beautiful vineyards, especially to the west around Nolay. Further south again more modest wines are generally found in the Côte Chalonnaise, leading down to the Beaujolais south of Maçon. *Régional* wines have an AOC for the whole of Burgundy, not a specific district, and generally refer to cheaper, simpler wines such as *Bourgogne aligoté*, a light white often mixed with cassis blackcurrant liqueur.

The **Loire Valley** is one of the most enjoyable regions for wine exploration. Not only does it produce fine reds and whites, but also France's best rosés (around Sancerre) and sparkling wines to challenge champagne (Crémant de Loire, around Saumur). The eastern Loire is dominated, as well as by rosés, by distinctive whites such as Pouilly-Fumé. The central area around Tours and Blois mostly produces characterful reds, with small, high-quality AOCs such as St Nicolas de Bourgueil and Chinon, but also has good whites, and its smaller vineyards are fascinating to visit, many with cellars in caves used for centuries. Towards the sea, white reasserts itself around Nantes with Muscadet and its higher-quality variant Muscadet-sur-Lie.

Champagne is France's oldest protected wine region *(see page 182)*. Like the food, the wines of the other northern French wine regions, **Moselle** and **Alsace**, are Germanic, with mainly Riesling and Gewürztraminer-based whites. The main vineyard area is between Strasbourg and Mulhouse.

Tourist offices in wine regions have abundant information on local *routes du vin*, and the best vineyards to visit.

Cider, calvados and beer

Until recently, no one in France's northernmost regions tried to grow vines. Instead, Normans, in particular, researched every possible use of the apple, producing some of the world's best ciders. Cider-making is still very much farm-based, making cider-hunting especially enjoyable (all tourist offices have leaflets, sometimes called a *route du cidre*, listing cider farms open for visits and sales). Normandy cider comes in two basic varieties, *doux* (sweet) and *brut* (dry), and the best is *cidre bouché* (corked), not with any kind of screw top. The Pays d'Auge around Cambremer is the most renowned cider district, the only one with an AOC, but excellent, slightly drier ciders are also found in the Perche and the Cotentin peninsula. Many farms also produce *poiré*, a similar drink made with pears. Brittany also produces enjoyable traditional ciders.

The other great Norman apple invention is calvados, crudely translated as apple brandy, one of the most subtle of all strong spirits. There are several grades, depending on how long the drink has been aged in a barrel, from "standard" varieties under five years old to *hors d'age* which can be up to 50 years old. *Pommeau* is a sweet liqueur made by mixing calvados and cider.

Thanks to its Germanic heritage, Alsace is France's largest beer producer, the home of major brands such as Fischer, Karlsbrau and Kronenbourg. Beer-lovers might find it more interesting to seek out the more characterful beers of smaller breweries in the Pas de Calais and Flanders such as Ch'ti in Benifontaine near Lens, or Trois Monts, from St-Sylvestre-Cappel, and the Brasserie d'Esquelbecq, in the village of the same name, both near Cassel. There are also good small breweries dotted across Normandy and Brittany, which often sell their wares at country festivals and markets. ❑

FAR LEFT: the Loire Valley produces fine whites and reds, as well as France's best rosés. **LEFT:** a vineyard in Montagny, Burgundy. **RIGHT:** cider farms throughout Normandy are open for tastings.

The Cheeses of Northern France

The delicious result of centuries of refinement, France's hundreds of cheeses each have a distinct personality

In one of his most memorable sayings General De Gaulle begged the question "How can anyone govern a nation that produces 246 different kinds of cheese." In fact, he underestimated. There are over 300, some say close to 400, cheeses produced in France today.

Most northern cheeses are made with cow's milk. Relatively little known are those of the Nord-Pas-de-Calais, powerfully pungent cheeses like Maroilles, Rollot and spicy Boulette d'Avesnes, excellent for cooking. Just east of Paris is the home of Brie, with its finest AOC *Brie de Meaux*, while the pride of southern Champagne and northern Burgundy is creamy, slightly mushroomy Chaource. Alsace cheeses like Munster are soft and strong, with an orange rind.

Brittany is a rare region not known for cheeses, while its neighbour Normandy is home to the most famous of all, Camembert (AOC *Camembert de Normandie* is the best kind). It's actually a relative newcomer, supposedly invented by milkmaid Marie Harel in 1791 on the basis of a recipe given to her by a priest fleeing the Revolution. Other Norman cheeses to sample are Livarot, Pont l'Evêque and white, subtle Neufchâtel from the Pays de Bray north of Rouen, documented since 1035. Burgundy's greatest cheese is the richly flavoured Epoisses, while in southern Burgundy and the Loire the goat's cheese regions begin, with many kinds of *chèvre* such as Sainte-Maure.

Above: a stunning range to try to choose from in a fromagerie in Montreuil-sur-Mer, in the Pas-de-Calais.

Below: Grès des Vosges, a soft, mildly pungent cheese from southern Alsace, with a characteristic fern leaf on the rind.

Left: the multi-varied labels of Camembert boxes are a real form of folk art.

THE CRAFT OF *AFFINAGE*

The quality of many cheeses is the result not only of the work of the original cheesemaker but also of *affinage*, or maturation in a cheese cellar. One of France's greatest inventions, this is an intricate, delicate process, in which cheeses are turned and washed in different liquids – beer, brine, *eau-de-vie* – over time to produce a complex range of subtle flavours. Some farm producers mature cheeses themselves, but the most distinctive come from the cellar of a *Maître Fromager Affineur* – a craft cheese merchant. This is one of the great French crafts that is now under threat from production-line methods, but there is still at least one in most French towns. Most are faithful to the idea of *terroir*, concentrating on cheeses from their own area.

Cheeses are *affiné* to be at their best at a certain time, so part of buying cheese is asking the *Fromager* when you should eat it. Most northern cheeses are soft and have a fairly short life, so usually need to be eaten within a week or two.

TOP: the affinage of cheese requires frequent, careful attention.

ABOVE: Valençay, Chabichou du Poitou, Sainte-Maure and other goats' cheeses from the Loire.

RIGHT: punchy, heart-shaped Rollot from Picardy and the Pas-de-Calais, was a favourite of Louis XIV.

RIGHT: both strong and creamy, pear-shaped Boulette d'Avesnes is flavoured with parsley and tarragon and clad in a rind rubbed with paprika.

THE ARCHITECTURE OF NORTHERN FRANCE

Romanesque churches and Gothic cathedrals, Renaissance châteaux and classical palaces, half-timbered cottages, medieval castles and motorway bridges all fit into a history of feverish experimentation

For 2,000 years northern France has been adding to the canon of Western architecture, often leading the way for other countries to follow. Sometimes it has built on home-grown inspiration; at other times ideas have been imported from abroad and adapted to French tastes and requirements.

In any history of architecture it is tempting to look for a single, evolving narrative, but simplicity can be a trap. Few buildings embody a pure style; most have been added to over their lifetimes so that with a little insight it is possible to read their history literally written in stone.

France's prehistoric inhabitants left no permanent structures behind them other than alignments, dolmens and chamber tombs, and the earliest surviving architecture in the true sense is therefore Roman, as especially seen in the south. The barbarian tribes who settled Gaul from the 3rd century AD, adopting Christianity, continued to build in the familiar Roman style with only a little variation, and they left behind them baptisteries, oratories and crypts. Some of these survive; others have been incorporated into later churches.

The medieval building boom

Then, shortly after the turn of the first millennium, something dramatic happened. A building boom began that would last three centuries and be as rich in innovation as in the quantity of magnificent buildings created. Between 1050 and 1350 France quarried more stone than Ancient Egypt in any equivalent period and used it to build 80 cathedrals and 500 large churches, as well as thousands of smaller ones.

LEFT: the Romanesque Fontevraud Abbey.
RIGHT: medieval timber-framed house, Angers.

Conventionally, the buildings of the Middle Ages are classed as Romanesque and Gothic but these are not discrete styles. They are rather convenient terms applied by architectural historians in hindsight to denote the start and finish of a continuum. One style merges into the other as builders, driven by ambition to build ever bigger, higher, more solidly, find solutions to technological problems that had defeated their predecessors.

As its name suggests, Romanesque builders were inspired by the remains of Roman buildings. The style spread to France from northern Italy by means of master-craftsmen from

Lombardy who provided the essential skills. The Roman basilica was the prototype, a simple structure with radiating aisles. However, in fertile French soil, the Romanesque soon developed its own vernacular forms that surpassed many Italian models. Romanesque buildings, dependent on the rounded arch, are generally simple, stout and majestic. Barrel-vaulting was the favoured system, a continuous vault of semicircular or pointed sections, unbroken by cross-vaults. If the architecture itself is simple, at least in comparison with what was to come, the decoration is not. It is in its stone carving that Romanesque excels. Capitals, tympanums and sometimes corbels show both religious scenes but also an inscrutable bestiary of real and imagined animals straight out of the mind of medieval man.

Some of France's best Romanesque architecture can be seen in Burgundy. Unfortunately, Cluny abbey has been reduced to little more than ruins, albeit majestic ones. But the pilgrimage church at Vézelay is a good introduction to the style.

Gothic and its risks

Early medieval building techniques imposed a limitation that builders in the north of France

MEDIEVAL CASTLES

"Fortification was the first architectural expression of social power," according to Pierre Lavedan, author of a seminal study of French architecture. The castle of the high Middle Ages, *château fort*, was the home of the local *seigneur*. In times of war it served as the key element in the defence of the town or village, and as a refuge for the common people when the enemy came too close.

The earliest preserved castles date from the 13th century but the Bayeux tapestry depicts late Carolingian castles largely made of wood. Returning Crusaders brought back with them oriental improvements to castle design.

A castle was always sited on a defensive position, ideally on a cliff or isolated hill and often on the bend of a river: a spot from which visibility was good and the approach of a besieging army rendered difficult on one or more sides.

Thick walls with few openings – a few loopholes or arrow slits – made for a strong castle and these were topped by battlements. Wooden overhanging galleries or hoardings were built from the battlements in order to drop missiles on attackers at the base of the walls. In some castles these became permanent stone features.

were anxious to overcome. Romanesque had essentially came from the south where there was a need to keep excess light *out* of a building. In the north, the goal was the opposite: to draw scarce sunlight in to illuminate the interior. The challenge was to create larger windows without the walls losing rigidity and strength. A succession of technical breakthroughs – including pointed arches, flying buttresses and rib vaulting – enabled Gothic naves to be stretched upwards and continued skywards by means of slender spires.

Experiments with the new methods can be seen already in several otherwise Romanesque churches, but St-Denis (1137–44) in the northern suburbs of Paris is considered the first Gothic building proper. It was followed in quick succession by the cathedrals of Sens, Laon, Notre Dame in Paris, Reims, Le Mans, Amiens, Strasbourg and Beauvais.

The stone structure established, windows could now expand within the slimmer walls to become features rather than mere pathways of light. A new skill developed to fill them with stained glass, as can be seen in all its glory in Bourges and, above all, Chartres.

LEFT: the Gothic nave of Laon cathedral.
ABOVE: the Renaissance Château de Chambord is the largest château in the Loire Valley.

Peace and the Renaissance

The frenzy of Gothic building and innovation began to slow down in around 1277 and there was no significant development in French architecture between the end of the 13th century and the turn of the 15th – a turbulent time in France's history characterised by war and famine. Then, as before, new inspiration came from Italy, brought back by the returning armies of Louis XII, to be adapted to French tastes.

The Renaissance style with its ideals of order, harmony and symmetry appealed to a new age casting off medieval preoccupations. It suited the hedonistic tastes of the wealthy and conditions were right for its implantation. Now that warfare had all but ceased on French territory, there was no need to build for siege and the *château fort (see box left)* could become the château in the sense of stately home.

The best examples of the Renaissance in France are in the Loire valley. At first classical motifs were added as ornament to existing buildings; interiors were updated; and Renaissance elements were grafted on to Gothic walls. The magnificent staircase added to the Château de Blois in 1515 is one of the first accomplished works of the French Renaissance. Soon, everyone with the means wanted to have a Renaissance newbuild or re-build, bringing into being such great houses as Chaumont, Azay-le-Rideau and Chambord.

French Classicism to Rococo

In Italy, the Renaissance was followed by a reaction against it in the form of the Baroque, which favoured drama and ornamentation over simplicity, reason and restraint. In France, however, there was little taste for dramatic buildings and a homegrown Classicism became dominant. It was pioneered by François Mansart who gave his name to a peculiarly French roof of double pitch (gentler in its upper part, steep below), but it reached its apogee during the reign of the Sun King, Louis XIV, in the *grand siècle* of the 17th century.

The divergence between Baroque and French Classicism is well illustrated by the visit of the great genius of Italian art and architecture, Gianlorenzo Bernini, to Paris in 1665. He was invited by the king to lay out his plans for rebuilding the Louvre. These were rejected in favour of a less daring French project for the building by Charles Perrault. Another architect, Louis Le Vau, also contributed to the revamped Louvre, but he is best remembered for his role in creating the palace of Versailles, the epitome of the new style.

Only later, in the early 18th century, did France develop a variant of Baroque, known as rococo, from *rocaille* (stone) and the *coquilles* (shells) used as motifs in its exuberant decoration.

Rural Architecture

France may have a prodigious amount of what is known as "polite" architecture – buildings of grand design – but it has an even greater amount of its opposite, the vernacular, the architecture of the common people.

All across northern France, farmers and villagers constructed houses that may look beautiful to us but were not designed with any academic principles in mind. Far more important to these anonymous builders was to make the best use of materials to hand – freely available and without the need to transport them. They built according to the needs of their families, crops and livestock and in response to the local climate with a windowless wall against the prevailing wind. But where they could they added aesthetic touches and charming, personalising details. There is an extraordinary amount of such informal, folk architecture left standing, particularly in the centre and south of the country where the bombs of World War II didn't reach.

The most abundant and most widespread building material was wood and hence the commonest type of medieval dwelling is the half-timbered house, found in abundance in Normandy, Alsace and Champagne, its walls filled up with brick or wattle and daub.

Some of these buildings are isolated and you only come across them by chance. Others cluster together in groups that are classified as among the *plus beaux villages* of France.

The Empire style

The vogue for French Classicism continued up until the Revolution only to be supplanted, after the upheavals, by Neoclassicism or the Empire style, a harking back to the models of Antiquity, which was favoured by Napoleon Bonaparte as a way of emulating the glory of his Roman predecessors.

The 19th century similarly looked backwards for its inspiration, reviving and mimicking lapsed and archaic styles. This was also the period in which heritage was discovered. In 1834, Prosper Merimée, author of the novel on which the operetta *Carmen* is based, became Inspecteur des Monuments Historiques and he commissioned his old schoolfriend Eugène Viollet-le-Duc to restore some of France's most eloquent ruins. The results, notably at Carcassonne, Notre-Dame and the Château de Pierrefonds, have been criticised for their fanciful "enhancements" but at least these buildings were preserved for posterity.

In the late 19th century, industrialisation began to provide new materials and lend its own aesthetic as epitomised by the Eiffel Tower with steel from Lorraine. The aim was no longer to impress with political power, but with technological prowess.

Into the modern age

French architecture of the 20th century is indebted to the work, but mostly the thought, of the Swiss-born Charles-Édouard Jeanneret-Gris, better known as Le Corbusier. A leading exponent of the Modern style, he famously described the house as "a machine for living" and illustrated his "five principles for a new architecture" in Villa Savoye in Poissy, near Paris, built during the inter-war years. A more popular building is his chapel at Ronchamp in the Franche-Comté.

After the destruction of World War II, the most pressing need was to reconstruct the shattered cities of the north which had lost irreplaceable medieval houses. The only quick and economic solution was to build with reinforced concrete in the Modern style. The rebuilt port of Le Havre, by Auguste Perret, is often held up as the exemplary achievement.

LEFT: apartment buildings in Paris. **RIGHT:** the new Georges Pompidou Centre in Metz, designed by Shigeru Ban and Jean de Gastines.

The security of the Fifth Republic and sustained decades of prosperity meant great state projects could once again be envisaged. The most controversial and the best-loved of these is the Pompidou Centre, the result of a collaboration between Renzo Piano and Richard Rogers. Their "inside out" design makes for light, space and flexibility.

The 1980s saw more *grands projets*, this time credited to the *dirigisme* of François Mitterrand. The Louvre was transformed by the addition of I.M. Pei's pyramid in 1989, and in the same year the Grande Arche de La Défense was erected.

The 21st century has seen two innovative

structures, the motorway viaduct at Millau and the new Pompidou Centre at Metz, both involving foreign architects. The best-known French architect of today, Jean Nouvel, has built his most stunning buildings abroad, but his work can be seen in Paris in the Institut du Monde Arabe and the new Musée du Quai Branly.

A greater preoccupation in present-day France than adding to the canon of architecture is the preservation of the back catalogue. Over 42,000 buildings are classified *monuments historiques* – 100 of them owned and managed by the state – and a further 147,000 other buildings are listed as of architectural value, giving them at least a notional level of protection. ❑

ART AND ARTISTS

Art in France has taken a long journey from regal grandeur to radical subversion. From the Renaissance court painters to the protagonists of the avant-garde, Paris was always, and remains, the country's creative hub

The Romans introduced individualised art to Gaul, in portrait figures and carvings. The invading Franks initially had little time for decorative refinement, but learnt fast, and by the Merovingian era produced fine gold chalices. Charlemagne sponsored a "Carolingian Renaissance", which produced stunning illuminated manuscripts with a visually original style, often with intricate carved ivory covers. After the collapse of Charlemagne's empire, work of similar quality was not seen in Europe for over 300 years.

As seen in the previous chapter, during the centuries that followed the first millennium, northern France achieved prodigious feats in architecture, with the building of the great monasteries and cathedrals, and exquisite sculptures. This outpouring of energy often appears to have deterred work in other arts, but beautiful free-standing sculptures in stone and wood also survive.

The first artists

The move to more individual art came in the 15th century, initially still within a religious setting. Around 1410 at Bourges, the Duc de Berry commissioned his *Trés Riches Heures du Duc de Berry* (now in the Musée Condé, Château de Chantilly), a prayer book, and the greatest of all medieval manuscripts, with detailed scenes of the duke's court depicted in jewel-like colours. Its creators, the three Limbourg brothers, were Flemish, as were the greatest painters of the time in northern Europe, Jan van Eyck and Rogier van der Weyden. Their patron was Philip the Good, Duke of Burgundy (1419–67), who maintained the most sophisticated court in Europe, which travelled between Burgundy and Flanders. Painting elsewhere in France followed Flemish influence, as in the work of the first court portraitist Jean Fouquet, employed by Charles VII from the 1440s.

The Renaissance exploded into France thanks to the enthusiasm of King François I, who bought Italian paintings and invited Italian artists to his court, including Leonardo da Vinci, by then too sick to work, but who came with the *Mona Lisa*. The king had more success with Rosso Fiorentino and Primaticcio, who decorated his new château at Fontainebleau.

LEFT: *St Jerome reading*, by Georges de la Tour, 17th century. **RIGHT:** portrait of Elizabeth of Austria (1554-1592) wife of Charles IX, by François Clouet.

French court painting, however, showed more formality than Italian vigour. François Clouet, court painter for several monarchs, produced remarkably precise portraits of figures such as Mary, Queen of Scots.

In the early 17th century France produced its first great painters, all very different. Georges de la Tour was born in 1593 in the Duchy of Lorraine, which only formally became part of France shortly before his death in 1652. His curiously modern paintings such as the exquisite *Newborn Christ* in Rennes have a wonderful stillness, with supreme light effects influenced by Caravaggio.

THE PUYS OF AMIENS

Among the most remarkable examples of early French art are the unique Puys of Amiens, commissioned by the *Fraternité de Notre Dame*, a charitable association of local merchants. Each Christmas, the Fraternity presented a painting, or *Puy*, to Amiens Cathedral. The oldest existing Puy (1437) is in the Louvre, but the largest collection, from the early 16th century, is in the Musée de Picardie in Amiens. Against a background often reminiscent of Brueghel, the paintings depict Fraternity members and their families gathered at the feet of the Virgin. It is a fascinating portrait gallery of the burghers of Amiens, many of whom look as if they would have been tough to do business with.

The three Le Nain brothers, Louis, Antoine and Mathieu – who all signed their work *Le Nain* – produced slightly austere paintings giving a dignified view of peasant life. Nicolas Poussin, born at Les Andelys in Normandy in 1594, was France's greatest Baroque painter, although he spent most of his life in Rome. Claude Gellée,

> *One of France's greatest and most original painters, Georges de la Tour, was almost completely unappreciated before the 20th century.*

known as *Claude Lorrain* as he was also from Lorraine, has gone through the opposite curve from Georges de la Tour. His misty landscapes were immensely influential for 300 years, but are now far less well regarded.

This same period saw a further growth of "official" art, led by Simon Vouet, court painter to Louis XIII. This naturally reached a peak under Louis XIV, when the role of painters such as Charles Le Brun, first head of the *Académie Royale* of painters and sculptors in 1663, and Hyacinthe Rigaud was to create majestic images of and around the Sun King. Court and aristocratic taste continued to dominate French art in the 18th century, although Baroque grandeur gave way to a more delicate charm in the paintings of Antoine Watteau, and a more sugary charm in the rococo work of Boucher and Fragonard, symbolising the unsuspecting frivolity of the *ancien régime*.

Artists as young men

The modern idea of art begins in France, like so many things, with the Revolution. Its foremost standard-bearer was Jacques-Louis David, who had already made an impact before 1789 with his monumental paintings of classical Greek and Roman subjects. He was notoriously adaptable, going from being chief propagandist for Robespierre to producing heroic images of Napoleon. David's exact style was emulated by his pupil Jean-Auguste Ingres, esteemed as a painter of portraits and voluptuous nudes.

The idea of the artist as rebel, a breaker of boundaries, gained hold in the years after 1815, with the combination of the Revolutionary mentality with Romanticism, seen in the dramatic work of Théodore Géricault, whose

Raft of the Medusa shocked Paris in 1819, and Eugène Delacroix, who created the classic image of Parisian revolution with his *Liberty Leading the People*, inspired by the July 1830 rising. Delacroix's expressive brush technique also laid the groundwork for Impressionism and later styles.

The 1840s saw the first realist art, with the socially aware paintings of Gustave Courbet. A different kind of realism was pursued by artists such as Théodore Rousseau, Camille Corot and Jean-François Millet, the first French artists to make a conscious move outside Paris, gathering in Barbizon near Fontainebleau to paint closer to nature. Millet moved on to paint scenes of peasant life, creating in *The Gleaners* and *The Angelus* some of the most famous images in French art. Around the same time Boudin also began painting seascapes in the open air at Honfleur.

At the time many of these artists were scarcely known. Far more celebrated were the painters of what was later dismissed as academic or *pompier* art ("firemen", because so many paintings featured classical scenes with men in Greek helmets that looked like those worn by French firemen). As well as classical topics they also often featured French historical subjects, and, especially during the decadent Second Empire, languorous mythological nudes. Nudes were even more sultry in the sculptures of Jean-Baptiste Carpeaux, who created the scandalous figures on the façade of the Paris Opera.

LEFT: *St Thomas the Apostle*, by Georges de la Tour, 17th century. **ABOVE:** *On the beach at Trouville*, by Eugene Boudin, c. 1865.

The Impressionist breakthrough

The radical tendencies of previous years came together in Impressionism. The name of the movement was first conceived as an insult, in a sneering 1874 review of Monet's *Impression, Soleil Levant* (Impression, Rising Sun). However, it stuck. The Impressionist painters had in common a wish to break out of the confines of studio painting to get close to real life and nature, and particularly movement, colour and light *(see box, page 82)*.

They first became visible as a group in the 1860s, when the work of Monet, Sisley, Pissarro and others was repeatedly rejected by the jury administering the annual Paris Salon for new painting. The jury was especially scandalised in 1863 by Edouard Manet's *Le Déjeuner sur l'Herbe*, showing two nude women not on a mythological rock but at a picnic with two fully clothed young men. However, Napoleon III raffishly decreed that those barred from the official Salon should be allowed to exhibit separately, and the resulting *Salon des Refusés* ("of the Rejected") was a sensation, launching these new artists for the world.

The origins of Impressionism were in Paris, the Seine valley and the Normandy coast. Pissarro and Monet, who lived for the last 43 years of his life at Giverny, his beloved home northwest of Paris, always stayed true to the region. The Provençal Paul Cézanne, on the other hand, returned to the south in search of more intense colour and light.

In the 1880s, the influence of Impressionism fragmented in several directions, with the Neo-Impressionist or pointillist works of Georges Seurat and Paul Signac, and the various kinds of "Post-Impressionist" styles, with more intense subject matter. This could cover Van Gogh, who spent the last month of his life before his suspected suicide in 1890 working intensively at Auvers-sur-Oise, and Paul Gauguin and the young artists known as the *Nabis* ("Prophet" in Hebrew), such as Paul Sérusier and Maurice Denis, who in the 1880s went to Pont Aven in Brittany in search of a simpler, wilder France, before Gauguin decided this was not primitive enough and went off to the Pacific islands.

Also sometimes classified as Post-Impressionists are Henri de Toulouse-Lautrec, who captured the spirit of the Belle Epoque in Paris in

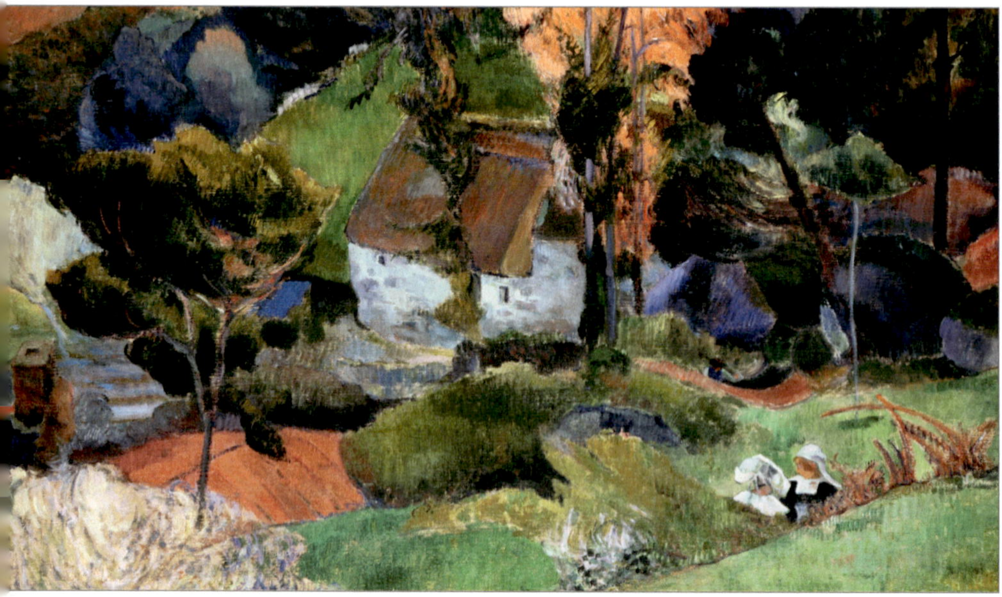

THE IMPRESSION OF NORMAN LIGHT

It's an idea that's almost intangible in itself, but yet made a major contribution to France's most famous artistic movement, Impressionism: that the light on the eastern Normandy coast, around the mouth of the Seine and along the Côte d'Albatre to Dieppe, has a specially limpid, translucent quality. It is most associated with Claude Monet, but the first artist to draw attention to it was the English painter, resident in France, Richard Bonington, who painted around Dieppe before his early death in the 1820s. The real founder of the "Seine estuary" school, though, was Eugène Boudin, born in Trouville but most associated with the coastal town of Honfleur, who began painting there *en plein air*, in the open air, in the 1830s.

Boudin's soaring, pearlescent skies had a huge influence, and he was a generous adviser to younger artists, especially Monet, whom he supposedly met in 1856 while painting on a beach, when Monet was 15, and whom he taught for some years. Monet, who felt that a landscape had no permanent appearance, since "the surrounding atmosphere brings it to life – the light and the air, which vary continually", was obsessed with the changing light of this coast, and painted particular points like the cliffs at Etretat time and again. One thing anyone can decide on, depending on where you're travelling to, is whether it really is true the light is so different from Normandy looking north than from the English side looking south.

his famous posters, and the unclassifiable Henri Rousseau, from Laval in the Mayenne, the most extraordinary of naïve painters.

Another influential movement which emerged at the end of the century was Symbolism, distinguished less by technique than subject matter. The symbolist paintings of Gustave Moreau, Odilon Redon and Pierre Puvis de Chavannes often featured dream-like, decadent images, combining religious mysticism with an interest in the erotic. Away from painting, in the 1870s Auguste Rodin had begun a transformation of modern sculpture.

> *Leading figure of the avant-garde, Marcel Duchamp, returned to Paris from the USA in the 1920s with the American photographer Man Ray, but then virtually gave up art for chess.*

Paris, cradle of the avant-garde

The 20th century began with another explosion of colour in the work of the *Fauves* or "Wild Beasts", exemplified by André Derain, Raoul Dufy and Henri Matisse, with a free, almost abstract, use of colour. By now Paris's position as the hub of everything new in art attracted artists from around the world, not just France, such as the young Picasso, the Italian Amedeo Modigliani and the Russians Ossip Zadkine and Marc Chagall. The way had been paved for Cubism, the decisive move towards abstraction by Picasso, Georges Braque, Juan Gris and others around 1907. Robert Delaunay with his Russian wife Sonia varied the Cubist repertoire with a strong use of colour and geometrical forms to express the dynamism of modern life.

One of the leading figures of the avant-garde was Marcel Duchamp, whose "readymades" – *Bicycle Wheel*, *Fountain* (a urinal) and *Bottle Rack*, made from 1913–17 – have been hugely influential on artists ever since. During World War I, which he spent in the United States, he also collaborated with the Dada group, a revolt against official art and the established order.

Perhaps the last great Parisian avant-garde movement, developing out of Dada, was Surrealism, which sought to link dreams with reality in the light of Freudian and similar ideas. Surrealism was entirely international, its most prominent artists being Max Ernst, Joan Miró, Man Ray and Salvador Dalí. Beginning in the 1920s, Surrealism was the motif behind some of the most exuberant years of the Parisian avant-garde, played out in the cafés and artists' studios of Montparnasse.

The current scene

By World War II Paris had lost its status as world artistic capital to New York. Artistic creativity continued, though, with the cartoon-like work of Jean Dubuffet, and in the 1960s with

the New Realism of Yves Klein, Niki de Saint Phalle and others. The current scene also owes much to movements like Fluxus, 1970s conceptual art, and to figures like Bruce Nauman, as well as to neo-pop art.

The contemporary art scene in France is amazingly open and international. Christian Boltanski creates sombre installations powerfully evoking themes of loss and death, while Daniel Buren produces conceptual installations that feature an entrancing use of stripes and colours. One of the last defined "movements" was *figuration libre*, led by Robert Combas in the 1980s, which reaffirmed the use of edgy, graffiti-like paintings of human figures in the face of the intellectualism of conceptual art. ❑

LEFT: *Landscape at Pont-Aven*, by Paul Gauguin, *c.*1888. **RIGHT:** *The Dead Swiss,* detail from an installation by Christian Boltanksi, 1990.

The English Channel – La Manche

It may be only a narrow strip of seawater, but it separates two worlds, and lures adventurers to cross it in challenging ways

On its southern shore it's called *La Manche*, "the sleeve", because of its tapering shape. To the north, however, it is proprietorially

known as "the English Channel". The different names suggest the relative importance of this international waterway to the two countries that face each other across it. For the British, "their" Channel is an obsession: a natural defence that separates their civilisation from "the continent", keeping invaders and undesirable cultural influences at bay. Conversely, it is also an obstacle that has to be crossed to get anywhere.

For the continental French, however, the Manche is mostly thought of as inconsequential, although historian Fernand Braudel warns his countrymen against underestimating it. Seas, he says, are rarely regarded as frontiers, "and yet if a frontier means a break, a discontinuity in space, what traveller, leaving Calais, or arriving in Dover, could fail to think that he was leaving one frontier and meeting another?"

The English Channel connects the North Sea with the Atlantic and is around 500km (300 miles) long. Its limits are taken to be a notional line drawn between L'Ile Vierge (off the north coast of Brittany) and Land's End in Cornwall in the west, and another line in the east between Walde lighthouse (near Calais) to Leathercote Point in Kent. Half a million years ago, there was no Channel and England was joined to France, but sometime in the Pleistocene period an earthquake – or simply water pressure – caused the North Sea to overflow across the isthmus and flood the land.

Since then, the Channel has kept the two countries at arm's length, but hasn't prevented the intermingling of their histories. Throughout the centuries, would-be invaders have looked across the waves with desires of conquest. But the crossing is almost the easy part: it is the landing that can be difficult. The Romans and William the Conqueror managed it with relative ease, but Hitler shelved his invasion in 1940 because he couldn't be sure of success without air supremacy, and Allied military planners in 1944 had to accept an immense loss of human life as the price of liberating occupied France.

At other times, the Channel has acted as a short but significant no-man's-land giving reassurance to exiles travelling in either direction. Fugitive Catholics would flee across it from Reformation England. Later, frightened aristocrats travelled in the opposite direction to escape from Revolutionary France. Voltaire and Zola both used England as a temporary home in times of trouble, while Oscar Wilde came to France to distance himself from his critics after he was released from prison.

Crossing the Channel

The usual way to cross the Channel is by ferry, plane or, since 1994, by train through the tunnel, but plenty of people have found other ways to cross it. As it funnels through the strait of Dover it reduces to 34km (21 miles/18.2 nautical miles) wide between Shakespeare Beach and Cap Gris Nez. This makes it just wide enough to be a worthwhile challenge but not so wide as to make the crossing impossible. On 7 January 1785 Jean Pierre Francois Blanchard of France and John Jefferies of the USA made the first aerial crossing on board a balloon. The first successful heavier-than-air (ie powered) cross-channel flight was achieved on 25 July 1909 by the aviator Louis Blériot. One year later a passenger-carrying aircraft made the same journey.

More recent aerial stunts have included crossing by human pedal power (1979), solar-powered glider (1997), parachute freefall using a wing suit (2003), jet pack (2008 – the crossing taking less than ten minutes) and "cluster balloon" (2010) – with the pilot hanging from a bunch of coloured balloons.

Swimming the Channel

But the greatest challenge is to swim the width of the Channel, a feat first performed by steamship captain Matthew Webb on 25 August 1875, taking 21 hours and 45 minutes. Since then around 800 people have swum the Channel, some of them more than once. The current "Queen of the English Channel" has made the journey 43 times. The record for the fastest crossing has fallen steadily and now stands at just under 7 hours. The record for the slowest swim, 28 hours and 44 minutes, was inadvertently set in 2010 by a 56-year-old woman who had to swim 65 miles to reach France because the tides kept pulling her off course.

Swimming the Channel is a feat of mental and physical endurance and takes months of training and meticulous planning. Every swimmer needs to be backed up by a boat with a pilot on board and an observer to validate the attempt. He or she also needs a support crew to supply feeds.

After 6 hours in the water, the body runs out of energy and starts to break down its own fat. The greatest threat, which has killed swimmers in the past, is hypothermia.

Maritime motorway

Apart from cold water, tides and currents, there is traffic to contend with. The Channel is the busiest shipping lane in the world, transited by over 400 commercial ships a day, plus numerous leisure craft. Following an accident in January 1971, the Traffic Separation Scheme (TSS) was set up by the International Maritime Organization to control shipping with the aid of radar. This turns the Channel into a maritime motorway, one lane of shipping going each way with a zone of separation in the middle in which ropes, buckets, seaweed and assorted detritus swirl about.

The British and French coastal authorities permit Channel crossing attempts which are properly organised but frown on publicity-seeking crossings using unorthodox craft which are "characterised by slow speed and poor or non-existent manoeuvrability, such as tyres, bathtubs, rafts and pedalos" because of the high possibility of mishap. One way to discourage foolhardy adventurers setting off is to deny them permission to land. The French coastguard strictly prohibits any unauthorised vessel from coming within 300 metres (330 yards) of the Pas-de-Calais shore. ❑

LEFT: the Opal Coast, Pas-de-Calais. **ABOVE:** Jackie Cobell swimming the Channel, 27 July 2010.

TRACES OF WAR

Moving testimony to some of the 20th century's most intense dramas, the battlefields of the Western Front and Normandy are also key to their understanding

The spoils of northern France have been fought over for centuries, as the presence of numerous castles, ramparts and other fortifications bears witness. But what draws many people here today is, of course, the region's central role in the two 20th-century conflagrations. Some of the sites from World Wars I and II are hugely atmospheric; some are beautiful, which makes the thought of what happened there even more telling.

The shock of 1914–18

The statistics of World War I are hard to take in: France lost 1,300,000 dead, Britain nearly 900,000, Commonwealth countries and India together 230,000. Germany had over 2 million dead. Most died on the muddy battlefields of the Western Front, curving from the Swiss border in Alsace north to Ypres in Belgium and the sea.

The principal explanation for such an appalling loss of life is simply that the conflict was marked by an unprecedented amount of new technology. It was the first machine-based war. Very few generals anticipated the effects of the machine-guns, the enormous increase in the rate of fire and accuracy of rifles and, above all, the destructive power of the new artillery – which could now rain down thousands of shells in a few minutes. In the damp country of northern France it could pound fields into a swamp where men disappeared without trace.

In the face of machine-guns, artillery and barbed wire, attackers were easily cut down, and armies became locked into immobility. If a breakthrough ever did come, the traditional way to exploit it was to send up the cavalry; vehicles were still unreliable, and tanks, invented by the British in 1916, very slow. Horses were even

more vulnerable than men. Dreadful communications led to huge numbers of unnecessary losses: phone lines were fragile, so often the way to contact the front line was with runners (messengers), who could easily get killed.

On the first day of the Battle of the Somme, 1 July 1916, the Newfoundland Regiment was in reserve at Beaumont-Hamel. By 8.45am many of the initial British assault force had been killed, but the division commander, having lost contact with the front line, assumed they had been successful, and ordered the Newfoundlanders forward. The communications trenches were blocked by the dead and wounded, and general chaos, so they were ordered to leave the trenches and advance over open ground, in full view of the German line. Out of 780 men, only 68 appeared for duty the next day.

The shape of the war

Huge numbers were lost in the first few months, when the front was still not set in trenches. The French army placed a great importance on "offensive spirit", and as soon as the war began launched frontal attacks in Lorraine – with horrific losses. The Germans meanwhile followed their own plan, marching through Belgium and turning south towards Paris before they were halted in the Battle of the Marne in September 1914. Then began the "Race to the Sea", with each side trying to outflank each other until they reached the Belgian coast in November, and the Western Front was created.

During 1915 there were fruitless offensives, as each side came to terms with static trench warfare. 1916 saw the worst slaughter of the war, beginning in February with the German attack on Verdun. The German commander later wrote that his intention had not been to take it, but to make France "bleed to death" defending the historic town. By November the French had lost 300,000 dead or wounded, in an area 20km (12 miles) wide. For France the defence of Verdun, hanging on for dear life, replaced heroic charges as the most powerful image of war.

> *Verdun became, according to one French officer, a place where one could not tell "where flesh were mud, or mud were flesh".*

On 1 July 1916, hoping to reduce the pressure on the French, Britain's new volunteer army unleashed its own offensive on the Somme. The first day was shattering, with 20,000 men dead within an hour. The campaign went on till November, struggling forward just metres at a time. Over two weeks in July Australians lost 23,000 casualties securing the village of Pozières.

In April 1917 the French General Nivelle launched his great offensive on the Chemin des Dames ridge, another of the great disasters. Mutinies began, as men refused to throw their lives away. Discipline was restored, but British and Commonwealth troops took on a larger role, with the successful Canadian attack on Vimy Ridge in April and another horrendous battle around Ypres and Passchendaele in Belgium.

There was a major change in 1917, with the entry of the USA into the war, which finally led

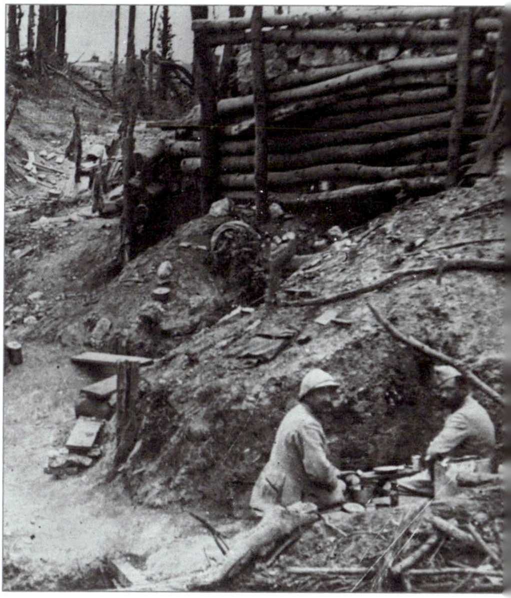

LEFT: a depiction of the Verdun battlefield, 1916. **ABOVE:** a ruined village by the Somme. **ABOVE RIGHT:** trench in a Somme wood.

to a return to a war of movement: the German commander Ludendorff saw he had to win before the Americans could arrive in any numbers, and after refining its tactics the German army broke through Allied lines in spring 1918 in an attempt to reach the sea. However, they were turned back, and by the war's end had been driven back into Belgium. Heavy casualties were suffered by both sides until the Armistice on 11 November.

The battlefields

Before visiting battlefields it's good to get some background. War museums come in two kinds – the larger ones giving an overview, while other, smaller museums focus on specific sites. The Historial de la Grande Guerre in Péronne *(see page 166)* on the Somme is the major modern museum covering the whole war.

Most sombre and awe-inspiring of all the battlefields is Verdun: nine villages were never rebuilt and remain as a silent forest of the dead, and the vast Ossuary at Douaumont contains the bones of 130,000 men, French and German. East and north of Verdun are St-Mihiel and the Argonne Forest, the main American sectors in late 1918. Although they only entered combat in May, the US forces suffered heavy casual-

BATTLEFIELD TOURS

For a deeper understanding of events in either World War, or to pursue a particular interest, many companies provide tours with expert guides speaking English and other languages. All give tours focusing on different nationalities on request. Some sites, notably the Canadian centres at Vimy, Beaumont-Hamel and Juno Beach, provide free tours, and the Caen Mémorial offers D-Day tours (charge). Some concentrate on one war or region, others offer a range; this is only a selection.

- Battlebus, Bayeux, tel: 02 31 22 28 82, www.battlebus.fr. D-Day and the Normandy battlefields.
- Battlefield Tours, Birmingham, UK, tel: 0121 430 5348, www.battlefieldtours.co.uk. British-based company giving military tours of all the battlefields of Europe and further afield.
- In the Footsteps Battlefield Tours, Ross on Wye, UK, tel: 01989 565599, www.inthefootsteps.com. Tours on request to all the battlefields of northwest Europe.
- Normandy Tours, Bayeux, tel: 02 31 92 10 70, www.normandy-landing-tours.com. Daily D-Day beaches tours other Normandy tours.
- Somme-Normandy Tours, Péronne, tel: 03 21 73 46 16, www.somme-normandy-tours.com. Based in the Somme, but covering both wars and different nationalities.
- Terres de Memoire, Péronne, tel: 03 22 84 23 05, www.terresdememoire.com. Bilingual guides focusing on the Somme and Western Front.

ties, with 116,000 dead, in part because they repeated mistakes the British and French had finally learnt to avoid and also because bullish US commanders wanted to take on as prominent a role as possible.

To the north, the Somme has powerful resonance for British and Australian visitors, while the Arras sector includes Vimy Ridge. Just west of Lille is Fromelles, where the remains of Australian and British troops killed in 1916 have only recently been located.

Around each site are cemeteries, which have national characteristics. A feature of the British and Commonwealth cemeteries is the effort made to enable families to place personal messages on graves. No country has done so much with its war sites, ceded by France in perpetuity, as Canada. The spectacular memorials at Vimy Ridge and Beaumont-Hamel are Canadian parks, providing excellent free tours. US cemeteries are monumental, precisely landscaped and give little individual information, while the French cemeteries are sometimes quite baroque, and by their sheer size give an aching sense of loss. Noticeable in German cemeteries, such as Neuville St-Vaast near Arras (44,833 graves), are the Stars of David among the crosses, since Jewish Germans fought in World War I just like other German citizens.

All *département* tourist offices produce guides to the war sites in their areas.

The Second War

World War II was very different. By this time, the full military implications of machines – tanks and aircraft – had been assimilated, although differently in different countries. The horrors of the first war had changed mentalities: in France, most generals felt their only option was to stay on the defensive, behind the fortified Maginot Line. In the long period of inactivity (the so-called Phoney War) following the declaration of war in September 1939, they waited for the Germans to do something, until on 10 May 1940 their foes unleashed the *Blitzkrieg* or Lightning War. The German army had understood the integrated use of tanks, infantry and aircraft, and drove rapidly westwards down the Somme to the sea, before turning north to push the British back to Dunkirk, and then south to Paris.

Having been expelled from France, the British, joined later by the Americans, spent the next few years trying to work out how to get back. One question was whether it was possible to take a Channel port directly, and in August 1942 several thousand Canadians landed at Dieppe in a costly experiment. When the Normandy invasion of D-Day, 6 June 1944, came, the British and Canadians on Sword, Juno and Gold beaches to the east and the Americans on Utah Beach landed successfully, supported by paratroop drops, but on the long beach now

known as Omaha (as shown in *Saving Private Ryan*) the Americans suffered such losses they considered turning back. Once the beaches were secured, two artificial harbours called "Mulberries" were built, at Arromanches (Gold Beach) and Omaha, although the latter was soon destroyed in a storm.

The battle for France

Allied commanders such as Eisenhower and Montgomery had not made extravagant forecasts, but they hoped that Caen, for example, would be taken on D-Day itself. As it was, the city was not fully in Allied control until 21 July. The battle of Normandy continued, ferociously, for nearly three months.

LEFT: war graves, Verdun. **RIGHT:** portrait of world war veterans in Colombey-les-Deux-Eglises, June 2010.

German equipment was superior, such as the famous 88mm gun, which could destroy a target at 1,000 metres (3,280ft), when most Allied tank guns were only effective at 500 metres (1,640ft). Normandy's *bocage* countryside of giant hedgerows and tiny fields gave them huge advantages, as fields had to be fought for one by one. The Allies' advantages were quantity rather than quality, and control of the air.

Slowly but surely, the British and Canadians fought their way through Caen, while the Americans struggled through the *bocage* across the Cotentin peninsula and took Cherbourg.

By the end of July they had reached Avranches, from where General Patton launched his breakout across Brittany before turning to the east. As the Canadians pushed south to Falaise, and the Americans arrived at Argentan, the German armies were trapped in the "Falaise Pocket". The Battle of Normandy came to an end on 19–20 August with the closing of the "Falaise Gap" at its mouth by Polish troops at Montormel.

After that, Paris was liberated on 25 August, Brussels by 2 September. Most of France – with the exception of Alsace and Lorraine – saw little fighting from that point onwards, but the battles to secure ports such as Brest and Le Havre continued for some time.

Visiting Normandy and other battlefields

There are 29 sites and museums in the well-organised *Espace Historique de la Bataille de Normandie*, with a *Normandie Pass* card providing discounts for several visits. All tourist offices provide comprehensive information. Again, museums come in two kinds. The two big museums are the Mémorial de Caen, which seeks to present the battle in a broader political context, and the Musée-Mémorial in Bayeux, which follows the actual events much more closely. Impressive among the smaller museums are Mémorial Pegasus, the Canadian Juno Beach Centre at Courseulles and Utah Beach; some private museums are quite tacky, with shop dummies in old uniforms.

> *The road junction of Tilly-sur-Seulles was the one Norman village actually obliterated, since British engineers decided there was so much rubble that it would be better just to bulldoze the remains so they could drive over them.*

The most famous American war cemetery outside the US is above Omaha Beach, with long, precise lines of over 9,300 graves. British and Canadian cemeteries, as for the first war, are smaller, and more garden-like, again with personal messages suggesting something of each life. The German cemeteries in Normandy, like that at La Cambe, near Omaha, are huge, dark and almost hidden.

Outside Normandy, there is little record of events in 1940, and only a modest museum in Dunkirk. Around the Pas-de-Calais, museums and preserved bunkers commemorate Hitler's Atlantic Wall. Near St-Omer are two oddities, giant bunkers built to launch V1 and V2 flying bombs and rockets against London.

Scars of war

The battles had lasting physical effects on the landscape. The devastation caused by artillery bombardments in 1914–18 stunned those who witnessed it, but the destruction of 1940–44, including that produced by aerial bombing,

LEFT: display inside the Caen Memorial Museum.
RIGHT: bunker overlooking the English Channel, in the Atlantic Wall Museum.

was on a whole new scale. In 1940 the Germans destroyed large parts of Amiens, Abbeville, Calais, Dunkirk and Rouen. From 1940 to 1944 many cities were targets for Allied bombers, notably ports such as Brest and Lorient that were German submarine bases. Then came the Normandy campaign, preceded by intensive bombing. Most of Caen was destroyed in the six-week battle for the city. Special mention is required of the Channel ports. The Germans were fully aware of the importance of denying the Allies a usable port. Hence Cherbourg, St-Malo and especially Brest and Le Havre were taken by siege, Brest by the Americans in several weeks, Le Havre in one massive British attack. The result was that these two were destroyed more comprehensively than any other cities in France. For many French people, "Liberation" evoked very mixed feelings.

Afterwards, the scale of reconstruction was daunting. A remarkable rebuilding programme was undertaken in St-Malo, while Le Havre was the focus of a radical architectural project. Elsewhere, in towns like St-Lô, or Calais, the solution was 1940s reconstruction architecture, the plain, grey, simple (and inexpensive) style that has become another part of the northern French landscape. ❑

GLOBAL WAR

World War I sites give a vivid idea of how global the conflict could be. Both France and Britain relied heavily on their empires, as reflected in the number of Muslim graves in French cemeteries, or the Indian Memorial at Neuve-Chapelle, west of Lille, with the names of over 4,700 men of the British Indian army (from India, Pakistan and Bangladesh) who died in France. Nearby at Richebourg is the Portuguese Military Cemetery. Portugal was dragged into the war in 1916 because of its traditional links with Britain, which put pressure on it to confiscate German assets in Portugal. When it did so, Germany declared war, and 55,000 Portuguese troops were attached to the British army in France. They had a particularly hard time in the German 1918 offensive, and 1,381 are buried in the cemetery.

Some of the most surprising graves are Chinese. In 1915 the British were already concerned at a likely shortage of men, and a call was sent to British diplomats in China to recruit labourers to take on fetching-and-carrying work behind the lines, to release soldiers for the front. Eventually the "Chinese Labour Corps" had 96,000 men in France. They were not asked to fight, but could be hit by artillery, and many died in the flu epidemic at the end of the war. Over 800 lie in the *Cimetière Chinois* at Noyelles-sur-Mer, by the Baie de la Somme.

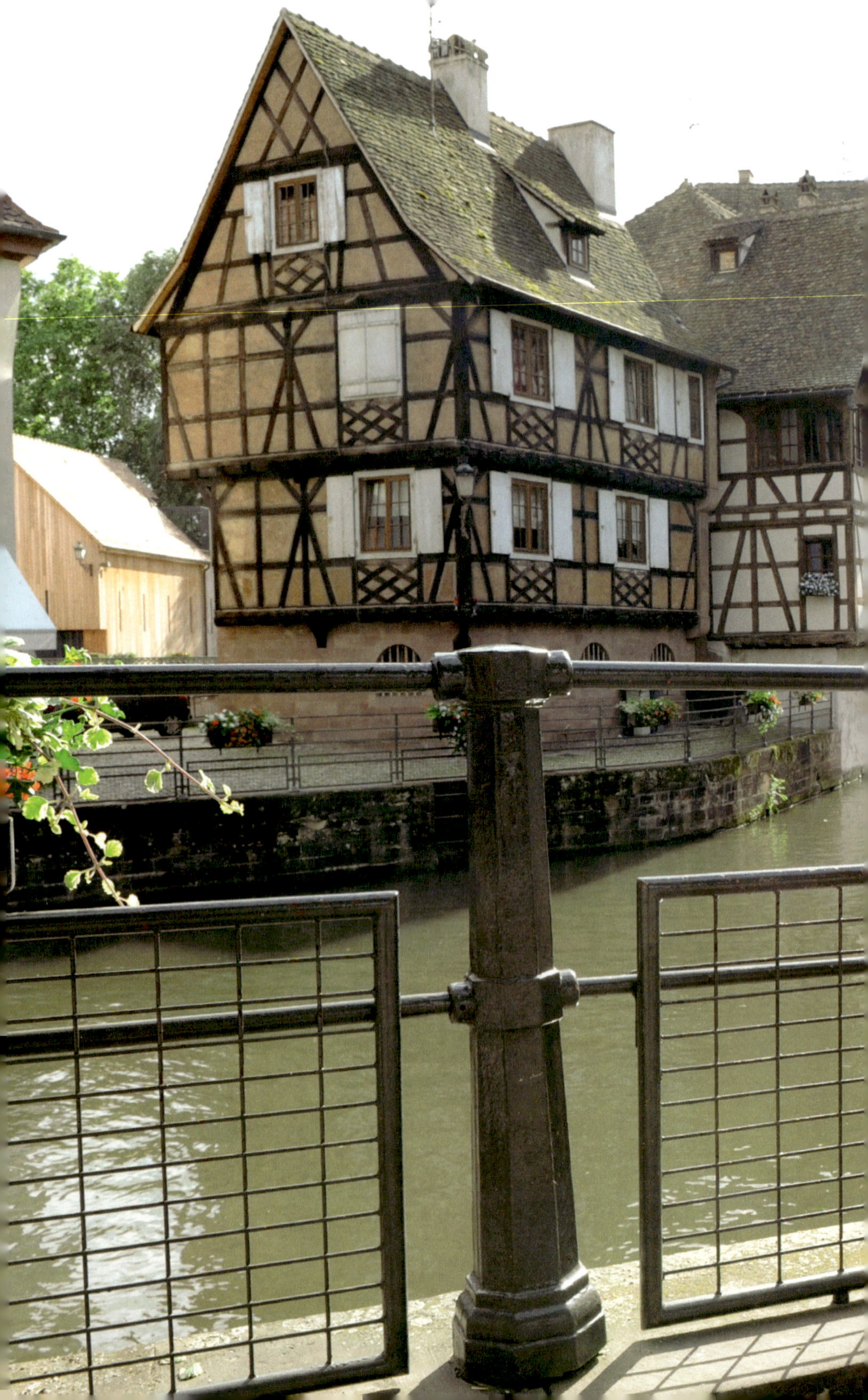

HOTEL DE FRANCE
Café
Le Bist
BAR
RESTAURANT
SALADERIE
GRILL
acier

PLACES

A detailed guide to the very best places to visit in northern France, with the principal sites clearly cross-referenced by number to the maps

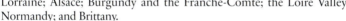

The north of France is densely packed with beautiful villages, historic towns and cities, great monuments and museums, and attractive countryside. So much so that the hardest part of any visit may be deciding where to start and how much to pack in.

For convenience, the 13 regions into which northern France is officially divided have been grouped into 10 chapters covering: Paris; its hinterland the Ile-de-France; the North (Nord-Pas-de-Calais and Picardy); Champagne; Lorraine; Alsace; Burgundy and the Franche-Comté; the Loire Valley; Normandy; and Brittany.

The obvious place to start is the capital, famous for its landmarks and romantic streets. It also makes a useful base for reaching much of the rest of the north. The choice opens up in all directions. Northern France gave the world Gothic architecture as seen in all its glory at Reims, Chartres and Amiens. Later it set the style for palace building with the great Renaissance châteaux of the Loire Valley and the legendary pleasure dome of Versailles. For battlefield tourism, there are the D-Day beaches of Normandy (with the famous Bayeaux tapestry close at hand) and the memorials of the Somme and Verdun from World War I. Further south, there is Champagne, Burgundy and Alsace – famous for their wine as well as exquisite food and some beautiful countryside. If, on the other hand, you just want to relax by the seaside, you'll probably find what you are looking for in Normandy and Brittany. These two regions also have attractive cliffs and islands, pretty seaports to visit, and restaurants specialising in fish and seafood. A visit to the atmospheric island abbey of Mont-St-Michel is a highlight of many trips.

In between these places are landscapes of quiet beauty. It is easy to see how writers and artists throughout the centuries, most notably the Impressionist painters, found inspiration across the region. All you have to do is choose where you want to see, and go. ❑

PRECEDING PAGES: the Louvre courtyard; the stunning Art Nouveau interior of the Galeries Lafayette, Paris; Petite-France, Strasbourg. **LEFT:** the Breton town of Josselin. **TOP:** detail from the Bayeux Tapestry. **ABOVE LEFT:** barrels of Veuve Clicquot champagne, Reims.

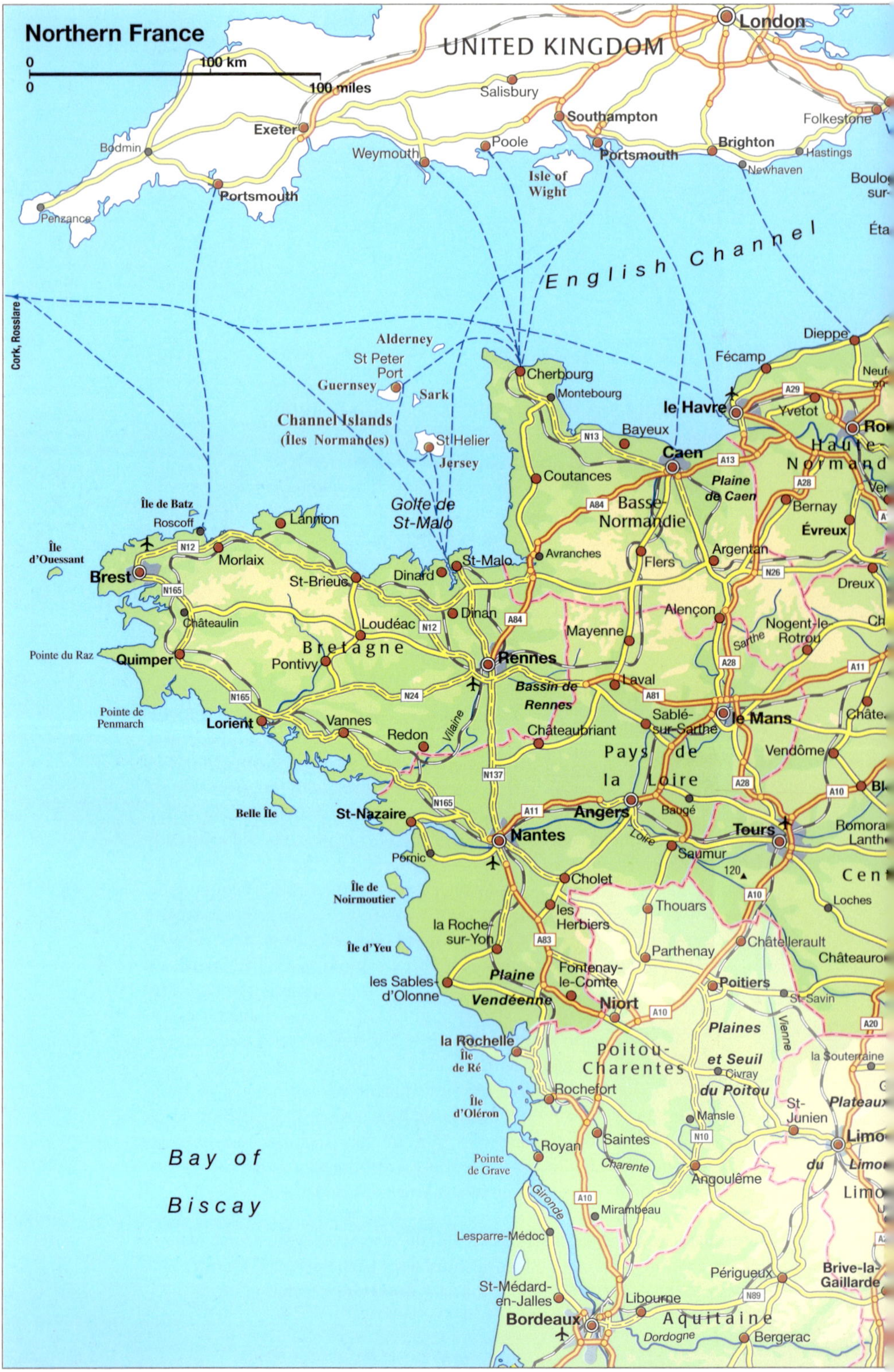
Northern France
0
100 km
0
100 miles
UNITED KINGDOM
London
Salisbury
Southampton
Folkestone
Exeter
Bodmin
Poole
Weymouth
Portsmouth
Brighton
Hastings
Newhaven
Isle of Wight
Penzance
Portsmouth
English Channel
Cork, Rosslare
Alderney
St Peter Port
Guernsey
Sark
Channel Islands
(Îles Normandes)
St Helier
Jersey
Golfe de St-Malo
Cherbourg
Montebourg
Dieppe
Fécamp
le Havre
Yvetot
Bayeux
Caen
Haute-Normandie
Coutances
Plaine de Caen
Basse-Normandie
Bernay
Évreux
Argentan
Flers
Avranches
Île de Batz
Roscoff
Lannion
Île d'Ouessant
Brest
Morlaix
St-Brieuc
Dinard
St-Malo
Dinan
Châteaulin
Loudéac
Bretagne
Pointe du Raz
Quimper
Pontivy
Rennes
Bassin de Rennes
Mayenne
Alençon
Dreux
Nogent-le-Rotrou
Sarthe
Laval
Pointe de Penmarch
Lorient
Vannes
Redon
Vilaine
Châteaubriant
Sablé-sur-Sarthe
le Mans
Pays de la Loire
Vendôme
Belle Île
St-Nazaire
Angers
Baugé
Nantes
Loire
Saumur
Tours
Pornic
Cholet
120
Île de Noirmoutier
les Herbiers
Thouars
Loches
la Roche-sur-Yon
Île d'Yeu
Parthenay
Châtellerault
Châteauroux
les Sables-d'Olonne
Plaine Vendéenne
Fontenay-le-Comte
Niort
Poitiers
St-Savin
la Rochelle
Île de Ré
Poitou-Charentes
Plaines et Seuil du Poitou
Vienne
Civray
la Souterraine
Rochefort
Île d'Oléron
Mansle
St-Junien
Saintes
Royan
Pointe de Grave
Charente
Angoulême
Bay of Biscay
Gironde
Mirambeau
Lesparre-Médoc
Périgueux
Brive-la-Gaillarde
St-Médard-en-Jalles
Libourne
Bordeaux
Aquitaine
Dordogne
Bergerac
N12
N165
N24
N13
A13
A84
A28
A29
N26
A81
A11
N137
N165
A83
A10
A20
N10
N89

NETHERLANDS
Knokke-Heist
Zeebrugge
Oostende
Antwerpen
Leverkusen
kerque
Gent
Mechelen
Roeselare
Köln
Bergisch Gladbach
Maastricht
St-Omer
Bailleul
Kortrijk
Bruxelles
Siegen
A16
A25
Roubaix
Aachen
Liège
rd-Pas-Calais
Lille
BELGIUM
Bonn
Tournai
Charleroi
Béthune
Verviers
GERMANY
Lens
Namur
Douai
Valenciennes
Koblenz
Frankfurt am Main
Arras
Dinant
Cambrai
Rhein
Wittlich
Amiens
Bastogne
Somme
A26
Bingen am Rhein
LUXEMBOURG
Mainz
Darmstadt
Hirson
St-Quentin
Trier
A16
Roye
Mosel
Charleville-Mézières
Laon
Luxembourg
Picardie
Mannheim
Beauvais
Compiègne
Merzig
Kaiserlautern
Vouziers
Longwy
Neunkirchen
Soissons
Ludwigshafen am Rhein
Meuse
Oise
Reims
Thionville
Saarbrücken
Château-Thierry
Verdun
Landau
A1
Marne
Châlons-en-Champagne
A4
Metz
Karlsruhe
toise
A4
PARIS
Meaux
A4
Pforzeim
Bar-le-Duc
Stuttgart
Créteil
A26
Sarrebourg
Toul
Nancy
Vitry-le-François
N4
Île-de-France
St-Dizier
Strasbourg
Provins
Lorraine
Lunéville
Champagne-Ardenne
A5
Alsace
Offenburg
mpes
Seine
Neufchâteau
Sélestat
Troyes
A31
N57
St-Dié
Nemours
Freiburg im Breisgau
Sens
Chaumont
Colmar
A5
Épinal
Vosges
éans
Montargis
Châtillon-sur-Seine
Grand Ballon
1424
A35
A6
Langres
Loire
Auxerre
Plateau de Haute-Saône
Mulhouse
Gien
N71
A31
Lure
Belfort
Rhein
Cosne-Cours-sur-Loire
Bourgogne
Selongey
Saône
Basel
Vesoul
Avallon
434
Mont Tasselot
598
Delémont
Zürich
N7
A10
Doubs
ierzon
A6
Dijon
Besançon
Biel
Dole
Bourges
Beaune
Bern
Haut-Folin
901
Franche-Comte
Luzern
Nevers
Autun
Pontarlier
Chalon-sur-Saône
Loire
mand-rond
FRANCE
Yverdon
Côte d'Or
Jura
Fribourg
A6
Lons-le-Saunier
Interlaken
Moulins
Tournus
Lausanne
SWITZERLAND
Digoin
Plaine de la Loire
A71
N83
Lac Léman
Montreux
Mâcon
Brig
Montluçon
Allier
Lapalisse
Genève
Sion
45
Le Buet
3099
N7
A71
Bourg-en-Bresse
Martigny
usson
Roanne
A6
Sallanches
Clermont-Ferrand
Thiers
A40
Annecy
Mt Blanc
4808
Puy de Dôme
1464
A89
Balbigny
Villeurbanne
Aosta
A41
Albertville
Lyon
A72
Rhône-Alpes
Auvergne
sel
Vienne
Chambéry
ITALY
Monts d'Auvergne
Puy de Sancy
1885
Issoire
St Étienne
Moûtiers
Alpi Graie
Grande Casse
3852
Bort-les-Orgues
Voiron
Vercelli
A75
N88
A7
Rhône
A41
Massif Central
A49
Grenoble
Modane
Torino
St-Flour
le-Puy-en-Velay
Massif du Pelvoux
Aurillac
Valence
Asti
Clelles
Briançon
Pradelles
Carmagnola
Alessandria
N

METROPOLITAIN
ABBESSES
VERY BAD TRIP

PARIS AND SURROUNDINGS

The city of romantics and art enthusiasts is fascinating at every turn. Easy day trips take you to magnificent palaces and other historic monuments

As Victor Hugo put it: "It is in Paris that the beating of Europe's heart is felt. Paris is the city of cities." Certainly, it is at the heart of France. In terms of urban sprawl, it is, in Europe, second only to London. Where matters of French administration, politics and cultural life are concerned, it plays an absolutely dominant role. It is also the world capital of chic. For all these reasons and more, Paris is so unlike much of the rest of its own country that it has been described as virtually a city-state in its own right.

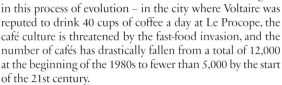

Largely undamaged by two world wars, Paris has been created by centuries of inspired planning. Its street corners reek of history, and its monuments and museums are well known to people from all over the world. Perfectly preserved though it is, Paris is a city unafraid of change. I.M. Pei's pyramid in front of the Louvre and the massive development at La Défense are evidence of that. But there are regrets in this process of evolution – in the city where Voltaire was reputed to drink 40 cups of coffee a day at Le Procope, the café culture is threatened by the fast-food invasion, and the number of cafés has drastically fallen from a total of 12,000 at the beginning of the 1980s to fewer than 5,000 by the start of the 21st century.

Paris has a reputation for being a city of romance, a city of arts par excellence and a city of fun. There's endless entertainment here for the observant, who will learn as much about Paris and its inhabitants from walking the streets as from visiting the great museums.

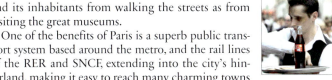

One of the benefits of Paris is a superb public transport system based around the metro, and the rail lines of the RER and SNCF, extending into the city's hinterland, making it easy to reach many charming towns and beautiful swathes of countryside. Chartres, the palaces at Versailles and Fontainebleau, Disneyland Paris, and other attractions within easy reach of Paris are profiled in the Ile-de-France chapter *(page 135)*. ❑

LEFT: Abesses metro station, one of just three original Art Nouveau entrances left in Paris. **TOP:** the signature neon windmill of the Moulin Rouge. **ABOVE LEFT:** Eiffel Tower souvenirs. **ABOVE RIGHT:** service may not always come with a smile, but Parisian waiters pride themselves on their professionalism.

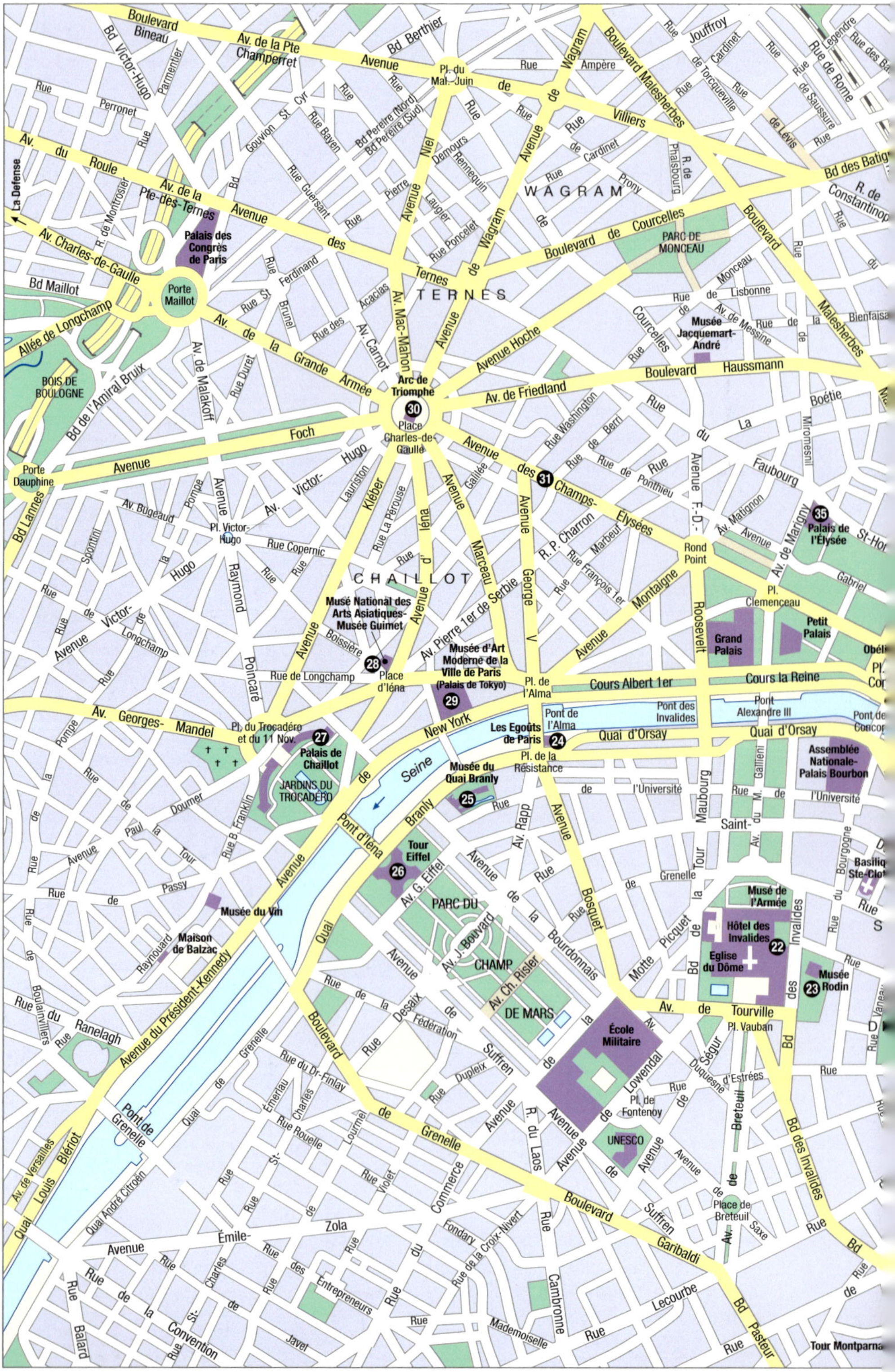
Boulevard Bineau
Av. de la Pte Champerret
Bd Berthier
Avenue
Pl. du Mal. Juin
de
Wagram
Boulevard Malesherbes
Rue Jouffroy
Rue Cardinet
Rue de Tocqueville
Rue de Rome
Rue de Saussure
Legendre
Rue des Ba
Rue Ampère
Villiers
de Lévis
Bd des Batig
R. de Constantinop
Bd Victor-Hugo
Parmentier
Rue Perronet
Gouvion St. Cyr
Rue Bayen
Bd Pereire (Nord)
Bd Pereire (Sud)
Niel
Demours
Rennequin
Rue Cardinet
Prony
R. de Phalsbourg
Av. du Roule
La Défense
R. de Montrosier
Av. de la Pte-des-Ternes
Avenue des Ternes
Rue Guersant
Rue Pierre
Laugier
Rue Poncelet
WAGRAM
Boulevard de Courcelles
PARC DE MONCEAU
Boulevard
Palais des Congrès de Paris
Av. Charles-de-Gaulle
Porte Maillot
Bd Maillot
Allée de Longchamp
Rue St Ferdinand
Brunel
Rue des Acacias
Av. Carnot
Av. Mac-Mahon
TERNES
Avenue Hoche
Rue de Lisbonne
Monceau
Av. de Messine
Musée Jacquemart-André
Courcelles
Malesherbes
Bienfaisa
BOIS DE BOULOGNE
Bd de l'Amiral Bruix
Av. de Malakoff
Rue Duret
Av. de la Grande Armée
Arc de Triomphe
30
Place Charles-de-Gaulle
Av. de Friedland
Boulevard Haussmann
Rue La Boétie
Miromesnil
Porte Dauphine
Avenue Foch
Victor-Hugo
Lauriston
Kléber
Rue La Pérouse
Avenue d'Iéna
Avenue Marceau
Galilée
Rue Washington
Rue de Berri
Rue de Ponthieu
Avenue des Champs-Élysées
31
Faubourg
Avenue F.-D.-Roosevelt
Av. Matignon
Avenue de Marigny
35
Palais de l'Élysée
St-Hon
Bd Lannes
Av. Bugeaud
Pompe
Pl. Victor-Hugo
Rue Copernic
Avenue George V
R. P. Charron
Marbeuf
Rue François 1er
Rond Point
Spontini
CHAILLOT
Raymond Poincaré
Musé National des Arts Asiatiques-Musée Guimet
Boissière
Av. Pierre 1er de Serbie
Avenue Montaigne
Pl. Clemenceau
Gabriel
Grand Palais
Petit Palais
Obél
Rue de Longchamp
28
Place d'Iéna
Musée d'Art Moderne de la Ville de Paris (Palais de Tokyo)
29
Pl. de l'Alma
Cours Albert 1er
Cours la Reine
Av. Georges-Mandel
Pl. du Trocadéro et du 11 Nov.
27
Palais de Chaillot
New York
Pont de l'Alma
Pont des Invalides
Pont Alexandre III
Pont de Concor
Les Egoûts de Paris
24
Quai d'Orsay
Pl. de la Résistance
Assemblée Nationale-Palais Bourbon
JARDINS DU TROCADÉRO
Seine
Musée du Quai Branly
25
Rue de l'Université
Av. Rapp
Maubourg
M. Gallieni
Doumer
Paul
Rue B. Franklin
Pont d'Iéna
Branly
Tour Eiffel
26
Avenue Bosquet
Saint-
Rue de Bourgogne
Basiliq Ste-Clot
Passy
Av. G. Eiffel
PARC DU CHAMP DE MARS
Bourdonnais
Grenelle
Musée du Vin
Av. J. Bouvard
Picquet
Motte
Musée de l'Armée
Hôtel des Invalides
22
Eglise du Dôme
Maison de Balzac
Raynouard
Quai
Av. Ch. Risler
Avenue Desaix
23
Musée Rodin
Rue de la Fédération
Av. de Tourville
Pl. Vauban
Boulainvilliers
Ranelagh
Avenue du Président-Kennedy
Boulevard de Grenelle
Suffren
Dupleix
École Militaire
Lowendal
Ségur
Duquesne
d'Estrées
Breteuil
Bd des Invalides
Rue du Dr-Finlay
Emeriau
Charles
Rue Rouelle
Lourmel
Pl. de Fontenoy
UNESCO
Pont de Grenelle
Av. de Versailles
Quai Louis Blériot
Quai André Citroën
Violet
Commerce
R. du Laos
Avenue de Saxe
Place de Breteuil
Avenue Émile-Zola
Rue des Entrepreneurs
Fondary
Rue de la Croix-Nivert
Rue Cambronne
Boulevard Garibaldi
Rue Balard
Rue de la Convention
St-Charles
Javel
Mademoiselle
Rue Lecourbe
Bd Pasteur
Tour Montparna

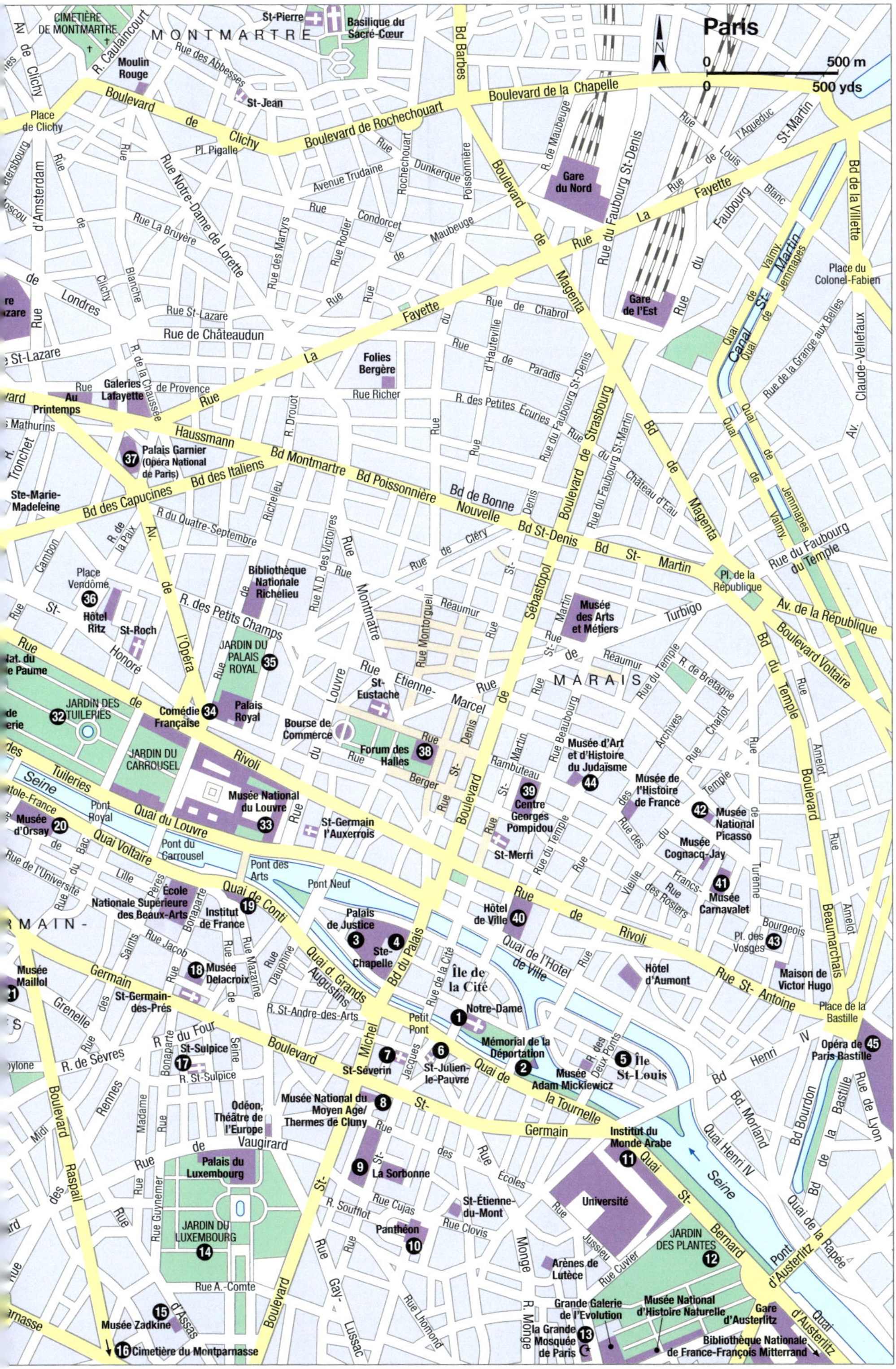

Paris
0
500 m
0
500 yds
N
CIMETIÈRE DE MONTMARTRE
MONTMARTRE
St-Pierre
Basilique du Sacré-Cœur
Moulin Rouge
St-Jean
Place de Clichy
Boulevard de Clichy
Pl. Pigalle
Boulevard de Rochechouart
Boulevard de la Chapelle
Bd Barbès
Gare du Nord
Gare de l'Est
Rue du Faubourg St-Denis
Boulevard de Magenta
Rue La Fayette
Avenue Trudaine
Rue Condorcet
Rue de Maubeuge
Rue Notre-Dame de Lorette
Rue des Martyrs
Rue La Bruyère
Rue de Londres
Rue St-Lazare
Rue de Châteaudun
Rue de Provence
Rue Richer
Folies Bergère
Rue de Paradis
Rue de Chabrol
R. des Petites Écuries
Galeries Lafayette
Au Printemps
Haussmann
Palais Garnier (Opéra National de Paris)
Bd des Capucines
Bd des Italiens
Bd Montmartre
Bd Poissonnière
Bd de Bonne Nouvelle
Bd St-Denis
Bd St-Martin
Boulevard de Strasbourg
Ste-Marie-Madeleine
R. du Quatre-Septembre
Place Vendôme
Hôtel Ritz
St-Roch
Bibliothèque Nationale Richelieu
R. des Petits Champs
JARDIN DU PALAIS ROYAL
Palais Royal
Comédie Française
JARDIN DES TUILERIES
JARDIN DU CARROUSEL
Musée National du Louvre
Rue de Rivoli
Quai des Tuileries
Quai du Louvre
Pont Royal
Musée d'Orsay
Quai Voltaire
Pont du Carrousel
Pont des Arts
Pont Neuf
St-Germain l'Auxerrois
Bourse de Commerce
St-Eustache
Forum des Halles
Rue Étienne-Marcel
Rue Réaumur
Rue Rambuteau
Centre Georges Pompidou
St-Merri
Musée des Arts et Métiers
MARAIS
Musée d'Art et d'Histoire du Judaïsme
Musée de l'Histoire de France
Musée National Picasso
Musée Cognacq-Jay
Musée Carnavalet
Pl. des Vosges
Maison de Victor Hugo
Place de la Bastille
Opéra de Paris Bastille
Hôtel de Ville
Hôtel d'Aumont
Rue St-Antoine
Pl. de la République
Av. de la République
Boulevard Voltaire
Bd du Temple
Boulevard Beaumarchais
Canal St-Martin
Quai de Valmy
Quai de Jemmapes
Rue du Faubourg du Temple
Place du Colonel-Fabien
Bd de la Villette
Rue de la Grange aux Belles
Av. Claude-Vellefaux
École Nationale Supérieure des Beaux-Arts
Institut de France
Quai de Conti
Quai d. Grands Augustins
Palais de Justice
Ste-Chapelle
Bd du Palais
Île de la Cité
Notre-Dame
Mémorial de la Déportation
Quai de l'Hôtel de Ville
Île St-Louis
Musée Adam Mickiewicz
Quai de la Tournelle
St-Séverin
St-Julien-le-Pauvre
Musée Delacroix
St-Germain-des-Prés
Boulevard St-Germain
Boulevard St-Michel
R. St-André-des-Arts
Petit Pont
Musée Maillol
St-Sulpice
R. de Sèvres
Odéon, Théâtre de l'Europe
Musée National du Moyen Age/ Thermes de Cluny
Rue de Vaugirard
Palais du Luxembourg
JARDIN DU LUXEMBOURG
La Sorbonne
Panthéon
St-Étienne-du-Mont
Rue des Écoles
Institut du Monde Arabe
Université
Quai St-Bernard
Seine
Quai Henri IV
Bd Henri IV
Bd Morland
Bd Bourdon
Rue de Lyon
Quai de la Rapée
Pont d'Austerlitz
Quai d'Austerlitz
JARDIN DES PLANTES
Arènes de Lutèce
Rue Monge
Grande Galerie de l'Evolution
Musée National d'Histoire Naturelle
Gare d'Austerlitz
La Grande Mosquée de Paris
Bibliothèque Nationale de France-François Mitterrand
Boulevard Raspail
Musée Zadkine
Cimetière du Montparnasse
Rue Gay-Lussac
R. Soufflot
Rue A.-Comte
Rue Guynemer
Rue d'Assas
Rue Lhomond

PARIS

Perhaps the grandest and certainly one of the most beautiful cities in the world, Paris is loved for its inimitable atmosphere and its many pleasures, from culture to cuisine

Paris is the hub of Europe, and its most densely populated capital. One-fifth of France's 64 million people live in and around the city, along with immigrants, students, artists, teachers, businesspeople and political refugees from around the world. The expatriate community is active; theatre, cinema, arts and news publications abound in various languages, including English. So many of the people living in the cosmopolitan region come from foreign lands and the provinces of France that the native *parisien* is a rare beast.

The first to arrive in this enchanted spot were the Parisii, a tribe of Gaulish fishermen and boatmen. The appearance of the Roman Empire brought about the strange mixture of Latin and northern civilisation that makes France unique. Though the Romans imposed their tongue, their official name for the city, Lutetia, disappeared from use over the years. Since then the number of emperors, philosophers, ambassadors, adventurers and outcasts who have arrived in this city is as uncountable as the lights bedecking it by night.

A city for strolling

Paris is a city ideal for strolling, tucked inside a 34km (21-mile) perimeter. It is divided into 20 *arrondissements*, or districts, which are used in postal codes and which begin in the centre with the *premier* (1er) *arrondissement* and spiral out like a snail shell in a clockwise direction, a pattern reflecting the city's historical development and successive enlargements. The River Seine weaves across Paris, dividing the north from the south into the *rive droite* (right bank) and *rive gauche* (left bank).

Everything is accessible by public transport. The metro is very efficient, but taking the bus, though slower, is a pleasant way to see the city and a good way to get your bearings.

LEFT: view from the Pont Alexander III.
RIGHT: romantic Montmartre moment.

Main attractions
- CATHÉDRALE NOTRE-DAME
- CONCIERGERIE
- SAINTE-CHAPELLE
- QUARTIER LATIN
- MUSÉE DE CLUNY
- PANTHÉON
- MUSÉE D'ORSAY
- LES INVALIDES
- TOUR EIFFEL
- ARC DE TRIOMPHE
- CHAMPS-ÉLYSÉES
- MUSÉE DU LOUVRE
- CENTRE POMPIDOU
- MONTMARTRE
- CIMETIÈRE PÈRE LACHAISE

The devilish gargoyles scowling down from Notre-Dame's upper gallery are not medieval nightmares but playful creations of the 19th-century Gothic revivalist architect, Viollet-le-Duc.

Notre-Dame

The Ile de la Cité in the middle of the Seine is the birthplace and topographical centre of Paris, and has been its spiritual and legislative heart for more than 2,000 years. Some of the ancient soul remains in its celebrated monuments.

The island is dominated by the soaring **Cathédrale Notre-Dame ❶** (Mon–Fri 8am–6.45pm, Sat–Sun 8am–7.15pm; free, charge for towers), which fills the eastern end of the island. The church of "Our Lady" was built during the 12th and 13th centuries, and extensively restored in the 19th. The original Madonna of the cathedral was a "black Virgin", a popular ancient fertility figure. This dark, hooded lady was already credited with several miracles before disappearing during the Revolution. A 14th-century statue of unknown origin stands in the same place (to the right of the choir) and is venerated still.

The building is a masterpiece of Gothic art. The tall central spire (82 metres/270ft) is flanked by two square towers. Visitors may climb all the way up during daylight hours and see the Bourdon, the 16-ton brass bell that the hunchback Quasimodo rang in Victor Hugo's novel, *Notre-Dame de Paris (The Hunchback of Notre-Dame)*. The view from the top, alongside the devilish stone gargoyles, is a heavenly reward after the long climb up the spiralling stone staircase.

Between the towers stretches a long gallery, and below this is the spectacular central rose window which has a diameter of 9 metres (31ft), forming a halo above a statue of the Virgin Mary. The window surmounts the Galerie des Rois, 28 modern statues of the kings of Judah and Israel. The statues were all decapitated during the Revolution *(see box below)*. Only recently were the heads discovered in a nearby construction site; they are now on display at the Cluny Museum. On a level with the parvis, the paved terrace in front of the cathedral, the three doorways of Notre-Dame are, left to right, the Virgin's Portal, the Judgement and St-Anne's Portal. Each is covered with intricate carvings relating biblical tales and the lives of the saints.

Lining the walls of the cathedral are 37 side chapels. Supported by flying but-

Notre-Dame through the ages

Even before it was finished, Notre-Dame had become the venue for state ceremonies, funerals and thanksgivings; in 1239 Louis IX deposited the Crown of Thorns and other relics acquired on crusade here, while Sainte-Chapelle was being built. Since then, Notre-Dame has been witness to a string of historical events. In 1589, Henri of Navarre was crowned in the cathedral, having decided to convert to Catholicism. The famous remark attributed to him – "Paris is worth a mass" – is almost certainly apocryphal. Come the Revolution, Notre-Dame was ravaged by looters, who melted down and destroyed anything that hinted of royalty, lopping off the heads of the kings of Judah along the top of the main portals.

By the time Napoleon decided to be crowned emperor in 1804, the cathedral was in such a shabby state that bright tapestries were hung up to cover the crumbling decor. Pope Pius VII attended reluctantly, and when he hesitated at the altar, Napoleon took the crown and – to cheers of "Vive l'Empereur!" – placed it on his head himself.

Another dramatic event took place at Notre-Dame in August 1944, at the thanksgiving ceremony for the Liberation of Paris, when the leader of the new government, General Charles de Gaulle, was shot at during the Te Deum.

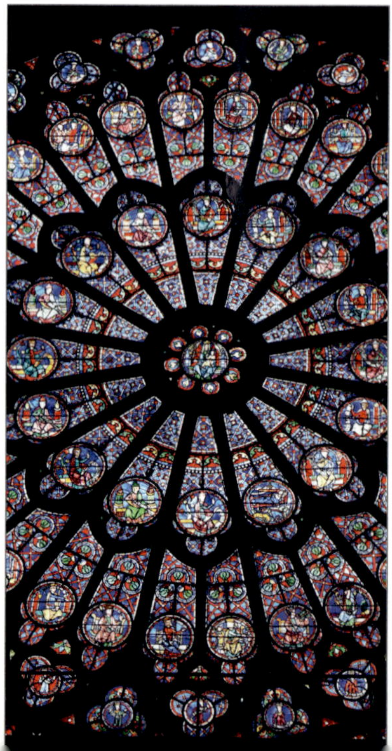

BELOW: rose window at Notre-Dame cathedral.

tresses, the vault of the chancel seems almost weightless, with stained-glass windows distributing rays of coloured light into the solemn shadows. The large main altar represents the *Offering of Louis XIII*, and commemorates the birth of the king's heir. To the left and right of the Nicolas Coustou *Pietà* are statues of Louis XIV (who completed the memorial) and Louis XIII.

In the **Crypte Archéologique** (Tue–Sun 10am–6pm; charge), underneath the parvis, are excavations of buildings dating back to the Roman city of Lutetia in the 3rd century, including parts of a house inhabited by the Gallic Parisii, amid the remains of medieval cellars.

Behind the cathedral, on the eastern tip of the Ile de la Cité, lies the bleak but moving **Mémorial de la Déportation** ❷ (9am–noon, 2–4.30pm) commemorating the 200,000 French deportees (Jewish, homosexual, or members of the Resistance) sent to their deaths in Nazi concentration camps. The chambers of this prison-like structure are engraved with quotations and the names of concentration camps.

A short walk west of Notre-Dame are the imposing walls of the Palais de Justice and Conciergerie.

The Conciergerie

At one time, the **Palais de Justice** ❸ (Mon–Fri 8.30am–6pm; charge) was a royal palace, and Louis IX had his bedroom in what is now the First Civil Court. In the 14th century, the monarchy, in the person of Charles V, moved his main residence to the new palace of the Louvre, and parliament, with full judiciary rights, moved in. Occupying the northeast wing, the **Conciergerie** (Mar–Oct 9.30am–6pm, Nov–Feb 9am–5pm; charge) looks like an intimidating castle, its four towers rising menacingly above impenetrable walls. It isn't hard to imagine this fortress as a merciless medieval prison, though it was originally built as a palace administered by the Comte des Cierges, or royal concierge, who was in charge of the king's seals, lodgings and taxes. The Conciergerie was made a prison in 1391, when his job changed to that of chief gaoler. The prison came into its own during the Revolution when

TIP

Every Sunday at 5pm, the organ master fills Notre-Dame with classical music, soaring out of the 112-stop instrument. Classical concerts are also given in Sainte-Chapelle.

BELOW: the Conciergerie.

TIP

Vedettes du Pont Neuf (tel: 01 46 33 98 38; www.vedettesdupont neuf.com) run cruises along the Seine lasting about an hour. Boats leave from the Square du Vert Galant, at the western tip of the Ile de la Cité (Métro: Pont Neuf), every half-hour in the high season.

it housed nearly 2,600 prisoners awaiting the guillotine, including Marie Antoinette. Ironically, her prosecutor, Danton, resided in the next cell before his trip to the guillotine as, in turn, did his nemesis, Robespierre.

Sainte-Chapelle

An ornate 18th-century gate next to the Palais de Justice opens onto the Cours de Mai, and the **Sainte-Chapelle** ❹ (Mar–Oct 9.30am–6pm, Nov–Feb 9am–5pm; charge), a glittering jewel of Gothic art, rising up amid the stark walls of the high court. The church was erected in 1246 to hold the Crown of Thorns bartered from the Venetians by Louis IX. Built in two tiers, the lower chapel was designed for the palace staff, and is consequently smaller and gloomier. From the shadows, climb the spiral staircase into the crystalline cavern of the upper chapel. The soaring windows catch the faintest of lights, creating kaleidoscopes of colour. Depicted are 1,134 scenes from the Bible which begin by the staircase with Genesis and proceed round the church to the 15th-century rose window. Regular concerts of chamber music are held in the chapel.

Three bridges

Several bridges link the Ile de la Cité to the river banks. The **Pont Neuf** (New Bridge) is, despite its name, the oldest bridge standing in Paris, having been completed in 1607. Linking the western end of the island to both the left and right banks, it was the first bridge to be built entirely in stone, the widest, and the only one to be equipped with raised pedestrian walkways. These qualities, plus its central location, made the Pont Neuf a popular meeting place for pedlars, acrobats, tooth-pullers, musicians, pickpockets and prostitutes. No small part of the Pont Neuf's charm are the 385 grotesque faces below its cornices, visible from the lower quai or aboard a *bateau mouche* tour boat *(see tip left)*.

The **Petit Pont**, which links the south side of the island to the left bank, is the shortest bridge in Paris but has the longest history, reaching back to the origins of Roman Lutetia. Originally a wooden bridge, it was burned

BELOW: the Pont Neuf, the oldest bridge in Paris.

Grand Paris

France has been described as a body with an over-swollen head. The capital sucks in inhabitants with a seemingly insatiable appetite and the built-up area expands in all directions. Yet even if Paris looks like a vast city, technically it is quite small in comparison with other major European cities. The Ville de Paris is a commune of just 105 square kilometres (41 sq miles) and it hasn't expanded its borders since 1860. It is surrounded by the *petit couronne*, a circle of 123 communes in 3 *départements*, each with its own mayor. Beyond them is the *grand couronne* of the other four Ile-de-France departments, bringing a great many more suburbs and satellite towns into the *agglomération parisienne* (conurbation). All this constitutes a metropolitan region of more than 11 million people divided into 1,500 independent but interrelated communes.

To inject some future cohesion into this huge and growing urban area, in 2007 president Nicolas Sarkozy announced a project for a "Grand Paris" to take shape over the following 30 or 40 years. Ten creative teams headed by architects, four foreign and six French, have been invited to work on the project. The aim is to make Greater Paris bigger, more dynamic and greener all at the same time, with tens of thousands of homes built each year, a fast automatic train line to link up business districts and a new forest planted to capture the carbon produced by the new metropolis.

down many times in the course of numerous battles. In 1718, the bridge and its surroundings blazed up once more, under strange circumstances. A custom of the times was to seek the repose of a loved one's soul by casting a bowl containing bread and a candle into the river. The mother of a drowned child did so, setting a barge piled with straw afire, and the bridge, packed with wooden houses, blazed out of control. This led to a law banning all buildings on bridges, which changed the face of the city.

Erected in 1970, the pedestrian **Pont St-Louis** is the seventh bridge built on the same site, joining the Ile de la Cité with the Ile St-Louis, a smaller island upstream.

Ile St-Louis

The **Ile St-Louis** ❺ is a privileged haven of peace and wealth. The island's elegance recalls the 17th century, the era of Louis XIII and Cardinal Richelieu, and its mansions are home to Paris's elite. Turning right along the south bank, you will come to the small **Musée Adam Mickiewicz** (by appointment, Thur 2.15–5.15pm; tel: 01 55 42 83 88; charge), former home of the Polish poet who lived in Paris from 1832–40 and devoted his work to helping oppressed Poles. The 17th-century building includes memorabilia of the Polish composer Frédéric Chopin, who often visited and played here.

Along the quiet streets of the island are small art galleries, intimate restaurants and tearooms, and Berthillon, home of what is reputed to be the best ice cream in Paris, which comes in over 100 delicious flavours. The main shop at 31 rue St-Louis-en-l'Ile stubbornly shuts in school holidays, but you can find its wares at many cafés nearby.

The Latin Quarter

Cross the river from either of the two islands on to the Left Bank and you step into the Quartier Latin (Latin Quarter), essentially the 5th *arrondissement*, a tangle of streets climbing the hill beside the boulevard St-Germain. The area is named after the lingua franca of students attending the university of the Sorbonne in the Middle Ages. The Latin Quarter is still a vibrant, studenty district and is served by innumerable small shops, bars, cafés and ethnic restaurants.

Close to the river bank is the church of **St-Julien-le-Pauvre** ❻ (9.30am–1pm, 3–6.30pm). Begun in 1170, it is small and squat, and tucked into a corner of its little garden where it looks like a humble country church which has somehow been transported to the city. The Italian poet Dante is said to have prayed here in 1304. In the garden you can sit under a 300-year-old false acacia. Behind it is the rue du Fouarre, named after the bales of hay on which students used to perch during open-air lectures in the Middle Ages. Round the corner, **St-Séverin** ❼ (11am–7.30pm) is another magical medieval church, famous for its palm-tree vaulting and twisting spiral columns, fine stained glass, and the oldest bell in Paris, dating from 1412. Its gargoyles thrust themselves out over the alleyway beside the church.

The convivial Brasserie de l'Ile St-Louis offers fine views of the Notre-Dame's soaring buttresses from its terrace.

BELOW: cycling around the Ile St-Louis.

TIP

The landmark English bookshop, Shakespeare and Company (37 rue de la Bûcherie; 10am–11pm), founded in 1956 by American George Whitman, stocks a wide range of literature, from the Bard to the Beatniks, and famous expatriate writers such as William Burroughs and James Baldwin, who were once frequent visitors.

The cluster of streets around here has been dubbed Little Athens because of its numerous Greek restaurants. At no 23 rue de la Huchette, parallel to the river, is the tiny **Theatre de la Huchette** which has been staging Eugene Ionesco's two short dramas *La Leçon (The Lesson)* and *La Cantatrice Chauve (The Bald Soprano)* nightly since 1957, and thus holds the world record for the longest-running play in the same theatre.

The Cluny Museum

At the corner of boulevards St-Michel and St-Germain is the **Musée National du Moyen Age/Thermes de Cluny** ❽ (Wed–Mon 9.15am–6pm; charge), France's national repository of all things medieval. The core of the building is a 15th-century *hôtel* (residence), one of the few medieval mansions remaining in Paris, but attached to this are the remnants of a Roman bath or frigidarium dating from between the 1st and 3rd centuries. The museum concentrates on the Romanesque and Gothic periods with items on display coming from across France and Europe. Exhibits include ivories, altarpieces, choirstalls, stained-glass panels, Visigothic crowns and carved stone heads from the statues adorning Notre-Dame's west portal.

The highlight of the museum is the dimly lit room on the first floor in which hangs a set of six tapestries known collectively as *La Dame à la Licorne* (The Lady and the Unicorn) after the two characters who are repeated in all of them. Richly detailed, the tapestries were woven in the 15th century and discovered in an obscure château in 1841. Five explore the realms of the senses: touch, taste, smell, sight and hearing; the sixth is on the more enigmatic title of "To My Only Desire".

Sorbonne to the Panthéon

At the heart of the Latin Quarter are the buildings of **La Sorbonne** ❾, one of the most celebrated and distinguished institutes of learning in the world, which was founded in 1253 as a college for poor theological students. Although the name is still used as shorthand for the University of Paris, the city now has thirteen indi-

BELOW: Gothic sculpture in the Cluny Museum.

vidual but connected universities, of which four make use of the premises of the old university. The facade of the Sorbonne looks on to the square of the same name (off the boulevard St-Michel) but its halls can only be entered by groups on a pre-arranged guided tour. The chapel, however, can be visited. Cardinal Richelieu is buried inside with his hat suspended above his tomb: it will fall, so legend has it, when he is released from hell.

Uphill from wherever you are in the Latin Quarter is the **Panthéon** ⑩ (Apr–Sept 10am–6.30pm, Oct–Mar 10am–6pm; charge), an 18th-century monument which sits on the top of Montagne Ste-Geneviève, the heart of the Roman city. Its crypt is the highly honoured resting place of the most illustrious French citizens, including Victor Hugo, Voltaire, Rousseau, Zola and Resistance leader Jean Moulin.

Close by, the attractive church of **St-Étienne-du-Mont**, with a superb rood screen, contains the remains of playwright Jean Racine (1639–99) and scientist and philosopher Blaise Pascal (1623–62), commemorated by plaques. It also has an ornate shrine to Ste Geneviève, patron saint of Paris.

Rue Mouffetard

Originally the road to Rome, **rue Mouffetard** is one of the oldest streets in Paris: narrow, crowded and full of cheap and cheerful places to eat. In its lower half is a street market (Tue–Sat, Sun am) around the Gothic church of **St-Médard**. Walk there via the picturesque place de la Contrescarpe (a few minutes from place du Panthéon eastwards), a lively place to sit and people-watch.

Besides the baths at Cluny, the only other Roman vestige in Paris is the nearby **Arènes de Lutèce**, the ancient arena, now used not for gladiatorial contests but for France's most popular outdoor game, *pétanque* or boules.

The far Left Bank

One of the most striking buildings on the Seine is the **Institut du Monde Arabe** ⑪ (10am–6pm Tue–Sun; charge), a high-tech blend of modern and traditional Arab styles, symbolic of the Institute's *raison d'être* – to deepen cultural understanding between the Western and Islamic worlds. A cultural centre and museum of Arab-Islamic art and civilisation, the nine-storey palace of glass, aluminium and concrete was designed by Jean Nouvel: its southern facade is a flat patterned wall of gleaming symmetry that recalls traditional Arab latticework. Views from the roof terrace-restaurant over the Seine and of Notre-Dame are exceptional.

The nearby **Jardin des Plantes** ⑫ is a good place for a stroll. Within the botanical garden is a small zoo (9am–6pm; charge), popular with children, and the Musée National d'Histoire Naturelle, France's official natural history museum. Its greatest attraction is the lavishly restored **Grande Galerie de l'Evolution** (Apr–Sept Mon, Wed–Fri 10am–5pm, Sat–Sun 10am–6pm; Oct–Mar Wed–Mon 10am–5pm; closed May; charge). The hall has retained elements of a 19th-century museum – parquet floors, iron columns, display cases

Foucault's original 67-metre (220ft) pendulum, designed to demonstrate the rotation of the Earth, hangs from the centre of the Panthéon dome.

BELOW: the Natural History Museum has an incredible collection of skeleton specimens.

Reading in the elaborately tiled Mosquée de Paris, the largest mosque in France and third largest in Europe.

– but has been completely modernised and equipped with the latest audiovisual techniques and interactive displays (mostly in French). The museum's pièce de résistance is the great herd of stuffed African animals that sweeps through the atrium.

Down the rue Quatrefages is **La Grande Mosquée de Paris** ⓭ (tours Sat–Thur 9am–noon, 2–6pm; charge). This green-and-white mosque was built in Hispano-Moorish style in 1922 by French architects to commemorate North African participation in World War I. The complex of buildings includes a museum of Muslim art, a patio inspired by the Alhambra in Granada, a delightful Moroccan tearoom and a Turkish bath.

Odéon and Luxembourg

The Odéon district acts as a buffer between the boisterous Latin Quarter (5th *arrondissement*) and the more refined St-Germain-des-Près (6th *arrondissement*). **Le Procope** on rue de l'Ancienne Comédie was the first ever café in Paris. Credited with introducing coffee to the city in 1686, it is still doing good business. Across the boulevard St-Germain, on place de l'Odéon, stands the neoclassical **Odéon-Théâtre de l'Europe**, one of France's leading theatres.

On the opposite side of the boulevard St-Michel from the Latin Quarter is the beautifully landscaped **Jardin du Luxembourg** ⓮, a haven of manicured greenery where young couples rendezvous under plane trees by the romantic Baroque Fontaine de Médicis, while children sail boats across the carp-filled lake in the middle. On Wednesdays and weekends, the famous Guignol puppet show is performed in the **Théâtre des Marionettes.** More serious entertainment is found by the corner with rue de Vaugirard, where people play chess under the trees. The **Musée du Luxembourg** (Tue–Thur, Sat 10.30am–7pm, Mon, Fri until 10pm, Sun 9.30am–7pm; charge) puts on crowd-pulling major exhibitions. Presiding over the gardens, the **Palais du Luxembourg**, built in the 17th century for Marie de Médicis after the murder of her husband, Henri IV, today houses the French Senate.

BELOW: playing chess and shooting hoops in the Jardin du Luxembourg.

Montparnasse

The once-rural area southwest of the Jardin du Luxembourg was christened Mount Parnassus – after the classical home of Apollo and his Muses – by a local poetry society in the 17th century, when they gathered on quarry mounds to recite verse. In the early years of the 20th century, the area became a magnet for artists, composers and revolutionaries, including Chagall, Picasso, Modigliani, Lenin and Stravinsky. Some decamped from Montmartre because of the inflated rents; others were émigrés in search of refuge or a new beginning, drawn to a place that embraced freethinkers and the avant-garde. They rented studios in the newly built-up area and gathered in cafés and brasseries on the boulevard Montparnasse such as **Le Select** (No. 99), **La Coupole** (No. 102) and the **Closerie des Lilas** (No. 171). After World War II, writers and philosophers such as Jean-Paul Sartre and Henry Miller moved in, patronising the same cafés – all still very much in business for those who wish to soak up the atmosphere over a cocktail and some classic brasserie fare.

The district – and the whole southern skyline – is dominated by the lumbering **Tour Montparnasse** (9.30am–11pm; charge). The 59-storey tower above Montparnasse train station was built in 1974 and is the only skyscraper in central Paris (as no more have been allowed since then). If you've a head for heights and the stomach for a lightening-fast lift, the roof terrace offers superb views of Paris.

As for art, the intimate **Musée Zadkine** ⓯ (Tue–Sun 10am–6pm; charge) displays the Cubist sculptures of the sculptor Ossip Zadkine, among the influx of émigrés from Russia, who moved into this tiny house and studio in 1928.

Boulevard Edgar-Quinet, which has some nice cafés and a lively morning market on Wednesdays and Saturdays, contains the third of Paris's giant cemeteries, with Père Lachaise and Montmartre. Among those buried in the **Cimetière du Montparnasse** ⓰ (April–Oct 8.30am–6pm, Sun from 9am; Nov–Mar until 5.15pm) are Baudelaire, Sartre, Simone de Beauvoir, Samuel Beckett and Alfred Dreyfus.

Beneath the Montparnasse tower is the Gare Montparnasse, which serves northwestern France. In the mid-19th century, thousands of Bretons emerged from this station, fleeing rural poverty and famine in Brittany, hence the many crêperies in the area.

BELOW LEFT: perusing the menu at the Atlas brasserie, rue de Buci. **BELOW:** Montparnasse mural, rue de la Gaité.

SHOP

Sandwiched between Café de Flore and Les Deux Magots is the sleek La Hune bookshop, crammed with literature and books on art, architecture and performing arts, in French and English. It stays open until midnight, and feels most "St-Germain" after dark.

Continuing the theme of death, under the lion at place Denfert-Rochereau stretch the **Catacombes** (Tue–Sun 10am–5pm; charge), miles of underground tunnels containing the skulls, femurs and tibias of some 6 million departed souls, stacked against the walls. The former Roman quarries were converted into ossuaries when cartloads of remains were removed from the overflowing cemeteries at place des Innocents and other areas *(see page 127)*.

Chic St-Germain

Historic heart of literary Paris, St-Germain-des-Prés covers an area roughly from St-Sulpice to the Seine. Its elegant streets now house chic boutiques, yet it retains a sense of animation, with cafés spilling out onto the pavements. In the 1940s the area became a breeding ground for literature and ideas. Existentialists, inspired by Jean-Paul Sartre, Simone de Beauvoir and Albert Camus, gathered in local cafés. The area has long since been colonised by designers and antique dealers.

Just north of the Jardin du Luxembourg looms the great bulk of **St-Sulpice** ⑰, one of the city's largest churches, harmonious except for its ill-matching towers on either side of its classical facade. Apart from one of the finest organs in Europe (used for many recitals) and Delacroix's *Jacob wrestling with the Angel*, inspired by the painter's own struggle with art, and an elaborate gnomon, the great cavern of a church has little to offer, but now draws throngs of fanatical readers of *The Da Vinci Code*, in which the church plays an important role.

The hub of St-Germain is the junction of boulevard St-Germain and rue Bonaparte in front of the 11th-century church of **Saint-Germain-des-Prés**, once one of the most powerful abbeys in the land. The legendary cafés **Flore** and **Deux Magots**, favoured by well-dressed intellectuals and tourists, face the **Brasserie Lipp**, where (rumour has it) only the most famous politicians and authors are invited to sit by the windows.

Behind the church, heading east down rue Jacob, filled with elegant antiques and design shops, you pass place de Furstenberg and the **Musée**

BELOW: a St-Germain café.

Metro Stations

It may sometimes be noisy, crowded, smelly and stuffy, but Parisians have an unconcealed affection for, and pride in, their underground rail system. For visitors it's usually a quick way to get around, but it's worth taking a breath en route and looking at your surroundings.

Several metro stations have been turned into authentic works of art. Abbesses has a mosaic by Montmartre artists down its staircase. Arts et Metiers is like being in a steampunk submarine. Concorde spells out the *Declaration of the Rights of Man and of the Citizen*. Other stations given a cultural makeover include Louvre-Rivoli, Bastille, Hotel de Ville, Tuileries, Parmentier, Pont-Neuf and Cluny-La Sorbonne. If you have nothing better to do, you could forget about the overground sights and spend a day exploring the Metro.

Delacroix 18 (Wed–Mon 9.30am–5pm; charge), where the Romantic artist lived from 1857 to his death in 1863, while he painted the murals in St-Sulpice. The museum has engaging sketches and memorabilia.

The streets around here are lined with chic boutiques. Rue de Buci throngs with shoppers in its colourful daily market (except Mon). Rue de Seine, rue Bonaparte, rue Jacob and rue des Beaux-Arts are full of modern art galleries.

Facing the river is the **Institut de France** 19 (guided visits only, Sat and Sun, 10.30am and 3pm; charge), the home of five "academies" grouping together the country's intellectual elite. The oldest and most august component of the Institute is the Academie Francaise which was founded in 1635 and always has forty members, known popularly as "the Immortals", who hold their seats until death, on which occasion a replacement is elected. The Academie's function is to rule over the all-important French language, regularising and standardising it as necessary. The other academies making up the Institute are watchdogs for Literature, Science, Fine Arts and Ethics, and Political Science.

In front of the Institute is the pedestrian **Pont des Arts** linking St-Germain-des-Prés with the Louvre *(see page 124)*, and a stroll across it is a good way to get a view of Paris without having to dodge cars. When it was first built, in 1801, it was the city's first iron bridge, but it has had to be rebuilt several times since then: in 1918 after a bombardment; again in 1944; and after damage by several boat collisions in the 1970s, it was rebuilt from the original plans and reopened in 1984.

Musée d'Orsay

No visit to Paris is complete without a pilgrimage to this spectacular former railway station, crammed full of the finest art spanning the period from 1848 to World War I. It was redesigned as a museum by Italian architect Gae Aulenti who preserved the building's Belle Époque architecture, redesigning the inner space, while keeping the airy majesty of the original train station. The **Musée d'Orsay** 20 (Tue–Sun 9.30am–6pm, Thur until 9.45pm; charge) is arranged on five levels around a vast central aisle, a grand setting for sculpture – the best pieces are by Carpeaux. Other artworks are displayed in chronological order starting on the ground floor with famous works by Ingres, Delacroix and Manet. The museum's biggest draw, its Impressionist paintings, hang on the crowded top floor, bathed in soft light from the glass-vaulted roof.

Not far from the Musée d'Orsay, housed in one of the many lavish 18th-century residences in this part of Paris, is the **Musée Maillol** 21 (Wed–Mon 10.30am–7pm, Fri until 9.30pm; charge). This more intimate museum focuses on paintings, sculptures and studies by Aristide Maillol, whose sculptures adorn the Tuileries *(see page 123)*, along with art by contemporaries Cézanne and Degas, collected by Dina Vierny, an art dealer and model for Maillol.

View across Paris to the Sacré Coeur from behind the old station clock on the upper level of the Musée d'Orsay.

BELOW: the skylit central aisle of the Musée d'Orsay.

TIP

Just east of the Invalides, in rue de Babylone, is La Pagode, Paris's most interesting cinema and tea house. The tea is strong, the gardens tropical and the films up to date. The building itself is a 19th-century replica of a Far Eastern pagoda whose main auditorium is lined with golden dragon motifs.

Invalides

The gleaming dome of the **Hôtel des Invalides** ㉒ is a masterpiece of French Baroque architecture and one of Paris's most prominent landmarks. Behind it is a set of 17th-century buildings commissioned by Louis XIV to house and care for retired and wounded soldiers. Napoleon, whose wars kept the hospital full, restored the institution to its former glory, making the church a necropolis and regilding the dome. The Eglise du Dôme, built as a royal chapel for Louis XIV, now contains Bonaparte's tomb. The emperor's body was returned to the city from St Helena in 1840, with much pomp and ceremony, and eventually laid to rest in the church crypt. His giant mausoleum is fittingly overblown.

Spread across either side of the Cour d'Honneur, the large **Musée de l'Armée** (Apr–Sept 10am–6pm, Nov–Mar until 5pm; closed first Mon of each month; charge) offers an extensive view of man's inhumanity to man and skill at warfare from the Stone Age to Hiroshima, with a terrifying selection of weapons and armour, and poignant displays on the two world wars.

Stretching to the Seine, the grassy **Esplanade des Invalides** is much loved by strollers, joggers, dogwalkers and rollerbladers. On its west side is a series of *pétanque* courts.

Rodin museum

A more peaceful place to visit is the nearby **Musée Rodin** ㉓ (Tue–Sun 10am–5.45pm; charge), in the Hôtel Biron, a fine 18th-century mansion where the sculptor lived and worked. Here, set in the charming garden of roses, trees and ponds, you can admire some of Rodin's most celebrated works including *The Thinker* (reputedly Dante contemplating inferno), *The Kiss*, *The Gates of Hell* and *The Burghers of Calais*. Inside, the various models for his statue of Balzac, which scandalised city officials, are alongside the collection of drawings, etchings and studies. Early critics accused the artist of making plaster casts of real bodies and pouring his bronze into them.

Included in the exhibition are works by Camille Claudel, the most famous of Rodin's mistresses and a gifted artist in her own right.

BELOW: the Jean Nouvel designed Musée du Quai Branly. **BELOW RIGHT:** Hôtel des Invalides.

On the river bank is the entrance to the city's least-likely-sounding tourist attraction, its sewers. Yet there is something fascinating about the subterranean working parts of great cities and **Les Egoûts de Paris** ㉔ (Sat–Wed June–Sept 11am–5pm, Oct–May 11am–4pm; charge), near Pont de l'Alma, have their particular charm. Half a kilometre of tunnels and chambers is visitable along with machines, models and displays on water supply and treatment for a teeming metropolis.

Quai Branly

Unlike his predecessor, François Mitterrand, President Jacques Chirac was not known for his *grands projets*, but in his last years in office he sponsored the **Musée du Quai Branly** ㉕ (Tue–Wed, Sun 11am–7pm, Thur–Sat until 9pm; charge), a popular new museum of world cultures which opened in 2006. It houses a vast collection of artefacts from Africa, Asia, the Americas and Oceania. With its colonial overtones, the collection has sparked some controversy, but the building itself – a striking foliage-covered maroon edifice by architect Jean Nouvel – has been more warmly received.

It is not far along the quai from here to Paris's trademark, the **Tour Eiffel** ㉖ (1st & 2nd levels mid-June–Aug 9am–12.45am, rest of the year 9.30am–11.45pm; charge). Erected for the Universal Exhibition of 1889, the 300-metre (985ft) tower designed by Gustave Eiffel was snubbed by intellectuals. But ordinary people grew fond of it as it rose up slowly, and cheered when Eiffel himself climbed up to plant a French flag on the top. The aesthetic debate raged on for years. Ultimately, telegraphic communications saved the tower, which became a relay station and is still used as a radio mast.

The view from the top is dynamite, the best city-gazing being about an hour before sunset. You can also visit the lift machinery and a small museum on the first floor which shows films about the tower. If you want to linger, there is a choice of places to eat, but expect to pay premium prices for the location.

The tower looks good from almost any angle. Even if you don't want to go

> *Gustave Eiffel epitomises all that is best of 19th-century architecture, heralding the Modern movement: inventiveness, lightness, structural expression, movement ... The Eiffel Tower still inspires us today.*
>
> Richard Rogers

BELOW: beneath the Eiffel Tower.

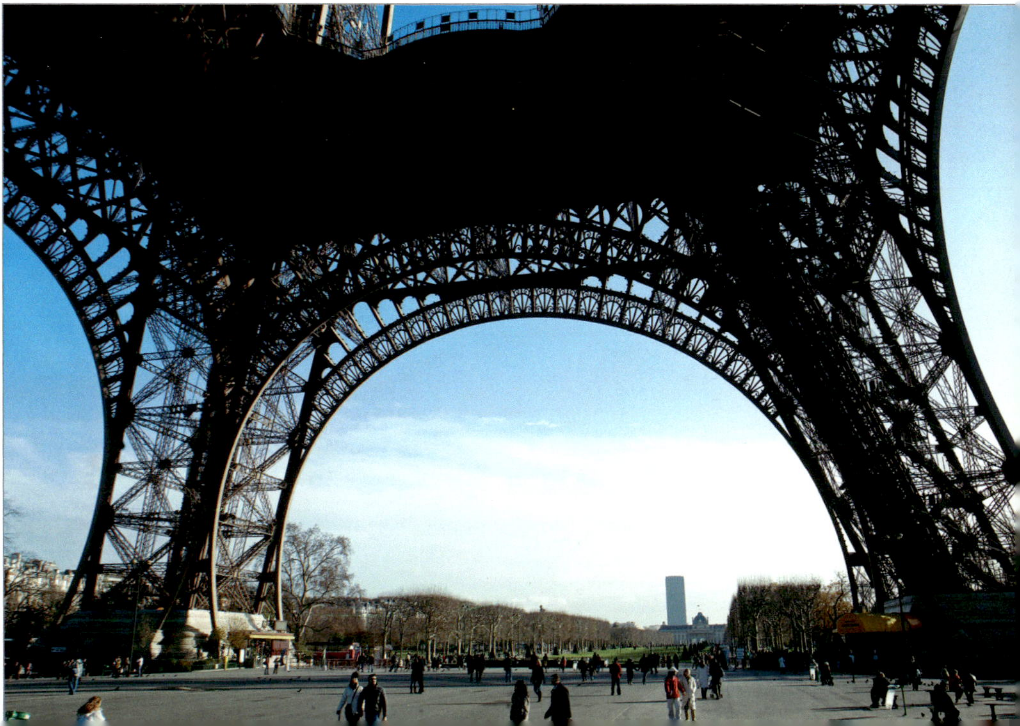

Paris Fashion

Its history as world couture capital is venerable, but globalisation has revolutionised the fashion world. Paris, London, New York and Milan now share equal status

French has been the language of fashion, and Paris its capital, since the Belle Epoque at the end of the 19th century. Since then, generations of designers have come and gone, preaching to people (women mainly) what they should be wearing.

The first of the style gurus was **Paul Poiret** (1879–1944), who opened his own house in 1903 and became famous as the man who released women from the corset – not for their comfort but in search of a look. After World War I, however, his clothes had begun to look dowdy in comparison with sleek and simpler creations of his new competitor, Gabrielle **"Coco" Chanel**, who dominated fashion in the interwar years.

World War II inevitably disrupted the world of fashion and after the conflict the world looked for change rather than a return to former styles. When **Christian Dior** presented his first collection (known as the "New Look") in 1947, he captured the mood of the post-war world and shot to fame, becoming, some would say, a dictator of fashion. Other designers of his generation were **Pierre Balmain**, with an instinct for sophistication and elegance, and the tall aristocrat **Hubert de Givenchy**, who dressed Audrey Hepburn in *Breakfast at Tiffany's*. Their success coincided with the rise of *Elle* magazine, founded in France in 1945, which would go on to be the largest fashion magazine in the world, printing 39 foreign editions.

French fashion was to face another shake-up in the 1960s, this time in response to the importation of youth culture from the USA and Britain. **Yves St-Laurent**, groomed as a successor by Christian Dior, is considered *the* man of the '60s and the inventor of *prêt a porter*. He once declared: *"the most beautiful way to dress a woman is with the arms of the man she loves"*, adding: *"but for those who haven't been lucky enough to find that happiness, I am here"*. **Pierre Cardin**, another doyen of French haut couture who started with Dior, is credited with the concept of unisex clothes and was instrumental in the '60s vogue for futuristic fashion. **Paco Rabanne**, born in Spain but raised in France because of the civil war, is sometimes called the "enfant terrible" of the decade because of his use of unconventional materials.

The 1970s and '80s brought with them the omnipresence of the mass media and consequently the overarching importance of image and branding. **Jean-Paul Gaultier**, sometime TV personality and also a friend of the camera-friendly Madonna, knew how to project the necessary new kind of cool: controversial, provocative and attention-grabbing.

In the last three decades, the world of French fashion has seen three fundamental changes. The first is globalisation. French fashion is now led by big business rather than maverick creativity: a French name and slogan are all that is needed to imbue any product with the kind of insouciant cachet, and hence profitability, that marketing people cannot invent. Simultaneously, Paris has seen the arrival of non-French designers at the head of its big couture houses – international stars transferred like football players between them. The third change is that Paris has become only one among several international capitals of fashion. It still has major fashion shows that attract the elite, but it takes its place in the calendar alongside its equals, London, New York and Milan. ❐

LEFT: modelling the mini dress and thigh boots, Paris 1969.

up the tower you can wander around the base and look at the iron framework whooshing overhead towards the vanishing point. A modern lighting system provides stunning illumination after dark.

The rectangular park at the foot of the tower is the **Champ de Mars**. For centuries this was a market garden supplying vegetables to Parisians. After the nearby Ecole Militaire was built, it became a parade ground, with capacity for 10,000 men. In 1790, it was the venue for the first-anniversary celebration of the storming of the Bastille.

Trocadéro

As you stand at the foot of the Eiffel Tower, your eye is carried across the river by the elegant span of the Pont d'Iéna. The buildings and terraces spread along the riverside on the far side of the bridge are known as the **Trocadéro**. The site was a wooded hill when Catherine de Médicis built a palace there, and Napoleon planned to build an imperial city, "a Kremlin a hundred times more beautiful than that of Moscow", on the spot.

Behind the Trocadéro lies the 16th *arrondissement*. This takes up a sizeable slice of western Paris and, like the 7th across the river, it is full of smart residences occupied by wealthy inhabitants. Not for those in search of the arcane or avant-garde. The reason most tourists and Parisians venture here is to visit the museums around place du Trocadéro, or to gaze at the magical views across the Seine to the Eiffel Tower.

The **Palais de Chaillot** ㉗ dates from the International Exhibition of 1937. The building holds three museums and the Théâtre National de Chaillot, devoted to productions of classical and modern plays. In the west wing are the **Musée de l'Homme** (closed for renovation until 2012), somewhat reduced since its collection of tribal art was transferred to the Musée du Quai Branly, and the **Musée de la Marine** (Wed–Mon 10am–6pm; charge), which charts the history of France as a seafaring nation. It holds a fine collection of paintings and models, but the centrepiece is the carved and gilded barge built for Napoleon. The east wing holds the **Cité de l'Architecture et du Patrimoine**, a museum and research centre which hosts large-scale exhibitions.

Major restoration of the Palais de Chaillot is ongoing, and parts of the complex may be inaccessible.

The **Musée National des Arts Asiatiques – Guimet** ㉘ (Wed–Mon 10am–6pm; charge) is one of the world's finest museums of Asian art. Its superb collection includes oriental art, statuary and textiles from China, Japan, India, Tibet, Nepal, Pakistan, Afghanistan, Korea and Vietnam – a reflection of France's colonial past. The prize exhibits are the Cambodian Buddhist sculptures from the temples of Angkor Wat.

Palais de Tokyo

Another monumental vestige of the 1937 Exhibition is the **Palais de Tokyo** ㉙, the east wing of which holds the **Site de Création Contemporaine** (Tue–Sun noon–midnight; charge), a

TIP

Queues for the Eiffel Tower can be up to two hours long in summer, so get there early. The best, and certainly most romantic place to see the Eiffel Tower is from Trocadéro at night, when it is gloriously lit up and in full view at the end of Champs de Mars.

BELOW: skateboarders practice their tricks around the Trocadéro.

TIP

The Champs-Élysées is made for parades and it looks its best during the Bastille Day (14 July) parade, and at night when the Arc de Triomphe and place de la Concorde are impressively floodlit.

state-funded contemporary arts centre, intended to serve as a laboratory for current art production. An adventurous, multi-disciplinary programme focuses on young artists through a dynamic mix of exhibitions, performances and workshops, and its fresh atmosphere, the hip "Tokyo Eat" restaurant-café, a stylish souvenir shop and the unique late-night opening hours have made it hugely popular.

In the same complex is the **Musée d'Art Moderne de la Ville de Paris** (Tue–Sun 10am–6pm; charge), an underrated modern art collection which gives a coherent survey of 20th-century art, especially relating to Paris, with works by Picasso, Matisse, Modigliani, Van Dongen, Soutine, and Raoul Dufy's gigantic mural, *La Fée Electricité* (Electricity Fairy), a celebration of light and energy commissioned for the 1937 Exhibition.

Adjacent is the **Pont de l'Alma** which was just another bridge across the Seine until the early hours of 31 August 1997 when a Mercedes travelling at high speed crashed in the underpass here killing three of its occupants including Diana, Princess of Wales, and her boyfriend, Dodi al-Fayed. Diana has become a legend and the Pont de l'Alma an ad hoc shrine to her memory.

On a lighter note, the Port de la Conférence next to the Pont de l'Alma, on the right bank, is the departure point for the nine open-top, glass-enclosed boats in the **Bateaux-Mouches** fleet. The standard riverborne sightseeing trip takes an hour and ten minutes. Some boats are floating restaurants for lunch or dinner cruises.

The Champs-Élysées

From the place de l'Alma, the avenue Marceau leads up to the **Arc de Triomphe** ㉚ (Apr–Sept 10am–11pm, Oct–Mar 10.30am–11pm; charge), at the top of the Champs-Élysées in the centre of place Charles de Gaulle-Etoile. It was commissioned by Napoleon in 1806, but the arch, ornately carved with heroic images of Revolutionary battles and the emperor's victories, was not complete until long after his death, in 1836. In 1920, an unknown soldier was buried beneath the arch and a flame

BELOW: the view down the Champs Élysées from the Arc de Triomphe.

marks his grave. The platform above the arch can be reached via a lift, and offers one of the finest Paris views.

The world's most famous street, the **Champs-Élysées** ㉛ leads you elegantly back towards the city centre, people-watching and window-shopping on the way. Its reputation has ebbed and flowed through the centuries: chic restaurants, cafés and nightclubs joined the fashion and luxury goods shops that appeared there through the 1990s, heralding the monumental avenue's comeback as one of the world's premier shopping destinations. The main shopping stretch of the avenue runs from the Arc de Triomphe to the Rond-Point. The lower half of the avenue runs through majestic chestnut trees down to the Tuileries gardens.

Between the Champs and the Seine stand the **Grand Palais** (Tue–Sat 9.30am–6pm, Sun 10am–7pm; charge for temporary exhibitions) and the **Petit Palais**, two distinctive glass-and-steel-domed museums which have changing exhibitions of 19th- and 20th-century paintings. Across the other side of the avenue, at the end of avenue de Marigny, the **Palais de l'Élysée** is the official residence of the President of the Republic.

Continue walking and you will emerge onto the **place de la Concorde**. The central Obelisk, which graced the tomb of Ramses II at Luxor 3,000 years ago, was erected on this spot in 1836. The greatest drama seen on the square was on 17 January 1793 when King Louis XVI was guillotined here.

The Tuileries

The **Jardin des Tuileries** ㉜ continues the line of the Champs-Élysées towards the Louvre. The Tuileries were designed by landscape artist André Le Nôtre, who also conceived the park at Versailles and other royal gardens. The wide paths and small lawns in the midst of trees are dotted with stately stone statues. At the Concorde end of the gardens, the small **Jeu de Paume** (Tue noon–9pm, Wed–Fri noon–7pm, Sat–Sun 10am–7pm; charge) puts on exhibitions of photography, and just opposite, the **Musée de l'Orangerie** (Wed–Mon 9am–5.45pm; charge) contains Monet's unforgettable "Water

Aristide Maillol (1861–1944) started sculpting at the age of 40, concentrating his efforts on large, bronze, nude female figures – 20 of which adorn the Tuileries.

BELOW: sunbathing in the Tuileries gardens.

The core of the Louvre's Egyptian collection originates from the victory spoils of Napoleon's Egyptian campaign.

Lilies" series, conceived especially for two oval rooms upstairs, alongside an impressive list of canvases by Cézanne, Renoir, Soutine, Matisse, Utrillo and Picasso among others.

Between the two wings of the palace which houses the Louvre is the **Jardin du Carrousel**, which ends in a square of the same name. Looking back, you have one of the longest architectural vistas in the world, stretching all the way from this small arch past the obelisk and Concorde, through the Arc de Triomphe to the Grande Arche at La Défense, ghost-like in the distance.

The Louvre

The queen of all art museums, the **Musée National du Louvre** ㉝ (Wed–Mon 9am–6pm, but until 10pm on Wed and Fri; admission charge) occupies a vast old palace which pivots around the modern Pyramid conceived by the Sino-American architect I.M. Pei and inaugurated, to much controversy, in 1989. Whether loved or despised, the design of the pyramid ingeniously disperses daylight round the foyer below, as well as providing multiple entrances to the Louvre's famous galleries.

BELOW: admiring the artwork in the Louvre.

The building is an accumulation of architectural projects. A fortress was erected on the riverside site in the 12th century by king Philippe-Auguste, the excavated remains of which can be visited. This was replaced in the 16th century by a Renaissance palace which was added to in the French classical style in the 18th century. The Louvre served as a royal residence until 1793.

Although the layout can be overwhelming at first, the museum has a relatively simple division into three wings: Richelieu (north), Denon (south, on the riverside) and Sully (around the courtyard of the Cour Carrée).

The Louvre's collections are divided into eight curatorial departments: Near Eastern antiquities (from Mesopotamia, Iran, Anatolia, Arabia and the Levant); Egyptian antiquities; Greek, Etruscan and Roman antiquities; Islamic art; sculpture; decorative arts (jewellery, tapestries, ivories, bronzes, ceramics and furniture); painting; and prints and drawings. The cut-off date for the Louvre's collection is 1848; art made after this date is allocated to the Musée d'Orsay across the river *(see page 117)*.

It would be folly to try to see all 35,000 works displayed in one go and, as with all large museums, it is essential to be selective and plan ahead. The Louvre is happy to dispatch visitors on a selection of self-guided themed routes, including one inspired by the plot of *The Da Vinci Code*.

Inevitably most visitors congregate around the best-known pieces, especially the "three ladies of the Louvre": the *Venus de Milo*, *The Winged Victory of Samothrace* and, most famous of all, Leonardo's *Mona Lisa* (La Joconde in French) with her enigmatic smile.

Forming part of the Louvre building, but independent of the main museum, is the **Musée des Arts Décoratifs** (Tue–Fri 11am–6pm, Sat–Sun 10am–6pm; charge). The 6,000 exhibits are arranged so as to act as a chronological guide to the decorative arts in France from the

Middle Ages to the present. All the main designers and manufacturers are represented and all styles illustrated: notably Gothic, Louis XVI, Directoire, Art Nouveau, Art Deco and Modernism. A fashion gallery, meanwhile, explores the evolution of costume from the Regency period to today.

Behind the Louvre is the **Eglise of St-Germain l'Auxerrois**, which has a dark secret in its past. The ringing of its bells was the signal for the start of what has become known as the St Bartholomew's Day Massacre on 24 August 1572, a frenzied orgy of assassinations and violence by Catholic mobs against the Huguenots (Protestants) of the city.

Palais Royal

Across the rue de Rivoli from the Louvre, overlooking two squares named after famous French writers, Colette and Malraux, is the **Comédie Française** ㉞, the revered classical theatre founded by Molière. Beside it, the **Palais Royal** was built by Cardinal Richelieu in the 17th century and willed to the king at his death. Anne of Austria moved here with her son, the future Louis XIV, because she preferred it to the gloomy Louvre. Today, the palace houses the Minsitry of Culture. In the main courtyard stand 250 black-and-white-striped columns of varying heights, erected by artist Daniel Buren in 1986. The **Jardin du Palais Royal** ㉟ behind the palace, once a meeting place for revolutionaries, is now a tranquil oasis, surrounded by arcades sheltering some fine restaurants , eccentric old shops and new top-end boutiques. In the shaded gallery at the north end, **Le Grand Véfour** is one of the most beautiful restaurants in Paris. It opened its doors in 1784 and has fed the likes of Napoleon and Victor Hugo. Today it serves grand classic haute cuisine.

At the far end of the park, cross the street to explore the Parisian *galeries*, picturesque shopping arcades built in the early 19th century. The best-preserved and most elegant of these are the **Galeries Vivienne** and **Colbert**. Spacious and quiet, covered with high glass roofs, they are an oasis in the crush of midtown. Tea or lunch at A Priori Thé in the Vivienne Gallery is guaranteed to soothe the most jangled nerves.

TIP

Each evening, 45 minutes before curtain-rise at the Comédie Française, 112 tickets are sold at low prices at the booth just off the square on rue de Montpensier behind the theatre. On the first Mon of the month, under 28s get in free.

BELOW: the elegant Galerie Vivienne shopping arcade.

Café Life

"You sit in a café and watch people walking up and down in front of it," wrote the humorist George Mikes of Parisian cafés in 1955. "Then you walk up and down in front of the café and give other people a chance to watch you. As a member of that strolling or surging crowd you have become one of the sights of Paris; you have become a rival of the Eiffel Tower."

The café has always been the Parisian's decompression chamber, easing the transition between *Métro-boulot-dodo* – commuting, working and sleeping. It provides a welcome pause in which to savour a *petit noir* (espresso) or an apéritif, to empty the mind of troublesome thoughts and to watch the people go by. The café is also the place to meet friends, have a romantic tryst or even to do business in a relaxed atmosphere.

There may be fewer authentic cafés around than there once were as Americanised coffee shops take their place, but there are still plenty left to choose from if you look. Several famous ones trade on their past glories, such as Le Procope (13 rue de l'Ancienne-Comédie; *see page 114*) which has moved upmarket since it started serving customers in 1686 thanks to its reputation as a meeting place for the literati. Other cafés are more shabby and authentic, remaining closer to the notion of the neighbourhood "zinc", named after the metal counter, and which have always been such an important part of the fabric of French life.

SHOP

South of place Vendôme, rue St-Honoré, and its even more elegant continuation, rue du Faubourg St-Honoré, form the traditional heartland of Parisian high fashion. St-Honoré has cutting-edge boutiques, while the really grand fashion houses are clustered on rue du Faubourg.

The Grands Boulevards

The **place Vendôme** ㊱, a short way up the rue des Petits Champs, is a 17th-century marvel of harmony and now lined with luxury jewellers. The Hôtel Ritz is well suited to its surroundings. Its opulence created the word "ritzy". Hemingway once hoped that heaven would be as good as the Ritz; his ghost still haunts the bar that is named after him. The luxury hotel is now most famous as the place where Princess Diana had her last meal before her fatal car crash in 1997.

The area north of here is known as the Grands Boulevards after its elegant avenues which were built straight and wide in the 19th century to replace untidy, crowded slums. It dates from Paris's great 19th-century face-lift under Baron Haussmann. The medieval city that succeeded ancient Roman Lutetia huddled close about the walls of the Louvre and was regarded by the upper and middle classes as a festering pit of poverty, crime and fomenting rebellion. In a few years, the area was transformed into one of the most elegant parts of the city.

BELOW: the grand staircase of the Palais Garnier.

The main axis is formed by three streets running into each other: the boulevards de la Madeleine, des Capucines and des Italiens. The glorious **Palais Garnier** ㊲ (daily 10am–5pm; guided tours in English Wed, Sat, Sun 11.30am; charge), designed by Charles Garnier and completed in 1875, occupies the central point where the great boulevards converge. The facade and exterior are covered in sculptures of great composers and allegorical figures representing spirits of music and dance, including voluptuous nudes that caused a scandal when first unveiled. The profusion of marble and gilt inside is almost oppressive in its excess, but the glamour of the Opéra's foyers is undeniable. The grand staircase was conceived by Garnier as the ultimate celebrity catwalk and the five-tiered auditorium drips with red velvet and gilt, its centrepiece a 6-tonne chandelier and the unexpected ceiling painting by Marc Chagall (1964).

In the nearby **Café de la Paix**, also designed by Garnier and a frequent haunt of Oscar Wilde, you can join the chic clientele enjoying coffee and croissants, or a glass of wine and oysters later in the day – though the prices match the luxurious setting.

The area behind the Opéra, along boulevard Haussmann, is dominated by the *grands magasins* (department stores). **Galeries Lafayette** (famed for its Art Nouveau central hall and stained-glass dome) and **Printemps**, both established in the late 19th century, have remained rivals ever since.

Beaubourg and Les Halles

South of the *grands boulevards*, sandwiched between the Louvre and Palais Royal to the west and the Marais to the east, this central chunk of the Right Bank is one of the city's most hyperactive commercial and cultural centres. Its epicentre is the **Forum des Halles** ㊳, a vast shopping and leisure complex. Built on the site of the historic food market that stood here from 1183 to 1969, it is an unsightly multistorey

Map on pages 104–5

blot on the landscape. But surrounding the shopping centre, some remnants of a bygone age remain, in the **Pied de Cochon** brasserie (rue Coquillière), which serves meals and hot onion soup night and day, as it did when the market kept the quarter lively around the clock; and in pedestrianised **rue Montorgueil**, where a colourful daily street market still operates. The Square des Innocents occupies the site of the city's oldest cemetery, dating from the Gallo-Roman period. A ghastly spot surrounded by charnel houses, the cemetery absorbed some two million corpses before it was emptied in 1786 *(see page 116)*.

There's always a colourful crowd around the **Centre Pompidou** 39, known locally as Beaubourg. Designed by an Italian-British team of architects (Piano and Rogers), the building presents a glass facade supported totally by an external skeleton. Though some Parisians claim to detest it, the inside-out museum rapidly became one of the most visited attractions in town. The **Centre National d'Art et de Culture Georges Pompidou** (Wed–Mon 11am–9pm; charge) is Paris's main showcase for modern and contemporary art and a dynamic arts venue. The gallery, which occupies levels four and five, holds a vast collection (roughly 50,000 works by 5,000 artists) and regular rehangs are intended to allow visitors to see as much of it as possible. Highlights of the modern period on the fifth floor include works by Picasso, Matisse, Kandinsky, Klee, Klein and Pollock, and sections on Dadaism and Surrealism. The excellent contemporary art collection includes pieces by Andy Warhol, Xavier Veilhan, Claude Viallat, Joseph Beuys, Gerhard Richter and Jean Dubuffet.

Also incorporated into the complex are a performance space, auditorium, cinema, library, and a space for children. There's a splendid view of Paris from the top floor, where the fashionable, but expensive, Georges restaurant is located. The precinct below buzzes with crowds and performers of all kinds. Included in the price of the museum ticket is entrance to the **Atelier Brancusi** (Wed–Mon; charge included in Musée National d'Art Moderne), a reconstruction of the sculptor's studio on the square.

The Marais

Stretching west to east from Beaubourg to Bastille, straddling the 3rd and 4th *arrondissments*, the Marais offers a wonderfully compact package of history and local colour. There's so much to recommend it: mansions and museums, chic boutiques and kosher groceries, gay bars and cosy cafés, all bundled together in a labyrinth of narrow streets and alleyways. It's hard to believe that the area was once a mosquito-infested swamp ("marais" means marsh). The marshes were drained, and in the 16th and 17th centuries sumptuous accommodations were built for nobles and courtiers. During the Revolution, the area was abandoned to the people, and the Marais's graceful *hôtels particuliers* fell into disrepair. In 1962 wide-scale renovation work was

The steel and glass façade of the Centre Pompidou, an icon of modern Paris.

BELOW: many of the old neighbourhood shops of the Marais now house chic boutiques.

Café Hugo on the place des Vosges is next door to Victor Hugo's former home, now a museum dedicted to the literary giant.

set in motion to preserve what had by then become a very run-down area. By the 1990s, the Marais had regained its status as one of the most fashionable – and costly – places to live in Paris. The Jewish and working class communities that once occupied the area have been marginalised by the relentless gentrification process. The character of the Marais is now defined by its designer boutiques, trendy bars and cafés and a thriving gay community.

The ornate neo-Renaissance **Hôtel de Ville** 40 on the rue de Rivoli is the most monumental reminder of the neighbourhood's heyday. The original 16th-century structure was burned to the ground on 24 May 1871 by angry communards. One year later, architect Viollet-le-Duc directed a scrupulous (though much enlarged) restoration.

Behind the Hôtel de Ville and off rue de Rivoli, rue Vieille du Temple winds into the oldest section of the Marais.

Marais museums

Many former private mansions in the area are now museums. The **Musée Carnavalet** 41 (Tue–Sun 10am–6pm) is a fascinating museum documenting the city's history from its beginnings as a Gallo-Roman settlement to its modern-day metropolis. The building occupies two mansions, the main 16th-century Hôtel Carnavalet and the neighbouring 17th-century Hôtel Le Peletier. Madame de Sévigné, whose celebrated letters provide an insight into 17th-century high society, lived here between 1677 and 1696, and there is a gallery devoted to her life.

More elegant Parisian interiors, along with paintings and decorative arts, can be seen in the **Musée Cognacq-Jay** (Tue–Sun 10am–6pm).

Nearby, at place Thorigny, the **Musée National Picasso** 42 (closed for renovation until 2012) occupies the 17th-century Hôtel Salé, built by a wealthy tax collector. Picasso's family donated a large collection of his works to the state, in lieu of huge inheritance tax payments due after the painter's death: 200 paintings, over 3,000 drawings and 88 ceramics, along with sculptures, collages and manuscripts.

The golden age of the Marais began in the reign of Henri IV (1553–1610)

BELOW: watching the tennis outside the Hôtel de Ville. **BELOW RIGHT:** buskers on the place des Vosges.

who built the magnificent **place des Vosges** 43 as a showcase for his court. The square comprised a garden surrounded by 36 arcaded residences. Today the arcades house restaurants and expensive commercial art galleries. In the southeast corner at No. 6 is **Maison Victor Hugo** (Tue–Sun 10am–6pm), the writer's Paris home for 15 years and now a small museum dedicated to his life and work.

The Jewish Quarter

At the southern edge of the Marais is rue des Rosiers, the hub of what remains of the Jewish quarter. Kosher delis and shops selling religious artefacts line this street. The history of France's Jewish community, along with items from all over the Jewish diaspora, is displayed in the beautiful Hôtel St-Aignan, now the **Musée d'Art et d'Histoire du Judaïsme** 44 (Sun–Fri; closed some Jewish holidays; charge) on rue du Temple. The synagogue in rue Pavée has an Art Nouveau facade by Hector Guimard.

Bastille

The eastern limit of the Marais is marked by the **place de la Bastille**. This was the site of the dreaded prison constructed in the 14th century, whose walls were about 11 metres (30–40ft) thick in some places, protected by high battlements and heavy artillery. Despite the apparently impregnable walls, the Bastille fell before the onslaught of the furious population on 14 July 1789. "Is it a revolt?" asked Louis XVI. "No sire," he was told, "a revolution." The hated jail was completely destroyed and in its place was eventually erected the towering **Colonne de Juillet** commemorating the victims of the 1830 and 1848 revolutions.

The modern place de la Bastille is a wide, busy traffic hub. Dominating the square, the giant glass-and-concrete **Opéra de Paris Bastille** 45 is now Paris's primary venue for opera and ballet, having taken over pride of place from its opulent predecessor, the Palais Garnier *(see page 126)*.

Montmartre

The most popular excursion from central Paris is up the hill north to Montmartre, a picturesque village apart from the rest of Paris which manages to be a living community, a magnet for gaping tourists and an artistic legend all at the same time. Painters Toulouse-Lautrec and Utrillo, and later Picasso, Matisse, poet Guillaume Apollinaire and pianist Eric Satie helped create the image of the freethinking hilltop and made it, for a time, the happiest and most conducive place for artists to live and work in Paris. Nowadays, there are still quiet corners of Montmartre where you can see what inspired these people, but some of its attractions must be taken with a pinch of postmodern salt.

An obvious first step is to go to the top of the hill crowned by the white domes of the **Basilique du Sacré-Cœur** A (7am–10pm; crypt until 6pm in winter, 7pm in summer; charge for crypt and dome), which was built from 1876–1914 on the site of the sparking point of the bloodily vanquished Commune de Paris. Parisians have acquired a grudging affection for the monument, which

The Mémorial de la Shoah, a centre devoted to the Holocaust, is in an underground crypt on rue Geoffroy l'Asnier. It is a poignant memorial to the Jews deported from France.

BELOW: the white domed basilica of the Sacré-Coeur.

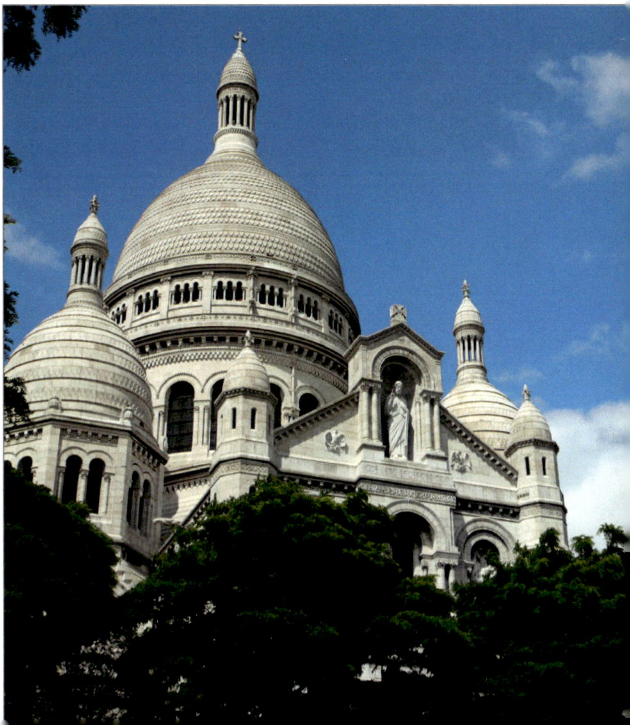

Pay tribute to Truffaut, Guitry, Dumas fils, Stendhal, Dalida, Berlioz, Degas, Najinsky, Zola and more in the shady groves of the Cimetière de Montmartre, just west of rue Lepic.

occupies the highest spot in the city.

Place du Tertre Ⓑ is the tourist trap of Montmartre, laden with kitschy, overpriced bistros and craft shops selling junk. It's far more appealing at night, when the coach parties have left and it is lit by fairy lights, retaining an animated charm. Leaving place du Tertre where it meets rue Poulbot, you will pass **Espace Montmartre Dalí** (10am–6pm; charge), home to over 300 works by Salvador Dalí, and a popular shop.

If you take the streets north from here, over the hill past the water tower, you should be able leave most of the tourists behind and get a feel for how Montmartre must once have been. Rue Cortot was home to Satie (No. 6) while he was composing his delightful piano pieces, and to Utrillo, who lived there with his mother, artist Suzanne Valadon. He captured many of La Butte's houses and cafés in his work.

At No. 12 is the **Musée du Montmartre** Ⓒ (Tue–Sun 11am–6pm; charge), which is housed in a 17th-century manor house, the oldest on the *Butte*. It chronicles the life and times of Montmartre and the artists' quarter. Its windows overlook the **Montmartre Vineyard**, planted in the 1930s in memory of the vineyards that once covered the hill.

Some of the old atmosphere still lingers in **Au Lapin Agile** Ⓓ, a cabaret on rue des Saules which puts on a nostalgic repertoire of popular French music.

On the corner of rue Lepic and rue Girandon stands the **Moulin de la Galette** Ⓔ. The windmill was made into a dance hall in the 19th century, and celebrated in a painting by Renoir. Van Gogh lived with his brother in a pretty little house, No. 54 rue Lepic, before moving south.

Rue Lepic turns into a **lively market street** that will carry you down the hill to lower Montmartre, or you may prefer to use the funicular, which runs from near place d'Anvers at the bottom of the hill to Sacré-Cœur at the top.

On the way down it's worth making a detour to **place Emile-Goudeau** Ⓕ to see the old piano factory, **Bateau-Lavoir**, which was where many of the great artists of the day had their extremely shabby, ill-equipped studios. In 1970

BELOW: Montmartre is awash with cafés and restaurants.

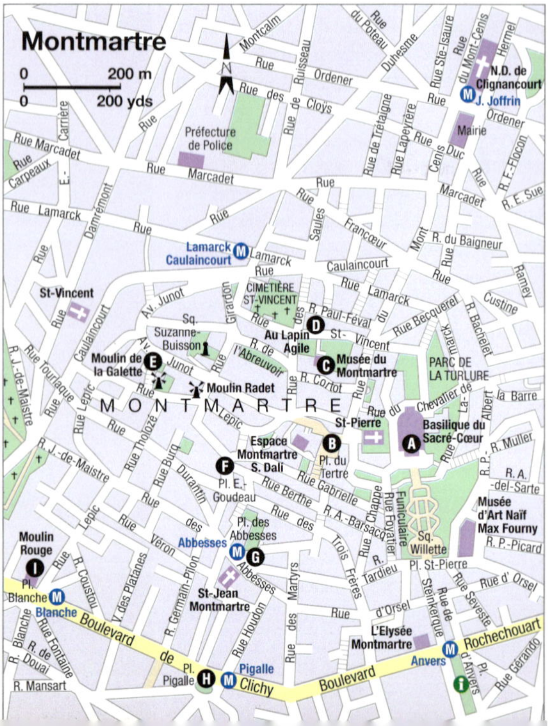

the original building burnt down, but it was replaced with a replica, in which modern-day artists rent studio space.

Further down, **place des Abbesses** Ⓖ, named after the nuns of the abbey which stood here in the Middle Ages, is a pretty square with a noteworthy Métro entrance, one of only two to retain its original glass roof. Designed by architect Hector Guimard, it is a picturesque evocation of early Art Nouveau.

Pigalle

Back down below the Butte **Pigalle** Ⓗ (Pig Alley to two generations of American and British soldiers), the city's red-light district is shedding its seedy reputation: it was the core of the Parisian sex trade for decades. Though sleaze still exists here, the cabarets that once occupied rue des Martyrs are being taken over by music clubs, such as **Divan du Monde**, at No. 75. Among the cabaret survivors is **Chez Michou** on rue des Martyrs, home of Parisian drag artists, and the **Moulin Rouge** Ⓘ on boulevard de Clichy, which has long since cleaned up its act and is now more cheesy than sleazy.

Père Lachaise

Edith Piaf, who became France's most popular entertainer during the war years and after, was discovered singing on the streets of Pigalle by a nightclub owner. She is among the celebrities buried in the **Cimetière Père Lachaise** Ⓙ, east of the city centre. This graveyard, with its streets and boulevards, above-ground monuments and regular visitors feeding the wild cats, is like a miniature city. You can buy a map of some of the many famous gravesites. These include the tombs of Rossini, Chopin, Gertrude Stein, Molière, Oscar Wilde, Sarah Bernhardt, Marcel Proust, Simone Signoret and Yves Montand, and The Doors' singer Jim Morrison. The French who visit the cemetery usually make a point of seeing the Mur des Fédérés: in 1871, the last of the insurgents from the Commune de Paris took a stand among the sepulchres of the hilly cemetery. They were trapped and executed against the wall, which still bears the marks of the fatal rounds.

Southeast of the cemetery is the **Château de Vincennes** Ⓚ (May–Aug 10am–6pm, Sept–Apr until 5pm;

TIP

Near Abbesses Métro station, rue des Abbesses is a focus of Montmartre life, with bustling cafés, grocery stores and wine merchants. The trio of streets east of the station – rue de la Vieuville, rue Yvonne-le-Tac, rue des Trois Frères – is lined with boutiques, little galleries supporting local artists, and "boho" bars.

Bohemianism

Paris has always been the spiritual home of Bohemianism, the living of an unconventional lifestyle in the company of like-minded souls, with a shared distain for the approval of society and a willingness to accept poverty as the price of freedom – often motivated by artistic or literary aspirations. The term *bohème* was first heard in 1659, but it didn't enter popular use until the mid-19th century. It originated in a derisory allusion to the unconventional customs, dress and attitudes of gypsies migrating from the region of Bohemia, now in the Czech Republic. Bohemianism quickly spread to other countries and had a profound influence on subsequent countercultural trends, particularly in the politically idealistic 1930s, the existentialist and Beat-driven 1950s, and during the hippy era of the 1960s.

BELOW: the grave of Edith Piaf, Père Lachaise cemetery.

According to legend, Edith Piaf was born under a lamppost at 72 rue de Belleville, and there is a commemorative plaque over the doorway. The tiny Musée Edith Piaf at 5 rue Crespin-du-Gast is a tribute to the queen of French chanson.

charge), built on the spot where the 13th-century Saint Louis, king of France, would sit under an oak tree in the forest and mete out justice to his subjects. The following century, Charles V erected a keep, along with ramparts and a chapel. The massive castle that grew up around these first ingredients was used as a royal residence and a suitable place for incarcerating important prisoners. The Marquis de Sade was detained here for debauchery.

Belleville

North of Père Lachaise cemetery is the vibrant district of **Belleville**. At one time a forge of working-class agitation, it is now home to more than 60 nationalities and, with its vendors of falafels and bagels, noodles and couscous, the area retains a laid-back charm, despite the encroaching gentrification.

Earlier in the 19th century, Belleville was a fertile country village, whose springs were tapped to channel water into Paris. There still remain a few old stone *regards* (control stations for the aqueducts), particularly around **Parc de Belleville** Ⓛ, a terraced crescent of green atop a hill with a panoramic view of Paris. The other park worthy of a detour is the **Parc des Buttes-Chaumont**.

Villette

From the place de la Bastille it is possible to skirt the city centre by boat in a two-and-a-half-hour trip along the **Canal St-Martin**, through a tunnel and several locks, to **Parc de la Villette** Ⓜ in the northeast of the city. Built on the site of a huge abbatoir, which was rendered obsolete by improved refrigeration techniques and poor design, are 55 hectares (136 acres) of futuristic gardens around a colossal science museum, the **Cité des Sciences et de l'Industrie** (Tue–Sat 10am–6pm, Sun 10am–7pm; charge), which celebrates human ingenuity with interactive exhibits. Other attractions in the park include **The Géode**, a huge geodesic dome covered with polished steel mirror surfaces, which houses a wraparound cinema; plus **L'Argonaute**, a retired naval submarine; and **Cinaxe**, a flight-simulator-cum-cinema.

The former slaughterhouse now houses a cultural and conference centre in the immense 19th-century

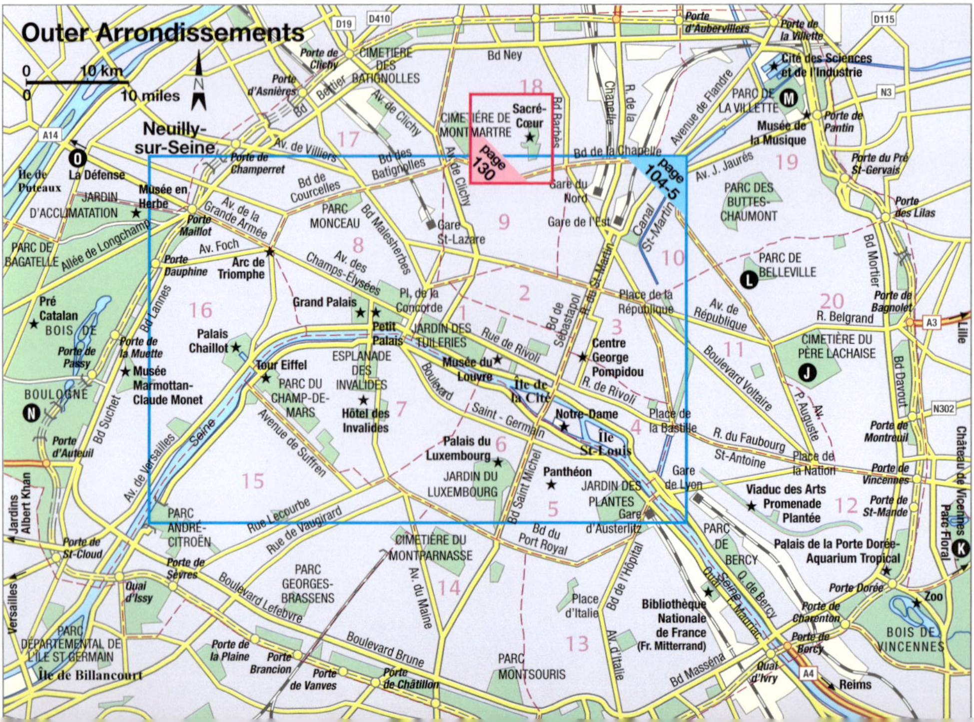

Grand Halle. Next door, the **Cité de la Musique** (Tue–Sat noon–6pm, Sun 10am–6pm; charge) includes a museum charting the development of classical, jazz and folk music and houses a collection of over 4,500 musical instruments.

The Bois de Boulogne

Across the other side of Paris is the city's green lung, the **Bois de Boulogne** Ⓝ. Embraced by an elbow of the Seine, this lovely 872-hectare (2,500-acre) expanse of woods and gardens has been the Sunday afternoon playground for generations of Parisian families. It offers gardens, lakes, wild woods, horse racing at two of France's most famous racecourses, **Longchamps** and **Auteuil**, a sports stadium, boating and restaurants (including **Le Pré Catalan**). On the northern edge is the **Jardin d'Acclimatation**, an amusement park for children. Outdoor theatre is performed at the Jardin Shakespeare during the summer. Be advised that walking through the park late at night, when it becomes a popular spot for prostitutes, is not advisable.

Located on the edge of the park, on rue Louis Boillu, the **Musée Marmottan-Claude Monet** (Tue 11am–9pm, Wed–Sun 11am–6pm; charge) holds more than 130 works by Impressionist painter Claude Monet. About 30 of the pictures represent his house at Giverny *(see page 267)*. Quite a few paintings from the series on Rouen Cathedral are hung here, too. Of particular interest is the painting entitled *Impression, Soleil Levant*, which gave the whole movement its name (*see page 81*).

La Défense

Further west beyond the Périphérique sprawls **La Défense** Ⓞ, Europe's largest business centre and a testimony to the French inclination to innovate. The district found a new focus with the opening in 1989 of the **Grande Arche de la Défense**, one of Mitterrand's *grands projets*, which mirrors the Arc de Triomphe. Glass elevators shoot up through a canvas "cloud" and into the roof, from where you can enjoy stunning views over the Bois de Boulogne and Paris (Apr–Sept 10am–8pm, Oct–Mar 10am–7pm; charge). ❑

Pre-schoolers (age 2-7) can put on tot-sized hard hats and construct or tear down a miniature building at the Cité des Enfants within the Cité des Sciences et de l'Industrie.

BELOW: the 'canvas cloud' and elevator shaft at the base of the vast Arche de la Défense.

Mesdames

ILE-DE-FRANCE

The region that encircles Paris is a rich mix of glittering palaces, castles and cathedrals, stately forests and quiet villages, all within striking distance of the city

Main attractions
CHÂTEAU DE VERSAILLES
DISNEYLAND PARIS
PROVINS
CHÂTEAU DE FONTAINEBLEAU

The region that surrounds Paris, the Ile-de-France, acquired its name in the 14th century, but the meaning is still debated. The "Ile" (island) may have been the territory delimited by the Seine, Marne, Oise and Beuvronne rivers which constituted the personal fiefdom of the Capetien kings around the turn of the first millennium; or it may refer to a linguistic island where French was spoken in contrast to the other local tongues of northern France. Another theory is that the name has nothing whatsoever to do with islands but comes instead from the Frankish *Liddle Franke or Little France*.

The area could convincingly claim to be the "original" France: the hub from which French culture has always radiated outwards. It is certainly – because of the city stuck in the middle – the epicentre of modern France – and everywhere beyond its borders is "the provinces". Because of this, *franciliens* (usually equated with Parisians) are often seen as smug and condescending when they travel elsewhere in their country.

For most travellers the Ile-de-France is a buffer zone to be hurried through or overflown on journeys to and from Paris rather than somewhere worth heading for in its own right. Daytripppers from the capital make it to Versailles and perhaps Fontainebleau, and families descend on Disneyland for short breaks from French culture, but the rest of the Ile is relatively undervisited.

It's true that this jigsaw of seven *départements* with hard-to-remember names doesn't start off with obvious appeal. It occupies the largely flat and fertile Paris basin, and while it has forests and nature reserves, its countryside is pleasant rather than spectacular and you are seldom able to leave civilisation behind. This is the most densely

LEFT: marble court, Palace of Versailles.
RIGHT: Sleeping Beauty Castle, Disneyland.

Suburban railways make the Ile-de-France well connected with the capital.

populated part of the country, home to around 20 percent of the national population. Many of the towns have been swallowed up in the "Paris effect" and reduced to dormitory suburbs or satellites providing services to the metropolitan hub.

But it doesn't take much to get beyond this first impression. There are plenty of interesting places to seek out even in the creeping built-up area of Paris. Much heritage has been preserved and anyone interested in architecture will find a fairly good summary of all the French styles within this small region. Some towns, meanwhile, have re-invented themselves as post-industrial tourist attractions, with character added by striking new 21st-century buildings.

Probably the best way to treat the region is to see it as an assortment of possible day or half-day trips to choose from if you have more than a few days in Paris, rather than as a place to undertake more lengthy tours.

Getting around

Where precisely the sights of Paris leave off and those of the Ile-de-France begin is an arbitrary distinction as far as most tourists are concerned. Certainly the public transport system doesn't see any difference, and the Ile-de-France benefits from the same light rail network as the capital itself. This is mainly designed for the benefit of commuters but it works just as well in reverse, making it possible to hop in and out of the city as you please.

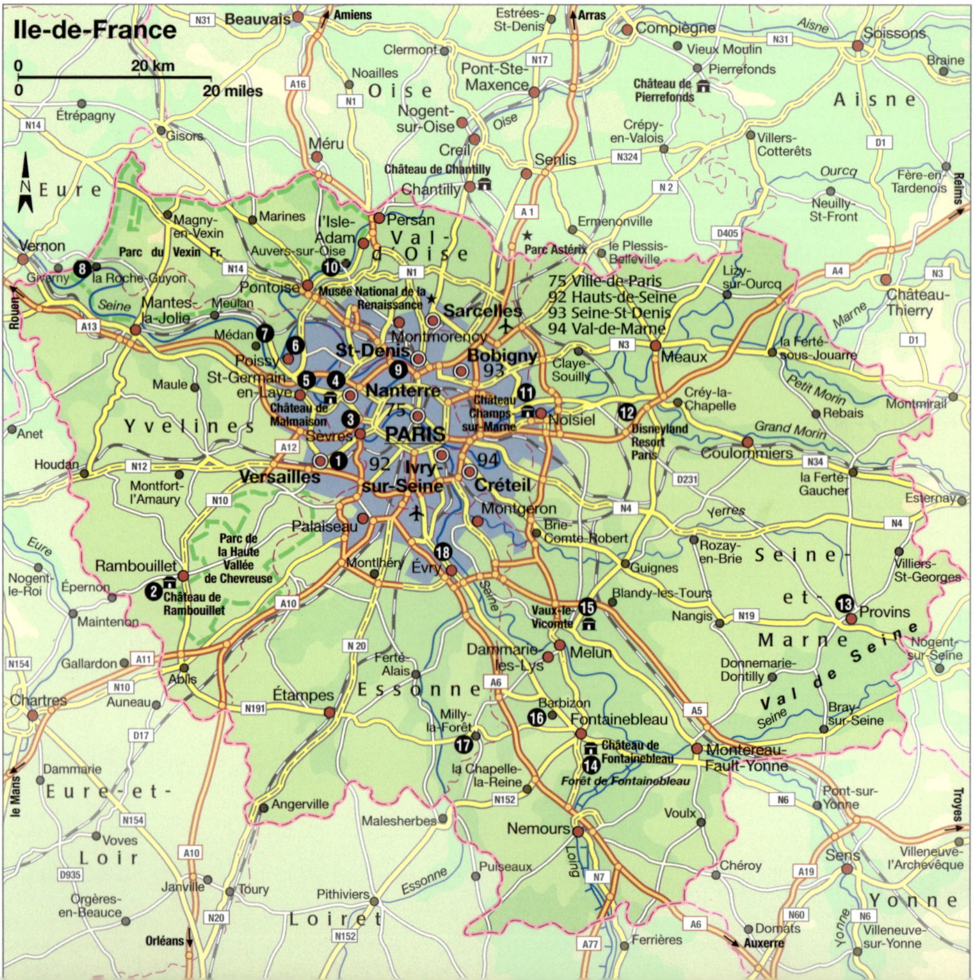

Where the metro gives out, the five lines of the RER (denominated A to E) take over and the two systems are integrated, sharing stations, and making it easy to switch between the two. The RER network is extended by the SNCF's Transilien lines (lettered H, J, K, L, N, P, R), departing from the main railway stations.

Versailles

For most visitors to the city there is one obvious and perhaps only excursion to be made and that is to the Sun King's **Château de Versailles** ❶ (Tue–Sun Apr–Oct 9am–6.30pm; Nov–Mar 9am–5.30pm; charge), glittering on the hilltop. Louis XIV (reigned 1643–1715) transformed the simple village and small château into an unequalled expression of wealth, privilege and absolute monarchy. At Versailles, the French court could amuse itself well away from the stench and conspiracy of Paris. As a result, the monarchy became out of touch: historians debate whether Marie Antoinette actually said of the starving people during the Revolution, "Let them eat cake", but angry crowds did drag Louis XVI and his wife to Paris, and later, in 1793, they were publicly executed. The château was ransacked, but saved from ruin.

Inside, the tour takes you through the **King's Apartments**, including his bedchamber, in the centre of the symmetrical palace. Other rooms include Marie Antoinette's quarters. The astonishing 70-metre (233ft) **Hall of Mirrors** is lined on one side by a series of arches filled with reflecting glass, and on the other by French windows overlooking the terrace.

The park (daily 8am–8.30pm, Nov–Mar Tue–Sun 8am–6pm) was designed by the landscape artist André Le Nôtre. From the palace steps, you can look down the length of the **Grand Canal** in the form of a fleur-de-lis, which divides the park in two. On each side of the central path leading to the garden's main focus, **Apollo's Pool**, the woods are sprinkled with delightful statues, secret groves, goldfish ponds, fountains and flowerbeds. Here nature is tamed, and the Sun King reigns supreme, represented as the god Apollo. On Sunday afternoons from April to September,

André Le Nôtre (1613–1700) is France's most celebrated gardener. Creator of the French formal garden, he designed those at Versailles, Vaux-le-Vicomte and the Jardin des Tuileries in Paris, where his family had gardened for three generations.

BELOW: Le Seine, in the Parterre d'Eau at the rear of Versailles palace.

TIP

The SNCF runs a bicycle rental service (Train + Vélo) at many stations – when you buy your train ticket, reserve a bicycle, which you pick up at your destination. This is the best way to visit Giverny (from Vernon station). Or SNCF runs a train/car hire service (Train + Auto).

the fountains are switched on to music in Les Grands Eaux Musicales.

The beauty of the palace is best appreciated from the bottom of the park, at the far end of the canal. The building floats on air, buoyed up by the fluffy mass of the trees on either side, capturing the sunlight in its bright windows and gilded ornaments. Don't be fooled by the tricks of perspective the gardens can play – it's nearly 5km (3 miles) around the canal.

On the northern side, Louis XIV built a smaller residence, the **Grand Trianon**, where he could escape from the stiff etiquette of the court. Nearby is the **Petit Trianon**, built by Louis XV, and the **Hameau**, a make-believe village where Marie Antoinette played milkmaid.

If this puts you in a mood to pamper yourself, try the tearoom at the top of the Grand Canal. From the Le Nôtre terrace there is a spectacular view of the Forêt de St-Germain.

Further out from Paris past Versailles, in the lovely *département* of Les Yvelines, is the ivy-clad **Château de Rambouillet** ❷ (guided visits only; Apr–Sept 10am, 11am, 2pm, 3pm, 4pm & 5pm; Oct–Mar 10am, 11am, 2pm, 3pm & 4pm; closed during official residence; charge), the summer home of the president of France.

Along the Seine

The landscape west of Paris is incised by the River Seine. As it flows towards Normandy and the sea it describes a series of exaggerated loops, flowing south then suddenly due north.

On the river between Versailles and Paris is **Sèvres** ❸, long famed for its manufacturing of fine porcelain, as can be seen in the **Musée National de la Céramique** (Wed–Mon 10am–5pm; charge) which displays French and foreign pieces on three floors. In the 19th century, when Sèvres was well beyond the Parisian urban area, it was chosen as a place of escape by the orator and statesman Léon Gambetta who retreated to the Maison des Jardies to enjoy the company of his mistress, Léonie Léon. It was here that he died tragically, from complications arising from a self-inflicted gunshot wound, two hours before midnight on 31 December 1882, aged 44.

BELOW: Marie-Antoinette's garden in the Petit Trianon. **BELOW RIGHT:** the Guard's House in the Hameau make-believe village.

The Seine now heads off north beside the Bois de Boulogne and the posh suburb of Neuilly-sur-Seine (of which Nicolas Sarkozy was once mayor) before returning as far south again. Not far from its banks stands the **Château de Malmaison** ❹ (Wed–Mon 10am–12.30pm, 1.30–5.15pm, open to 5.45pm at weekends in winter and 6.15pm in summer; charge). The name "evil house" either derives from a hideout for Norman invaders or a leper colony that once occupied the site, depending on which story you listen to. The château was bought by the Empress Josephine Bonaparte in 1799 for 325,000 francs, three years after her marriage to Napoleon Bonaparte. After her divorce in 1809, she retreated home and eventually died of pneumonia on 29 May 1814 three days after her ex-husband – now remarried and blessed with the male heir that Josephine had been unable to give him – had been shipped off to exile on the isle of Elba.

The stretch of the river around **Chatou** is associated with the Impressionist painters, mostly because Pierre-Auguste Renoir made a riverside restaurant, or *guinguette*, the setting for his most famous painting, *Luncheon of the Boating Party* (*Le Déjeuner des Canotiers*, 1881). The restaurant is now the **Maison Fournaise** (Wed–Fri 10am–noon, 2–6pm; Sat–Sun 11am–6pm; charge), a museum visited more for its artistic memories rather than its exhibits.

St-Germain-en-Laye ❺, perched above the Seine, is one of the city's most chic and affluent suburbs, with a **château** that was another royal retreat, gloomily rebuilt by Napoleon III as the **Musée des Antiquités Nationales**, the state archaeological collection (Wed–Mon 10am–5.15pm; charge).

Standing between St-Germain-en-Laye and the river is the **Château de Maisons-Lafitte** (Wed–Mon 10am–12.30pm, 2–5pm, closes 6pm in summer; charge), built by Mansart in 1651 as a "maison de plaisance" or country house, on the edge of Paris, which is often cited as one of the most perfect examples of French classical architecture. Even though it lost its outbuildings and park during the course of the 19th century, its decor is still intact.

Detail from the ornate gateway to the Château de Maisons-Lafitte, a perfect example of French baroque architecture.

BELOW: Château de Rambouillet.

Houseboats line the quayside at Conflans-Sainte-Honorine, a major hub of France's network of inland waterways.

Round the next bend of the river is **Conflans-Sainte-Honorine**, a traditional centre for waterway transport, where one of the boats moored at the quayside is marked with the words "Je sers" ("I serve"). This, surprisingly, is a church for the spiritual use of boatmen and boatbuilders. Conflans also has a museum explaining all things to do with rivers and canals, the **Musée de la batellerie** (Mon, Wed–Fri 9am–noon, 1.30–6pm, Tue 1.30–6pm, Sat and Sun 3–6pm in summer, 2–5pm in winter; charge).

Le Corbusier and Zola

Continuing downstream, **Poissy** ❻ has one of the signature buildings of the 20th century. The Villa Savoye (Tue–Sun May–Aug 10am–6pm; Mar–Apr and Sept–Oct 10am–5pm; Nov–Feb 10am–1pm, 2–5pm) by Le Corbusier may not be as well known as his chapel at Ronchamp in the Franche-Comté *(see page 227)* but it is rated more highly by architectural cognoscenti. It was built between 1929 and 1931 and embodies its creator's "Five Points towards a new architecture": a free plan; pilotis (structural piles); a free facade; ribbon windows; and a roof garden.

The novelist Emile Zola spent the last 24 years of his life, from 1878 to 1902 (apart from a period of unhappy exile in England), in his house at **Médan** ❼ downstream from Poissy, which is now the **Maison Zola** (open for guided tours Sat 3pm, 4.30pm, Sun 2.30pm, 3.30pm, 4.30pm, 5pm). Faithful to his motto, "never a day without a line", here he wrote *Nana*, *Germinal* and *La Bête Humaine*. Much of his original furniture is still *in situ* and some of the photographs on the walls were taken by the writer himself. It was here, also, that he weathered the storm of the Dreyfus Affair (explained in newspaper cuttings and caricatures) which brought him plaudits from one half of France and abuse from the other. On 28 September 1902 he returned from Médan to his town house in Paris but that night succumbed to asphyxiation caused by the fire in his bedroom, possibly assassinated by anti-Dreyfusards.

BELOW: the Villa Savoye, one of Le Corbusier's most important works.

Last den of the Desert Fox

The Seine flows northwestwards through Mantes-la-Jolie before executing another meander which is guarded by the attractive village of **La Roche-Guyon** ❽, on the frontier between the Ile-de-France and Normandy. It is overlooked by the ruins of a medieval castle keep that stands on a wooded cliff riddled with tunnels. In Renaissance times, a more stately **château** (Apr–Oct Mon–Fri 10am–6pm, weekends 10am–7pm; Nov–Mar daily 10am–5pm; charge) was built on the flatter ground below by the Silly family who entertained François I, Henri II and Henri IV during the hunting season. The château was redesigned in the age of enlightenment when stables, pavilions and a kitchen garden were added. In February 1944 the castle was chosen as a headquarters by Field-Marshal Erwin Rommel, "the Desert Fox", commander-in-chief of Army Group B which was charged with the defence of occupied Europe. La Roche Guyon was liberated on 18 August 1944, but not before it had been bombed by mistake, needing 20 years of reconstruction.

North of Paris

Heading north from Paris, you are soon into the region of Picardie *(see page 153)* but on the way there are three sights worth seeing. An easy visit from central Paris is to **St-Denis** ❾, a formerly industrialised commune in the northern suburbs which has two distinguishing features. The more recent is France's most important sports stadium, the **Stade de France**, built for the 1998 football World Cup. More significantly, however, at least for anyone interested in the history of architecture, is the **Basilique St-Denis** (Apr–Sept Mon–Sat 10am–6.15pm, Sun noon–6.15pm; Oct–Mar Mon–Sat 10am–5.15pm, Sun noon–5.15pm; charge for royal tombs), which is considered to be the first church built in Gothic style. It became the mausoleum of French kings and holds the tombs of most monarchs from Clovis (died 511) to Louis XVIII (died 1824).

A little way beyond St-Denis is the superb **Musée National de la Renaissance** in the **Château d'Ecouen** (Wed–Mon 9.30am–12.45pm and 2–5.15pm; charge), which displays

TIP

Make sure you have the right ticket before you get on a train or metro in Paris headed for the outer limits. Fares jump once you get outside zones 1 and 2 and an ordinary "t+" metro ticket will not do. You need to buy a "billet Origine-Destination" for the specific journey you are making. If you buy a go-as you-please *mobilis* ticket, make sure it covers the zones you will be travelling to.

BELOW: St-Denis cathedral tower.

The Fateful Last Summer of Erwin Rommel

Rommel knew that it was only a matter of time before the Allies would mount an invasion to retake occupied Europe and he worked hard to prepare the fortifications of the "Atlantic Wall" which stretched from Holland to the Loire. By early summer 1944, however, he was badly in need of a rest and on 4 June he drove to Germany to celebrate his wife's birthday. Forty-eight hours after his departure, the long-awaited invasion was launched and Rommel's absence from the theatre of war until late in the afternoon on D-Day was an unexpected stroke of good luck for the Allies.

As the Allies advanced through Normandy towards his headquarters in the summer of 1944, Rommel was persuaded to join the conspiracy to assassinate Hitler and stage a military coup d'etat "for the good of Germany". Several covert meetings took place at La Roche Guyon. Three days before the plotters struck, Rommel's car was touring the front line when it was strafed by a Spitfire and the field-marshal was injured in the head.

When it came on 20 July, the attempt to kill Hitler by planting a bomb under a conference table failed spectacularly and the conspirators were hunted down. By this time, Rommel had returned to Germany where he was arrested, but because he was considered a national hero he was given the choice of facing disgrace or committing suicide by cyanide. He chose the latter option, killing himself on 19 October 1944.

The Church at Auvers *by Vincent Van Gogh, 1890.*

rich collections of art, tapestries and furnishings from the 16th century.

Further out of the city heading northwest is **Auvers-sur-Oise ⑩**. Although the Dutch post-Impressionist painter Vincent Van Gogh is most often associated with Provence, his final days were spent here, in Auvers, where he came in May 1890 so that he could be close to his physician Dr Gachet, and his brother Theo. He continued to paint – producing canvases of Gachet and Auvers church among other subjects – but was pursued by the same inner demons that had caused him to fight with his best friend Gauguin a year and a half before, and to cut off part of his own ear in a brothel.

One of his last and most haunting works is *Wheatfield with Crows* which, with the benefit of hindsight, is pregnant with foreboding. On 27 July 1890, when he was still only 37, Vincent Van Gogh walked into a field brandishing a revolver and shot himself in the chest. He survived his wounds and managed to return to his rented room in the Auberge Ravoux (now known as the Maison de Van Gogh) where he died two days later, on 29 July, with Theo by his side. His last words are said to have been "La tristesse durera toujours": "*This sadness will last forever*". Theo only survived his brother by six months and the two are buried side by side in Auvers' cemetery.

Out East

The eastern suburbs of Paris are bisected by the river Marne on its way to join the Seine. On one of the meanders of the lower reaches of the river stands the splendid **Château of Champs-sur-Marne ⑪** (house closed for restoration until 2012, grounds May–Sept Wed–Mon 9.45am–6.30pm, Oct–Apr closes at 5.30pm, Nov–Jan open weekends only; charge), renowned not so much for its architecture as for one of its tenants. In 1757, Jeanne-Antoinette Poisson, known to history as Madame de Pompadour, rented this neoclassical house and lived in it in a style befitting the

BELOW: well-known Disney characters roam Fantasyland to the delight of awestruck children.

The Banlieues

Historically, the word "banlieue" ("outskirts") referred to the loop of land within a distance of one league ("lieue") from a city's perimeter. Nowadays the word applies to any residential area in the orbit of Paris or any other large city. Whereas some *banlieues* are affluent and picturesque complexes of detached and semi-detached houses, mostly the term puts French people in mind of "cités": estates of high-rise blocks of flats, often built as HLMs: *habitation à loyer modéré*, which provides social housing at affordable prices for tenants on low incomes.

The grimmest *banlieues* were built in the 1960s and 70s to provide cheap housing for a growing workforce, in particular, immigrants from former French colonies in Africa. The first arrivals lived in the *banlieues* only long enough to earn the means to move on to somewhere better. But when industry slumped from the mid-1970s onwards, the children and grandchildren of the migrants found they couldn't accumulate the wealth to move out as their predecessors had done.

And so began a vicious circle whereby disadvantaged people have accumulated in out-of-town ghettos where they are unseen and ignored by policy makers who have no clear idea how to tackle the problem. Poor facilities fuel local resentment; and chronic vandalism gives the state the perfect excuse not to invest in these neglected communities.

official chief mistress of Louis XV. Although somewhat altered after the Revolution, including a redesign of its landscape gardens, it still gives a good idea of the fashionable pleasure house of the 1700s.

Almost next door is the industrial town of **Noisiel**, where there is a singular old chocolate factory, the Ancienne chocolaterie Menier (open Sat only for guided tour at 11am lasting one and a half hours), built at the end of the 19th century and listed for its experimental decoration.

Disneyland

Disneyland Resort Paris ⓬ (daily from 10am; closing times vary throughout the year, for details call 0825 30 02 22) at Marne-la-Vallée, 32km (20 miles) east of the city is like a little piece of America dropped into the French countryside. It is built around a fun park divided into five themed areas: Main Street USA, Frontierland, Adventureland, Fantasyland and Discoveryland (high-tech wizardry). Alongside it is Walt Disney Studios Park with shows and activities about the business of film-making.

The site is accessed via RER line A, or a TGV train from Roissy-Charles de Gaulle airport (15 minutes). There is also a shuttle bus from Orly airport. It's not a place to drop in for a casual visit – you need at least a whole day there – and many people visit it separately to Paris. The best way to benefit fully from your time here is to plan ahead: decide what you want to do in order of priority and get there early, as by midday queues at the most popular rides can be up to 45 minutes long.

Once through the turnstiles, you enter **Main Street USA**. City Hall, on the left, is the central information centre, a contact point for lost children and property. Here, too, is the Main Street station, from where the Disneyland train circles the park. The station is often quite crowded, so it is a good idea to get on the train at one of the other stations en route. What many small children love best is the daily parade of Disney characters, which goes round both parks each afternoon.

Frontierland, to the left of Main Street, evokes dreams of the Wild West. Its centrepiece, **Big Thunder Mountain**, is a towering triumph of red rock reminiscent of every Western film you have seen. **Adventureland** contains another top attraction, the **Pirates of the Caribbean**, whose water ride through tropical swamp to the open sea is orchestrated by jovially barbaric Disney workers.

Le Temple du Péril, near Explorers' Club Restaurant, is a stomach-churning ride in carts that plunge through rainforest and turn upside down above a mock archaeological dig inspired by the *Indiana Jones* sagas.

The most popular land for younger children is **Fantasyland**, containing Sleeping Beauty's Castle – the centrepiece of the park – and Snow White and the Seven Dwarfs. **Discoveryland** provides an assortment of futuristic high-tech experiences.

A masterpiece of Renaissance architecture, the Château d'Ecouen is the fitting home of the French Renaissance collection of decorative and fine art.

BELOW: the Big Thunder Mountain roller coaster.

The rocks of Fontainebleau forest are a popular training ground for climbers.

Walt Disney Studios begins with **Front Lot**, an elaborate film set, complete with hundreds of film props. **Animation Courtyard** is Disney's homage to the art of the cartoon. In **Production Courtyard**, shows and productions take place almost every day in the Walt Disney Television Studios.

Back Lot is where most of the thrills are: the special-effects facility, the music recording stages and the stunt workshops. The highlight of the Back Lot is the **Stunt Show Spectacular**. Staged up to five times a day in front of 3,000 people, the live action trashes cars, motorcycles and jet-skis in a crescendo of film stunts performed in a Mediterranean village seaside set.

Provins

Southeast of Paris and somewhat remote from it is **Provins ⓭**, part of the historical county Champagne but now in the Ile-de-France, It is one of France's lesser-known World Heritage Sites, honoured as such for having once been a "town of medieval fairs". It looks down on the valley of the Seine from a ridge and has formidable 12th- and 13th-century ramparts. Its most splendid monument is the castle keep, the Tour de Cesar, which, despite its name and the legend attached to it, was built more than a millennium after Julius Caesar passed this way.

Fontainebleau

After Versailles, the other most popular sightseeing day trip out of Paris is to another royal palace, slightly further away, the **Château de Fontainebleau** ⓮ (Wed–Mon Apr–Sept 9.30am–6pm; Oct–Mar 9.30am–5.30pm; charge), in the town of the same name, which, in turn, is shrouded by the beautiful **Forêt de Fontainebleau**, 200 sq km (77 sq miles) of oak, beech, birch and pine, incorporating 300km (185 miles) of walking trails. There are weird giant rock formations in the forest, complete with local alpinists and climbers who stay in shape by scurrying up them. The station (reached from Gare de Lyon) is in the suburb of Avon, in the heart of the woods, and is a starting point for cyclists, picnickers, mushroom hunters and birdwatchers.

BELOW: Château de Provins.

The first royal residence was erected in the 12th century and every subsequent royal inhabitant left his mark on the hunting palace. The most remarkable work was commissioned by François I in the 16th century. In the long, airy gallery and ballroom, you can almost hear the swish of voluminous skirts, the satin dancing slippers, and the music drifting out to mingle with the sounds of the forest.

Perhaps the château bid *adieu* to regal splendour in 1814, when Napoleon I, who fled here from Paris when his government collapsed, parted company with the Imperial Guards in the aptly named **Cour des Adieux**. Tourists can witness the haughty magnificence of his **Throne Room** (private apartments only on guided visits).

Fontainebleau town is joined to a smaller neighbour, **Avon**, which had a most unusual resident for a time in the 1920s. George Ivanovitch Gurdjieff, an exiled Armenian, widely regarded as either an enlightenened spiritual teacher or a charlatan (with few opinions favouring anything in between), installed his Institute for the Harmonious Development of Man in the château of Prieuré des Basses Loges in 1922. It was, by all accounts, a frenetic community of 70-odd people drawn to learn about Gurdjieff's technique for self-knowledge which he called "Hurry Up Yoga". The New Zealand short-story writer, Katherine Mansfield, lived her last months at the Institute before dying suddenly of tuberculosis in 1923 at the age of 35. Almost two years later, Gurdjieff himself had a near-fatal car accident near Fontainebleau after which he peremptorily closed the Institute down.

Around Fontainebleau

There are several other interesting sights not far from Fontainebleau which can be grouped together in a small tour. The most obvious one is the **Château de Vaux-le-Vicomte** ⓯ (July–Aug daily 10am–6pm; Apr–Nov Mon, Wed–Sun 10am–6pm; charge), commissioned by Nicolas Fouquet who was appointed treasurer to Sun King Louis XIV in 1653 and used his privileged position to amass a fortune. A patron of the arts, he supported

Fontainebleau has been called "a rendezvous of châteaux" because it incorporates buildings of so many different periods.

BELOW: the frescoed corridor of François I, Fontainebleau Palace.

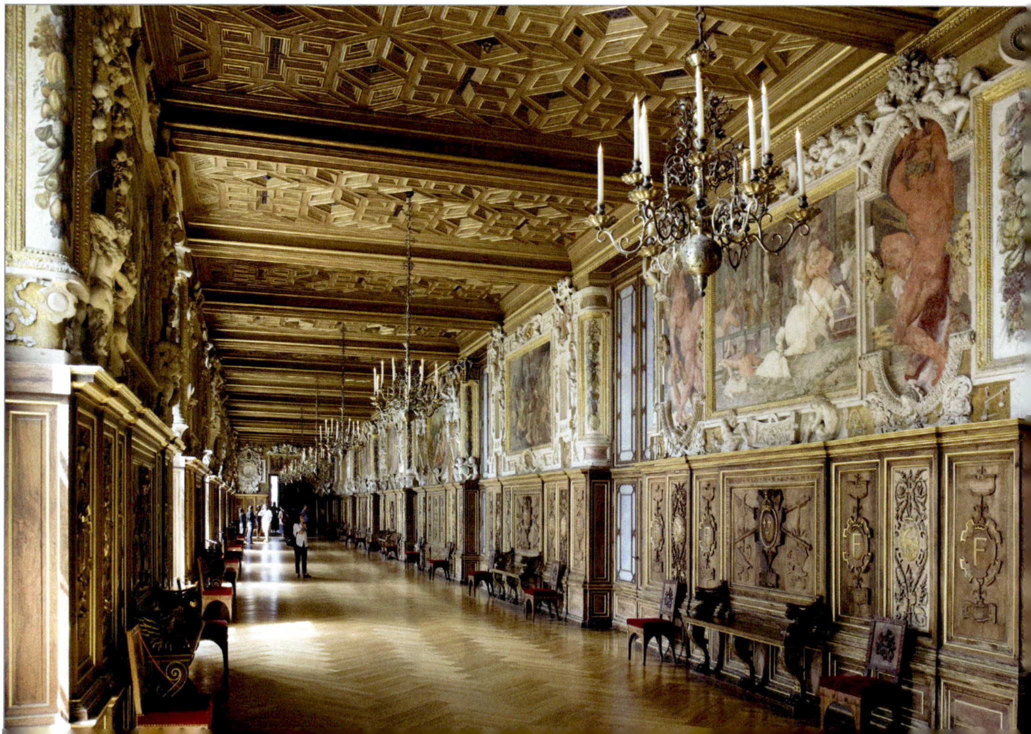

Statue gracing the formal gardens of Vaux-le-Vicomte.

Molière and Jean de la Fontaine, and organised extravagant parties that were the talk of the town. When he decided to build a country palace, he called on the finest designers: architect Le Vau and landscapist Le Nôtre.

They chose a site near the ancient town of Melun, on the northern edge of Fontainebleau forest. The park was Le Nôtre's first major work and the elegant symmetry of the garden is echoed by the château. The blue water in the pools, the green velvet lawns and the sandy pathways set off to perfection the warm stone and slate-blue roofs of the building.

When it was completed in 1661 Fouquet organised a grand *fête* to celebrate the king's birthday and inaugurate his exquisite new home. The fountains sprayed, musicians played, torches sparkled everywhere. A fantastic show, including dancing horses (some of them drowned in the moat), was given for the king's enjoyment. But Louis was not amused. He was outraged at the display of Fouquet's wealth and panache. His aide Colbert assured him that the treasurer's fortune had been stolen from the king's own coffers. Fouquet was arrested and imprisoned at Vincennes. But Louis's pride still wasn't satisfied. He ordered Le Vau and Le Nôtre to build another, bigger palace, sparing no expense. They did, and while Fouquet grew old and died in prison, the Sun King and his court shone at Versailles. Visitors can relive the château's history in candlelit visits on Saturday nights from May to mid-October.

If you can't take any more stately homes, across the A5 motorway is **Blandy-les-Tours** which has the only complete medieval fortress (Wed–Mon Apr–Oct 10am–12.30pm, 2–6pm; Nov–Mar 10am–12.30pm, 1.30–5pm; charge) in the Ile-de-France, having been reconstructed by the departmental council of Seine-et-Marne. It was originally built in 1206 but added to during the Hundred Years War. It is hexagonal in plan and has five round towers and one square one.

Following the eastern edge of Fontainebleau forest you come to **Barbizon** ⓰, a village famed for its links with 19th-century artists, when landscape painters Rousseau and Millet

BELOW: Château de Vaux-le-Vicomte, considered to be the forerunner to Versailles.

settled here and formed the École de Barbizon. The **museum** of the school is located in the Auberge du Père Ganne (Wed–Mon 10am–12.30pm, 2–5.30pm; charge), while Rousseau's studio is open for occasional exhibitions.

Milly-la-Forêt ⓱ also has artistic connections, as well as being a lovely town with an impressive wooden *halle* (covered market hall) built in 1479.

An old tradition in the area is the cultivation of medicinal herbs and flowers. These plants, known as *simples*, were first grown around a 12th-century leprosarium. When it was demolished, only the **Chapelle St-Blaise** remained (Apr–Nov Wed–Mon; Dec–Mar Sun & public holidays; tel: 01 64 98 84 94 for opening times; charge), and it still stands today. Poet Jean Cocteau decorated the chapel in 1958. Painted flowers grow up the walls, around tiny stained-glass windows, and a frisky cat is poised to leap into the holy water font. Above the altar, Cocteau painted the resurrection of Christ in pure lines and delicate colours.

La Maison de Jean Cocteau (Wed–Sun 10–7pm summer, closes 6pm in winter; charge) is the house in which the artist lived and worked.

In the woods outside Milly-la-Forêt stands **Le Cyclop** (guided tours May–Oct Sat 2–5pm, Sun 11am–12.30pm and 2–5.45pm; charge), a massive kinetic iron and mirror sculpted monster created by Jean Tinguely, which can be clambered over thanks to a series of ladders and galleries.

Not an obvious tourist destination, but refreshing for that, is the new town of **Evry** ⓲ in Paris's southeastern suburbs which is fast becoming France's interfaith capital. Not only does it have the only cathedral built in the country in modern times but also one of Europe's largest mosques and a synagogue located on the delightfully named "allée du pourquoi pas" ("Why not? Street"). One day it will also have Europe's biggest Buddhist temple. The Pagode Khanh-Anh is being built at the rhythm that donations come in and that craftsworkers in the Far east can supply the materials and adornments. It will eventually serve as the centre of Vietnamese Buddhism in Europe and be looked after by monks. ❑

Jean Cocteau is buried in Chapelle Ste Blaise. The inscription on his tomb is moving in its simplicity: "Je reste avec vous" – "I am still with you".

BELOW: Auberge Ganne, museum of the Barbizon school of artists.

Al Patat Rie
PUB

La Queue de Vache
LA ROSE DU VENT

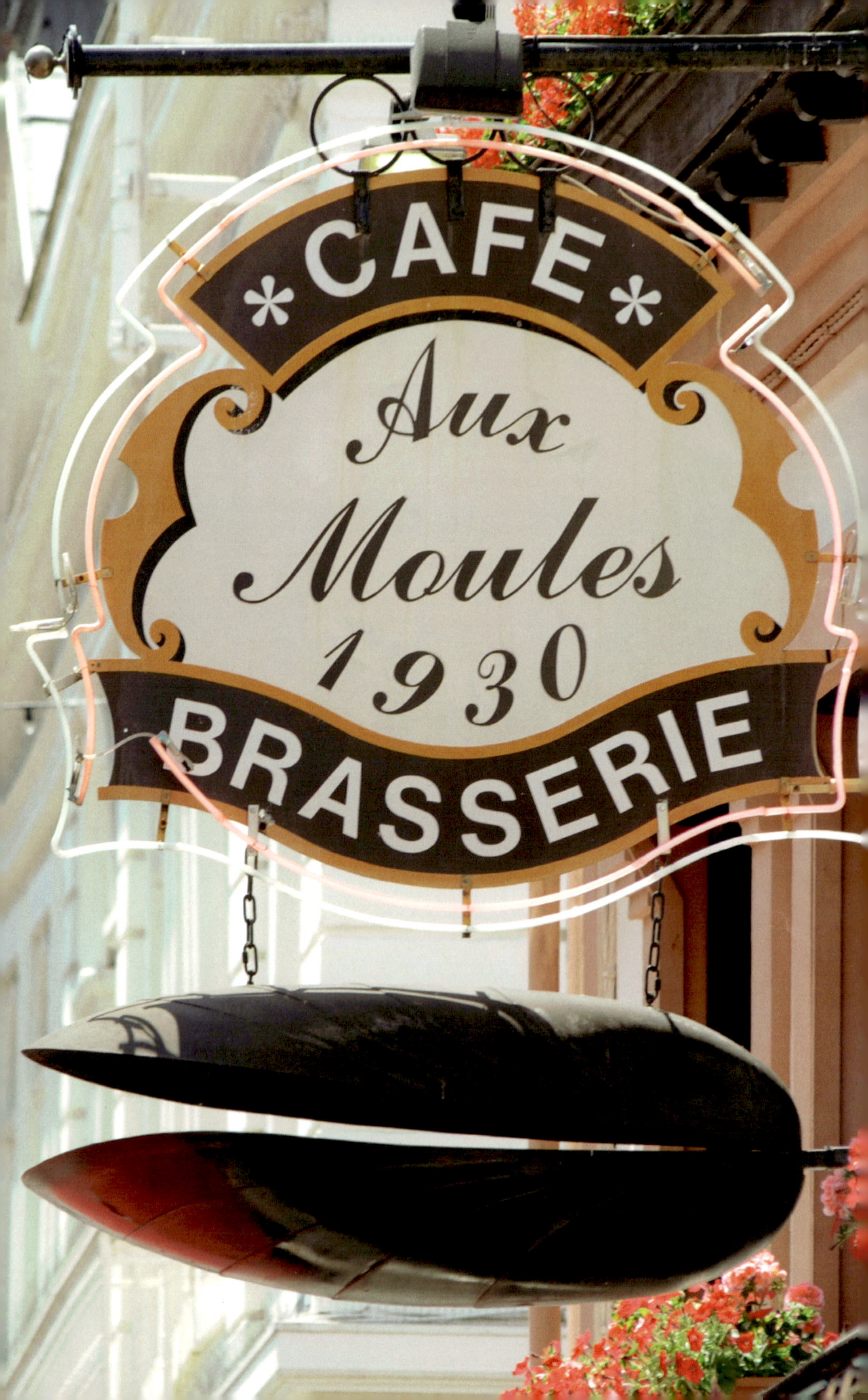
CAFE
Aux
Moules
1930
BRASSERIE

THE NORTH

A true historical crossroads, France's northeast corner has not just memories of war but also charming cities and supreme works of Gothic builders

France's northeast regions of Picardy and the Nord-Pas de Calais are sometimes dismissed as places to be passed through rather than to visit. Lille and its neighbouring towns were major centres of 19th-century industry, a landscape of coal mines and textile mills; much of the industry has, of course, disappeared, but the region is still widely perceived as grey and uninteresting. Yet, if you know where to look, there is plenty of charm and a wealth of historical attractions. The Channel ports of Boulogne, Calais and Dunkerque have very individual characters. Just inland are small-town gems such as St-Omer and Cassel, and the cultural mix of French Flanders. Lille itself is a vibrant city with a historic core that's excellent for food- and fashion-shopping. The Nord's artistic heritage is well displayed in fine museums. To the south, Arras is a fascinating small city with one of the most beautiful and largest 17th-century market squares in Europe.

This region was also one of the great theatres of World War I, the battlelines of which can be traced from Flanders to Vimy Ridge and Arras, the Somme battlefields and the Chemin des Dames east of Soissons. The battlefields and cemeteries are intensely moving.

On the coast south of Boulogne, long sandy beaches extend to the nostalgically upmarket resort of Le Touquet. Beyond are the peaceful wetlands of the Baie de la Somme. Two walled towns, Montreuil-sur-Mer and St-Valery-sur-Somme, are rich in the past and immensely charming. Inland is Amiens, France's "little Venice", with its riverside *quartiers* and one of the most glorious of all Gothic cathedrals. Further south across Picardy, one of the great cradles of Gothic, there is more superb architecture in Noyon, Laon and Senlis, and the mock-medieval castles of Compiègne and Pierrefonds. Finally, there is the elegant capital of French horse racing in Chantilly, and a must-see for kids in Parc Astérix theme park. ❑

PRECEDING PAGES: waterside restaurants, St-Leu, Amiens. **LEFT:** Brasserie Aux Moules, Lille. **TOP:** a French icon, the Citroën 2CV. **ABOVE LEFT:** seagull on the Calais docks. **ABOVE RIGHT:** World War I memorial grave, Vimy.

THE NORTH AND PICARDY

Small characterful towns, wild, empty wetlands, an abundance of historic sites and superb art collections all make up the map of the north

France's northernmost region is a borderland, a meeting point of French and Flemish cultures much of which only became part of France in the 17th century. Its towns were among Europe's first great centres of medieval trade and wealth, but it was also often a battlefield, from Roman times to the 20th century. The region has also been closely marked by its proximity to England.

Ports of entry

The sizeable town of **Boulogne-sur-Mer ❶**, buffeted by the damp westerly winds that blow in from the Channel, has been a well-established port for over two millennia. It served as the launchpad for Julius Caesar's first invasion of Britain in 55 BC, and in 1214 King Philippe Auguste made it the first outpost of French royal power in the north. He entrusted it to his unruly second son Philip "Frizzy-Hair", who in the 1220s began building the massive walls that, remarkably, still surround the hilltop old town – **Haute-Ville** – today. A walk around the ramparts is recommended for the wonderful views. In one corner, the **Château-Musée** (Mon, Wed–Sat 10am–12.30pm, 2–5.30pm, Sun 10am–12.30pm, 2.30–6pm; charge) has many Egyptian artefacts, donated by the Boulogne-born 19th-century Egyptologist Auguste Mariette.

LEFT: the walled town of Bergues, 'the other Bruges'. **RIGHT:** Boulogne old town.

Down the hill, the centre of town is an attractive ensemble of period buildings (interspersed with some remarkably ugly post-war eyesores). **place Dalton** has lively cafés and restaurants, and hosts the area's best traditional **market** on Wednesdays and Saturdays. Boulogne is now France's foremost fishing port, and its seafood restaurants are renowned. Beside the harbour, the **Nausicaa** sealife centre (9.30am–6.30pm, July–Aug closes at 7.30pm; charge) is a big hit with children.

Main attractions

- BOULOGNE-SUR-MER
- CASSEL
- LILLE
- ARRAS
- MUSÉE MATISSE, LE CATEAU-CAMBRÉSIS
- MONTREUIL-SUR-MER
- BAIE DE LA SOMME
- AMIENS
- SOMME BATTLEFIELDS
- LAON
- COMPIÈGNE
- PARC ASTÉRIX

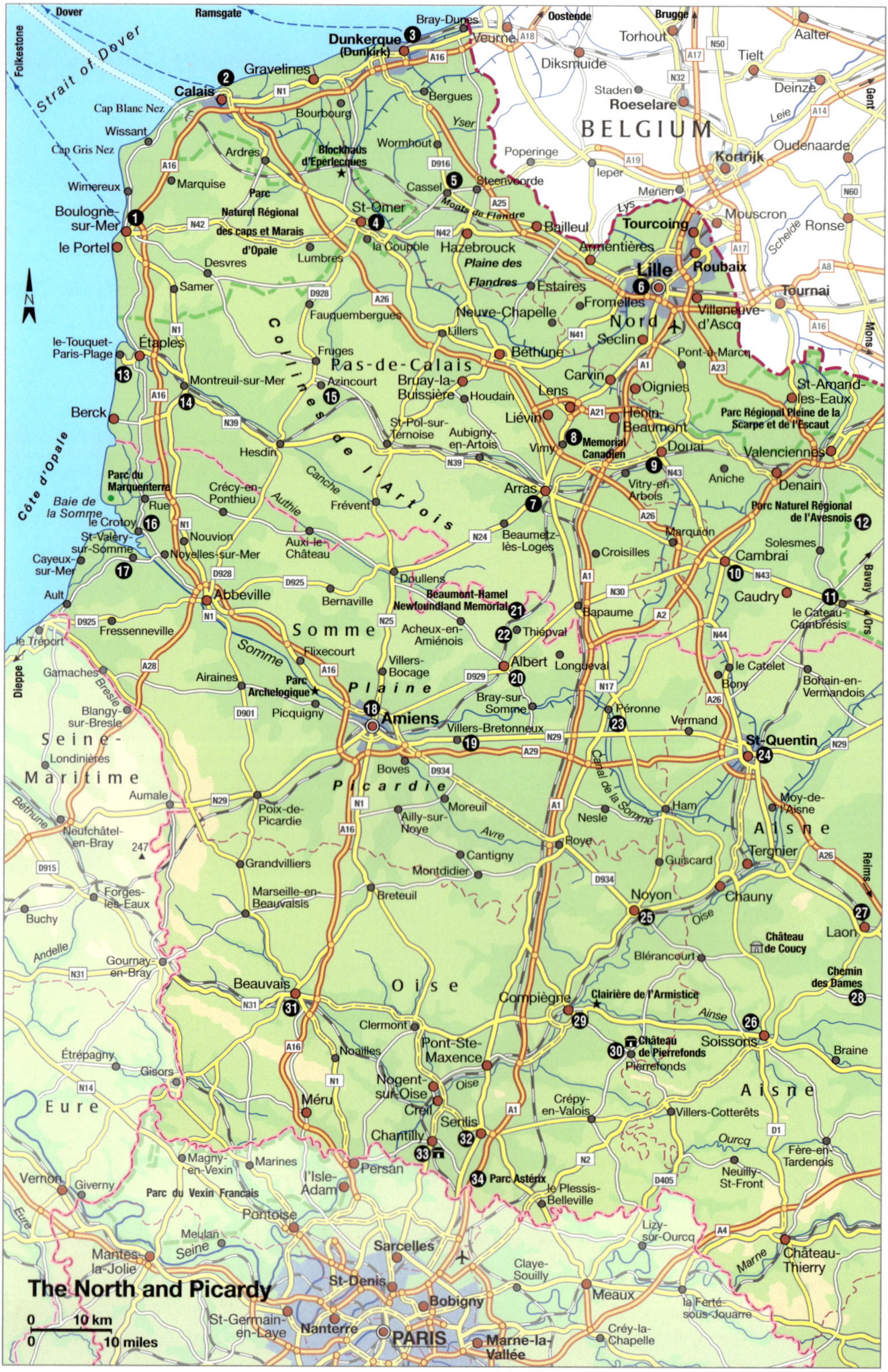

Dover
Ramsgate
Folkestone
Strait of Dover
Oostende
Brugge
Bray-Dunes
Dunkerque
(Dunkirk)
Veurne
Torhout
Aalter
Tielt
Diksmuide
Gravelines
Calais
Bergues
Staden
Roeselare
Deinze
Gent
Cap Blanc Nez
Bourbourg
Yser
Leie
Wissant
BELGIUM
Cap Gris Nez
Ardres
Blockhaus d'Eperlecques
Wormhout
Poperinge
Ieper
Kortrijk
Oudenaarde
Marquise
Wimereux
Parc Naturel Régional des caps et Marais d'Opale
Cassel
Steenvoorde
Menen
Lys
Mouscron
Boulogne-sur-Mer
St-Omer
Monts de Flandre
Bailleul
Tourcoing
Schelde
Ronse
le Portel
la Coupole
Hazebrouck
Armentières
Plaine des Flandres
Lumbres
Lille
Roubaix
Desvres
Samer
Estaires
Tournai
Fromelles
Villeneuve-d'Ascq
Fauquembergues
Neuve-Chapelle
Nord
Collines de l'Artois
Lillers
Seclin
Mons
le-Touquet-Paris-Plage
Étaples
Fruges
Béthune
Pont-à-Marcq
Pas-de-Calais
Carvin
Azincourt
Bruay-la-Buissière
Houdain
Lens
Oignies
St-Amand-les-Eaux
Montreuil-sur-Mer
Parc Régional Pleine de la Scarpe et de l'Escaut
Berck
Liévin
Hénin-Beaumont
St-Pol-sur-Ternoise
Aubigny-en-Artois
Vimy
Memorial Canadien
Douai
Côte d'Opale
Hesdin
Valenciennes
Parc du Marquenterre
Canche
Arras
Vitry-en-Artois
Aniche
Denain
Crécy-en-Ponthieu
Authie
Baie de la Somme
Rue
Frévent
Parc Naturel Régional de l'Avesnois
le Crotoy
St-Valery-sur-Somme
Beaumetz-lès-Loges
Marquion
Nouvion
Auxi-le-Château
Solesmes
Cayeux-sur-Mer
Noyelles-sur-Mer
Croisilles
Cambrai
Ault
Doullens
Abbeville
Bernaville
Beaumont-Hamel Newfoundland Memorial
Caudry
Bavay
Bapaume
le Cateau-Cambrésis
Ors
Fressenneville
Somme
Thiépval
Acheux-en-Amiénois
le Tréport
Flixecourt
Villers-Bocage
Albert
Longueval
le Catelet
Bony
Bohain-en-Vermandois
Dieppe
Gamaches
Bresle
Airaines
Parc Archelogique
Plaine
Blangy-sur-Bresle
Picquigny
Bray-sur-Somme
Péronne
Vermand
Amiens
Villers-Bretonneux
Seine-Maritime
St-Quentin
Londinières
Boves
Canal de la Somme
Aumale
Picardie
Ham
Moy-de-l'Aisne
Poix-de-Picardie
Moreuil
Béthune
Ailly-sur-Noye
Nesle
Aisne
Neufchâtel-en-Bray
247
Avre
Roye
Tergnier
Cantigny
Guiscard
Reims
Grandvilliers
Montdidier
Forges-les-Eaux
Marseille-en-Beauvaisis
Breteuil
Noyon
Chauny
Buchy
Oise
Laon
Château de Coucy
Andelle
Blérancourt
Gournay-en-Bray
Chemin des Dames
Beauvais
Compiègne
Clairière de l'Armistice
Ainse
Clermont
Soissons
Étrépagny
Pont-Ste-Maxence
Château de Pierrefonds
Pierrefonds
Braine
Gisors
Noailles
Eure
Nogent-sur-Oise
Méru
Crépy-en-Valois
Villers-Cotterêts
Creil
Senlis
Chantilly
Ourcq
Fère-en-Tardenois
Magny-en-Vexin
Marines
Vernon
Giverny
l'Isle-Adam
Persan
Parc Astérix
Neuilly-St-Front
Parc du Vexin Français
le Plessis-Belleville
Pontoise
Lizy-sur-Ourcq
Meulan
Seine
Sarcelles
Mantes-la-Jolie
Château-Thierry
Marne
Claye-Souilly
St-Denis
Meaux
la Ferté-sous-Jouarre
Bobigny
St-Germain-en-Laye
Nanterre
Créy-la-Chapelle
PARIS
Marne-la-Vallée
The North and Picardy
0 10 km
0 10 miles
N

Northwards, **Wimereux** is an utterly charming traditional French beach resort, complete with the necessary brasseries along its promenade. Around **Cap Gris Nez** there are superb vistas over the Channel, and some of the German Atlantic Wall bunkers are open as museums. Now popular with sand-yachters, tiny **Wissant** was also once a Channel port, before its harbour silted up around 1500.

Flanked by the Channel Tunnel complex at Sangatte, **Calais** ❷, so often dismissed as drab by British visitors, would also be a historic town were it not for its devastation in 1940. This destroyed nearly all its medieval architecture from the time when it was an English possession, from 1347 to 1558. In front of the Flemish-revival town hall, the siege of 1346 is commemorated by Rodin's magnificently moving statue *The Burghers of Calais*, commissioned by the city in 1885. More Rodin work is on show in the **Musée des Beaux-Arts** (Apr–Oct Tue–Sat 10am–noon, 2–6pm, Sun 2–6pm; Nov–Mar closes 5pm; charge), and a Calais speciality, fine lace, is showcased in the **Cité Internationale de la Dentelle** (Wed–Mon Apr–Oct 10am–6pm, Nov–Mar closes at 5pm; charge).

Dunkerque ❸ (Dunkirk) also required extensive reconstruction after 1945. Long a Flemish-speaking town, definitively part of France since 1662, it has a long maritime history, inventively recalled in the **Musée Portuaire** (July–Aug daily 10am–6pm, Sept–June Wed–Mon 10am–12.45pm, 1.30–6pm; charge). Dunkerque also holds one of France's biggest **Carnival** celebrations each spring, and is unusually well endowed with art museums: the **Musée des Beaux-Arts** (Wed–Mon 10am–12.15pm, 2–6pm; charge) has fine 17th–18th-century paintings, and the **LAAC** centre (Wed–Mon Apr–Oct 10am–12.15pm, 2–6.30pm; Nov–Mar closes at 5.30pm; charge) focuses on cutting-edge contemporary art, and has a sculpture garden.

The events of May–June 1940, when over 300,000 British and French troops were evacuated off the Dunkerque beaches to England, are commemorated in the **Mémorial du Souvenir** museum (Apr–Sept daily 10am–noon, 2–5pm; charge), in a former bunker. Eastwards, fine sand-dune beaches run for 16km (10 miles) through **Bray Dunes** to the Belgian border.

Flatlands

St-Omer ❹ stands out as a classic French small town, with a broad square occupied by an excellent market on Saturdays, and a majestic Gothic **Cathedral** with intricately carved porch. The **Musée de l'Hôtel Sandelin** (Wed–Sun 10am–noon, 2–6pm; charge), in an archetypically French 18th-century town mansion, is an especially attractive local museum, with ceramics, furniture and decorative arts as well as Flemish and other paintings.

Just outside the town is an expanse of wetlands, the ***Marais Audomarois***, famed for producing fine vegetables, which can be explored on boat trips. Also nearby are two of the most awe-inspiringly bizarre of France's many

The Dunkerque war memorial bears the simple inscription 'Souvenez-vous' – 'Remember'.

BELOW: Dunkerque docks.

Sign welcoming tourists to the top of Mont Cassel, the tallest of the group of hills overlooking the plains of Flanders.

World War II sites, the **Blockhaus d'Eperlecques** (May–Sept 10am–7pm, Apr, Oct 10am–noon, 2.15–6pm, Mar 11am–5pm, Nov 2.15–5pm; charge) and **La Coupole** (10am–6pm, July–Aug until 7pm; charge). Both are bunkers built as launching sites for German flying bomb and V2 rocket attacks on London. The dark concrete pit of La Coupole, especially, has tremendous macabre fascination.

East of St-Omer one enters **French Flanders**, where place names – Zuytpeene, Godewaersvelde – immediately show this is not the most conventionally French part of the country. It became French mainly because it contains the ***Monts de Flandre***, the only substantial hills in a famously flat region; when Louis XIV was pushing his frontiers northeast in the 1670s, his generals recognised their strategic value. This is a corner of France that retains an engaging distinctness, its foremost symbols of identity being boisterous festivals, traditional games, very un-French cuisine, fine beer and quaint pub-like bars called *estaminets*. The traditional hub is the marvellously unusual walled town of **Cassel ❺**, on the tallest of the *Monts* and commanding breathtaking views across the landscape of hills, fields and woods all excellent for walking.

Another characteristic of old Flemish towns is their giant belfries, a good example being the massive Gothic **Beffroi** in **Bailleul**, rebuilt after World War I – when many towns here formed part of the front line. **Fromelles**, a little to the west of Lille, is the site of the first new Commonwealth war cemetery in France in over 50 years, recently opened for the Australian and British troops killed in a disastrous attack here in 1916. Nearby at **Neuve-Chapelle** is the **Indian Memorial**, commemorating the thousands of Indian troops who died serving in the British army.

Urban pleasures: Lille

The city of **Lille ❻** lies at the centre of a sprawling conurbation labelled *Lille-Metropole*, whose overall urban area is the fourth-largest in France. One of the great trading and weaving cities of medieval Flanders, it flourished under Spanish governors in the 16th and 17th

BELOW: the Grand'Place, Lille.

centuries (the area was part of the Spanish Habsburg lands that extended up to Holland; *see page 39*), and its citizens were not enthusiastic about becoming French when Louis XIV seized the city in 1667. Lille's long-established textile traditions contributed to the town becoming a centre of industry in the 19th century, with many Paris fashion houses having their products made here. This, together with imaginative renovation, its role as a hub of the Eurostar and TGV rail network, and a chic shopping centre, has helped make lively modern Lille an accessible and enjoyable place to visit.

The main downtown focus is the broad **Grand'Place**, home of the famed *Braderie* flea market each September as well as a lovely Christmas fair. Separating it from place du Théâtre are the red and gold facades of the **Vieille Bourse** **A**, a classic of Flemish merchant Baroque by architect Julien Destrez from 1652–3, which now contains small shops and book stalls. Across the Grand'Place on adjacent place Rihour, the **Palais Rihour** is the last remaining vestige of Lille's medieval town hall, ravaged in World War I, which now hosts the **tourist office**.

The narrow streets of **Vieux Lille**, north of the main squares, are also the best area for window-shopping. Among the fashion and design outlets there are fabulous food shops. On rue des Chats Bossus, **A l'Huitrière**, with its 1928 Art Deco tiles, is France's most spectacular fishmonger as well as being a gourmet restaurant; the **Patisserie Meert** on rue Esquermoise is an 1840s temple to the French love of cakes and chocolate.

Lille's cathedral, **Notre-Dame de la Treille** **B**, is a strange anomaly of 19th-century vintage which was given a much-criticised modern facade in 1999. On delightful rue de la Monnaie, the **Musée de l'Hospice Comtesse** **C** (Mon 2–6pm, Wed–Sun 10am–12.30pm, 2–6pm; charge) is housed in a former hospital founded by a Countess of Flanders in 1237; within its spectacular Baroque chapel are art and craftwork from the 14th to the 17th centuries. On place Louise de Bettignies are several of Lille's finest 17th-century Flemish houses, while the **rue de Gand** has old Lille's most

TIP

Lille has two Metro lines, which meet in the centre at Gare Lille-Flandres and Porte des Postes and run across Lille Metropole, as well as tram and bus routes. The same tickets are used on all systems, and the City Pass, available from Lille tourist office, gives unlimited access to public transport and free entry to many museums and attractions for 1–3 days, for €20–45. Lille also has a public cycle rental scheme, Vélopole, with bikes available at points around the city for any period from 1 hour upwards.

BELOW: bustling thoroughfare of Vieux Lille.

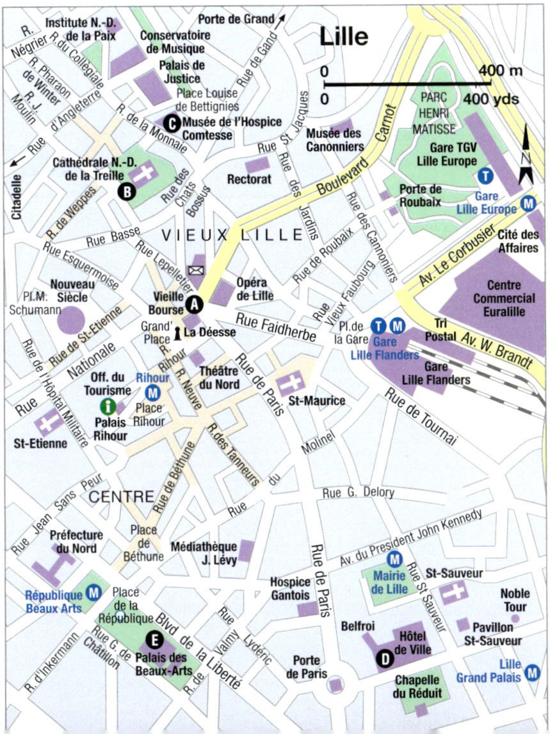

SHOP

Lille's Braderie is the largest flea market in Europe, and is held on the first weekend of each September. It dates back at least to the 13th century, and one of its roots is said to be a law that allowed servants to sell their masters' old clothes for a few days each year. It now attracts some 2 million visitors. There are food stands as well as junk stalls, and stopping for some *moules-frites* is part of the ritual.

popular restaurant row, leading to the **Porte de Gand** or Ghent Gate, built by the Spanish governors in 1621.

After 1667 Lille was given a more French look. Marshal Vauban *(see page 42)* built one of his largest fortresses, the **Citadelle**, to the northwest to keep the city in France. These days it serves as an enjoyable park. Rue de Paris extends south to the 1680s Porte de Paris, overshadowed today by the extraordinary 1920s **Hôtel de Ville** **D**, in a style that could be called Art Deco Flemish Gothic. There are also relics of older Lille in the 1460s **Hospice Gantois**, now a hotel. One of France's best regional museums, the **Palais des Beaux-Arts** **E** (Mon 2–6pm, Wed–Sun 10am–12.30pm, 2–6pm; charge) features sumptuous Flemish and Dutch art, notably by Rubens, with major works by David, Courbet and Goya, as well as ceramics and various other decorative arts.

The idea of spreading cultural venues throughout Lille-Metropole is reflected in the location of two other striking museums. **LaM – Musée d'Art Moderne** (Tue–Sun 10am–6pm; charge), focusing on contemporary art, is in Villeneuve d'Ascq, to the east; **La Piscine – Musée d'Art et d'Industrie** (Tue–Thur 11am–6pm, Fri 11am–8pm, Sat–Sun 1–6pm; charge), at Roubaix, is stunningly located in an Art Deco former swimming pool, and presents an opulent collection of applied arts, notably textiles. Both are easily accessible by Metro and bus.

Lens, Vimy, Arras

Cultural decentralisation is also intended to transform the profile of **Lens**, previously known as the capital of the mining district and home of one of France's best-supported football teams. The **Louvre-Lens** (www.louvrelens.fr) is set to open in 2012 in a cutting-edge all-glass building on a former mining site. It will exhibit some of the vast holdings of *the* Louvre not often shown, and thematic exhibits not practicable in the Paris building. The project's capture by Lens was a surprising coup.

More often Lens is passed over in favour of its gem of a neighbour, **Arras** **7**. It has been a major market town

BELOW: Palais des Beaux Arts, Lille.

since (at least) 828, and its **Grand'Place** is truly stunning, one of the largest squares in Europe and ringed by 16th- and 17th-century arcaded houses topped with Flemish gables. Next to it, the **place des Héros** or *Petit Place* is more intimate, home to the grand Gothic **Hôtel de Ville** with its lofty belfry, first completed in 1506 (and which now also contains the tourist office). More remarkable still is the fact that both squares and the town hall had to be painstakingly reconstructed, brick by brick, after World War I. Arras stands on chalk, and the ground beneath it has been excavated since Roman times to create a fascinating labyrinth of tunnels, called ***Boves***, used for every kind of purpose, from wine cellars and prisons to secret chapels. *Boves* tours *(see below)* are run from the tourist office.

The *places* of Arras with their cafés, restaurants and individual shops are wonderful places to soak up the atmosphere, and on Wednesdays and Saturdays they continue their historic function with one of the region's most richly varied traditional **markets**. In December there's also a lovely Christmas fair. Away from the squares, Arras' **Musée des Beaux-Arts** (Wed–Mon 9.30am–noon, 2–5.30pm; charge), in the 18th-century Abbey of St-Vaast, has exceptional porcelain and medieval sculptures, and a rare example of the once-famous Arras tapestries. 'Arras' was once the English word for tapestry – hence Hamlet stabs Polonius 'behind the Arras'.

The Arras sector saw fierce fighting throughout World War I. On **Vimy Ridge** between Arras and Lens, taken by Canadians in April 1917, is the **Canadian National Memorial** ❽, perhaps the most dramatically impressive of all the Western Front memorials. The excellent **visitor centre** (Apr–Oct 10am–6pm; Nov–Mar 9am–5pm) provides enlightening free tours of the preserved trenches and tunnels on the ridge, from where its strategic value is evident as it overlooks the whole mining district to the east. Nearby are several British cemeteries, the giant French cemetery at **Notre Dame de Lorette**, and the German cemetery at **Neuville St-Vaast**. In Arras itself, the city's *boves* chalk tunnels gave shelter

A new branch of the Paris Musée du Louvre is due to open in the former mining town of Lens in 2012.

BELOW: the Vimy Ridge memorial commemorates Canadian soldiers who lost their lives in World War I.

Welcome to the Ch'tis

The inhabitants of the Nord-Pas de Calais have not traditionally been treated with respect by the rest of France, especially by Parisians and anyone from further south. They are often referred to as *ch'tis* probably – there are other possible explanations – because in the local dialect *ch* and *sh* sounds are more common than in standard French. The fact that the northerners entered fully into the first industrial revolution goes against the grain in a country that likes to define itself with Parisian boulevards and neat small towns. They are thought to live in dark towns and have coarse, un-French habits, such as not knowing how to dress, and almost English levels of beer consumption.

In the north, meanwhile, *ch'ti*-dom is brandished with pride: Lille's entertainment guide is *Le Chti*, and one of the best local beers is simply named *Ch'ti*. Moreover, in 2008, the comedy *Bienvenu chez les Ch'tis* ("Welcome to the Ch'tis") became the most successful film in French history. The core of the film's story is that a post-office worker from Provence is sent as a punishment to Bergues, near Dunkerque; the joke is, he finds he likes it. That the film was such a hit perhaps shows how outlandish many people felt this idea to be.

EAT

Two specialities of Arras are *coeurs d'Arras*, heart-shaped ginger biscuits, and *rats d'Arras*, chocolate rats. Rats have been a symbol of the city since at least the 14th century, possibly just as a pun on the name "Arras". The best place to find them is Patisserie Thibaut, on the place des Héros.

for months to British troops, and British and New Zealand miners extended them towards the German lines. These tunnels can be visited at the **Carrière Wellington** (10am–12.30pm, 1.30–6pm; charge).

Mines and Matisse

Even by the standards of the region, **Douai** ❾ – another centre of mining and industry – has been especially battered in military conflict: the medieval town was burnt during the wars of Louis XIV, which made it part of France, and it was bombarded again in World Wars I and II. Its elaborate 80-metre (262ft)-high Gothic **belfry**, first built in 1380, has been carefully restored. Douai's university, founded by Philip II of Spain, was for two centuries the leading centre for the education of English, Scottish and Irish Catholics escaping persecution.

Around 40km (25 miles) to the south, **Cambrai** ❿ is a historic weaving town. Its light cotton cloth, *cambric* in English, was copied across Europe. Cambrai was also the scene of the first large-scale tank attack in history, by the British in November 1917. Nevertheless, a surprising amount of its Flemish historic architecture has been restored. The **Musée de Cambrai** (Wed–Sun 10am–noon, 2–6pm; charge), in an 18th-century *hôtel*, has art by Ingres, Rodin, Boudin, Van Dongen and others, and large archaeological collections.

Over the fields to the east, **Le Cateau-Cambrésis** ⓫ is a plain little town that in 1869 was the birthplace of Henri Matisse. Though he moved away to Paris and the south in 1952 – two years before his death – he endowed a museum in his home town, with personal instructions on how it was to be run. Installed in the Palais Fénelon, built for an 18th-century Archbishop of Cambrai, the **Musée Matisse** (Wed–Mon 10am–6pm; charge) has the third-largest Matisse collection in France, with over 170 works. An immersion in colour, its highlights include his 1951 *Woman in a Blue Gandourah*. There are also works by other artists, and temporary shows.

In the Communal Cemetery in **Ors**, east of Le Cateau on the Sambre-Oise canal, is the grave of the poet Wilfred Owen, killed five days before the war's end on 4 November 1918. In 2011 the **Forester's House**, where he wrote his last letters in the preceding days, is to be opened as a museum.

To the east the landscape becomes increasingly wooded and hilly into the **Parc Naturel Régional de l'Avesnois** ⓬, around the charming town of **Avesnes-sur-Helpe**. Stretches of beech forest run between small farms, hedgerows and villages almost like the Normandy *bocage*, and equally known for fine cheeses; town-dwellers come here to walk, cycle, swim or sail at the family holiday centre on **Val Joly** lake. The **Maison du Parc** information centre is in a fine old farm in **Maroilles**, home of the renowned cheese. **Bavay**, in the north of the park, contains the remains of *Bagacum*, capital of the Gaulish *Nervii* and later a Roman town. The site can be seen along with fascinating finds from the excavations at the

BELOW: Douai's grand Gothic belfry.

Musée-Site Archéologique (Apr–Sept Wed–Mon 9am–6pm; Oct–Mar Mon, Wed–Fri 9am–noon, 2–5.30pm, Sat–Sun 10.30am–12.30pm, 2–6pm; charge).

The Opal Coast

Back on the coast, 30km (19 miles) south of Boulogne is **Le Touquet-Paris-Plage** ⓭, the full name of an artificial resort inaugurated by a Parisian developer in the 1870s, in imitation of Deauville. It enjoyed its golden age in the 1920s and '30s, when Noël Coward and London high society came here for weekends, using Le Touquet's own little airport. British influence (grand hotels with names like "The Westminster", the golf course), combines with French (the casino, the restaurants). Eccentrically old-fashioned, Le Touquet has never given up its air of indulgent luxury, and has recently enjoyed revived popularity, particularly among fans of Art Deco. The beach is enormous, especially at low tide, and slides in the **Aqualud** water park are huge fun for kids.

Other beach towns nearby are more low-key, leading down to charming **Berck-sur-Mer**, popular with windsurfers and sand-yachters. Next to Le Touquet but completely different is **Etaples**, a gritty fishing town.

Just 15km (9 miles) inland is one of the north's most attractive towns, **Montreuil-sur-Mer** ⓮. It is still officially "sur-Mer" even though its port on the River Canche dried up over 500 years ago. Built high on a rock to dominate the river, Montreuil continued to be an important stronghold in France's wars with the Spanish Netherlands even after its harbour became unusable, and the walls around the upper town (*ville-haute*) were last rebuilt in the 1540s. They still enclose it today, providing gorgeous views from the path around the top, while inside the walls is an old town of enormous charm and character. A popular stopover ever since it was a halt for Paris-Calais mail coaches, Montreuil has particularly good restaurants, and an impressive **market** each Saturday.

East of Montreuil are the ***Sept Vallées*** or "Seven Valleys" of Artois, snug green valleys of glittering little rivers and red-roofed villages leading off the main Canche valley. Their centre is **Hesdin**, with another fine **market**, on Thursdays. When Montreuil was a French stronghold, Hesdin was a bastion of the Spanish Netherlands, a status reflected in Flemish-style buildings such as the **Hôtel de Ville**, with a Baroque porch from 1629 with Spanish coat of arms. Hesdin fell to the French just ten years later.

Nearby are two older battlefields. **Azincourt** ⓯, English Agincourt, is the site of Henry V of England's victory over the French in 1415, celebrated in Shakespeare. The battlefield is remarkably easy to distinguish, and the **Centre Historique Mediéval** (Apr–Oct daily 10am–6pm, Nov–Mar Wed–Mon 9am–5pm; charge) vividly fills in the background. To the south, just inside Picardy, is **Crécy-en-Ponthieu**, site of the battle of Crécy in 1346, where a viewing tower stands on the site of the mill from which Edward III supposedly watched the battle.

Pedalling round Le Touquet, a relaxing coastal resort that blends old English charm with French style.

BELOW: Le Touquet beach on a warm summer day.

TIP

Guided walks across and around the Baie de la Somme at low tide, including seal-watching trips, are provided by Rando-Nature en Somme (www.rando nature-baiedesomme.com) in St-Valery and Noshoes Club (www.noshoes-baiedesomme.com) in Le Crotoy, among others. No one should every try walks into the bay without an experienced guide, as the changing tides are very dangerous. Noshoes Club also rents sandyachts, bikes and kayaks.

Far horizons

After entering Picardy the coast opens up into the **Baie de la Somme**, a giant arc of sand flats, salt marsh and immense skies. At low tide the sea recedes to the horizon, leaving behind placid pools and expanses of marsh grasses with subtle colours and deep silence, a landscape ideal for walkers, cyclists and birdwatchers. In the dunes north of the bay is the **Parc du Marquenterre** (Apr–Sept 10am–7.30pm, last ticket issued 5pm; Oct–Mar until 6pm, last ticket issued 4pm; charge), a bird reserve with well-planned viewing paths of varying length.

On the north side of the bay, **Le Crotoy** ⓰ grew up as a modest Belle Epoque seaside resort, loved by Jules Verne. Since there is often not much water due to the tide, its vast beach is popular for activities such as sand-yachting. Le Crotoy's great seafood restaurant terraces remain weekend favourites for the people of Amiens, without any Le Touquet-style stuffiness.

St-Valery-sur-Somme ⓱, on the southern side of the bay, seems almost impossibly old, with flowers sprouting from gnarled towers around its walled *Ville-Haute*. Located next to an abbey founded in 611 by an Irish monk called St Valerius, it was a fortress by the 10th century. It has long been said that this was where Harold of Wessex, sent to Normandy by Edward the Confessor, was held after he was shipwrecked and captured by the Count of Ponthieu, as recounted in the Bayeux Tapestry *(see page 275)*. When William, his later nemesis, heard of this he paid for Harold's release, one of the origins – according to the Normans – of his indebtedness to the Norman Duke. An ancient tower is accordingly known as **Tour Harold**. Joan of Arc was imprisoned in St-Valery in 1430.

St-Valery wears its history quite lightly, and despite being slightly "discovered" by weekending Parisians, generally maintains the same calm that emanates from the bay. There are wonderful views beside the 16th-century church of **St-Martin**, with walls in a Picard chessboard pattern. In the lower town are some eccentric Belle Epoque mansions and a quayside promenade, and the bay's best market on Sundays

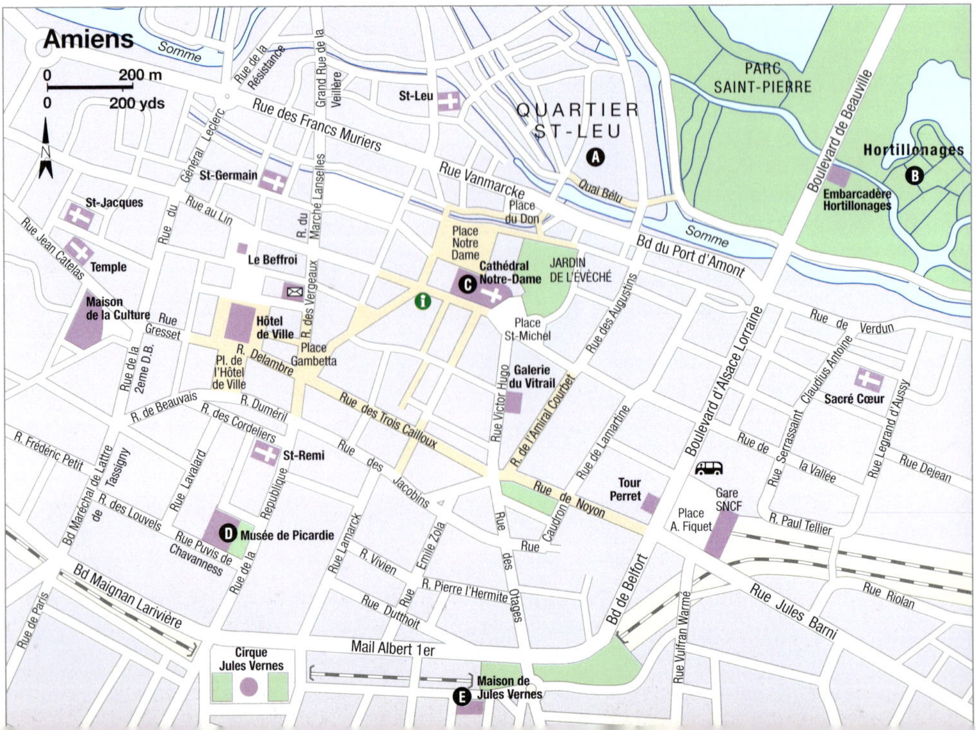

and Wednesdays. A lovely longer walk runs west along the bay shore, eventually leading to the tiny isolated village of **Le Hourdel**.

A steam railway line, the **Chemin de Fer de la Baie de Somme**, puffs up and down between Le Crotoy St-Valery and Cayeux from April to November. Outside **Noyelles-sur-Mer** is one of the more unusual war cemeteries, the **Cimetière Chinois**, where the dead of the Chinese Labour Corps employed behind the lines by the British in World War I are buried.

Abbeville had the sad fate of being the French town most devastated by the German *Blitzkrieg* in May 1940, and the giant Gothic church of **St-Vulfran** remains heavily bomb-scarred. The town's 1950s brick-and-concrete reconstruction architecture, once radical, is now more like a period piece.

Amiens: the Canals and the Cathedral

In the 1470s King Louis XI of France called **Amiens** ⓲ "my little Venice", and the sobriquet has stuck ever since to describe the city's watery charm. The Somme runs through Amiens in channels, creating islets linked by footbridges, most notably in the **Quartier St-Leu** Ⓐ, while along the quays are tiny houses with tall gables and up-and-down rooflines, and woodwork in a paintbox of colours. Many now contain antique shops and other places to attract browsers. A weavers' and dyers' district since the Middle Ages, St-Leu was protected by its canals from the fires that devastated much of the city after German incendiary raids on 18–19 May 1940. The restaurant-lined **Quai Bélu** and **place du Don** on the south bank are social and nightlife hubs.

Amiens' other, unique, water feature is to the east in the **Hortillonages** Ⓑ. Extending over several hectares, these marsh-gardens, crisscrossed by tiny canals, have been cultivated since Roman times, and remain highly prized for the high-quality vegetables they produce (sold from boats every Saturday in the *marché d'eau* or water market, opposite Quai Bélu). Tours are run by the plot-holders *(Hortillons)* from the **Embarcadère** on boulevard Beauvillé (tel: 03 22 92 12 18; Apr–Oct daily from

The west facade of Amiens cathedral is carved with hundreds of figures and biblical scenes.

BELOW: Quartier St-Leu, Amiens.

Sunset over the Somme valley.

2pm, according to demand; charge), in silent electric boats. The gardens form a magical wet, green, tranquil environment in the heart of the city, and *hortillons* personalise their plots with all sorts of quirky decorations.

From Quai Bélu's terraces there is a fine view up to the **Cathédrale Notre-Dame** Ⓒ. A major Gallo-Roman city as *Samarobriva* (Bridge over the Somme), Amiens flourished again as another of the north's great medieval trading and textile cities. Begun in 1220 to house the head of St John the Baptist, supposedly brought back from the Crusades, Amiens Cathedral is one of the great Gothic masterpieces. The **West Front** is astonishing, covered in superb carvings of Christ, saints and biblical stories. As fascinating as these major dramas are, look out for small details such as the images around the lower levels of the portals showing aspects of 13th-century life, and curiosities such as a plump hedgehog. Inside, the endlessly tall nave has a wonderful luminosity, and the carvings, this time in plaster and wood, are again spectacular. As in other medieval cathedrals the West Front was originally painted, and every evening from June to September and around Christmas its colours are stunningly re-created in an unmissable Laser show, *La Cathédrale en Couleurs*.

Many of the streets south of the Cathedral were reconstructed after 1945, and renovated again in recent years. The **Musée de Picardie** Ⓓ (Tue, Fri–Sat 10am–noon, 2–6pm, Wed 10am–6pm, Thur 10am–noon, 2–9pm, Sun 2–7pm; charge), in an extravagant Second-Empire building, has more character than many French regional museums: its most distinctive exhibits are local – the *Puys*, remarkable paintings commissioned by Amiens' guilds in the 16th century. Contemporary art includes a multicoloured room by Sol LeWitt, and there is also a wonderfully ornate café.

Across central Amiens' ring of boulevards is the **Maison de Jules Verne** Ⓔ (Apr–Oct Mon, Wed–Fri 10am–12.30pm, 2–6.30pm, Tue 2–6.30pm, Sat–Sun 11am–6.30pm; Nov–Mar same hours but closed Tues; charge), former home of Amiens' famous resident writer, which engagingly illuminates his multifaceted world. Nearby

BELOW: Jules Verne, father of science fiction.

The Sage of Amiens

Born in Nantes in 1828, Jules Verne, the father of science fiction, moved to Amiens, the home town of his wife Honorine, on her wishes in 1871. Beyond his devotion to his wife, to whom he was married for over 50 years, Verne stood out among French writers by becoming a determined provincial, who after spending his early writing years in Paris felt no more need for the "sterile agitation" of the capital. In Amiens, he was a local institution for 34 years.

He was also by far the wealthiest author in France: not only did his novels sell worldwide, but his science and geography textbooks were in every school in the country. He bought a series of magnificent yachts, the *St Michel I, II* and *III*, which he kept at Le Crotoy or Le Tréport and with which he sailed around Europe and the Mediterranean. In Amiens, an invitation to the Vernes' weekly *soirées* was highly prized, and he involved himself in every area of local life, serving on the city council and the boards of the local industrial society, horticultural society and savings bank, among others. In 1875 he produced a pamphlet titled *An Ideal City: Amiens in the Year 2000*, a vision of the future including mechanised communal child-rearing. One of his enthusiasms was the circus, and in 1889 he persuaded his fellow councillors into giving Amiens a permanent circus hall, with very Verne-esque architecture.

is the **Cirque Jules Verne**, the grand circus hall that he badgered his fellow citizens into building.

Outside Amiens, a short way west is **Samara** (July–Aug daily 10am–7pm, Sept–June Mon–Fri 9.30am–5.30pm, Sat–Sun 10.30am–6pm; charge), an "archaeological park" situated next to Roman ruins. With reconstructions of Neolithic and Gaulish huts and demonstrations of ancient crafts, it's a popular family attraction.

The Battlefields

East of Amiens are the battlefields of the Somme, where Britain's volunteer army (with Commonwealth units) faced its baptism of fire on 1 July 1916, losing 20,000 dead in the first hour. By November at least another 75,000 British and Commonwealth soldiers had died, along with 50,000 Frenchmen and 160,000 Germans. There was more fighting here in spring 1918, when the Germans made their desperate attempt to break through to the sea. Tourist offices provide abundant information, and a "Circuit of Remembrance" is indicated around the main sites, but one can of course visit them in any order. Every village has historical resonances, and many have war cemeteries.

Nearest to Amiens is **Villers-Bretonneux** ⓳, where the Australians halted the German advance in April 1918, with the **Australian National Memorial** and cemetery and the **Musée Franco-Australien** (Mon–Sat Mar–Oct 9.30am–5.30pm, Nov–Feb 9.30am–4.30pm; charge). Another Australian memorial is nearby at **Le Hamel**.

The 1916 battlefields are to the northeast. In **Albert** ⓴, British headquarters in the battle, the **Musée Somme 1916** (June–Sept 9am–6pm; Oct–mid-Dec Feb–May 9am–noon, 2–6pm; charge) occupies tunnels used by the troops, and is a traditional museum with a lot of militaria. A vivid site is the **Beaumont-Hamel Newfoundland Memorial** ㉑ (Apr–Oct 10am–6pm, Nov–Mar 9am–5pm; free), where part of the front where the Newfoundland Regiment was virtually wiped out on 1 July has been preserved, and which, like other Canadian memorials, provides impressive free tours.

TIP

A comprehensive guide to visiting the Somme battlefields and the many sites in the area can be found on www.somme-battlefields.com.

BELOW: "In Flanders fields the poppies blow."

Apart from for the cathedral, Laon and the Ardon valley are famed for artichauts gros verts, *giant artichokes, said to have been introduced during the Crusades. They feature in many local dishes, and an artichoke festival is held in the village of Chivy-les-Etouvelles at the end of August.*

At **Thiepval** ㉒ is the main **Franco-British Memorial**, an awe-inspiring giant arch designed by Sir Edwin Lutyens in 1928–32 inscribed with the names of over 72,000 British and South African troops who died on the Somme with no known grave. The modern **Visitor Centre** (Mar–Oct 10am–6pm, Nov–Feb 9am–5pm; free) is informative. Still visible at **La Boiselle** is the "Lochnagar Crater", created by a British mine dug beneath the German trenches, and at **Pozières**, taken at appalling cost by Australians in July–August 1916, there's another Australian memorial, as well as one to the first-ever use of tanks. A **South African Memorial** is at **Longueval**, while little **Rancourt** has British, French and German cemeteries.

The Somme's principal museum is the **Historial de la Grande Guerre** (10am–6pm; charge), in the 13th-century castle in **Péronne** ㉓, which was itself dreadfully damaged in the war. Inaugurated in 1992, the museum opens up the battles and the whole context of World War I with wide-ranging, imaginative displays. Péronne is also an attractive, historic town, ringed by small lakes or *étangs*.

St-Quentin ㉔, founded by the Romans, was a major trading centre during the Middle Ages. The site of many earlier battles, it was also ravaged by World War I. However, its 13th-century **Basilica** and grand Gothic 1509 **Hôtel de Ville** have been carefully restored, and it has many splendid 1920s Art Deco buildings. To the north at **Bony** is another World War I site, an **American Cemetery** where the graves include men who died in the first action by US troops in the war at **Cantigny** south of Amiens on 29 May 1918.

Bohain-en-Vermandois, some 20km (12 miles) northeast of St-Quentin, is where Henri Matisse spent his youth after his family moved from Le Cateau–Cambrésis, and the **Maison d'Henri Matisse** (Tue–Fri 10am–noon or 1pm, 2–6pm, Sat–Mon 2–6pm; charge) can be visited. Matisse left Bohain well before he became an artist, but the house and the family's grain shop have been attractively restored to evoke the years of his childhood, and there's a pretty café and temporary exhibition space.

BELOW: Thiepval Memorial to the Missing of the Somme.

Map on page 154

Gothic glories

Eastern and southern Picardy is one of the historic heartlands of France, and of Gothic architecture. The coronations of both Charlemagne, crowned King of the Franks in 768, and Hugues Capet, crowned King of France in 987, took place in the first Cathedral at **Noyon** ㉕. Its replacement **Notre-Dame de Noyon**, built from 1145, finely represents the transition from Romanesque to Gothic, with a soaring twin-towered facade. Its grandeur presumably did not impress Noyon's most famous son, John Calvin, born here in 1509. The **Musée Jean Calvin** (Tue–Sun Apr–Oct 10am–noon, 2–6pm, Nov–Mar 10am–noon, 2–5pm; charge) is a reconstruction of the long-demolished birthplace of the founder of strict Protestantism, built in the 1920s.

To the east are the dramatic hilltop remains of what was once one of the largest of all France's castles, the **Château de Coucy** (May–Aug 10am–1pm, 2–6.30pm, Sept–Apr 10am–1pm, 2–5.30pm; charge), built for a local lord, Enguerrand III, in the 1220s. Already partly ruined before 1914, it was blown up by the Germans in 1917.

Soissons ㉖, capital of a Gaulish people called the *Suessiones* conquered by Julius Caesar, became the seat of one of northern France's first bishops around the year 300, and from the 480s was one of the capitals of the Merovingian kings. Pepin the Short was crowned here in 752. Its prominence declined, but it still acquired fine Gothic buildings. Soissons was devastated in 1914–18, but its giant Gothic **Cathedral**, built over three centuries from 1176, was restored, and the majestic facade of the abbey of **St-Jean-les-Vignes** – mostly destroyed after the Revolution, not in the war – stands as a spectacular ruin.

One of the first great masterpieces of true Gothic, the **Cathedral** at **Laon** ㉗ was built from around 1160 to 1230, the same time as Notre-Dame in Paris. Majestically tall, with flat-topped towers, it shows a fascinating advance in style from Noyon. Its carvings are superb – notably the towers' famous oxen, supposedly representing beasts sent from heaven to help with their construction – and inside the stained glass and rose window are especially beautiful. Situated on a steep ridge, Laon was relatively fortunate in the World Wars, and around the Cathedral many of its old buildings and charming medieval streets survive.

East of Soissons and south of Laon is the **Chemin des Dames** ㉘, the "Ladies Road", so-called because it was built in the 18th century for the daughters of Louis XV to get to their châteaux. It runs along a ridge above the River Aisne, which was occupied by the Germans in 1914. It saw vicious fighting many times but above all in April 1917, when General Nivelle's Aisne offensive led to such horrendous losses and had such a total lack of success that the French Army mutinied. More fighting went on following the German spring 1918 offensive, involving British and American as well as French troops. There are memorials, battle sites and cemeteries at many

The monument to French tanks on the Chemin des Dames sits on the point of departure for France's first tank unit in April 1917. Tanks first appeared on the battlefields in 1916 and played an increasingly important role in the latter stages of the war. The tank in the picture is a World War II model at the site.

BELOW: medieval gateway to Laon.

The sumptuous Musée Condé gallery in the Château de Chantilly features works by Poussin, Watteau, Delacroix, Van Dyck and Ingres, among others.

BELOW: the moated Château de Chantilly.

points on and around the ridge. The **Musée du Chemin des Dames** is in the **Caverne du Dragon** (May–Sept 10am–6pm, Oct–Apr Tue–Sun 10am–6pm; charge) at **Oulches-La Vallée**, deep caves in a quarry used as a shelter by German troops. To the south near **Château-Thierry** is **Belleau Wood**, site of the first major American World War I battle in June 1918, with a **US War Cemetery** and memorial.

Napoleon to Astérix

Between its towns southern Picardy is often – like so much of France – green and placidly rural, and nowhere more so than in the **Fôret de Compiègne**, a magnificent oak and beech forest that was a royal hunting reserve, with wonderful walks and cycle routes well-used at weekends. On its north side is the **Clairière de l'Armistice**, where the Armistice ending World War I was signed in Marshal Foch's railway carriage in November 1918, and where Hitler insisted on coming to formalise the defeat of France in 1940. He then had the carriage destroyed, but a **museum** (Wed–Mon Apr–mid-Oct 9am–12.30pm, 2–6pm, mid-Oct–Mar 9am–noon, 2–5.30pm; charge) has a reconstruction and other exhibits.

The town of **Compiègne** ㉙, where Joan of Arc was captured in 1430, has an air of grandeur, reflecting centuries of royal patronage and its good fortune in recent wars. Dominating the scene is the **Château de Compiègne** or **Palais Impérial** (Wed–Mon 10am–6pm; charge). A royal residence since the Middle Ages, it was entirely rebuilt for Louis XV in the 1750s, and was a favourite of Marie Antoinette, and both Napoleons. Napoleon III and his Empress Eugènie made Compiègne their country seat, redecorating many of its over 1,000 rooms to suit their grandiose tastes. Other rooms were created for the first Napoleon, and there is a museum of the Second Empire and one of carriages and vintage vehicles.

Napoleon III's taste for extravagance and self-glorification was also expressed across the forest in the extraordinary **Château de Pierrefonds** ㉚ (May–Aug daily 9.30am–6pm, Sept–Apr Tue–Sun 10am–1pm, 2–5.30pm; charge). In 1857 Napoleon gave Viollet-le-Duc, apostle

of the Gothic Revival in France, free rein to rebuild the ruined castle as the medieval retreat the Emperor would have wanted in his dreams. The result is pure romantic fantasy, with fairy-tale turrets, a wonderfully mad folly.

To the west, **Beauvais** ❸❶, badly damaged in 1940, has a special monument to the wild ambition of medieval builders – its cathedral. Begun in 1225, it was to have been the tallest of all Gothic cathedrals, but the roof of the choir collapsed and had to be rebuilt, and an immensely tall central tower fell down in 1573. It remains unfinished, with no nave, but the soaring choir is stunning. **Senlis** ❸❷, in contrast, has the more conventional – but still majestic – cathedral of **Notre-Dame de Senlis**, another early Gothic jewel. Around it there is still a part-medieval walled town, encased within medieval ramparts built on a Gallo-Roman base.

South of Senlis is more lush woodland that was once an aristocratic hunting reserve, in the **Forêt de Chantilly**. The original 16th-century **Château de Chantilly** ❸❸ was from the 1630s the home of the Prince de Condé, the *Grand Condé*, a cousin of Louis XIV, great General and patron of the arts. Much damaged, the château was rebuilt in the 1870s in a slightly mock style. Within an exquisite park, it contains the **Musée Condé** (Wed–Mon Apr–Oct 10am–6pm, Nov–Mar 10.30am–5pm; charge), one of France's great collections of historic art. It includes many masterpieces, especially by Italian masters such as Raphael and Botticelli, but its most celebrated treasure is the *Tres Riches Heures du Duc de Berry*, the finest of medieval illuminated manuscripts (visitors normally can only see a facsimile).

Southern Picardy is celebrated horse country, and Chantilly is now most famous for the **Hippodrome de Chantilly**, home of French horse racing. Should the track not attract, one of Europe's most distinctive theme parks lies nearby at **Parc Astérix** ❸❹ (tel: 0826 30 10 40, www.parcasterix.fr; Apr–Aug and Oct, Christmas holidays 10am–6.30pm, also occasional late nights, check website for closing days and details; charge), a mini-village with great rides given a special Gaulish slant. ❑

Chantilly and its château were such a byword for luxury and grand living that its name was attached to a style of fine lace – even though much of it was made in Normandy – and to crème Chantilly, whipped cream with a little sugar and vanilla, which some say was invented in the château's kitchens, although the first record of it being served is at Versailles in 1784.

BELOW: Asterix and Obelix.

Cream of Chantilly

A Republic France may be, but French horse racing maintains an aristocratic style, helped by its roots in the Grand Écuries or "Great Stables" of the Château de Chantilly, built between 1719 and 1740 by the eminent architect Jean Aubert for horse-obsessed Louis-Henri de Bourbon-Condé. The story goes that Louis-Henri was convinced he was going to be reincarnated as a horse, and wanted a future home worthy of his rank. He was so proud of his Écuries that he held banquets for royal guests in them, surrounded by his horses. The most palatial stables in the world, they now form the **Musée Vivant du Cheval** (Wed–Mon Apr–Nov 10am–5pm; Dec–Mar 2–5pm; charge), where you can admire horses of various breeds and see dressage and other shows.

Modern horse racing, like sea-bathing, was introduced from England, and the track next to the château held its first race in 1834. The background architecture gives special cachet to races at Chantilly, especially its two classics the Prix du Jockey Club and Prix de Diane, both in June. It was also seen that the park and local countryside gave ideal conditions for training, and today thousands of horses are prepared around Chantilly and on the celebrated gallops through the forest, forming the largest horse training ground in the world. For information on French racing, see www.francegalop.com.

CHAMPAGNE
CAFÉ d'HA
2
Plat du Jour
Restauration
Glaces...

TVILLERS
HAUTVILLERS
LICENCE
Champagne
à la Coupe
Ratafia
Marc
de

THE EAST

Frontier France is greatly influenced by its cross-border neighbours. Where once battles were fought, now international connections are being forged

The three regions that run alongside France's northeastern border with Belgium, Luxembourg and Germany – Champagne, Lorraine and Alsace – share one thing in common. They have all played significant roles in the modern history of France, especially in the two world wars of the 20th century which have left behind them memorials, museums and fortifications as sobering reminders of difficult times.

Champagne needs no introduction for its chief item of export. Since the 17th century, the most northerly wine-producing area of France has been specialising in high-quality fizz which is expertly marketed both at home and abroad. Its capital, Reims, has a remarkable Gothic cathedral that was the traditional place of coronation for the kings of France.

Lorraine, next door, is currently re-inventing itself as a post-industrial region. Its two largest cities, Metz and Nancy, are packed with historical monuments. The latter specialises in both 18th-century Baroque finery and Art Nouveau. Less obvious sights to see are Verdun, scene of historic resistance in 1916–18 and the redundant forts of the Maginot Line built between the wars. Lorraine is also the birthplace of Joan of Arc.

Squeezed between the hills of the Vosges and the mighty Rhine River is Alsace, which stands slightly apart from the other regions of France with a strong identity of its own. It has many pretty – almost too pretty – towns and villages to explore. It also has a highly regarded cuisine and manages to produce both fine white wines and excellent beers.

Alsace is much influenced by its associations with Germany, although its capital city Strasbourg prefers these days to think of itself as an international metropolis that happens to be in France. In fact, this attitude could easily symbolise the whole of the northeast. Warfare may have made the region vulnerable in the past, but today it lies at the heart of the new Europe. ❑

PRECEDING PAGES: Café d'Hautvilliers, in the heart of Champagne.
LEFT: Strasbourg cathedral. **TOP:** Strasbourg saucisson. **ABOVE LEFT:** Mercier champagne vineyard. **ABOVE RIGHT:** quaint crafts from Alsace.

CHAMPAGNE

Globally famous for its sparkling wine, the Champagne region is rich in forests, lakes, picturesque towns and history in abundance

Main attractions
ÉPERNAY
REIMS
TROYES
HALF-TIMBERED CHURCHES
COLOMBEY-LES-DEUX-EGLISES

The name may be used across the world as a generic name for any sparkling wine, but to the French such loose talk is sacrilege: the only true champagne comes from designated vineyards in a specific area of dry, chalky hillsides. The significance of Champagne, however, goes much further than celebratory drinks. This could be said to be the spiritual omphalos of the country. Every schoolchild in France is taught that the baptism of Clovis, chieftain of the Franks, in Reims on 25 December 496 was the first step in uniting France and thus is effectively the birthday of their country. From then on it was a rite of passage for the kings of France to come to the city for their coronations in order to legitimise their regimes.

In the Middle Ages, Champagne grew to be a powerful and prosperous region ruled over by a dynasty of counts who made good money by holding annual trade fairs. These brought together merchants from the Low Countries and Italy and gave an impetus to Europe's developing economy.

In more recent times, though, it has been one big battlefield. Nudging up to the Belgian border, the region was strategically important during each of the wars fought against invading German armies. The region is consequently full of memorials, war museums and cemeteries.

The modern region of Champagne-Ardenne is composed of four *départements*. It is geographically divided into two broad zones: the *champagne crayeuse*, dry, chalky land just right for growing vines; and the *champagne humide*, a much wetter area of farmlands, forests and lakes.

BELOW: vineyards of Hautvillers.

Heartland of Champagne

The natural place to begin a tour of Champagne is in the abbey church of **Hautvillers** village ❶ where the monk Dom Pérignon (1639–1715) lies buried. Put in charge of the abbey's wine cellars, he earned a great reputa-

Map on page 176

tion for himself as a skilled wine maker and he is popularly regarded as the inventor of the *méthode Champenoise*. "I am drinking stars…" he is supposed to have pronounced in a eureka moment, although this quote is almost certainly a later addition to the legend. He probably didn't invent champagne alone. By injecting passion and patience into his craft, he made a number of crucial improvements to the production process and gradually perfected the quantity and quality of the abbey's wines. The reputation of Champagne for unwavering high standards, built over the following centuries, rests on his contribution. It is ironic, however, that the selfless labours of a reclusive monk should provide the world with the drink associated with idle, self-indulgent wealth, glamour and libertinage. *Dom Pérignon* is James Bond's brand of choice.

The centre of gravity of the champagne industry has moved a little south since Dom Pérignon's time, to **Epernay** ❷, where Moët et Chandon, one of the largest and most famous houses, has its premises (open for guided tours 9.30–11.30am and 2–4.30pm; Feb–Mar & mid-Nov–Dec Mon–Fri only; admission charge, including a glass of wine). Tours of the cellars include a tasting session, and if you pay a little more you get to sample a higher-quality vintage. The town also has a museum explaining the champagne production process.

A good way to get an impression of the vineyards is to make a detour on the way to Reims via the **Phare de Verzenay** (Tue–Fri 10am–5pm, Sat–Sun 10am–5.30pm; charge), a "lighthouse" which was built in the early 20th century as an advertising gimmick. From the top there is a view over the sea of vines.

The sacred city

The city of **Reims** ❸ was largely destroyed by the fighting that raged around it in World War I, and the magnificent **Cathédrale Notre-Dame**, begun in 1211, was left standing in 1918 as a hollow shell. Its restoration has been lengthy and meticulous. Though badly scarred, the cathedral's west front is once again covered in 13th-century carvings – look for the

> *Champagne is the only wine which makes a woman more beautiful after drinking it.*
>
> Madame de Pompadour

BELOW LEFT: Epernay. **BELOW:** Veuve Clicquot cellars, Château les Crayères, Reims.

Established in 1743 in Epernay, Moët & Chandon is the world's largest and most famous champagne house.

Smiling Angel and attendants on the north portal. A further surfeit of statuary decorates the interior wall, and richly carved friezes encircle the pillars in the soaring but otherwise simple nave. The stained glass is superb, from the 13th-century rose window to the 20th-century windows by Chagall in the ambulatory, with their luminous blues and purples.

That so much attention was lavished on the restoration of the cathedral testifies to its symbolic importance. Clovis' baptism in the 5th century was an astute political move as much as a religious one, uniting various tribes into a proto-state with the blessing of the Catholic Church. It invested the cathedral with a legitimising function, and 26 subsequent kings of France elected to be crowned in the city. Most notably, in 1429, Joan of Arc made a point of accompanying the would-be Charles VII to Reims so that he could be seen as the rightful heir to the throne and the man capable of uniting the French against the English.

Next door to the cathedral, the former archbishop's residence, **Palais du Tau** (May–early Sept Tue–Sun 9.30am–6.30pm; mid-Sept–May 9.30am–12.30pm, 2–5.30pm; charge) was the residence of royalty during their sojourns in Reims. It is now a museum of precious objects and tapestries.

At the **Musée des Beaux-Arts** (Apr–June Mon, Wed–Fri 10am–noon, 2–6pm, Sat–Sun 11am–6pm; opening times vary the rest of the year; charge),

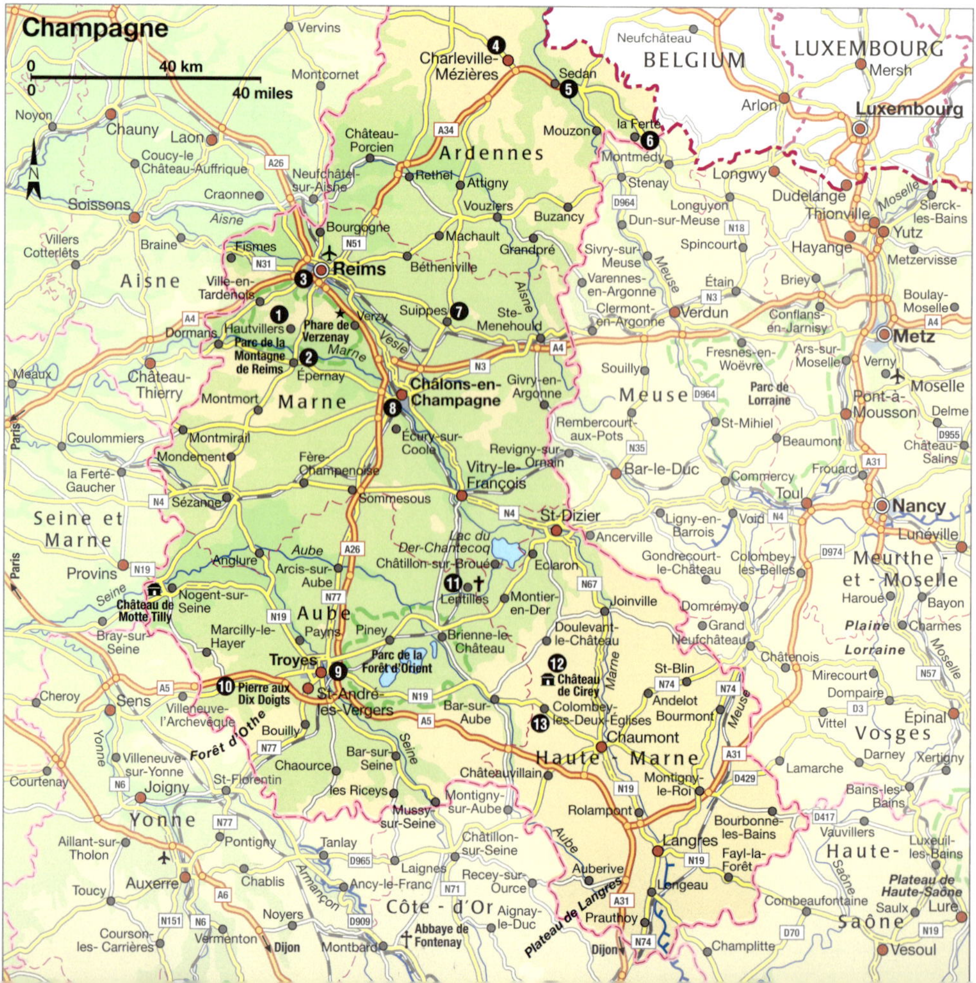

not far from the cathedral on rue Chanzy, you can relive the coronation rites through the paintings that were hung in the streets in honour of the royal arrival.

The **Musée-Hotel de la Vergeur** (Tue–Sun, 2–6pm; charge) is a private Renaissance residence (not a hotel) whose 13th-century Gothic hall houses 15 woodcut panels of the Apocalypse of St John by Albrecht Dürer.

Altogether different is the **Musée de la Reddition** (Museum of the Surrender; Wed–Mon 10am–noon, 2–6pm; charge), behind the railway station, which occupies the room in the city's technical college which served as the map room of General Eisenhower's supreme allied command during World War II. It was here that the commanders of the German army agreed to meet with representatives of the Allies to sign a document of surrender on Monday 7 May 1945, eight days after Hitler's suicide and the day after the last German garrison had surrendered to Soviet troops. The surrender came into effect on 8 May which became known as VE (Victory in Europe) Day.

Reims also has a number of the most important champagne houses, which can be visited (ask for details in the tourist information office), including Taittinger Pommery, Krug, Martel, Mumm, Piper-Heidsieck and Veuve-Cliquot.

Northern Champagne

The thickly wooded hills of the Ardennes make up the north of the region, with the Meuse River wriggling through them as it leaves the main town of **Charleville-Mézières** ❹. This was the home town of the poet Arthur Rimbaud. Despite having claimed to hate the place, he is honoured in the **Musée Rimbaud** (Tue–Sun 10am–noon and 2–6pm; charge), housed in an old water mill, and the Maison Natale Arthur Rimbaud, where he was born.

This is frontier country and as such has seen frequent battles. One place which has seen more than its share is **Sedan** ❺, which has one of the biggest castles in Europe. In 1870, Emperor Napoleon III and his army were surrounded here by the Prussians and forced to surrender, leaving the way clear for the

Stylised signs like this one illustrating the theme of wine production can be seen around the main champagne producing centres.

BELOW: the grape harvest.

Marianne, the symbolic figure of France and revolutionary icon.

invader to besiege and eventually take Paris. During World War II, Sedan was identified as the weak point in France's northern defences, the "hinge" between two defending armies, and as such it was the principal target of Hitler's strategy to take France by pushing a column of armour through the Ardennes.

La Ferté ❻ (July–Aug daily 2–6pm; Apr–June & Sept–Oct Sun and public holidays 2–6pm; charge), near Villy to the southeast of Sedan, marks the western end of the Maginot Line *(see page 200)* and was the only one of the line's forts to be attacked in 1940 and fall into German hands. Its strategic significance was negligible, but the action was intended to prompt French military commanders to reinforce their border fortifications at points which would not be attacked, thus weakening their forces elsewhere.

Battles of the Marne

Thirty years previously, the whole of the Champagne region had been swept up in the struggles of World War I, in particular the two battles of the Marne. The story is told in the visitors' centre at **Suippes** ❼ (July–Aug daily 10am–7pm; Apr–June & Sept 10am–1pm, 2–6pm; Oct–Mar Tue–Sun 2–6pm; charge) southeast of Reims.

Each of two battles, fought from 6–12 September 1914 and 15 July–15 August 1918 respectively, constituted a turning point in the action of the war. In the late summer of 1914 the German army succeeded in advancing as far as Meaux, 40km (25 miles) from Paris. It looked certain that the capital would be besieged. After ten days in retreat, French and British troops were exhausted and many people feared that the Western Front was as good as lost. As the French government decamped to Bordeaux, however, Allied commanders counterattacked. The tide of the battle is famously supposed to have been turned by the arrival of reinforcements from the reserves ferried to the front line from Paris by a fleet of 600 city taxis.

The Germans were now forced to retreat and they dug themselves into a line of trenches. Thus began an almost four-year war of attrition which continued until, in early 1918, the Germans

BELOW: Canal de la Marne.

launched a new offensive intended to break the deadlock and gain victory. They managed to split the defending forces and cross the Marne but the presence of American troops had tipped the balance of forces in the Allies' favour and the Germans were driven back to where they had started. The German failure to win the Second Battle of the Marne left the momentum with the Allies, and 15 weeks later the Armistice was signed.

Chalons

Although smaller than Reims, **Chalons-en-Champagne** 8 (called Chalons-sur-Marne until 1998 and still marked as such on some maps) sits roughly in the middle of the region of Champagne-Ardenne, and is its capital. It is a harmonious collection of preserved half-timbered houses which are at their best on place de la Republique, the old market square. One good way to see the town is by boat on a canal which runs through the centre.

The cork-shaped town

Troyes 9 is the capital of the *département* of the Aube – named after the river but also meaning "dawn". Under the rule of the medieval counts of Champagne, Troyes enjoyed almost equal political and economic status with Reims. Because of its strategic position between the Mediterranean and the north of Europe, between Italy and Flanders, it became the site of two important annual trade fairs which brought together merchants from both north and south.

It also played its part in French history. At the Council of Troyes in 1128, held in the cathedral under the auspices of St Bernard of Clairvaux, the order of the Knights Templar was given the approval of the Church. The 12th century also produced two famous sons: the romancier Chrétien de Troyes (probably 1135–83), purveyor of grail legends, and Jacques Pantaléon (1185–1264), who became Pope Urban IV.

Later, following the Battle of Agincourt during the Hundred Years War, Troyes was the location for the 1420 treaty-signing which gave Henry V sovereignty over France.

In 1524 a great fire raged through the town, destroying many of its half-timbered houses and thereby creating an opportunity for artists and craftsmen to assemble and apply their skills to the reconstruction. A reborn Troyes became the centre of the French hosiery industry.

The tourist information office likes to point out that the ancient town centre is in the shape of a Champagne cork, with the river Seine running around the crown. The **cathedral** is in the bulging mushroom-shaped part of the cork. Built in the 13th century, it is unusually bright inside thanks to its prodigious 1,500 sq m (16,000 sq ft) of stained glass.

The cathedral is sandwiched between two museums. The **Musée St-Loup** (Tue–Sun 9am–noon, 1–5pm; charge) is housed in the buildings of an 18th-century abbey and has collections of both fine art and archaeology, as well as the remains of a Gallo-Roman villa.

The well-preserved medieval streets of Troyes are lined with half-timbered houses.

BELOW: Troyes cathedral.

Sculpture at the Musée d'Art Moderne.

BELOW: Troyes' Museum of Modern Art is set inside the historic bishop's palace.

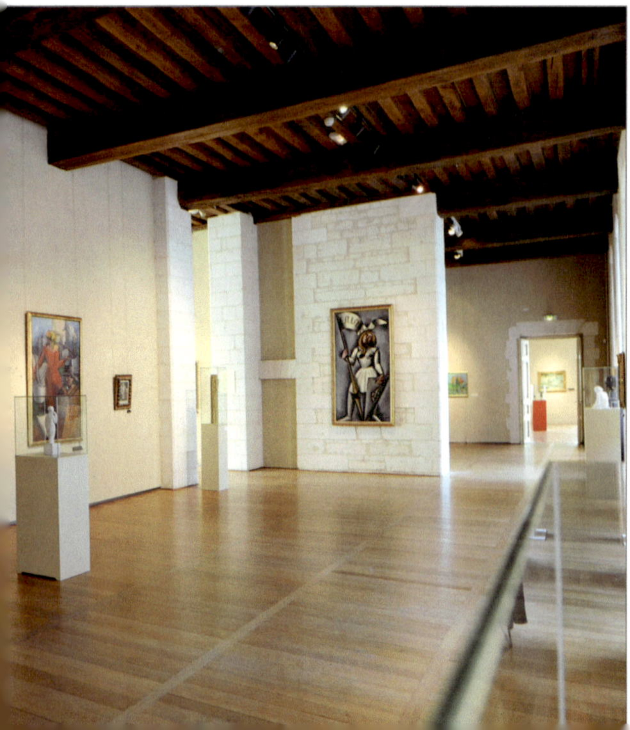

Its paintings and sculptures range from the 15th to the 20th centuries, the highlghts from the 17th and 18th centuries. On the other side of the cathedral is the **Musée d'Art Moderne** (Tue–Sun 10am–1pm, 2–6pm; charge), occupying the former bishop's palace. Art from Courbet (1850) to Staël (1950) is presented in 2,000 exhibits, including works by Matisse, Modigliani, Delacroix, Picasso, Cézanne and Seurat.

The streets and squares in the "neck of the cork" are more rewarding to explore. The almost unbelievably narrow alleyway of **ruelle des chats** gives a good impression of what pre-1524 Troyes must have been like. The oldest and finest church is the **Eglise Sainte-Madelaine**, begun in the mid-12th century. It has an exquisitely ornate rood screen *(jubé)*, made from 1508–17 by Jean Gailde, and forming a "bridge" of *ogee* arches overhead. Another church worth seeing (mainly for its stained glass) is the **Basilique Saint-Urbain**, founded by Pope Urban IV on the site of his father's cobbler's workshop.

Some 12km (7½ miles) northwest of Troyes along the Aube is the small village of **Payns**, fiefdom of Hugues de Payns, co-founder and first Grand Master of the Knights Templar, who is depicted several times larger than life on the municipal watertower. A museum (Wed, Thur & Sun 2–6pm, Fri–Sat 9am–noon, 2–6pm; charge) explores the history and legends related to Payns, and the Templars in general.

The northwest corner of Aube *département* has rich megalithic monuments left by Stone Age agrarian peoples. As well as dolmens and menhirs, whose functions are still unknown, there are a number of stones of more prosaic purpose. *Polissoirs*, literally "polishing stones", were blocks of sandstone used to sharpen flint axes and arrow heads. It took great physical pressure and hours of hard labour to work the edges of such tools, and over time deep parallel grooves were incised into the rock. One of the best surviving *polissoirs* is the **Pierre aux Dix Doigts** ❿ in the woods near Villemaur-sur-Vanne, so-called because St Flavian is said to have fallen asleep on the stone and left the marks of his fingers *(doigts)* on it when he woke up.

The **Château de Motte Tilly** (May–Sept Wed–Sun 10am–noon, 2–6pm; Oct–Apr Wed–Sun 2–5.30pm; charge), on a bend of the Seine near Nogent-sur-Seine, was built from 1754 for Abbot Terray, minister in charge of national finances to Louis XV, whose career was suddenly checked by the accession of Louis XVI. It is a typical house of the Enlightenment built by a high state official not far from the source of power. It was restored and repaired by an aristocratic family between 1910 and 1970. There are opulent 18th-century interiors and pleasant gardens on the banks of the upper Seine.

Half-timbered churches

Between Troyes and Brienne-le-Château to the northeast is Aube's lake district, a loose cluster of three reservoirs: the Lac du Temple, the Lac d'Amance and the much larger Lac du Der-Chantecoq. Part of the area is classed as the **Parc Naturel Régional de la Forêt d'Orient**.

Scattered around the landscape are 10 half-timbered churches and one chapel built between the late 15th and 18th centuries using the locally available materials of oak, clay and straw. The finest is the Eglise Saint-Jacques et Saint-Philippe at **Lentilles** ⓫, which dates back to the 16th century.

Also in the lakes area is **Montier-en-Der**, with its Benedictine monastery established in 672; only the church remains after the place was turned into a national stud farm. It has a 10th-century pre-Romanesque nave, a Gothic choir and stained glass from various periods.

The area around the lakes was made a regional nature reserve, the Parc Naturel Régional de la Forêt d'Orient, in 1970 – one of the first such reserves created in France. It is a stopover for migratory birds including cranes, ducks, geese and various raptors. The information centre (July–Aug 10am–6pm; Apr, May, June, Sep & Oct 10am–12.30pm, 1.30–5.30pm, Nov–Mar 1–5pm) is at the D79 and D43 junction, close to the Lac d'Orient.

To the southeast is the **château de Cirey** ⓬ (open for guided tours daily 2.50pm, 4pm, 5.10pm, 6.10pm in July and Aug, Sun in May, June and Sept; charge) where the writer Voltaire lived for 15 years from 1734 to 1739. He took refuge here in the house of a friend, the Marquise du Chatelet, after his *Philosophic Letters* or *English Letters* brought persecution for his criticism of the institutions of France. The house has one of France's 30 remaining private or court theatres.

The War Hero

South from Cirey a huge double-barred Cross of Lorraine in pink granite stands on a hilltop, visible from far across the rolling, chalky plain. It beckons the visitor to the village of **Colombey-les-Deux-Églises** ⓭, where Charles de Gaulle had his country home, La Boisserie; he lies buried in the humble churchyard. The house is now a museum (Apr–Sept daily 10am–6.30pm; Oct–Mar Wed–Mon 10am–1pm, 2–5.30pm; charge). More impressive, however, is the new **Mémorial Charles de Gaulle** (May–Sept 9.30am–7pm; Oct–Apr 10am–5.30pm; charge), a visitor centre beneath the cross which has exhibitions about the man and his times. ❑

> *I always thought I was Joan of Arc and Bonaparte. How little one knows oneself.*
>
> De Gaulle replying to the suggestion that he was like Robespierre, 1958

BELOW: Charles de Gaulle (1890–1970).

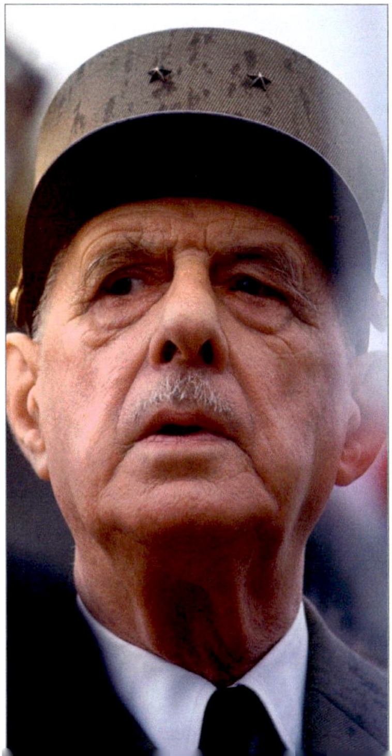

Charles de Gaulle

General Charles de Gaulle was a largely unknown figure when he delivered a stirring broadcast from London on 18 June 1940 urging his fellow Frenchmen and women not to capitulate to the invading Germans but to keep their dignity, unite with Britain and fight on. The wavering French government holed up in Bordeaux disagreed and the controversial regime of Vichy was born out of the impasse.

De Gaulle then dedicated himself to aiding the Allies in the liberation of France. After the war, he appealed to the nation to create a new republic which relied on a strong president rather than the instability of parliamentary parties. He failed, retreating from public life to Colombey to write his memoirs – and wait for the summons to come and save the nation.

When the Fourth Republic ran into trouble, he agreed to help on the condition that a new constitution would be passed to give him full presidential powers. The Fifth Republic was effectively tailor-made to his requirements in 1958, and for the next decade he dominated French politics.

His authority was tested by the events of May 1968 which made some of his supporters feel that he had become politically out of date. The following year he vowed to resign if a referendum on reform of the Senate went against him. He lost the vote and, true to his word, withdrew for the last time to Colombey-les-Deux-Églises where he died in November 1970.

CHAMPAGNE

Benedictine monk, Dom Pérignon, is widely credited with the invention, albeit accidental, of sparkling wine, a drink so unique and wonderful that it was named after a whole region

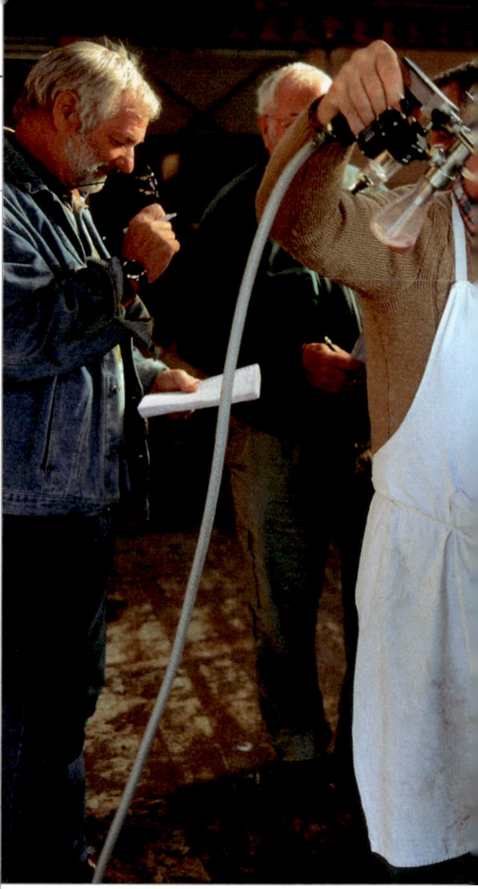

ABOVE: champagne cellarcraft is an elaborate and time-consuming business. The base wines undergo an initial fermentation before being blended. After a secondary fermentation, each bottle is riddle by gradual tilting and turning to remove the remaining yeast residu

BELOW: the vineyards of Champagne are the northernmost in France. The soil and chilly climate give the wine its unique flavour.

The world's most famous effervescent wine was supposedly the result of an experiment conducted in the 17th century by Dom Pérignon, head cellarer of Hautvillers Abbey (between the two most important champagne-producing towns of Reims and Epernay).

For a long time it was the drink of royalty, aristocracy and the rich, but in the 19th century, feverish promotion led to it becoming more widely marketed. On the eve of the Revolution 300,000 bottles were being filled and corked; by the outbreak of World War I this had risen to 30 million. Today, the supply is greater than ever, with over 300 million bottles produced to meet demand each year, but champagne has kept its expensive price tag all the while. A third of the production goes for export: one of the singular qualities of champagne is that it travels well.

It never has been and never will be just another drink to compete with the rest. Champagne is associated with special occasions, with winning, with celebration, seduction, impressing people, flaunting wealth and devil-may-care hedonism. Each bottle is estimated to have 50 million bubbles which rise to the surface forming "a delicate pearl necklace".

Connoisseurs recognise five flavours (flowers, fruit, vegetable, dried fruit and gourmet) and four types of champagne according to whether the wine has body (powerful and intense), heart (generous and smooth), spirit (light and vivacious) or soul (rich and complex).

LEFT: champagne must be served chilled, at 6–9° C. The bottle is turned, not the cork, which mustn't pop – or gas and flavour will be lost.

THE FUNDAMENTALS OF FIZZ

The name of champagne is strictly policed, and for it to be on the label of a bottle, the rules of the *appellation d'origine contrôlée* must have been adhered to.

Champagne can only be made from three types of grapes – Chardonnay, Pinot Noir and Meunier – and these can only be grown in the designated wine region by the 15,500 officially recognised growers. There are rules on how the vines are cultivated and the production allowed per hectare.

Some growers make their own champagnes but most pass their crops on to *negociants* (champagne houses) who must stick to the *méthode champenoise*, which involves precise ways of assembling, manipulating and ageing the wines.

The label of the bottle tells you who is responsible for what: RM stands for *recoltant-manipulant*, meaning that the wine has been made by the grower; NM *(negociant-manipulant)* signifies that it has been made by a champagne house; CM indicates a cooperative effort between grower-producers.

The result is a tightly controlled industry producing 9,716 brands, several of them world-famous.

BOVE: the great champagne producers mature their wines in ıcient subterranean chalk quarries which provide the necessary ɾen temperature. **BELOW:** champagne labels of the past.

ABOVE: bottles of champagne ready for export.
RIGHT: champagne is best drunk out of a flute, in order to avoid concentrating the flavour.

LORRAINE

Two fine historic cities, the birthplace of the nation's heroine and monuments to the horrors of war contrast with unspoilt countryside hugging the slopes of the Vosges

Main attractions

- VERDUN
- HACKENBERG
- METZ
- NANCY
- THE VOSGES

The territory now known as Lorraine, a medium-sized region of four *départements*, ultimately owes its existence to the pivotal Treaty of Verdun (843) which divided up the empire of Charlemagne into three kingdoms. The middle of these was Lotharingia, an impossible isthmus some 1,600km (1,000 miles) long and only 200km (125 miles) wide stretching from Holland to Italy across the Alps, like a wedge between France and Germany. Its disintegration was inevitable and one of its constituent parts became the duchy of Lorraine which was finally incorporated into the French Crown in 1788. Northern Lorraine – along with neighbouring Alsace – was later claimed by an expansionist Germany, and the two regions shuttled backwards and forwards between the rival states between 1871 and 1944.

Lorraine was a particulary prized commodity because it was one of the industrial heartlands of France, sitting as it does on the southern Saar coalfield and able to draw on large deposits of iron ore for steelmaking. Since the 1970s, the mines and steelworks have closed, many of them reinventing themselves as tourist attractions.

In stark and beautiful contrast to the post-industrial north and the Moselle corridor between Nancy and Luxembourg is eastern Lorraine, dominated by the forested Vosges mountains.

The national heroine

To the French, Lorraine represents heroic resistance against the foreign aggressor in two formative episodes of their history – the Hundred Years War and World War I. **Domrémy-la-Pucelle** ❶ is as good a location as any to begin a tour of the region. The national heroine Joan of Arc (Jeanne d'Arc) was born here in 1412. When she was 13 she left the village after claiming to have heard voices telling

LEFT: the Vosges foothills.

her to go and eject the English from France. Her house still stands, and the 12th-century font in which she was baptised can be seen in the church. The national monument to Joan's memory is the half-religious, half-patriotic **Basilique Du Bois Chenu**, built at the end of the 19th century on a nearby hillside, Domrémy. Inside, it is decorated with mosaics and paintings showing the saint's life. The crypt contains the polychrome statue of Our Lady of Bermont which Joan prayed before.

Bar-le-Duc and the Sacred Road

Northeast of Domrémy is **Bar-le-Duc** ❷, with its *ville haute* (upper town) of 16th–18th-century houses and a much earlier clock tower remaining from the defences of the château. Inside the church, the Eglise de Saint-Etienne, there is an unusually grisly funerary monument, the Transi or Squelette. Made by Ligier Richier, it is the memorial to René de Chalon, prince of Orange, who died in battle in 1544, aged 25.

Head north along the N35 or RD1916, officially termed the **Voie sacrée** in reference to the Via Sacra in ancient Rome, because it formed the vital logistical artery for supplying the besieged fortresses of Verdun during World War I. In the critical year of 1916 it is estimated that one truck loaded with men or munitions travelled up the road every thirteen seconds night and day. To keep the road open, impromptu quarries were dug along it and teams of navvies would shovel stones continuously into the ruts formed by the vehicles. There was no time or need to flatten the new material: the next wave of trucks did the work of the steam roller.

Resistance at Verdun

More than any other battlefield, **Verdun** ❸ represents the horrors of World War I for the French: a hell hole which sucked in an unimaginable number of lives; but it is more than that. This was French soil and as such it was considered a sacred duty to defend it at all costs.

By early 1916, both sides were desperate to end the stalemate of trench

Grave of an unknown soldier, one of 13;000 crosses that adorn the field of Verdun. Overlooking the war graves, the Douaument Ossuary holds the unidentified remains of some 130,000 soldiers killed on the battlefield.

BELOW: Verdun war graves.

Joan of Arc's symbol was the double-armed Cross of Lorraine and because of this it became also the symbol of the Free French Forces, under Charles de Gaulle, during World War II.

warfare and inflict a decisive defeat on the enemy. The Germans feared that an Allied attack was immiNent and decided to pre-empt it with an attack of their own that would force the French to sue for peace. They chose Verdun as a target because it formed a salient in the front that was vulnerable from three sides. The only railway line supplying the town was within range of German artillery.

The battle lasted almost the entire year, from 21 February to 26 December 1916, or "300 days and 300 nights of fighting" From February to July, the German army attacked French positions and after that the French counterattacked. At the end, no significant territory had been gained, but a staggering 378,777 French soldiers were dead, wounded or missing – against 333,000 German casualties. "On ne passe pas" had been the watchword of the battle: "they will not get through". A middle-aged Philippe Pétain emerged as the hero of Verdun, lending him a sheen of prestige he would draw on in 1940. The young Charles de Gaulle also won his spurs at Verdun: he was wounded and taken prisoner.

It is not hard to imagine these events in the hills northeast of Verdun, above the River Meuse, which are scattered with memorials of various kinds. A visit to the giant forts, the grassy remains of trenches, and the towering ossuary of **Douaumont** is an immensely moving experience (May–Aug 10am–6.30pm, Apr 10am–6pm, Feb–Mar and Oct–Dec 10am–5pm; charge). The Musée de la Citadelle Militaire gives a good idea of life in the trenches.

As a more unusual, and especially poignant, memorial, six villages on the former battlefield were left un-rebuilt and unpopulated, yet still officially communes, each with its nominal mayor and local council.

Today the theme of Franco-German reconciliation dominates, and Verdun styles itself as a "ville de paix", the home of the **Centre Mondial de la Paix, des libertés et des droits de l'Homme** (World Centre for Peace, Freedom and Human Rights; July and Aug daily 9.30am–7pm; Jan–June and Sept–Dec Tue–Sun 9.30am–noon, 2–6pm;

Joan of Arc

Joan of Arc (Jeanne d'Arc, in French, and also known as La Pucelle, the Maid of Orléans, the Maid of Heaven and various other names) was born in Domrémy on 6 January 1412, the youngest of five children, during the Hundred Years War. At the age of 13 she began to hear voices directing her to throw the invading English army out of France, and in 1429, dressed in men's clothes, she set off "into France".

She went to Chinon where she successfully identified the claimant to the throne, Charles of Ponthieu, who had disguised himself as a courtier to test her. Jean was given the nominal leadership of an army which lifted the siege of Orleans and defeated the English in battle, thus removing their aura of invincibility. She then escorted Charles to Reims where he was crowned king. However, on 23 May 1430 she was taken prisoner by the Burgundians at Compiègne and handed over to the English. She was tried as a witch in Rouen, convicted and burnt at the stake on 30 May 1431, still not twenty years old. She was subsequently declared "innocent" by the Catholic Church, and a martyr. After the Revolution she became a symbol of French nationalism and resistance against the foreign invader, a status she has retained ever since. The final stage in her long road to sainthood was achieved two years after the end of World War I, in 1920.

BELOW: Joan of Arc, the Iron Maiden martyred in 1431.

charge) which occupies the Episcopal palace built by the royal architect Robert de Cotte in 1723.

The Flight to Varennes

Varennes-en-Argonne ❹ played a pivotal part in an earlier epoch of French history. In June 1791 Louis XVI and his family were forced to flee Paris to escape the Jacobins. They headed northeast, disguised as the servants of a Russian baroness. They were almost certainly attempting to get to either the royalist stronghold of Montmedy or across the border to Belgium – which at the time belonged to Austria, and was ruled by the brother of Marie Antoinette, Emperor Leopold II. The ultimate aim was probably to launch a counter-revolution, but wherever they were headed, they only managed to get as far as Varennes.

There are many versions of the story of how their party was recognised; one improbable one has it that the king's face was compared to his portrait on a coin as he tried to buy something from a shop. In Varennes they were stopped and arrested by one Citizen Drouet, and returned to Paris.

Three Frontiers

The north of the region, around Thionville, north of Metz, is known informally as "the land of the three frontiers" because here Lorraine becomes the only French region to have three international borders – with Belgium, Luxembourg and Germany. Nudging up to these borders are the pretty village

Only in France – a roadside warning of "No Food".

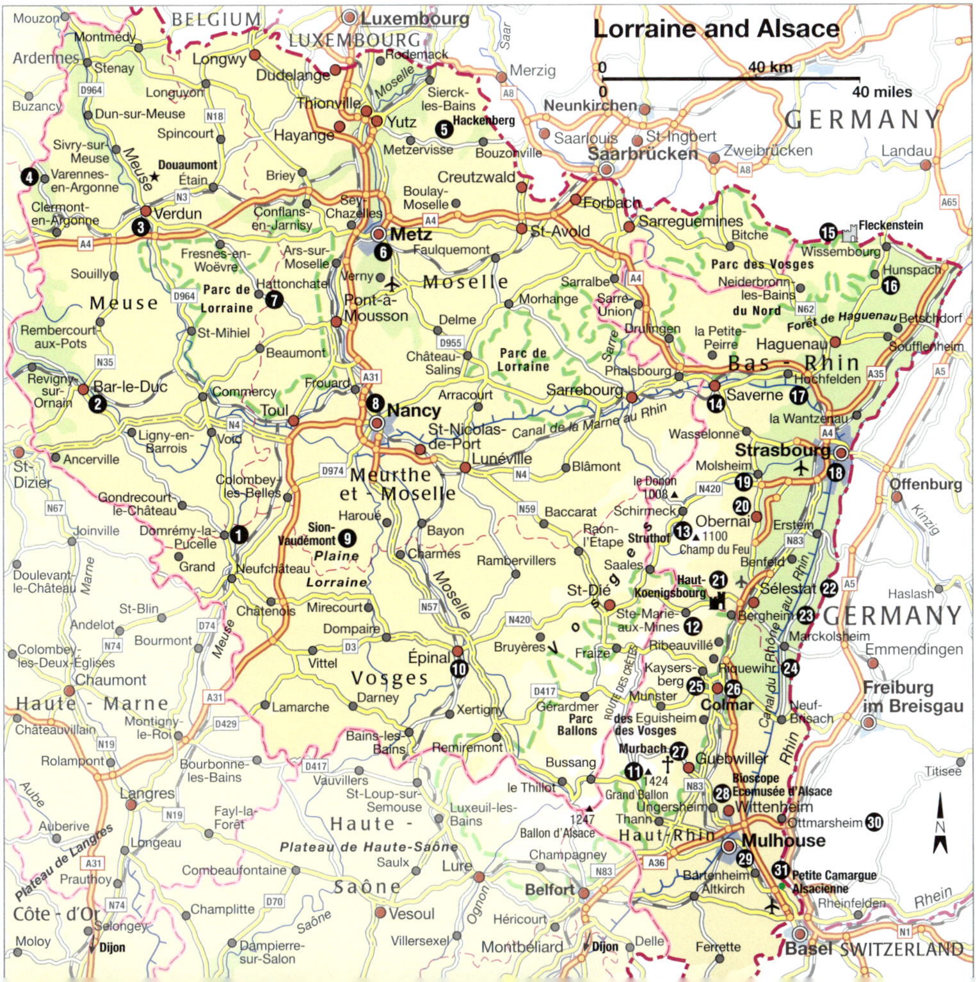

Choucroute, *an Alsatian speciality.*

of **Rodemack** with its 15th-century ramparts, and **Sierck les Bains**, whose intact château walls date back a further four centuries.

In the interwar years, this area became one of the principal sections of the Maginot Line. The Line's largest fortress is **Hackenberg** ❺ (open for guided visits only; June–Sept Mon, Tue, Thur & Fri at 3pm; Nov–Mar Sat at 2pm; Apr–Oct Sat–Sun and public hols at 2pm; enquire about tours in English at the entrance; charge) outside Veckring, southeast of Thionville. The access road is marked by a parked American tank, which can be visited on a guided tour. The fortress is a complex of 10km (6 miles) of underground galleries with a power station capable of supplying a town of 10,000 people. Here, 1,000 battle-ready men could be kept self-sufficient for up to 3 months. The visit is on board an electric train which was used for transporting munitions.

Metz

Lorraine's regional capital, **Metz** (pronounced "Mess") ❻, stands near the confluence of the rivers Seille and Moselle, at the intersection of the trade routes linking Paris with Germany and the Low Countries with Burgundy (and hence Provence). As Dividorum, it was an important Roman city, and later became capital of the Frankish kingdom of Austrasie: as such, it is considered the birthplace of the Carolingian dynasty. Always French-leaning, for centuries it formed part of the Holy Roman Empire but was only incorporated into France after a great siege in 1552. Metz then developed as the military supply centre for the defence of the vulnerable northern frontier, and later as an industrial conurbation.

The old city is built on two hills between the rivers overlooking three islands in the much-branched Moselle, and the best way to get a sense of the layout is to walk along the river bank below the old town and cross one of the bridges onto the small island dominated by the graceful **Temple Neuf**. The **place de la Comedie** adjacent has France's oldest opera house, functioning since 1752.

Back across the river and up the hill is the **Cathédrale St-Etienne**, which

BELOW: the new outpost of Paris' Pompidou Art Centre in Metz.

can claim to have the largest expanse of stained glass in the world. Some of the designs are by Marc Chagall. A few streets away is the lively complex of the **Musées de la Cour d'Or** (Museums of the Golden Court; Mon–Fri 9am–5pm, Sat–Sun 10am–5pm; charge), which exhibits archaeological, architectural and fine-art collections.

Across the shopping district from the old town is the sprawling square of the **place de la République**. Just off the square is the old arsenal and next to it the city's two most interesting churches, both open only for exhibitions and concerts (ask for details at the tourist information office). The Ancienne Abatiale **St-Pierre-aux-Nonnains** was begun in the 4th century and is a contender for the oldest church in France. The diminutive and easily overlooked **Chapelle des Templiers** was built for the Knights Templar in 1180.

If Metz has suffered somewhat from the decline in its military and industrial significance, its cultural reputation has grown since the opening of the **Centre Pompidou** (Mon and Wed 11am–6pm, Thur and Fri 11am–8pm, Sat 10am–8pm, Sun 10am–6pm; charge), a provincial branch of the famous cultural centre.

Scy-Chazelles, in the outskirts of Metz, was the home of Robert Schuman (1886–1963), the former French prime minister who played an instrumental role in creating what is now the European Union and as such is known as "the father of Europe" (a title also bestowed upon Jean Monnet – *see page 52*). He is buried in the 12th-century church of the village where he lived, and his house is now a museum.

Hattonchatel ❼, 30km (19 miles) southwest of Metz, has a handsome château founded in the 9th century but destroyed in World War I and subsequently rebuilt. **Toul** is another historic town which produces "vin gris": "grey wine" – white wine made from red grapes, in this case Gamay and Pinot Noir. It also makes *eau de vie* flavoured with Mirabelle plums.

Nancy

The city of **Nancy** ❽, 40km (25 miles) due south of Metz, was the capital of the Duchy of Lorraine until this was

The steelworks of Pompey, to the north of Nancy, supplied the 7,300 tonnes of steel needed to build the Eiffel Tower.

BELOW: Temple Neuf and the Moselle River, Metz.

Stanislas

Stanislas Leszczynski may have bequeathed his name to the main square of Nancy but he didn't much care for the city, and it was only the result of a failed career that he ended up in Lorraine. He was born the son of a provincial governor in what is now Ukraine in 1677, and was to lead an eventful life – first as serial monarch, later as Enlightenment philosopher. He was placed on the Polish throne by Sweden in 1705 but was forced to abdicate in 1709. He survived an assassination attempt in 1716, and in 1725 his daughter Maria married Louis XV, for whom it was a convenient alliance involving royal blood but without rival strings of power attached.

Stanislas lived in the Château de Chambord in the Loire until in 1733 he was placed on the Polish throne for a second time, this time by the French. In 1736 he abdicated again and as a consolation was given the Duchy of Lorraine with the proviso that it would revert to France on his death. While he was responsible for the beautifying of Nancy, he preferred to live in his palace at Lunéville. There he was surrounded by one of the last independent princely courts in Europe. The last years of his life were spent engaged in scholarship, philosophising and the writing of books. He died in 1788, aged 88, having seen the birth of his great-great-grandaughter.

The ornate wrought iron work on place Stanislas, Nancy.

swallowed up by the French Crown in 1766. Now a modern university city, it is notable for two styles of architecture which sit incongruously side by side: the aristocratic monuments of the 18th century and the Art Nouveau buildings created by the École de Nancy. The city is divided up into zones according to its history. In the 18th century its old medieval core (Vieille-Ville) was sidelined in favour of what is now called the "Espace XVIIIe siècle". The last duke of Lorraine, Stanislas, reorganised the city centre even if he didn't care to live here.

The hub of the city and the place to begin a tour is the eponymous **place Stanislas** Ⓐ. This spacious, pedestrianised 18th-century square is distinguished by its gilded wrought-iron grillework, particularly impressive in the corner fountain, and the handsome buildings in the style of French classicism: the town hall, a theatre, and the **Musée des Beaux-Arts** (Wed–Mon 10am–6pm; charge), a gallery of fine arts.

A monumental arched gateway on the northwest side of the square, the **Arc de Triomphe**, gives on to the broad **place de la Carrière** which ends in the **Hemicycle du General de Gaulle**. Parallel to these two squares runs the rather subdued main street, the **Grande Rue**, with the 15th-century residence of the Dukes of Lorraine, the **Palais Ducal** Ⓑ, now part of the **Musée Lorrain** (Tue–Sun 10am–12.30pm and 2–6pm; closed public hols; admission charge), which also occupies a former Franciscan monastery. Further on, the Grand Rue ends at the **Porte de la Craffe** Ⓒ, a twin-towered medieval gateway remaining from the city's fortifications.

Nancy is also noted for its collection of home-grown Art Nouveau art and architecture. The tourist information office publishes a map of all the surviving buildings. Some of the best examples are in the city quarter confusingly known as the New Town of Charles III, southwest of the place Stanislas. Three buildings are fairly close together, on or just off the rue St-Georges: the **Credit Lyonnais Bank** Ⓓ (7 rue St-Georges), with its large stained-glass ceiling; the **CCF building** Ⓔ (2 rue Bénit), built on an iron structure; and the **BNP Bank** Ⓕ (9 rue

BELOW: Porte de la Craffe, Nancy.

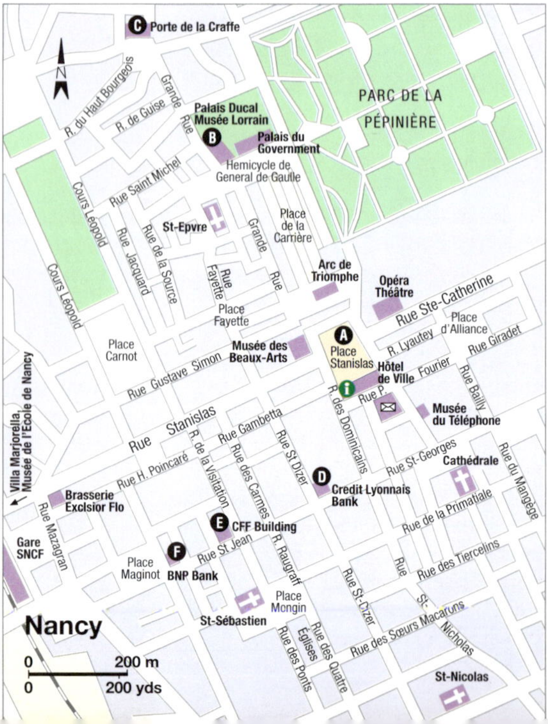

Maps page 187 & opposite

Chancy). An ideal place to stop for coffee during an Art Nouveau tour of the city is the **Brasserie Exclsior Flo** (3 rue Mazagran), a fine old bar with original furniture, fittings and stained glass.

Further out are the **Villa Marjorelle** (1 Louis Majorelle), the home of Nancy's leading Art Nouveau architect, and the **Musée de l'École de Nancy** (Wed–Sun 10am–6pm; charge), which brings together many works of the city's brand of Art Nouveau.

A few kilometres east of Nancy is the basilica of **St-Nicolas-de-Port**, dedicated to the patron saint of Lorraine. The **Parc Régional de Lorraine,** near Sarrebourg, has extensive forests that harbour wild boar and roe deer.

The sacred hill

Northeast of the spa town of Vittel is the L-shaped hill of **Sion-Vaudémont** ❾, looking down on the Saintois plateau. It is at once beauty spot, mystical location, Catholic and nationalistic shrine, and paradise for fossil-hunters who come here looking for star-shaped crinoids, the remains of plant-like animals that lived 200 million years ago.

At one end of the hill is the village of **Sion**, built around a basilica. At the other extreme of the mound are the remains of the medieval town of **Vaudemont**, once an important place but demolished on the orders of Cardinal Richelieu in 1639.

Between the two is a monument to the local author who became a parliamentary deputy, Maurice Barrès (1862–1923). Barrès turned Sion into a mystical site with his 1913 historical novel, *La Colline Inspirée (The Sacred Hill)*, which declared in its early pages, "there are places where spirit blows." During his political career, Barrès shifted from left to right and infamously articulated the anti-Semitic case during the Dreyfus Affair. In 1921 he was subjected to a mock trial by Dadaist radicals, accused of abandoning the principles of youth for later conservative conformity. He was "convicted" and sentenced to 20 years forced labour. In reality, the only result of the trial was to destroy the Dadaist movement itself.

The Vosges in Lorraine

In the southeast, Lorraine is joined to Alsace by the Vosges mountains – the highest land in northern France (unless the Jura, abutting the Swiss border, are included). From the Lorraine side, the slopes rise quietly in dark, green forests. **Épinal** ❿, the chief town, is synonymous with a distinctive kind of popular print, naïve, sentimental and flattering to the subject, which has been produced by the **Imagerie d'Epinal** (July–Aug 9am–12.30pm, 2–7pm, Sun pm only; Sept–June Mon–Sat 9am–noon, 2–6.30pm; charge) since the 18th century. The first prints were hand-coloured woodcuts, but in the 19th century the printing works switched to lithography.

The best of the scenery of the Vosges is arguably over the ridge in Alsace, but on the Lorraine side the two hill resorts of **Bussang** and **Gérardmer** make good bases for exploring the range. From either it is an easy climb to the spectacular Route des Crêtes. ❑

TIP

For information about walking and wildlife-spotting in the southern Vosges, shared between Lorraine and Alsace, see www.parc-ballons-vosges.fr. Other useful sites for exploring the range are www.massif-des-vosges.com and www.tourismevosges.fr.

BELOW: a chamois in the Vosges mountains.

Ville Haute
Quartier Pittoresque

ALSACE

Wedged in between the Rhine and the Vosges, France's smallest region is cosy and compact, with a picture-postcard prettiness, an excellent cuisine and fine wines

Main attractions
THE VOSGES
HUNSPACH
STRASBOURG
SÉLESTAT
ALSACE WINE ROUTE
HAUT-KOENIGSBOURG
PARC DE CIGOGNES, HUNAWIHR
RIQUEWIHR
COLMAR
MULHOUSE

Although it is clear on any map which country Alsace belongs to, it hasn't always been so. This strip of land extending along the left bank of the Rhine has a long history of toing and froing between France and Germany, leaving it with an enchanting mix of the two rivals' cultures.

Alsace was originally integrated into the Alemannic kingdom of Charlemagne's succession and did not become part of France until 1648. Meanwhile, its capital Strasbourg retained the right to levy its own taxes and finance a Protestant university. Later, following the French defeat in 1871, Alsace and part of Lorraine were annexed by Bismarck and not returned to France until the peace settlement of 1919.

In 1940, Alsace, along with part of Lorraine, was not so much occupied by the Nazis along with the rest of France as forcibly annexed to the Third Reich. In 1945 it reverted once again to France and its people are nowadays clearly turned towards Paris rather than Berlin. It now lives in peace, doubly endowed with the cultures of both countries – and, with Strasbourg now one of the seats of the European Parliament, lies at the heart of the new integrated Europe.

Alsace is France's smallest mainland region, a densely populated plain squeezed between the Vosges mountains in the west and the Rhine in the east. Small it may be, but it is crammed with sights and exquisite, well-kept, flower-filled villages. A stay here is made all the more pleasant by the food, specialities of which include *choucroute* (sauerkraut), Munster cheese and the ubiquitous *tarte flambée*, a "flame-grilled" pizza. Unusually, the region produces both renowned wines (dry, white and fruity) and beers.

The influence of Germany continues to be seen in the place names, architecture, cuisine and local patois. Around

LEFT: place de l'Hôtel de Ville, Ribeauvillé.
RIGHT: half-timbered houses are the pride of their Alsatian dwellers.

This sculpture of a woman in traditional Alsace costume is symbolic of the area's strong regional identity.

two-thirds of the population speak their own dialect, Alsatian or Elsässisch, giving it a claim to be the second most spoken tongue in France after French.

The Vosges

The backbone of Alsace is the **Massif des Vosges**, a range of low mountains covered with mainly coniferous forests which separates the region from Lorraine. In many ways the massif mirrors the Black Forest on the other side of the Rhine. While the German range has its cherry gateau, the restaurants of the Vosges invariably offer bilberry tart on their dessert menus.

The Vosges is a favourite place for walking. The GR5 long-distance footpath, linking the North Sea to the Mediterranean, runs north to south through the hills and intersects with the east-west-running GR7. Altogether, there are 18,000km (11,000 miles) of footpaths signposted and maintained by enthusiasts of the Club Vosgien.

By car, the best way to get the flavour of the Vosges is to follow the **Route des Cretes** (**Route of the Crests**) between Cernay and the Col de la Schlucht, along a road built to facilitate troop movements during World War I. The route skirts around the highest peak, the **Grand Ballon** ⓫ (1,424m/4,672ft). The summit, which is topped by the white ball of a radar station, can be easily ascended on foot. Still more accessible is **Mt Hohnek** (1,362m/4,468ft), from where there are views over the Rhine Valley and into Germany.

The Route des Cretes continues north, though not as scenically, to **Ste-Marie-aux-Mines** ⓬ where the old silver mines have been converted into a museum, **Tellure** (July–Aug 10am–7pm; Apr–June and Sept–Oct 10am–6pm), giving an insight into the life of a miner in the 16th century.

Midway up the length of the Vosges, near Schirmeck, is **Struthof** ⓭, the site of KL-Natzweiler, the only Nazi concentration camp in France. It was a labour camp, established in 1941 to hold political prisoners from all over Europe as well as Jews, gypsies and homosexuals. Among those who came here were the rebels rounded up in the occupied territories under the "Nacht und Nebel" (Night and Fog) orders, the

BELOW: the Vosges around Mt Hohnek. **BELOW RIGHT:** the European white stork, a symbol of good luck, is often seen nesting in urban areas.

Nazis' infamous programme of "forced disappearance". An estimated 52,000 deportees passed through the camp or its annexes and 22,000 of them died, including 86 Jews who were executed in a gas chamber so that their bodies could be used for scientific experiment. The camp is now the **European Centre of Deported Resistance Members** (May–Sept 9am–6.30pm; Mar–Apr and Oct–Dec 9am–5pm; admission charge), a museum and memorial to those who suffered, died or simply vanished.

The peak of **Donon** (1,009 metres/ 3,308ft), northwest of Schirmeck, has been a sacred site since at least Celtic times. An imitation Greco-Roman temple now stands on the summit, from which there are tremendous views. There is a footpath from the car park on the D993 below. It takes about two and a half hours to walk the 4.2km (2½ miles) to the top and back again.

The main town in the north of the Vosges is **Saverne** ⓮, where the noble Rohan family built an extravagant and ostentatious château complemented by an immense rose garden. It houses a **museum** (Wed–Mon 10am–noon, 3–6pm; charge) investigating local archaeology and the château's history.

La Petite-Pierre is the information centre for the **Parc Régional des Vosges de Nord**, where trails wander off through a wildlife reserve.

Lower Alsace

The north of Alsace is a land of ancient forests and razed castles. The **Forêt de Haguenau** shelters hamlets of wooden houses, renowned for their colourful festivities during which men and women dress in the typical folk costumes of Alsace and perform traditional dances.

The most impressive of the ruined castles is, perhaps, **Fleckenstein** ⓯ (July–Aug 10am–6pm; Mar–June and Sept–Oct 10am–5.30pm; Jan–Feb Sun noon–4pm; charge). Built in the 12th century, its crumbling masonry now blends into the rock outcrop it perches on, looking somewhat like a ruined stone ship.

More recently constructed fortresses mark the course of the Maginot Line *(see page 200)*, built in the 1930s in a vain attempt to stave off attack by

> *I went on horseback to Saverne, where in fine weather the little friendly place seemed to smile at us most charmingly.*
>
> J.W. von Gorthe

BELOW: Château Saverne.

The hors d'oeuvre tarte flambée is the Alsatian equivalent of pizza, traditionally made with crème fraîche, cheese and onions, and baked in a wood-fired oven.

Nazi Germany. The forts in Alsace never fired a shot in anger while they waited for an invasion that took an unexpected route. They then became a tourist attraction for the occupying German forces.

The most delightful village in the north, indeed one of the most beautiful in France, is **Hunspach** 16, a harmonious cluster of three- or four-storey traditional black-and-white half-timbered houses. Many of the windows have rounded panes of glass to allow the occupants inside to see out without being seen themselves.

Betschdorf and **Soufflenheim** are renowned for their potteries. Betschdorf pottery is made according to a method that hasn't changed since 1717. Pieces are made from grey clay, decorated with cobalt blue and varnished using salt. Soufflenheim produces cooking dishes, moulds and pitchers mostly in yellow, green or brown. Betschdorf has a museum (Easter–Oct Mon–Sat 10am–noon, 1–6pm; Sun 1–6pm; charge).

Hochfelden 17 is the lone outpost of Alsace's last independent brewery, Météor, which struggles to compete with the four giants that supply half of the beer consumed in France. Beer is considered equal to wine in this part of the country, and a favourite aperitif is beer with a shot of *amer*, a liqueur made from bitter herbs. Special beers are brewed in spring, drawing on the last barley harvest, and at Christmas a strong rich ale is traditionally made to use up the brewery's leftover ingredients.

Strasbourg

Strasbourg 18, France's seventh-largest city, the capital of Alsace and the home of several international institutions, stands close to (but not quite alongside) the River Rhine which forms the border with Germany. It grew up on the site of a Roman camp on an island in the Rhine's tributary, the Ill, at a strategic intersection of east-west and north-south trade routes. Indeed, its name means "the town at the crossroads".

The city has changed hands several times in the course of its history and has always been a place of passage. Two important German innovators spent

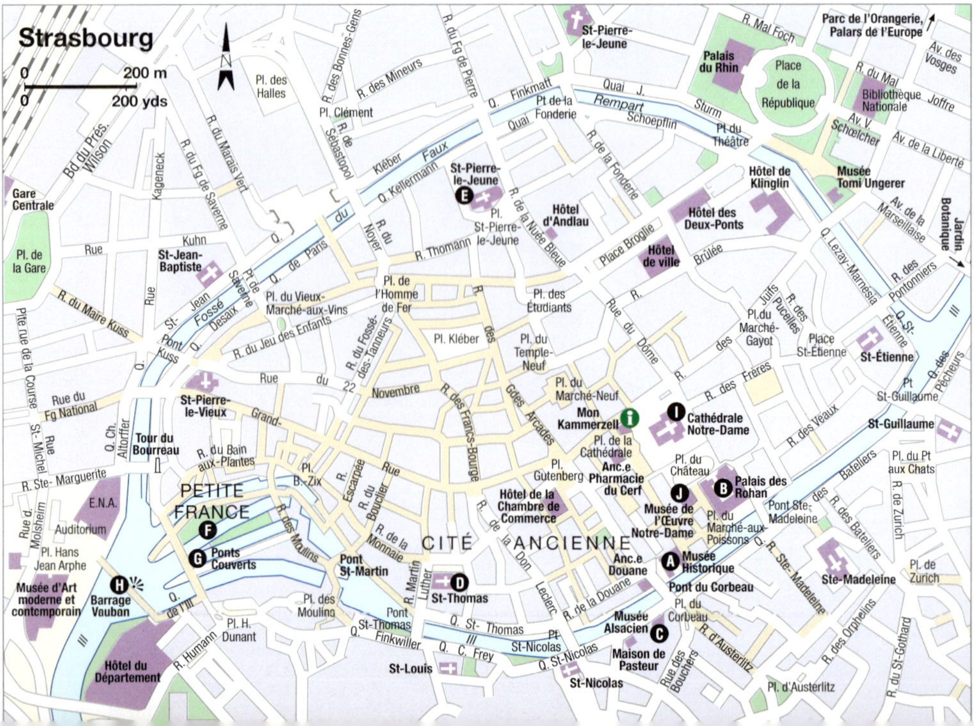

formative sojourns here. The biography of the pioneering printer Johannes Gutenberg is patchy, but it is known that he spent the years 1434–44 in Strasbourg, during which time he carried out trials which would lead him to perfect his printing press. Three centuries later, the literary polymath Johann Wolfgang von Goethe came here in 1770 after a period of illness and stagnation to resume his studies in law. A chance meeting with Johann Gottfried von Herder awakened an interest in Shakespeare and folk poetry. It was a pivotal moment that turned Goethe into a major writer and laid the foundation of the "Sturm und Drang" (Storm and Stress) literary movement. Goethe also had a brief romance with a pastor's daughter, Frederike, in Sessenheim, to the northeast of Strasbourg, and she became the inspiration of some of his poems.

Another visitor who found inspiration in the city, this time French, was Claude Joseph Rouget de Lisle. While stationed here on a military tour of duty in 1792, he was asked to write a rousing battle hymn. On the night of 25–26 April he came up with the "War Song for the Army of the Rhine". Three months later volunteer troops from Marseille marched into Paris singing it, and its popularity turned it into a rallying call for the Revolution. It has been better known ever since as *La Marseillaise*.

Strasbourg is also a good city for cycling, with an efficient bike-hire scheme and around 500km (300 miles) of cycle tracks within the urban area. For more leisurely travel, there are five tram lines, a mini-tram and riverboats.

The city is particularly atmospheric at Christmas time when the city centre is illuminated and the air perfumed with the scent of spices and mulled wine. A giant Christmas tree is installed in place Kleber and a colourful market sprawls across two other main squares, the place de la Cathedrale and place Broglie. Through the rest of the year, the district bustles during the twice-weekly flea market (Wed and Sat).

Old city sights

Within outer rings of modern developments, Strasbourg's historic city centre is entirely confined to the **Grande Île**, standing in a river transformed into a series of basins and canals to regulate boat traffic and water flow. Because it is so small, the area is easy to explore on foot. No two buildings on the evocatively named streets of the old neighbourhood appear exactly alike. The half-timbered houses seem to have been inflated to giant proportions. Above wide fronts to two or three storeys, the roofs carry up to five gabled windows, one above the other, diminutive in the distance.

The late 16th-century **Ancienne Grande Boucherie**, or Great Butcher's shop, by the river, houses the **Musée Historique** Ⓐ (Tue–Fri noon–6pm, Sat–Sun 10am–6pm; charge), with displays on the history of the city from the Middle Ages to the 19th century. In

Christmas markets are a big tradition in Alsace, with illuminations and stalls selling mulled wine, Christmas decorations, food specialities and handcrafted gifts. The best-known are in Strasbourg, Colmar and Kaysersberg.

BELOW: Christmas in Strasbourg.

Occupying several traditional half-timbered houses, the Musée Alsacien in Strasbourg is filled with distinctive artefacts documenting the customs and folklore of the region.

rue Hans Jean Arphe, the **Musée d'Art moderne et contemporain** (Tue, Wed and Fri noon–7pm, Thur noon–9pm, Sat–Sun 10am–6pm; charge) has a fine collection of modern art within a superb glass building on the river.

The 18th-century **Palais des Rohan** **B** (Mon and Wed–Fri noon–6pm, Sat–Sun 10am–6pm; charge) – which includes museums of fine art, decorative art and archaeology – amazes the eye with princely chambers of gilt and velvet. Across the river on Quai St-Nicolas, the **Musée Alsacien** **C** (Mon and Wed–Fri noon–6pm, Sat–Sun 10am–6pm; charge) is installed in a typical 16th-century Strasbourg dwelling. Its 30 rooms display distinctive Alsatian artefacts, such as ovens made of green tiles, wooden furniture, ceramics and toys, which represent the traditions of various occupations including farming, wine-growing and arts and crafts.

In keeping with a humanist tradition, Strasbourg is noted for its prominent Jewish and Protestant minorities. Protestant congregations are numerous, and their properties likewise. Two of these churches are particularly notable. **St-Thomas** **D** has a cloister and the splendid mausoleum of the royal Marshal de Saxe (Count of Saxony). Across town, **St-Pierre-le-Jeune** **E**, founded in 1035, also has a cloister, along with 14th-century frescoes.

The jewel of Strasbourg is the picturesque, traffic-free **Petite France** quarter **F**, a central knot of traditional houses that is impeccably maintained, with fresh paint and flowers applied regularly. In fact, it is so picturesque that it seems a little unreal, like a film set or an oversize doll's house. Along the rue des Moulins, where the river is divided into several channels for the running of mills, buildings have doors at water level. The **Ponts Couverts** **G** are no longer covered bridges as their name suggests, but the square towers of the 14th-century fortifications still stand. Just upstream is the **Barage Vauban** **H**, a dam or lock which could be closed in case of attack in order to flood the fields south of the city, turning them into marshes and rendering them useless to the enemy.

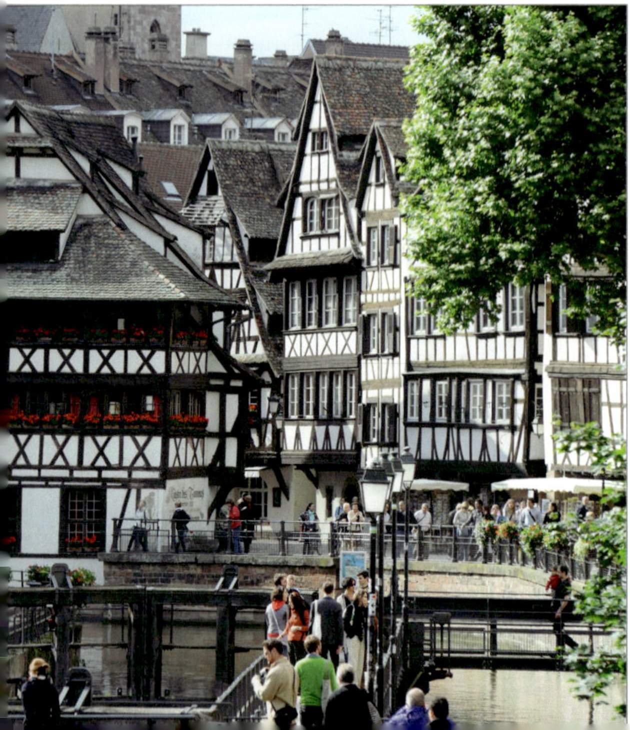

BELOW: picturesque Petite France.

The cathedral

The quais and cobbled lanes of the Grande Île converge on the **Cathédrale Notre-Dame** **I**. The building, in rosy sandstone dappled with cream, has been compared to an immense marble cake. When it was finished in the 15th century, the 142-metre (465ft) steeple was the highest in Europe, although it looks somewhat forlorn without its missing twin – the south tower that was never built.

This is a cathedral laden with decoration, taking the Gothic idea to its natural limit. Incessantly modified during its construction, the exterior is layered with lacy spires and innumerable statues. On the inside, the pulpit and the celebrated Column of Angels are flights of a sculptor's fancy. The astronomical clock was installed in the 16th century, a multifaced mechanism tracing hourly, daily and yearly celestial movements. When it strikes at 12.30pm, figures of ancient and biblical mythology execute their ordained rounds. You can ascend the 330 steps to the platform at an altitude of 66 metres (216ft) to see the view from the top and visit the workshops for the restoration (Apr–Sept 9am–7.15pm; Oct–Mar 10am–5.15pm; charge).

The **Musée de l'Oeuvre Notre-Dame** ❶ (Tue–Fri noon–6pm, Sat–Sun 10am–6pm; closed public hols; charge) was created during the 13th century to supervise the building of the cathedral, and has been in continuous existence since. Due to this lengthy life span, its museum is brimming with treasures. In a Renaissance mansion of lovingly polished wood, the displays range from a rare series of pre-14th-century Jewish epitaphs to a superb collection of late medieval art, especially paintings of the Lower Rhine School. Most exceptional of all, the museum shows the original master plans for the construction of the cathedral. On 2-metre (6ft) scrolls of parchment the artists drew and coloured each section of the facades exactly as they were to appear.

European Centre

Modern Strasbourg is one of the three non-capital cities in the world (along with New York and Geneva) to be the headquarters of major international institutions. A purpose-built Euro-quarter of flagpoles and luxury hotels, inhabited by bureaucrats and interpreters, contains the seats of the Council of Europe and European Court of Human Rights, and is a regular host to the European Parliament, whose 736 members occupy the enormous Palais de l'Europe once a month.

Next to the European institutions is the city's largest green space, the **Parc de l'Orangerie**, which has a lake, a stork breeding centre and the Buerehiesel, a beautiful Alsatian half-timbered house rebuilt here in 1885 and since turned into a smart restaurant.

A more tangible sign of the era of European cooperation is another park, the **Jardin de Deux Rives**, which straddles the Rhine by way of a pedestrian and cycle bridge connecting Strasbourg to Kehl across the border in Germany.

The Alsatian plain

Many of the towns and villages on the plain between the Vosges and the Rhine south of Strasbourg are

Symbolic statue outside the European Court of Human Rights. Its mission is to enforce the Convention for the Protection of Human Rights and Fundamental Freedoms.

BELOW: the European Parliament, Strasbourg.

The Maginot Line

For centuries the fear of invasion through the porous northeast frontier haunted the French psyche and dictated military thinking

While France has strong boundaries – mountains and seas – on four of its six sides, to the north and northeast its territory merges into Germany and the Low Countries without any means of natural defence. In 1870 the country was invaded by Germany through this vulnerable northern frontier, and again in 1914. After World War I it was felt that something had to be done to prevent a repetition of this catastrophic scenario.

The experience of static trench warfare between 1914 and 1918 was fresh in the minds of the military planners of the early 1930s who believed the only answer was to build a permanent line of fortifications from the Swiss border to the North Sea. It was particularly important to protect the vulnerable regions of Nord and Lorraine where much of the country's heavy industry was located. Thus was born the line of defence which was finished in 1935 and named after the minister for War, André Maginot.

The 58 great fortresses, 400 casemates and assorted forward observation posts, tank obstacles, machine-gun nests, anti-tank gun emplacements and infrastructure for supply and communications were built at enormous expense. They were not merely there to repulse any attack but to act as a deterrent, or at least to prevent surprise attack – to give the French army the two or three weeks breathing space it needed to mobilise and reinforce the frontiers.

By the late 1930s, however, the Maginot Line had become redundant. In hindsight, it is easy to dismiss it as a preparation for the previous war not the one to come, but it is important to understand the times in which it was built. The line formed part of a strategy which presumed that Belgium would remain allied to France and thus there would be no need to fortify the heavily industrialised and populated "iron frontier" from the Meuse to the coast. In 1936, however, Belgium switched from ally to neutral country, thus handing a gift to any unscrupulous dictator ready to take advantage of it.

In any case, modern warfare had moved on with technological progress. Nazi Germany was preparing not another war of infantry attrition but a swift-moving Blitzkrieg. In the invasion of France in the early summer of 1940, German tanks and aircraft were dispatched across the Benelux countries (violating their neutrality) into northern France, skirting around the western end of the Maginot Line which was effectively ignored.

The fortresses which proved useless when the long-expected invasion arrived remained intact and became tourist attractions for occupying German troops. After the war, the French state kept the Line maintained until 1964. By then, European cooperation and the existence of nuclear weapons had made it seem even more obsolete. ❑

ABOVE: English soldiers at the Fort de Sanghain on the Maginot Line. **LEFT:** an underground tunnel.

stops on the Alsace wine route. First of interest is **Molsheim** ⓳, a walled town enclosing preserved traditional houses. Particularly worth seeing is the Metzig, a beautiful Renaissance building with a double staircase and sculpted balconies.

Obernai ⓴ is distinguished by a central, covered marketplace and an elaborate 16th-century fountain equipped with six buckets. A few kilometres from the town, on a winding road that leads into the Vosges, is **Mont Ste Odile**. From pre-Christian times this spot was both sacred and strategically important, as the 10km (6-mile) -long "pagan wall" attests. This presumably defensive installation (although no one is certain what it was built for) continues almost without interruption through the forest, with views towards the remnants of surrounding fortresses. Two chapels remain from the 11th and 12th centuries.

Medieval castles

Alsace's most visited tourist sight – it's also in the top league for all of France – is the castle of **Haut-Koenigsbourg** ㉑ (July–Aug 9.15am–6pm; Apr–May and Sept 9.15am–5.15pm; Mar and Oct 9.30am–5pm; rest of the year 9.30am–noon and 1–4.30pm; charge). Standing proud on an outcrop of rock at an altitude of 757 metres (2,483ft), it may look from afar as every medieval castle should, but it is not quite as authentic as it seems. The first fortress on the site was built in the 12th century. A rebuilt version was destroyed in 1633 by Swedish artillery during the Thirty Years War and it then lay in ruins for two centuries until Kaiser Wilhelm II decided to restore the fortress to its original grandeur at the beginning of the 20th century – Alsace being in those days in the hands of the Germans. Although he let himself be guided by the historical and archaeological knowledge of his time, there is evidently a large amount of his own taste in the finished product. It is also a political statement: Haut-Koenigsbourg is intended to look like a castle in Germany. All the ingredients of a medieval castle are there – drawbridge, curtain walls, *cour d'honneur*, battlements – but there are also primly pointed turrets and touches of neo-Gothic fantasy.

The nearby **Château de Kintzheim** (daily Apr–Oct 10am–5pm; charge), meanwhile, has been turned into the Volerie des Aigles, dedicated to the protection of birds of prey, where you can see eagles, condors and vultures in flight above the ruined medieval castle.

Sélestat ㉒ is one of the old independent cities of Alsace that grouped themselves together as the Decapole in order to defend the privileges accorded them by the Holy Roman Emperor. A traditional market town, it has a medieval section including two city gates. The church of Ste Foy is of dusky yellow-pink stone with a slightly bulging central hexagonal tower. In the same stone is the Gothic St-Georges. The city is proud of its Bibliothèque Humaniste (July–Aug Mon, Wed–Sat 9am–noon and 2–6pm, Sun 2–5pm; Sept–June Mon and Wed–Fri 9am–noon and 2–6pm, Sat 9am–noon; charge), one

Mosaic in the Chapel of Tears, one of four chapels in the shrine of Mont Sainte Odile, dedicated to the patron saint of Alsace.

BELOW: the imposing fortress of Haut Koenigsbourg.

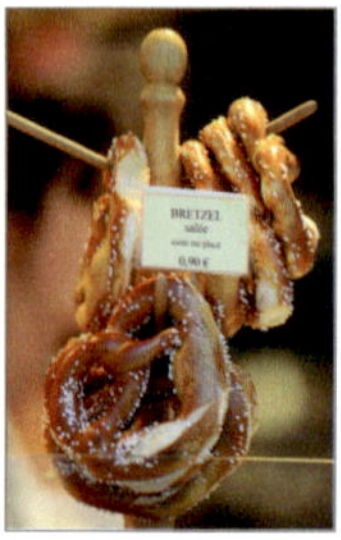

Freshly baked Alsatian bretzels. These savoury knot-shaped biscuits, sprinkled with salt and caraway seeds, are the traditional accompaniment to a glass of beer.

of the most important cultural treasures of Alsace. It houses the library of Beatus Rhenanus (1485–1547), a friend of Erasmus and leading light in Sélestat's influential humanist school. Illuminated manuscripts and rare tomes dating back to the 7th century are displayed alongside 15th-century carvings and faïence.

Museum of Witchcraft

If Sélestat is a town built on reason, **Bergheim** ㉓, to the south, recalls a different aspect of human development. The intriguing **Musée de la Sorcellerie** (Museum of Witchcraft; July–Aug Wed–Sun 2–6pm; charge), housed in a 16th-century school for boys, deals with the irrational side of human nature and attitudes to it. The focus of the museum – and the reason for its location – is the witch trials which took place in the town between 1582 and 1683. Between these dates, 43 people were tried and executed, the majority burnt at the stake. To give the subject a human face, the museum tells the story of Catherine Bassler, the maid of the local priest, who was accused of murder. She was treated leniently by the magistrate: he had her beheaded before the body was thrown onto the pyre.

Another documented case is that of Apolonia Schaeffer of Molsheim (which had its own series of witch-trials). In 1589 she was accused of causing a woman to fall ill so that she refused to eat or talk, and also of robbing her son-in-law of his virility and turning him into a wolf. Under interrogation, she confessed to all accusations just as long as the torture would stop.

What comes across from the museum is a picture of the transition that took place between the Middle Ages and more enlightened times; of the fears widespread in rural society; and the uncertainty of how to react to the vicissitudes of life. Anything could attract suspicion and bring down the judgement of the Church and the criminal authorities: cooking a chicken during Lent, knowledge of the healing powers of herbs, failure to attend church, walking around after nightfall, or just the wrong way of looking at someone in the eye. In an era of high infant mortality, midwifes were especially

BELOW: Place de la Sinne, Ribeauvillé. **BELOW RIGHT:** a pampered pooch.

susceptible. And when life or death depended on the health of herds and crops, an argumentative neighbour was a more obvious culprit to blame than the weather.

Picturesque towns

A string of beautiful wine towns begins south of Bergheim with **Ribeauvillé**. The town extends in a thin line along the Grand Rue, rising through the busy new town (18th century) to the tower guarding the medieval city. About halfway up the main street, the half-timbered houses pull back to form a plaza of several Renaissance stone facades. Look out for details such as the curve of an enclosed staircase, a dog's head carved on a beam end, or a date set in the lintel over the door. At the end of the street there is an ancient fountain.

From the town a footpath leads on a circuit of three ruined châteaux: **St-Ulrich** (the oldest and most important), **Girsberg**, and, located on higher ground, **Haut-Ribeaupierre**. The tour of the three castles takes about an hour and gives splendid views of the Vosges and the Rhine valley.

Hunawihr possesses a stork and otter rescue centre, the **Parc des Cigognes et des Loutres** (June–Aug 10am–6pm or 7pm, rest of year 10am–12.30pm and 2–5.30pm or 6.30pm; charge). A century ago, thousands of white storks (*Ciconia ciconia*) would fly north from Africa to spend each summer feeding in the fertile fields of Alsace. The stork was such a familiar sight that it became a symbol for the region, its presence taken for granted. But in the post-war years, numbers declined rapidly. A conservation programme was initiated, led by the Hunawihr rescue centre, which has at least halted the decline.

The best preserved and most stunning of this group of towns is **Riquewihr** ㉔, enclosed in its protective walls. The town is a tourist heaven, and to keep it so cars are parked outside the centre. Practically every house is a delight of colours, tiles, balconies and flower boxes. Many have cobbled courtyards multiplying the possibilities of little turrets or intricate woodcarvings. Riquewihr's most distinctive trait is its tradition of shop signs of forged iron, old ones as in the **Postal**

TIP

The Alsace Wine Route is best trodden in autumn, just before the wine harvest, when the huge volume of tourists and tour buses has died down and the pretty villages are quiet once more.

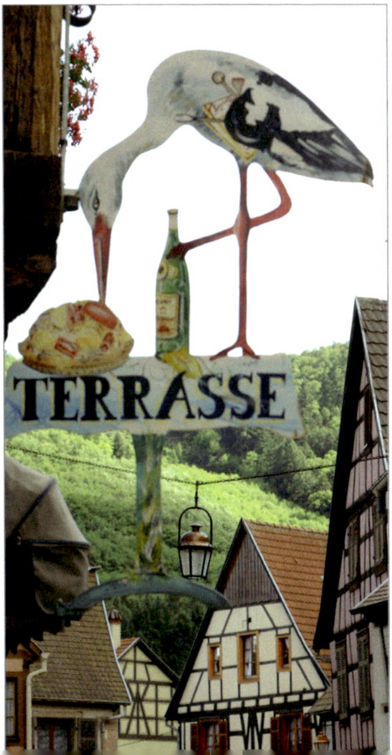

BELOW LEFT: the white stork is a symbol of the region.

The Alsace Wine Route

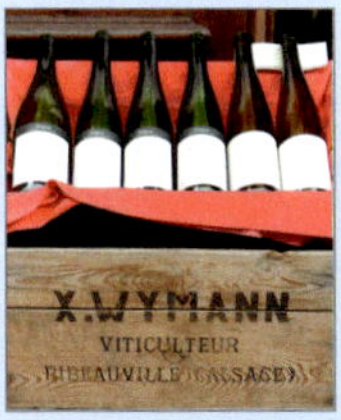

A good way to get to know the wines of the region is to follow the the **Alsace Wine Route**, which winds through the vineyards at the foot of the Vosges mountains for 170km (110 miles) from Marlenheim in the north to Thann in the south. It is well signposted, with 103 stops at places of interest, mostly wineries but also churches, castles and picturesque views. Among the vineyards are orchards of cherries and plums destined for the region's potent fruit brandies. Many wine producers are open for visits and tastings except during the grape harvest, which takes place between late September and late October. The centre of the wine region, and the main stop on the route, is Colmar, where you can visit the Maison des Vins d'Alsace (Mon–Fri 9am–noon, 2–7pm).

Alsatian wines often smell sweet but in fact taste dry. They are intense and powerful with mouth-filling exotic fruit flavours. In the informal taverns known as *winstubs* they are served in attractive glasses with long green stems, and are very popular choices with fish, seafood and Alsatian specialities such as tarte flambée, choucroute, foie gras and sweet cheese pie.

Alsace is renowned for its fine white wines, divided into three appellations d'origine contrôlée. *The bulk is classed as AOC Alsace. Choicer wines come under the stricter AOC Alsace Grand Cru. These wines must stipulate the grape, the vintage and the producer on the label. AOC Cremant d'Alsace are the region's sparkling wines. Only seven varieties of grape are used: Sylvaner, Pinot Blanc, Pinot Gris, Pinot Noir, Riesling, Muscat and aromatic Gewürztraminer.*

BELOW: the ideal form of transport in Colmar's "Little Venice".

Museum (in the château; Apr–Oct & Dec 10am–5.30pm; charge) and modern ones in the streets. There are also a large number of wine cellars.

The town of **Kaysersberg** ㉕ is also seductive. Birthplace of Albert Schweitzer, Nobel Peace Prize winner, the old quarter has the narrow form typical of the region, enhanced by the presence of the River Weiss. Near the top of the town, the river traverses a circular plaza united by a fortified bridge and a stone altar, in the shadow of the castle keep perched on the mountain above. The 16th-century houses in narrow alleys are served by Renaissance fountains. The main thing to see is the **Musée Albert Schweitzer** (126 rue du Général de Gaulle, Apr–Nov 9am–noon, 2–6pm; charge), the building where the doctor was born, which has been turned into a museum to his memory.

Colmar

A business centre for wine professionals, **Colmar** ㉖ is also Alsace's second-largest tourist town, and particularly pretty in December during the Christmas market. The sculptor Bartholdi, creator of New York's Statue of Liberty, was born here, and his works are prominent in the town's parks.

The old town is a large pedestrian zone of irregularly shaped plazas connected by short streets that wind around historic buildings and churches. The **Dominican church** is the site of the altarpiece *Madonna with the Rose Bush* (1473), which hangs in the choir; it is an expressive masterpiece executed by 15th-century artist Martin Schongauer, a native of Colmar. The **Musée d'Unterlinden** (May–Oct daily 9am–6pm; Nov–Apr Wed–Mon 9am–noon and 2–5pm; charge) features a phenomenal Issenheim altarpiece by Mathias Grünewald. The central tableau is surrounded by double panels, painted on both surfaces and emitting a strange glow which vividly re-creates the saints' tortures and demons.

The stroll through Colmar leads to the quarter called La Petite Venise, in honour of the little River Lauch and adjacent canal where tanners once cleaned their pelts. Here, as throughout the city, the balconies are lined with flowers, and each half-timbered house has an individualistic touch, a gabled turret or unusual sculptures such as the heads on the Maison des Têtes. The Ancienne Douane or Koifhus is covered in glazed tiles arranged in patterns of green and yellow.

Heading south

Neuf-Brisach, southeast of Colmar, towards the Rhine, is a perfect piece of military town planning guarding the German border. The star-shaped citadel was designed by the Marquis de Vauban *(see page 42)*.

Back on the wine route heading south, **Eguisheim** was the birthplace of the 11th-century Pope Leon IX. It is a fortified town of concentric streets lined with half-timbered houses decorated with flowers. In the hills behind Guebwiller is **Murbach** ㉗, a Benedictine monastery founded in 727 and given a Romanesque church in the 12th century. This was partially destroyed in the 18th century to make way for a new church that was never built – although the transept and two towers of the old building remain.

At the fascinating open-air **Bioscope Ecomusée d'Alsace** 28 (daily July–Aug 10am–7pm; Apr–Oct 10am–6pm; charge) north of Mulhouse, traditional timber-framed houses and farm buildings have been regrouped to form an Alsatian village.

Mulhouse and the Rhine

Mulhouse 29 is an industrial city whose historical monuments from its time as an independent republic were erased by wartime bombing. To make up for this, it has become a city of museums with a technological focus. The unique **Musée de l'Impression sur Etoffe** (Tue–Sun 10am–noon, 2–6pm; charge) is devoted to the techniques and arts of printed cloth and wall paperings. Another legacy of industrial wealth is the **Musée de l'Automobile** (Apr–Oct daily 10am–6pm; Jan Mon–Fri 1–5pm, Sat–Sun 10am–5pm; rest of the year 10am–5pm; charge), with its collection of over 500 antique and rare cars, while the **Cité du Train** railway museum (daily Apr–Oct 10am–6pm; Jan Mon–Fri 10am–2pm, Sat–Sun 10am–5pm; rest of the year 10am–5pm; charge) presents vintage locomotives.

The traditional buildings of Colmar and other Rhineland towns are embellished with sculptures and stone reliefs.

A few kilometres east is a Romanesque marvel, the octagonal church of **Ottmarsheim** 30. This is also, surprisingly, one of the few points of interest on the Rhine, one of the defining rivers of Europe which forms the entire Franco-German border. It is hard to get an idea of the natural river. Before 1800 it ran in so many rivulets and around so many islands that it was impossible to map. In the age of industrialisation, however, the river was straightened and confined to a single channel between dykes to prevent flooding. The development of river ports and the building of dams for generating hydroelectric power further transformed the flow. The **Petite Camargue Alsacienne** 31, a wetland nature reserve and fish farm south of Ottmarsheim, gives a hint of how the natural ecosystem once appeared. ❑

BELOW: fine *charcuterie* is a speciality of Alsace.

The Dreyfus Affair

Captain Alfred Dreyfus, born in Mulhouse in 1859, had two handicaps to overcome if he was to succeed as an officer in the French army during the Belle Epoque. Not only was he Jewish, but he was also from Alsace, a region which had been part of Germany since the disastrous war of 1870–1. At that time, Alsatians had to choose allegiance to one of two bitter enemies, France or Germany, locked in a glowering feud of mutual scorn.

When secret messages destined for German hands were found in a wastepaper basket in the French General Headquarters, who better to blame, therefore, than an Alsatian Jew? And there was only one person who fitted the description: the young, high-flying Dreyfus. The irony was that, *because* of his background, Dreyfus was more zealously patriotic than his accusers – but that didn't prevent him facing a kangaroo military court which dispatched him to prison on Devil's Island. The evidence against him had been fabricated, but few people in France were concerned about fairness when what was needed was a scapegoat.

The miscarriage of justice was finally exposed by another Alsatian army officer, Colonel Marie-Georges Piquart. For his pains, Piquart was expelled from the army and imprisoned, then exonerated on the same day as Dreyfus (who was still unshakeably loyal to France after all he had been through) and went on to become a minister for war.

The Art of the Alsatian House

Half-timbered houses are seen throughout northern France, but they are most plentiful and picturesque in Alsace. Decoding the decorative symbols adds to their fascination

Timber-framed houses were built in profusion because of the supply of wood from the Vosges mountains. As well as being cheap, they also resisted earth tremors because of their innate suppleness and could be rebuilt quickly after a war. For this reason, the Alsatian half-timbered house was considered a "portable" possession rather than an immovable one.

The earliest surviving examples of timber houses date from the 15th century and are generally distinguished by their long corner posts stretching from ground to eaves. During the Renaissance, particularly in well-to-do towns and wine growing villages, innovative techniques enabled builders to go higher, fit larger windows and incorporate balconies.

The Alsatian house reached its apogee in the 18th and early 19th centuries when proud owners treated them to lavish decorations: even the timbers were arranged so as to be aesthetically pleasing as well as structurally sound.

Around 1870, however, the advent of industrial methods of building using stone and brick caused the half-timbered house to fall abruptly out of fashion. Nowadays, the Alsatians take great pride in preserving their stock of half- timbered houses, as can be seen particularly in Strasbourg's Petite France, Colmar's Petite Venise, Eguisheim, Riquewihr and other towns.

LEFT: improved methods of construction meant that timber-framed houses could be built up to four storeys high.

ABOVE: no two half-timbered houses are exactly alike and when clustered together the result is extremely picturesque, as here in Colmar.

BELOW: the spaces between the timbers were filled with wattle and daub and covered with rendering. A coat of limewash added a vivid colour.

WRITING ON THE WALL

The half-timbered houses of Alsace are not just beautiful buildings. Many also tell a story in symbols if you know how to read them. Some of the symbols are there to attract happiness and prosperity to the inhabitants; others are meant to keep malevolent forces away. Almost always they combine layers of ancestral meaning derived from both pagan and Christian tradition.

Sometimes the exposed timbers are arranged to represent a tree of life; a lozenge; St Andrew's cross (both of these invocations of fertility); or a circle with a cross through it (the sun combined with a crucifix); a stylised man with legs apart and arms outstretched as if holding the house together; or else a curule chair – the folding stool of a magistrate in Ancient Rome, perhaps indicating the prestige of the house's owner.

Other symbols carved into the timbers, engraved on stone door posts or painted on to the limewash of the walls, include five-pointed stars (signifying earth, air, fire, water and spirit), hearts (happiness), swastikas (the sun) and recumbent figure "8"s representing infinity.

BOVE: where there was a quarry nearby, ɔne was often used in the ground floor of ɪouse.

BOVE: some houses are personalised by pithy or tty inscriptions set into the facade.

RIGHT: decorative wrought iron shop sign projecting over the street

LEFT: many houses are embellished with details such as this carved wooden figure in Strasbourg.

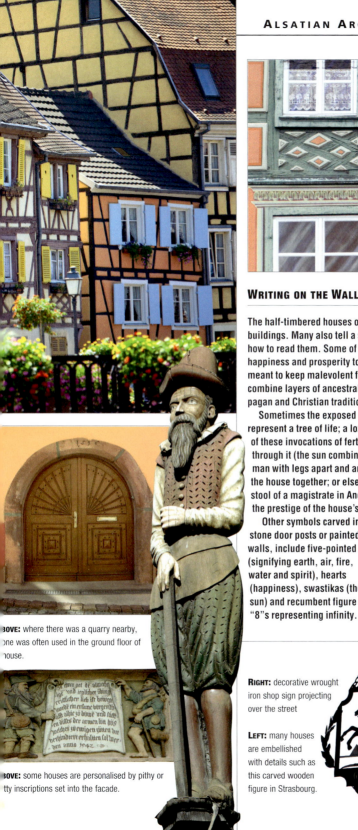

THE CENTRE

A privileged area of châteaux, vineyards, monasteries and beautiful countryside stretching from the mouth of the Loire to the Jura mountains

Four regions extend like a belt across the upper middle of France, from the Atlantic coast to the mountains of the Jura, and these have been grouped together in the following two chapters.

The regions of Pays de La Loire and Centre are better summed up as the Loire Valley as they are given cohesion by the longest river in France. In them you might find all you want from a holiday: easy travelling, a picturesque view at every turn, and good restaurants to punctuate the day.

The Loire is the very picture of sedate and beautiful countryside, and it is stuffed with history. Little wonder that it is associated with writers and artists attracted by the peace and inspiration it has to offer. Its prize possession is a string of splendid Renaissance châteaux – Azay-le-Rideau, Blois, Chambord Chenonceau – bristling with beautiful architectural touches, striding proprietorially over watercourses, or standing in magnificent formal gardens. As well as these stately homes, the Loire has ancient castles of the warlike kind. Bourges and Chartres have great cathedrals famous for their stained-glass windows.

The other two regions, in the east, are Burgundy and its neighbour Franche-Comté. Burgundy is synonymous with wines – some of the world's best are produced here – and also has a prodigiously lauded cuisine. It has been a prosperous place for centuries, as can be seen from the number of Romanesque churches, such as at Vézelay. Two great monastic movements were launched in Burgundy and great abbeys were built, notably Cluny and Fontenay. The chief city is Dijon, but more charming is Beaune with its multicoloured rooftops and winding streets.

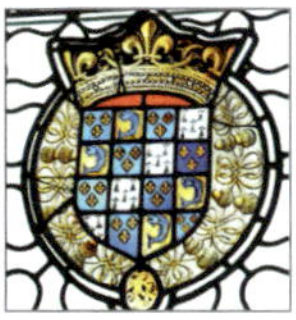

Less well known is the Franche-Comté whose chief asset is its scenery. Sharing the Jura mountains with Switzerland, it is a quiet region of forested hills, upland pastures and verdant river valleys. ❏

PRECEDING PAGES: Saumur's graceful château. **LEFT:** the formal gardens of Château de Villandry, the last of the grand Renaissance châteaux to be built on the banks of the Loire. **ABOVE LEFT:** sign to Villandry. **ABOVE RIGHT:** Château de Blois. **BELOW RIGHT:** coat-of-arms in stained glass at Chaumont sur Loire.

BURGUNDY & THE FRANCHE-COMTÉ

The "heart of France" is an opulent region, blessed with glorious architecture, world-renowned vineyards, fine cuisine and beautiful landscapes. To the east lies often-overlooked Franche-Comté

Less than an hour from the roar of Paris traffic, the calm, spacious countryside, immaculate vineyards and prosperous towns of Burgundy (Bourgogne) come as a welcome surprise to many a visitor. Some of France's best food and wine add further to the appeal.

Burgundy has had a long and eventful history, much of it independent from the rest of France. Settled in prehistoric times, the region witnessed the last act of resistance by native tribes against the invading Roman legions before becoming an important component of Gaul. Around the turn of the first millennium, it emerged as the cradle of European monasticism, engendering the Cluniac and Cistercian orders and radiating the Romanesque style across France.

In the 13th century the duchy of Burgundy was created as a semi-autonomous feudal unit by the French king John II for his son Philip the Bold. He could not have known that he was setting up a rival dynasty in his own backyard. For the next century, from 1364 to 1477, four skilful dukes of the Valois dynasty cultivated their domain, exploiting its position on the crucial trade route between northern and southern Europe. They extended their territory and power until Burgundy was an independent state, a kingdom in all but name, extending through Luxembourg, Belgium, Artois, Flanders and Holland. For a time it looked as if Burgundy would become a third great power interposed between France and Germany.

At the height of its prestige, ducal Burgundy was able to broker treaties between the English and French during the Hundred Years War. Meanwhile, the dukes lived in high style, maintaining a lavish court, promoting the arts and entertaining ambassadors in full-blown royal fashion.

Main attractions
- ABBAYE DE FONTENAY
- MUSEOPARC, ALISE STE REINE
- BASILIQUE STE MADELEINE, VÉZELAY
- DIJON
- HÔTEL-DIEU, BEAUNE
- CLUNY
- BESANÇON
- CASCADES DU HÉRISSON
- CHAPELLE NOTRE-DAME, RONCHAMP

LEFT: Montagny vineyard with premier cru status, Burgundy. **RIGHT:** Beaune resident.

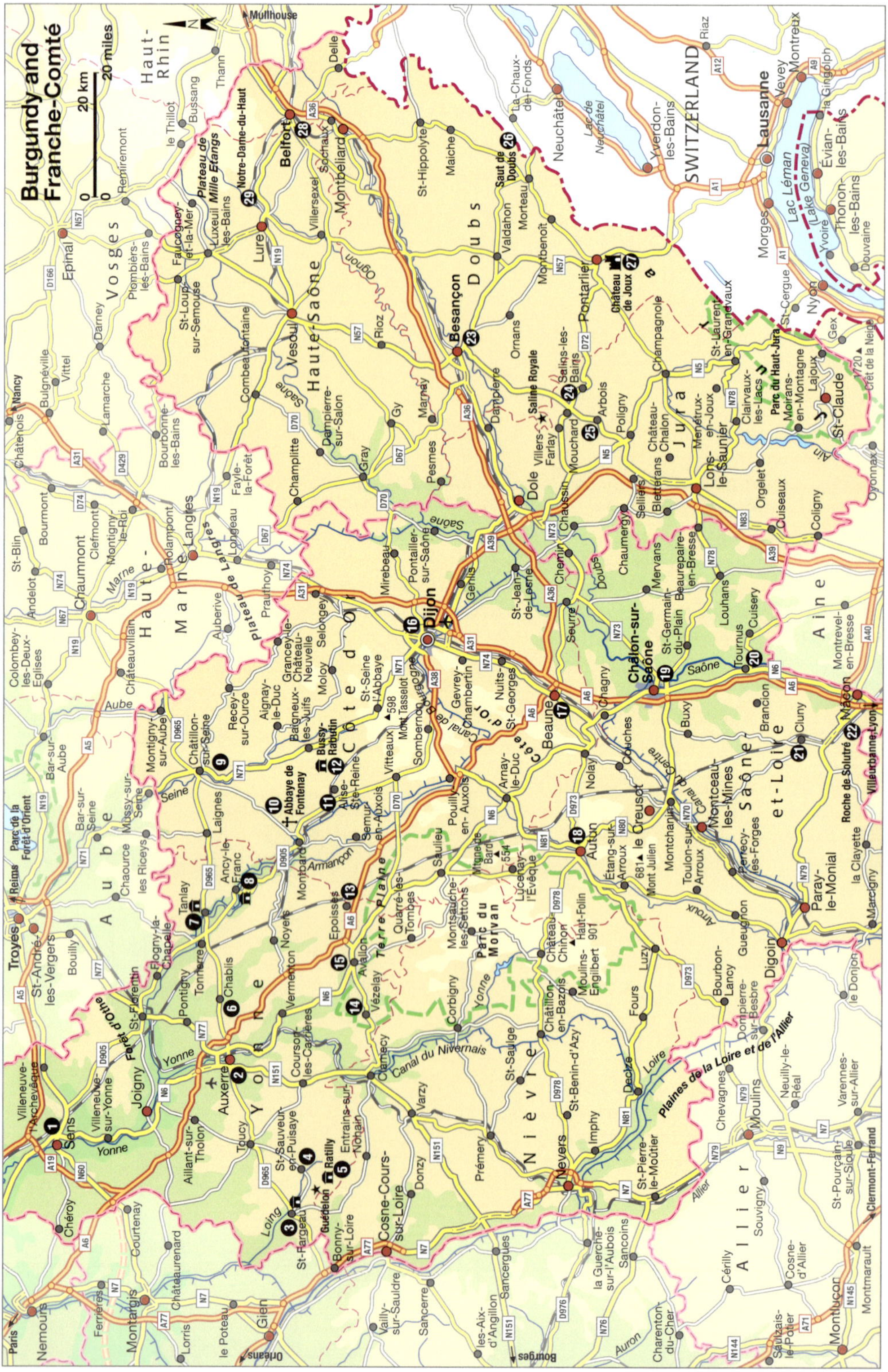

Burgundy and Franche-Comté
0 20 km
0 20 miles
Haute-Saône
Doubs
Jura
Côte d'Or
Yonne
Nièvre
Saône-et-Loire
Haute-Marne
Aube
Vosges
Haut-Rhin
Allier
Ain
SWITZERLAND
Lac Léman (Lake Geneva)
Lac de Neuchâtel
Lausanne
Neuchâtel
Dijon
Besançon
Belfort
Montbéliard
Vesoul
Lure
Dole
Pontarlier
Lons-le-Saunier
St-Claude
Chalon-sur-Saône
Mâcon
Beaune
Autun
Auxerre
Sens
Nevers
Avallon
Montbard
Châtillon-sur-Seine
Langres
Chaumont
Troyes
Épinal
Le Creusot
Montceau-les-Mines
Paray-le-Monial
Digoin
Cluny
Tournus
Louhans
Moulins
Cosne-Cours-sur-Loire
Vézelay
Joigny
Gray
Arbois
Salins-les-Bains
Saline Royale
Château de Joux
Notre-Dame-du-Haut
Plateau de Mille Étangs
Abbaye de Fontenay
Bussy-Rabutin
Guédelon
Ratilly
Parc du Morvan
Parc du Haut-Jura
Parc de la Forêt d'Orient
Plaines de la Loire et de l'Allier
Forêt d'Othe
Plateau de Langres
Terre Plaine
Canal du Nivernais
Canal de Bourgogne
Canal du Centre
Roche de Solutré
Saut du Doubs
Mont Tasselot 598
Haut-Folin 901
Mont Julien 681
Crêt de la Neige 1720
Paris
Reims
Nancy
Mulhouse
Orléans
Bourges
Clermont-Ferrand
Villeurbanne, Lyon

But the good times were not to last. When Charles the Bold was defeated and killed in battle in 1477, Burgundy was incorporated into the French Crown. Burgundy's empire was dismembered and the region demoted to a province administered by a governor. For a time it acted as a buffer state between France and the German states. The creation of the *départements* after the Revolution weakened its cultural identity and it was only with the grouping of the *départements* into regions in 1972 that Burgundy regained a measure of cohesion. All the while, however, it prospered economically because of its strategic location and good communications, and on the back of its prestigious wine industry.

Wines of Burgundy

Modern Burgundy continues to be a prosperous place laying great store on preserving its heritage and traditions, particularly those to do with food and wine. It is impossible to visit the region without being aware of the importance of wine which is treated with reverence to the point of snobbery.

The Burgundy wine region is the fourth-largest area of vines in France and claims to be the first in "the number, variety and quality of its *appellations*" – although the wine makers of Bordeaux might beg to differ. Burgundy is France's most northerly area for red wine but also produces renowned whites, notably Chablis.

Its prime vineyards are planted on stony, well-drained hillsides facing east away from the prevailing west winds, its vintages nurtured by the warm summers of the quasi-Continental climate. The 100 *appellations* are organised in a pyramid system on four hierarchical levels. Just over half the wines produced are classified under 23 "regional" labels. Next up are wines that come from particular communes or villages. The finest are the *premier crus* from 645 individually named plots and, most presitigious of all, *grand crus* which account for only 1.4 percent of the wine produced.

Gothic splendour

Until 1622, the Archbishop of **Sens** ❶ lorded over an area extending all the way to Paris. His palatial lodgings house two museums (June–Sept daily 10am–6pm; Oct–May Wed, Sat and Sun 10am–noon, 2–6pm; Mon, Thur and Fri afternoon only; charge) with collections devoted to local history showing a variety of artefacts dating from the Bronze Age to 18th-century artwork, and the Collection Marrey, which includes 19th- and 20th-century ceramics and paintings.

The **Cathédrale St-Etienne** was the first in France to be built in the Gothic style. Construction began in the 12th century and work was not completed until 500 years later. In the course of time, this monumental structure was embellished with intricate sculpture, high arches and an impressive series of stained-glass windows. In the adjoining buildings, the Trésor de la Cathédrale St-Etienne is remarkable for rare liturgical garments.

Auxerre ❷, one of the oldest cities in France and the ancient capital of northwestern Burgundy, resounds with

The Route des Grands Cru (www. route-des-grands-crus-de-bourgogne.com) covers 60km (37 miles) from Dijon to Santenay and passes through 38 Burgundy wine-making villages. One of the largest vineyards, at Clos de Vougeot, has a small château which was built to house wine presses. Today it is the home of the Chevaliers du Tastevin.

BELOW: Tour de l'Horloge, Auxerre.

The first recorded mention of mustard in Burgundy was at a banquet for Philip VI, when, according to the account book, 66 gallons (300 litres) were consumed.

history. Renaissance houses follow a semicircular pattern around the 15th-century Tour de l'Horloge, which once guarded the ramparts. The unusual clock has two dials, one for the time and the other for tracking the movement of the sun and stars. Two churches rival one another for attention. The **Cathédrale St-Etienne** is recognised by the sharp slope of its asymmetric facade. The medieval sense of Christianity is vivid in this church, from the tympanum's three-tiered life of Christ, to the lives of the saints depicted in jewel-like red and blue stained glass. The abbey church dedicated to **St Germain**, also Gothic, is built on an extraordinary hive of underground chapels. Parts of the structure date from the time of Charlemagne and the frescoes of St Stephen go back to AD 850, the oldest in France. The ancient dormitory houses a **museum** (June–Sept Wed–Sun 10am–12.30pm, 2–6.30pm; Oct–May Wed–Sun 10am–noon, 2–6pm; charge).

La Puisaye

Southwest of Auxerre, the spires adorning the brick and stone **Château de St-Fargeau** ❸ (Mar–Nov 10am–noon, 2–6pm; closes at 7pm July and Aug; charge) appear like minarets on the horizon. This is where the Grande Mademoiselle, Louis XIV's sister, once lived. Dating from the 15th century, the château was renovated in the mid-17th century by Le Vau, the architect of Versailles.

St-Fargeau is situated in an area known as La Puisaye. This is rural Burgundy at its best. In summer, the hills shimmer in the early afternoon heat and tall, shady trees line the banks of rivers such as the Loing. Gentle and watery, it is a perfect region to explore by bicycle or on foot.

The area's most celebrated native daughter is the author Colette (1873–1953), whose writings remain popular in France and abroad and whose birthplace can be seen in rue des Vignes in the centre of the little town of **St-Sauveur-en-Puisaye** ❹. The **Musée Colette** (Apr–Oct Wed–Mon 10am–6pm; Nov–Mar Sat–Sun 2–6pm; charge), housed in a beautifully furnished château, is dedicated to her life and work.

BELOW: Château de St-Fargeau.

Nearby are two châteaux, one ancient and the other modern. The superb 13th-century **Château de Ratilly** ❺ (June–Sept daily 10am–6pm; Apr–May, Oct Mon–Fri 10am–noon, 2–6pm (4.30pm in Oct), Sat and Sun 3–6pm; charge) lies hidden in a brambly wood. From the outside it seems like nothing but towers, yet inside the arched entrance a cheerful grassy courtyard opens onto a pottery school. **Guédelon**, on the other hand, is a château-in-the-making, an amazing construction site, where a medieval château (July–Aug daily 10am–7pm; Mar–June and Sept–Oct Thur–Tue 10am–6pm; charge) is being built by 35 craftsmen and women, using only 13th-century materials, techniques and equipment – a project which started in 1997 and is expected to last 25 years.

Across the North

The Serein (Serene) river valley, east of Auxerre, is a quiet haven that merits its name. A major attraction is the small town of **Chablis** ❻, mainly because of its world-famous vineyards, stitched like patchwork quilts over the hills. Upstream, cradled in a bend of the river, the little town of **Noyers** has preserved all the charm of its medieval history. The rampart wall is guarded by no fewer than 16 towers circling the arcades of the central square.

The Renaissance **Château de Tanlay** ❼ (Apr–Nov Wed–Mon 10am–12.30pm, 2.15–6pm; charge), 11km (7 miles) east of Tonnerre, is a fine sight, ensconced as it is in a series of moats, arcades and iron grilles. Another château gem, **Ancy-le-Franc** ❽ (Apr–Nov Tue–Sun guided tours only at 10.30am, 11.30am, 2pm, 3pm, 4pm and 7pm; charge), presents an austerely symmetrical exterior, but the inner courtyard and furnishings are of sumptuous splendour inspired by the Italian Renaissance.

Châtillon-sur-Seine ❾ is worth a detour for its **Musée du Pays Châtillonnais** (July–Aug 10am–7pm; Sept–June 9am–noon, 2–6pm; charge), built around an extraordinary prehistoric treasure trove unearthed in 1953. The centrepiece of the Trésor de Vix is an extremely large bronze urn, discovered in the grave of a priestess or princess who had been buried in a ceremonial chariot with its wheels removed.

Abbaye de Fontenay

Solitary and independent, at the bottom of a small valley near Montbard is the **Abbaye de Fontenay** ❿ (Apr–Oct 10am–6pm; Nov–Mar 10am–noon, 2–5pm; charge), founded by Saint Bernard in 1118 and Burgundy's most complete surviving medieval monastery. In the 19th century it was sold off and turned into a paper mill, but later rescued and restored – and also added to – by a private owner. All the buildings from the time when the abbey housed an active community of "white monks" have been preserved.

The church and cloister in particular show the Cistercian ideal of simplicity, without ornamentation of any kind to distract from a life of piety

Artisans reconstructing a medieval wall.

BELOW: Château de Ratilly.

Developed by monks in the Middle Ages, the pungent Epoisses de Bourgogne is a French Appellation d'origine controlée (AOC) cheese, said to have been a favourite of Napoleon.

and contemplation. The bare paving stones and immaculate columns have acquired, in the course of time, a look of grandeur. The church is often the setting for classical music concerts in the summer months.

Attached to the church are various functional buildings including an infirmary, bakery and, oddly, the oldest ironworks in Europe, where a reconstruction of a hydraulic hammer, invented here around 1220, has been installed.

The defeat of Vercingétorix

Just south of Fontenay is the site of a battle decisive in French history and of which it has been rather dramatically stated "It is here that Gaul died and France was born." Mont Auxois, above the village of **Alise-Ste Reine** ⓫, is generally accepted as the site of the battle of Alésia, where the Gauls under Vercingétorix were defeated by Julius Caesar. A monumental statue of Vercingétorix overlooks the Gallo-Roman city where excavations have been under way since 1906. Among the foundations uncovered are those of an early Christian church dedicated to the martyred Reine. Objects from the site are on display at the MuséoParc, a new museum opening in 2011.

BELOW: the gardens of Fontenay Abbey.

Almost adjacent is the **Château de Bussy-Rabutin** ⓬ (Tue–Sun 9.15am–noon, 2–5pm, closes 6pm in summer; charge), arguably Burgundy's most absorbing stately home. It was rebuilt in 1649 by Roger de Bussy-Rabutin, who was banished to the countryside by Louis XIV for his satirical commentaries on court affairs. In exile, he decorated the house with contemporary portraits: there are 25 women onlookers in his bedchamber, including Madame de Sévigné (his cousin) and Maintenon.

Semur-en-Auxois, to the west, still retains the flavour of a medieval fortress town, guarded by imposing dungeon towers that overlook the peaceful Armançon River and the Pont July which crosses it. The architecturally eclectic church of Notre Dame (1218) offends purists but delights others. Beyond Semur lies **Epoisses** ⓭, less known for its medieval château (July–Aug Wed–Mon 10am–noon, 3–6pm; charge) and Renaissance houses than for its cheese. Creamy, pungent and soft, its orange rind is washed with brandy (marc de Bourgogne) as it matures in the cellars. It's the region's finest cheese and is best enjoyed with a glass of red Burgundy.

Vézelay

Occupying a prominent hilltop 16km (10 miles) west of Avallon, **Vézelay** ⓮ is one of the principal shrines of France and a departure point for one of the main routes of pilgrimage to Santiago de Compostela in Spain. The possession of Mary Magdalene's supposed relics made Vézelay an extremely popular destination in the Middle Ages, a focal point of Christendom, and it was from here that St Bernard of Clairvaux launched the Second Crusade in 1146.

A steep road climbs up through the town to the majestic **Basilique Ste Madeleine** (sunrise–sunset; free) which was founded in the 9th century as an abbey but rebuilt in its present form after a fire in 1120. The church was damaged in the Hundred Years War, the Wars of Religion and in the Revolution, but was saved and restored in the 19th century. Not only does it continue to be an important Christian monument, reoccupied by a religious order, but it also fascinates enthusiasts of esotericism who see it riddled with symbolic meaning.

The building is considered to be one of the masterpieces of Romanesque architecture and sculpture. The doors in the west facade lead into a narthex (entrance hall or porch) which shelters the main portal. The tympanum of the central doorway shows Christ in glory surrounded by the Apostles, while the people of the earth parade across the lintel. The outer achivolt shows the signs of the zodiac and labour in the fields.

Beyond this portal is the nave, flanked by striped arcades. Over 100 of the column capitals are decorated, some of them too high to be seen from ground level. The themes of these carvings are mainly biblical, including sin and its consequences. The most famous of the capitals, on the fourth pillar on the right as you go down the nave, is known as the "mystical mill". Moses, representing the Old Testament, is shown pouring grain out of a sack into another sack held by St Peter, on behalf of the New Testament. In the background is a millwheel.

Many people use the town of **Avallon** ⓯ as a base for visiting Vézelay. There are remains of fortifications, a handsome bell tower (the Tour de l'Horloge, 1456) and a church, the Collegiale Saint-Lazare, which dates partly from the 1th century. One theory equates Avallon with the Avalon of the Arthurian legends. The figure of Arthur may have derived from Riothamus, a military leader who lived around 470.

South of Vézelay and Avallon the landscape changes dramatically. The sparsely inhabited uplands of the **Parc Natural Régional de Morvan** are the first spurs of the Massif Central and are popular for hiking, canoeing and fishing. The Celtic name Morvan, meaning "Black Mountain", derives from the dense forest cover.

The forge at Fontenay Abbey was used by the Cistercian monks to make iron tools sold in the area.

BELOW: an aerial view of Vézelay abbey, a masterpiece of Romanesque architecture.

The Canal de Bourgogne, designed to link Paris and Dijon, was begun in 1775 but only completed in 1883.

Canal country

Burgundy's centre of economic gravity has always been focused on the more populated east of the region, and one sign of this is the **Canal de Bourgogne** which connects the River Saône with the Yonne, forming part of an inland fluvial transport network effectively joining the Mediterranean to the Atlantic. It was built to carry freight but is now used by pleasure cruisers. There is a visitor's centre, Cap Canal, at the highest point between the two rivers (378m/1,240ft), **Pouilly-en-Auxois.**

Dijon

The capital of Burgundy, **Dijon** ⑯ is both a handsome and functional city. There are many old buildings in the centre, dominated by the massive **Palais des Ducs** Ⓐ (guided tours arranged by tourist office), on the semicircular place de la Liberation, seat of power of the dukes and now the city hall. Arched passageways give access to its spacious courtyards where the light colour of the wide, regular paving stones echoes the pale facades. One wing of the building is occupied by the **Musée des Beaux-Arts** Ⓑ (Wed–Mon, May–Oct 9.30am–6pm, Nov–Apr 10am–5pm; charge), one of the finest in France, which displays French, German and Italian statuary and art from the 14th–18th centuries. Much of the vast collection, the most significant outside Paris, was acquired during the Revolution from the homes of local nobility, as well as churches and monasteries. The Salle des Gardes contains the museum's prized tombstones of three members of the ducal dynasty, sculpted in alabaster and black marble. The 14th-century kitchen has six huge fireplaces, recalling the splendour of banquets in times past.

Behind the ducal palace is a cluster of old streets and small squares around the 13th-century Gothic church of **Notre Dame** Ⓒ, itself full of delightful curiosities, such as the family of figures animated by a clock mechanism. Down the narrow street beside the church, the rue de la Chouette, the small, barely recognisable figure of an owl is carved

BELOW: a Burgundian brasserie.

Burgundian Cuisine

The Burgundians' near-religious devotion to food is long-established. To prove that the high quality of the region's cuisine is a result of their innate understanding of food, Burgundians will point to ancient culinary inscriptions in the Dijon archaeological museum and tell of their dukes, whose kitchens were vast and whose meals took on the aura of religious ceremonies, with hand-held torches lighting the dishes' way to the duke's table, and pointed allusions to the sacramental properties of bread and wine.

Dijon's two main culinary specialities, mustard and *pain d'épice*, have long historical associations, as do some of the great cheeses of the region: Chaource and the brandy-washed Epoisses were first made in the abbeys of Pontigny and Fontenay, while the delicately flavoured Cîteaux is still only made in its eponymous monastery. Yet it is not only tradition, but also the quality and variety of the local ingredients which shape Burgundian cooking. Wild produce is prized: crayfish, snails, boar, quail, thrushes and woodland mushrooms, while Bresse chickens are reared on a special diet. Then there are the charcuterie from Morvan, pork dishes such as *jambon persillé*, *gougère* made with cheese, kidneys with mustard, and the great stews, such as the classic boeuf bourguignon, liberally doused in red wine.

into the wall. It is supposed to bring good luck to those who touch it and as result has been almost worn away. It is used as a symbol of the city.

One of the old streets, the **rue des Forges D**, was, until the 18th century, the main street of Dijon. It is named after the goldsmiths, jewellers and knife-makers who had their workshops there. The Hôtel Chambellan is the most striking of a series of Renaissance residences that line the street, with elaborate balconies and staircases hidden away in interior courtyards.

Work your way west to reach a group of three churches, the first of which, the **Cathédrale St-Bénigne E**, draws the eye with its tall spire and multicoloured octagonal towers. The church itself is somewhat disappointing but the crypt (charge) holds a surprise: the last fragment of a much earlier, round church, possibly dating from the 6th century, in a primitive Romanesque style. It contains the sarcophagus of the eponymous saint Benignus, a 2nd-century martyr.

Next to the cathedral is the **Archaeological Museum F** (Musée Archéologie June–Sept Wed–Mon 9am–12.30pm, 1.30–6pm; Oct–May Wed–Sun 9am–12.30pm, 1.35–6pm; charge). Exhibits include Bronze Age treasures, 1st century AD tributes left by pilgrims at the sanctuary of Les Sources de la Seine, and a 14th-century bust of Christ by Claus Sluter.

Hills of gold

Dijon is also the prefecture of one of France's most favoured *départements*, which goes by the evocative name of the Côte d'Or, or the "hills of gold". This is where all the great vineyards are located. Some say the name comes from the gold-coloured leaves that cover the hills in autumn, while others maintain that it is from the great wines or "bottled gold" they produce. No matter, the hills are beautiful and the wines excellent. The vineyards are quite easy to visit since most of them line the western edge of the D974 that runs from Dijon southwards to – and beyond – Beaune. Here, the names of the towns evoke great wines: Gevrey-Chambertin, Vougeot, Vosne-Romanée, Nuits-St-Georges. Roadside signs invite

Learn about the history of wine in Beaune's wine museum housed in the former residence of the Dukes of Burgundy.

BELOW: some of the finest vineyards in France are in hills around Dijon.

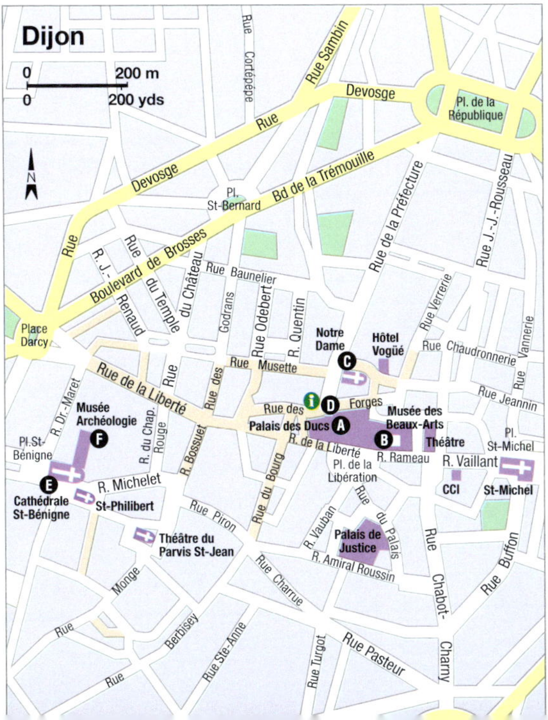

In the 1930s the mock medieval Confrérie des Chevaliers du Tastevin, was formed as a way of promoting wines. It organises the Tres Glorieuses, three annual autumn festivals to celebrate the new vintage. The biggest and most popular of these is the Hospice de Beaune wine auction in the Hôtel-Dieu.

passers-by to stop and sample the wine; you will be expected to buy at least a few bottles if you taste.

Rooftops of Beaune

It's a short drive either by main road or motorway from Dijon to **Beaune** ⓱, where the jewel-like roof of the **Hôtel-Dieu** (Apr–Nov 9am–6.30pm; Dec–Mar 9–11.30am, 2–5.30pm; charge), made of multicoloured tiles, can be seen glimmering in the distance as one approaches. Since the 18th century, Beaune has been the heart of the Burgundian wine trade, and the auction of the Hospices de Beaune in the Hôtel-Dieu, a charity hospital historically supported by the wine produced on lands donated by benefactors, is still the high point in the local wine calendar. Under its splendid multicoloured roof, the long ward contains the original sick beds. The halls off the courtyard house a collection of artwork and tapestries crowned by a painting of the Last Judgement by Rogier van der Weyden.

The wine culture in Beaune is all-pervasive. Every other shop peddles wine, books on wine, cellar equipment or wine glasses; every other café or restaurant proclaims its loyalty to the vinous tradition. The big Beaune *négociants* (wine merchants) lure tourists into their cellars with free tastings. The **Musée du Vin de Bourgogne** (Apr–Nov 9.30am–6pm; Dec–Mar Wed–Mon 9.30am–5pm; charge) is in the Hôtels des Ducs de Bourgogne, on rue d'Enfer.

Just outside the town centre, at 31 Faubourg Bretonnière, is **La Moutarderie Fallot**, the last independent manufacturer of Dijon mustard left in Burgundy (visits Mar–Nov, Mon–Sat and some Sun: 10am and 11.30am; extra visits June–Aug: 3.30pm and 5pm; charge).

BELOW: Les Hospices de Beaune.

Autun

The ancient town of **Autun** ⓲, south-west of Beaune, has been an administrative centre ever since Augustus defeated the Gauls. Traces still remain of the Roman roads that led to the town, and the quadruple-arched gates of this small provincial city bear witness to its imperial past. The amphitheatre, the largest in Roman Gaul, held up to 15,000 spectators. Medieval prosperity left behind the Cathédrale St-Lazare, whose white sculpted doorway contrasts with the more rustic rock of the church itself. Opposite is the **Musée Rolin** (Apr–Sept Wed–Mon 9.30am–noon, 1.30–6pm; Oct–Mar 10am–noon, 2–5pm; Sun 10am–noon, 2.30–5pm; charge), where it is hard to choose between the seven rooms of Gallo-Roman archaeology and the collections of medieval painting and sculpture. Behind the cathedral the remaining ramparts make a lovely stroll to the ancient Ursulines' keep.

The Saône Valley

South of Beaune, **Chalon-sur-Saône** ⓳ sits in the middle of the Saône valley amid scattered vineyards. Although an industrial centre today, half-timbered houses still crowd around the Cathédrale St-Vincent in the old quarter of town. Chalon is also the birthplace of Nicéphore Niépce, the inventor of photography, and has a museum, the **Musée Nicéphore Niépce** (July–Aug 10am–6pm; Sept–June Wed–Mon 9.30–11.45am, 2–5.45pm; charge), dedicated to him and the history of photography.

Further south in the Saône valley, **Tournus** ⓴ is the remarkably quiet site of one of Burgundy's greatest Romanesque churches. St-Philibert owes its special beauty to the unretouched surface of its small irregular stones. The exterior, with a square tower and almost no decoration, has a forbidding military appearance. Inside, massive columns of the same yellow stone carry three parallel systems of arches. This austerity is the hallmark of the church, cloister and surrounding monastery buildings (11th–12th centuries). Old streets lead to the river and from the bridge there's a splendid view of the church and its buildings.

Perched on a narrow crest of rock, **Brancion** is a delightful feudal burg. Above the old quarter of the church and marketplace is the crumbling château, one of the few such examples in Burgundy where the dukes' power countered individual fiefdoms.

Cluny and the south

During the Middle Ages, Burgundy gave birth to two great monastic orders whose fervour and organisational zeal revived the spiritual life of Europe while also contributing to its political and economic development.

The first and greatest of these orders arose in **Cluny** ㉑. In 910 William the Pious of Aquitaine decided to found an abbey at Cluny, and twelve monks led by Abbot Bernon settled a piece of land near Mâcon to create an abbey under the Benedictine rule. Cluny came under the direct jurisdiction of Rome and its abbot was so important that he acted as mediator between the pope and secular political authorities. At its height in the 12th century, Cluny had 1,400 houses depending on it. The abbot presided over an "empire" of 10,000 monks.

Cluny's great church, the Maior Ecclesia, begun in 1088, was the largest structure erected in the Middle Ages,

Dining alfresco in Cluny.

BELOW: part of Cluny Abbey, once the largest church in Christendom.

Medieval monasticism in Burgundy

There are two orders that express the greatness of Burgundian monasticism: Cluny and Citeaux. The Cluniac order was founded in 910 by William I (the Pious) at Cluny in southern Burgundy. The abbey was subject only to the pope's authority, and became the most far-reaching religious reform in the Middle Ages. Hundreds of priories and abbeys were attached, all directly under the supervision of the abbey of Cluny. The Cluny order became the wealthiest in the Western world permitting the monks to live an elaborate lifestyle. Weakened by this prosperity, Cluniac zeal diminished in the 12th century, with the Cistercians taking over as the zealots spurring monastic reform.

The Cistercian order was founded at Cîteaux, south of Dijon, in 1098 by a small group of monks from Cluny. The Cistercians believed in simplicity and poverty and it was the first order to directly manage and work its own land, including vineyards. The Cistercians also pioneered the iron-smelting industry, and evidence of this can be seen at Fontenay. Cluny, which was the largest church in Christendom before St Peter's basilica in Rome, was heavily plundered in the years following the French Revolution, and little remains of its splendour today. Cîteaux was partially destroyed during the French Revolution, but it is still home to a small community of monks.

The Romanesque Basilique du Sacré Coeur in the quiet town of Paray-le-Monial on the River Bourbince.

surpassed only by St Peter's in Rome in the 16th century. It was supposedly inspired by the dream of a monk and accounts of it make clear that it was a masterpiece of Romanesque art. Cluny continued to expand until the 18th century (when a cloister was built), but its glory came to an abrupt end with the Revolution when it was sold off and its stones used to build local houses.

Of the church that was for five centuries the largest in all Christendom, only a small group of chapels and spires, the cloister, and five of the original fifteen towers, remain. Still, imaginative presentation of the site makes it possible to get a good idea of the great **abbey** (May–Aug 9.30am–6pm; Sept–Apr 9.30am–noon, 1.30–5pm; charge) that once had its headquarters on the site, radiating secular and spiritual power across Western Christendom. The best platform for an overview is the **Tour de Fromages** (May–Sept daily 9.30am–7pm; Oct–Apr Mon–Sat 10am–12-.30pm, 2.30–5 or 6pm; charge), outside the abbey grounds.

In the town there are Romanesque houses on rue de la République and rue Lamartine, while the **Musée d'Art et d'Archéologie** (Palais Jean de Bourbon; same opening hours as abbey; charge) offers an overall view of the dramatic rise and fall of Cluny.

Paray-le-Monial, 50km (31 miles) west of Cluny, is an important site of pilgrimage, and its Sacré Coeur basilica, built in the 12th century, gives an idea of what the great church of Cluny would have looked like in its pomp.

Further south is the highly distinctive rock outcrop, the **Roche de Solutré** 22 (492m/1,614ft), which makes for a good climb. It also forms part of modern French political history. When François Mitterrand was president, Solutré became the focus of a media circus. He would climb the rock on Whit Sunday pursued by courtiers and a pack of puffing journalists in expectation of a sound bite from the great man at leisure. At the base of the rock there is the **Musée départemental de Préhistoire** (Apr–Sept 10am–6pm; Oct–Mar 10am–noon, 2–5pm; charge).

The Franche-Comté

To the east of Burgundy, the Franche-Comté is a rare case of a French region which corresponds to an ancient province, having survived the Revolution's determination to make a break with the past. The "free county" probably acquired its name in the 12th century when its lord, the count of Burgundy, refused to pay homage to the Germanic emperor. When Burgundy became a part of France in 1477, the Franche-Comté passed into the hands of the Austrian emperor and it was only in 1678 that it was subsumed under the French Crown. The modern region of four *départements* is dominated by the Jura mountains, which straddle the border with Switzerland.

Besançon

Sitting in the crook of the Doubs River, the capital of the Franche-Comté, **Besançon** 23 developed into a major town due to its position on the Rhine-Rhône trade route. Formally a religious

BELOW: vineyards at the foot of La Roche de Solutré.

town, and later a military stronghold, today it is an industrial and technological centre. Reputed to be France's leading watch- and clock-making town the **Musée du Temps** (Tue–Sat 9.15am–noon, 1–6pm, Sun 10am–6pm; charge), housed in the Renaissance Palais Granvelle, exhibits an impressive collection of timepieces. Another tribute to the trade is found in the bell tower of the Cathédrale St-Jean, whose **Horloge Astronomique** is a magnificent astronomical clock dating from 1858, with 57 faces and 62 dials, giving the time in 16 places around the world. Also worth seeing is the **Musée des Beaux Arts** (Wed–Mon 9.30am–noon, 2–6pm, closes 8pm Thur; charge).

On a hilltop above the town is the **citadel** (Jul–Aug 9am–7pm; Apr–June and Sept–Oct 9am–6pm; Nov–Mar 10am–5pm; charge), financed by Louis XIV and built by Vauban between 1688 and 1711. Within the fortress walls there are 11 hectares (27 acres) of grounds with a zoo, an insectarium, a noctarium, an aquarium and two museums. Within the citadel, the **Musée Comtois** relates local history while the **Musée de la Résistance et de la Déportation** bears witness to the events of the German occupation between 1940 and 1944.

Salt

One of the Franche-Comté's most important industries of old was the extraction of rock salt, and two adjacent towns are especially associated with the process. **Salins-les-Bains** ㉔, in the Vallée de la Furieuse, has 18th-century subterranean galleries where salt was mined (guided tours 10.30am, 11.30am, 2.30pm, 3.30pm and 4.30pm; extra tours in July and Aug; charge) and a museum of salt (10am–noon, 2–5pm, admission included with guided tour of saltworks).

The **Saline Royale** (Royal Saltworks; Apr–Oct 9am–6pm, closes 7pm July–Aug; Nov–Mar 10am–noon, 2–5pm; charge) at **Arc et Senan** testifies to the wealth produced by salt. Built by Claude-Nicolas Ledoux for Louis XV in 1779, the works speak more of enlightenment philosophy than industrial requirements. They consist of 11 monumental buildings laid out in a

Louis Pasteur was born in Dole, southwest of Besançon, and his childhood home La Maison Natale (Apr–Oct daily; Nov–Mar Sat–Sun pm; charge) displays artefacts from his youth, including his university cap and gown. Later he settled with his family in Arbois where his laboratory is exhibited in La Maison de Louis Pasteur (June–Sept daily; Apr–May daily pm; charge).

BELOW: Besançon is cradled within a loop of the Doubs river.

In February more than 3,000 skiers take part in the Transjurienne, a 76km (47½ mile) ski race through the Jura from Lamoura to Mouthe with a short incursion into neighbouring Switzerland.

semicircle in imitation of a sun dial, which were to form the nucleus of an ideal town.

Wine and cheese

Arbois ㉕ is the centre of the Jura wine region, France's smallest viticultural area, which stretches to Lons-le-Saunier and takes in the attractive town of **Château-Chalon**. The most distinctive produce is known as *vin jaune*, "yellow wine", which is made from Savagnin grapes and has a strong flavour. Other wines made here are *cremant de Jura*, a sparkling wine from Chardonnay grapes, pale reds and the sweet white, *vin de paille*.

To go with the wine there is one of France's tastiest cheeses, Comté, flavoured by the grasses and herbs that grow in the upland pastures of the region. The **Maison du Comté** in Poligny (July and Aug daily 10–11.30am, 2–5.30pm; Apr–June, Sept–Oct Tue–Sun 2–5pm; charge) explains all.

The Jura

Southeastwards, the landscape gradually rises into the Jura mountains which stretch down the Franco-Swiss border in an oblique line of around 300km (180 miles), separating Besançon and Geneva. One way to approach the mountains is the scenic train route, the **Ligne des Hirondelles** ("Swallow Line"), between Dôle and St-Claude. However you get there, the best place to orient yourself is the visitor centre of the Parc Naturel Régional du Haut Jura nature reserve at **Lajoux**.

The Jura reach their maximum height of 1,720 metres (5,643ft) at **Le Crêt de la Neige** which looks down over Lake Geneva and the subterranean, trans-frontier Large Hadron Collider where scientists are busy searching for the mysterious micro-particles that make up existence. Another fine viewpoint is **Mont d'Or**, around 20km (12 miles) south of Pontarlier, with views across to Mont Blanc.

These green mountains have many beauty spots. The most accessible is the **Région des Lacs** and, in particular, the River Hérisson which tumbles down the valley forming a series of seven waterfalls (the Cascades du Hérisson) near Menétrux-en-Joux before flowing

BELOW: Château de Joux in winter.

into Lakes Val and Chambly. A there-and-back 7.4km (5-mile) footpath links the cascades (allow about 3 hours), the highest of which are the 65-metre (213ft) l'Eventail and 60-metre (196ft) Grand Saut.

Further north in the Jura is the Franche-Comté's prime scenic spot, **Saut de Doubs** 26. There are boat trips from Villers-le-Lac that take passengers down the meandering Doubs, across Lake Chaillexon and through gorges before mooring within walking distance of two viewpoints over the falls.

The most impressive human addition to the Jura is the **Château de Joux** 27 (July–Aug 9.30am–6pm; Apr–June, Sept–Nov 10am–11.30am, 2–4.30pm, charge) at Le Cluse-et-Mijoux. Originally built in the 11th century to guard a mountain pass, the castle was reworked by Vauban in the 17th century and revamped again by Joffre two hundred years later. In its time it has served as a prison for the moderate revolutionary aristocrat Mirabeau, and Toussaint Louverture, the leader of the Haitian independence movement who died here in 1803 but whose remains were subsequently lost.

As for oddities, it is hard to beat the **Saugeais Republic** northeast of Pontarlier, a "micronation" which grew out of a joke between the local innkeeper of Montbenoit, Georges Pourchet, and the visiting prefect in 1947. Pourchet proclaimed himself president, a title which has been inherited by his daughter. The "republic" has its own prime minister, customs officers and ambassadors. It also has a flag, a national anthem and issues its own stamps.

Territoire de Belfort

The northern part of the Franche-Comté is the Territoire de Belfort, essentially the French-speaking part of Alsace which held out against annexation by Germany in 1871 to become France's 90th *département* in 1922. **Belfort** 28 itself, a city of 145,000 inhabitants, has a citadel built by Vauban. To the south of it is the industrial complex of Montbeliard, including, on its outskirts, **Sochaux**, home to the car manufacturer, Peugeot. The **Musée de l'Aventure Peugeot** (daily 10am–6pm; charge) displays 100 vehicles out of a collection of 450 cars and 50 motorbikes.

Northwest of Belfort is one of France's best-known works of modern art, the **Chapelle Notre-Dame-du-Haut** 29, in the former mining town of **Ronchamp**. Designed by Le Corbusier and completed in 1955, this surreal building, with its curved white walls and vast swell of concrete roof, is a masterpiece of contemporary architecture.

Away to the north stretch the Vosges. Below them, between the valleys of the Ognon and Breuchin, is the **Plateau des Mille Etangs** where the "1,000 lakes" of the name can be explored. They are not natural, but were made by monks and peasants from the 11th century onwards in order to farm fish. There is an information centre for the area in Faucogney-et-la-Mer. ❑

Nuits-Saint-George, a robust yet elegant Burgundy made with grapes from the Côtes de Nuits wine region, known for its reds.

BELOW: Le Corbusier's Chapelle Notre-Dame-du-Haut.

THE LOIRE VALLEY

The wealth and beauty of this lush valley were once denied to all but a privileged few. Today, the private domains of the Loire are a public showcase of French civilisation

Main attractions
BOURGES
CHARTRES
CHAMBORD
BLOIS
AMBOISE
CHENONCEAU
TOURS
AZAY-LE-RIDEAU
VILLANDRY
CHINON
FONTEVRAUD L'ABBAYE
SAUMUR
ANGERS
NANTES

At 1,012km (630 miles), the Loire is France's longest river. It rises in the Ardèche, on the eastern edge of the Massif Central near the industrial city of St-Etienne, and flows through 12 *départements*, draining a fifth of the land surface of France before meeting the Atlantic Ocean at St-Nazaire.

The name "Loire Valley" is often used to refer to a relatively short stretch of the river between Orléans and Angers which is sometimes also called "the Valley of the Kings" because of its extraordinary Renaissance châteaux built by princes and courtiers. Amboise, Blois, Azay-le-Rideau, Chambord, Chenonceau and Villandry, amongst others, were once the preserve of the privileged and powerful few, but are now open to all to enjoy. A broader definition, meanwhile, takes in much of the area now covered by the two modern regions of Centre and Pays de la Val de la Loire but once broken up into the feudal domains and provinces of Berry, Sologne, Orleanais, Touraine, Anjou and others.

Apart from the great châteaux there are many other places to see, including castles built for defence rather than pleasure (Angers, Chinon, Loches), great cathedrals (Bourges and Chartres), historic cities (Orléans, Tours, Nantes), monasteries, nature reserves, viewpoints and innumerable quaint towns and villages scattered about the expansive landscape. Here, too, there is also a definable literary landscape inhabited by the ghosts of Honoré de Balzac, Marcel Proust, François Rabelais and George Sand.

Wherever you go in this part of France, water is the common denominator. The Loire is joined by a host of tributaries including the Cher, Indre, Vienne, Sarthe, Mayenne and the confusingly named Loir. One of the greatest joys of visiting this part of France is simply to sit on a river bank and watch the "*avenue qui marche*" flow slowly by

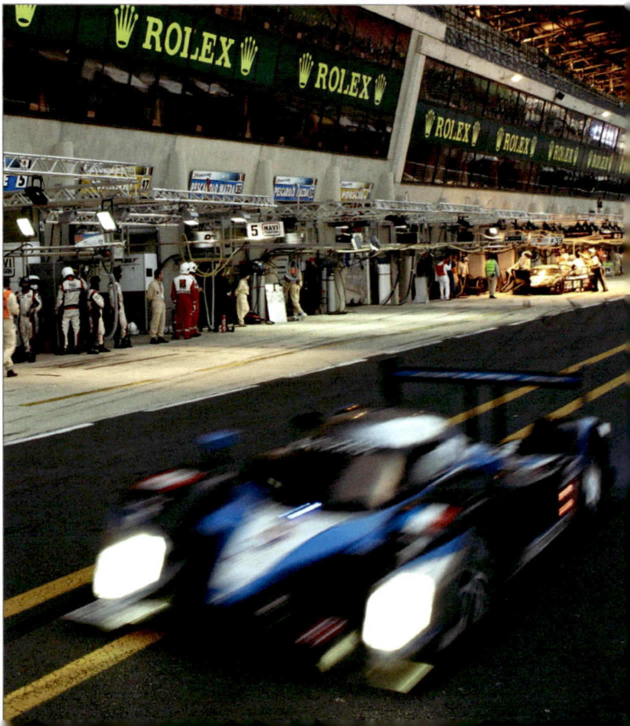

LEFT: Chambord is one of the most impressive châteaux. **RIGHT:** Le Mans race track.

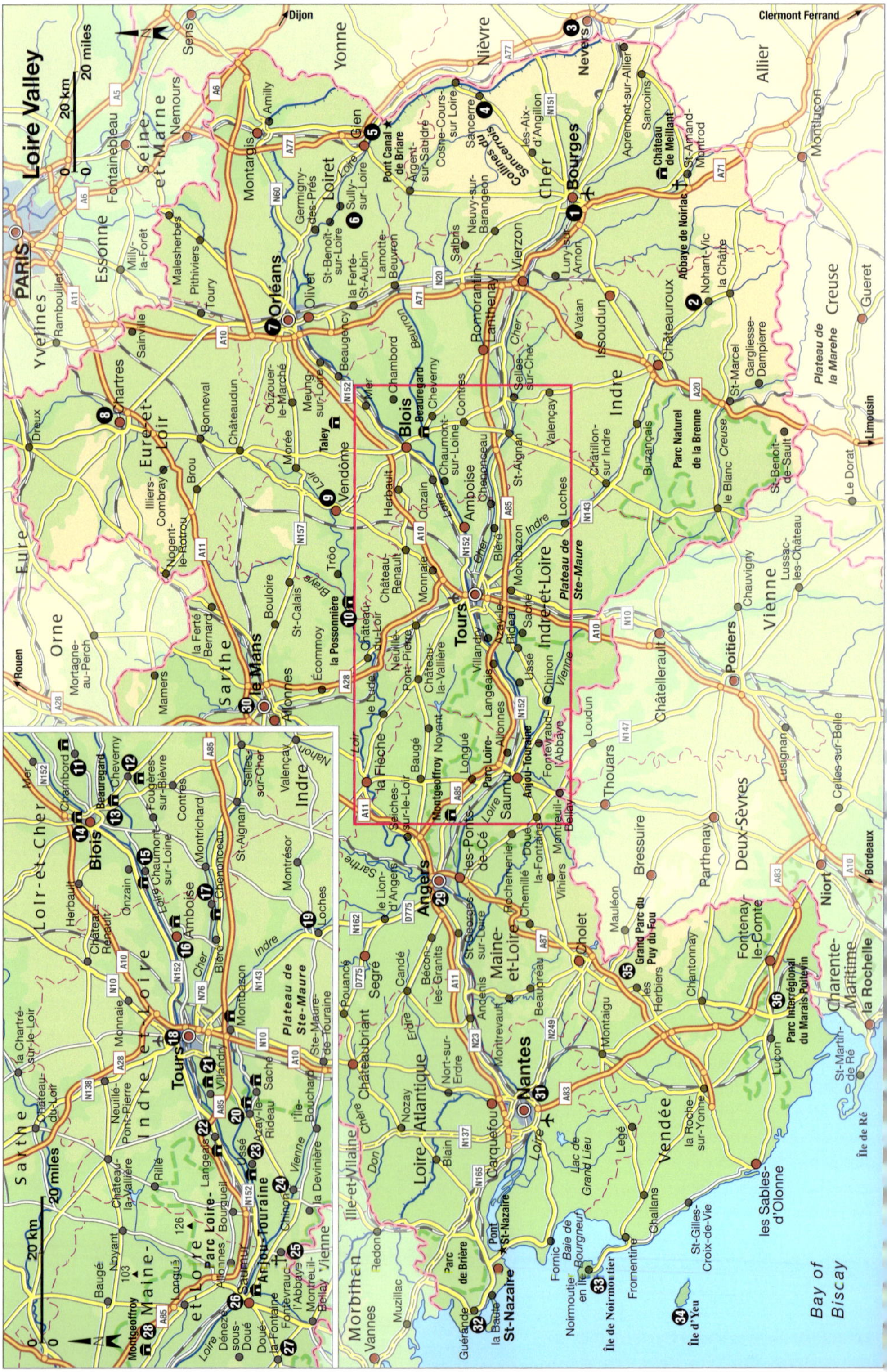
Loire Valley
0 20 km
0 20 miles
PARIS
Dijon
Clermont Ferrand
Rouen
Limpusin
Bordeaux
Yvelines
Essonne
Seine-et-Marne
Yonne
Nièvre
Allier
Loiret
Cher
Creuse
Indre
Eure
Eure-et-Loir
Orne
Sarthe
Loir-et-Cher
Indre-et-Loire
Vienne
Deux-Sèvres
Maine-et-Loire
Loire-Atlantique
Ille-et-Vilaine
Morbihan
Vendée
Charente-Maritime
Bay of Biscay
Plateau de Ste-Maure
Plateau de la Marche
Parc Naturel de la Brenne
Parc de Brière
Parc Interrégional du Marais Poitevin
Grand Parc du Puy du Fou
Collines du Sancerrois
Île de Noirmoutier
Île d'Yeu
Île de Ré
Orléans
Tours
Blois
Angers
Nantes
Bourges
Le Mans
Poitiers
Chartres
Vendôme
Amboise
Saumur
Chinon
Loches
Cholet
Niort
La Rochelle
St-Nazaire
Nevers
Gien
Sancerre
Sully-sur-Loire
Chambord
Cheverny
Chenonceau
Chaumont-sur-Loire
Villandry
Azay-le-Rideau
Langeais
Ussé
Fontevraud-l'Abbaye
Montgeoffroy
Beauregard
Talcy
La Possonnière
Château de Meillant
Abbaye de Noirlac
Pont Canal de Briare
Vierzon
Romorantin-Lanthenay
Châteauroux
Issoudun
Montargis
Fontainebleau
Nemours
Sens
Dreux
Rambouillet
Châtellerault
Loudun
Thouars
Bressuire
Parthenay
Fontenay-le-Comte
les Sables-d'Olonne
la Roche-sur-Yonne
Châteaubriant
Vannes
Guérande
la Baule
Ancenis
Segré
la Flèche
Montlucon
Gueret
Le Blanc

on its inexorable journey to the sea – or, better still, take to the water yourself.

In between the rivers, the countryside is attractively varied. The Loire Valley has been dubbed the "garden of France" for its lush, fertile farmland characterised by sunflowers, wheat fields and vineyards, but it also has extensive areas of woodland, marsh and bleak plateaux.

Bourges

Leaving the Massif Central behind, the Loire flows between Burgundy to the east and the ancient province of Berry to the west. This latter straddles the *départéments* of Cher and Indre, the former with its capital at **Bourges ❶**. At the heart of this venerable city, close to the geographical centre of France, is the 13th-century Cathédrale de St-Etienne, one of the finest Gothic buildings in France and visible for many kilometres across the surrounding countryside. Supported by majestic flying buttresses placed at regular intervals, its high, narrow nave is a symphony of vertical lines culminating in superb stained glass.

The finest example of Bourges' Renaissance domestic architecture is the 15th-century **Gothic Palais Jacques Coeur** (rue Jacques Coeur; July–Aug 9.30am–12.30pm and 2–6.30pm; Sept–June 9.30 or 10am–noon or 12.30pm, 2–5.15 or 6pm; charge), named after its first occupant, a wealthy merchant and royal treasurer to Charles VII. More fine Renaissance residences line rue Bourbonnoux, including **Hôtel Lallemant** (Tue–Sun July–mid-Sept 9.30am–12.30pm and 1.30–6.30pm; Feb–June, mid-Sept–Oct 10am–noon, 2–6pm; Nov–Jan 2–5pm; free), which houses the Musée des Arts Décoratifs. Nearby is place Gourdaine, with its half-timbered medieval houses.

Around Berry

If Berry is known at all beyond its borders it is as the birthplace and residence of one of France's most celebrated novelists, Amandine Aurore-Lucie Dupin (1804–76), who separated from her husband and adopted a bold new persona under the pen name of George Sand. After a stint as a journalist in Paris and wanderings in Spain with her lover Frédéric Chopin, she settled in the grand house she had inherited at **Nohant-Vic ❷**, a short way northwest of La Châtre. This is now open to the public as the **Maison de George Sand** (July–Aug 9.30am–6.30pm; Sept–Jun 10am–12.30pm, 2–6pm, closes 5pm in winter; charge). She called her corner of Berry, la Vallée Noire (the Black Valley), and spoke for it with the words, "Look at me if you wish; it matters little. If you continue on your way, Godspeed; if you stop, so much the better for you."

To the southwest, near the River Creuse, is the beautiful village of **Gargliesse-Dampierre**, with its 12th-century Romanesque church containing frescoes. The village describes itself as the capital of the harp, which features in a summer festival here.

Further west, beyond Châteauroux, are the 2,000-odd lakes and ponds which constitute the **Parc Naturel Régional de la Brenne**, one of the

The soaring nave of Bourges cathedral, one of the finest Gothic buildings in Europe.

BELOW: whiskered terns, La Brenne.

The Coeur de France wine route covers the central Loire taking in the vineyards and cellars of Sancerre, Menetou-Salon, Quincy, Reuilly, Giennois and Château de Meillant.

most important wetlands in France. Among the reserve's 2,300 species of birds, mammals, butterflies, fish, reptiles and amphibians is the diminutive European pond terrapin, which can live to be 60 or 70 years old. The park's information centre is at **Le Bouchet** near Rosnay (July–Aug 9am–7pm; Sept–June 10am–6pm; free).

Towards the southern extent of the park is the village of **St-Benoit-de-Sault**, an assembly of 15th- and 16th-century houses built on an outcrop of granite overlooking the Portefeuille valley. It grew up around a Benedictine priory of which the Romanesque church survives.

There is another religious house to the east, the **Abbaye de Noirlac** (Apr–Sept 10am–6.30pm; Feb–Mar and Oct–Dec 2–5pm; charge). It is a rare example of a perfectly intact Cistercian abbey, and its 12th-century church of light-coloured stone conveys a powerful simplicity through its total lack of decoration, which the monks regarded as frivolous and distracting. It makes an ideal setting for summer concerts.

Located in the lordly seclusion of its wooded grounds near St-Amand-Montrond, the splendid **Château de Meillant** (July–Aug 9.30am–6pm; Sept–June 9.30am–noon, 2–6pm; charge) shows how the sophisticated Renaissance style could be grafted on to a medieval castle complete with moat. Its courtyard is pure Renaissance, with its free-standing chapel.

Nevers

On a hill above the Loire river stands **Nevers ❸**, historically part of Burgundy but included in this chapter for the sake of convenience. In the middle ages a pottery industry grew up here, taking advantage of the river for transporting the finished product to market. When Italian craftsmen arrived in the 16th century, the town began to specialise in faïence. One of its workshops, Au Bout de Monde (now Faïencerie Montagnon), was founded in 1648 and is still in business, making it the oldest ceramics factory in France.

The old town centre is distinguished by the *palais ducal* (duke's palace), built at the end of the 15th century, and three churches. **St-Etienne** is a superb exam-

BELOW: aerial view of Gien.

ple of Cluniac Romanesque. The **cathedral** also has Romanesque elements but was rebuilt in the Gothic style after a fire in 1211. Pilgrims flock to the third church, that of the convent of St-Gildard, to see the embalmed body of Bernadette Soubirous (1844–79), who was born into poverty but became famous after seeing apparitions of the Virgin Mary in a cave at Lourdes in the Pyrenees. Bernadette spent her last 13 years as a nun in Nevers and was canonised in 1933. The tomb forms part of the **Espace Bernadette** (open Apr–Oct 7am–12.30pm, 1.30–7.30pm; Nov–Mar 7.30am–noon, 2–6pm) which includes a museum dedicated to her life.

Just to the southwest of Nevers, **Apremont-sur-Allier** stands close to the confluence of the Allier River with the Loire. Originally a village of quarry workers, in the pursuit of harmony in the early 20th century it was purged of any house not deemed to be in the regional medieval style. It has a beautiful botanic garden, inspired by Vita Sackville-West's garden at Sissinghurst, which is scattered with delightful pavilions and a pagoda-style bridge.

Pleasant roads meander 60km (37 miles) downstream to **Sancerre** ❹, marking the easternmost extent of the vineyards of the diffuse Val de Loire wine area, an amalgam of 63 distinct *denominations d'appellation contrôlée* extending from here to the coast. Sancerre and Pouilly-sur-Loire, across the river, are renowned for their distinctive dry white wines made from Sauvignon Blanc grapes.

Parallel to the Loire is a lateral canal that at one point crosses the river by means of a handsome bridge, the **Pont-Canal de Briare**. Gustave Eiffel had a hand in its construction. It was inaugurated in 1896 and at 662 metres (2,172ft) remained the longest canal bridge in the world until 2003.

Downriver to Orléans

The Loire curves around the forested region of the Sologne as it heads towards Orléans. The small town of **Gien** ❺ owes much of its beauty to Anne de Beaujeu, daughter of Louis XI. She was responsible for building the château, the bridge, the cloisters and church in the late 15th century. The château now

Every year on 7–8 May, Orléans celebrates its liberation from the English by Joan of Arc with a pageant and a service of dedication in the cathedral.

BELOW: the château of Sully-sur-Loire.

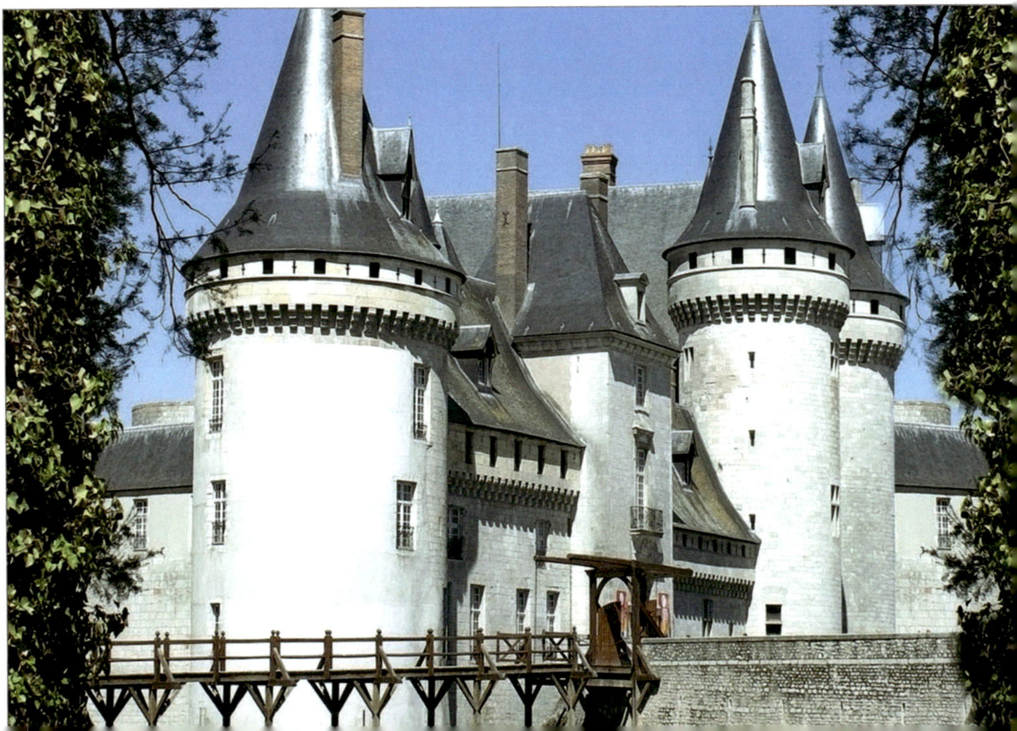

The Gothic vaulted nave of St-Benoît-sur-Loire was added to the Romanesque church in the early 13th century. The original ceiling was probably made of wood.

houses a museum of hunting, the **Musée International de la Chasse** (Wed–Mon 10am–6pm; closed Jan; charge).

The red-and-black brick of the château, laid in geometric patterns, is one of the typical styles of the valley, while the streets of the bustling little Renaissance town are hung with flags and lined with flowers. *Faïencerie de Gien* (glazed earthenware), founded in 1821, is well known for its bright designs; the riverside factory can be visited only by request (write in advance or telephone 02 38 67 00 05; museum daily except Jan–Feb Mon–Sat; shop Mon–Sat, also Sun in July–Aug; charge).

Some 23km (14 miles) downstream from Gien lies the château of **Sully-sur-Loire** ❻ (10am–6pm; closed Jan; charge). Seemingly afloat along with the ducks and swans around it, the castle has two distinct parts: the early 14th-century fortress and the 17th-century wing added by Sully, finance minister to Henry IV. In the older section, three vast rooms on succeeding floors tell of life in the Middle Ages. Furniture was reduced to large chests which served for storage, seating, and even sleeping; dining tables were planks laid over simple trestles; the court slept as many as 12 to a bed. The big draughty rooms were lined with tapestries, which were also used as hanging partitions.

The high, keel-shaped timber roof, made of chestnut, is 600 years old. The great tree trunks were soaked and salted, heated and bent, a process which took as long as 50 years. In the 17th-century wing, the rooms are of more human proportions. The beams are hidden by ornamental ceilings and the floors panelled in wood. Sully-sur-Loire is a rare example of a château with the contrasting architecture of both medieval fortress and Renaissance pleasure palace.

A little way downstream is the church of **St-Benoît-sur-Loire**, one of the finest Romanesque buildings in France. Most remarkable is the square bell tower which forms the porch, embellished with three aisles of arches decorated with carved capitals. The crypt contains the relics of St Benedict, brought from Italy in the 7th century – a monastery was founded here in AD 650.

A little further along the river is **Germigny-des-Prés**, a diminutive

BELOW: the intricate stained glass of Chartres cathedral.

Stained Glass

The windows of thick-walled Romanesque churches were so small that no ray of light could be wasted on frivolity or else the interior would be impenetrably gloomy. Gothic architecture removed this limitation. The audaciously large openings in the walls that it made possible meant that there could be light to spare. The building could be illuminated in spectacular fashion at the same time as glorifying God.

Hesitant experiments were made with stained glass around the 9th century but they were confined to simple portraits and other rudimentary compositions. But by the early 12th century the technique of fitting coloured shapes of glass held together by lead canes into intricate sockets of stone tracery had been perfected, and a new breed of medieval craftsman pushed the possibilities of their art to the limit.

The great medieval stained-glass windows invariably recount biblical anecdotes in picture form for the benefit of the illiterate. They are generally designed to be read from left to right and bottom to top, with the conclusion of the story pointing towards heaven. Such skilled and laborious work did not come cheap. Commissions were from wealthy patrons, or in some cases by craft guilds who would record their acts of pious generosity by getting the artist to depict the tools or practice of their profession in some discreet but not inconspicuous pane of glass.

 Map on page 230

church dating from the time of Charlemagne (9th century, except for the 11th-century nave). It contains a wonderful Byzantine glass mosaic, also 9th century, which was uncovered in 1840. Glowing with colour, it depicts the Ark of the Covenant.

The Maid of Orléans

At the northernmost point of the Loire's meandering course stands **Orléans** ❼, a modern city whose heart was bombed out during World War II. Its soul, however, lives on in the cult of Joan of Arc; it was here that she successfully resisted the English Army before being burnt at the stake at Rouen. Deprived of its historic buildings except for the **Cathedral**, built and rebuilt in Gothic style over hundreds of years, Orléans is now strewn with memorials to the national heroine. In the handsome, if desolate, **place du Martroi** there is an equestrian statue, while the site where she stayed in 1429 has become the **Maison Jeanne d'Arc** (3 place du Général de Gaulle; May–Oct Tue–Sun 10am–12.30pm and 1.30–6.30pm; Nov–Apr afternoons only; charge).

The glory of stained glass

Chartres ❽ is close enough to Paris (97km/60 miles) to make it a popular day trip from the capital. This attractive medieval town sits on the banks of the Eure, on a plateau of gigantic wheat-fields. The first glimpse of the lofty spires of the **Cathedral** (8.30am–7.30pm; charge for tower) rising above the plain – exactly as 13th-century pilgrims must have seen them – is magical.

Begun in 1194, the gigantic edifice took just 30 years to construct, lending it an architectural unity and an air of perfection. Before you enter, take a look at the intricate carvings on the door known as the Portail Royal. Once inside, look down to see the ancient, circular labyrinth inlaid in the nave floor. It is not known exactly what it was used for, but it is possible that penitents followed its serpentine path on their knees in symbolic pilgrimage. It is not a maze as such, rather a tortuous path without dead ends.

The incontestable glory of Chartres is its 176 **stained-glass windows**, measuring a total of 2,499 sq metres (26,900 sq ft) and representing the world's

The Loire Valley landscape is one of rolling vineyards and sunflower fields.

BELOW: the quiet town of Illiers was a source of inspiration for Proust.

The Loire is crossed by 165 bridges of various ages carrying roads, railways, pedestrians and even canals. The adjective for all things to do with the river is ligerien(ne), *from the ancient name for the Loire, the Liger.*

most remarkable ensemble. The three large rose windows on the south, north and west walls respectively depict the Apocalypse, the Virgin Mary and the Last Judgement. Most of the windows date from the 13th century, but three over the Portail Royal predate a fire of 1194 which badly damaged the building. The glass has been cleaned in contemporary times. Most of the windows illuminate biblical themes, but here and there in them are glimpses of medieval life such as two men playing dice in one of the scenes depicting the Prodigal Son. Where a window was donated by a trade guild it is often "signed" in the corner by one or two men carrying out the relevant craft.

Because of its cathedral windows, Chartres styles itself as the world capital of the glazier's and glass painter's art, a theme which is expounded on in the **International Stained Glass Centre** (Mon–Fri 9.30am–12.30pm, 1.30–6.30pm; Sat 10am–12.30pm, 2.30–6pm; Sun 2.30–6pm; charge), located in a medieval storehouse.

The rest of the city is worth exploring, too. The old district is a medieval maze of streets winding down from the cathedral to the River Eure. It is characterised by the "tertre", a steep and often stepped passage. Aside from the cathedral, the town's finest building is the **Maison du Saumon** on the place de la Poissonerie, built in the early 16th century and adorned with sculptures. The city's oldest house dates from the 12th century and stands at No. 29 rue Chantault.

BELOW: the Château de Chambord.

The Loir Valley

Chartres is the prefecture of the *département* of Eure-et-Loir, which, as its name implies, has two principal rivers. The Loir (without the e) flows north of its famous near-namesake and eventually joins it at Angers. It is a less spectacular, more tranquil, stream, but it does have its points of interest.

The source of the Loir is near a curious town which claims to be a source of another kind. In 1971, on the centenary of the birth of Marcel Proust, **Illiers** became the first and only commune in France to name itself after a fictional place, when it acquired the suffix of Combray, the setting for much of the action in *A la recherche du temps perdu* (*In search of Lost Time*). Some literary critics argue that Illiers does not have as strong a claim on the name as it thinks – that Proust's holiday retreat was just one source of inspiration – but that hasn't stopped the locals playing on the literary theme and peddling "Proust's little madeleine cake" as the local culinary speciality.

After flowing through Châteaudun, the Loir reaches **Vendôme** ❾, a sophisticated and attractive old town full of elegant shops and restaurants. Its centrepiece is the abbey church of **La Trinité**, which encompasses architectural styles from the 11th to the 16th centuries. The bell tower is the earliest part of the building; the most spectacular is the facade, resplendent in Flamboyant Gothic tracery.

Here the prettiest part of the Loir begins. The village of **Trôo**, 55km (34 miles) southeast of Le Mans, is known for its maze of subterranean dwellings.

One or two are open to the curious, and the owners will show you how comfortably and snugly you can live underground.

The manor of **La Possonnière** ⑩, birthplace of the poet Ronsard, is a beautiful Renaissance building of white stone (June–Sept Wed–Mon 10am–1pm and 2.30–7pm; Apr–May, Oct Thur–Sun 2–6pm; charge).

The Valley of the Kings

The most interesting stretch of the Loire Valley proper begins downstream from Orléans. Just 18km (11 miles) west of the city is quiet **Beaugency**, where an 11th-century bridge provides a view of the river and the town, and whose tiny streets still exude a medieval feel. Market days, with local produce and handicrafts, the smell of roast meats and fresh bread, are particularly atmospheric. The 15th-century **Château de Dunois** has certainly remained unchanged, except for slight damage sustained during the French Revolution.

A little way northwest of the river is the **Château de Talcy** (May–Aug 9.30am–12.30pm, 2–6pm; Sept–Apr 10am–12.30pm, 2–5pm; charge), built in the 16th century as a fortified country residence for a royal adviser. It was subsequently acquired by one of the Florentine financiers of François I's Italian wars. In the 18th century its grounds were landscaped and formal walled gardens created.

Chambord and Cheverny

Over the other side of the river is the **Fôret de Chambord**. Deer, wild boar and other animals roam the national game reserve freely, and observation towers have been set up for the public. In all, the park covers 5,463 hectares (13,500 acres), surrounded by the longest wall in France.

In the middle of this forested domain stands the **Château de Chambord** ⑪ (mid-June–mid-Aug 9.30am–7.30pm; Apr–mid-June and mid-Aug–Sept 9am–6.15pm; rest of the year closes 5.15pm; charge), the largest château on the Loire. It was built in 1519 as a glorified hunting lodge for François I and added to in subsequent reigns. From afar, the roofline cuts an extraordinary silhouette of gables, pinnacles, turrets and ornamented chimneys which has been called "the skyline of Constantinople on a single building". Chateaubriand saw it as "...an arabesque... like a woman with her hair blowing in the wind." Inside, 90 of the 440 rooms, including the chapel, are open to visitors, some of them decorated with the salamander, emblem of François I. The most striking feature of the building is the double-spiralled staircase in the centre of the castle, where lords and ladies once played games of hide-and-seek and visitors amuse themselves ascending and descending in view of each other but their paths never crossing.

From Chambord to Blois, the traveller can take a delightful route past some less grandiose châteaux of white tufa stone and slate. At the end of a long avenue of stately trees, the **Château de Cheverny** ⑫ (Apr–Sept 9.15am–6.15pm; Oct–Mar 9.45am–5pm; charge) rises up gracefully. Though it is still inhabited – by the same

This stone relief at the entrance of the Château de Blois depicts a porcupine, emblem of Louis XII.

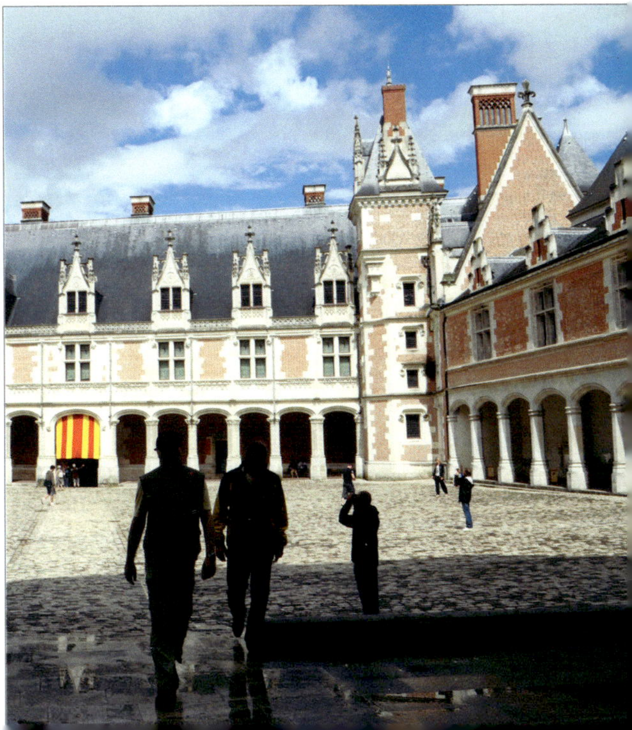

BELOW: courtyard of the Château de Blois.

In 1516, François I invited Leonardo da Vinci, whom he greatly admired, to stay at the Manoir du Clos Lucé, a short walk from the Château d'Amboise. Leonardo spent the last three years of his life here and his remains lie in the chapel of St-Hubert on the castle grounds.

BELOW: seating installation at the Chaumont garden festival.

family since the early 16th century – visitors can tour the sumptuous 17th- and 18th-century rooms, richly hung with Aubusson and Flemish tapestries.

More intimate is the **Château de Beauregard** ⓭ (May–Sept 10am–7pm; Mar–Apr, Oct 2–6pm; charge) in the nearby village of Cellettes, with its 17th-century Galerie des Portraits, containing the charmingly naive depictions of 327 famous men and women; the tiny Cabinet des Grélots, with marquetry of bells; and a lovely modern walled garden, at its best in May.

A short distance away is **Fougères-sur-Bièvre**, a charming village off the tourist trail, with a 15th-century feudal château built for the treasurer of Louis XI (mid-May–mid-Sept daily 9.30am–12.30pm, 2–6pm; mid-Sept–mid-May Wed–Mon 10am–12.30pm, 2–5pm; charge).

Elegant Blois

To the north, the town of **Blois** ⓮ was a central stage for courtly intrigue. Louis d'Orléans was assassinated in the **Château de Blois** (July–Aug 9am–7pm, Apr–June, Sept closes 6.30pm, Oct closes 6pm; Jan–Mar and Nov–Dec 9am–12.30pm, 1.30–5.30pm; charge), as was the Catholic Duc de Guise, suspected of plotting against Henry III. His mother, Catherine de Medici, gave up the ghost in the castle after a lifetime of subterfuge and power play; her gorgeous apartments are riddled with secret hidey-holes. Each of their stories is told in the spectral *son et lumière* (Apr–mid-Sept).

In the clear light of day, Blois is a pleasant place. The château's monumental octagonal staircase and its sculpted balconies are superb examples of early French Renaissance design. Although the town itself suffered severely during World War II, the reconstruction successfully preserved the regional style, with slate roofs and brick chimneys. The pedestrian areas near the castle are paved in colourful stone.

At nearby **Chaumont** ⓯ the Loire is particularly wide, and the round towers of the **Château de Chaumont** (Apr–Oct 10am–6.30pm; Nov–Mar 10am–5pm; charge) look down upon it from the top of a wooded hill. It was acquired by Catherine de Medici in 1560 after the death of her husband, Henry II; she forced his mistress, Diane de Poitiers, to reluctantly give up her residence at Chenonceau and move here. Visiting the richly furnished rooms and the large, attractive gardens, it is hard to relate to Diane's distress. Today Chaumont is perhaps best known for its adventurous **International Garden Festival**, when experimental themed gardens by leading garden designers, architects and artists transform the grounds each summer (Apr–Sept; charge). As you cross the river, the park and the Loire form a lovely scene.

Leonardo's last home

Downstream, the town of **Amboise** ⓰ nestles around its impressive **château** (Mar–Aug 9am–7pm; rest of the year 9am–12.30pm, 2–5.30pm; charge). Rich in history, Amboise belonged to the Counts of Anjou and Berry before becoming a part of the French throne in 1434. Charles VIII died here of a concussion he inflicted on himself passing through a low doorway. Visitors take note – and duck.

After the failure, in 1560, of the Amboise conspiracy – an attempt by the Huguenots to abduct the young king François II – the château fell from royal favour. Napoleon handed it over to politician Roger Duclos, who demolished two-thirds the building; later, World War II damaged most of what was left. Only the facade facing the river reveals the original Renaissance charm. Nonetheless, the château is still beautiful and contains several unique features, notably the **Tour des Minimes**, with its spiral ramp for mounted horsemen, and the **Chapelle St-Hubert**, where Leonardo da Vinci is buried.

The town seems to be a natural extension of the château. The **rue Nationale** is the colourful main market street, reserved for pedestrians. The essence of a provincial French town is captured in this lively thoroughfare: the sing-song of the merchants, the cafés, the aromas and abundance of fresh produce.

A short walk from the château is **Clos Lucé** (July–Aug 9am–8pm; Feb–June and Sept–Oct 9am–7pm; Nov–Jan 10am–6pm; charge), the red-brick manor house where Leonardo spent the last three years of his life, invited to join the royal court by his patron and admirer, François I. It has been made into a museum, displaying scale models of his precocious inventions, based on the master's drawings. Outside, the family-oriented **Parc Léonard da Vinci** (combined ticket with Clos Lucé; same hours) is dotted with lifesize interactive maquettes of Leonardo's inventions, such as the helicoidal screw, the multi-barrelled cannon and the armoured car.

If you leave the banks of the Loire, and follow instead its southern tributary, the Cher, you will come to the **Château de Chenonceau** ⓱ (July–Aug 9am–8pm; Feb–June, Sept–Oct 9/9.30am–6/7pm; Nov–Jan 9.30am–5pm; charge). This is perhaps the most elegant of all the Loire valley jewels, renowned for the arches that carry it across the water. The building rests on pillars planted in the river bed, but the design is so light and delicate it might as well be floating on air, and the beauty of the interior complements this elegance. At night, a *son*

TIP

Tours of Chenonceau are self-guided, so you can wander at will. Don't miss a visit to the kitchens, housed in the feet of the bridge, with their very effective waste-disposal system.

BELOW: the incomparable Château de Chenonceau.

> *This town is laughing, loving, fresh, flowery, more perfumed than all the other towns in the world.*
>
> Honoré de Balzac on Tours

et lumière recounts the story of Diane, Henry II's favourite, and his jealous wife, Catherine de Medici, who couldn't bear to see so much perfection and not own it.

The tumultuous events of the 20th century touched the château, when owner Gaston Menier set up a military hospital in the gallery during World War I. During World War II, a number of people benefited from the particular situation of Chenonceaux village: the southern exit was in the free zone, while the château entrance was in German-occupied territory.

The Touraine

Amboise and Chenonceau are on the eastern edge of the **Touraine** region. This "Garden of France" has been described by novelist Honoré de Balzac in *The Lily of the Valley*: "Each step in this land of enchantment allows a fresh discovery of a picture, the frame of which is a river or a tranquil pool in whose watery depths are reflected a château and its turrets, parks and fountains."

The prime stretch of the valley is dominated by the city of **Tours** ⓲, a Gallo-Roman settlement sited between the Loire and the Cher, and named after its prehistoric tribal inhabitants, the Turones. Its early history is associated with Saint Martin of Tours, who was born in Hungary in 316. He joined the Roman army and was sent to Gaul, and later became a bishop of the city. After his death in 397, a cult grew up around his sepulchre, and the great basilica built over it became an important place of pilgrimage.

Tours grew rich on the manufacture of silk. It reached its apogee under Louis XI and his successors, and for a century from around 1450 to 1550, it was the capital of France. Nowadays, it's a handsome university city and the fulcrum of the Loire wine region.

The place to begin a visit is in the **Cathédrale St-Gatien** Ⓐ (Apr–Sept daily 10am–6pm; Oct–Mar Wed–Sun 10am–6pm; charge), a Gothic building with a fine cloister, the Cloitre de la Psalette, and scriptorium. Next to it is the **Musée des Beaux-Arts** Ⓑ (Wed–Mon 9am–noon and 2–6pm; charge) with its interesting collection of paintings and decorative arts. On the other

BELOW: rose window, St-Gatien cathedral.

Les Compagnons

Tours is considered the mecca of the Compagnons de la Tour de France (not to be confused with the bike race). *Compagnons* are skilled craftsmen belonging to one of three organisations which claim to maintain the traditions of the medieval guilds of brotherhoods that built the great Gothic cathedrals. Membership requires an apprenticeship involving a working tour of France, demanding tests of ability and personality. The successful applicant is rewarded with a name which cites one of his virtues or personality traits, such as Jacques le Resolut ("Jacques the Determined").

It is claimed that the knowledge and traditions of the *compagnonnage* derive from three figures, the biblical king Solomon, the legendary stonemason Maître Jacques and carpenter Père Sourbise.

side of the cathedral, meanwhile, is the **Château Royal de Tours** Ⓒ (Wed and Sat 2–6pm; charge), a former royal residence which now houses displays on the history of Tours and temporary art exhibitions.

From these three buildings it's a short walk down rue Colbert, the main street of the medieval town, to the surviving core of old Tours. On the way are two museums. One of these is the **Musée des vins de Touraine** Ⓓ, at 16 rue Nationale (Fri–Sun 9am–noon, 2–6pm; charge), with displays on the local wine industry arranged in the cellars of 13th-century Abbaye Saint-Julien.

The other museum to see is the **Musée du Compagnonnage** Ⓔ (June–Sept daily 9am–12.30pm, 2–6pm; Oct–May Wed–Mon 9am–noon, 2–6pm; charge), which is full of masterpieces by apprentices in craft guilds ranging from slate-working to chocolate. A short way further on, on the corner of rue Commerce and rue Constantine, is the **Hotel Gouin** Ⓕ, housing an archaeological museum (closed for works) which has a handsome Renaissance façade.

The core of the medieval town is **place Plumereau**. The finest surviving old building is the 15th-century **Maison de Tristan** Ⓖ, located on a street off the north side of the square. Going the other way (ie away from the river) you emerge from the pedestrianised streets near the **Tour Charlemagne**, a surviving tower from the great basilica that was built over the tomb of St Martin; the edifice was ransacked by Protestants in the 16th century and then destroyed by Revolutionaries in 1793. It was replaced in the late 19th century by the "new" **Basilique St-Martin** across the road.

St Martin's remains may have suffered the vagaries of fortune but his reputation lives on, even in the wine industry. According to legend, the monks of his monastery discovered to their dismay that their errant donkeys had found a way into the vineyard planted in the grounds of the saint's monastery and chewed off most of the tender young branches. The following year's harvest, however, was the best on record – and *la taille* (pruning) has been an essential chore in the vineyards ever since.

Haute cuisine at the Château d'Artigny, a luxury hotel in Montbazon.

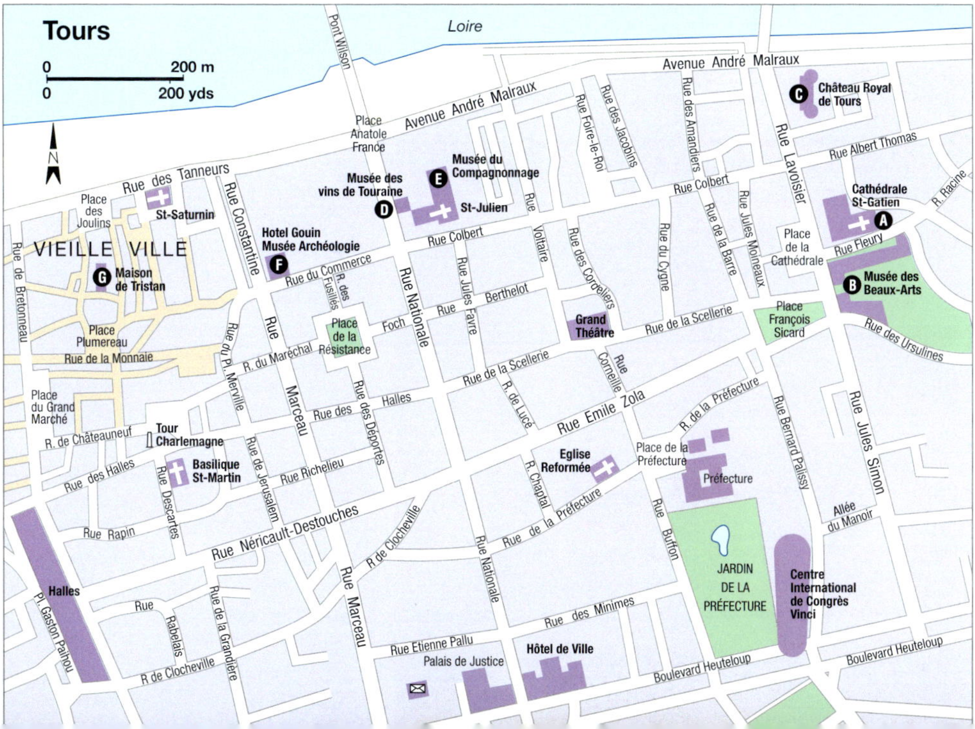

In Villandry's kitchen garden you will find many vegetables, both exotic and common, but no potatoes: they were not introduced until the 18th century.

Loches

On the banks of the Indre 38km (22 miles) to the southeast of Tours is the remarkably preserved royal town of **Loches** ⓳. Around the year 900, it became the property of the counts of Anjou before passing into the hands of the kings of France and becoming a place of royal sojourn.

The fourth count of Anjou, Foulques Nerra, built the **castle** at the southern end of the walled citadel that covers the rocky promontory above the town, between 1010 and 1035. The **donjon** (Apr–Sept 9am–7pm; Jan–Mar, Oct–Dec 9.30am–5pm; charge) is one of the oldest surviving keeps in Europe. Inside is a torture chamber and royal apartments decorated with tapestries and paintings.

Also within the walls of the citadel is the **Eglise St-Ours**, built in the 11th century and enlarged in the 12th, when it was given a Romanesque portal. Its other distinguishing marks are two pyramidal cupolas over the nave. Inside is the tomb of Agnès Sorel, a famed beauty and mistress of King Charles VII.

A single gateway, the **Porte Royale**, dating from the 13th century but rebuilt in the 15th, leads from the citadel into the lower old town which is protected by another set of ramparts. Here two more handsome gateways survive: the militaristic **Porte Picois** and the decorated **Porte des Cordeliers**.

The finest building in Loches is the palace of the **Logis Royal**, erected in the 15th century, now standing beside a large public park. The Renaissance period is represented further by the town hall, the Tour St-Antoine (a belfry) and private mansions such as the one known as La Chancellerie ("the Chancellery").

South and west of Tours

The **Château d'Artigny**, directly south of Tours and now converted into a luxury hotel, was designed by the perfumier François Coty in pure 18th-century style with spacious lawns and terraces. Nearby, the 10th-century **Château de Montbazon** is mostly in ruins. The eccentric American painter Lillian Whittaker once lived here, and fond tales of "La Dame de Montbazon" may still be heard. A small crêperie at the foot of the ruins is a pleasant place for lunch.

BELOW: French literary giant, Honoré de Balzac (1799–1850).

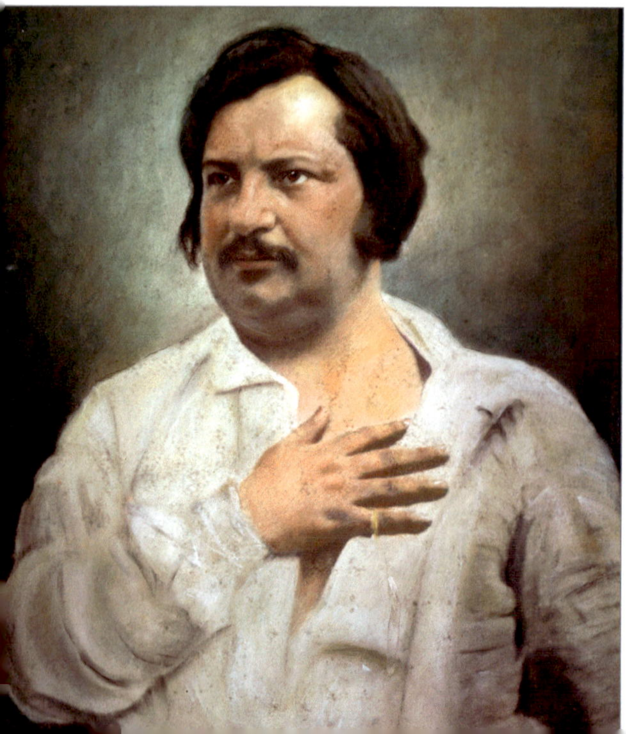

Honoré de Balzac

Described as "by turns a vagrant and a hermit" and possessed with "superhuman energy and vitality", Balzac was almost as exaggerated as one of his characters. In 20 years he churned out 85 novels, mostly in his ambitious series, La Comédie Humaine, which aimed to cram all of French life within it. He was a slow and meticulous worker who often rose at midnight and worked for 15 hours at a stretch, fuelled by black coffee. While at Saché, he worked in a small room on the second floor and it was here that he wrote his masterpiece, *Le Père Goriot* (1835). Despite his enormous success – he dominated his contemporaneous world of letters – Balzac was dogged by debt throughout his life. Late in life he married a wealthy Polish widow, but died five months after the wedding.

The River **Indre**, southern tributary of the Loire, was described by Honoré de Balzac as "unravelling like a serpent in a magnificent emerald basin". The writer loved the valley dearly, spending his most prolific days between 1830 and 1837 in the **Château de Saché** (July–Aug daily 10am–7pm; Apr–June and Sept daily 9am–6pm; Oct–Mar Wed–Mon 10am–12.30pm, 2–7pm; charge), which belonged to friends of his parents. Devotees can admire a wonderful collection of Balzac memorabilia here, including letters and portraits of his lady loves, his manuscripts (which he edited at such length that typesetters refused to work on them more than one hour a day – and that at double pay) and his room, exactly as it was. The first-floor salon has also retained its character, in part due to the surprising optical illusion of the hand-painted wallpaper. The arrangement of the furniture and game tables makes it easy to imagine the drawing-room intrigues so often described in novels of the period.

Downstream along the Indre is **Azay-le-Rideau** ⓴, a small château of exquisite proportions (July–Aug daily 9.30am–7pm; Apr–June, Sept daily 9.30am–6pm; Oct–Mar 10am–12-.30pm, 2–5.30pm; charge). The river forms a wide moat around this epitome of Renaissance grace and perfection. The influence of medieval defence architecture is clear, but at Azay all is designed for pleasure. The four turrets are slim and elegant, the crenellations ornamental, and the outlook better for observing clouds reflected in the water than advancing enemies.

A short distance to the north, not far from the confluence of the Cher and the Loire, stands the **Château de Villandry** ㉑ and its famous 16th-century **gardens** (July–Aug 9am–6.30pm; rest of the year 9.30am–5.30pm; gardens are open daily all year; charge). The three tiers of the garden (the pond, the decorative gardens, the kitchen garden) can be viewed at once from the high terrace of the château. Planted with low box-wood and yew hedges enclosing flowerbeds, the gardens represent the four faces of love on one side, music on the other. The kitchen gardens and herb garden were designed according to documents preserved by medieval monks, and the former is like something from *Alice Through the Looking Glass:* each square describes a different geometric design in contrasting colours that change from year to year in the course of crop rotation. The standard red roses sweetening the air represent the monks tending the vegetable plots.

Langeais and Ussé

North of Villandry, back on the Loire, the **Château de Langeais** ㉒ presents a much more severe image (July–Aug 9am–7pm; Feb–Mar 9.30am–5.30pm; mid-Nov–Jan 10am–5pm; rest of the year 9.30am–6.30pm; charge). Built in the 15th century by Louis XI as a defensive fortress on the site of a 10th-century stronghold, it has never been altered or added to. The last owner, Jacques Siegfried, oversaw the complete furnishing of the castle in wonderful period pieces before donating it to the

Modern sculpture at Azay-le-Rideau.

BELOW: Villandry castle gardens.

Canals & Rivers of France

Rural France looks different from the deck of a boat, going at the lazy pace of the river's flow

France has 8,500km (5,000 miles) of navigable inland waterways, including 100 canals, the most extensive network of any country in Europe. The first canals were built in the 17th century to link the major rivers, and by the height of the Industrial Revolution in the 19th century they had become a highly efficient waterborne transport system. The coming of the railway rendered many canals obsolete, but since 1945 there has been a massive revival of interest in them as a resource for leisure boating.

There are many ways to get afloat. The easiest is to take an organised cruise down a river. Paris has its famous Bateaux Mouches and other sightseeing areas have their own cruise vessels. In some places, large boats have been turned into floating restaurants or hotels.

But nothing can beat being your own captain for a few days. Many inland ports in northern France have reinvented themselves as tourist centres with specialised companies renting out modern cruisers. The typical houseboat ranges from under 9 metres (30ft), sleeping 2 people, to over 14 metres (45ft), with 10 to 12 berths.

Everything is geared towards making cruising easy for the novice. Your hire company will issue you with a temporary riverboard "licence" and provide information on how to operate the boat. Instruments are kept to a minimum – essentially a steering wheel, throttle, lever, indicator and horn – leaving you with the main tasks of steering and stopping.

You will need to learn the basics of the aquatic highway code. Boats in France, like cars, travel on the right and pass each other port side to port side. Upstream traffic gives preference to downstream and all pleasure craft must give way to commercial vessels. There are speed limits to observe and a set of "road" signs to be aware of. You'll also have to get used to using locks. Some of these are automatic; some you have to operate yourself; but a few still have lock-keepers who are invaluable sources of information on where to go and what to see.

The key to a good boating holiday is to plan your route, take your time and not be too ambitious. Five hours a day sailing on average is plenty for most people, leaving time for sightseeing, strolling and enjoying leisurely lunches to the sound of lapping water.

The only drawback to getting around by boat is that you can only see the sights within reach of the waterside on foot, by bicycle or by public transport; but this limitation can make you appreciate all the more the journey rather than the destinations. The pace of travel on a boat is slow and gentle, and that gives you time to take in more scenery, impressions of human life and wildlife than you'll ever see through a car window. ❐

ABOVE: manoeuvering a boat through a lock.
LEFT: moored at Verdun.

 Map on page 230

Institut de France in 1904. Those who are particularly interested in the transition from medieval to Renaissance life will enjoy the authentic interiors, the 15th-century Flemish and Aubusson tapestries and the unequalled collection of furniture, everything immaculately maintained.

In 1491, Charles VIII married Anne de Bretagne in the Langeais chapel. Her dowry was the realm of Brittany, which thus became united with France. Her reputation for piety is unsurpassed, and her humility and strength of character shine through the ages in the handsome wedding portrait of the couple as well as in her motto, which she had inscribed on the walls: "If God is with us, who can be against us?"

Cross the Loire and head down the D7, where the many turrets of a tall white castle loom up against the background of the tenebrous forest of Chinon. This is the **Château d'Ussé** ㉓ (Apr–Aug 10am–7pm; Feb–Mar, Sept–Nov 10am–6pm; charge), the castle which inspired Charles Perrault to write *Sleeping Beauty of the Woods.* The furnishings are in poor repair, but young children will want to visit the wax figures of fairy-tale characters.

Chinon and Fontrevraud

On the other side of the dark forest lies Chinon, on the banks of the River Vienne. This is the heart of the **Rabelaisie**, the name given to this locality in honour of the 16th-century humanist and author, François Rabelais. His satirical works, *Gargantua* and *Pantagruel*, are recommended for those who would appreciate a less stuffy perspective of the Renaissance. Particularly juicy passages of *Gargantua* describe rather unholy activities at the imaginary Thelème Abbey, where the entrance gate bore the motto: "Do What You Will!".

You can visit his house, **Maison Rabelais**, in nearby **La Devinière** (July–Aug daily 10am–7pm; Apr–June and Sept Wed–Mon 10am–12.30pm and 2–6pm; rest of the year closes 5pm; charge). The well-preserved, historic town of **Chinon** ㉔ itself has an imposing, though largely ruined, 12th-century **château fort** (daily Apr–Sept 9am–7pm; rest of the year 9.30am–5pm; charge) running along the top of a steep ridge overlooking the Vienne. The English Plantagenet kings spent much time at Chinon, and Charles VII met Joan of Arc here in 1429.

Now turn back towards the banks of the Loire, passing by **Fontevraud l'Abbaye** ㉕ (July–Aug 9.30am–7.30pm; Apr–May, Sept–Oct 9.30am–6.30pm; rest of the year 9.30am–5.30pm; charge). In this rather over-restored 12th-century abbey lie the remains of the earliest Plantagenet kings. Four recumbent funeral effigies are the only decoration in the vaulted 90-metre (295ft) -long church. Three of the stone sculptures represent Henry II, his wife Eleanor of Aquitaine and their son Richard the Lionheart. Henry was buried here at his request, though English interests would have preferred that he rested closer to the heart of his kingdom. Richard, who succeeded his father to the English throne, also chose to be buried here, next to his beloved parents. The three polychrome sculptures lie side by side. The fourth

Fontevraud Abbey, burial place of the Plantagenet kings, was once the most powerful monastic complex in France.

BELOW: tomb of Henry II Plantagenet, King of England from 1154 to 1189, at Fontevraud Abbey.

A gargoyle fountain at Saumur.

figure is that of Isabelle of Angoulême, wife of King John Lackland (Richard's brother), and the oldest known wooden monument of this type.

Eleanor had been the abbess and royal protector of Fontevraud and lived an extraordinary life. Determined and strong-willed, yet also beautiful, cultured and capricious, she dominated the 13th-century affairs of both England and France. After the annulment of her marriage to King Louis VII of France in 1152, because of consanguinity, she married Henry Plantagenet, Count of Anjou and Duke of Normandy, who succeeded to the English throne in 1154 as Henry II. Their union meant that England, Normandy and the west of France became one powerful empire. Eleanor bore Henry five sons, two of whom became kings of England. All the while she played an active part in administering the kingdom, and in later life even led an army to put down a rebellion in Anjou. Eventually she retired to Fontevraud to live out her last days. The nuns described her as a queen "who surpassed almost all the queens of the world."

Architecturally, the abbey is celebrated for its large Romanesque kitchens in the **Tour Evraud**, with 21 chimneys constructed entirely of stone; the restoration here was, however, completed with some disregard for historical accuracy.

Saumur and the troglodyte caves

The route from Fontevraud to **Saumur** ㉖ (D947) sums up the Loire valley. Besides the numerous châteaux perched above the majestic river, prehistoric dolmens and Roman churches and baths testify to a long history of human community in this region at the crossroads of Anjou, Poitou and Touraine. Saumur is mainly known for its **château** (July–Aug 10am–6pm; Apr–June, Sept–Oct Tue–Sun 10am–1pm, 2.30–6pm; charge) and for the **Cadre Noir Cavalry School**; you can visit the school and its stables (guided visits 9.30–11am, 2–4pm; charge) and watch the morning training sessions.

While the grand Renaissance château may seem like a typical Loire palace, there is another side to the story

BELOW: the Loire at Saumur.

altogether – underground. Anjou, in particular south of the river between Saumur and Doue-la-Fontaine, has Europe's highest concentration of cave dwellings. There are estimated to be over 1,000km (600 miles) of excavated passages carved out of the soft tufaceous limestone (tufa for short). Many of these are now abandoned, but plenty have been put to new use, or have been in continual use for centuries. During the Middle Ages it has been estimated that a quarter of the population lived underground. Some caves are used to age sparkling Saumur wines (a number of producers will give you a guided tour), or to grow crops of whitecap mushrooms: the Saumur region is the world's leading mushroom producer. Just outside Saumur, in St-Hilaire-St-Florent, the **Musée du Champignon** (Feb–Nov 10am–7pm; charge) offers guided visits of the underground galleries where all the various uses of the caves are demonstrated.

Other caves have been converted into restaurants, hotels, art galleries and nightclubs. Many are simply inhabited by ordinary people, out of choice rather than necessity. These so-called troglodyte dwellings have several advantages over a house. It is cheaper to dig a hole than to build walls and throw a roof over them. At the same time, the excavated stone can be sold: many of Anjou's buildings, including churches and fine châteaux, are made from tufa. A cave also makes a comfortable place to live since it maintains a constant temperature, warm in winter, cool in summer. For centuries, people didn't think about whether they wanted to live in a cave or not; it was just the done thing, the easiest alternative. In the last decades there has been a revival of interest in troglodyte dwelling, partly as a way of preserving local heritage but mostly because caves make practical places to live or to keep as a holiday home.

Two villages and one town near to Saumur make a good introduction to the underbelly of the Loire. The easiest place to start a tour is **Doué-la Fontaine** 27, 20km (12 miles) southwest along the D960 from Saumur, which has its own special variety of limestone laid down by the Faluns Sea 20–25 million years ago. **Troglodytes et Sarcophages** (June–Aug daily 2.30–7pm, May 2.30–7pm Sat–Sun only; charge) is believed to be the oldest cave in the Anjou. It was dug as a quarry in Merovingian times (first millennium AD), and in the past the local aristocracy would come here to order their sarcophagi. Different in character are the **Cathédrales Troglos des Perrières** (July–Aug 10.30am–6-.30pm; Apr–June, Sept–Oct 2–6.30pm; charge), gigantic arched chambers dug for the extraction of rock in the 18th and 19th centuries.

Rochemenier, to the north of Doué, describes itself as a "village troglodyte" and is the largest group of accessible caves in the Anjou. It has two subterranean farms, a chapel and a restaurant.

La cave aux sculptures (Apr–Oct 10.30am–1pm, 2–6.30pm for guided tours, lasting one hour; charge) at **Dénézé-sous-Doué**, a few kilometres away, has hundreds of figures carved into its walls in the late-16th/early-17th

France's best rosé wines are produced in the Loire Valley.

BELOW: Saumur wine cellar.

Aside from the château, Angers has a number of historic buildings, including some unusual 15th- and 16th-century wooden houses, with interesting architectural details worth seeking out.

BELOW: botanical theme park, Terra Botanica.

centuries by unknown persons and for reason unknown.

Bringing the theme of underground art up to date is the **Helice Terrestre de l'Orbiere** (May–Sept daily 11am–8pm, Oct–Apr Sat and Sun only 2–6pm) at **St-Georges-de-Sept Voies**, northwest of Doué. It was dug and sculpted by Jacques Warminski and is used to hold exhibitions and concerts.

West to Angers

Returning to the main route west along the Loire, continue from Saumur towards Angers along the D74 to reach the distinguished 18th-century **Château de Montgeoffroy** ㉘ at Maze, and its long, tree-lined drive. The château, resplendent with Louis XIV furnishings, is still inhabited but open to visitors (mid-Mar–mid-Nov daily 10am–noon and 2.30–8pm, but mid-June–mid-Sept 10am–6pm; charge).

The medium-sized city of **Angers** ㉙ is the ancient capital of Anjou and fiefdom of the Plantagenets. The **Château** (May–Aug 9.30am–6.30pm; Sept–Apr 10am–5.30pm; charge) took 100 years to build. The 17 turrets are built in local stone and slate in a striking striped pattern. Formidable from the exterior, the battlements have only a few small openings at the top. From within the castle, the view of the grassy moat alongside the deer and flowers softens the image somewhat.

Angers is home to an impressive collection of tapestry. Most famous is the **Apocalypse of St John**, displayed inside the château in a specially constructed building. The world's largest tapestry, it extends for some 107 metres (350ft) and was commissioned by the dukes of Anjou in the 14th century. It is an astonishing show of complexity, technique and imagination. Each of the 75 wonderfully detailed and coloured panels reveals John, in a small Gothic structure, observing and reacting to his fantastic visions.

On the other side of the river, the **Musée Jean Lurçat** holds that artist's reply to the Apocalypse, *Le Chant du Monde* (Song of the World). Woven at the Aubusson studios from 1957 to 1966, the 10 tapestries are on display in the Gothic **Hôpital St-Jean** (June–Sept daily 10am–6.30pm; Oct–Mar Tue–Sun 10am–noon, 2–6pm; charge), built by Henry II Plantagenet in repentance for the death of Thomas à Becket at Canterbury Cathedral in 1170. Angers' **Musée des Beaux-Arts** (June–Sept daily 10am–6.30pm; Oct–May Tue–Sun 10am–noon, 2–6pm; charge) displays art from the 15th to the 20th centuries in a sumptuously restored Renaissance house and other buildings.

Outside Angers is a new botanical theme park, **Terra Botanica** (Apr–Aug 10am–7pm, Sept–Nov 9am–6pm; charge), a combination of gardens, greenhouses, ponds, theme-park rides and activities all related to plant life.

North to Le Mans

North of the Loire are two of France's lesser-known *départements*, both named after the respective rivers that flow through them – Mayenne and Sarthe. Together they comprise the ancient province of Maine, which bequeathed its name to the state in New England via early French colonists.

Together they make up a somewhat nebulous region of gentle countryside merging into southern Normandy, for the most part sparsely populated. The only large centre is the city of **Le Mans** ㉚, whose conurbation contains more than half the population of Sarthe *département*.

Le Mans has some lovely old streets lined with houses dating from the 15th and 16th centuries southwest of the Cathédrale St-Julien, but is best known for the world's most famous endurance sports car race, held here in June. The 24 Heures du Mans takes place on the Circuit de la Sarthe, using stretches of public roads. The object is to do as many laps as possible within 24 hours. Since a serious crash in 1955, each car has had to have a minimum of three drivers to avoid errors due to fatigue. Technology has been steadily pushing up the performance of cars since the race was inaugurated in 1923, and these days the winners will clock up over 5,000km (3,100 miles) at an average speed of over 220km/h (130 mph). Le Mans has a permanent **museum** of the race (Musée des 24 heures; Apr–Sept daily 10am–6pm; Oct–Mar Wed–Sun 11am–5pm; charge).

Nantes

Around 75km (47 miles) west of Angers is the river port of **Nantes** ㉛, emotionally and economically attached to Brittany but no longer officially part of that region since local government reorganisation in 1972 made it instead the capital of the Pays de la Loire. Nantes made its fortune in the 18th century from the proceeds of sugar and slavery (referred to in polite society as "the ebony trade"). Ships would set sail from here to ply a triangle linking Africa and the West Indies, going out loaded with African slaves and returning with sugar to be refined in France.

The city's most conspicuous building is the **Château des Ducs de Bretagne** Ⓐ (July–Aug daily 9.30am–7pm; rest of the year Tue–Sun 10am–6pm; charge), commissioned by Duke François II and continued by his daughter, the Duchess

Five of the 12 planned long-distance Eurovelo cycling routes pass through northern France. Eurovelo routes are for the most part surfaced. They avoid steep gradients and busy roads, and link up towns and villages offering food and accommodation.

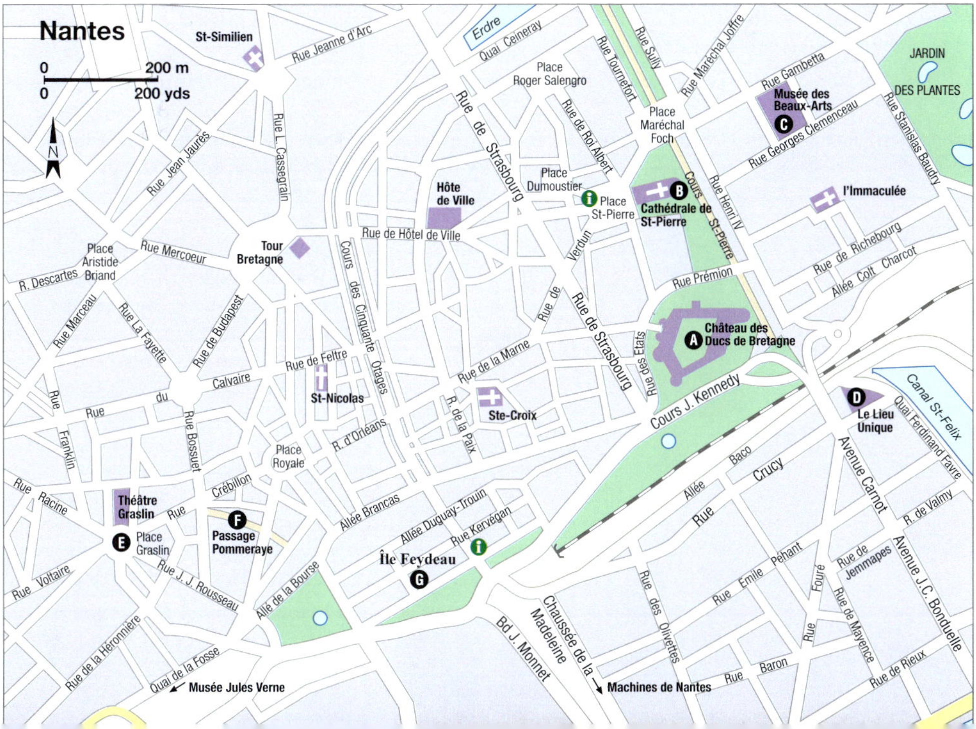

Exhibition at the Musée d'Histoire de Nantes, an enlightening museum of local history sited within the castle.

BELOW: Château des Ducs de Bretagne.

Anne – who married King Louis XII of France in its chapel in 1499, thereby uniting France and Brittany. It was during a stay at the castle in August 1598 that Henry IV issued the crucial Edict of Nantes, granting a measure of tolerance to France's Calvinist protestants – the Huguenots – and ending the fratricidal Wars of Religion. The Revocation of the Edict of Nantes by Louis XIV in 1685 would later cause the Huguenots to decamp en masse to neighbouring Protestant countries.

To the north of the château is the beautiful, austere **Cathédrale de St-Pierre** Ⓑ, built of the same pale stone as Canterbury cathedral. On the other side of the tree-lined avenue of Saint Pierre is the **Musée des Beaux-Arts** Ⓒ (Wed–Sun 10am–6pm; charge), featuring a collection of fine art from the 13th to the 19th centuries.

The old Lu biscuit factory on Quai Ferdinand Favre has been turned into an intriguing arts centre, **Le Lieu Unique** Ⓓ (Tue–Sat 1–7pm, Sun 3–7pm) which includes a theatre, bar, shop and hammam. Best of all, the tower can be ascended for a view of the city from the **gyrorama** (charge), a visitor-operated moving platform.

Roughly following the line of the river through the shopping streets brings you to the **place Royale** and then the **place Graslin** Ⓔ, on which stands a theatre of the same name, and a famous brasserie, La Cigale. Between the place Royale and the river is the **Passage Pommeraye** Ⓕ, an unusual three-storey 19th-century covered shopping arcade linking two streets.

The island of **Île Feydeau** Ⓖ was imperceptibly joined to the rest of the urban area on the river bank in the 1930s. Ship owners and slave merchants built themselves large houses, many of which have decorative wrought-iron balconies and *marcarons*, exotic ornaments featuring grotesque faces.

Downstream is the Île de Nantes where the former shipyards have been turned into the fascinating workshop **Machines de Nantes** (Tue–Fri 10am–6pm, Sat and Sun 10am–7pm; charge). Like something out of a science fiction film, a team of machine buildings inspired by their experience with street theatre work on extraordinary creations under the public gaze. Children love it. The workshop's flagship is a giant engine-driven hydraulic elephant, 12 metres (39ft) high, 8 metres (26ft) wide and weighing 50 tonnes. Travelling at a top speed of a quarter of a kilometre per hour, it takes 49 passengers for a 45-minute ride. Current projects include a three-storey carousel called Marine Worlds, and The Branch of the Heron Tree – a monumental hanging gardens and viewing platform.

The machines certainly owe a debt at least in spirit to the imagination of Jules Verne, who was born in Nantes. The **Musée Jules-Verne** (Wed–Mon 10am–noon, 2–6pm; charge), close to the river just west of the Ile de Nantes, is dedicated to his memory.

The mouth of the Loire

Just before the river meets the Atlantic it passes under the 3.3km (2-mile) length of the cable-stayed **Pont St-Nazaire**, the last and longest of the 165 bridges over the Loire, and the longest bridge in France.

To the northwest of the port of **St-Nazaire**, the coast bulges out in a peninsula, the **Presqu'île de Guérande**, renowned for its production of sea salt. The Guérande salt marshes are worked in the traditional way – mainly by hand, using basic tools. Over winter the saltpans are purged of rainwater and cleaned of algae ready for the harvest which takes place between June and September. Twice a day, the high tide enters the marshes by channels, and gates are opened to allow the water to fill reservoirs. Here heavy impurities, especially sand and clay, are allowed to settle out. Finally, the water is fed into thousands of smaller ponds – *oeillets* – where the wind and sun cause the brine to evaporate, leaving behind crystallised salt. While the water is evaporating, a fine skin of salt crystals known as *fleur de salt* (literally "the flower of the salt"), esteemed by chefs, forms on the surface and is scooped off in the evening before the dew falls. The salt residue at the bottom of the pans is dug out and processed according to its intended use. Table salt must be dried and crushed before being packed.

The handsome, well-preserved town of **Guérande** 32 was fortified at the end of the Middle Ages by the dukes of Brittany, and is still surrounded by a complete set of ramparts connecting six towers and four gateways.

Inland the peninsula is mainly marshy and much of it is conserved under the auspices of the **Parc Naturel Régional de Brière**, created in 1970 in an effort to harmonise the needs of man and nature. The marshes, water channels and wetlands are on the principal west-coast route of bird migration between Africa and northern Europe, and the rich fauna includes such species as the purple heron, black stork, spoonbill and bittern. The traditional crafts of the marshlands are reed gathering and peat cutting.

The peninsula's coast is dubbed the Côte Sauvage (the Wild Coast), a name which belies its sprawling tourist resorts, the largest at **La Baule**.

Coat of arms on the Château des Ducs de Bretagne, Nantes.

BELOW: the Guérande salt marshes.

Jules Verne

As a young boy growing up in the busy port of Nantes, Jules Verne (1828–1905) was inspired by the sight of so many great ships arriving and departing for mysterious destinations. When he was 12 he stowed away on the Coralie, bound for the West Indies, but only got a short way down river before his father caught up with him. As a consequence he is said to have declared "From now on I shall only travel in my imagination."

On leaving home, he became a lawyer and stockbroker, but his heart was always in writing. His first success was *Five Weeks in a Balloon* (1863), set in Africa and written at a time when aeronautics was still in its infancy. *A Journey to the Centre of the Earth* (1864) brought him further fame. In *Twenty-thousand Leagues Under the Sea* (1870) he returned to his nautical roots, envisaging a submarine, the Nautilus, powered by electricity several years before the first successful electric motor had been perfected. *Around the World in Eighty Days* (1873) describes an attempt to circumnavigate the globe in what was then an impossibly short time. He wrote many more books after these classics, some of them published posthumously, but his later works are less well known.

Verne is often called the father of science fiction, and while it is true that he was fascinated by the advance of scientific knowledge, above all he was a writer of good adventure stories.

During the repression after the Vendée uprising, it is said that a favourite form of execution was a "republican marriage" in which a naked man and naked woman were tied to each other and drowned in the Loire.

The Vendée

South of the Loire is the department of the Vendée, one of the less well-known regions of France. Economically dependent on farming, fishing and tourism, it has little to distinguish it except that large stretches of its coastline have been saved from development. Its principal significance in mainstream French history took place in 1793, when an uprising of Royalists and conservative peasants challenged the central Revolutionary government in Paris and was put down with brutality and bloodshed. This traditionalist corner of rural France had not welcomed the overthrow of the Ancien Regime in 1799. It was staunchly Catholic and its peasantry did not consider itself in conflict with the local nobility. The introduction of conscription finally provoked the Vendeans to take up arms and form an army. Initially they had some success, taking Thouars, Parthenay, Fontenay and Saumur, but a siege of Nantes failed. The rebels were defeated in battle first at Cholet on 17 October, and then, decisively, at Savenay on 23 December. Resistance continued in the Vendée after this, but on a smaller, less organised, scale that never seriously challenged the authority of Paris.

Along the Vendée coast are several modest-sized resorts and two interesting islands. **Noirmoutier** ❸❸ is a tidal island at the mouth of the Baie de Bourgneuf, linked to the mainland by a main road across a bridge: a more appealing short cut is to take the 4.5km (3-mile) causeway, the Passage du Gois (the D948), which is useable for a few hours a day at low tide – a sign indicates when it is safe to cross.

Smaller and further offshore is the **Île d'Yeu** ❸❹, accessed by ferry from Fromentine, Saint-Giles-Croix-de-Vie and Les Sables-d'Olonne in summer. Its most famous – or infamous – inhabitant was sent here against his own volition, never to return. After the war, the leader of the Vichy regime, Marshal Pétain, was tried for collaboration, cashiered, stripped of his rank and sentenced to death. This was commuted to life imprisonment on the grounds of age and his heroic service in World War I. In November 1945 he was sent

BELOW: Passage du Gois causeway at low tide.

to the Citadel or Forte de Pierre Levée on the Île d'Yeu where he remained until his death on 23 July 1951. He is buried in a cemetery near the castle, although there has been a campaign to move his remains to Verdun.

History shows

The wooded estate around the remains of a 15th-century château near Les Epesses, in the eastern Vendée has been turned into one of France's largest theme parks, the **Grand Parc du Puy du Fou** ㉟ (Apr–Sept 10am–7pm, later in peak summer months). The theme here is the history of the Vendée, brought to life in a replica medieval village, 18th-century hamlet and town from the 1900s. The emphasis is on spectator shows, which include a Roman chariot race, a Viking raid and the storming of a castle. All this culminates in the *son-et-lumière* extravaganza of Cinéscénie (June–Sept, Fri and Sat; separate reservation and charge), billed as "the biggest nighttime show in the world". A cast of 1,200 local actors in 6,000 costumes presents the history of the Vendée in an hour and forty minutes on a vast open-air stage.

Green Venice

The beautiful, man-made marshlands of the **Marais Poitevin** ㊱, or Venise Verte (Green Venice), extend across the southern reaches of the Vendée. In the 11th century, monks decided to tame what was then a natural expanse of water at the mouth of the River Sèvre Niortaise by building canals, fisheries, dykes, locks, channels and water mills. In the 17th century, Dutch engineers were brought in to drain the land further, and the present landscape developed: an agreeable labyrinth of still-flowing green channels and high banks under a canopy of poplar and oak. The best way to explore the Marais is by traditional flat-bottomed boat. Other good ways to get around are on foot, by bicycle or on horseback.

Arçais and **Coulon** are the best towns to use as a base for a tour. Both have companies offering bicycles and rowing boats for hire. Another good way to travel is on board a traditional wooden punt boat steered by an oarsman-guide. For more information see www.marais-poitevin.com or www.parc-marais-poitevin.fr. ❑

The windmill at Jard sur Mer in the Vendée.

BELOW LEFT: exploring the Marais Poitevin.

The Tour de France

The Vendée has been chosen as the starting point of the 2011 Tour de France, which will attract world attention for at least a brief while. Every year in July a razzmatazz of advertising and tourist hype sweeps through rural France. The route changes every year…France's greatest sporting event takes up three weeks in July and receives saturation media coverage with action followed live by cameras mounted on motorbikes and on-board helicopters. The route around the country varies but always culminates in a showy ride down the Champs Élysées on the last day, by which time the overall winner, wearing a yellow jersey, has usually been decided. Most attention is focused on big-name riders, but the Tour de France is a contest of teams, not just individuals. Each of the 20-odd daily stages concentrates on one of three different tests: mountain climbing, flat racing, or pedalling against the clock in a time trial. The race is unashamedly commercial with an advertising "caravan" of vehicles preceding the cyclists, blasting sponsors' messages to the captive crowds lining the route.

RESTAURANT - PIZZERIA - SALON DE

THE WEST

Stunning beaches and seascapes, luxuriant green countryside and a dense web of historical resonances: Normandy and Brittany are two of France's most enjoyable regions

France's northwest contains two of its most distinctive and beautiful regions, taking the visitor from the domesticated countryside of central France to much wilder landscapes on the Atlantic coast. Settled by Celts and the descendants of Vikings, Normandy and Brittany have played special roles in French history and each has a very rich, idiosyncratic character.

Normandy is exceptionally rich in historical associations with the English-speaking world, from the castles and abbeys built by the Anglo-Norman dukes and the Bayeux Tapestry to the battlefields of World War II. The Norman landscape can seem impossibly green and lush, and inspired artists such as Monet. Rural Normandy is a land of apples and cows, producing the most refined ciders, its own great speciality, calvados, and world-renowned cheeses. By way of contrast are the lively city of Rouen, with its majestic Gothic architecture, buzzing resorts like Trouville and Deauville, and easy-going beach towns like those of the Cotentin peninsula, as well as the spellbinding Mont-St-Michel.

Around the long granite spur of Celtic Brittany, the coastline is so consistently spectacular, from the bizarre rock formations of the Côte de Granit Rose to the massive cliffs and sweeping views of the Pointe de Raz and the idyllic "inland sea" of the Golfe du Morbihan, that one can run the risk of getting blasé about each stunning vista. This is an ancient land, and around Carnac in the south – and to a lesser extent across Brittany as a whole – there is one of the largest and most spectacular concentrations of Stone Age standing stones and other monuments in Europe.

Brittany's historic Celtic culture also gives the country a special character, reflected in the folklore attached to the landscape and the traditional music and dance seen at its many festivals. Its cuisine includes fabulous seafood, as well as the omnipresent Breton crêpes and galettes. It has highly idiosyncratic traditional architecture, in the strange 16th-century parish closes of Finistère or the fairy-tale streets of small Breton towns. Its coastal cities and towns, such as St-Malo or Douarnenez, have strong character, and a strong tang of the sea. ❑

PRECEDING PAGES: Mont-St-Michel. **LEFT:** Josselin, a typical town of rural Brittany. **TOP:** chambres d'hôtes are often a better, more characterful choice than hotels in Normandy and Brittany. **ABOVE LEFT:** Breton costume.

NORMANDY

Sophisticated, yet often rustic, Normandy has an intense, emotive history, and a landscape of stunning, green abundance

Main attractions
- ROUEN
- ETRETAT
- FÉCAMP
- DIEPPE
- GIVERNY
- HONFLEUR
- TROUVILLE-DEAUVILLE
- PAYS D'AUGE
- BAYEUX
- D-DAY BEACHES
- COTENTIN COAST
- MONT ST-MICHEL

Land of apples, cider, cream and cheese, a sumptuous countryside of a thousand shades of green, Normandy was also the home of ferocious warriors who conquered England and carved out kingdoms for themselves in Italy. Now famous as the great battleground of 1944, this was also the region that inspired the Impressionist painters and writers such as Flaubert and Maupassant. Its architectural heritage, culminating in the magic mountain of Mont-St-Michel, is stunning, and its coastline runs from the neat chic of Deauville to the wild and windblown dunes of the Cotentin peninsula.

Rouen, the half-timbered survivor

Rouen ❶ was founded at a natural crossing point over the Seine, a broad gap in the steep chalk cliffs that line the river to the east and west. As Rotomagus, it grew into one of the most important cities of Roman Gaul. The Vikings attacked and seized it in the 9th century, and then, after they settled down and became the Normans, made it the first capital of their Duchy, in 911; in the next century, William the Conqueror paid more attention to his own preferred city of Caen, but after the French Crown seized control of Normandy in 1204, Rouen was restored as the region's centre of government and trade. Despite its distance from the sea, it continues to be a river port to this day.

The Anglo-Norman Dukes, French monarchs and the Church all built lavishly in Rouen, which has left the city with an extraordinary range of medieval architecture. It expanded particularly after the Hundred Years War, when new wealth from the textile and river trade was reflected in the creation of major buildings in the extravagantly intricate late Gothic Flamboyant style, many by a local architect-mason, Rolland le Roux.

LEFT: cliffs at Etretat. **RIGHT:** remains of the Mulberry artificial harbour, Arromanches.

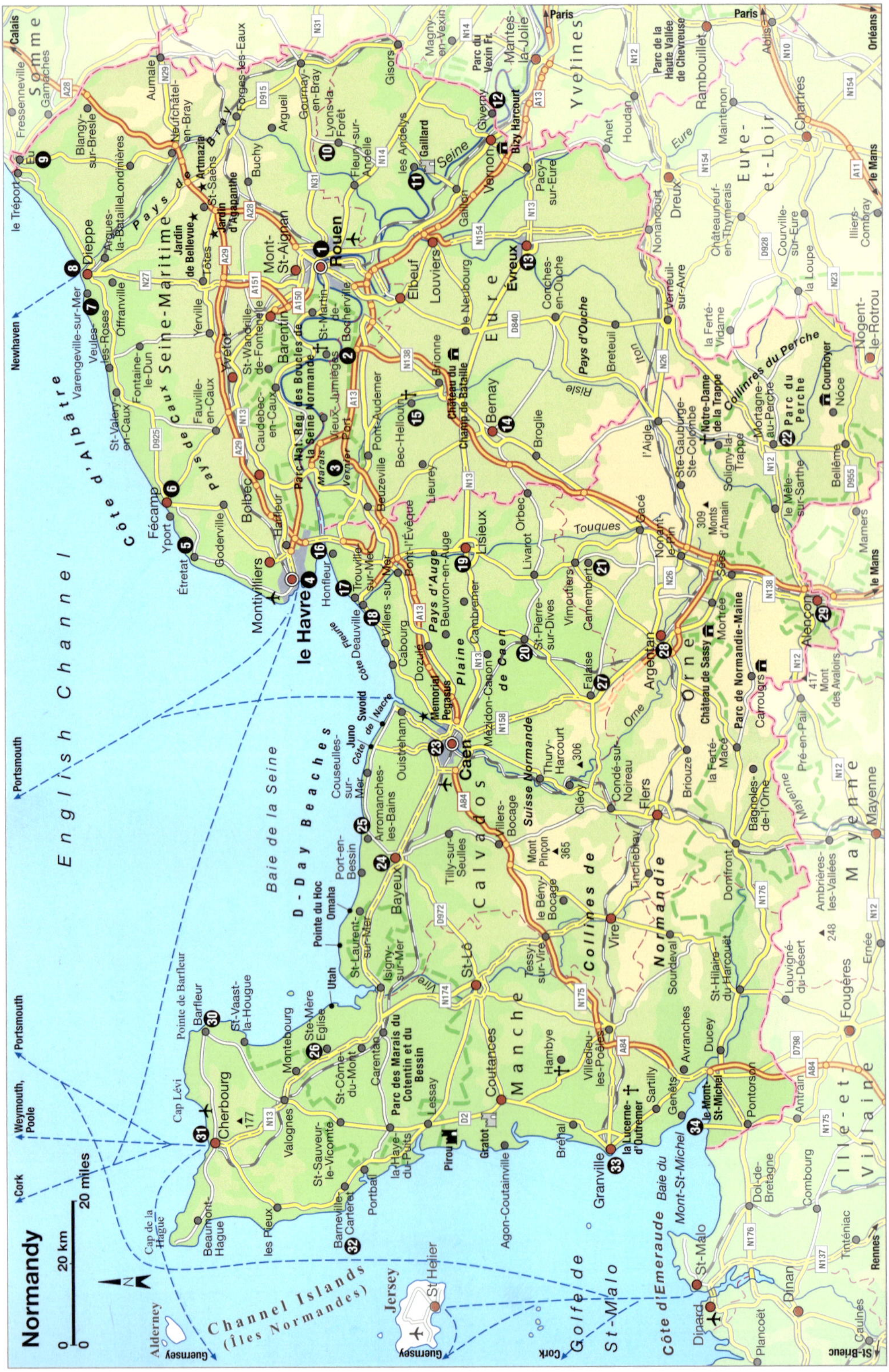
Normandy
0 20 km
0 20 miles
N
English Channel
Baie de la Seine
D-Day Beaches
Channel Islands (Îles Normandes)
Golfe de St-Malo
Baie du Mont-St-Michel
Côte d'Emeraude
Côte d'Albâtre
Côte de Nacre
Côte Fleurie
Pays de Caux
Pays de Bray
Pays d'Auge
Pays d'Ouche
Plaine de Caen
Suisse Normande
Collines de Normandie
Collines du Perche
Seine-Maritime
Eure
Calvados
Manche
Orne
Somme
Yvelines
Eure-et-Loir
Mayenne
Ille-et-Vilaine
Alderney
Guernsey
Jersey
St Helier
Newhaven
Portsmouth
Weymouth, Poole
Cork
Calais
Paris
Orléans
le Mans
Rennes
St-Brieuc
Rouen
le Havre
Caen
Cherbourg
Dieppe
Fécamp
Étretat
Honfleur
Deauville
Trouville-sur-Mer
Lisieux
Bayeux
St-Lô
Coutances
Granville
Avranches
le Mont-St-Michel
St-Malo
Dinard
Dinan
Fougères
Vire
Flers
Argentan
Falaise
Alençon
Évreux
Vernon
Giverny
les Andelys
Louviers
Elbeuf
Bernay
Dreux
Chartres
Rambouillet
Mantes-la-Jolie
Gisors
Forges-les-Eaux
Neufchâtel-en-Bray
Eu
le Tréport
Yvetot
Bolbec
Montivilliers
Cabourg
Ouistreham
Arromanches-les-Bains
Port-en-Bessin
Omaha
Utah
Juno
Sword
Pointe du Hoc
Barfleur
St-Vaast-la-Hougue
Ste-Mère-Église
Valognes
Carentan
Pont-l'Évêque
Pont-Audemer
Jumièges
Mortagne-au-Perche
Nogent-le-Rotrou
Domfront
Bagnoles-de-l'Orne
Villedieu-les-Poêles
Parc des Marais du Cotentin et du Bessin
Parc Nat. Reg. des Boucles de la Seine Normande
Parc de Normandie-Maine
Parc du Perche
Parc du Vexin Fr.
Parc de la Haute Vallée de Chevreuse
Memorial Pegasus

Old Rouen had the misfortune to be battered and burnt twice in World War II, in 1940 and 1944, and restoration was long and difficult. Nevertheless, in among plainer post-war architecture it retains more of its old *maisons de pans de bois*, half-timbered houses, original or restored, than virtually any other large city in Europe, making a night-time walk especially atmospheric.

City sights

Monet painted the west front of the **Cathédrale Notre-Dame** Ⓐ over 30 times, catching the shifts of light at different times of day (a sign marks the site of the building where he worked, destroyed in World War II). It is a classic medieval accumulation of history in stone. On the left, most of the **Tour St-Romain** survives from an earlier Norman-Romanesque cathedral, built around the 1150s; on the right the **Tour du Beurre** (Butter Tower) is elegant 15th-century Gothic, while the stunningly elaborate central portal was added from 1509–21 by architect Rolland le Roux. Among the tombs inside are those of Rollo, the Viking chief who founded the Duchy of Normandy in the early 10th century, and the heart of Richard the Lionheart.

The cathedral also shows the marks of bomb damage in its carvings, and the clear windows mixed in among its superb 13th-century stained glass.

Opposite the cathedral, the 1509 **Hôtel des Finances**, now the **tourist office**, incorporates Italian Renaissance influence and is one of Rouen's most attractive old buildings. Close by, lovely rue St-Romain leads to **St-Maclou** Ⓑ, second of Rouen's three great Gothic temples, dedicated to the same saint as the city of St-Malo, and with a fabulous *Flamboyant* portal. A narrow passageway off rue Martainville leads into the **Aître St-Maclou** Ⓒ, a broad half-timbered courtyard carved with skulls and skeletons, as it was first created as a plague cemetery. Curiously, it now serves as an art school.

More old alleys lead to the huge abbey church of **St-Ouen** Ⓓ, third in the "trinity" and a glorious example of earlier, more restrained *Rayonnant* Gothic. Its richly coloured, mostly 16th-century, stained glass had been put into storage before 1940, and so survived.

Broad rue Jean Lecanuet leads to the **Musée des Beaux-Arts** Ⓔ (Wed–Mon 10am–6pm; charge, free under-26s and first Sun of each month), an impressive collection that includes a fine display of the Impressionists (including, of course, several Monets) as well as major works by Caravaggio, Velázquez, Géricault and others, including local artistic revolutionary Marcel Duchamp. Around it are two other museums showcasing ceramics and applied arts.

To the south, streets such as rue Ganterie form Rouen's main shopping centre, with attractive small food- and fashion shops. In amongst them on the rue aux Juifs (Jews' Street) is the magnificent **Palais de Justice**, built as the Exchequer and *Parlement* of Normandy by Le Roux from 1499–1526 and one of the largest non-religious *Flamboyant* buildings in France. Part of a 12th-

The Pont Gustave Flaubert is an impressive 86-metre vertical lift bridge. It is the last crossing in Rouen before the river flows into the sea, enabling traffic to bypass the city centre.

BELOW: interior staircase, Rouen cathedral.

Colombiers, dovecotes or pigeon lofts, were a major sign of status in medieval and Renaissance Normandy, since only aristocrats were allowed to have this important source of meat and fertiliser. They became increasingly elaborate as lords competed to show off their wealth, and it was no surprise that the non-noble ex-pirate Jehan d'Ango, having been given a special exception to have one, went on to build the largest in France at his Manoir d'Ango.

century synagogue has been discovered underneath the building (tours Tue 3pm only, check with tourist office).

Above a parallel street is a symbol of Rouen, the **Gros Horloge** **F**, a sumptuously ornate Renaissance clock built as a bridge across the street in the 1520s, and once again in working order following delicate restoration. The historic **place du Vieux Marché** **G**, where Joan of Arc was burnt at the stake in 1431, is now buzzing with cafés. The radically modern 1970s church of **Jeanne d'Arc**, built to replace the former, medieval, church destroyed in the war, is an effective memorial.

Down river

Over 100km (62 miles) from the sea, Rouen is the last point upriver on the Seine open to ocean-going shipping. In spite of this occasional traffic – mostly heavy-duty barges – this stretch of water generally appears very leisurely, making its way through giant meanders known as *bouclés* (curls). The banks are lined with wooded hills, chalk cliffs and somnolescent villages. At various points tiny river ferries called *bacs* link up minor roads, the most famous at lovely **La Bouille**, with riverside restaurants that fill up at weekends. The only bridges below Rouen are three giants, the **Pont de Brotonne**, **Pont de Tancarville** and the immense, arching **Pont de Normandie** (tolls are charged for the last two).

The Vikings sailed up the Seine to carve out their new home, and its valley has always been a highway. Testimony to its medieval importance are the three great abbeys along the north bank, each in an exquisite setting. The abbey church of **St-Georges-de-Boscherville** (Apr–Oct 9am–6.30pm; Nov–Mar 2–5pm; charge) in **St-Martin-de-Boscherville**, built between 1113 and 1140, is one of the finest works of pure Norman Romanesque architecture: lofty, white and flooded with light, and remarkably intact. More celebrated is **Jumièges** **2** (mid-Apr–mid-Sept 9.30am–6.30pm, mid-Sept–mid-Apr 9.30am–1.30pm, 2.30–5.30pm; charge). Founded in 654, the abbey was sacked by the Vikings, but rebuilt by the Normans themselves on a far larger scale in the 11th century.

BELOW: St-Valéry-en-Caux.

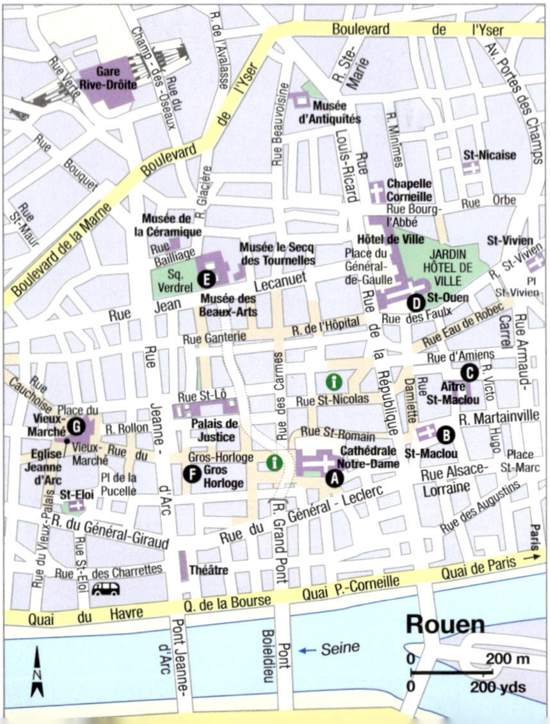

Dissolved after the Revolution, it's now a majestic ruin, but its immense size is still apparent, with two churches. Every Saturday in July and August the ruins are lit up in an impressive *son et lumière* (check for times; charge).

St-Wandrille-de-Fontenelle (usually 5.30am–1pm, 2–9pm; guided tours available, charge), in a Monet landscape near Caudebec-en-Caux, still performs its original function, since a community of Benedictine monks returned to the abbey in 1931. Visitors are free to wander around the ruined Gothic church and 17th-century buildings, and attend services in the chapel, a former barn, with Gregorian chant.

Beyond the next big bend in the Seine, close to the Tancarville bridge, a silent expanse of marshland extends along the south bank, the **Marais Vernier** ❸. Loved by walkers, cyclists and birdwatchers, the *marais* is also known for its tumbledown thatch-roofed cottages called *chaumières*, some of the prettiest of which are in **Le Vieux-Port**.

In the 1900s Raoul Dufy frequently painted his home city of **Le Havre** ❹, France's largest Atlantic port, at a time when its boulevards were often compared to those of Paris. Physically, very little of this city survives; Le Havre was devastated in September 1944, when British and Canadian forces took the port rapidly with maximum force, including massive bombing. Post-war, the adventurous decision was made not to attempt restoration but to entrust the "re-creation" of Le Havre to modernist architect Auguste Perret, a long-time proponent of the use of concrete. The result is a city of long wide avenues, massive concrete edifices – such as Perret's astonishing skyscraper church of **St-Joseph** – and radical creations like Brazilian architect Oscar Niemeyer's 1970s **Espace Niemeyer** square and cultural centre. Lovers of modern architecture delight in Le Havre, while most others detest it. Old Norman quaintness can still be found in the suburb of **Harfleur**, the original rivermouth port (and as such attacked by Henry V of England in 1415), before King François I decreed that a much larger harbour of Le Havre be created in 1517.

Clusters of wind turbines dot the farmland around north Normandy.

BELOW: the Bassin du Commerce dock, Le Havre.

Beach huts at the small beach of Yport.

One of France's foremost art museums, the **Musée Malraux** (Wed–Fri, Mon 11am–6pm, Sat–Sun 11am–7pm; charge), by Le Havre waterfront, is exceptionally strong on Impressionists and Post-Impressionists, with wonderful collections of artists born or resident in Le Havre (Monet, Dufy, Boudin and others).

The Alabaster Coast

A near-continuous line of white chalk cliffs runs northeast from Le Havre to Normandy's border at the River Bresle, the *Côte d'Albâtre* or Alabaster Coast. Harbours appear in gashes in the cliffs, with pebble beaches. Inland, the limestone plateau of the Caux is broad, green and open, except for clumps of trees planted as barriers against the Atlantic wind. Where village or inlets are sheltered, though, they can be surprisingly lush, with mild microclimates. This coast is equally celebrated for its limpid light, treasured by the Impressionist painters.

The most often-painted cliffs in all France are at **Etretat** ❺, especially the **Falaise d'Aval** to the west, with its rock arch and *Aiguille* (needle), associated above all with Monet. Walks along them and the **Falaise d'Amont** to the east are unmissable towards sunset. Etretat sits in a particularly deep, protected coastal cleft, and its climate was recommended as healthy to 19th-century high society. Russian aristocrats and a deposed Queen of Spain stayed here, and the valley filled with elaborate villas, all pinnacles and intimate gardens, which give the town an enjoyably whimsical feel despite the summer crowds.

Nearby **Yport** is a charming miniature harbour that also attracted many painters. **Fécamp** ❻ (15km/9miles east of Etretat), with its harbour mouth between towering cliffs, is a fascinating mix of charm, eccentricity and grittiness. Fécamp Abbey, founded in 1001 around a shrine said to hold some of the Precious Blood of Christ, was one of Normandy's largest, and William the Conqueror celebrated his conquest of England here in 1067. The Gothic abbey church or **Abbatiale de la Trinité** is magnificent, with the Precious Blood in a 1510 reliquary. Fécamp later became a deep-sea fishing port, and a

BELOW: Etretat.

Alexander the Great

Alexander Le Grand, creator of Bénédictine liqueur, was both a great fantasist and a founder of modern marketing. The son of a Fécamp wine merchant, he was looking through some old papers acquired by his grandfather when Fécamp Abbey was dissolved during the Revolution, and found a recipe for a herbal liqueur said to have been made by the monks since 1510. Rather than simply refining it and selling it in the family shop, Le Grand created a prestige image for his new product, emphasising its roots in a (possibly fictitious) monastic past, and exporting it to Britain and America. It was a huge success. He also decided that his distillery, the centrepiece of his advertising, should not be some dull factory but a kind of neo-Gothic palace, which purchasers were encouraged to think was some sort of continuation of the ancient abbey.

Le Grand appears to have believed some of his own propaganda. Part of the Palais is a museum filled with his own extraordinary collections of Renaissance wooden carvings, medieval paintings, illuminated manuscripts, antique doorlocks and more. When the first Palais Bénédictine burnt down in 1892, he promptly rebuilt it on a larger scale. Local architect Camille Albert was encouraged to use the finest materials and a wild mix of styles – Gothic, Renaissance, Baroque, Art Nouveau. Le Grand never saw it at its best, dying in 1898 two years before its completion.

seafront museum recalls its seamen's lives (due to transfer to a new venue by the harbour; check with tourist office for details). Fécamp also became a modest resort in the later 19th century, with promenade and shingle beach.

Fécamp's unique feature is the neo-Gothic wonderland of the **Palais Bénédictine** (tours daily July–Aug 10am–7pm; Apr–June, Sept–Oct 10am–1pm, 2–6.30pm; Feb–Mar, Nov–Dec 10.30am–12.45pm, 2–6pm; charge), the home of Bénédictine liqueur *(see panel, below left)*. As well as a sumptuous private museum, this is still a working distillery, and very enjoyable tours end with tastings in the shop.

The fishing and yachting harbour of **St-Valery-en-Caux** suffered heavy war damage in June 1940. Tucked away to the west is impossibly pretty **Veules-les-Roses**, on "the smallest river in France", which runs very fast for under a kilometre, lined by tiny, half-timbered water mills. The effect is somewhat like that of a model village.

The coast rises to discreetly lovely **Varengeville-sur-Mer** ❼, where villas spread among the woods. Cubist artist Georges Braque lived here, designing exquisite stained glass for the 12th-century clifftop church, beside which he is buried. There are also two fascinating house-and-garden combinations. The 1530s **Manoir d'Ango** (Apr–Sept daily 10am–noon, 2–6pm; Oct Sat–Sun only; charge) is a mix of rustic manor and Renaissance château, built for Dieppe's pirate-prince Jehan Ango *(see below)*; the **Bois des Moutiers** (tel: 02 35 85 10 02; gardens mid-Mar–mid-Nov daily 10am–noon, 2–6pm, house tours by appointment; charge) was built in 1898 by English architect Edwin Lutyens for anglophile banker Guillaume Mallet, with gardens by Gertrude Jekyll. Below Varengeville, the beach at **Pourville** was another spot loved by Monet.

Dieppe and Le Tréport

The name **Dieppe** ❽ comes from the same Norse word as English "deep", and its harbour is the best on this coast. In the 16th century its seamen, like those of St-Malo *(see p283)*, marauded on the high seas as privateers, notably one Jehan (or Jean) Ango, who raided

Writer Guy de Maupassant was born in the château of Miromesnil, just south of Dieppe, in 1850. This was partly by accident, as his father rented several châteaux around the area to keep up an image of grand living.

BELOW: the pebble beach at St-Valéry-en-Caux.

An Avenue Verte *cycle and walking track runs along a former rail line from Dieppe to Forges-les-Eaux, through beautiful stretches of Bray countryside. This forms part of a projected cycleway all the way between Paris and London. For information see www.voievertes.com.*

Brazil and became a local hero by sharing out much of his wealth in his home town; later Dieppe became France's first seaside resort, and a contact point between the French and British art worlds. It has never lost its blend of seaport tanginess and raffishness.

Dieppe's unusually broad seafront was damaged by the Dieppe Raid of August 1942, when thousands of Canadian troops were lost in an "experiment" at taking a Channel port by direct assault, and by unimaginative post-war reconstruction. Behind it, however, the old town is largely intact. The old port is right in the centre, with cafés and seafood restaurants all along **Quai Henri IV**. Streets west of the harbour contain superb food and wine shops, and on Saturdays a fabulous **market** fills the squares beneath the lordly Gothic church of **St-Jacques**. One essential site of Dieppe is the grand **Café des Tribunaux**, where Oscar Wilde spent many hours when he took refuge near Dieppe after his release from prison in 1897. The **Château-Musée** (June–Sept daily 10am–noon, 2–6pm, Oct–May Wed–Mon 10am–noon, 2–5pm; charge) in the brooding 14th-century keep above the town has work by artists associated with Dieppe – Pissarro, Braque, Walter Sickert – but also commemorates its maritime past, especially with an astonishing collection of carved ivories, a traditional craft of Dieppe seamen.

Le Tréport, 30km (19 miles) further northeast, is a busy fishing port and weekend seaside town, with great-value seafood restaurants. Just inland, charming **Eu** ❾ offers a wealth of unusual historical associations. Its majestic Gothic **Collégiale** church guards the tomb of the Irish Saint Laurence O'Toole, who died here in 1180 on a futile quest to persuade Henry II of England and Normandy to halt the invasion of Ireland. In the 1570s the Catholic leader the Duke of Guise built just one wing of a projected vast Renaissance château; 250 years later this was the favourite home of Louis-Philippe of Orléans, who became king of France in 1830, and welcomed Queen Victoria and Prince Albert here in 1843. Now officially known as the **Château-Musée Louis-Philippe** (Mar–Oct Wed–Thur, Sat–Mon 10am–noon, 2–6pm; Fri 2–6pm; charge), the rambling mansion is a delightful house of surprises.

BELOW: Place du Marché, Lyons-la-Forêt.

The Pays de Bray

Only a little south of Dieppe and Eu is the **Pays de Bray**, one of those corners of France that despite their proximity to cities and highways remain deeply, unalterably rural. A landscape of soft, deep-green valleys, munching cows, and old brick farms with low-hanging roofs, this is the home of the oldest and, to some, finest of Normandy cheeses, Neufchâtel. Small towns such as **Neufchâtel-en-Bray** and **St-Saëns** unfussily go about their business as local markets, and it's enjoyable to wander in no particular direction, seeking out local produce. North of St-Saëns are the beech woods of **Forêt d'Eawy**, with beautiful tracks for riding and walking.

There are also more remarkable gardens, notably near St-Saëns. The **Jardins de Bellevue** (10am–6pm; charge) at Beaumont-le-Hareng has exotic plants from around the world, while the **Jardin d'Agapanthe** (Apr–Oct Thur–Tue 2–7pm; charge) near Grigneuseville is a ravishing display mainly of agapanthus.**Artmazia** (May–Aug daily 2.30–6.30pm; Sept Sat–Sun 2.30–6.30pm; charge) outside Massy is a garden and "art maze" created by British artist Geoff Troll, with lots of fun things for kids.

To the south the beech trees become denser again into the **Forêt de Lyons**, once a hunting reserve of the Norman dukes. At its heart is another of France's great beauties, **Lyons-la-Forêt** ⑩, with a famous village square of contrasting black-and-white Norman half-timbering. In 1135 Henry I of Normandy and England died in Lyons castle – demolished after the Revolution – supposedly due to eating too many lampreys or river eels. Crowded on some weekends, Lyons has delightful places to stay and eat, and makes a great base for exploring the forest on foot, horseback or by bike.

Henry I also built much of the **Château** (tours Apr–Sept Wed–Mon 10–11am, 2pm, 3.30pm, 5pm; Feb–Mar, Oct–Nov Sat–Sun 10.30am, 2.30pm, 4pm; charge) at **Gisors** on Normandy's eastern edge, now one of the most intact Norman castles. More awe-inspiring, however, is the ruined **Château-Gaillard** (free access to site; keep Mar–Nov Wed–Mon 10am–1pm, 2–6pm; charge), on a mighty crag with a breathtaking view over the Seine valley above **Les Andelys** ⑪. It was built in just one year, 1196–7, by Richard the Lionheart to keep King Philippe Auguste of France out of Normandy. It did so while Richard was alive, but after he was succeeded by his brother John a fresh French siege in 1204 took Château-Gaillard, and brought the rule of the Anglo-Norman kings over Normandy to an end. Below it, the charming riverside quarter of **Le Petit Andely** has restaurant terraces with beautiful views of the Seine.

Château-Gaillard, Richard the Lionheart's stronghold at Les Andelys.

Giverny

A road beside the river leads to the most renowned of all Normandy's gardens, at **Giverny** ⑫, where Claude Monet lived

BELOW: *Garden path at Giverny*, by Claude Monet, 1902.

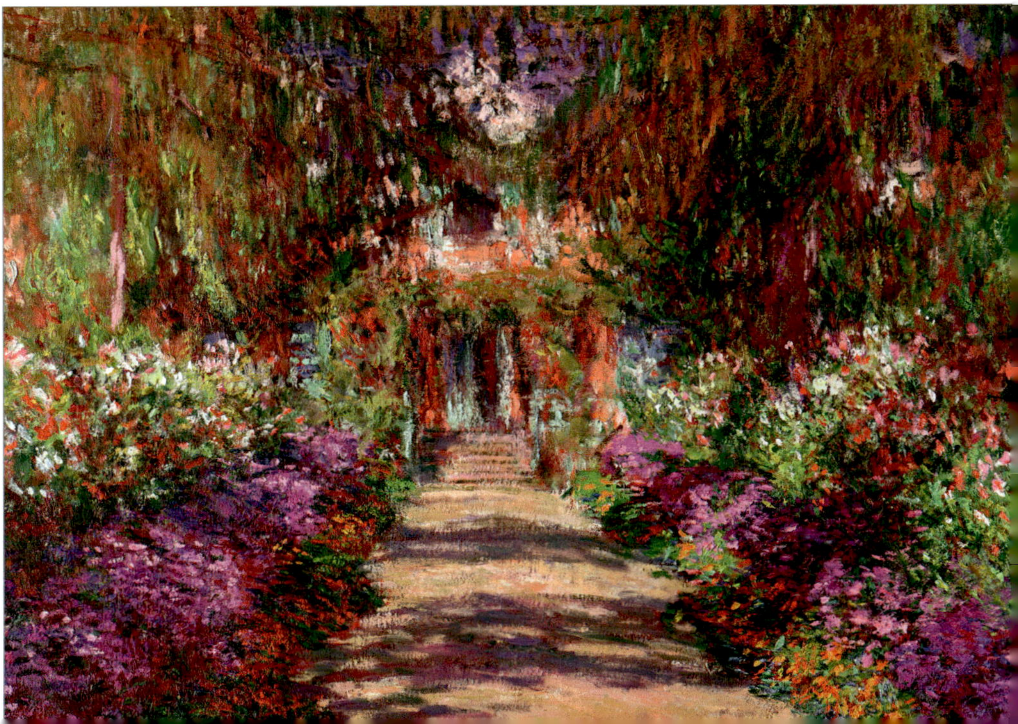

The town of Bernay survived largely unscathed from World War II.

from 1883 until his death in 1926. His wonderfully warm family house and very personal garden are beautifully maintained as the **Fondation Claude Monet** (Apr–Oct daily 9.30am–6pm; charge). Monet's love of light and nature are apparent throughout, in the Japanese pond where he painted his *Nymphéas* or waterlily pictures, in the bright yellow kitchen and blue dining room, and in his stunning collection of Japanese prints. Giverny receives huge numbers of visitors (try to avoid visiting at midday and at weekends) but the gardens with their changing swathes of colour are still ravishing. Further along the main street are the **Musée des Impressionismes** (Apr–Oct daily 10am–6pm; charge), which presents exhibitions on Impressionism and related art, and the churchyard where the Monet family is buried. Giverny is a very seasonal attraction; when the Monet house is closed from November to March, it scarcely stirs.

The Eure and the Risle

Still standing beside the busy Seine bridge at **Vernon** are three arches of a 12th-century equivalent, topped by a mill cottage, the **Vieux Moulin**. On the hill west of the town is the **Château de Bizy** (Apr–Oct Tue–Sun 10am–noon, 2–6pm; Mar Sat–Sun 2–5pm; charge), a "little Versailles" built in 1741 by the fashionable architect Constant d'Ivry for one of Louis XV's ministers, the Duc de Belle-Isle.

Running semi-parallel to the main river, the Eure is a picturesque mini-Seine valley, a placid stretch of water popular for fishing and gentle boating. Much of **Evreux** ⓭, 70km (43 miles) south of Rouen, was rebuilt after 1945, but its **Cathedral** was remarkably undamaged, with a magnificent *Flamboyant* Gothic facade added to a 12th-century Norman nave, and stunning early stained glass. The **Musée d'Evreux** (Tue–Sun 10am–noon, 2–6pm; charge), in the medieval Bishop's Palace, has an exceptional array of local Gallo-Roman relics.

West of Evreux, the heart of the Eure *département* is a relatively little-visited stretch of bucolic Norman countryside, with engaging towns such as **Conches-en-Ouche**, dominated by a romantically crumbling ruined castle. **Bernay**

BELOW: recumbent cows in a field near Honfleur.

⓮ was fortunate in the Norman lottery of 1944; it escaped serious bombing, and so remains one of the region's most stunning ensembles of half-timbered town-houses, at their prettiest near the River Charentonne and its tributaries. The abbey church of **Notre-Dame**, with its exhilaratingly lofty arches, is one of the oldest Norman Romanesque churches, begun in 1017, while the former abbey buildings contain the **Musée des Beaux-Arts** (Tue–Sun June–Sept 11am–6pm; Oct–May 2–5.30pm; charge), with a surprisingly varied art collection and fine Rouen porcelain. Bernay's old streets host engaging small antique and food shops, and a vibrant market on Saturdays.

The Charentonne runs into the Risle, another of Normandy's historic river-thoroughfares. Charming little **Brionne** once dominated the valley, due to its hilltop castle, now a ruin. Nearby are two mostly intact but contrasting *châteaux*. The **Château du Champ de Bataille** (July–Aug daily 10am–6pm; May–June, Sept daily 2–6pm; Apr, Oct Sat–Sun 2–6pm; charge) is a palace built in the grand manner in the 1650s for a Marquis banished from Paris. Moreover, in 1992 it was acquired by theatre designer Jacques Garcia, who has spent fortunes on restoring the château, filling it with sumptuous period furnishings and re-creating huge Le Notre-style gardens.

The **Domaine d'Harcourt** (Jun–Sept daily 10.30am–6.30pm; Mar–May, Oct–Nov Wed–Mon 2–6pm; charge), between Brionne and Le Neubourg, takes you back to the Middle Ages again with a classic Norman castle of moat, keep and outer bailey begun around 1025 for the Harcourt clan, one of whom fought with William the Conqueror in 1066. Exhibits in the keep trace the history of the Harcourts, and around the castle there is a delightful arboretum.

In a setting of fabulous lushness is the one-time intellectual hub of the Norman empire, the abbey of **Le Bec-Hellouin** ⓯. Founded in 1039, it gained prominence due to the originally Italian scholar Lanfranc, whom William the Conqueror appointed as his first Archbishop of Canterbury. Only one Gothic tower survives of the medieval abbey, but since 1948 the 18th-century buildings have again housed a community of monks. Visitors are free to walk around the grounds, buy articles made by the monks in the shop and attend services, and guided tours are also available (Wed–Mon, check for times, tel: 02 32 43 72 60). Beside it, Le Bec-Hellouin village is a gorgeous collection of flower-bedecked half-timbered houses.

The Risle rolls down to attractive **Pont-Audemer**, not far from the Seine. The town didn't escape war damage but still has old former leather-tanners' houses along the little streams in the centre, and plenty of lively character. Its Monday and Friday markets are among the area's biggest.

Seaside chic

A different Normandy appears in the *Côte Fleurie*, the "Flowery Coast", Parisians' favourite quick seaside escape for over 150 years. At its eastern end is **Honfleur** ⓰, an old port which has

Land-yachting is a popular sport on Normandy's broad, sandy beaches.

BELOW: Quai Ste-Catherine, Honfleur.

The Invention of the French Seaside

Belle Epoque villas, grand hotels, promenades and seafood brasseries have been assembled over the years to create a genteel but seductive cocktail

In 1824 the Duchesse de Berry, niece of Louis XVIII, caused a stir by visiting Dieppe to go bathing, in the way already fashionable across the Channel in Brighton. For French royalists she was a tragic heroine, whose husband had been assassinated when she was only 19. Bright and vivacious, the Duchesse was an arbiter of fashion. She returned to Dieppe every year until her father-in-law Charles X was deposed in 1830, and by then the town's status as France's first *station balnéaire* was firmly established. Nearby Etretat was also recommended for longer stays due to its balmy climate, and saw the first large-scale appearance of the seaside villa as an opportunity for whimsical architecture, with extra curlicues and other touches of neo-Gothic fantasy.

Dieppe maintained its position for several years, and remained popular with the British – it had the first regular Channel ferry service, in 1825 – but as rail links developed, Parisians discovered that the long sand beach of Trouville, in the Baie de la Seine far to the west, was much nicer for swimming than the shingle of Dieppe. Trouville's success was ensured under the Second Empire, when Napoleon III visited regularly, along with Impressionist painters and growing crowds, who all mingled along its newly created promenade.

In 1860 Napoleon III's half-brother, the Duc de Morny, notorious for dubious business ventures, looked across the River Touques with his associates and saw, amid the empty dunes, a perfect location for an entirely new, more profitable, resort. Deauville was born. Its development took time, interrupted by the Empire's fall in 1870 and its promoters' lack of cash, and it was not until the 1900s, under a new promoter called Eugène Cornuché, that it took definitive shape with the completion of its vast grand hotels. Being purpose-built, Deauville brought a much more defined sense of style and exclusivity to the French resort, a clearer distinction between society spots and others for the hoi polloi. Another feature of the town is that, since it was artificial, its promoters could insist on a building style, the fantasy variation on traditional Pays d'Auge manors called *Anglo-Normand*, producing giant mock-half-timbered "cottages" that brought a new level of extravagance to the seaside villa.

Cornuché also highlighted Deauville's casino as the centre of town, and hundreds of French resorts have since followed suit – with pleasure palaces ranging from luxury venues on the Côte d'Azur to the slightly shabby places in towns like Luc-sur-Mer. Another essential feature of the French seaside is that one goes there to eat, as much as for the beach. It would be sad to visit the sea without sampling local fish or *fruits de mer*, and so a resort without its seafood brasseries, chic or homely, is inconceivable.

One last, specifically French, element is *Le Thalasso*, the thalassotherapy centre. Thalassotherapy, essentially high-pressure bombardment with seawater and similar treatments, was first identified by a Dr De la Bonnardière in Arcachon, near Bordeaux, in 1865. It's a very French fad: it has an aura of science and medical rigour, but is also very much to do with toning the skin, and looking good. The women who greet you at top-end *thalasso* centres consequently emit a suitably perfect, slightly unearthly glow. ❑

LEFT: Le Touquet beach.

played a role in French life out of all proportion to its size: Samuel Champlain sailed from here to found Quebec in 1608, and it can dispute with Etretat and Rouen the title of birthplace of Impressionism. There are lovely places to stay, fine shops and scores of restaurants, and despite the weekend crowds the place never loses its charm.

Honfleur makes a strong visual impression, in no small part due to the impressively tall, slate-fronted 17th-century houses along **Quai Ste-Catherine** on the old harbour, the **Vieux Bassin**. Opposite, the lower-level medieval **Enclos** district is a knot of little alleys and courtyards. Twin museums, the **Musée d'Ethnographie** and **Musée de la Marine** (both Apr–Sept Tue–Sun 10am–noon, 2–6pm; mid-Feb–Mar, Oct–Nov Tue–Fri 2.30–5.30pm, Sat–Sun 10am–noon, 2.30–5.30pm; charge), present entertaining exhibits on all areas of local life, and enable you to visit the old town prison.

In a lovely sloping square above Quai Ste-Catherine is Honfleur's astonishing half-timbered wooden "cathedral", **Ste-Catherine**, built in the 1460s by local shipwrights after a stone church had been destroyed by the English. The roof has the structure of two upturned ships' hulls. Nearby is the **Musée Eugène Boudin** (Mar–Sept Wed–Mon 10am–noon, 2–6pm; Oct–Feb Mon, Wed–Fri 2.30–5.30pm, Sat–Sun 10am–noon, 2.30–5.30pm; charge). Delightfully airy, the museum has work by Boudin himself, Monet, Jongkind and later painters such as Dufy. Honfleur was also the birthplace of composer Erik Satie, and his first home is now the **Maison Satie** (Wed–Mon May–Sept 10am–7pm; mid-Feb–Apr, Oct–Dec 11am–6pm; charge). Rather than a conventional collection, it consists of rooms evoking Satie's very particular world, with plenty of his music, forming a hugely original, stimulating "museum".

A tree-shrouded corniche road leads to the long beaches of **Trouville** ⓱ and Deauville, separated by a bridge across the River Touques. One of Deauville's labels is the "21st *arrondissement* of Paris". In Paris, historically, respectable society congregated on the right bank of the Seine, artists and radicals on the left; on the Touques they change places. Trouville on the right bank is bohemian and arty, with narrow streets, unfussy beach cafés and buzzing *quai*-side brasseries. It has a fabulous **market** on Wednesdays and Sundays, with spectacularly fresh fish and seafood (unfortunately awkward with nowhere to cook it).

Deauville ⓲, meanwhile, is neat and *comme il faut*, a planned resort *(see opposite)* with wide avenues designed to create a feel of ordered luxury. Its hubs are the **Casino**, the two vast grand hotels either side of it, the Normandy and the Royal (a third, the Hôtel du Golf, sits on Mont Canisy behind the town, with its golf course), and the beach-front promenades or ***planches*** with their café terraces. The resort has never lost its fashionable cachet, and hosts all kinds of concerts and events each season, culminating in the **Festival du Cinéma Américain** each September, which draws in Hollywood names. It is also a

Among Deauville's main attractions are the racing tracks at La Touques and Clairefontaine.

BELOW: the Casino, Deauville.

SHOP

In addition to the regular weekly markets, extra *marchés à l'ancienne* are held in the Pays d'Auge in summer, where farmers dress up in traditional costumes and demonstrate country crafts as well as selling their produce. The best are held every Sunday in July and August in Pont l'Evêque and Cambremer (which also holds them around Easter), and there is a cheese fair in Livarot at the end of July.

centre of French horse racing, with two tracks, **Clairefontaine** for trotting races and exclusive **La Touques** for flat racing, and buyers from across the world attend the October horse sales.

More Trouvillesque **Villers-sur-Mer** sits beside the cliffs of the *Vaches Noires*, known for fossils, which explains the giant model dinosaur on its seafront. More traditionally staid are **Houlgate** and especially **Cabourg**, which trades on its associations with Marcel Proust, who returned to its stately Grand Hôtel each year to write and recall his youth. Half-hidden by the *Côte Fleurie* is historic **Dives-sur-Mer**, from where William the Conqueror set sail for England, and which boasts a superb 15th-century market hall.

Land of plenty

Of all the idyllic green landscapes in Normandy, nowhere are the leaves more lush, the valleys more softly curving or the cows more contented-looking than in the **Pays d'Auge**, due south of the Côte Fleurie. Its half-timbered houses or *maisons de colombage* are made with more and thinner wooden uprights than in other styles, allowing the use of varied patterns that give them an extra charm. It is the only area with *appellations contrôlées* for both its calvados and its ciders. Three of the great Norman cheeses are also from here: Pont l'Evêque, Livarot and Camembert.

The town of **Pont l'Evêque** suffers from being a major road junction, but still has a fine market every Monday. The heart of the Auge cider country lies just to the south. It's most enjoyable simply to wander down the criss-crossing lanes or follow the *Route du Cidre* maps from tourist offices, showing cider and calvados farms open for direct sales. **Cambremer** is the district's (still very low-key) main town, with its main market on Fridays. To the northwest is **Beuvron-en-Auge**, a celebrated extravaganza of half-timbering so outrageously pretty it could be hard to believe even as a film set.

The only large town in the Auge, **Lisieux** ⓳ was transformed in the 1890s, when a local girl called Thérèse Martin showed such obsessional religious devotion that she was made St Thérèse of Lisieux. A vast neo-Byzantine **basilica**, completed only in the 1950s, now dominates the town. This is the largest Catholic pilgrimage site in France after Lourdes, but for non-pilgrims Lisieux has few attractions.

While the northern Pays d'Auge is prime cider country, the south is most obsessed with cheese. Cheese producers are harder to visit than cider farms, due to modern health regulations, so the best places to find farm products are local markets. The area's agricultural hub is **St-Pierre-sur-Dives** ⓴, where the Monday market has been held since medieval times in and around the giant **Halles** timber-frame market hall. Next to the serene **Abbatiale** church the other remaining parts of St-Pierre's abbey include a cloister and beautiful Gothic chapterhouse, and contain the tourist office, above which is a museum that tells you all you ever wanted to know about cheesemaking.

BELOW: the basilica of Lisieux.

Nearby are two contrasting visions of the French 18th century. The **Château de Canon** (gardens only June–Sept Wed–Sun 2–6pm, Easter–May Sat–Sun 2–6pm; charge) at **Mezidon-Canon** was rebuilt in the 1770s by J-B Elie de Beaumont and his wife Anne-Louise, believers in Enlightenment ideas who held democratic festivals of *Bonnes Gens* ("Good People") with their workers, and laid out delightful gardens, with a Chinese summerhouse and other curiosities. To the south, the 1750s **Château de Vendeuvre** (May–Sept daily 11am–6pm; Oct Sun 2–6pm; charge) is all *ancien régime* extravagance. It was gutted in 1944, but the Comtes de Vendeuvre have succeeded in lavishly restoring it in all its pastel-coloured glory. There is also the world's largest museum of miniature furniture, and a fanciful modern water garden.

More can be found out about cheese at the likeably quaint **Musée du Camembert** (Apr–Oct Thur–Mon 2–5.30pm; charge) in **Vimoutiers**, with a vast collection of cheese-label art. Nearby is the idyllic hilltop village of **Camembert** ㉑ itself, where little Marie Harel supposedly first made the famous cheese. The hard-sell **Maison du Camembert** (May–Aug daily 10am–6pm; Mar–Apr, Sept–Oct Wed–Sun 10am–6pm; charge) museum and shop is quite tacky, however. A few kilometres away is the **Mémorial de Montormel** (May–Sept daily 9am–6pm; Oct–Apr Wed, Sat–Sun 10am–5pm; charge), where Polish troops fought the last battle of the Normandy campaign in August 1944.

Deep south

The hills rise southwards into the **Perche**, a broad area that extends into Maine (the Parc Naturel Régional du Perche is shared with the *Région du Centre*), with a more remote feel than the Auge. At **Soligny-la-Trappe** is the **Abbaye de Notre-Dame de la Trappe**, first abbey of the silent Cistercian order of monks, or Trappists. Dissolved by the Revolution, it was reoccupied and rebuilt after 1815. There is a shop, and visitors are welcome on retreats; the setting amid forests and lakes is exquisite.

The Perche hills provided many of Quebec's colonists in the 17th century, a link that is still maintained. **Mortagne-**

Trappist monks only.

BELOW: Soligny-la-Trappe abbey.

Bayeux cathedral.

BELOW: the Bayeux Tapestry.

au-Perche ㉒, the main town, has a backwater tranquillity, with a fascinating accumulation of historic buildings. This is also Normandy's capital of *boudin noir*, black pudding, and its *charcuteries* are eye-opening. To the south, **Bellême** is a gem of a small town, around a tiny hilltop walled core.

The Perche is also home to the Percheron horse and very fine dry ciders, and is renowned for its fortified manor houses, mini-castles built by local squires when this was a lawless area in the 15th century. One of the grandest is the **Manoir de Courboyer** near **Nocé**, now part of the **Maison du Parc** (July–Aug 10.30am–6.30pm; Apr–June 10.30am–6pm; Sept–Mar 10.30am–5.30pm; charge for manor), where as well as the manor itself there are exhibitions, Percheron horses and a shop for local produce.

Caen and Bayeux

The Normandy coast west of the River Orne naturally has a much older, broader identity than as a giant stage for the landings of June 1944. **Caen** ㉓ was the favourite city of William the Conqueror, who made it Normandy's "second capital" after Rouen. He and his wife, Matilda, each endowed giant abbeys on opposite sides of Caen, the **Abbaye aux Hommes** (for men) and **Abbaye aux Dames** (for women), to atone for their marriage, which had been questioned since they were cousins. Their churches of **St-Etienne** and **La Trinité**, jewels of Norman Romanesque, both survived the onslaught of 1944. The city was a battlefield for over a month, and as a result much of the urban area today has the typically bland, grey appearance of post-war reconstruction.

The massive walls of the Norman dukes' **Château** now enclose a park, and two fine museums, the **Musée de Normandie** (June–Oct daily 9.30am–6pm; Nov–May Wed–Mon 9.30am–6pm; charge) on the region's history, and **Musée des Beaux-Arts** (Wed–Mon 9.30am–6pm; charge), with major works of Italian and Flemish art but surprisingly few Impressionists.

Caen's most visited museum is by the ring road north of the city, the **Mémorial de Caen** (Feb–Oct daily 9am–

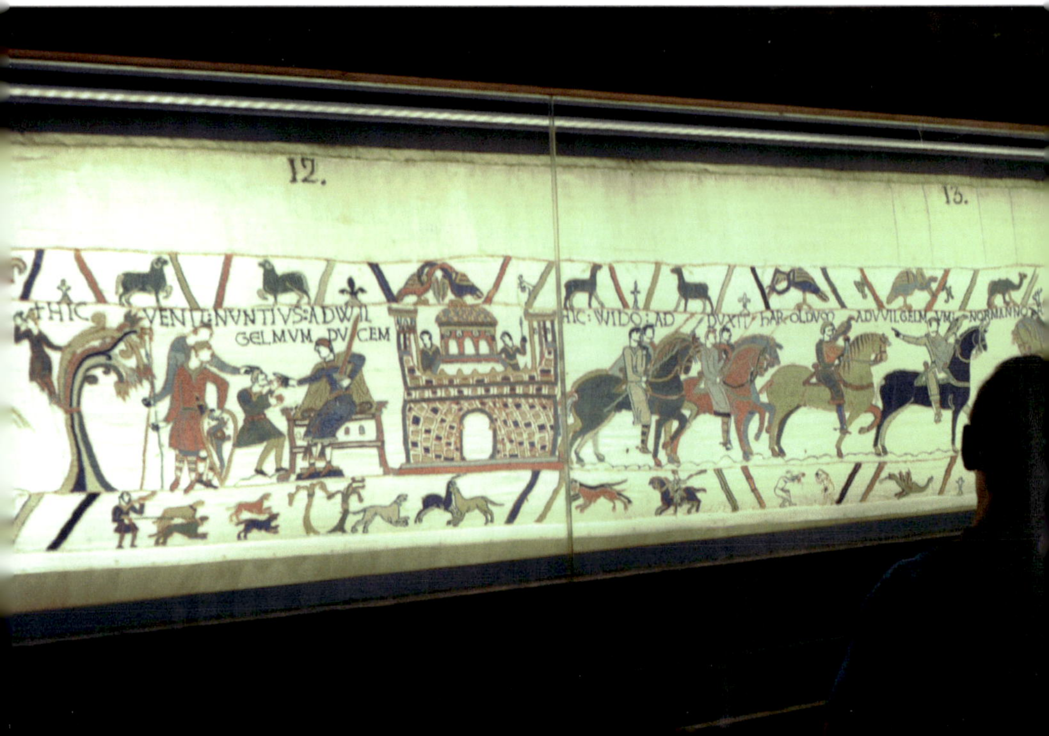

7pm; Nov–Jan Tue–Sun 9.30am–6pm; charge), a multimedia "peace museum" that seeks to present the events of 1944 within a broader political context.

Bayeux ㉔, older and once larger than Caen, had the great fortune to fall to British troops on 7 June, and so emerged near-unscathed as a model Norman country town, with medieval and 18th-century houses on its long main street. The glorious **Cathedral**, consecrated by Odo, Bishop of Bayeux and William's troublesome half-brother, in 1077, has one of the most beautifully serene of Norman naves. Bayeux's unique treasure, of course, is the **Bayeux Tapestry**, superbly presented in the **Centre Guillaume-le-Conquérant** (May–Aug 9am–7pm; Mar–Apr, Sept–Nov 9am–6.30pm; Dec–Feb 9.30am–12.30pm, 2–6pm; charge), with a museum to set the historical context *(see panel, below)*.

On the south side of Bayeux are the largest **British War Cemetery** in Normandy, and the **Musée-Mémorial de la Bataille de Normandie** (May–Sept 9.30am–6.30pm; Oct–Apr 10am–12.30pm, 2–6pm; charge), second of the two big 1944 museums, which those closely interested in the actual events of the campaign often prefer to the Caen Mémorial.

The D-Day beaches

The D-Day landing beaches stretch over 95km (60 miles) west from **Ouistreham**. One striking site is at **Pegasus Bridge** over the Caen Canal, where the **Memorial Pegasus** (May–Aug 9.30am–6.30pm, Feb–Apr, Oct–Nov 10am–5pm; charge) commemorates the British paratroopers who took the bridge on the night of 5–6 June 1944. The alter ego of the British **Sword** and Canadian **Juno** beaches is the *Côte de Nacre* or "mother-of-pearl coast", a line of never-very-fashionable seaside towns like **Lion-sur-Mer**. At **Courseulles-sur-Mer** the **Juno Beach Centre** (Apr–Sept 9.30am–7pm; Mar, Oct 10am–6pm; Nov–Dec, Feb 10am–5pm; charge) is, like other Canadian memorials, a model combination of information and sensitivity. The villas thin out towards **Arromanches** ㉕, aka **Gold Beach**, where the British built the Mulberry artificial harbour, remains of which lie

There is a total of 29 museums and historic sites connected with the Normandy campaign in the Espace Historique de la Bataille de Normandie. *A full list is on leaflets available at all tourist offices and on www.normandiememoire.com. The Normandie Pass card (www.normandiepass.com), available for €1, gives discounts on admission to many sites.*

The Norman Comic Strip

The Bayeux Tapestry is one of the earliest and most vivid examples of visual propaganda. Almost certainly made in England in the 1070s and commissioned by Odo of Bayeux to hang in his new cathedral, it presents the Norman case for William's right to be King of England. Earl Harold, the Saxon claimant, is shown being sent to Normandy by King Edward the Confessor to tell William he is his chosen successor; Harold then fights alongside William in Brittany, and swears on holy relics to support William as king, so that by then claiming the throne himself he broke a sacred oath and committed a crime against God. The scenes then gather pace, with superb visual verve, to climax in William's victory at Hastings. How much is entirely true is impossible to know, since no contrary Saxon version exists.

Beyond the main events, the great fascination of the Tapestry – really an embroidery – lies in all the details it gives of 11th-century life: the way ships are built, the gathering of stores for the invasion, the moustaches of the English,the peasants stripping their clothes off the dead after the battle. The margins at top and bottom of the main panel are filled with all kinds of images, of peasant life, strange animals, legends, before the dead and the dying from the main panel spill over into them in the dramatic final scenes.

TIP

In among the eastern *bocage* country around Vire is the Viaduc de la Souleuvre, a 62-metre (205ft) -high railway viaduct designed by Gustave Eiffel. Closed to trains since the 1960s, its towers are now one of Europe's foremost bungy-jumping destinations (www.ajhackett.fr).

offshore like sleeping whales. Its **Musée du Débarquement** (May–Sept 9am–6/7pm; Oct–Apr 9.30/10am–12.30am, 1.30–5.30/6pm; charge) is one of the most-visited museums.

The coast is interrupted by the charming fishing harbour of **Port-en-Bessin** before **Omaha Beach**, where the US force suffered horrendous losses on 6 June. Broad and open, it's actually the most beautiful of all the beaches. Above it at **Colleville-sur-Mer** is the **American Military Cemetery**, and nearby there's a choice of three museums. Another American memorial is at **Pointe du Hoc**, where the US Rangers scaled the cliffs on D-Day.

A larger interruption comes with the **Marais du Cotentin**, a protected expanse of bird-filled marsh and wetland. The **Ponts d'Ouve** centre at **St-Côme-du-Mont** near Carentan gives information on activities.

Beyond are the long dunes of **Utah Beach**, with the illuminating **Musée d'Utah Beach** (June–Sept 9.30am–5pm, Feb–May, Oct–Nov 10am–5.30/6pm; charge). Just inland, **Ste-Mère-Eglise** ㉖, centre of the drop zone for the US airborne divisions, has the popular **Musée Airborne** (Apr–Sept 9am–6.45pm; Feb–Mar, Oct–Nov and Christmas 9.30am–noon, 2–6pm; charge). On Ste-Mère's stout church tower a dummy of a US paratrooper hanging by a parachute commemorates Private John Steele, who was caught on the tower for most of 6 June, while the Germans thought he was dead.

BELOW: Omaha Beach.

Falaise to Alençon

Falaise ㉗, 35km (22 miles) south of Caen, is the birthplace of William the Conqueror in 1028; his existence was the result of a liaison between Robert, second son of the Duke of Normandy, and a 17-year-old tanner's daughter, Herleva (or traditionally Arlette), hence his earlier title of "William the Bastard". In August 1944 Falaise was also one of the great anvils of the Battle of Normandy, as the northern side of the "Falaise Pocket", trapping the German armies. The **Musée Août 1944** (Apr–mid-Nov daily 10am–noon, 2–6pm; charge) recalls the battle. Despite war damage, Falaise retains plenty of character, and William's home, the **Château Guillaume-le-Conquérant** (July–Aug 10am–7pm; Sept–June 10am–6pm; charge), has a wonderfully dramatic location atop a rocky crag.

The Orne valley above **Thury-Harcourt** is dubbed **La Suisse Normande**. It's scarcely Alpine, but the rugged granite gorge stands out amid the Norman woods and fields, and is popular for walking, cycling, climbing and other activities. The views are gorgeous around **Clécy** and **Le Vey**.

Argentan ㉘, on the southern rim of the Falaise pocket, retains much of its historic centre, including the *Flamboyant* Gothic-Renaissance church of **St-Germain**. The Orne is celebrated horse country, and east of Argentan is the **Haras National du Pin** (tours Apr–Sept daily 10am–6pm; Mar, Oct Sat–Sun 2–5pm; charge), the august national stud farm founded by Louis XIV, with regular horse shows. To the south, the **Château de Sassy** (tours mid-

June–mid-Sept daily 10.30am–12.30pm, 2–6pm, Easter–mid-June, late Sept Sat–Sun 3–6pm; charge) is an elegant, well-filled Louis XV mansion still owned by an aristocratic horse-breeding family.

Little, medieval **Sées** has in its midst an extraordinary early Gothic Cathedral, with superb rose windows. **Alençon** 29 has been famous for centuries for its lace, a tradition commemorated with exquisite work in the **Musée des Beaux-Arts et de la Dentelle** (July–Aug daily 10am–6pm; Sept–June 10am–noon, 2–6pm; charge). It also presents demonstrations of lace-making, although Alençon's production is now a tiny fraction of its 18th-century peak. On the town's *Grande Rue*, the church of **Notre Dame** has a spectacular *Flamboyant* porch.

To the west is the red-brick, moated 15th-century château of **Carrouges** (tours mid-June–Aug 9.30am–noon, 2–6.30pm; Sept–mid-June 10am–noon, 2–5/6pm; charge), an intriguing transition point between fighting castle and luxury residence. Beyond, an open plain extends to the hilltop fortress-town of **Domfront**. North and west is the Normandy *bocage*, extending from the Vire area across the Cotentin peninsula, a landscape of woods, tree-shrouded lanes and tiny fields divided by massive hedgerows. Naturally picturesque, it caused misery to the Allied troops in 1944, when the hedgerows had to be taken one by one.

The wild Cotentin

The Cotentin peninsula has a wilder, more remote feel than much of Normandy, with granite cliffs or windswept dunes along the coast and impenetrable *bocage* inland, punctuated by austere villages of grey stone. In its northeast corner, **St-Vaast-la-Hougue** is a delightful harbour from where boats run to **Ile Tatihou**, with a Vauban fort that hosts varied events each summer. Tiny **Barfleur** 30, amazingly, was once a major communication link for the Anglo-Norman empire, but is now a placid fishing and leisure port. There are superb views all around this coast, especially at **Cap Lévi**.

Cherbourg 31 grew up as a navy port under the *ancien régime* and Napoleon. In 1944 it was a major Allied objec-

The Goury lighthouse at the northwestern point of the Cotentin peninsula, a beacon in treacherous waters.

BELOW: Barfleur.

As you plan your visit to Mont-St-Michel, be prepared to share the experience with hundreds of other tourists.

tive, which fell to the Americans after a fierce battle on 30 June. The **Musée de la Libération** (May–Sept Tue–Sat 10am–noon, 2–6pm, Sun–Mon 2–6pm; Oct–Apr Wed–Sun 2–6pm; charge) occupies the battle-scarred **Fort du Roule** above the port. Cherbourg harbour runs into the city centre, and its most popular attraction is the **Cité de la Mer** (July–Aug 9.30am–7pm; Apr–June, Sept 9.30am–6/6.30pm; Oct–Dec, Feb–Mar 10am–6pm; charge) a multi-faceted sea-life centre in the former transatlantic liner terminal. Exhibits include a vast aquarium and a (decommissioned) nuclear submarine.

To the west the city gives way to the spectacularly rugged cliffs of the **Cap de la Hague**, a granite spur that's at its most dramatic when the Atlantic winds are up. On the south side of the cape is the controversial Beaumont-La Hague nuclear plant, but even this cannot mar the majesty of the scenery.

Barneville-Carteret 32, a combination of country town, fishing port and easy-going beach resort, makes an excellent base in the area. Many kilometres of empty dune beaches run to the north and south. Further south, **Lessay** has a stunningly beautiful Romanesque church, carefully restored after 1944. In the countryside beyond are two very old castles, at **Pirou** (Wed–Mon Apr–Sept 10am–noon, 2–6.30pm; Feb–Mar, Oct–Nov 10am–noon, 2–5pm; charge) and **Gratot** (10am–7pm; charge); both are of the type of castle that appears in children's drawings, and are great fun to explore.

The great treasure of **Coutances** is its 13th-century cathedral, with its almost modernistic facade of tall, narrow columns. Inland, **St-Lô** was one of the main 1944 battlefields, and reconstructed post-war. The *bocage* is at its densest in the southern Cotentin, and getting lost among the hills and green-tunnel lanes is part of the enjoyment. Amid exquisite woodland are two 12th-century abbeys, the ruined **Hambye** (July–Aug daily 10am–noon, 2–6pm; Apr–June, Sept–Oct closed Mon; charge) and **La Lucerne d'Outremer** (Apr–Sept Mon–Sat 10am–noon, 2–6.30pm, Sun 2–6.30pm; Mar, Oct–Nov Mon–Sat 10am–noon, 2–5pm, Sun pm only; charge), which

BELOW: La Mère Poulard, traditional Mont-St-Michel biscuits.

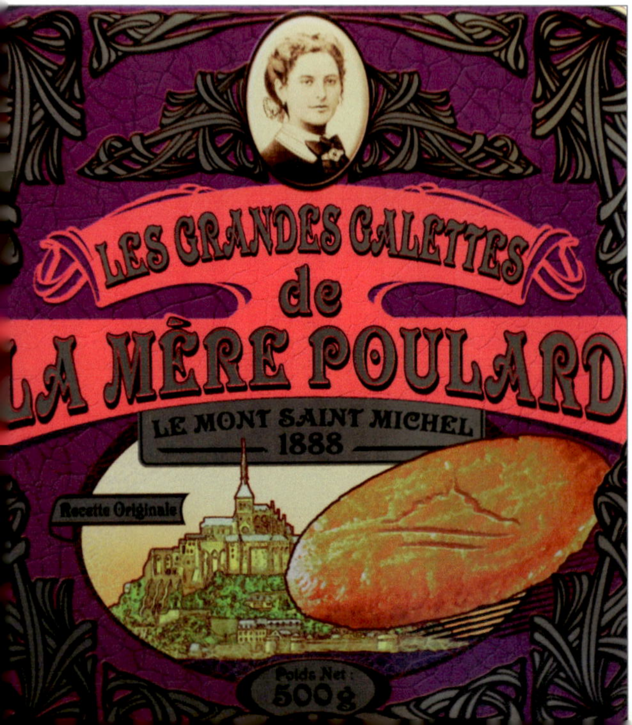

The Norman Hole

Normans were long renowned for the amount they ate – in *Madame Bovary*, the wedding feast goes on for 16 hours, with chicken, steaks, a suckling pig, cakes, custard, cream, cider and wine. To help all this down there was the institution of the *trou normand* or "Norman hole", a shot of calvados that men would take between courses to "make a hole" for the next round. Calvados was of course a healthy *digestif*, not an indulgence and believed to stave off any threat of heartburn and properly revive the appetite.

Today the old-style *trou* is mostly confined to the most traditional country dinners. A more delicate modern variation is to serve a little scoop of apple sorbet between courses, doused in calvados. Be sure to sniff the *calva* just before swallowing, for a transcendental experience.

remarkably is being slowly rebuilt by a private foundation.

On the coast, the old town of **Granville** ㉝ occupies a rocky headland, with some good seafood restaurants along the harbourside below it. The main attraction is the **Musée Christian Dior** (May–mid-Sept daily 10am–6.30pm; charge), in the villa that was the great couturier's childhood summer home.

Magic Mountain

The vast **Baie du Mont-St-Michel**, where the sea disappears for 15km (9 miles) at low tide, seems expressly designed around its magical abbey. The sight of the mount and its soaring spire, glimpsed across the sands like a giant magnet, is a central part of any visit. At **Genêts**, from where medieval pilgrims walked to the mount, guides still take groups across, and the **Maison de la Baie** provides extensive information.

Avranches, on a granite hill with more superlative views, is also inseparable from the mount. The **Scriptorial d'Avranches** (May–Sept daily 10am–6/7pm; Oct–Apr Tue–Fri 10am–12.30pm, 2–5pm, Sat–Sun 10am–12.30pm, 2–6pm; charge) provides a striking modern setting for the surviving manuscripts from Mont-St-Michel.

The causeway built to **Mont-St-Michel** ㉞ in 1877 distorted the movement of silt in the bay, and its replacement with a bridge is supposed to be completed in 2012. The town of Mont-St-Michel, smallest municipality in France, is incorrigibly tacky, with overpriced restaurants, but neither this nor the crowds detracts from the **Abbaye** (May–Aug 9am–7pm, Sept–Apr 9.30am–6pm; charge). A shrine was first built on the island in the 8th century, after St Aubert, Bishop of Avranches, was told to do so by the Archangel Michael in a vision, but was expanded hugely by the Normans. It is an astonishing work of medieval engineering: the great church is not built *on* the mount but *above* it, around four massive pillars. Later sections, such as the delicate Gothic ***Merveille*** or marvel, are intricately intertwined around this central structure. Don't miss a chance to return at night for the excellent *son et lumière* presentations, which allow you to appreciate all the abbey's mystery. ❑

TIP

Walking across to Mont-St-Michel at low tide is the most memorable way to visit the mount. Guided walks are led from Genêts by Découverte de la Baie (www.decouvertebaie.com), Chemins de la Baie (www.cheminsdelabaie.com) and some other groups. Night walks, special-interest walks, horse rides and other options are also available. No one should ever try these walks without an experienced guide; the tides in the bay are famously quick to change.

BELOW: Mont-St-Michel, "God's pyramid".

Celtic Brittany

Brittany's Celtic heritage has populated the region with myths and legends, and left a wealth of traditions in its culture, language and music

An extraordinary number of prehistoric menhirs and stones testifies to Brittany's long history of occupation. Its Celtic character was reinforced in the 5th to 6th centuries AD with the settlement of migrants from Wales and Cornwall, fleeing Anglo-Saxon invasions. Brittany and Celtic parts of Britain share much in common historically and culturally, including figures of Celtic mythology. Stories of King Arthur are prominent in Breton folklore. The mythical forest of Brocéliande, said to be the Paimpont forest in the east of Brittany, is Arthur and Merlin's Breton home.

A popular Breton legend tells of the sunken city of *Ys*. King Gradlon, one of the mythical founders of Brittany, had a beautiful but depraved daughter, Dahut. She demanded a city of her own by the sea, and her devoted father built her a dazzling citadel in the Bay of Douarnenez. Ys became a centre of debauchery, until it was swallowed up by the sea. Gradlon fled the deluge on his magic horse Morvarc'h and tried to carry Dahut with him, but Saint Guénolé appeared to the king and bade him to release his daughter and her sinful city to the sea. A granite statue of the legendary king stands outside the Gothic Cathedral of St-Corentin in Quimper.

Other key figures of Breton folklore are *Ankou*, King of the Dead, represented by the grim reaper figures seen in Brittany's parish closes, *Korrigans*, malicious elves that live in the woods, and the *Bugul Noz*, another forest spirit who is not evil but so ugly no one can look at him.

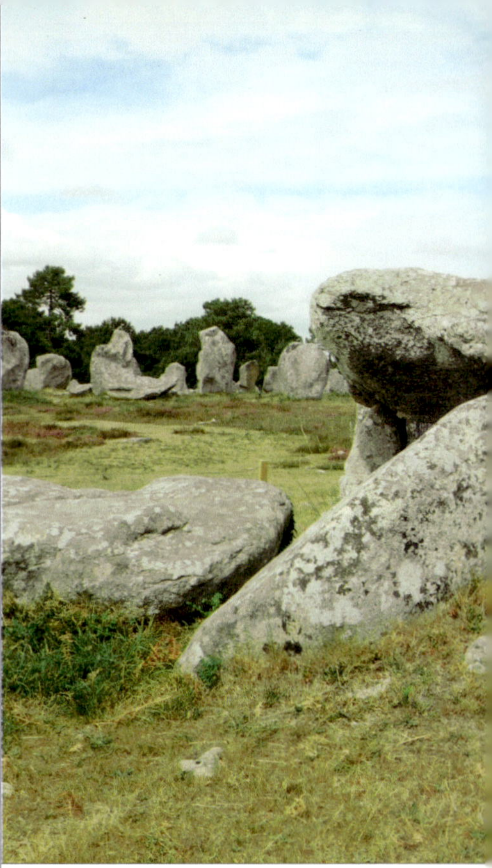

Above: over 3,000 years old, the long lines of standing stones at Carnac provide extraordinary testimony to Brittany's long history of human occupation.

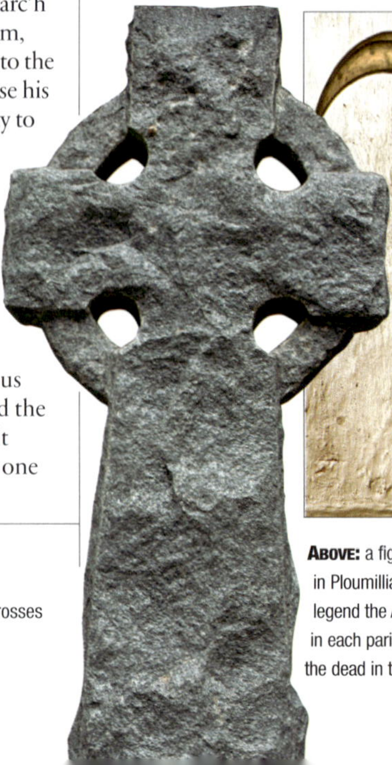

Left: dressed for the parade at the Interceltique Festival in Lorient, 2010.
Right: traditional Celtic-style stone crosses can be seen in churchyards and on monuments throughout Brittany.

Above: a figure of Ankou from the church in Ploumilliau, near Lannion. In one legend the Ankou is the last person to die in each parish in a year, who then collects the dead in the following year.

LEFT: fourth-century AD Celtic vase from St-Pol-de-Léon, near Roscoff.
BELOW: Celtic motifs reproduced on modern souvenirs.

BELOW: the Kermaria standing stone.

BELOW: guiding spirit of Breton traditional music, harpist Alan Stivell.

LIVING CULTURE

The use of the Breton language may have declined precipitously since the 1920s, but Celtic Breton culture thrives in many ways. Rural Brittany's most traditional festivals are the *pardons*, processions to a shrine of a saint in traditional dress with elaborate banners, usually followed by music, food and traditional games. The *pardons* in St Yves in Tréguier (third Sunday in May) and Notre Dame in Le Folgoët (first Sunday in September) are particularly well observed.

Music is at the heart of the Breton cultural revival, sparked by master-harpist Alan Stivell in the 1970s. Towns and villages host *Fest-noz,* local music and dance parties similar to Scottish ceilidhs. Dances are performed in lines or rings, music is played on traditional instruments like the harp, the Breton bagpipe *(biniou)* and oboe-like *bombarde*, and there is a variety of singing styles, from unaccompanied ballads to call-and-response songs. Many music and culture festivals are held in Brittany each year (some more traditional than others), especially during the summer (a full list is on www.gouelioubreizh.com), but the best event to experience traditional Celtic music, and its more contemporary interpretations, is the Interceltique festival at Lorient, held in August.

TOP: a *pardon* in Locronan, Finistère

RIGHT: local styles feature many colourful variations.

BRITTANY

Soaring cliffs, wind-blasted rocks, gorgeous beaches and exquisite sheltered harbours succeed each other around the Breton coast, an ideal setting for the legends and rich traditions of a distinctive Celtic culture

Main attractions
- St-Malo
- Dinan
- Rennes
- Paimpol and Goëlo Coast
- Côte de Granit Rose
- Parish Closes
- Crozon Peninsula
- Pointe du Raz
- Pont Aven
- Josselin
- Carnac
- Golfe du Morbihan

A great granite tongue jutting out into the Atlantic, Brittany has France's most spectacular coastline, while inland lies a deep-green rural world of lonely hills, forest and idiosyncratic little towns. Thanks to the fickle Atlantic weather, the Breton landscape can change completely in the course of a single day; grey and austere in the thin light and winds of morning, gold and subtle shades of green against a dazzling sunset.

With its isolation, Celtic language, traditions and folklore, Brittany is quite unlike the rest of France, and avoided incorporation into the realm until the 1530s. The architecture of its lofty old town houses and multi-spired churches strays off from usual styles recognised further east, and its manor houses with their up-and-down pointed towers have an extra Gothic-fantasy quality. All this adds to the feeling that Brittany is a distinctive, rather strange world of its own.

The Pirate City

The best way to get a first sight of **St-Malo** ❶ is from the sea. The old walled city, known as *Intra-Muros* or "within the walls", appears almost like a giant granite ship at the mouth of the River Rance, surrounded by surf-capped rocky islands. This fortified stronghold has been famously, belligerently, independent. It long played the kings of France and dukes of Brittany off against each other, and in the 1490s declared itself an independent republic, with the motto *Ni Français, ni Breton, Malouin Suis* ("Neither French, nor Breton, I am Malouin"). To win its loyalty French kings gave St-Malo special privileges, including *Lettres de Course* (origin of the word *Corsaire*), allowing mariners to raid on the high seas and keep most of the profits, so long as they only did so against the enemies

LEFT: Château de Josselin. **RIGHT:** the Grand Turk, figurehead of the three-masted frigate, *L'Etoile du Roy*, moored at St-Malo.

Brittany
0 20 km
0 20 miles
N
English Channel
Golfe de St-Malo
Manche
BAY OF BISCAY
Plymouth, Cork
Cork
Jersey, Guernsey
Portsmouth
Cherbourg
Caen
le Mans
Angers
Poitiers
Île d'Ouessant
Île Molene
Île de Sein
Île de Batz
les Sept Îles
Île de Bréhat
Île de Groix
Belle-Île
Île d'Houat
Île d'Hœdic
Côte de Granit Rose
Côte de Goëlo
Côte d'Emeraude
Baie de St-Brieuc
Baie du Mont-St-Michel
Baie de Douarnenez
Baie d'Audierne
Presqu'île de Crozon
Presqu'île de Quiberon
Pays de Léon
Pays Bigouden
Cornouaille
Finistère
Côtes-d'Armor
Ille-et-Vilaine
Morbihan
Loire-Atlantique
Parc d'Armorique
Parc de Brière
Monts d'Arrée
Landes de Lanvaux
Forêt de Paimpont
Bassin de Rennes
Canal de Nantes à Brest
Brest
Rennes
Nantes
Quimper
Lorient
Vannes
St-Malo
St-Brieuc
Dinan
Dinard
Fougères
Vitré
Redon
Lannion
Morlaix
Roscoff
Concarneau
Douarnenez
Quimperlé
Pontivy
Loudéac
Lamballe
Guingamp
Paimpol
Tréguier
Perros-Guirec
Carnac
Auray
Quiberon
Josselin
Ploërmel
St-Nazaire
Guérande
la Baule-Escoublac
Châteaubriant
Cancale
Dol-de-Bretagne
Combourg
Pont-Aven
Locronan
Pointe du Raz
Pointe de Penmarch
Pointe St-Mathieu
Le Mont-St-Michel
Granville
Avranches
Pontorson
Cap Fréhel
Fort de la Latte
Château de Kerjean
Château de Suscinio
Château de la Bourbansais
Château de Merguéhennec
Menhir de Champ Dolent
Cairn de Barnenez
Parc Floral de Haute Bretagne
1
2
3
4
5
6
7
8
9
10
11
12
13
14
15
16
17
18
19
20
21
22
23
24
25
26
27
28
29
30
31
32
33
34
35
36
37

of France. St-Malo's privateers brought great wealth, and the most famous – Duguay-Trouain, Robert Surcouf – are commemorated all around town. Local mariners sailed to every corner of the world, and from the 17th century St-Malo grew wealthier still from the profits of the slave trade.

Various wars brought attacks from foreigners, notably the English and the Dutch. In 1689 Marshal Vauban began replacing the port's medieval defences with the ramparts that define *Intra-Muros* St-Malo today, completed by his lieutenant Siméon de Garangeau. In addition, following a catastrophic fire in 1661, new building within the walls was only allowed in stone. Space was scarce, so new houses were built unusually tall, like clusters of granite towers.

The natural point of entry into *Intra-Muros* is **Porte St-Vincent** Ⓐ in the southeast corner, outside which is the tourist office. Beyond is **place Chateaubriand**, old St-Malo's main square, with its broad café terraces. The 15th-century **Château** Ⓑ, incorporated into Vauban's ramparts, contains the **Musée d'Histoire de la Ville** (Apr–Sept daily 10am–12.30pm, 2–6pm, Oct–Mar Tue–Sun 10am–noon, 2–6pm; charge), an old-fashioned celebration of St-Malo's seafaring history. The castle's ramparts and dark passageways are great fun to explore.

The Château is also a good place to start a walk around the **ramparts**. At every point there are superb views, outwards over ever-changing seascapes and the Rance, inwards over narrow streets. Outside the walls two small fortified islands can be visited at low tide (consult the tourist office for a schedule; charge), the **Fort National** and **Petit Bé**. The adjacent island of **Le Grand Bé** contains the tomb of the extravagant writer-politician Chateaubriand, who demanded that his home town give him a grand funeral there in 1848.

Intra-Muros St-Malo also has beaches, mainly along the northwest side, with an enclosed saltwater swimming pool, reached from the **Porte des Bés** Ⓒ, next to the **Tour Notre-Dame**. On the landward side are the great drum towers of the 15th-century **Grande Porte** Ⓓ, the main gate until Vauban added the Porte St-Vincent. St-Malo has one of France's largest concentrations of seafood restaurants, and many (though not the best) are all in a row on either side of the gate, along rue Cartier and rue de Chartres.

Although old St-Malo seems such a historic city, much of it is a remarkable replica, painstakingly reconstructed after *Intra-Muros* was devastated in the siege of 1944. A walk up rue Chateaubriand leads to one of the oldest surviving buildings, the 15th-century **Maison de la Duchesse Anne** Ⓔ. The surrounding streets, such as **rue de la Corne de Cerf**, make up one of the most charming parts of the old city. Along the southern wall of the largely reconstructed **Cathédrale** Ⓕ is the **Maison Guella**, renowned purveyors of chocolates, biscuits and other specialities.

A must-see is the Hotel d'Asfeld or **Maison du Corsaire** Ⓖ (tours July–Aug daily 10–11.30am, 2.30–5.30pm,

EAT

A great place to stop on a walk around St-Malo's ramparts is the *Corps de Garde* crêperie, next to the Tour Notre-Dame. As the only restaurant actually on the walls, it's also the only one with a terrace with a sea view.

BELOW: seagull on the lookout at St-Malo harbour.

Cancale, on the north-east coast of Brittany, is famous for its oysters. There are plenty of opportunities in the little resort town to sample the shellfish.

Feb–June, Sept–Nov Tue–Sun 3pm; charge). Its original owner François-Auguste Magon probably wouldn't have appreciated being labelled a *corsaire*, since he was a more respectable shipowner, but the *Maison* gives a vivid idea of life in an 18th-century merchant's home, with giant cellars for merchandise below, and elegant rooms above.

Outside the walls, a walk south past the Channel ferry terminal leads to the little promontory of **Cité d'Aleth**, site of the original settlement founded in the 6th century by the Welsh monk Maclow or Maclou, who became Saint Malo. A gorgeous footpath runs all around the Aleth rock. On the Rance side, the 15th-century **Tour Solidor** tower contains a maritime museum. East of the old city in **Rotheneuf** is the fascinating **Musée Jacques Cartier** (tours July–Aug daily 10–11.30am, 2.30–6pm, June, Sept Mon–Sat 10–11.30am, 2.30–6pm, Oct–May Mon–Sat 10am, 3pm; charge). In 1534 Cartier discovered the St Lawrence River and so began French involvement with Canada, but was passed over on later voyages because he was not an aristocrat, and retired to this humble manor house. Very little in it is original, but it is still highly evocative.

Brittany's fortified frontier

The Rance estuary runs inland due south from St-Malo, past coves and reed beds and – as so often in France – as soon as you leave the main highways, everything feels deeply rural. Boat trips provide the most leisurely way to appreciate the green placidity of Brittany's loveliest river.

Arrival in **Dinan** ❷ gives an immediate introduction to the sheer oddity of Brittany's historic towns. Old walled Dinan is almost impossibly picturesque, and the view from the north ramparts in particular, over the winding stairway-street of **rue du Jerzual**, seems far too much like a medieval fantasy to be actually real. Dinan was a centre of power for the Breton dukes in their struggles with their neighbours (a Norman siege of Dinan is shown in the Bayeux Tapestry). Its walls, the longest medieval ramparts in the region, are no longer entirely complete, but a walk around them

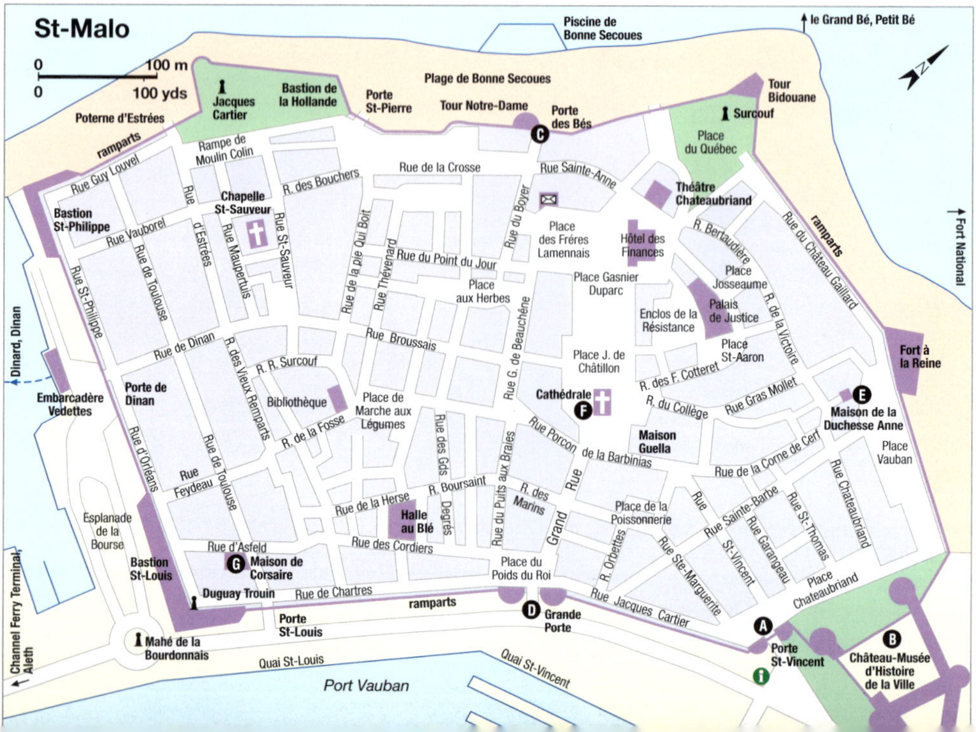

 Map opposite & page 284

still gives a feel of the enclosed city, and there are beautiful views over the Rance gorge. The hub of the old town is **rue de l'Horloge**, with the busiest cafés and souvenir shops, around the **Tour de l'Horloge**, a soaring 1490s bell- and clock tower.

East of St-Malo lies the Breton half of the Bay of Mont-St-Michel, and the charming fishing and resort town of **Cancale** ❸, famous for its oysters and as a holiday spot loved by the author Colette. Further east around the dead-flat bay the eye is caught by an abruptly steep hill, with a windmill and crêperie at the top, **Mont Dol**. Once one of the three granite islands across the bay, it was surrounded long ago by the expanding silt. On the southern edge of the marshes, **Dol-de-Bretagne** ❹ was the seat of one of Brittany's oldest bishoprics. Soaring up in the middle of the little town is a stunning Romanesque and early Gothic **Cathedral** with fabulous, little-known 13th-century stained glass.

In a field south of Dol is the **Menhir de Champ Dolent**, nearly 10 metres (33ft) high, one of the most famous of Brittany's many prehistoric standing stones. Believed to have stood here for 6,000 years, it features in many local legends, and is also recognisable as the model for the menhir that Astérix's friend Obélix carries behind his back.

Because eastern Brittany remained a military frontier until the 1530s, the rolling green countryside is peculiarly rich in castles of the massive-walled variety that were clearly built to mean business. One of the most dramatic is at **Combourg** ❺ (park July–Aug daily 10am–12.30pm, 2–6pm; Apr–June, Oct Sun–Fri 10am–12.30pm, 2–5/6pm; château tours at more limited times; charge), forever associated with Chateaubriand, who spent part of his childhood here and in his memoirs presented Combourg as a symbol of Gothic gloom.

A short way to the west, the **Château de la Bourbansais** (Apr–Sept daily park 10am–7pm, château tours 11.15am, 2–5pm; Oct–Mar park daily 1.30–5.30pm, château tours Sun 3–4pm; charge) is more of a 17th-century stately home, on an estate held by the Lorgeril family since the early Middle Ages. The

Brittany has two traditional languages. Breton, descended from the language of 6th-century Cornish and Welsh migrants, was historically spoken in western Brittany; northeast Brittany around Rennes and Fougères spoke Gallo, a romance language related to French. Well over half the people of western Brittany spoke Breton – and often knew scarcely no French – in 1900. Today, fewer than 10 percent know any Breton at all, while Gallo has largely disappeared.

BELOW: Rue du Petit Fort, Dinan.

TIP

Rennes has one partly overground Metro line, which runs from north to south, with a central stop at place de la République. The bus network is centred on the same square. The Rennes City Pass, available from the tourist office, gives reduced fares on public transport and admission to various attractions for two days, for €13. Like other French cities, Rennes also has a public cycle-access scheme, Vélostar; for details ask at the tourist office or see www.levelostar.fr.

BELOW: Château de Fougères.

house itself is extraordinary, with rare 1750s painted-wood panelling; around it, the elegant park is now a **zoo** and wildlife park.

The most dramatic fortifications are at **Fougères** ❻, which from around 900 to the 1530s was the eastern bastion of independent Brittany. Built unusually not on a hilltop but almost in a ravine, to guarantee its water supply, the **Château de Fougères** (July–Aug daily 10am–7pm, May–June, Sept daily 10am–1pm, 2–7pm, Oct–Apr Tue–Sun 10am–12.30pm, 2–5.30pm; charge) is partly in ruins, but what remains is still one of the largest surviving medieval castles in Europe. It's a very organised attraction, with interpretative displays and audioguides, but you can just wander around and soak up the atmosphere at will.

Fougères itself is a likeable town, with a typically French centre rebuilt after 18th-century fires, and a snug medieval quarter by the castle. To the north near Le Châtellier is the **Parc Floral de Haute Bretagne** (July–Aug daily 10.30am–6.30pm; Apr–June, Sept Mon–Sat 10am–noon, 2–6pm, Sun 10.30am–6.30pm; Mar, Oct–mid-Nov daily 2–5.30pm; charge), a lovely set of gardens that draw from some of the same inspiration as Monet's famous garden at Giverny (but without the crowds).

South of Fougères is another border fortress at **Vitré**, described by Victor Hugo as "a complete Gothic town". Most of the steep-roofed streets he enthused over can still be seen in the tightly packed walled town or *Ville Close*, leading up as usual to the **Château**, with the town hall and local museum (Apr–Sept daily 10.30am–12.30pm, 2–6.30pm; Oct–Mar Tue–Sat 10.30am–12.15pm, 2–5.30pm, Sun 2–5.30pm; charge).

City interlude

Given the rural or coastal feel of most of Brittany, the urbanity of its capital, **Rennes** ❼, can be a bit of a shock. An important Roman city, in the Middle Ages it became one of the residences of the Dukes of Brittany, who surrounded it with fortifications. Its medieval heart has been damaged not by recent wars but by fire, especially a giant conflagration in 1720. The centre was rebuilt in a classically French, rational style, with peculiarly long, straight streets of stone facades. Today these form the city's shopping and business hubs, while socialising seems to go on more in the surviving squares and narrow lanes of old Rennes. It is one of France's fastest-growing cities, with two universities and a varied cultural scene.

The central axis of modern Rennes is formed by the quais along the River Vilaine, either side of the huge **place de la République** Ⓐ. A short walk leads to another typical French-official grand square, **place de la Mairie** Ⓑ, with the 1730s **Hôtel de Ville** facing the 1830s **Opéra**. For more intimate spaces, head west to the excellent **Tourist Office** Ⓒ, in the former St-Yves chapel, which is also an attractive free city **museum**. Beside it, **rue Dottin** leads into a lovely knot of streets of multicoloured timber-frame houses, many with ornate carved details and many now serving as attractive restaurants, or, as in the case of the 1505 **Ty-Coz** on rue Guillaume, a bar-club, El Teatro. A short detour leads to Rennes' sombre **Cathédrale St-Pierre** **D**, mostly rebuilt after the 1720 fire, near which, oddly part-hidden down an alley, are the **Portes Mordelaises** **E**, the only survivors of Rennes' 15th-century gates.

Place des Lices **F** – "Place of Lists", since medieval jousts were held here – has along its north side Rennes' most spectacular giant half-timbered town houses, built for merchants in the 16th and 17th centuries. The square is best known as the location for one of France's largest weekly food **markets**, a showcase for Brittany's best produce held every Saturday in two giant halls, the **Halles aux Lices**. A few steps away, **place St-Michel** **G** forms with nearby **place du Champ-Jacquet** one of the social hubs of Rennes, lined with studenty cafés, small shops and restaurants at the foot of timber-frame towers.

The apparently endless straight streets to the east are most interesting as an exercise in perspective, anchored around the **Parlement de Bretagne** **H**, designed in 1618 by Salomon de Brosse, architect of the Paris Luxembourg, and now used as law courts. The present building is actually a restoration; it survived the 1720 fire, but rioting fishermen protesting over EU fishing policy managed to set it on fire in 1994.

Rennes' **Musée des Beaux-Arts** **I** (Tue 10am–6pm, Wed–Sun 10am–noon, 2–6pm; charge) has the typically eclectic collection of French regional museums, with some stand-out masterpieces such as Georges de la Tour's exquisite *Nouveau-Né* (New-Born) and Picasso's 1928 *Baigneuse* (Bather), painted at Dinard. Graphic arts are also a highlight, especially Italian Renaissance drawings. The city's contemporary *grand projet*, **Les Champs Libres** **J** (July–Aug Tue–Fri noon–7pm, Sat–Sun 2–7pm, Sept–June Tue noon–9pm, Wed–Fri noon–7pm, Sat–Sun 2–7pm; charge), is a multi-space arts complex by architect Christian de Portzamparc, opened in 2006. Within it the **Musée de Bretagne** presents Breton history and traditions in state-of-the-art style.

Rennes old town has some attractive half-timbered houses dating from the 17th century.

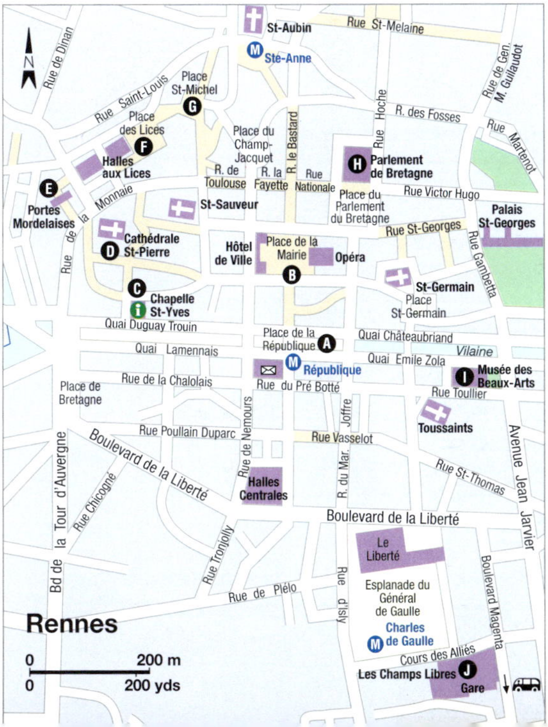

BELOW: Rennes town hall, place de la Mairie.

Breezy seaside café terrace, Dinard.

Dinard and the Emerald Coast

Facing St-Malo across the Rance, **Dinard** ❽ has a shorter but much more respectable history. It was scarcely a village before the 1850s, when the English Faber family built the first large villa here. Over the next decades it acquired all the features of a fashionable resort, as the wealthy of France joined the British in building villas on the cliffs, mostly in extravagant neo-Gothic style and carefully placed to catch the views. The villas, some with a distinct resemblance to the house in *Psycho*, can be seen on the lovely walk around the *Chemin de Ronde* footpath. Dinard also attracted artists; Debussy began his *La Mer* here in 1902, and Picasso came in the 1920s. Today it retains its air of slightly eccentric gentility, and deep tranquillity. Its **Festival of British Film** each October is much appreciated by all the British media types who get invited.

While Dinard was developing, the coast westwards was dubbed the *Côte d'Emeraude* (Emerald Coast), due to its unquestionable greenness. Turn off seawards and you find rocky inlets and sheltered sandy beaches, with cosy family-oriented resorts that, like Dinard, have long been particularly popular with the British. Pretty **St-Cast-le-Guildo** is known for its seven beaches, some of which have very placid waters while others offer surfing and windsurfing.

To the west the giant slab of the Cap Fréhel peninsula juts out into the sea, with the most spectacular of all Brittany's many castles, **Fort de la Latte** ❾ (early July–Aug daily 10am–7pm, Apr–early July, Sept daily 10am–12.30pm, 2–6pm, Oct–Mar Sat–Sun, holidays 2–6pm; charge), on one tip. It's the most castle-ish castle you could imagine, on a mighty crag above the ocean, with enough battlements, dark chambers and winding staircases to fire anyone's imagination. Much-used as a film set, La Latte was built in its apparently impossible location in the 1340s, and restored in the 1930s by a local family. From the massive keep and walls there are fabulous views along the cliffs to **Cap Fréhel**

BELOW: Breton woman donning a *coiffe* or lace cap.

Coiffes and Striped Jerseys

Alongside rocks and ocean, Brittany's traditional costume is one of its foremost symbols. Elements of it date back centuries, but it actually became more elaborate in the 19th and early 20th centuries, when traditional dress was disappearing as everyday wear in most of France, possibly as a deliberate reaction against the imposition of uniformity by Revolutionary and later governments. Lace, embroidery, and the differences in styles between districts, villages, trades and social classes became ever more intricate.

Black and white are the basic colours: men generally wear breeches, an embroidered waistcoat and short jacket and round-brimmed hat. The centrepiece for women is the *coiffe* or lace cap, which reached its peak in the exaggerated starched decorative *coiffes* – often taken as symbols of Brittany as a whole – of the Bigouden in south Finistère, which could be 35cm (1ft) tall. Until the 1980s it was quite common to see old ladies who wore *coiffes* every day. Today this is rare, but they reappear at every festival.

The other garment identified with Brittany – of course – is the striped Breton top sold in countless *Vêtements Bretons* shops. Its origins are unrecorded, but it may just be an adaptation of the striped shirts of the French Navy.

itself, with a lighthouse, more views and teeming seabird colonies.

Beyond the cape is a windblown coastline of cliffs topped by heather and wild flowers, with sweeping views and paths leading down to sandy coves that are generally empty off-season. Cosiness returns at **Sables-d'Or-les-Pins**, which as its name suggests has the area's prettiest beach, and is backed by pine woods. Created in the 1920s, it never grew into a major resort, and its villas, modest hotels and restaurants offer complete, low-key relaxation. West again, the little port of **Erquy** sits beside a vast beach, popular for sand-yachting. Even broader are the sands at **Pléneuf-Val-André**, backed by a promenade over 2km (1¼ miles) long, leading to the snug marina at **Dahouët**.

Land of pink granite

St-Brieuc was founded by a Welsh monk called Brieuc or Briog around the year 485, but is now a plain city. Most visitors head north and west, to Brittany's most extraordinary granite coastline. Known as **Goëlo** after a historic Breton lordship, the west side of St-Brieuc bay is more lush than Cap Fréhel, but the further one goes north the more jagged are the rocks and the more dramatically beautiful the vistas, whether in a north wind or against evening sunlight. All along the coast are well-sheltered harbours, now all with their crop of yacht masts. **Binic** is one of the busiest, with a long tidal beach and plenty of waterfront restaurants. Anyone wanting to miss the crowds, though, can find plenty of space by wandering down lanes to places such as **Le Palus**, with three crêperies, a campsite and a sand-and-shingle beach.

West from **Plouha** road signs are written in French and Breton, since this is the traditional frontier between Breton- and *Gallo*-speaking Brittany. Just outside Plouha, the 13th-century chapel of **Kermaria-an-Iskuit** has carved wooden figures of the 12 Apostles in the porch and rare frescoes of a "dance of death".

Paimpol ❿ was famous as a hardy deep-sea fishing port, a time recalled in the **Musée de la Mer** (mid-June–Aug daily 10.30am–12.30pm, 2–6.30pm,

It is said that buckwheat, sarrasin *or* blé noir *(black wheat) in French, was first brought back to Brittany from Asia during the Crusades, but there is evidence that it was already known much earlier. Disregarded in much of Europe, buckwheat grows well on relatively poor, rocky soils like those of Brittany. The buckwheat* crêpe *or* galette *was for centuries the staple diet of Breton peasants.*

BELOW: old rigging boats in Paimpol harbour.

Creach lighthouse.

mid-Apr–mid-June, early Sept daily 2–6pm; charge). Today it attracts plenty of tourists and has the obligatory marina, but also retains an inshore fishing fleet, and has an easy-going, genuine feel, with an excellent market filling the streets every Tuesday. In the surrounding villages there are impressively craggy granite chapels with fine carvings, and just east is the **Abbaye de Beauport** (daily mid-June–mid-Sept 10am–7pm, mid-Sept–mid-June 10am–noon, 2–5pm; charge), a part-ruined, part-restored Benedictine monastery founded in the 13th century as a subsidiary of La Lucerne in Normandy *(see page 278)*, in an atmospheric setting on a sheltered inlet.

From tiny **L'Arcouest**, north of Paimpol, boats run to **Île de Bréhat** ⓫, a 10-minute crossing that is an easy ride in good weather, and much more like an adventure when the wind is up. The island with its two villages was once a wild, isolated spot, but now gets pretty crowded in high summer.

Directly west, **Tréguier** ⓬ has been called the archetypal Breton town. It certainly meets the requirements, with little streets and alleys around **place du Martray**, spectacular stone and half-timbered houses and a placid waterfront on the River Jaudy. The 14th-century **Cathedral**, with typically bizarre Breton spire, contains the tomb of one of Brittany's most revered saints, Saint Yves. For more seascapes, head up any of the lanes north either side of Tréguier through villages such as **Plougrescant** to find rocky beaches, empty inlets and reed beds.

The most celebrated coastline of all is the **Côte de Granit Rose** ⓭ ("pink granite"), so called because its rocks have a distinctive pinkish hue. Often immense, battered over centuries into weird shapes, they lie along the coast like giant abstract sculptures. All human habitation has been built around and between them, from prehistoric shelters to neat Art Deco villas. The main town is **Perros-Guirec** ⓮, a mix of fishing-and-leisure port and unfussily old-fashioned resort town, although its Trestraou beach has also become popular for surfing. Some of the craziest rock formations, one like a giant baboon, are along the *Sentier*

BELOW: the distinctive pink rocks of the Côte du Granit Rose.

des Douaniers, the coastal footpath round to the gorgeous beach inlet of **Ploumanac'h**, which has a more chic feel, with a boutique hotel-restaurant. Boats also run from Perros-Guirec around the **Sept-Îles**, uninhabited islands that are breeding grounds for thousands of seabirds. One, the **Île aux Moines** (where boats land), has a medieval hermitage and 18th-century fort.

The coves further around the coast all have their sets of monster rocks, especially **Trégastel Plage**, where one has a strangely kitsch figure of Christ on top. Tiny **Île Grande**, linked to the shore by a causeway, contains one lovely village, and a bird reserve. On a clear day the combination of sea, rocks and crystalline light is ravishing all around this coast, and west-facing coves benefit from stunning sunsets.

Off the road west of **Lannion** a winding detour leads to **Le Yaudet**, where the remains of a Gallo-Roman fort and Iron Age settlement occupy a crag above the wooded Léguer estuary. Although the Romans were here, this isolated spot is said to be the model for Astérix's Gaulish village.

Land's End

Morlaix ⓯ sits in a gorge-like valley at the head of an estuary that made it an excellent refuge from enemies and winter storms. Its most prominent structure is an immense 1861 **viaduct**, which strides over the town carrying the Paris–Brest rail line, and now looks down on a forest of masts, for Morlaix has one of Brittany's best-equipped yacht harbours.

On the east bank of the river is the **Cairn de Barnenez** (May–Aug daily 10am–6.30pm; Sept–Apr Tue–Sun 10am–12.30pm, 2–5.30pm; charge), one of the largest Neolithic stone burial mounds in Europe, over 72 metres (236ft) long and dating from 4500–3900 BC. On the west bank the estuary ends at **Roscoff** ⓰, a rugged little granite sea town that was surprisingly prominent in cross-Channel affairs even before it became a port for British and Irish ferries. Mary, Queen of Scots landed here, aged six, in 1548 on her way to marry the French Dauphin, and in the 19th century Roscoff became the main port of departure for the Breton "Johnny Onion" men who for decades

Decorative mural near the port entrance of Le Conquet, departure point for boats to the islands of Ouessant and Molène.

BELOW: Ploumanac'h lighthouse.

TIP

Ferries to Brittany's offshore islands and trips around the coast are provided by several companies. Among the most prominent are Les Vedettes de Bréhat (tel: 02 96 55 79 50, www.vedettesdebrehat.com; Île de Bréhat, and tours); Penn Ar Bed (tel: 02 98 80 80 80, www.pennarbed.fr; Brest and Le Conquet to Ouessant and Molène, and Audierne–Île de Sein); and Compagnie Océane (0820 056 156, www.compagnie-oceane.fr; Lorient–Île de Groix and Quiberon to Belle Île, Houat and Hoëdic).

left every year with their bikes to sell their famous onions around Britain. An engaging museum, the **Maison des Johnnies** (tours June–Sept Mon–Sat 11am, 3pm, 5pm; Oct–Dec, Feb–May Tue, Thur, Fri 3pm; charge), tells their story. Boats run to the **Île de Batz**, often wind-blasted but one of the most engaging Breton islands, with beaches and lovely walks.

The prow of northern Finistère is more austere than areas further east, with few trees to stand against the Atlantic wind, and long, empty beaches backed by rocks and grassy dunes. The tendency to strangeness in Breton church architecture seems to become more accentuated in these parts, especially in the multi-towered spires. A cathedral-sized Gothic basilica dwarfs **Le Folgoët** ⓱, focus of one of the most famous *Pardon* religious processions each September. The countryside is also dotted with granite manors with more towers than one would ever think necessary, ideal places for declining aristocrats to go mad, such as the **Château de Kerjean** (July–Aug daily 10am–7pm; Apr–June, Sept–Oct Wed–Mon 1/2–5/6pm, Feb–Mar, Nov–Dec Wed, Sun only 2–5pm; charge), now an exhibition centre.

Mainland France's westernmost point, its true *Finistère*, is **Pointe de Corsen**, near St-Renan. To the south is **Le Conquet**, departure point (boats also run from Brest) to the islands of **Molène** and **Ouessant** ⓲, known to British sailors as **Ushant** and feared for its storms and terrifying rocks. The days when its 1,000 people – mostly women and children, since men were usually away at sea – really lived in isolation "at the end of the world" have gone (places to stay in the one village, **Lampaul**, are in short supply in summer), but it's still a wildly atmospheric spot, ringed by lighthouses. Bike rental shops help exploration.

Below Le Conquet the coast turns sharply eastwards into the ***Rade*** or roadstead of Brest, a superb natural harbour that makes it self-evident why this was chosen as one of France's main naval ports in the 17th century. One fact is most significant about modern **Brest** ⓳: in the whole city there is just one street, rue de St-Malo, that was not

BELOW: Ouessant Island.

destroyed or badly damaged in the siege of August–September 1944. Afterwards, no attempt was made at a St-Malo-style reconstruction, and so Brest today is an entirely modern city, a slice of contemporary France with its tower blocks and edgy suburbs. Its main visitor attractions are the 15th-century **Château**, which survived the war and is now a navy museum (**Musée National de la Marine**; Apr–Oct 10am–6.30pm; Sept–Mar 1.30–6.30pm; charge), and **Océanopolis** (May–Aug daily 9am–6-/7pm; Sept–Apr Tue–Sun 10am–5pm; charge), an ultramodern, very popular sea-life centre.

Fantasy churches and the Monts d'Arrée

Rural Brittany reasserts itself a short way inland at **Landerneau** ⓴, centred on the 1510 **Pont de Rohan** over the River Elorn, one of few inhabited bridges left in Europe, and the location for one of the largest Breton culture festivals, the *Kann al Loar*, every July. Around the countryside to the east and south are the ***Enclos Paroissiaux***, the church closes built from the 15th to the 18th centuries *(see page 296)*. One of the most extraordinary creations of the *Enclos* builders is only just south of Brest, in **Plougastel-Daoulas**, where the calvary, separate from the church, illustrates every aspect of the Easter story with over 150 carved figures, some of which look to have strayed in from the children's fantasy *Where the Wild Things Are*. Much older, the **Abbaye de Daoulas** (July–Aug daily 10.30am–6.30pm, late Mar–June, Sept–Nov Sun–Fri 1.30–6.30pm; charge) is a part-restored former Augustinian abbey, founded in 1130, amid large, peaceful gardens, including a delightful herb garden.

The most famous *enclos* are along the Elorn valley to the east. **La Roche-Maurice**, beneath a ruined 13th-century castle, has a Baroque ossuary from 1639 incorporating very Breton carvings of "the dance of death". **Lampaul-Guimiliau** church has a massive porch leading to a stunningly ornate interior, with wonderfully intricate altarpieces depicting the life of John the Baptist and other Gospel stories, a giant font that looks like a fairground attraction, and a 15th-century *Deposition of Christ* carved from a single piece of wood. In **Guimiliau** the most impressive work is in the grand Gothic porch and the calvary, from 1588, crowded with strange figures. **St-Thégonnec** ㉑ has one of the largest and most extravagantly Baroque enclosures, and the carving of the figures on its calvary is especially moving and dynamic.

To the south, the *enclos* at **Sizun** has an ossuary in pink stone, lined with figures of saints. One of the most atmospheric *enclos* is in lonely **Commana**, on the slopes of the **Monts d'Arrée**, the ridge of ancient mountains that runs across Finistère. The people of the surrounding valleys long avoided these bleak, wild hills, the land of fairies and giants. Along the crest are moors of rock, bog and heather, swept by what seem like continuous winds; then, drop down into one of the sheltered clefts, and you are surrounded by over-

Sculptural detail from the Enclos Paroissal de Pleyben, a fine example of a parish close (see box page 296).

BELOW: a typical Breton Calvary.

Kouign-amann is a Breton cake featuring buttery pastry and caramelised sugar. A speciality of Douarnenez, the name comes from the Breton words for cake ("kouign") and butter ("amann").

whelmingly dense woods. In a particularly luxuriant dip west of Commana, the **Ecomusée des Monts d'Arrée** occupies a 1610 mill, the **Moulin de Kerouat** (July–Aug daily 11am–7pm; Mar–June, Sept–Oct Mon–Sat 10am–6pm, Sun 2–6pm; charge), and recalls the life of the hill villages. The museum has a second location in a 1702 manor, **Maison Cornec** (July–Aug 11am–7pm; June 2–6pm; charge), to the south in **St-Rivoal**. Both lichen-clad buildings seem as much carved from the landscape as built.

Nowadays the Monts d'Arrée are popular walking territory, and together with Ouessant and Crozon form part of the **Parc Naturel Régional d'Armorique**, Brittany's largest protected area. From the highest point, **Roch'h Trévezel** (383m/1,256ft), there are immense panoramic views, and a *circuit des rochers* path links it to other crags such as **Montagne St-Michel**, with its rugged chapel. **Botmeur** and **Brasparts** are good places to begin walks. Villages south of the ridge are more sheltered and leafy, notably pretty **Huelgoat**, renowned for its huge boulders said to have been thrown down by Celtic giants.

Crozon and Pointe de Raz

South of Brest two giant spurs dart out into the ocean, the *Presqu'île* or "almost an island" of the **Crozon Peninsula** and **Cap Sizun**. Crozon forms the south side of the *Rade de Brest* (parts of it are military reserves), but the bay appears more like a vast inland sea, the city a streak in the distance. Snug inlets and tree-shrouded beaches lead out to majestic seascapes at the peninsula's end.

The northern entrance to Crozon is **Le Faou** ㉒, another almost ridiculously quaint Breton town, its *Grande Rue* lined with 16th-century slate-shingled houses. In a glorious location by the mouth of the River Aulne is the **Abbaye de Landévennec** (July–Aug daily 10am–7pm; Sept daily 10am–6pm; Apr–June Sun–Fri 10am–6pm; Oct–Nov, Feb–Mar Sun 10am–5.30pm; charge). Founded in the 5th century by

BELOW RIGHT: aquamarine waters off the rocky Crozon Peninsula.

The Parish Closes of Finistère

The idiosyncrasy of Brittany's religious architecture reached a peak in the *Enclos Paroissiaux* (Parish Closes) of central Finistère. Deeply Catholic, the area underwent a religious revival in the 16th century, at a time when many villages were prosperous thanks to the leather and linen trades. For decades, their merchants vied with each other in building ornate monuments in a unique local style.

An *Enclos* typically consists of a walled enclosure with an elaborately carved arched gateway, containing a church, a cemetery, a calvary and an ossuary for the bones of the dead. The ossuary was sometimes the grandest part, for a cult of the dead was a particular Breton feature. Inside, in contrast to the grey granite outside, churches have exuberantly colourful painted wooden fonts and altarpieces, with scores of figures in biblical scenes.

Created far from artistic centres, these remote churches are a European equivalent of the folk-Baroque churches of Latin America, built by local artisans who had vague ideas of "official" Gothic and Renaissance styles but mixed and adapted them to suit their own needs. The results could be erratic – when the proportions of a Baroque ossuary seem all wrong, or a church porch, as at Le Martyre, bends inwards – but they express an intense, distinctly Celtic religiosity with a rare inventiveness.

Saint Guénolé or Winwaloe, a monk of Welsh or Cornish descent, the abbey was only dissolved just before the Revolution. It is now an atmospheric ruin, with a very effective museum on monastic life and early Breton history. In 1950 a new Landévennec Abbey was founded nearby.

Further along the coast, **Le Fret** is a sleepy little harbour from where boats run to Brest and around the bay. At its end Crozon appears like a splayed hammerhead, with capes spreading north, west and south. Jabbing north, **Pointe des Espagnols** is so-called because Spanish soldiers occupied it in 1594 in an unsuccessful attack on Brest. **Camaret-sur-Mer**, westernmost town on the *presqu'île*, is a relaxed little harbour dominated by the pink stone **Tour Vauban**, built from 1689–94. Directly west, **Pointe de Tourlinguet** is wild and open; more famous is **Pointe de Penhir**, with a massive memorial to the Free French forces in World War II, and dramatically jagged rocks – popular with climbers – pointing out to a line of crags offshore known as the *Tas de Pois* ("string of peas"). The coast turns in around the **Anse de Dinan**, a glorious curving beach, to **Pointe de Dinan** and, much further on, **Cap de la Chèvre**, with a lighthouse, another war memorial and more immense views. The walks between the capes are among the most unforgettable stretches of the coastal footpath.

Beyond the modest beach resort of **Morgat**, more long beaches line the coast southwards. Just inland, **Locronan** ㉓, named after St Ronan, a 6th-century Irish missionary saint, is one of Brittany's most celebrated (and visited) beauty spots, an often-filmed town of granite houses built by 18th-century merchants.

Douarnenez ㉔ is a town with beauty and character. Its bay is said to be the site of the mythical city of Ys. From the 19th century it was France's foremost sardine fishing and canning port, an industry that made it a centre of left-wing agitation. It still is a significant fishing harbour, with plenty of ozone-scented movement. The imaginative **Port-Musée** (July–Aug daily 10am–7pm, Sept–June Tue–Sun 10am–12.30pm, 2–6pm; charge)

TIP

The GR34 footpath runs virtually all the way around Brittany's coastline, and walking at least part of it is an unmissable part of any visit. There are also many other long-distance footpaths, plus *Voie Vertes*, "Green Ways" or cycle trails, and the Equibreizh network of bridle paths for horse riding. Details are on www.brittanytourism.com or (in French) www.randobreizh.com for walks or www.equibreizh.com for riding.

BELOW: Douarnenez harbour.

TIP

Some of the most elaborate traditional Breton costumes can be seen at the *Fête des Brodeuses* or Embroiderers' Festival in Pont l'Abbé in early July. This four-day festival of music, dance and traditional arts culminates in the election of the "Queen of the Embroiderers" on the final Sunday.

is a combination of static museum and historic working boats. To the west villas cluster on the cliffs of the tranquil suburb of **Tréboul**, with irresistible views across to Crozon. The corniche path back to Douarnenez is delightful.

France's actual westernmost point may be at Corsen, but it's no surprise that many French people think it is **Pointe du Raz** ㉕ at the end of Cap Sizun, since it's so much more spectacular, a massive blade of granite cliffs. A great view of it can be had from its neighbour **Pointe du Van**. Between the two points the beach of **Baie des Trépassés** (Bay of the Dead) is so-called because of the ghosts of shipwrecked sailors said to gather here. Pointe du Raz is such a famous landmark that admission is charged for vehicles, and there is a big visitor centre with shops and restaurants, but there is still plenty of space on the paths around the point, full of birds. Visible in the distance is tiny **Île de Sein.** It holds a special place in modern French history; when its fishermen heard General de Gaulle's appeal from London to continue the fight in June 1940, they sailed their boats to England to volunteer. Ferries run from **Audierne**, on the south side of Cap Sizun.

Southern Finistère

Southern Finistère is known as *Cornouaille*, or Cornwall (the British county is written *Cornouailles*), since it was populated by migrants from across the Channel in the 5th and 6th centuries. Its southwest corner, the **Pays Bigouden**, is famed as a home of Breton culture and tradition, epitomised by the extravagantly tall lace *coiffes* of *Bigoudène* women. The Bigouden coast is part of wild Brittany, lined by austerely magnificent windswept beaches down to the lighthouses at **Penmarc'h**. In the main town of **Pont l'Abbé** ㉖, the **Musée Bigouden** (June–Sept daily 10am–12.30pm, 2–6/6.30pm; Apr–May Tue–Sun 2–6pm; charge) covers the area's language, dress and culture.

Said to have been founded by legendary Breton king Gradlon – although a settlement existed here in Roman times – **Quimper** ㉗ is the capital of *Cornouaille* and Finistère *département*,

BELOW: Quimper in bloom.

and plays a role as a Breton cultural centre Brest could never occupy. Its old centre is still a medieval fairy-town of massive houses jutting out over narrow streets; a spacious square opens up around the soaring **Cathedral of St Corentin**, mostly built from the 1230s to the 1490s. On either side are two impressive museums. The attractively modernised **Musée des Beaux-Arts** (July–Aug daily 10am–7pm, Sept–June Wed–Mon 10am–noon, 2–6pm; charge) has a range of European painting, but more distinctive is its display of art from (or connected with) Brittany, from Romantic portrayals of Breton folklore to the Pont Aven artists and contemporary art. The **Musée Départemental Breton** (June–Sept daily 9am–6pm; Oct–May Tue–Sat 9am–noon, 2–5pm, Sun 2–5pm; charge), in the former Bishop's Palace, covers Brittany's history and culture, from Iron Age stones to traditional dress, Art Deco furniture and Quimper's own colourful *faïence* pottery.

Brittany's southern coast has a much softer quality than the ocean-battered north and west. Village architecture has a more varied – and more conventionally French – look, and creek-sized estuaries form delightful little harbours, flanked by beach villages. The natural attention-grabber is **Concarneau** **28**. Its walled town or ***Ville Close***, fortified in the 14th century and renovated by Vauban in the 17th, is entirely intact on a little island in the middle of the harbour. A walk around the ramparts is fascinating, but because it is separate from the rest of the town the *Ville Close* is largely a prettified museum piece, with crêperies and often-tacky shops nose-to-tail along its one main street and packed crowds in summer. Around it, modern Concarneau is a substantial fishing port, with a giant yacht marina.

Its surprising fame as one of the birthplaces of modern art also attracts crowds to **Pont-Aven** **29**, and at times it can appear to have more biscuit shops than are humanly possible. But, it has a lived-in feel, too, and the beauty that drew painters here is still evident. Discreet signs help identify the locations of specific pictures, such as the mills along the exquisitely leafy River Aven.

The Ville Close de Concarneau.

BELOW LEFT: Quimper cathedral. is an imposing backdrop to the town's pretty medieval streets.

The Artists of Pont-Aven

Artists first began to visit Pont-Aven in the 1860s, drawn to western Brittany by its remoteness and archaic feel, epitomised by the traditional dress still worn by village women. It was also cheap to stay as long as one liked. Pont-Aven was happy to serve them, and soon the village had art supplies shops and two competing hotels.

Though called "the Pont-Aven School", individual artists were very different, but many had in common a use of symbolism, blocks of colour and simplified, primitive forms. Its most consistent members were Emile Bernard and Paul Sérusier, but the most famous was Paul Gauguin. He came first in 1886, honing his style in contact with the Breton landscape. Returning in 1889, he found Pont-Aven already too commercial, and moved to Le Pouldu on the coast. His last visit was in 1894, after his first voyage to the Pacific. He arrived with his Javanese mistress, Annah. This was too much for conservative Bretons. At a *fête* in Concarneau some sailors threw stones at Annah, and the ensuing fight left Gauguin with a broken leg. After months convalescing in the Hotel Gloanec in Pont-Aven (now the Ajoncs d'Or), he left France for good.

EAT

For a gourmet experience in an irresistible setting, try the *Moulin de Rosmadec* in Pont-Aven, in a wonderful old mill beside the glittering little River Aven (Venelle de Rosmadec, tel: 02 98 06 00 02; *see page 337*).

The excellent **Musée de Pont Aven** (July–Aug 10am–7pm; Apr–June, Sept–Oct 10am–12.30pm, 2–6.30pm; other months 10am–12.30pm, 2–6pm; charge) has works by all the Pont-Aven painters, and presents high-quality exhibitions.

Along the coast is the old-fashioned beach village of **Le Pouldu**, which was very remote in 1889 when Gauguin, Sérusier and Dutch painter Meijer de Haan came to avoid the crowds in Pont-Aven. The evocative **Maison-Musée du Pouldu** (June–Sept Tue–Sun 10am–6pm; Apr–May, Oct Sat–Sun 2–6pm; charge) is a partial reconstruction of the little hotel run by Marie Henry (who became De Haan's lover) where they stayed. As payment they painted the walls of the dining room, which has been faithfully copied.

The interior

Historically, the people of coastal Brittany, the *Ar Mor* or "land of the sea", had little contact with the people inland in the *Ar Goat*, "land of the forest", regarding them as semi-savage. Modern roads and agriculture have taken away most of the impenetrable, silent woods of the Breton interior, but an idea of the life once lived there can be gained at **Poul-Fetan** ㉚ (July–Aug 10.45am–7pm; June, Sept 11am–6-.30pm; Apr–May 2–6.30pm; charge), a village, abandoned like many others in the 20th century, that has been rather cutely restored as a "living museum" of rural life. Finding it is an experience in itself, winding down lanes through great swathes of green. A still older era is recalled at **Melrand** in the **Village de l'An Mil** (July–Aug daily 10am–7pm; Mar–June, Sept–Oct Mon–Fri 11am–5pm, Sat–Sun 11am–6pm; charge), a reconstruction of a Breton village from AD 1000.

In the very middle of Brittany, **Pontivy** ㉛ is an intriguing combination of two towns in one. One is a venerable Breton town, home to the vast 1450s **Château des Rohan** (Wed–Sun June–Sept 10.30am–6pm; Apr–May 10am–noon, 2–6pm; Feb–Mar, Oct–Nov 2–6pm; charge). In the 1790s, Pontivy, almost alone in central Brittany, opposed the Chouan rebellion against the Revolution, and so in the next

BELOW: Château des Rohan, Josselin.

decade Napoleon, deeply suspicious of the reactionary Bretons, set out to reward its loyalty by making it a stronghold of Parisian power, renaming it "Napoléonville" and designing a new town himself with enormously long streets and barrack-like public buildings. It was never finished, but its straight lines and disproportionately vast main square stand as a monument to the Napoleonic ego.

Little **Josselin** ㉜ is perhaps the prettiest of all Brittany's fairy-tale towns, with steep streets of 16th-century houses brimful of quirky details, a handsome Gothic church and an animated Saturday market. Its riverside **Château** (tours mid-July–Aug daily 11am–6pm; Apr–mid-July, Sept daily 2–6pm; Oct Sat–Sun 2–5pm; charge) has enough tall towers for any fairy story, and is still owned by the Rohan family, descendants of its 14th-century builders. They also have a doll museum (**Musée des Poupées**). Tours are given in English.

British visitors can be surprised to find that the **Fôret de Paimpont**, east of Josselin, is the home of King Arthur. It is traditionally identified with the mythical forest of **Brocéliande**, which in Breton legends and many medieval romances is the magical home of Merlin and the site of many other stories. Local lore and Arthurian enthusiasts have identified spots around the forest with legendary sites ("Merlin's Tomb", the "Spring of Eternal Youth", and more). The tourist office in **Paimpont** village provides excellent maps, and finding them adds to the enjoyment of beautiful walks through an intact stretch of Breton forest.

In the countryside between Pontivy and Vannes, the park around the elegant 18th-century **Château de Kerguéhennec** has been made into an attractive modern **sculpture garden**, with work by major international artists and temporary exhibitions (July–Sept daily 11am–7pm; Apr–Jun, Oct Fri–Sun 2–6pm; charge for château, park free; www.art-kerguehennec.com).

Lorient and Quiberon

Lorient was founded only in 1666, as a port for trade with India and the Orient *(L'Orient)*. In 1940 the Germans made it their main U-Boat submarine base, so the city was heavily bombed by the Allies. Ferries run from Lorient to rocky **Île de Groix**, with two villages and secluded beaches.

The rocky spike of the *Presqu'île* of **Quiberon** is linked to the mainland by a long neck of sand. Today tourism rather than fishing is its main business. Benign beaches spread along its east side, down to Quiberon harbour. The west side is barren and windswept, although its label "*côte sauvage*" rather overstates this. Beaches along the sand spit are a mecca for surfers and windsurfers.

Quiberon is the main port for passenger and (expensive) car ferries to **Belle-Île** ㉝, largest of Brittany's islands. There are superb walks around its coast, past forts built by Marshal Vauban in the 1680s, sheltered beaches on the mainland side and jagged cliffs

Upturned dinghies at Quiberon, a popular seaside resort and departure point for ferries to Belle-Île.

BELOW: cycling along the Canal de Nantes.

TIP

A Pass Découverte is available for several sites in the Morbihan *département* (including Poul Fetan, Melrand, the Cairn de Gavrinis, Petit Mont and Suscinio), with which you pay full price for the first one visited but reduced admission for the rest. A separate Pass des Mégalithes in the Carnac area also includes Gavrinis and the Petit Mont together with the Carnac museum, the Maison des Mégalithes tours and Locmariaquer. They are available from participating venues.

to the south and west, including the rocks of **Port Coton** painted by Monet. Ferries also run to tiny **Houat** ("duck" in Breton) and **Hœdic** ("duckling"). Until the early 20th century they were priestly autocracies, as the *curé* of each island controlled all the money, doling out a little to any islanders who ever needed to visit the mainland.

Carnac and the southeast

Carnac ㉞ is Brittany's busiest single holiday resort, with plenty of restaurants, bars and buzz along its *Grande Plage*. It is more famous as the centre of the densest concentration of megalithic stone monuments in Europe, and above all for the **Carnac Alignments**, awe-inspiring parallel lines of over 3,000 standing stones that extend like a great barrier for over 4km (2½ miles) behind the town. They were erected around 4000–3000 BC; there are many theories as to their purpose – from the legend that they were Roman soldiers turned to stone for persecuting Christians, to the idea that they formed ceremonial entries to temples – but none is established as definitive. The **Maison des Mégalithes** (May–Aug 9am–7/8pm; Sept–Apr 10am–5pm; charge) by Ménec alignment has a lively explanatory exhibition, and provides guided tours. In the town, the **Musée de Préhistoire de Carnac** (July–Aug daily 10am–6pm; Sept–June Wed–Mon 10am–12.30pm, 2–5/6pm; charge) has remarkable archaeological finds but tells the story in drier fashion, and mostly only in French. There are more prehistoric stones, including flat dolmens or "table stones", all around the area.

Vannes ㉟, capital of Morbihan *département*, has, like Quimper, a charming old town of winding shopping streets, with 14th- to 15th-century ramparts above the park of Promenade de la Garenne. The Romanesque–Gothic **Cathédrale St-Pierre** has an unusually plain, austere interior. Opposite it, **La Cohue**, a former covered market, hosts Vannes' **Musée des Beaux-Arts** (June–Sept 10am–6pm; Oct–May Mon–Sat 1.30–6pm; charge, free Sun), with Délacroix's *Christ on the Cross* and contemporary Breton art.

BELOW: the Carnac Alignments.

Other attractions of Vannes include its cafés around its yacht basin, which leads down to the **Golfe du Morbihan** ❸❻. Over 20km (12 miles) wide, this magical "little sea" (*Mor Bihan* in Breton) is dotted with over 40 islands, and frequented by vast fleets of seabirds. It is tidal, shallow and very sheltered – its mouth at Locmariaquer is no wider than a modest river – and so is ideal for lazy sailing, canoeing and other boating from idyllic villages around the shoreline. Some islands are privately owned, but boats run across to the largest two, **Île d'Arz** and the mini-paradise of **Île aux Moines**; others can be reached simply by walking across at low tide. Tourist offices provide very easy-to-use free guides to local walks.

There are also more prehistoric sites. Near **Locmariaquer**, the **Site des Mégalithes** (May–Aug 10am–6/7pm; Sept–Apr 10am–12.30pm, 2–5.15pm; charge) contains the **Grand Menhir Brisé** (Broken Menhir), an immense rock once 20 metres (65ft) tall that now lies in four pieces, a tomb barrow and the **Table des Marchands**, a carved dolmen.

Accessed by boat from **Larmor-Baden**, the **Cairn de Gavrinis** (Apr–Sept daily 9.30am–12.30pm, 1.30–6.30/7pm; Mar, Oct–Nov Thur–Tue 1.30–5pm; charge, includes boat; reservation advisable; www.gavrinis.info) is a tomb barrow on a Gulf island, with chambers carved with unexplained spiral patterns.

Right around the Gulf at **Arzon** ❸❼ is the **Petit Mont** (July–Aug daily 11am–6.30pm; Apr–June, Sept Thur–Tue 2.30–6.30pm; charge), a cairn-barrow with the novelty of a concrete bunker inside, built by the Germans in 1943 in the hope that Allied aircraft would not notice it.

By comparison to all the ancient stones, the 13th- to 15th-century **Château de Suscinio** (Apr–Sept 10am–7pm; Feb–Mar, Oct 10am–noon, 2–6pm, Nov–Jan 10am–noon, 2–5pm; charge) near **Sarzeau** is a complete newcomer. In a glorious setting within a moat, it's a fitting representative of all the pepper-pot-turreted Breton castles. ❑

The western side of the Quiberon peninsula, the 5-mile (8km) -long Côte Sauvage (wild coast) is ideal for a bracing walk past caves and coves – but the sea is far too treacherous for swimming.

BELOW: Locmariaquer beach.

GARAGE

INSIGHT GUIDES TRAVEL TIPS

NORTHERN FRANCE

Transport

Accommodation

Eating Out

Activities

A – Z

Language

Further Reading

TRANSPORT

GETTING THERE AND GETTING AROUND

GETTING THERE

By Air

Paris-Charles de Gaulle (CDG) airport is France's great air hub, especially for long-distance services.

From the UK and Ireland

Due to the convenience of Paris there are relatively few flights from the UK or Ireland to other airports in northeast France. Ryanair flies to Beauvais (which it calls "Paris-Beauvais") from Scottish and Irish airports, and there are more low-cost services to airports in Brittany and the Loire valley, with Ryanair or Flybe. As with all low-cost airlines, fares change greatly depending on the season. The following currently fly regularly to France, but timetables change frequently.

Aer Lingus flies to Paris CDG from Dublin and Cork, and to Rennes from Dublin.

Air France flies to Paris CDG from London Heathrow and London City, and from Birmingham, Manchester, Bristol, Southampton, Edinburgh, Aberdeen and Dublin.

bmibaby flies to Paris CDG from East Midlands airport.

British Airways flies to Paris CDG from London Heathrow, Birmingham and Manchester.

easyJet flies to Paris CDG from Luton, Bristol, Liverpool, Newcastle, Edinburgh, Glasgow and Belfast International, and to Nantes from London Gatwick.

Flybe flies to Paris CDG from Birmingham, Cardiff, Manchester, Southampton, Exeter, Glasgow and Belfast City, to Paris Orly from Southampton, to Rennes from Birmingham, Manchester, Southampton, Exeter and Edinburgh, to Brest from Birmingham, Manchester and Southampton, and to Nantes from London Gatwick.

Ryanair flies to Beauvais from Edinburgh, Glasgow, Dublin and Shannon, to Dinard from London Stansted and East Midlands airport, to Brest from Luton and Dublin, to Nantes from East Midlands, Leeds, Dublin and Shannon, to Tours from Stansted and Dublin (summer only), and to Poitiers from Stansted and Edinburgh.

Main Airlines

Aer Lingus
Tel: (IR) 0818 365000; (France) 0821 230 267; www.aerlingus.com

Air Canada
Tel: (Canada and USA) 1-888-247 2262; (France) 0825 880 881; www.aircanada.com

Air France
Tel: (France) 0820 320 820; (UK) 0845-084 5111; (USA) 1-800-237 2747; (Canada) 1-800-667 2747; www.airfrance.com

American Airlines
tel: (USA and Canada) 1-800-433-7300; (France) 0826 460 950; www.aa.com

bmibaby
Tel: (UK) 0905 828 2828; www.bmibaby.com

British Airways
Tel: (UK) 0844 493 0787; (France) 0825 825 400; (USA and Canada) 1-800-247-9297; www.britishairways.com

Delta Airlines
Tel: (USA and Canada) 1-800-241-4141; (France) 0811 640 005; www.delta.com

easyJet
Tel: (UK) 0871 244 2366; www.easyjet.com

Flybe
Tel: (UK) 0871-700 2000; www.flybe.com

Ryanair
Tel: (UK) 0871-246 0000; (IR) 0818 30 30 30; (France) 0892 780 210; www.ryanair.com

From the USA and Canada

Travellers from North America can obtain direct flights to Paris with Air France and several major airlines, particularly Air Canada, American Airlines, Continental, Delta, Northwest Airlines and United. Prices are competitive, so check around.

Paris Airports

Paris has two airports:

Roissy–Charles de Gaulle (CDG), 23km (15 miles) northeast of the city via the A1 or RN2, which handles all long-haul and most international flights.

Orly (ORY), 14km (9 miles) south of the centre via the A6 or RN7, which handles French domestic and some short-haul international flights.

Information for both airports tel: 3950, from outside France +33 1 70 36 39 50, www.aeroportsdeparis.fr.

Airport Transport

From Charles de Gaulle Airport

The airport has two main terminals, CDG1 and CDG2, and the smaller CDG3 mainly used for charter flights, with a free shuttle bus between them. The quickest and most convenient way into central Paris is on the suburban **train line** (RER), line B. There are stations at both terminals; the main station, at Terminal 2, also has TGV high-speed train services from outside Paris. RER trains stop at Gare du Nord and Châtelet-Les Halles in central Paris, where you can transfer onto the Métro. Trains run every 15 minutes from 5am to 11.58pm. Average journey time is 50 minutes and the fare €9.40.

There are several **bus** services. **Roissy Bus** runs to rue Scribe, near place de l'Opéra, calling at all Terminals every 15–30 minutes 6am–11pm; journey time is 45–60 minutes and fares similar to those of the train. **Air France** buses serve Charles de Gaulle-Etoile and Montparnasse and leave from both Terminals every 30 minutes 5.40am–11pm; journey time is 40 minutes and the fare around €15. From 12.30–5.30am the *Noctilien* Nightbus runs from Terminals 3 to Paris Gare de l'Est every 60 minutes. A shuttle bus service to **Disneyland Paris** departs every 20 minutes usually 8.40am–10.25pm.

Taxis to central Paris will cost about €50, with higher rates after 5pm and on Sundays. The journey will take around 1 hour, depending on traffic. It is customary, though not required, to tip, usually about 10 percent of the fare.

From Orly Airport

There are two terminals, Orly-Sud and Orly-Ouest. To get a **train** into Paris take the shuttle bus from either terminal to Pont de Rungis station on RER Line C, which stops at Gare d'Austerlitz, Champ de Mars-Tour Eiffel and other points in central Paris. It runs every 15 minutes from 5.50am–11.30pm. The journey takes about 35 minutes and the fare is about €6.30. Alternatively, take the **Orlyval** automatic shuttle train to Antony station on RER line B, for Châtelet-Les Halles and the Gare du Nord. Trains run about every 5 minutes from 6am–11pm. The journey takes about 30 minutes and the fare is about €13.

There are two main bus services. **Orlybus** goes to place Denfert-Rochereau near Montparnasse and leaves from both terminals every 15 minutes 6am–11.30pm. Journey time is about 30 minutes and the fare €6.60. **Air France Buses** go to Invalides and Gare Montparnasse, leaving from both terminals every 30 minutes from 6am–11pm. The journey takes about 35 minutes and the fare is €11.50. A bus service to **Disneyland Paris** runs every 45 minutes, 8.30am–7.30pm.

A taxi from **Orly** to central Paris will cost around €40 (more after 5pm and on Sundays) and take about 45 minutes.

ABOVE: the five-line Strasbourg tram network is an efficient transport system.

Between Paris Airports

Air France buses: Route 3 links Charles de Gaulle and Orly, leaving each airport every 15 minutes 5.55am–11.30pm. The journey takes about 1 hour and a single fare is €19.

Other Airports

Regional airports have dedicated bus services to their cities, such as the Navette Aéroport in **Nantes** (every 30 minutes Mon–Sat 5.30am–11.15pm, Sun 6.15am–11.15pm; €7), or local bus line 57 in **Rennes** (every 20–30 minutes Mon–Fri 5.26am–12.07am, Sat 6am–12.07am, every hour Sun 11.53am–12.08pm; €1.20).

By Sea

Several ferry services operate between the UK, the Republic of Ireland, the Channel Islands and France. Most carry foot passengers as well as cars. Prices change by season, time of day and from weekdays to weekends so check around when booking. Dover–Calais and Dover–Boulogne, parallel to the Channel Tunnel, are the busiest routes; Dover–Dunkerque takes a little longer but is cheaper. The western Channel routes (to Dieppe, Le Havre, Caen, Cherbourg, St-Malo or Roscoff) are more expensive but the crossings are longer and very comfortable, and depending on where you are going in France can save a lot of driving time. Ferry crossings from Ireland are overnight sailings and take about 18–19 hours.

Brittany Ferries: Portsmouth to Caen, Cherbourg and St-Malo, Poole to Cherbourg and Plymouth and Cork to Roscoff. Sailing times on UK routes are generally 5–9 hours, but fast catamarans operate on the Cherbourg routes from May–Oct in 2–3 hours. Tel: (UK) 0871 244 0744; (France) 0825 828 828; (IR) 021 4277 801, www.brittany-ferries.com.
Condor Ferries: Portsmouth–Cherbourg, and Poole and Weymouth to St-Malo via Guernsey and Jersey. Tel: (UK) 0845-609 1024; (France) 0825 135 135; www.condorferries.co.uk.
Irish Ferries: Rosslare to Roscoff and Cherbourg. Tel: (IR) 0818 300 400; (France) 01 70 72 03 26; www.irishferries.com.
Norfolkline: Dover to Dunkerque in a little under 2 hours, and Rosyth, Scotland to Zeebrugge in Belgium, conveniently close to the French motorway network. The Dunkerque route often has some of the lowest prices. Tel: (UK) 0871-574 7235, (from France) 0044 20 8127 8303; www.norfolkline.com.
P&O Ferries: very frequent Dover – Calais services, and also Hull–Zeebrugge. Tel: (UK) 0871 664 5645; (France) 0825 120 156; www.poferries.com.
SeaFrance: Dover–Calais. Tel: (UK) 0871-423 7119; (France) 03 21 17 70 33; www.seafrance.com.
Transmanche Ferries/LD Lines: Dover Boulogne, Newhaven–Dieppe, Portsmouth–Le Havre. Tel: (UK) 0844 576 8836; (France) 0825 304 304; www.transmancheferries.com.

By Rail

Around 20 **Eurostar** trains each day run through the Channel Tunnel between London St Pancras station and the Gare du Nord in Paris, with a journey time of just 2hrs 15 minutes, reaching top speeds of 300kph (186mph). Several also stop at Ebbsfleet or Ashford in Kent, Calais-Fréthun and the dedicated station for Disneyland Paris Resort. Like air and ferry prices, Eurostar fares vary a lot by season and time of day, so check alternative times when booking.

Eurostar trains also stop at Lille, which is a hub of the French **TGV** high-speed rail network, with direct services to many parts of the country. If you are not actually heading for Paris changing trains in Lille is much quicker than doing so in the capital, where you have to travel between the main stations. Tickets combining Eurostar and internal French trains can be booked through **Rail Europe** *(see page 309)*.

There are also high-speed train services to France from other parts of Europe. **Thalys** trains run to Paris from Germany, Belgium and Holland; **TGV Lyria** from Switzerland; **Artesia** trains from Italy; and **Elipsos** trains (not yet TGV) from Spain. Many stop at other cities en route. Details are on the Rail Europe or French railways (**SNCF**) websites.

If you arrive in Paris, you will come into one of its seven major stations. Going clockwise, they are: for Britain on Eurostar, Belgium, Holland, north Germany and northeast France the station is the **Gare du Nord**; for central and southern Germany, Lorraine and Alsace the **Gare de l'Est**; for Italy, Switzerland, Burgundy, the Rhône valley, the Mediterranean and eastern Spain, **Gare de Lyon** or nearby **Gare de Bercy**; for most of Spain, the eastern Loire valley and most of the southwest, Gare d'Austerlitz; for Brittany and western and southwest France, **Gare Montparnasse**; and for Normandy **Gare St-Lazare**. *For more on French railways and tickets, see below.*

Eurostar: Tel: (UK) 08432 186 186; (Fr) 0892 353 539; www.eurostar.com.

By Bus

Eurolines provides bus services throughout Europe. There are seven daily between London Victoria coach station and Porte de Bagnolet bus station (Galliéni Metro) in eastern Paris, and less frequent services to other French cities. This is one of the cheapest ways of reaching France, with single fares from about £15. Connections can be made with everywhere in the UK via Victoria.

Eurolines: Tel: (UK) 08717 818 179; (Fr) 0892 899 091; www.eurolines.com.

By Car

Cars can be taken to France from the UK by ferry or the **Eurotunnel** shuttle through the Channel Tunnel from Folkestone to Sangatte, just west of Calais. Eurotunnel runs 24 hours a day, all year, and the journey time is about 35 minutes. You stay with your car during the trip. Eurotunnel and the ferry companies compete keenly on fares, and so Tunnel fares similarly vary widely between peak and off-peak times, so you can save money by travelling at night or in the early morning. The Tunnel's great advantage is in bad weather. Reservations are not essential but advisable to get the best deals, in peak seasons and to travel at a certain time. The Tunnel connects with the M20 motorway in the UK, and the A16 in France.

Eurotunnel: Tel: (UK) 08443 353 535; (France) 0810 630 304; www.eurotunnel.com.

Driving requirements

To take your car to France, you will need a valid driving licence, the vehicle registration document and insurance documents. US, Canadian, Australian, New Zealand and many other licences are valid in France. Vehicle insurance policies issued in the EU include basic third-party cover in any EU country automatically, but it is advisable also to take out fully comprehensive European cover, which most insurance companies provide for a small extra charge, and additional breakdown cover. It is also a **legal requirement** to carry a warning triangle and a yellow reflective waistcoat for use in case of breakdown; if you have to pull over by the roadside, you must put on the reflective jacket, and place the warning triangle 30m (98ft) behind the car. With a right-hand-drive car you must get headlamp deflectors for your lights, and it is a good idea (but not obligatory) to carry replacement light bulbs. Triangles, jackets and headlamp deflectors are on sale at the Tunnel Terminal, ferry ports and on-board ferries. *For more on driving in France, see page 309.*

Getting Around

By Air

Given the efficiency of the rail network, internal flights are not of great use for getting around northern France, but there are regular regional services from Paris-Orly.

By Rail

France has a very efficient and comprehensive rail network operated by the **SNCF** *(Société Nationale des Chemins de Fer)*. Unless you have a car, trains will be the best way to cover long distances. In areas where rail services have been closed, the SNCF operates replacement buses. There are various types of train; the fastest are naturally more expensive, but fares are still reasonable. The **TGV** *(train à grande vitesse)* ultra-comfortable high-speed trains are the stars of the system, with journey times from Paris or via Lille shorter than flight times for most destinations (3 hours 20 minutes, Paris–Strasbourg). Some regions, notably Normandy, are still not on the TGV network, but train services are still efficient.

Intercités and **Téoz** trains are more standard express trains, but still fast and comfortable, and **Corail Lunéa** are long-distance sleeper trains. Lastly, **TER** trains (or *Transilien* in the Ile de France around Paris) are regional services that stop at every station, with local lines in each region. Seat reservations are required for the top four types of train but not for TER trains, though you must still validate your ticket *(see box above)*.

Validating Tickets

Rail tickets and seat reservations (if issued separately) bought in France must be validated (date-stamped) just before you get on the train, using the yellow or orange machines by station platforms. Failure to do so may incur a fine. These machines are marked *compostez votre billet*. E-ticket printouts are the only ones that do not have to be *composté*.

Tickets and Information

Tickets can be bought at all SNCF stations, and by phone and online. As well as ticket counters most stations have ticket machines *(billetterie automatique)* that take cash and credit or debit cards. Tickets for trains that require reservation (TGV, Intercités) can be bought from 90 days ahead and until 5 minutes before departure. There are various fares for each train, depending on the seat class, the train time and when you book; check too if there are discount fares available in the same period (usually called *Prem*'s). If you book online you may be sent an email confirmation, which you should print out, or you can collect the ticket at the station. Except with email tickets you must always remember to **validate** your ticket just before boarding the train *(see box above)*.

You can also pre-book a rental car *(Train + Auto)*, bike *(Train + Vélo)* or hotel *(Train + Hôtel)* at your destination. Disabled travellers can arrange assistance through the Accès Plus programme; details (in French) are on the main SNCF website.

SNCF tickets can be booked outside France through **Rail Europe**, which has separate websites for the UK, USA and other territories and can include train connections throughout Europe. You can also book with the English-language pages of www.voyages-sncf.com, but it is often simpler to use Rail Europe.

Timetable and other information is available in English on the **SNCF** websites www.sncf.com and www.voyages-sncf.com, and from **Rail Europe**. Station information offices also provide timetable leaflets. Invaluable extra information on how to get the best out of all European railways is on **The Man in Seat 61** website.

Rail Europe

UK: Tel: 0844 848 5848; www.raileurope.co.uk
USA: Tel: 1-800 622 8600; www.raileurope.com
Canada: Tel: 1-800 361 7245; www.raileurope.com
From other countries, check www.raileurope-world.com
SNCF
tel: 3635; www.sncf.com (information); www.voyages-sncf.com (bookings)
The Man in Seat 61: www.seat61.com.

Rail Passes

A range of rail passes is available to foreign visitors, giving unlimited rail travel for a set time. They must be purchased ahead, outside France. Be aware, though, that unless you use trains a lot it can be cheaper to get single tickets, and that pass holders still have to pay supplements to use certain trains, such as the TGV. Hence it's worth checking on the benefits before buying a pass. Rail passes can be ordered through **Rail Europe**.

From the UK, InterRail Passes offer EU residents unlimited rail travel in France alone or several European countries on standard trains (not TGV or Eurostar) for a specified number of days within a month.

For visitors from outside the EU, the main rail pass is **Eurail**, which comes in various country combinations and time slots within a two-month period. Other options include the **EurailDrivePass**, combining train travel and car rental, and a **France Day Pass** for a day excursion from Paris. Full details are on Rail Europe websites.

By Bus

There are relatively few long-distance bus services, but **Eurolines** *(see page 308)* operates some from Porte de Bagnolet in Paris. Every region and *département* does have a network of local buses serving small towns and villages, centred on the bus station *(gare routière)* in the main town or city, often close to the railway stations.

By Car

Motorways/Autoroutes

Most French motorways are toll roads *(autoroutes à péage)*. Toll rates vary, but to get from Calais to Paris by *autoroute*, for example, costs around €19 in tolls. Some stretches of *autoroute* are toll-free, notably the ring roads around big cities like Paris and Lille, the A84 from Caen to Rennes and all the motorway-standard highways in Brittany.

On toll *autoroutes*, you collect a ticket from a machine when you enter the motorway, and pay at a toll gate when you exit. On some short toll sections there is a fixed toll, but usually the toll varies according to the distance travelled and type of vehicle. You can pay by cash or credit card. Regular users can subscribe to the *Liber-t* prepayment scheme, with which you get discounts and can get more quickly through electronic toll gates.

Full information, including a toll calculator for all routes, is provided in English on the *Societé d'Autoroutes* website.
Societé d'Autoroutes: www.autoroutes.fr.

Other Roads

Non-motorway main roads are *routes nationales*, identified by N or RN. Except at busy times – particularly the peak French holiday travelling times, the first and last weekends in August and the 15 August holiday – most are rarely congested, so driving can be very relaxing. Look out for green holiday route signs (BIS) indicating alternative routes, part of a national network of *Bison Futé* routes to avoid congestion at peak periods. To explore the countryside, get off main routes completely down the D *(Départementale)* roads.

Signposting is reliable, and some signs are especially helpful in navigating towns. When arriving in any French town, *Centre Ville* signs will take you to the middle of town; when you want to leave, look for signs for *Toutes Directions* (all routes) which will take you to the main trunk routes out of town. If one main city is signposted, an *Autres Directions* sign will point to others.

Rules of the Road

- The **minimum age** for driving in France is 18.
- Full or dipped **headlights** must be used in poor visibility and at night.
- The use of **seat belts** (front and rear) in cars, and crash helmets on motorcycles is compulsory. Children under 10 are not permitted to ride in the front seat unless the car is fitted with a rear-facing safety seat or has no rear seat.
- The French **drink-driving limit** is 0.5 mg alcohol per litre of blood.

Speed Limits

Speed limits are as follows, unless otherwise indicated:
Toll motorways: 130kph (80mph)
Urban motorways and dual carriageways; 110kph (68mph)
Other roads outside towns: 90kph (56mph).
Built-up areas unless there is a specific extra restriction 50kph (31mph).
There is also usually a minimum

Priorité à Droite

Give Way to the Right
Traffic on major roads in the French countryside normally has the right of way, with traffic being halted on minor approach roads by a white line across the road and one of the following signs.

- ***Stop***
- ***Cédez le passage*** – give way
- ***Vous n'avez pas la priorité*** – you do not have right of way
- ***Passage protégé*** – no right of way

A yellow diamond sign beside the road indicates that you have the right of way; with a diagonal black line it indicates you do not.

Be careful in small towns, villages and some rural areas where an older French system still applies: there may not be any road markings at all, and you are expected to give way to any traffic coming from the right, even if the road this refers to is only a tiny lane. Watch out especially for farm vehicles, whose drivers are the most used to this system.

If an oncoming driver flashes headlights it is to indicate that he or she is claiming the right of way, not that they are letting you go.

speed limit of 80kph (50mph) on the outside lane of motorways. Speed limits are reduced in wet weather as follows: toll motorways 110kph (68mph), dual carriageways 100kph (62mph), other roads 80kph (50mph).

Fines can be levied on the spot; if you pay immediately the fine will be lower than if you delay payment.

Highway Information

The official *Bison Futé* service provides all kinds of information on road conditions, including upcoming roadworks. The phone line is French-only, but the website is also in English.
Bison Futé: tel: 0800 100 200; www.bison-fute.equipement.gouv.fr.

Petrol

Sans plomb is unleaded petrol (gas); most stations have two grades, 95 and 98 octane, and diesel fuel (*gazole* or *gas-oil*), sometimes with high-grade *gasoil+*. Petrol is generally slightly less expensive than in the UK, and diesel is about 20 percent cheaper. The most economical places to fill up are the petrol stations attached to big supermarkets. In country areas many petrol stations are closed on Sundays, so fill up before a weekend.

Parking

In most medium-sized towns parking is restricted in the centre, with spaces marked out in blue and pay-and-display machines *(horodateurs)*. Charges are usually quite low, and parking is often free during French lunchtime (usually noon–2pm).

In cities street-parking spaces are much more scarce, so it's generally much more convenient to find one of the large pay car parks around all city centres (indicated with a large "P") and leave your car there for the day. *Libre* signs indicate if there are spaces available.

Accidents and Emergencies

It is compulsory to carry a luminous reflecting jacket to wear, and a red triangle to place at least 30 metres (100ft) behind the car in case of breakdown or accident for all vehicles *(see below)*.

In an emergency, call the police (tel: 17) or use the free emergency telephones sited every 2km (1 mile) on motorways. If you take out European insurance cover you will be given copies of a European Accident Statement Form, which both drivers should complete in case of an accident. Insurance companies also arrange breakdown cover, for an additional charge.

Car Rentals

Booking a car ahead with a hire company or through an internet booking service is now nearly always the way to get the best rates. Terms can vary, but usually the minimum age to hire a car in France is 21, and you must have held a full licence for at least a year, and present your licence, passport and a credit card. Some firms will not rent to people under 26 or over 60. Nowadays it's normal practice to include all taxes and unlimited mileage in the deal, but check that this is so. Collision damage waiver (CDW) is also usually included, and extra insurance cover is available for an additional charge.

Check that your car has the equipment obligatory by law in France, a warning triangle and luminous jacket.

Avis, tel: 0820 05 05 05
www.avis.com
Budget, tel: 0825 00 35 64
www.budget.com
Europcar, tel: 0825 358 358
www.europcar.com.
Hertz, tel: 0825 861 861
www.hertz.com
Rentacar, tel: 0891 700 200
www.rentacar.fr

Walking Tours & Holidays

A big range of walking holidays with camping or hotel accommodation is available, through tour operators outside France and some French tourist offices. Independent travellers can take advantage of low-priced accommodation offered in *gîtes d'étapes*, hostels offering basic facilities. For more information see the Gîtes de France website *(see page 313)*.

A good basic guidebook for serious walkers is Bruce Lefavour's **France on Foot** (Attis Press, 1999). Sigma Publishing produce a series entitled **Holiday Walks in...**, which includes Brittany, Loire Valley and Normandy. Useful websites on walking in France include:

www.randosbalades.fr Online version of a French bimonthly magazine about walking in France.
www.abc-of-hiking.com A listing of websites about walking with links to blogs and discussion forums.
www.ffrandonnee.fr French Walking Association or FFRP, which produces excellent trail guides.
www.franceonfoot.com General and regional information on planning a walking holiday.
www.sentiersdefrance.com Offers a wide variety of pre-planned but unguided walks in France.

Motorbikes and Mopeds

Rules of the road are largely the same as for car drivers, with the addition that helmets are compulsory, and dipped headlights must be switched on at all times. The minimum age for driving machines over 80cc is 18 years.

Inner-City Transport

Paris: Métro, RER and Bus

The Paris **Métro** is quick, efficient and generally the most convenient way to get around the city. There are 14 lines that operate daily 5.30am–12.30am (Sat till 2.20am). Lines are identified by number, a colour and the names of the last station in each direction. Supplementing the Métro is the **RER**, five suburban rail lines, identified as A–E, which run out from the centre to destinations such as the airports, Disneyland Paris and Versailles. In the centre RER lines have fewer stops than the Métro, so are faster.

There is a comprehensive **bus** network, with most routes operating from 6am–midnight, and *Noctilien* night buses through the night. Route details are posted up at bus stops. If you're not in any hurry, Parisian buses are a particularly good and cheap way to sightsee. Many are now wheelchair-accessible. In Paris, as on city buses everywhere in France, you board the bus at the front, and get off at the middle or rear doors. Paris also now has some **tramway** lines outside the centre, and is due to build several more.

The RATP transport authority has common tickets for all systems. The same T-Tickets are valid for Métro, buses and RER trains within the city, and can be bought at Métro and RER stations, airports, tourist offices and tobacco shops *(tabacs)*. Métro/RER stations have ticket machines as well as staffed booths.

Buying a ticket every time you travel wastes time and money, so it's better to buy a *carnet* of 10 tickets. There are lower fares for children aged 4–9, and free travel for those under 4.

Another option specially for tourists is the *Paris-Visite* card, which is valid for from 1 to 5 consecutive days on the Métro, bus and rail lines in Paris and the Ile de France, in zones 1–3 or 1–6. Card holders also get discounted entry to many museums and other attractions, and again there

ABOVE: *vélos* for hire.

are reduced rates for children. Cards can be bought from Métro and SNCF stations, the airports and tourist offices. Free Métro and other maps are provided at all stations, and full information on all tickets and cards is available from the RATP.
RATP: tel: 3246; www.ratp.info.

Other Cities

Lille has an underground Métro system that serves the whole of the Lille-Métropole conurbation, and Rennes and Rouen have urban rail lines. Many cities, such as Caen, Nantes and Strasbourg, have comfortable modern tramway systems, and all cities also have local buses.

Provincial cities have integrated ticket systems similar to those of Paris, with the same tickets valid for local Métros, trams and buses, and usually available as single tickets or in *carnets* of 10 for lower prices. They are generally sold from tourist offices, Métro or tram stops and tobacco shops. Most larger cities also offer some kind of city pass giving unlimited local travel and other benefits for one or more days, details of which are available from tourist offices.

Taxis

Taxis are most readily available at airports and railway stations. In Paris there are almost 500 taxi ranks, but be careful to hail only a genuine taxi (with a light on the roof). Paris taxis operate with three tariff bands: **Tariff A** (the lowest) 10am–5pm Mon–Sat; **Tariff B** (higher) 5pm–10am Mon–Sat and 7am–midnight Sunday and public holidays; **Tariff C** (the highest) midnight–7am Sun within the city and 7pm–7am Mon–Sat and all day Sun in suburban areas. There is now a single number for phoning for Paris taxis. Taxis with full disabled facilities should be available on request.
Paris Taxis: tel: 01 45 30 30 30.

In other cities, taxis are less numerous but still not hard to find. Each city has its own phone cab numbers.

Hiring Bicycles

Bicycles *(vélos)* are readily available for rent in cities, and in country towns near areas good for mountain-biking. Local tourist offices provide information on hire facilities, and French Railways rent bikes at some stations, which do not necessarily have to be returned to the same station. Bikes can be carried free on buses and on some trains.

Many French cities now have public-access bike rental schemes on the model of the *Vélib'* in Paris, although there has been a falling-off in their popularity (the scheme in Lille has closed). Bikes are kept at "stations" around the city, from where you can rent a bike usually for any period from one hour upwards, and then leave it at any other "station" in the city. Charges are low, and visitors can subscribe for as long as they want; instructions are given at bike stations and tourist offices.

Outside cities, there are extensive regional networks of *Voie Vertes* or "Green Ways", cycle routes that allow you to cover long distances, such as across Brittany from Nantes or St-Malo to the Rade de Brest. All tourist offices have details of those in their area, and regional offices provide handy guides on paper and on their websites.

On Foot

All the main footpaths in France form part of the national network of long-distance footpaths *(Sentiers de Grandes Randonnées* or *GR)*. The routes are numbered for easy identification, e.g. the GR1 takes you around Paris and the Ile de France, covering 630km (395 miles).

Local tourist offices provide excellent guides to the main paths in their areas, and many walking guides are available. The official IGN *(Institut Géographique National)* Blue series maps, at a scale of 1:25,000, are ideal for walkers.

Hitchhiking

Hitchhiking is not generally recommended. **Allostop** is a nationwide organisation that aims to connect hikers with drivers (you pay a registration fee and a contribution towards the fuel), tel: 01 53 20 42 42, www.allostop.net.

Inland Waterways

One of the most pleasant ways of exploring a corner of France is on a narrowboat or one of the other craft that can be hired on the country's navigable canals and rivers. Choices range from piloting your own hired boat to enjoying the luxury of "hotel barges".

Burgundy is particularly well favoured with waterways; the longest is the Canal de Bourgogne, which connects the River Yonne in the north to the Saône in the south. Other popular options in northern France include the **Loire** and its tributaries, the Nancy–Strasbourg canal in **Lorraine** and **Alsace**, and, especially, the Nantes–Brest canal and the River Rance and the rivers and canals that connect St-Malo to Nantes, both in **Brittany**.

Some companies offering canal or river holidays are the following:

Outside France

Le Boat
UK: Tel: 0844 463 3594;
www.leboat.co.uk.
USA: Tel: 1-800 734 5491;
www.leboat.com.
Offers a wide range of cruisers on all the main waterways.
European Waterways
Tel: (UK) 01784-482 439;
www.gobarging.com.
France Afloat
Tel: (UK) 0870-0110 538;
www.franceafloat.com.
French Country Waterways
Tel: (USA) 1-800-222 1236;
www.fcwl.com.

In France

This is just a small selection of the operators available; *département* tourist offices have full local lists *(see Useful Addresses, page 352)*.
France Fluviale
Tel: 03 86 81 54 55,
www.bourgogne-fluviale.com.
Specialists in Burgundy and the Loire.
Locaboat Plaisance
Tel: 03 86 91 72 72; www.locaboat.com.
MS Niagara
Tel: 03 80 49 76 00; www.msniagara.com
A luxuriously converted barge that cruises the canals of Burgundy.
Paris Canal
Tel: 01 42 40 96 97; www.pariscanal.com.
Quite luxurious cruises on the canal network around Paris.

ACCOMMODATION

HOTELS, YOUTH HOSTELS, BED & BREAKFAST

Hotels

Hotels are plentiful in cities and along main highways, but the most attractive are often in small towns and coastal locations. All hotels in France carry national star ratings, from 1 to 5, set down by the government, but these can be very deceptive, since they are based on a checklist of facilities and rarely take into account such things as charm, individuality or overall quality of service. Many individual hotel and B&B associations have their own classification systems, which are more reliable. Overall, especially in country areas, good *chambres d'hôtes* (French for bed-and-breakfast) are now often a more attractive option, and better value, than hotels.

Hotel and other accommodation prices nearly always vary by season: in most of the country, peak season is July–August, perhaps also including Easter and the Christmas season, and lower prices apply the rest of the time, although many places also have a "mid-season" and then one with the lowest prices, generally October–November and February–March. Paris seasons are broadly similar but more variable: there are price hikes during such things as the fashion weeks in spring and autumn, and some business hotels (as in other cities) are actually cheaper in summer. In general, though, if you can avoid travelling in France in July and August your costs can drop a great deal.

Hotel prices are charged per room, rather than per person, and breakfast is usually charged for separately (in contrast to *chambres d'hôtes*). Many traditional hotels also have restaurants, and offer half-board *(demi-pension)* or full board *(pension complète)* as well as room-only bookings. Some hotels, especially in beach towns, may require you to have at least one meal in the hotel *(demi-pension)* in peak summer seasons. Hotels are required to display their room prices and menus outside, and details of room prices should also be visible either in reception or on the back of bedroom doors.

Lists of hotels for each area are provided in booklets and online by French Tourist Offices abroad and (more comprehensively) by regional, *département* and city tourist offices in France *(see page 352)*. Several regional and local websites have booking services.

Hotel Groups

Several hotel chains and associations offer central booking services.

Accor Hotels, tel: (UK) 0871 702 9469, (France) 0825 012 011, www.accor.com. France's biggest hotel group (and one of the biggest in the world), with several brands covering every comfort grade: Sofitel, Pullman and the more boutique-ish MGallery are all luxurious; Novotel, Mercure and Ibis hotels are reliable, good-value mid-range hotels, and Novotels in particular have superior provision for children; Suitehotels and Adagio are self-contained apartments, for slightly longer stays; and Etaphotel and Formule 1 are bargain-basement minimalist hotels for keeping to tight budgets. The group also has spa and casino hotels. Accor hotels, found all over France, are not associated with great character but are very professionally run, and reliably good value.

Logis de France, tel: (France) 01 45 84 83 84, www.logishotels.com. Very different from the hotel corporations, Logis are an association, not a chain, of independent, usually family-run, small hotels where the owner must live on or near the premises. They include a large proportion of France's traditional small-town hotels, and while some are quite elderly they guarantee a level of individuality and often great charm the chains cannot. With their own grading system of from 1–4 *cheminées* (chimneys), they maintain high standards at very reasonable prices, and most have restaurants that are committed to maintaining and presenting local cuisine. Four-chimney Logis are called Logis d'Exception, and can be gorgeous.

Louvre Hôtels, tel: (France) 01 64 62 48 64, www.louvrehotels.com. Another large group with several brands from the upscale Royal Tulips to the functional mid-range Tulip Inns and the motel-like Campanile hotels.

Relais et Châteaux, tel: (UK) 00 800 2000 00 02, (France) 0825 825 180, www.relaischateaux.com. Representing most of the *premier cru* of French luxury hotels and many gourmet restaurants, with indulgent opulence guaranteed.

Relais du Silence, tel: (UK) 020 7295 0301, (France) 01 44 49 79 00, www.relaisdusilence.com. Another luxury hotel group that particularly represents country-house hotels.

Bed & Breakfast

There is a broad range of bed and breakfast or *chambres d'hôtes* accommodation across France from simple rooms on farms to magnificent old manor houses, elegant town houses and even châteaux. They can have a maximum of only five or six rooms, and breakfasts, usually very generous, are included. Prices are usually lower than for comparable hotels in the same area. Staying in *chambres d'hôtes* is commonly the most enjoyable as well as the best-value way to see the French countryside, an ideal opportunity really to get to know an area and its people. Some, especially in country areas where the nearest restaurant may be a good drive away, offer *table d'hôtes* as well on request, home-cooked evening meals of local dishes.

Nearly all *chambres d'hôtes* are registered with one of three organisations. Most rural *chambres d'hôtes* are part of the national **Gîtes de France** federation, which coordinates and takes bookings for farmhouse and other rural accommodation across France. It has its own classification system for its *chambres d'hôtes*, from 1 to 4 *épis* ("ears of wheat"). The other main organisation is **Clévacances**, which crosses over *Gîtes de France* in some country areas but also has B&Bs in many towns and around the coast. Its grading system uses from 1 to 4 *clés* ("keys"), and is sometimes better at identifying really attractive places than the *épis* of *Gîtes de France*. In either system, anywhere with 3 or 4 *épis* or *clés* will be pretty and very enjoyable, and those graded 4 are often additionally classed as *gîtes de charme*, which are usually ravishing. Lastly, **Fleurs de Soleil** is a small association that only handles *gîtes de charme*. In most areas, the more attractive *chambres d'hôtes* will probably cost around €60 or more in mid-season for a double room.

Tourist offices all have regional and local guides of available *chambres d'hôtes*. Bookings can be made through all the associations' websites, which also indicate which proprietors speak English and other languages. For peak seasons and summer weekends, good *chambres d'hôtes* are in great demand, so book early.

Clévacances, tel: (France) 05 61 13 55 66, www.clevacances.com.
Fleurs de Soleil, tel: (France) 0826 620 322, www.fleursdesoleil.fr.
Gîtes de France, tel: (France) 01 49 70 75 75, www.gites-de-france.com.

Self-Catering: Gîtes

France has what is probably Europe's best network of self-catering holiday cottages (*gîtes*). They are regulated by the same organisations as B&Bs – **Gîtes de France** and **Clévacances** – which handle bookings and grade their cottages in the same way *(see above)*. *Gîtes* are extremely popular as an inexpensive way of enjoying a holiday in rural France. As with B&Bs, the properties range from very simple farm cottages to grand manor houses and even the odd château. Many *gîtes* are off the beaten track, and a car, or at least a bicycle, is usually essential. Bicycles can often be hired locally or sometimes from *gîte* owners. *Gîtes* are completely self-catering (in many cases expect to supply your own bed linen), but most have owners living nearby who will tell you where to buy local produce. One other thing to note is that many *gîtes* are, naturally, on working farms, so having livestock close by will be part of the experience.

Regional, *département* and local tourist offices have lists of *gîtes* and may be able to arrange bookings. Bookings are best made well ahead for the July–August season, when the best *gîtes* are highly prized.

Camping

There is a good choice of campsites in France, many near lakes or rivers. Regional and local tourist offices *(see page 352)* produce lists of all recognised sites, with details of star ratings and facilities. As with other accommodation, sites can get booked up in high season, so consider advance booking. The Michelin *Camping/Caravanning Guide* lists sites which accept (or insist on) pre-booking.

Campsites, like hotels, have official classifications from one-star sites (minimal comfort, water points, showers and sinks) to four-star luxury sites with more space to each pitch, and above-average facilities, often including a restaurant or takeaway food, games areas and swimming pools. The majority of sites are two-star. Some farms offer "official" sites under the auspices of the *Gîtes de France (see above)*, which are designated *camping à la ferme*; facilities are usually limited but farmers are only allowed to have six pitches and if you are lucky you will get to know the farm and some of its produce.

Packaged camping holidays are popular and very convenient, as all the camping paraphernalia is provided on the site. Many sites offer facilities for sports such as windsurfing, which can be included in the package, and many offer kids' clubs and other activities for children. Some sites are very large, however, and might not suit those who wish to get away from it all.

Campsites designated ***aire naturelle de camping*** are grounds where facilities are absolutely minimal and have prices to match. These have a maximum of 25 pitches so they offer the opportunity to stay away from some of the more commercial sites. The **FFCC guide** *(see below)* lists over 2,000 of these sites nationwide.

Camping Reservations and Information

Alan Rogers Travel Service, tel: (UK) 01580-214 4000, www.alanrogers.com.
Camping and Caravanning Club, tel: (UK) 0845 130 7632, www.campingandcaravanning club.co.uk.
French Federation for Camping and Caravanning guide (FFCC), tel: 01 42 72 84 08, www.ffcc.fr. Lists 11,000 sites nationwide, and indicates which have facilities for disabled campers.
Michelin Green Guide – Camping/Caravanning France is very informative and also lists sites with facilities for the disabled.
Caravan Club, tel: 01342-326 944, www.caravanclub.co.uk.

Youth Hostels

Holders of accredited Youth Hostel cards can stay in French hostels run by either of two separate organisations: **Fédération Unie des Auberges de Jeunesse (FUAJ)**, tel: 01 44 89 87 27, www.fuaj.org, or the smaller **Ligue Française pour les Auberges de Jeunesse (LFAJ)**, tel: 01 44 16 78 78, www.auberges-de-jeunesse.com. Expect to pay around €9 per night.

The British **Youth Hostel Association (YHA)** provides comprehensive information on hostels around the world, as well as supplying Youth Hostel cards; contact tel: 0800 0191 700, www.yha.org.uk. In the US apply to **Hostelling International-USA**, tel: 301-495 1240, www.hiusa.org.

Gîtes d'etapes offer hostel accommodation in country areas, particularly in national parks, and are popular with ramblers, climbers and horse riders. Prices are similar to youth hostels – around €8 per night for basic accommodation, but €17-plus in more luxurious establishments which may be on farms offering riding facilities and/or stabling. You do not have to be a member of any organisation to use them. For information and reservations, see *Gîtes de France*, above.

Accommodation Listings

Paris

Hôtel de l'Abbaye
10 rue Cassette, 75006
Tel: 01 45 44 38 11
www.abbaye-paris-hotel.com
A tastefully converted abbey. The public rooms are comfortably large and filled with fresh flowers and there is a lovely conservatory-style breakfast room/bar in the old chapel, with French windows opening out onto the courtyard garden. **€€€**

Hôtel d'Angleterre
44 rue Jacob, 75006
Tel: 01 42 60 34 72
Formerly the British Embassy (Benjamin Franklin refused to enter to sign the Treaty of Paris because he considered it to be British soil), the hotel maintains a faintly British air. Elegant rooms, often with splendid bathrooms and a lovely courtyard garden. **€€€**

Hôtel de Banville
166 boulevard Berthier, 75017
Tel: 01 42 67 70 16
A 1930s Art Deco-style town house with an elegantly furnished piano bar and excellent old-fashioned service. **€€€€**

Hôtel Chopin
10 boulevard Montmartre, (46 Passage Jouffroy), 75009
Tel: 01 47 70 58 10
Well back from the main road at the end of a 19th-century glass-and-steel-roofed arcade, this is a quiet and friendly hotel. **€€**

Hôtel Cluny Sorbonne
8 rue Victor Cousin, 75005
Tel: 01 43 54 66 66
Small hotel in a quiet street opposite the Sorbonne, close to the Pantheon and the Luxembourg gardens. **€–€€**

Price Categories

Price categories are for a double room without breakfast:
€ = under €100
€€ = €100–150
€€€ = €150–200
€€€€ = over €200

Hôtel Duc de St-Simon
14 rue de Saint-Simon, 75007
Tel: 01 44 39 20 20
A charming hotel in the heart of St-Germain. There is a little secret garden and a courtyard. The salon is beautifully furnished and the bedrooms elegant yet cosy. **€€€**

Hôtel Ducs de Bourgogne
19 rue du Pont-Neuf, 75001
Tel: 01 42 33 95 64
Furnished with antiques, the public rooms are warm and welcoming. Bedrooms are modern and well appointed. Ideally situated for the Louvre. **€€€**

Ermitage Hôtel
24 rue Lamarck, 75018
Tel: 01 42 64 79 22
Tucked away behind the Sacré-Cœur, a friendly little hotel filled with surprises, including a garden and a great rooftop view over the city; an old-fashioned antique-filled parlour; walls, skirtings and doors painted with scenes of Montmartre. Spacious bedrooms with tiny bathrooms and lots of floral wallpaper. **€**

Hôtel de Fleurie
32 rue Grégoire-de-Tours, 75006
Tel: 01 53 73 70 00
A very popular, family-run hotel which combines elegance and cosiness. There is a sitting room with stone walls and exposed beams, a bar and breakfast room and bedrooms are prettily decorated. **€€–€€€**

Four Seasons George V
31 avenue George V, 75008
Tel: 01 49 52 70 00
Fabulous antiques, paintings and tapestries adorn this vast famous hotel, beautifully restored and celebrated for its lavish style and sumptuous flower arrangements. There's a fashionable bar and Le Cinq restaurant has three Michelin stars. **€€€€**

Hôtel George Sand
6 rue des Mathurins, 75009
Tel: 01 47 42 63 47
Located between La Madeleine and the Opéra, and a short walk from the Louvre and the Champs-Élysées. Its bedrooms are fresh and harmonious and staff are very helpful. **€€€**

Grand Hôtel des Balcons
3 rue Casimir-Delvigne, 75006
Tel: 01 46 34 78 50
A wrought-iron balcony-fronted hotel with simply furnished rooms on an Art Nouveau theme. The buffet breakfast is substantial. **€€**

Grand Hôtel Levêque
29 rue Cler, 75007
Tel: 01 47 05 49 15
A modest, modern hotel located on a lively market street on the Left Bank. Simple rooms with air conditioning in summer. No restaurant; 24-hour reception. **€€**

Hôtel du Jeu de Paume
54 rue Saint-Louis-en-Ile, 75004
Tel: 01 43 26 14 18
A 17th-century building that began life as a palm-game court (the forerunner of tennis) and is now a very unusual hotel with stone walls, exposed beams and a glass-walled lift. There is a courtyard garden and a sauna. **€€€–€€€€**

Hôtel Le Crillon
10 place de la Concorde, 75008
Tel: 01 44 71 15 00
Built for Louis XV in the 18th century, on the beautiful place de la Concorde, the Crillon is one of Paris's truly grand hotels. A splendid mansion with marble reception hall, winter-garden tea room, presidential suites, piano bar, fitness centre and two restaurants, Les Ambassadeurs and L'Obélisque, all on a most luxurious scale. **€€€€**

Hôtel Le Sainte Beuve
9 rue Sainte Beuve, 75006
Tel: 01 45 48 20 07
Discreet, cosy hotel with fireplace and antiques in the salon, tastefully decorated and hung with contemporary paintings.

Excellent policy of upgrading guests to a more expensive room than booked whenever possible. **€€€**

Hôtel Lutetia Paris
45 boulevard Raspail, 75006
Tel: 01 49 54 46 46
Opulent Art Nouveau hotel on the Left Bank, exquisitely decorated in 1930s style. Bar is a fashionable literary venue with live jazz. **€€€€**

Hôtel Montalembert
3 rue de la Montalembert, 75007
Tel: 01 45 49 68 68
Beautifully restored hotel with immaculate designer furnishings. You can choose between antique or sleek modern decor in the bedrooms. Splendid views from the eighth floor. **€€€€**

Murano Urban Resort
13 boulevard du Temple, 75003
Tel: 01 42 71 20 00
This hip, high-tech designer hotel on the edge of the Marais has novelties such as furry lifts, fingerprint recognition doorpads to bedrooms, a bar and Mediterranean restaurant, and a health spa. Two suites have their own private outdoor pools on the balcony. **€€€€**

Hôtel de Nesle
7 rue de Nesle, 75006
Tel: 01 43 54 62 41
A laid-back, student and backpackers' hotel (reservations by phone only), basic facilities and spotless bedrooms with vibrant murals on various themes. Some overlook a garden. **€**

Hôtel de Nice
42 bis rue de Rivoli, 75004
Tel: 01 42 78 55 29
The delightful result of

collectors-turned-hoteliers, featuring antique mirrors and doors, and period engravings, prints and fabrics. Basic amenities and small bathrooms but a wealth of charm and character. Choose your room carefully: some of them are cramped and noisy; those overlooking the courtyard are nicer and quieter. **€€**

Pavillon de la Reine
28 place des Vosges, 75003
Tel: 01 40 29 19 19
The best hotel in the Marais, ideally located on the place des Vosges, but with a quiet courtyard. Beautifully furnished with antiques. **€€€€**

Plaza-Athénée
25 avenue Montaigne, 75008
Tel: 01 53 67 66 65
A magnificent 19th-century hotel built and furnished in the Empire style. Close to the Théatre des Champs-Élysées and a favourite with performers and musicians. Fitness club, beauty parlour and five restaurants, all under the supervision of Alain Ducasse. **€€€€**

Regina
2 place des Pyramides, 75001
Tel: 01 42 60 31 10
Antique furnishings and flamboyant decor make this delightful hotel by the rue de Rivoli a favourite for film sets. **€€€€**

Relais Christine
3 rue Christine, 75006
Tel: 01 40 51 60 80
Tranquillity in the middle of St-Germain-des-Prés in this hotel in the cloisters and chapel of a 16th-century abbey. Tiled reception hall, stone-vaulted breakfast room with massive fireplace and large bedrooms, some of which overlook the lovely garden and courtyard. **€€€€**

Relais Hôtel du Vieux Paris
9 rue Gît le Coeur, 75006
Tel: 01 44 32 15 90
A 19th-century hotel which was a favourite in the 1950s and 60s with American Beat Generation writers William Burroughs and Allen Ginsberg. Today, it is a more luxurious establishment, all exposed beams, marble bathrooms, floral wallpaper and limousines. **€€€**

Hôtel Ritz
15 place Vendôme, 75001
Tel: 01 43 16 30 30
Guaranteed elegance with original marble and chandeliers, the Ritz is still the place to stay for many of the world's wealthiest people. Unashamed luxury on one of the most famous squares in the capital. Famed as the setting for the last supper of Princess Diana and Dodi Al Fayed. **€€€€**

Hôtel St-André-des-Arts
66 rue Saint-André-des-Arts,75006
Tel: 01 43 26 96 16
A late 16th-century hotel, originally built to house the king's musketeers, sporting an old shop-front facade. In the entrance, you will find an old choir stall (complete with misericords) and a listed staircase. The warren of thin-walled bedrooms are all individually styled, with exposed beams. Note that there is no lift or air conditioning. **€**

Hôtel Saint-Germain
50 rue du Four, 75006
Tel: 01 45 48 91 64
In the heart of St-Germain, close to the Sorbonne and the Luxembourg Gardens, the hotel has a warm and friendly atmosphere and comfortable bedrooms. **€€**

Hôtel St-Louis
75 rue Saint-Louis-en-Ile, 75004
Tel: 01 46 34 04 80
Smart, old-fashioned hotel on the Ile St-Louis, with warm, rustic decor and furnished with antiques. Close to the Marais and Notre Dame, and good value for the area. **€€**

Hôtel St-Louis-Marais
1 rue Charles-V, 75004
Tel: 01 48 87 87 04
Sister hotel to the Saint-Louis, with exposed beams, tiled floors and attractively decorated rooms. **€€**

Hôtel St-Thomas-d'Aquin
3 rue Pré-aux-Clercs, 75007
Tel: 01 42 61 01 22
In the heart of the Left Bank close to the Louvre and Musée d'Orsay. An attractive town house with plain, modern interiors. **€€**

AROUND PARIS (ILE-DE-FRANCE)

Disneyland Paris

Disneyland Paris
Sequoia Lodge
77777 Marne-la-Vallée
Tel: 0825 30 02 22
One of the seven hotels in Disneyland Paris, all playing on American themes. This one is inspired by a national park lodge. **€€€**

Kyriad à Disneyland® Paris
10 avenue de la Fosse des Pressoirs, 77700 Magny le Hongre
Tel: 01 60 43 61 61
A chain hotel with a free shuttle bus to the theme park. Reasonable prices if you book ahead. **€€**

Flagy

Hostellerie du Moulin
2 rue du Moulin, 77940 Flagy
Tel: 01 60 96 67 89
Imaginatively converted 13th-century mill with garden, cosy sitting room and wood-beamed rooms. Convenient for Fontainebleau or Sens. **€**

Fontainebleau

Aigle Noir
27 place Napoleon Bonaparte, 77300 Fontainebleau
Tel: 01 60 74 60 00
A grand 15th-century building with French Empire-style rooms. **€€€–€€€€**

La Demeure du Parc
6 rue D'Avon, 77300 Fontainebleau
Tel: 01 64 22 24 24
A renovated 17th-century building in the town centre, with its own grounds and a swimming pool. **€€**

Napoléon
9 rue Grande, 77300 Fontainebleau
Tel: 01 60 39 50 50
Fine old hotel with elegant salon, open fire, charming garden and restaurant.

Monfort l'Amaury

Saint Laurent
2 place Lebreton, 78490 Monfort l'Amaury
Tel: 01 34 57 06 66
Small but smart hotel north of Rambouillet. **€€–€€€**

Montigny-le-Bretonneux

Auberge du Manet
61 avenue du Manet
78180 Montigny-le-Bretonneux
Tel: 01 30 64 89 00
A hotel and restaurant in a restored seigneurial residence by the waterside. Cosy individual rooms. Terrace for outdoor dining in summer; fireplace in winter. **€–€€**

Saint Ouen sur Morin

Auberge de la Source
8 place Saint Barthélémy,

77750 Saint Ouen sur Morin
Tel: 01 60 24 80 61
A comfortable hotel with spa bathrooms attached to the rooms. Situated in the Vallée du Petit Morin, 75km (50 miles) east of Paris. **€–€€**

St-Germain-en-Laye

Pavillon Henri IV
19–21 rue Thiers, 78100 St-Germain-en-Laye
Tel: 01 39 10 15 15
Grand hotel with views over Paris from the airy dining room. **€€€**

The North and Picardy

Amiens

Hotel Mercure Amiens Cathédrale
21–23 rue Flatters, 80000 Amiens
Tel: 03 22 80 60 60
Conveniently located by the cathedral and the Quartier St-Leu, this hotel has more character than most in the Mercure chain, but still has its good-value facilities. **€€**

Hotel Le Prieuré
17 rue Porion, 80000 Amiens
Tel: 03 22 71 16 71
The most characterful place to stay in Amiens, this historic Logis hotel has been extensively but sympathetically renovated to keep up with modern needs. Right by the cathedral and plenty of restaurants. **€**

Arras

La Maison d'Hôtes– La Corne d'Or
1 place Guy Mollet, 62000 Arras
Tel: 03 21 58 85 94
An exceptional urban *chambre d'hôtes* in an 18th-century town house lovingly restored to make the most of its architecture, with five gorgeous guestrooms and very welcoming owners. **€€**

Ostel Les Trois Luppars
49 Grand Place, 62000 Arras
Tel: 03 21 60 02 03
The oldest house on Arras' fabulous Grand Place, with a Flemish gable facade from 1467, is also its most memorable hotel. Rooms are small, but many have fine views (go for the upper floors). Great value. **€**

Baie de la Somme

Hôtel Picardia
41 Quai du Romerel,
80230 St-Valery-sur-Somme
Tel: 03 22 60 32 30
A traditional hotel on the harbourside in St-Valery that has been given a very fresh modern makeover by its young owners. Rooms are well equipped and very airy, and there are especially good family rooms. **€€**

Hôtel Les Tourelles
2–4 rue Pierre Guerlain,
80550 Le Crotoy
Tel: 03 22 27 16 33
The views across the bay from this imaginatively modernised, easy-going hotel are entrancing, and the seafood at the restaurant sets them off perfectly. A bargain. **€**

Beauvais

Hôtel Le Chenal
63 boulevard Général de Gaulle,
60000 Beauvais
Tel: 03 44 06 04 60
Atmospheric little hotel with colourful rooms and a friendly bar, well located for the station and buses to Beauvais airport. **€€**

Boulogne-sur-Mer and Wimereux

L'Enclos de l'Evêché
6 rue de Pressy,
62200 Boulogne-sur-Mer
Tel: 03 91 90 05 90
An exceptional *chambre-d'hôtes* in the old walled town of Boulogne, with five individually decorated, very comfortable rooms and a pretty terrace restaurant. **€€**

Hotel Atlantic
Digue de Mer, 62930 Wimereux
Tel: 03 21 32 41 01
This Art Deco hotel on Wimereux's seafront is a classic piece of the French seaside, with superb views from its best rooms and the reputed La Liégoise restaurant. Prices for seaview rooms go up a band in peak seasons. **€€–€€€**

Calais

Hotel Meurice
5–7, rue Edmond Roche,
62100 Calais
Tel: 03 21 34 57 03
Rebuilt after World War II, the Meurice nevertheless maintains some of the classic grand-hotel style that has made it the best in Calais since the 1770s. Reasonable prices. **€€€**

Chantilly

Château de la Tour
Chemin de la Chaussée,
60270 Chantilly-Gouvieux
Tel: 03 44 62 38 38
Regal comforts are guaranteed on this opulent estate in the forest of Chantilly – not actually a historic château, but a Belle Epoque mansion – ideal for an overnight stay after a day at the races. Sumptuous restaurant and pool. **€€€**

Compiègne

Hostellerie du Royal-Lieu
9 rue de Senlis, 60200 Compiègne
Tel: 03 44 20 10 24
A grand old half-timbered hotel between Compiègne town and the forest. Rooms are generously sized, and there's a lovely garden into which the restaurant extends in summer. **€€**

Coucy-le-Château

Hôtel Bellevue
2 Porte de Laon, 02380 Coucy-le-Château-Auffrique
Tel: 03 23 52 69 70
In the old town beneath the dramatic ruins of the Château de Coucy, this charming hotel and its reliably good restaurant makes an excellent base for exploring the Aisne region. **€€€**

Dunkerque

Hôtel Borel
6 rue de l'Hermitte,
59140 Dunkerque
Tel: 03 28 66 51 80
A traditional hotel near Dunkerque harbour, built in the 1950s, and stylishly renovated. At most times of year rates are near the bottom of this price band, and very good value. **€€**

Ermenonville

Château d'Ermenonville
60950 Ermenonville
Tel: 03 44 54 00 26
A superb château hotel in the countryside east of Senlis, in a magnificent 18th-century mansion where Jean-Jacques Rousseau stayed for several months, invited by its enlightened aristocratic owner, and where he died in 1778. The rooms and restaurant are delightful. **€€–€€€**

Hesdin/7 Valleys

La Cour de Rémi
1 rue Ballet, 62130 Bermicourt
Tel: 03 21 03 33 33
The stables of a modest château in the countryside east of Hesdin have been converted with great flair to create this very attractive, stylishly modern hotel, which also has a great restaurant with creative modern cooking and an exceptional wine list. One room is in an especially romantic treehouse. **€€**

Laon

Hôtel de la Bannière de France
11 rue Franklin-Roosevelt,
02000 Laon
Tel: 03 23 23 21 44
Cosy, traditional hotel in the centre of Laon's medieval old town. Its similarly styled restaurant offers fine local cuisine. **€–€€**

Lille

L'Hermitage Gantois
224 rue de Paris, 59000 Lille
Tel: 03 20 85 30 30
One of the city's classic

Price Categories

Price categories are for a double room without breakfast:
€ = under €100
€€ = €100–150
€€€ = €150–200
€€€€ = over €200

Flemish buildings, a former hospital partly dating from the 1460s, has been beautifully restored and converted into this original luxury hotel. The Hermitage restaurant and Estaminet Gantois bar are an added attraction. **€€€**

Hôtel de la Treille
7–9 place Louise de Bettignies, 59000 Lille, Nord
Tel: 03 20 55 45 46
A good-value modern hotel in the middle of old Lille, well placed for the shopping streets, the rue de Gand restaurants and Eurostar, with nice views from its best rooms. **€€**

La Maison Carrée
29 rue Bonte Pollet, 59000 Lille
Tel: 03 20 93 60 42
This very stylish B&B in a big Belle Epoque town house with garden has five striking and comfortable rooms with all sorts of extras. It's some way from the centre, along the Métro to the west. **€€**

Montreuil-sur-Mer

Coq Hôtel
2 place de la Poissonerie, 62170 Montreuil-sur-Mer
Tel: 03 21 81 05 61
In a fine old town house in one of the region's prettiest towns, this veteran, family-run hotel has been modernised without losing its personality. Le Cocquempot restaurant also serves generous cuisine from the local *terroir*. **€€**

Recques-sur-Hem

Château de Cocove
avenue de Cocove, 62890 Recques-sur-Hem,
Tel: 03 21 82 68 29
This restored 18th-century château is situated in a wooded park between Calais and St-Omer, with a refined restaurant looking onto well-managed gardens. There is also a very comprehensive wine cellar. **€€**

CHAMPAGNE

Bazeilles

Château de Bazeilles
Rue Galliéni, Bazeilles, 08140
Tel: 03 24 27 09 68
Peaceful rooms in the rebuilt stables of a château just outside Sedan, built as a summer residence in 1750. Slightly run down, but there is a delightful restaurant in the Orangery. **€€**

Châlons-en-Champagne

Hôtel d'Angleterre
19 place du Mgr Tissier, 51000 Châlons-en-Champagne
Tel: 03 26 68 21 51
Small, elegant hotel close to the church of Notre Dame-en-Vaux, with four-star restaurant. Closed mid-July–mid-Aug and Christmas. **€€**

Colombey-les-Deux Eglises

Hostellerie de la Montagne
52330 Colombey-les-Deux-Eglises
Tel: 03 25 01 51 69
A charming hotel in a stone house with a pleasant garden. It has just eight bedrooms and a suite but a very well-known restaurant. **€€**

Condé-Northen

La Grange de Condé
41 rue des Deux Nieds 57220
Tel: 03 87 79 30 50
The 20 rooms in this hotel and restaurant northeast of Metz, on the road to Boulay, include three luxury suites. Among the facilities are a jacuzzi and sauna, heated outdoor pool and cigar cellar. **€€€**

Dolancourt

Moulin du Landion
5 rue Saint-Léger 10200
Tel: 03 25 27 92 17
A converted water mill 40km (25 miles) from Troyes. Fireplaces are lit in the lounge and bar in winter. There is a riverside terrace for use in good weather. **€€**

Epernay

Le Clos Raymi
3 rue Joseph de Venoge, 51200
Tel: 03 26 51 00 58
Delightful hotel in a 19th-century manor house, with seven bright and comfortable bedrooms decorated with great attention to detail. **€€–€€€**

Fagnon

Abbaye de Sept Fontaines
08090 Fagnon
Tel: 03 24 37 38 24
On the A4 from Reims, just 9km (5 miles) from Charleville-Mezières. Peaceful château set in a large park in the Ardennes countryside, with 9-hole golf course; close to large forest where you can walk and cycle. **€€**

Langres

Grand Hôtel de l'Europe
23–25 rue Diderot, 52200 Langres
Tel: 03 25 87 10 88
A charming old hotel with a good traditional restaurant. Closed Sunday evening in low season. **€–€€**

Reims

Le Boyer Les Crayères
64 boulevard Henri Vasnier, 51100 Reims
Tel: 03 26 24 90 00
A luxurious Relais et Châteaux hotel set in its own park close to the centre of town. The château offers beautiful rooms and has a renowned restaurant. Closed end Dec–mid-Jan. **€€€**

Grand Hôtel du Nord
75 place Drouet d'Erlon, 51100 Reims
Tel: 03 26 47 39 03
The pick of the hotels on this lively restaurant-lined square in the heart of Reims offers bright, well-tended rooms (those at the front are more spacious) and a helpful English-speaking welcome. **€€**

Ste-Menehould

Le Cheval Rouge
1 rue Chanzy, 51800 Ste-Menehould
Tel: 03 26 60 81 04
Charming, rustic hotel with functional, renovated rooms, brasserie and restaurant. **€**

Troyes

Hôtel de la Poste
35 rue Emile Zola, 10000 Troyes
Tel: 03 25 73 05 05
Centrally located in historic town; comfortable, with a bar and restaurant next door. **€€–€€€**

La Maison de Rhodes
18 rue Linard Gonthier, 10000
Tel: 03 25 43 11 11
Handsome half-timbered building in the town centre. The attic rooms are especially characterful. **€€€**

Villars-Montroyer

Le Carré Rouge
Route de Santenoge
52160 Villars-Montroyer
Tel: 03 25 84 22 10
Incongruously set in the countryside near Langres, the "red cube" is the minimalist creation of artist Gloria Friedmann. One of the most unusual hotels in France – it doesn't have running water or electricity, but uses pumped rainwater and firewood for cooking and heating. Sleeps up to six. **€€**

ALSACE/LORRAINE

Ballon des Vosges

Chalet Hotel du Grand Ballon
68760 Willer-sur-Thur
Tel: 03 89 48 77 99
Incomparably located near the top of Alsace's highest peak on the Route des Cretes, this chalet is owned by the Club Vosgien Strasbourg. If the decor and facilities are somewhat plain it's because the place is meant principally to serve the needs of walkers. The restaurant serves simple meals, including a vegetarian menu. **€**

Bergheim

La Cour du Bailli
57 Grand Rue, 68750 Bergheim
Tel: 03 89 73 73 46
Hotel and restaurant in a brightly painted building which is arranged around a pretty, flower-filled courtyard. The restaurant is in a 16th-century wine cellar. Some bedrooms are in an annexe a short way from the main building. **€€**

Colmar

Grand Hôtel Bristol
7 place de la Gare, 68000 Colmar
Tel: 03 89 23 59 59
Grand, traditional hotel with two restaurants specialising in Alsatian food and fish and game. **€€**

Le Maréchal
Quartier Petite Venise, place des Six Montagnes Noires, 68000 Colmar
Tel: 03 89 41 60 32
A classy small hotel in 16th-century building near the river, in the romantic "Little Venice" area of the old town. Rooms are decorated with antiques, in Louis XV and Louis XVI style. There is also a gourmet restaurant. **€€–€€€**

Gérardmer

Hostellerie des Bas-Rupts
181 route de la Bresse, 88400 Gerardmer
Tel: 03 29 63 09 25
Popular large chalet-style hotel, with swimming pool and restaurant, in a peaceful mountain setting. Part of the Relais et Châteaux group. On the D486, 3km (2 miles) from town. **€€€**

Kientzheim

Abbaye d'Alspach
2 et 4 rue Foch 68240
Tel: 03 89 47 16 00
The adapted buildings of a former abbey in a medieval village set in the vineyards. It has been in the owners' family since the 18th century. The rooms offer three different levels of comfort and price. One is equipped for guests with reduced mobility. **€€**

La Wantzenau

Relais de la Poste
21 rue du Gal de Gaulle 67610
Tel: 03 88 59 24 80
Hotel in a small town a short distance northeast of Strasbourg. The 18 tastefully decorated rooms are arranged on two floors with an elegant restaurant (closed Sat lunch, Sun dinner, all day Mon) downstairs. **€€**

Les Monthairons

Hostellerie du Château des Monthairons
26 route de Verdun, 55320 Les Monthairons
Tel: 03 29 87 78 55
An elegant château hotel, restaurant and spa (with hammam, jacuzzi and sauna). Three types of room are available: "château style", with high ceilings and canopied beds; "floral touch", on the second floor and in the attic; and more modern rooms called "Meuse la Vallée". **€€–€€€€**

Metz

Citadelle
5 avenue Ney 57000
Tel: 03 87 17 17 17
This luxury hotel of 44 rooms, 33 apartments and 3 suites occupies one of the last fragments of the citadel of Metz built in 1559. It has a well-known restaurant, the Magasin aux Vivres which gives cookery lessons. **€€€–€€€€**

Hôtel de la Cathédrale
25 place de Chambre, 57000 Metz,
Tel: 03 87 75 00 02
Charming small hotel in an 18th-century golden-stone building on a square near the cathedral. **€€**

Montbard

Hotel Ecu
7 rue Auguste Carré, 21500 Montbard
Tel: 03 80 92 11 66
A hotel with a gourmet restaurant, well placed for visiting the Abbey at Fontenay, which is just 6km (4 miles) away. **€**

Mulhouse

Hôtel Bristol
18 avenue de Colmar, 68100 Mulhouse
Tel: 03 89 42 12 31
Large, comfortable hotel with Art Deco salon, near the old town but on a main road. No restaurant. **€€–€€€**

Murbach

Hostellerie Saint Barnabé
53 rue de Murbach, 68530 Buhl
Tel: 03 8962 14 14
A complex of hotel, restaurant (Le Jardin des Saveurs) and spa set in extensive grounds of its own just outside Murbach. Surrounded by greenery and silence. **€€–€€€**

Nancy

Grand Hôtel de la Reine
2 place Stanislas, 54000 Nancy
Tel: 03 83 35 03 01
Majestic 18th-century hotel on place Stanislas, named after Marie Antoinette who stayed here on the way to marry the future Louis XVI. **€€€**

Hotel de Guise
18 rue de Guise, 54000 Nancy
Tel: 03 83 32 24 68
An old mansion conveniently located for exploring the centre of the city and reasonably priced but not suitable for a long stay. Popular with business travellers which means that you can get a very early breakfast (the only meal served). **€€**

Obernai

Les Jardins d'Adalric
rue du Maréchal Loening, 67210 Obernai
Tel: 03 88 47 64 47
A charming hotel in the heart of Obernai, with a swimming pool, tennis court and peaceful garden. Rooms are understated and stylish. An excellent breakfast is served. **€€**

Osthouse

À la Ferme
10 rue du Château, 67150 Osthouse
Tel: 03 90 29 92 50
Hotel with seven double rooms and a restaurant (L'Aigle d'Or), located in a village between Obernai and the Rhine. The bedrooms are delightfully decorated in plain colours, with wooden furniture, and exposed beams overhead. **€€**

Ottrott-le-Haut

L'Ami Fritz
8 rue du Château
67530 Ottrott-le-Haut
Tel: 03 88 95 80 81
Beautiful stone building dating from the 18th century just outside Obernai, at the foot of Mont Ste Odile. The restaurant serves Alsatian specialities. **€€**

Râon-l'Etape

Museumotel L'Utopie
Ile Haüsermann
88110 Râon-l'Etape
Tel: 03 29 50 48 81
Retro chic or dated nostalgia: you decide. This curious hotel consists of 9 "bubble-bungalows" built in 1967 on an island by a would-be utopian and visionary architect Pascal Haüsermann. Each bungalow sleeps 1 to 5 people. **€–€€**

Riquewhir

Couronne
5 rue de la Couronne,
68340 Riquewhir
Tel: 03 89 49 03 03
A prettily restored 16th-century house, located in the middle of the old town, with a cobbled courtyard. Some rooms have beamed ceilings and hand-painted walls and furniture. **€**

Strasbourg

Dragon
12 rue du Dragon,
67000 Strasbourg
Tel: 03 88 35 79 80
This hotel is in a renovated 17th-century building with a central patio near the cathedral. It is decorated in a contemporary style. Some rooms have views of the cathedral. **€€**

ABOVE: chalet-style hotel, Les Bas Rupts, in the Vosges mountains.

Hannong
15 rue du 22-Novembre,
67000 Strasbourg
Tel: 03 88 32 16 22
Charming town-house hotel, convenient for the old town, with a good wine bar. **€€–€€€**

Monopole-Métropole
16 rue Kuhn,
67000 Strasbourg
Tel: 03 88 14 39 14
Elegant wood-beamed hotel. Some of the bedrooms are furnished with antiques. Close to the Petite France historic area. **€€€**

Thionville

L'Horizon
50 route du Crève-Cœur,
57100 Thionville
Tel: 03 82 88 53 65
Modern hotel, with an old-world elegance. The restaurant has a lovely terrace for alfresco dining. **€€**

Verdun

Hostellerie Le Coq Hardi
8 avenue de la Victoire,
55100 Verdun
Tel: 03 29 86 36 36
This friendly hotel offers individually styled rooms and a very good restaurant. **€€–€€€**

Château des Monthairons
26 rue de Verdun,
55320 Les Monthairons,
Dieve-sur-Meuse, nr Verdun
Tel: 03 29 87 78 55
A grand 19th-century château, complete with turrets, set in parkland by the River Meuse (on the D34 south from Verdun). The rooms are spacious and elegant and there is a spa and an excellent restaurant. **€€€**

BURGUNDY AND FRANCHE-COMTÉ

Autun

Hôtel Saint-Louis et de la Poste
6 rue de l'Arbalète,
71400 Autun
Tel: 03 85 52 01 01
Elegant old coaching inn with airy bedrooms and a lovely dining room. Napoleon stayed here. Closed Jan. **€€**

Auxerre

Hôtel Normandie
41 boulevard Vauban,
89000 Auxerre
Tel: 03 86 52 57 80
Attractive 19th-century country house with quiet rooms overlooking the garden or terrace. **€€**

Beaune

Hôtel Central
2 rue Victor Millot,
21200 Beaune
Tel: 03 80 24 77 24
Comfortable central hotel with character. Traditional and modern decor. Modern bedrooms and a good restaurant. **€€**

Besançon

Charles Quint
3 rue Chapitre,
25000 Besançon
Tel: 03 81 82 05 49
Charming 18th-century mansion with a lovely garden, situated at the foot of the Citadel.The nine elegantly furnished bedrooms, with well-equipped bathrooms, have either a view of the garden or the cathedral. No restaurant. **€€**

Château de la Dame Blanche
1 route de la Goulotte,
25870 Geneuille
Tel: 03 81 57 64 64
Standing in its own leafy grounds, this handsome château, a 10-minute drive from the city, has bright, stylish bedrooms (some of them suites) and a gourmet restaurant offering regional

PRICE CATEGORIES
Price categories are for a double room without breakfast:
€ = under €100
€€ = €100–150
€€€ = €150–200
€€€€ = over €200

specialities. A romantic place to stay. **€€–€€€**

Chablis

Hostellerie des Clos
18 rue Jules Rathier, 89800 Chablis
Tel: 03 86 42 10 63
A peaceful hostelry, formerly part of the Chablis Hospices, with comfortable, if spartan, modern rooms. Excellent restaurant. Closed mid-Dec–mid-Jan. **€€**

Cluny

Hôtel de Bourgogne
Place de l'Abbaye, 71250 Cluny
Tel: 03 85 59 00 58
French poet and politician Lamartine was a regular guest at this stone-built *hôtel particulier*, which stands next to the famous abbey ruins. Simply furnished traditional bedrooms, plus three good-sized apartments, a cosy lounge and pretty patio garden. Copious buffet breakfast and a reliable restaurant. Closed Dec–Feb. **€€**

Dijon

Le Jacquemart
32 rue Verrerie, 21000 Dijon
Tel: 03 80 60 09 60
Friendly, inviting hotel in the old quarter; no restaurant. **€**

Nitry

Hôtel de la Beursaudière
5–7 rue Hyacinthe Gautherin, 89310 Nitry
Tel: 03 86 33 69 69
A delightful priory and attendant buildings transformed into a hotel and restaurant. Full of charm and fun – it even has its own theme song. **€€**

Nuits-St-Georges

Hostellerie la Gentilhommière
13 Vallée de la Serrée, 21700 Nuits-St-Georges
Tel: 03 80 61 12 06
A 16th-century former hunting lodge in a large park with a river. Beautiful rooms, all with garden views; a summer pool, tennis courts and optional dining under the pergola. Excellent restaurant. Closed Jan. **€€**

Sens

Hôtel de Paris et de la Poste
97 rue de la République, 89103 Sens
Tel: 03 86 65 17 43
Close to the cathedral, a hotel with charming public areas and comfortable, modern bedrooms. There is a large terrace, a pretty garden and a good restaurant. **€€**

Vézelay

Le Compostelle
Place du Champs de Foire, 89450 Vézelay
Tel: 03 86 33 28 63
An economical option for a visit to the famous pilgrimage church. Some of the bedrooms overlook the village, others have views of the garden or the valley. The cheapest ones are in the attic. **€**

Villers-le-Lac

Auberge Sur la Roche
Le Chauffaud
25130 Villers-le-Lac
Tel: 03 81 68 08 94
An 18th-century mountain farmhouse standing at an altitude of 1,150m (3,773ft) not far from the Saut du Doubs waterfall. Rooms for 2–6 people and a small dormitory sleeping up to 8. **€**

Vougeot

Hotel de Vougeot
18 rue du Vieux Château, 21640 Vougeot
Tel: 03 80 62 01 15
Simple hotel set in a wine town between Dijon and Beaune and ideal for visiting them both as well as the vineyards. There are 16 rooms distributed across three buildings giving a sense of independence and privacy. Below is a beautiful wine cellar. **€–€€**

LOIRE VALLEY

Amboise

Château de Pray
Route de Chargé, 37400 Amboise
Tel: 02 47 57 23 67
A historic turreted château just outside Amboise, with fanciful fireplaces and some romantic canopied beds. There's a swimming pool and a restaurant. Closed mid-Nov–2 Dec and Jan. **€€–€€€**

36 quai Charles Guinot, 37400 Amboise
Tel: 02 47 30 45 45
Beautiful, refurbished 18th-century mansion overlooking the river, with a pretty garden and swimming pool. There's a good restaurant too. A member of the Relais et Château group. Closed mid-Dec–mid-Jan. **€€€**

Angers

Hôtel d'Anjou
1 boulevard Maréchal Foch, 49100 Angers
Tel: 02 41 21 12 11
Old hotel restored and modernised with large, well-equipped rooms. Restaurant Salamandre serves traditional French food. **€€–€€€**

Hôtel du Mail
8 rue des Ursules, 49100 Angers
Tel: 02 41 25 05 25
Built in the 17th century as part of a convent; a charming hotel in a central yet quiet location. **€**

Azay-le-Rideau

Le Biencourt
7 rue Balzar, 37190 Azay-le-Rideau
Tel: 02 47 45 20 75
This budget hotel on the road to the château occupies a renovated 18th-century school. **€**

Le Grand Monarque
3 place de la République, 37190 Azay-le-Rideau
Tel: 02 47 45 40 08
Close to the château, the hotel has been charmingly renovated to combine the rustic atmosphere of an old manor house with modern comfort. A pretty courtyard and a good restaurant. Closed Dec–mid-Feb. **€€**

Blois

Anne de Bretagne
31 avenue Jean-Laigret, 41000 Blois
Tel: 02 54 78 05 38
A popular and cheerful little hotel quietly located close to the château. No restaurant. Closed Jan. **€**

Holiday Inn Garden Court
26 avenue Maundory, 41000 Blois
Tel: 02 54 55 44 88
A contemporary chain hotel on the outskirts of Blois, offering standard modern comforts. **€–€€**

Buzançais

Château du Boisrenault-Indre
36500 Buzançais
Tel: 02 54 84 03 01
This hotel in a Renaissance-

style château built in the 19th century stands in the countryside near a little town between Tours and Châteauroux. It makes a handy base for visiting the Brenne nature reserve. The rooms are spacious. Two are suites. There are also two self-catering apartments. **€€**

Chinon

Hôtel de France Chinon
47 place du Général de Gaulle,
37500 Chinon
Tel: 02 47 93 33 91
This historic inn in the heart of the old town has been renovated to a good standard. A maze of rooms have exposed stone walls, beams and ancient niches; many have balconies with views of the castle. There's also a good restaurant. Closed two weeks in Feb and two weeks in Nov. **€€**

Conflans Sur Anille

Château de la Barre
Château de la Barre
72120 Conflans sur Anille
Tel: 02 43 35 00 17
The count and countess de Vanssay, 20th generation of one of France's oldest noble families, welcome guests to this marvellous 15th-century château in the hills of the Perche (between Tours and Chartres). Normally only breakfast and afternoon tea are served, but candlelit dinners can be arranged on request. A cottage in the grounds has been converted into two apartments for longer stays. **€€€€**

La Flèche

Le Relais Cicero
18 boulevard d'Alger,
72200 La Flèche
Tel: 02 43 94 14 14
A peaceful 17th-century house with garden. No restaurant. Closed first two weeks in Aug. **€€**

Fontevraud-l'Abbaye

Le Domaine de Mestré
Mestré, 49590 Fontevraud l'Abbaye
Tel: 02 41 51 75 87
The abbey's 13th-century farmhouse offers a warm welcome and the farm's own produce for the table. Closed mid-Dec–Easter. **€€**

Hostellerie de la Croix Blanche
7 place des Plantagenets,
49590 Fontevraud l'Abbaye
Tel: 02 41 51 71 11
Delightful old coaching inn with wooden beams and stone fireplaces, close to the abbey. Good food and a pub. **€–€€**

Loches

George Sand
39 rue Quintefol, 37600 Loches
Tel: 02 47 59 39 74
An old coaching inn under the castle ramparts, full of medieval character. **€–€€**

Montreuil-Bellay

Splendid Hôtel and Relais du Bellay
96 rue Nationale,
49260 Montreuil-Bellay
Tel: 02 41 53 10 10
Elegant hotel (43 rooms in total) in its own grounds with a swimming pool, fitness suite and sauna and view of the château. Comfortable rooms, good food. **€**

BELOW: the charming Hotel Le Choiseul overlooks the Loire.

Nantes

Astoria
11 rue de Richebourg,
44000 Nantes
Tel: 02 40 74 39 90
A comfortable, traditional hotel, close to the château, museums and the botanical gardens. **€**

La Villa Hamster
2 rue Malherbe
44000 Nantes
Tel: 06 64 20 31 09
A bizarre and original place to stay for a night – not more than that: a flat equipped to make you appreciate what it is like to be a hamster, complete with wheel. **€€**

Orléans

Jackhotel
18 rue du Cloître Saint-Aignan,
45000 Orléans, Loiret
Tel: 02 38 54 48 48
Small, central hotel in a former cloister behind the church. **€**

Rochecorbon

Les Hautes Roches
86 quai de la Loire
Tel: 02 47 52 88 88
This luxury hotel consists of an 18th-century manor house glued to the side of a cliff in which caves have been excavated. Of the 14 bedrooms, 12 are in the rock. The house contains the restaurant and the remaining two bedrooms. Within easy reach of Tours. **€€€–€€€€**

Saumur

Anne d'Anjou
32–33 quai Mayaud,
49400 Saumur
Tel: 02 41 67 30 30
Lovely hotel set in a charming, 18th-century building with an internal courtyard and gardens beneath the château and beside the River Loire. Rooms have been renovated but some have original Empire decor. **€–€€€**

Les Terrasses de Saumur
2 rue des Lilas, Saint-Hilaire-Saint-Florent,
49400 Saumur
Tel: 02 41 67 28 48
Hotel and restaurant in a peaceful setting, overlooking the town and river. **€€**

Tours

Hôtel du Théâtre
57 rue Scellerie,
37000 Tours
Tel: 02 47 05 31 29
Small but charming rooms lead off a half-timbered 15th-century stairwell at this friendly hotel on the antiques dealers' street of Tours. **€**

Turquant

Demeure de la Vignoble.
3 impasse Marguerite d'Anjou
49730 Turquant
Tel: 02 41 53 67 00
This semi-subterranean hotel is a short way up the river bank from Saumur. It has one room and one family suite underground and a choice of more conventional rooms. What sets it apart is the heated swimming pool in its own open-ended cavern. **€€**

Vendôme

Le Vendôme
15 Faubourg Chartrain,
41100 Vendôme
Tel: 02 54 77 02 88
Built on the site of an old *auberge* (inn) used by pilgrims on their way to Santiago de Compostela, close to the centre of the old town. **€–€€**

PRICE CATEGORIES

Price categories are for a double room without breakfast:
€ = under €100
€€ = €100–150
€€€ = €150–200
€€€€ = over €200

NORMANDY

Alençon

La Louvière
Le Fault, 61420 St-Denis-sur-Sarthon, nr Alençon
Tel: 02 33 29 25 61
A stunning *chambre d'hôtes* in a beautifully restored farmhouse in the countryside west of Alençon, with five guest rooms, each with their individual touches of opulence, and an equally impressive garden with swimming pool. The owners' care for their house is also expressed in their hospitality. **€€**

Barfleur

Hôtel Le Conquérant
16–18 rue St-Thomas Becket, 50760 Barfleur
Tel: 02 33 54 00 82
An impressively solid granite edifice in old Barfleur that contains spacious, pleasant rooms, and has a nice garden at the back for summer breakfasts. There's no restaurant, but there are plenty of possibilities around the town. **€–€€**

Barneville-Carteret

Hôtel des Isles
9 boulevard Maritime, 50270 Barneville-Carteret
Tel: 02 33 04 90 76
Right on the beach in the cosy little resort of Barneville-Carteret, the Hôtel des Isles has been attractively renovated to make the most of the wonderful coastal light, with relaxing rooms in blues and whites. The friendly staff maintain an easy-going atmosphere and the restaurant has a modern approach to traditional seafood favourites. Closed Feb. **€–€€**

Bayeux

Churchill Hotel
14–16 rue St-Jean, 14400 Bayeux
Tel: 02 31 21 31 80
In the heart of old Bayeux, close to the cathedral and tapestry museum, this traditional hotel with cosy bedrooms is a long-running favourite with visitors to the Normandy beaches, and provides ample information. **€€**

Hôtel d'Argouges
21 rue St-Patrice, 14400 Bayeux
Tel: 02 31 92 88 86
This 18th-century town mansion, with grand antique-filled public rooms and bedrooms, is one of the most elegant options in Bayeux. Despite its grandeur, the atmosphere is very relaxed and it's centrally located. **€€**

Beuvron-en-Auge

Aux Trois Damoiselles
Place Michel Vermughen, 14430 Beuvron-en-Auge
Tel: 02 31 39 61 38
This half-timbered inn is actually only a few years old, but you'd never know it – to blend in with the celebrated village square (Beuvron is classified one of the "most beautiful villages of France") it was built entirely with traditional techniques. The five rooms, with equally traditional, cosy decor, are all lovely and excellent value, and there's a *salon de thé* showcasing local produce. If you like cider and Calvados, this is the place for you. **€–€€**

Cambremer

Château Les Bruyères
Route du Cadran, 14340 Cambremer
Tel: 02 31 32 22 45
An elegantly opulent country-house hotel in a small château amid lush Norman countryside outside Cambremer, with ample gardens, a swimming pool, and an equally smart restaurant. A very relaxing retreat. **€–€€**

Cherbourg

Hôtel du Louvre
28 rue de la Paix/2 rue Henri-Dunant, 50100 Cherbourg
Tel: 02 33 53 02 28
Close to the port in central Cherbourg, this traditional hotel has been attractively modernised with airy, white rooms and good facilities. Excellent value. **€**

Clécy

Hôtel-Restaurant Au Site Normand
2 rue des Châtelets, 14750 Clécy
Tel: 02 31 69 71 05
Fine food is a particular attraction at this bright little hotel in the heart of the Suisse Normande district, as it not only has a restaurant but also a *traiteur* (deli) producing irresistible ready-made meals. Rooms are very pleasant, and it makes a tranquil base for exploring one of Normandy's most scenic districts. **€**

Crépon (D-Day Beaches)

Ferme de la Rançonnière
Route de Creully, 14480 Crépon
Tel: 02 31 22 21 73
A distinctive hotel in one of the finest of the Bessin district's medieval fortified stone farmhouses, with beautiful, in some cases palatial, rooms dotted around the ancient complex. It feels remote, but is only a short distance from Bayeux, Arromanches (Gold Beach) and Courseulles (Juno). The superb restaurant is a showcase for inventive Norman cooking. **€€**

Dieppe

Mercure Dieppe La Présidence
1 boulevard de Verdun, 76200 Dieppe
Tel: 02 35 84 31 31
One of several big 1960s hotels along the beachfront in Dieppe, with fine sea views, the Présidence has gone up a notch with its renovation by the Mercure group. It offers good facilities and bright modern decor. **€€**

Villa des Capucins
11 rue des Capucins, 76200 Dieppe
Tel: 02 35 82 16 52
An especially charming B&B in a former convent. The small garden enclosed by high walls is a peaceful haven and the guest rooms that give onto it are snug and pretty. **€–€€**

Etretat

Domaine St-Clair-Le Donjon
Chemin de St-Clair, 76790 Etretat
Tel: 02 35 27 08 23

BELOW: room at the beachfront Mercure Dieppe hotel.

Eccentric architecture is a trademark of Etretat, and "The Keep" – a mock-medieval, cliff-top *château* from the 1860s – is one of its most whimsical buildings. In its new incarnation as a luxury hotel it makes the most of the architecture, with plush rooms named after famous Etretat visitors such as Proust and Offenbach, and the gourmet restaurant is equally sumptuous. **€€–€€€**

Eu

Hôtel-Restaurant Maine
20 avenue de la Gare, 76260 Eu
Tel: 02 35 86 16 64
Once the station hotel of this idiosyncratic little town in the Baie de Somme, this hotel has plenty of personality too, from the Art Nouveau dining room to the individual decor of each of its 19 rooms. The restaurant serves excellent Norman cuisine. **€–€€**

Giverny

Le Moulin des Chennevières
34 chemin du Roy, 27620 Giverny
Tel: 06 81 13 77 72
A magnificent 17th-century mill a short walk from Monet's house, with four lovely B&B rooms and one gîte: the suite, in a tower, is spectacular. Breakfast is served in a baronial chamber, and delicious *table d'hôte* meals are also available. **€–€€**

La Réserve
34 chemin Blanche, 27620 Giverny
Tel: 02 32 21 99 09
Gracious and generously sized B&B rooms furnished with antiques in a beautiful country house, set in spacious gardens in the woods above Giverny. **€€–€€€**

Hambye

Auberge de l'Abbaye
5 route de l'Abbaye, 50450 Hambye
Tel: 02 33 61 42 19
In a lovely rural setting by the River Sienne deep in the heart of the wooded Cotentin countryside, this unassuming Logis hotel, a short walk from the ruined abbey of Hambye, has been a favourite among travellers to the area for decades. The restaurant serves generous Norman fare, and once there urban life seems very far away. **€–€€**

Honfleur

L'Absinthe
1 rue de la Ville, 14600 Honfleur
Tel: 02 31 89 23 23
Impressive renovations are a characteristic of old Honfleur, and the integration of luxurious modern fittings into one of the historic port's oldest buildings (16th century) is impressive. Some rooms are quite manorial, others show a lighter touch. In a separate building there's also a very superior restaurant *(see page 335)*. **€€–€€€**

La Cour Ste Catherine
74 rue du Puits, 14600 Honfleur
Tel: 02 31 89 42 40
In a quiet hillside street, with a little café beside a flower-filled garden, this very cosy, very charming spot has a choice of B&B rooms or self-contained apartments, all at bargain prices. **€–€€**

Hôtel des Loges
18 rue Brûlée, 14600 Honfleur
Tel: 02 31 89 38 26
Chic and charming with all mod cons, this is the most appealing of Honfleur's boutique hotels, with modern design skilfully blended into the historic building. The breakfasts are delicious. **€€**

Le Havre

Hôtel Vent d'Ouest
4 rue de Caligny, 76600 Le Havre
Tel: 02 35 42 50 69
Le Havre's severe post-war architecture can feel oppressive, but this hotel is an imaginative pocket of boutique style, with softly furnished, comfy rooms and excellent service. **€€**

Lyons-la-Forêt

Hôtel La Licorne
27 place Isaac Benserade
27480 Lyons-la-Forêt
Tel: 02 32 48 24 24
One of the most historic buildings on Lyons' picture-book half-timbered square. An inn since 1610, La Licorne's interior has been daringly transformed into a stylish boutique hotel, with subtle design and state-of-the-art fittings in its grandly spacious rooms. The Licorne Royale restaurant offers gourmet Norman cuisine *(see page 335)*, and there's a garden and pool. Equally well placed for the Forêt de Lyons, Rouen and Giverny. **€€**

Mont-St-Michel

Hotel Croix Blanche
Grand Rue, 50170 Mont-St-Michel
Tel: 02 33 60 14 04
Hotels on Mont-St-Michel are always pricier than equivalent places on the mainland, and tend not to provide much in the way of good service to justify their rates, but if you want to stay over on the rock this is a decent option, with pleasant rooms that have been well modernised. Closed mid-Nov–mid-Feb. **€–€€**

Manoir de la Roche-Torin
La Roche Torin, 50220 Courtils
Tel: 02 33 70 96 55
A much better option than any of the hotels on Mont-St-Michel itself, this grand, ivy-shrouded old house sits beside the marshes on the south side of the bay, with spellbinding views of the mount from its restaurant, gardens and best rooms. The most attractive – with view, of course, and some with garden terraces – are quite luxurious, and the food is excellent. **€€**

Mortagne-au-Perche

Hôtel des Tailles
9 rue des Tailles, 61400 Mortagne-au-Perche
Tel: 02 33 73 69 09
A discovery in apparently remote Mortagne, this Louis XV-style town mansion has been carefully restored and now has four exquisite B&B rooms, all in period style. **€–€€**

Hôtel du Tribunal
4 place du Palais, 61400 Mortagne-au-Perche,
Tel: 02 33 25 04 77
The archetypal French small-town hotel, looking like something out of a Victor Hugo novel, the Tribunal has nevertheless benefited from some modernisation, including the addition of Wi-fi. The traditionally pretty restaurant is a renowned showcase for local cuisine (the town is renowned for its *boudin noir,* blood sausage). **€–€€**

Rouen

Best Western Hôtel de Dieppe
Place Bernard-Tissot, 76000 Rouen
Tel: 02 35 71 96 00
A classic town hotel by the train station, with well-sized, comfortable rooms. Its restaurant is famed for its traditional local dishes, particularly *caneton à la Rouennaise,* Rouen duck. **€€**

Hôtel le Cardinal
1 place de la Cathédrale, 76000 Rouen
Tel: 02 35 70 24 42
Rooms at this venerable hotel have been rather blandly if comfortably modernised, but the best, at the front and especially on the upper floors, have one great thing to recommend them: stunning views of Rouen Cathedral. It's also well located for all the other attractions in the city centre. **€–€€**

PRICE CATEGORIES

Price categories are for a double room without breakfast:
€ = under €100
€€ = €100–150
€€€ = €150–200
€€€€ = over €200

Le Vieux Carré
34 rue Ganterie, 76000 Rouen
Tel: 02 35 71 67 70
An informal, relaxed hotel with small but comfortable rooms within an old half-timbered building around a courtyard (the *Carré*). The breakfast room becomes a popular *salon de thé*, with delicious light lunches. Exceptional value. **€**

Saint-Saëns

Le Logis d'Eawy
1 rue du 31 Août, 76680 Saint-Saëns
Tel: 06 19 15 52 04
A delightful B&B in a lovingly restored half-timbered inn just off St-Saëns main square, in a likeable slice of Norman countryside. The four rooms are full of character, and breakfast can be served in a garden courtyard. **€**

Trouville

Hôtel Le Central
5–7 rue des Bains, 14360 Trouville-sur-Mer
Tel: 02 31 88 80 84
A classic but fun hotel in a stately Belle Epoque building on the seafront, with one of the town's most buzzing brasseries on the ground floor. Ideally placed for Trouville's raffish street life and its superlative seafood. The bedrooms are on the small side but have been given an imaginative and chic makeover. Those facing the port cost a little more, but are worth it. **€€**

BRITTANY

Belle-Ile-en-Mer

Hôtel Atlantique
Quai de l'Acadie, 56360 Le Palais, Belle-Ile-en-Mer
Tel: 02 97 31 80 11
Presiding over the snug little harbour of Belle-Ile's main village, this traditional small hotel offers delightful sea views from its best rooms, which have been attractively modernised in a light, airy style. The restaurant is one of the island's best, with delicious fish and seafood. Rooms are only available on a half- or full-board basis in peak seasons. **€€**

Brest

Hôtel de la Corniche
1 rue Amiral Nicol, 29200 Brest
Tel: 02 98 45 12 42
A charming small hotel in a traditional stone house on the outskirts of the city, with fine views over the bay. Excellent for coastal walks. **€**

Carnac

Les Ajoncs d'Or
56340 Plouharnel, near Carnac
Tel: 02 97 52 32 02
An ivy-clad farmhouse set in a pretty garden just a few minutes from the centre of Carnac. Its traditional rooms are tranquil and comfortable. The rustic restaurant serves local specialities. Closed mid-Oct–Mar. **€**

Concarneau

Hôtel Les Sables Blancs
Plage des Sables-Blancs, 29900 Concarneau
Tel: 02 98 50 10 12
Chic Art Deco hotel on a sandy beach outside Concarneau with contemporary-style rooms and an equally attractive seafood restaurant. The sea views can be enjoyed from the lounge terraces and the room balconies. **€€**

Le Conquet

Hôtel au Bout du Monde
Place Llandeilo, 29217 Le Conquet
Tel: 02 98 89 07 22
At "the end of the world", near France's own Land's End, and the quay for Ouessant ferries, this little hotel can never lack for atmosphere. Its 20 rooms have been given a colourful makeover. Wonderful for walking and taking in the sea air. **€–€€**

Crozon-Morgat

Grand Hôtel de la Mer
12 rue d'Ys, 29160 Morgat
Tel: 02 98 27 02 09
At the water's edge, this big 1920s Art Deco hotel is now a family-oriented "holiday club", with tennis courts as well as functional bedrooms with lovely views of the sea or a palm-tree-lined garden. Most guests stay on half- or full-board terms. Good value. Closed Oct–Mar. **€€**

Dinan

Hôtel d'Avaugour
1 place du Champ Clos, 22100 Dinan
Tel: 02 96 39 07 49
On Dinan's ramparts, with the medieval city behind it, the Avaugour has a lovely garden where breakfast and tea are served, with gorgeous views. The brasserie-restaurant is in a 15th-century former guardroom. **€€**

Dinard

Villa Reine Hortense
19 rue de la Malouine, 35800 Dinard
Tel: 02 99 46 54 31
Ideal for appreciating Dinard's Belle Epoque atmosphere, an elegant villa with plush, period-style rooms offering fine sea views from their balconies. Closed Nov–Mar. **€€€**

Douarnenez

Le Clos de Vallombreuse
7 rue d'Estienne-d'Orves, 29100 Douarnenez
Tel: 02 98 92 63 64
An elegant hotel in a Belle Epoque villa surrounded by a garden with a large pool, overlooking the bay. Rooms in the main house are traditionally opulent, while those in the annexe are more modern. The restaurant serves gourmet cuisine. **€€**

Hôtel Ty Mad
Plage St-Jean, Tréboul, 29100 Douarnenez
Tel: 02 98 74 00 53
One of the oldest hotels in Douarnenez, in a beautiful location above the quiet beach of Tréboul, the Ty Mad ("Good House" in Breton) has been refurbished in a bright but unfussy boutique style, with superior facilities

and a great modern restaurant. The views at sunset are stunning. **€€**

Landerneau

Le Clos du Pontic
3 rue du Pontic, 29800 Landerneau, Finistère
Tel: 02 98 21 50 91
In a 19th-century villa with garden, a short distance from Landerneau's historic bridge, this charming, relaxed hotel has comfortable modern rooms and an excellent, creative restaurant. **€–€€**

Locquirec

Grand Hôtel des Bains
15 rue de l'Eglise, 29241 Locquirec
Tel: 02 98 67 41 02
Luxury spa hotel on a headland just east of Morlaix. The modern rooms are beautifully furnished, and most have fine views. There's a smart restaurant, a lounge bar with open fire, a saltwater pool, jacuzzis and steam rooms, and various thalassotherapy treatments are available. **€€€**

Ouessant

Hôtel Ti Jan ar C'hafé

ABOVE: the grounds of the elegant Grand Hôtel des Bains.

Kernigou, 29242 Ouessant
Tel: 02 98 48 82 64
A place to get away from it all in comfort on lonely Ouessant, with eight stylish, pampering rooms. No restaurant, but nothing on Ouessant is far away. Rooms on the island are in huge demand in summer, and need to be booked very early. Closed mid-Nov–mid-Feb except over Christmas/New Year. **€€**

Paimpol–Ploubazlanec

Le Relais de Launay
18 rue de l'Arcouest, 22620 Ploubazlanec
Tel: 02 96 55 86 30
A low-key, friendly small hotel with fine sea views, on the roadside between Paimpol and the smaller village of Ploubazlanec and Ile de Bréhat. Rooms are simple but cosy, some with separate bathrooms, and so very low prices; the restaurant is a crêperie, with Breton specialities. **€**

Perros-Guirec and Côte de Granit Rose

Hôtel Castel Beau Site
Plage de St-Guirec, 22700 Ploumanac'h
Tel: 02 96 91 40 87
On the Pink Granite Coast's most beautiful cove, this veteran hotel has been given a smart boutique-style makeover. The Côte restaurant is similarly stylish with innovative, light cuisine. The views are always ravishing. **€€–€€€**

Hostellerie Les Feux des Iles
52 boulevard Clémenceau, 22700 Perros-Guirec
Tel: 02 96 23 22 94
Some of the Granite coast's loveliest views are the main attraction of this traditional hotel high on the corniche above the port and old town of Perros-Guirec. Rooms are light and comfortable, the dining room neatly pretty. **€€**

Ploermel

Hôtel Le Roi Arthur
Le Lac au Duc, 56800 Ploermel
Tel: 02 97 73 64 64
There are plenty of things to do in central Brittany's "King Arthur" country, especially for walkers, but this multifaceted retreat beside a lake aims to offer everything on-site, including a golf course, spa, fitness centre, extensive grounds, creative restaurant and more. Rooms are plainer than the public areas, so rates can be surprisingly low. **€€–€€€**

Pont-Aven

Les Ajoncs d'Or
1 place de l'Hôtel de Ville, 29930 Pont-Aven
Tel: 02 98 06 02 06
The long-established hotel where Gauguin, Sérusier and many other artists laid their heads is still going strong, and retains much of its Belle Epoque character – as well as an easy-going, family feel, and low prices. Floors may creak a bit, but the rooms have all the necessary modern comforts; the restaurant serves excellent classic French and Breton fare. **€**

Quiberon

Hôtel Europa
Port-Haliguen, 56173 Quiberon
Tel: 02 97 50 25 00
A traditional beach-front hotel that blends excellent facilities – including a spa and a great indoor swimming pool – with individuality and a relaxed atmosphere. The rooms have been imaginatively modernised, and the terrace restaurant is high quality. Closed mid-Nov–Mar. **€€**

Quimper

Hôtel Gradlon
30 rue de Brest, 29000 Quimper
Tel: 02 98 95 04 39
Just two minutes' walk from the cathedral and the streets of historic Quimper, the Gradlon has bright, charming rooms, and a cosy lounge bar. **€€**

Rennes

Hôtel Lecoq-Gadby
156 rue d'Antrain, 35000 Rennes
Tel: 02 99 38 05 55
An original city boutique hotel and restaurant with chic, comfortable rooms, very relaxing lounges and a pretty garden. Other facilities include an organic spa and a shop with local produce. **€€€**

Roscoff

Hôtel du Centre – Chez Janie
Le Port, 29680 Roscoff
Tel: 02 98 61 24 25
Even in windblown Roscoff there's a stylish option: this little hotel has 16 bright, fresh modern rooms, and an equally attractive bar-restaurant, focusing, naturally, on fish and seafood. **€–€€**

St-Brieuc

Hôtel Ker Izel
20 rue du Gouët, 22000 St-Brieuc
Tel: 02 96 33 46 29
A modest hotel not far from the centre of town, with peaceful, cosy rooms and the unusual extra at this price of a swimming pool in the garden. **€**

St-Malo

Hôtel Elizabeth
2 rue des Cordiers, 35400 St-Malo
Tel: 02 99 56 24 98
A venerable hotel in one of the oldest houses of St-Malo, next to the ramparts, with a fascinating stone cellar where breakfast is served. The 17 bedrooms are spread over two buildings; the best are in *Les Armateurs*. **€€**

Hôtel Le Nautilus
2 rue de la Corne de Cerf, 35400 St-Malo
Tel: 02 99 40 42 27
Great-value youth-oriented budget hotel, with 15 bright, comfortable rooms squeezed into one of St-Malo's fine old town houses. Staff are very friendly, and the bar is lively. **€**

Le Mont Fleury
2 rue du Mont-Fleury, 35400 St-Malo
Tel: 02 23 52 28 85
A special B&B in a Malouinière, an 18th-century shipowners' mansion. The five nautically themed rooms are spacious and attractive, there's a large garden, and owner Bob Haby is very helpful. **€–€€**

Vannes

Hôtel Manche-Océan
31 rue Lieutenant-Colonel Maury, 56000 Vannes
Tel: 02 97 47 26 46
Part of the Inter-Hôtel chain, this modern hotel nevertheless has plenty of character to go with its bright, very comfortable rooms, and is exceptional value. It's conveniently located for the old town, theatre and museums. **€**

PRICE CATEGORIES

Price categories are for a double room without breakfast:
€ = under €100
€€ = €100–150
€€€ = €150–200
€€€€ = over €200

Eating Out

Recommended Restaurants, Cafés & Bars

France is full of wonderful restaurants, from the grand classics to the tiny country *auberge* (inn) and busy city *brasseries*. Despite the recent onset of modern convenience and fast foods, most French people pay serious attention to their food, and whenever they are not in a hurry are notably selective about where they will eat. It could be argued, though, that the French have always enjoyed convenience foods of a different kind – provided by their splendid *pâtissiers* (bakers), *traiteurs* (delicatessens) and *charcutiers* (butchers), where you can pick up a selection of prepared dishes for dinner or a delicious picnic.

Each region has its own specialities: the creamy and cider sauces of Normandy, *choucroute* (sauerkraut) in Alsace, *coq au vin* (chicken in red wine sauce) in Burgundy and wonderful seafood all around the coast.

Prices have been rising, but in general, and certainly in most of the north outside Paris, eating out in France is still excellent value for money. It is always worth seeking out the local regional food, since thanks to the very French idea of *terroir* *(see page 67)* these will nearly always be the dishes made with the most skill, and the best, local produce. This is also of course the best way to get the flavour of a region, complemented by the local wine, cider, beer or other drinks.

Regional cooking has been the most fashionable in France for several years now, and many of the most popular restaurants in Paris specialise in the cuisine of the provinces. Vegetarianism, however, hasn't really taken off; while in cities you may find more modern-style restaurants that provide vegetarian options, in traditional country restaurants, especially, non-meat eaters may find choices limited.

For a brief guide to the different types of French restaurant, see page 64. In addition to those listed here, most French hotels also have restaurants, so many of the addresses listed under Accommodation *(see page 312)* will also have excellent places to eat. In small country towns, particularly, the restaurant in the local hotel is commonly the best in town.

It is always advisable to book ahead at any upscale or particularly popular restaurant for evening meals, or at restaurants of all kinds for Friday and Saturday evenings and Sunday lunchtimes. Even if you call just an hour or so in advance the same day (as many French people do), this will generally be better than just turning up. City and seaside brasseries operate on a more flexible basis. In small towns and rural areas, particularly, not many restaurants are open on Sunday evenings, so make up for it with a long lunch.

Below: chalkboard *ménu du jour.*

Wine – Reading the Label

Wines are graded according to quality, and this is shown on the label. The grades are as follows:

- *Vin de table:* usually inexpensive everyday table wine. The quality can vary.
- *Vin de pays:* local wine; higher quality than *vin de table*.
- *VDQS (vin délimité de qualité supérieure):* wine from a specific area; higher quality than *vin de table*.
- *AOC (appellation d'origine contrôlée):* The top category where the wines are made to regulations covering vineyard yields, grape varieties, geographical boundaries and alcohol content.
- *Mis en bouteille au château:* bottled at the vineyard. Also indicated by the words, *récoltant* or *producteur* around the cap.
- *Négociant:* a wine that has been bought by a dealer and bottled away from the estate. This is not necessarily to the detriment of the wine; there are many excellent *négociants* in business today.

Restaurant Law and Lore

Smoking is now banned in public places in France and the rule is generally respected. Menus must be displayed by law outside any restaurant. Most places will offer a *prix fixe* menu – a set meal at a particular price – which is usually just called a *menu* or, if it is particularly cheap, a *formule*. Otherwise you order separate items from *La Carte*. The set menu is usually excellent value.

For more on Food and Drink, see pages 63–69.

RESTAURANT LISTINGS

PARIS

Auberge Nicolas Flamel
51 rue de Montmorency
Tel: 01 42 71 77 78
The oldest house in the city, formerly the residence of the eponymous alchemist. Choice dishes include fried lobster with vanilla and porterhouse steak with morels, tender aubergine and sweet potato crisps. Closed Sun except by arrangement. **€€**

Au Chien qui Fume
33 rue du Pont Neuf, 75001
Tel: 01 42 36 07 42
Porcelain dogs and pictures of dogs decorate this popular and friendly Parisian restaurant founded in 1740. It serves traditional French cuisine, particularly seafood, and has a terrace for outdoor dining. **€€**

Au Pied de Cochon
6 rue Coquillière, 75001
Tel: 01 40 13 77 00
Venerable Les Halles brasserie open around the clock for onion soup, pigs' trotters and seafood. **€€**

Brasserie Bofinger
5–7 rue de la Bastille, 75004
Tel: 01 42 72 87 82
Hugely popular brasserie with exquisite Belle Epoque decor, serving specialities including foie gras, oysters and *choucroute*. Reserve in advance, especially if you want to sit beneath the beautiful glass dome. **€€**

Café Beaubourg
43 rue Saint Merri, 75004
Tel: 01 48 87 63 96
This trendy café with a spacious terrace beside the Centre Pompidou is popular with locals and tourists alike and it serves brunch at any time of the day. **€€**

Café de la Nouvelle Mairie
19 rue des Fossés Saint-Jacques
Tel: 01 44 07 04 41
Bistro in the Latin Quarter with an original 1920s facade and an agreeably old-fashioned feel to it. The cuisine is drawn from the Aveyron in southwest France. Wines are available by the glass, some of them from small, little-known wine makers. Closed Sun.

Café de la Paix
5 place de l'Opéra, 75009
Tel: 01 40 07 36 36
This beautiful café/brasserie with decor by Charles Garnier is classified as a historic monument; great people-watching from the terrace. **€€–€€€**
€–€€

Chez Georges
11 rue du Mail, 75002
Tel: 01 42 60 07 11
A family-run bistro near La Bourse, serving traditional bourgeois cuisine, very popular with the stock-exchange crowd. Try the sole filet with a wine sauce and fresh cream. Closed Sat and Sun. **€€**

Dans le Noir
51 rue Quincampoix, 75004
Tel: 01 42 77 98 04
Be prepared for a new dining experience in this restaurant where you eat in pitch darkness to appreciate both the flavours of the food and what it is like to be blind. Book 3 to 5 days ahead. **€€€**

Jules Verne
Eiffel Tower, 75007
Tel: 01 45 55 61 44
There are three choices of where to eat on the Eiffel Tower. This is the highest and best, being on the 2nd stage, at 125m (410ft), but you pay for the location. A second best is **58 Tour Eiffel** (tel: 0825 566 662, **€€**) on level 1 which has only a modest view. **€€€**

Le Chalet des Iles
Lac Inferieur du Bois de Boulogne, Porte de la Muette, 75016
Tel: 01 42 88 04 69
A beautiful and secluded restaurant, inaugurated in 1880, on the edge of a lake in the Bois du Boulogne. It is reached by a short ride in an old-fashioned boat and it is the perfect location for a romantic summer evening. **€€€**

Le Dôme
108 boulevard du Montparnasse, 75014
Tel: 01 43 35 25 81
Along the road from the other famous café, La Coupole, this is one of the grandest seafood restaurants in Paris. Try the *bouillabaisse* (fish stew). **€€€**

Le Grand Véfour
17 rue de Beaujoulais, 75001
Tel: 01 42 96 56 27
This exquisite 18th-century restaurant has been catering for artists, writers and politicians for more than two hundred years. Closed Fri evening, Sat, Sun and Aug. **€€€€**

L'Hôtel
13 rue des Beaux-Arts, 75006
Tel: 01 44 41 99 00
The gourmet restaurant of this hotel in which Oscar Wilde died in 1900 is located on a quiet back-street, set back from the bustle of St-Germain-des-Prés. It has been awarded a Michelin star. **€€€**

Le Meurice
228 rue de Rivoli, 75001
Tel: 01 44 58 10 10
Yannick Alléno's very good "revisited" classical cooking is presented in flamboyant style in this grand hotel dining room. A place for a special occasion under a blowsy rococo painted ceiling. Closed Sat lunch, Sun, Mon and two weeks mid-Aug. **€€€€**

Le Pamphlet
38 rue Debellyme, 75003
Tel: 01 42 72 39 24
You'll find very fine cooking and remarkable value for money at this discreet and comfortable restaurant in the northern Marais, including superb fish and seasonal game. Closed Mon and Sat lunch, Sun, and two weeks in Jan and Aug. **€€**

Le Petit Zinc
11 rue St-Benoit, 75006
Tel: 01 42 86 61 00
An Art Nouveau restaurant in St-Germain-des-Prés which includes among its signature dishes shoulder of lamb flavoured with pink garlic from the town of Lautrec in the Tarn. An agreeable calm reigns

BELOW: classic Left Bank restaurant, Le Petit Zinc.

PRICE CATEGORIES

Price categories are per person for a three-course meal:
€ = under €20
€€ = €20–45
€€€ = €45–90
€€€€ = over €90

inside. In good weather there are tables on the terrace. **€€–€€€**

Le Train Bleu
Gare de Lyon, 75012
Tel: 01 43 43 09 06
An extravagant and luxuriously decorated restaurant on the first floor of the Gare de Lyon train station, with painted ceilings, red curtains, gilded mouldings, mirrors and solemn waiters. A bit pricey, but for atmosphere, this place is hard to beat. **€€€**

Le Troquet
21 rue François-Bonvin, 75015
Tel: 01 45 66 89 00
Creative modern bistro fare with a Basque accent in an animated, friendly setting. Closed Sun and Mon, and three weeks in Aug. **€€**

Lucas Carton
9 place de la Madeleine, 75008
Tel: 01 42 65 22 90
A beautiful Art Nouveau setting, perfect service and the refined cooking of Alain Senderens. The extravagant can choose the *carte* with its suggested wine for each dish, but there's also a superb lunch menu. Advance reservation essential. **€€€€**

Violon d'Ingres
135 rue St-Dominique, 75007
Tel: 01 45 55 15 05
Fashionable restaurant serving traditional cooking with a modern twist. Closed Sun and Mon lunch. **€€€**

ILE-DE-FRANCE

Chatou

Maison Fournaise
Ile des Impressionnistes
3 rue du Bac, 78400 Chatou
Tel: 01 30 71 41 91
The location is the big attraction here as this is where Renoir sat down to paint the *Luncheon of the Boating Party*, an icon of Impressionism. Weather permitting, you can sit on the terrace beside the Seine to enjoy the same vantage point, but you will pay for the privilege. The cuisine is mainly French with some international influences. €€

Disneyland-Paris

Auberge de Cendrillon
Fantasyland, Disneyland
Tel: 01 60 30 40 50 70
(reservations for all Disneyland restaurants)
It's worth planning where you are going to eat before arriving in Disneyland, which has 70 restaurants, including 30 in the park, 12 in the village and 8 in Walt Disney studio. Broadly the choices are between where you are likely to be at lunchtime; whether you want to sit down or eat fast food on the move (which is cheaper); American food or something international; and whether or not your kids want to be served by cartoon characters. This is the only French restaurant in the park, a faux historical house on the theme of Cinderella (Cendrillon in French). **€€**

Fontainebleau

Hostellerie du Moulin
2 rue du Moulin,
77940 Flagy
Tel: 01 60 96 67 89
On the banks of the Orvanne, around 20 minutes from Fontainebleau, set in a beautifully converted 18th-century flour mill. Enjoy adventurous cooking by candlelight in winter or dine by the river in summer. **€€–€€€**

Saint Prix

Hostellerie du Prieuré
74 rue Auguste Rey,
95390 Saint Prix
Tel: 01 34 27 51 51
Small auberge consisting of a restaurant and a hotel of 8 rooms in a village of the Val d'Oise, just outside the northern suburbs of Paris. The owners are great wine-lovers and offer a choice of 200 appellations. **€€**

Versailles

Gordon Ramsay au Trianon
1 boulevard de la Reine,
78000 Versailles
Tel: 01 30 84 50 00
The celebrity Scottish chef directs this 2-Michelin starred restaurant in the Trianon Palace. The decor is elegant and intimate and the innovative food inspired by French tradition. La Veranda is a more casual alternative for those on a smaller budget. **€€€€**

THE NORTH AND PICARDY

Amiens

Le Bouchon
10 rue Alexandre Fatton,
80000 Amiens
Tel: 03 22 92 14 32
In a rather plain street, this restaurant stands out for its imaginative, high-quality cooking, featuring rich classic elements – especially fine foie gras – combined with fresh seasonal ingredients, Service is obliging. **€€**

Brasserie Jules
boulevard Alsace Lorraine,
80000 Amiens
Tel: 03 22 71 18 40
This grand, spacious restaurant expresses a very French nostalgia for the Belle Epoque – when grand brasseries were all the rage – as well as paying *hommage* to Amiens' own distinguished resident Jules Verne. The decor is plush traditional, and the menu features all the great brasserie classics: steaks, salads, fabulous seafood platters and much more. Hugely enjoyable. **€€–€€€**

Le Pot d'Etain
15 quai Bélu, 80000 Amiens
Tel: 03 22 72 10 80
One of the most consistent of the several restaurants with riverside terraces along the Quai Bélu by Quartier St-Leu, with a fine view of the cathedral back across the Somme. Fish and meat grills are mainstays of the menu, but there are nice salads and lighter dishes too, and a well-organised wine selection. **€€**

Arras

La Faisanderie
45 Grand Place, 62000 Arras
Tel: 03 21 48 20 76
This lovely restaurant occupies one of the Boves cellars beneath Arras' Grand Place, and once you're down below it feels like a snug refuge, far away from any urban bustle. The refined seasonal menus make great use of northern ingredients, and there's a superior wine selection. **€€**

Le Grand Bleu
rue Henry Robert, 62118 Roeux
Tel: 03 21 55 41 74
An unusual restaurant next to a lake – actually a flooded quarry – just east of Arras, where one of the region's best young chefs, Gaetan Citerne, plies his trade with great flair. Menus are strictly seasonal; in autumn or winter, anything with forest mushrooms is fabulous. **€€–€€€**

Baie de la Somme – Le Crotoy

Chez Mado
41 quai Léonard, 80550 Le Crotoy
Tel: 03 22 27 81 22
The biggest of several

ABOVE: a steaming dish of *moules marinières*.

appealing informal traditional seafood restaurants along Le Crotoy's seafront, with giant terraces and a *salle panoramique* from which to admire the view while tucking into mussels, lobster, local sole and pollock *(lieu)* – a Somme Bay speciality. A place to see a slice of French family life. Despite its size, tables need to be booked well ahead for summer weekends to avoid disappointment. **€€–€€€**

Hôtel Les Tourelles
2–4 rue Pierre Guerlain, 80550 Le Crotoy
Tel: 03 22 27 16 33
A little way back and uphill from the seafront, and so with even better views, Les Tourelles is equally outstanding as a hotel *(see page 316)* and a restaurant. Their fresh seafood platters are outstanding value, and more original dishes such as swordfish brochette with seaweed sauce are beautifully done. **€€**

Boulogne-sur-Mer

Chez Jules
8 place Dalton, 62200 Boulogne-sur-Mer
Tel: 03 21 31 54 12
A perfect multi-purpose town brasserie, right on Boulogne's market square. Downstairs is the terrace, café, and bustling brasserie, while above is a rather more comfortable dining room. The menu covers everything from small snacks to magnificent seafood platters and refined cooking, all freshly prepared. A wonderful local institution. Closed two weeks Sept. **€–€€**

Aux Pêcheurs d'Etaples
31 Grande Rue, 62200 Boulogne-sur-Mer
Tel: 03 21 30 29 29
The "Pecheurs" are one of the north's largest fishing cooperatives, and as well as having an eye-catching fish shop, they also have a bright, quite refined fish restaurant above it to showcase their catch. Freshness is naturally unbeatable, the options, whether on set menus or single platters of *moules*, fish stews and even Provençal *bouillabaisse*, leave you spoilt for choice. **€€–€€€**

Calais

La Pléiade
32 rue Jean Quéhen, 62100 Pas-de-Calais
Tel: 03 21 34 03 70
Amid the plain streets of central Calais, just off the main square, Eric Mémain prepares some of the north's finest cuisine in his unassuming, very comfortable restaurant, with an array of original dishes such as skate wings with coriander and a delicate mango and ginger seasoning. Ideal for a fine meal on arriving in France, or just before you leave. **€€–€€€**

Cassel

Het' Kasteelhof
8 rue St-Nicolas, 59670 Cassel
Tel: 03 28 40 59 29
Within sight of the Belgian border, at the very top of Mont Cassel, the highest point in Flanders, this is a very different, distinctly un-French eating spot – the model of a cosy Flemish Estaminet or pub, with all sorts of knick-knacks around the walls, fabulous beer, and hearty food such as tartine open sandwiches, *potjev'leesch* (mixed cold meats) or beef in beer, all served with chips. A very convivial place, with soaring views from the main room or an outside terrace. Closed Mon–Wed. **€–€€**

Compiègne

Restaurant L'Endroit
14 rue des Pâtissiers, 60200 Compiègne
Tel: 03 44 40 83 38
Traditional without being stuck in its ways, this comfortable restaurant in a modernised old house doesn't fail to present attractive menus with market-fresh ingredients, full of satisfying flavours. Food and wines are excellent value. **€€**

Laon

La Petite Auberge
45 boulevard Brossolette, 02000 Laon
Tel: 03 23 23 02 38
A very stylish restaurant in central Laon where chef Willy-Marc Zorn prepares adventurous, internationally influenced cuisine in line with market and seasonal availability. As in so much fine French cooking, the charm is in the superb details, such as the *amuse bouches* and fabulous home-baked bread. The wine cellar is exceptional too. **€€€**

Lille

A l'Huîtrière
3 rue des Chats Bossus, 59000 Lille
Tel: 03 20 55 43 41
One of the curious sights of Lille is to see well-dressed diners making their way past the magnificent Art Deco-tiled fish shop – surely one of the world's most spectacular – to the stairs up to the equally grand dining rooms. A destination for a foodie pilgrimage, it's a temple of the very best in fish and seafood, superbly prepared. Closed Sun eves. **€€€€**

L'Assiette du Marché
61 rue de la Monnaie, 59000 Lille
Tel: 03 20 06 83 61
In a distinguished 17th-century building in the heart of old Lille, this striking restaurant has a chic, modern decor, relaxed atmosphere and offers light, varied menus ideally suited to contemporary tastes. As the name suggests, they change frequently in line with market availability and seasons, and the quality of cooking is exceptional. Great value, too. **€€**

La Cave aux Fioles
39 rue de Gand, 59000 Lille
Tel: 03 20 55 18 43
One of the most popular of the many restaurants along rue de Gand, with snug, dark decor and plenty of intimate corners that make it a favourite for dinners-for-two. Menus are enjoyably rich, but have their subtle points too. **€€**

Le Compostelle
4 rue St-Etienne, 59000 Lille
Tel: 03 28 38 08 30
A short walk from the Grand'Place, in a

PRICE CATEGORIES

Price categories are per person for a three-course meal:
€ = under €20
€€ = €20–45
€€€ = €45–90
€€€€ = over €90

beautiful Flemish Renaissance building, this comfortable restaurant serves a delicious mix of Mediterranean and northern regional dishes. **€€€**

Montreuil-sur-Mer

Auberge de Grenouillère
La Madeleine-sous-Montreuil, 62170 Montreuil-sur-Mer
Tel: 03 21 06 07 22
A beautiful Picard-style farmhouse by a stream, below the old town of Montreuil, decorated by an English visitor in the 1920s with whimsical paintings of frogs, is the location for this lovely restaurant where young chef Alexandre Gauthier presents inventive dishes with wonderfully delicate, original flavours. There are also four bright and pretty guest rooms. Closed Jan. **€€€–€€€€**

Froggy's Tavern
51 bis place du Général de Gaulle, 62170 Montreuil-sur-Mer
Tel: 03 21 86 72 32
Alexandre Gauthier of the gourmet Grenouillère is also a partner in this very different modern bistro in Montreuil itself. The style is informal, with dishes marked up on a blackboard: a rotisserie forms a centrepiece, with fresh-roasted pork a menu highlight, but there are several other meaty options too, plus some fish choices. **€€**

St-Quentin

Brasserie L'Imprimerie
10 place de l'Hôtel de Ville, 02100 St-Quentin
Tel: 03 23 05 50 40
This ever-busy brasserie has won the hearts of locals with a modern look and a menu that covers every option, from delicious mixed salads, crêpes and even pizzas and Chinese dishes to hefty steaks and seafood dishes. Plus it's open every day, and excellent value. **€€**

Senlis

Le Scaramouche
4 place Notre Dame, 60300 Senlis
Tel: 03 44 53 01 26
This restaurant by the cathedral is as timeless as its unchanging, romantic location in the old streets of Senlis. Its classic dishes such as home-made terrines of duck are very nicely done. **€€–€€€**

CHAMPAGNE

Charleville Mézières

Abbaye de Sept Fontaines
08090 Fagnon
Tel: 03 24 37 38 24
Château hotel in the Ardennes countryside, which offers regional cuisine in elegant surroundings. **€€–€€€**

Colombey-les-Deux Eglises

Restaurant Natali
Hostellerie La Montagne, 52330 Colombey-les-Deux-Eglises
Tel: 03 25 01 51 69
In this restaurant on the first floor of the Hôtel La Montagne, garlanded chef Jean-Baptiste Natali serves gourmet seasonal cuisine using mainly produce sourced from local farmers. The fish comes fresh from Roscoff once a week. **€€–€€€**

Etoges

Château d'Etoges
4 rue Richebourg 51270 Etoges
Tel: 03 26 59 30 08
The restaurant of this elegant château (converted into a 28-room hotel) enjoys a view of the house and the parkland. Vegetarian menu available. **€€€**

Mesnil-Saint-Père

Au Vieux Pressoir
5–7 rue du 28 Août 1944 10140
Tel: 03 25 41 27 16
Restaurant of Auberge du Lac, located by the shore of the Lac d'Orient. Foie gras, scallops and truffles are among the many fine things on the menu. The atmosphere can be a little stuffy. **€€–€€€**

Piney

Le Tadorne
5 place de la halle
Tel: 03 25 46 30 35
A half-timbered house renovated under the direction of the chef himself who is passionate about the local vernacular architecture. Home cooking with fresh ingredients varying according to the season. **€**

Reims

Les Crayères
64 boulevard Henry Vasnier, 51100 Reims
Tel: 03 26 24 90 00
Haute cuisine in a luxurious château with an excellent selection of vintage champagnes to accompany the gourmet dishes. There is a large terrace giving onto the garden. For a slightly cheaper and less formal option try the more modern Brasserie le Jardin, in the château's garden, which specialises in regional cuisine. Reservation essential. Closed Sun, Mon and August. **€€€€**

Sedan

Le Saint-Michel
3 rue Saint-Michel, 08200 Sedan
Tel: 03 24 29 04 61
Restaurant, hotel and gift shop (selling local crafts and culinary produce) at the foot of the castle. On the menu are some of the specialities of the Ardennes: wild boar, pork and cured ham. **€–€€**

Soulaines-Dhuys

La Venise Verte
rue du Plessis, 10200 Soulaines-Dhuys
Tel: 03 25 92 76 10
Restaurant and hotel in the lakes region east of Troyes. Specialities include duck and beef. The fish is also good. **€€**

Troyes

La Grille Saint-Jean
21 rue Champeaux, 10000 Troyes
Tel: 03 25 73 52 26
Traditional cooking in a half-timbered 16th-century building on a pedestrian street in the centre of town. **€**

BELOW: fine dining at Les Crayères.

ALSACE/LORRAINE

Colmar

A l'Echevin
Quartier Petite Venise, place des Six Montaignes Noires, 68000 Colmar
Tel: 03 89 41 6032
The cosy restaurant of the hotel Le Marechal occupies a converted 16th-century inn on the waterside in Colmar's "Little Venice". It serves gourmet cuisine, combining regional dishes with modern flair. Try the *filet mignon de veau* or the *foie gras d'oie cuit en terrine*. **€€€**

Domremy-la-Pucelle

La Table de Jeanne
6 rue Principale
88630 Domremy-la-Pucelle
Tel: 03 29 94 74 88
Over the road from the house in which Joan of Arc was born is this restaurant named after her. The decor is minimalist, the food stylish and the wine list varied. Children's menu available. Closed Sun and Mon evening and all day Tue. **€€**

Eguisheim

Auberge Alsacienne
12 Grand Rue, 68420 Eguisheim
Tel: 03 89 41 50 20
Restaurant on the main street of town serving Alsatian and French cusine. Also a hotel: upstairs are pretty bedrooms decorated in bright colours. **€–€€**

Epinal

Le Bistrot Gourmand
5–7 rue du Chapitre, 88000 Epinal
Tel: 03 29 34 20 77
Located on a quiet pedestrianised street near to the church. Good-value lunch menu Tue–Fri. Peaceful terrace for outdoor meals in summer. **€€**

Longuyon

Le Mas
65 rue Augistrou, 54260 Longuyon
www.lorraineetmas.com
An elegant family-run place to have lunch or dinner. Children's menu available. The restaurant of the Hotel Lorraine which has 14 delightful bedrooms. **€€–€€€**

Hunspach

Au Cerf
5 rue de la Gare, 67250 Hunspach
Tel: 03 88 80 41 59
Perhaps the best option for a meal while visiting one of the prettiest villages of Alsace. Among the dishes on the menu are sauerkraut, onion tart, veal and snails. **€–€€**

Metz

Brasserie Flo
2 bis, rue Gambetta, 57000 Metz
Tel: 03 87 55 94 95
A very pleasant brasserie outside the train station, decorated in Belle Epoque style, with mirrors and plush velvet. Perfect for a drink or a bite before or after the opera or theatre. **€€**

Maire
1 rue du Pont des Morts, 57000 Metz
Tel: 03 87 32 43 12
A gourmet restaurant combining traditional and modern cuisine. It's located near the cathedral and has a terrace on the banks of the River Moselle. Closed Tue and Wed lunch. **€€€**

Mittelbergheim

Winstüb Gilg
1 route du Vin, 67140 Mittelbergheim
Tel: 03 88 08 91 37
Traditional half-timbered *winstüb* (restaurant) on the Alsace wine route where you can complement wine tasting with a range of fish dishes. Closed Tue–Wed and two weeks in January. **€€**

Mulhouse

Chez Auguste
11 rue Poincaré, 68100 Mulhouse
Tel: 03 89 46 62 71
Classic French cuisine using only fresh ingredients is served in this bistro near the station in which the menu is renewed each season. Closed Sun and lunch Sat and Mon. **€€**

Nancy

Le Capucin Gourmand
31 rue Gambetta, 54000 Nancy
Tel: 03 83 35 26 98
This restaurant in the city centre is a meeting point for the city's gourmets. There is a good-value set menu at lunchtime. Cooking courses are held on Saturdays. Closed Sun. **€€€€**

Excelsior Flo
50 rue Henri-Poincaré, 54000 Nancy
Tel: 03 83 35 24 57
One of the excellent chain of Flo brasseries, decorated in Art Nouveau style and specialising in oysters. **€€**

Riquewihr

Trotthus
9 rue des Juifs, 68340 Riquewihr
Tel: 03 89 47 96 47
Typical Alsatian cuisine, including *choucroute* and a variety of *tartes flambées* served in a pleasant *winstüb* towards the top of the town. **€€**

Selestat

L'Acoustic
5 place du Marché, 67600 Selestat
Tel: 03 88 92 29 40
Only 100 percent organic food is served in this restaurant beneath a brick vault in the centre of town. Half the choices on the menu are vegetarian. The wholemeal bread is home-made. **€**

Strasbourg

Au Crocodile
10 rue de l'Outre, 67060 Strasbourg
Tel: 03 88 32 13 02
An elegant restaurant near the cathedral, in the historic part of town, which serves a refined and sophisticated cuisine. Closed Sun and Mon. **€€€**

Buerehiesel
4 parc de l'Orangerie, 67000 Strasbourg
Tel: 03 88 45 56 65
This reconstructed Alsatian farmhouse in Strasbourg's Orangerie Park is home to one of the city's best restaurants. **€€€€**

Maison Kammerzell
16 place de la Cathédrale, 67000 Strasbourg
Tel: 03 88 32 42 14
Excellent food and wine in one of the oldest houses in Strasbourg, next to the cathedral. The historic building, dating back to the Renaissance, is decorated with frescoes, a deserving backdrop to its exquisite Alsatian dishes ranging from the signature *choucroute* with three fish to seasonal game. Special lunchtime deals for families. **€€€**

L'Eveil des Sens
rue des Dentelles, 67000 Strasbourg
Tel: 03 88 32 81 81
Little gem of a restaurant among the more touristy establishments of the Petite France area. It's the culinary fiefdom of chef Antoine Huart, voted Alsace's best young talent, 2011, by Gault et Millau. The interior is tastefully decorated, Alsatian-style. There is an intimate dining room upstairs. Good value for money. **€€–€€€**

Tantonville

La Commanderie
1 rue Pasteur, 54116 Tantonville
Tel: 03 83 52 49 83
Smart, but warm and welcoming restaurant close to the hill of Sion-Vaudemont. Very reasonable *menu du jour* if you can avoid the temptations of *à*

PRICE CATEGORIES

Price categories are per person for a three-course meal:
€ = under €20
€€ = €20–45
€€€ = €45–90
€€€€ = over €90

la carte. Children's menu available. Closed late Aug to early Sept. **€€**

Uttenhoffen

Jardins de la Ferme Bleue,
21 rue Principale,
67100 Uttenhoffen
Tel: 03 88 72 84 35
This *salon du thé* serves delicious sweet-and-savoury brunches on Sunday mornings in summer and around Christmas, between 10.30am and 2pm. The rest of the time, it's a great place for tea and cakes. **€–€€**

Verdun

Hostellerie du Coq Hardi
avenue de la Victoire,
55100 Verdun
Tel: 03 29 86 36 36
This Verdun institution, in a beautiful half-timbered house, has been serving up refined cuisine since 1827. Its gourmet restaurant has a young chef whose specialities include *marbré de pied d'agneau* with piquillo peppers. There is an extensive wine list. Closed Fri, Sat lunch and Sun eve. **€€€**

Burgundy and Franche-Comté

Avallon

Capuchins
6 avenue du Président Doumer – avenue de la Gare, 89200 Avallon
Tel: 03 86 34 06
Well-run restaurant with brightly painted walls and functional bedrooms available upstairs. Straightforward regional cuisine in an agreeable setting. **€–€€**

Beaune

La Bouzerotte
21200 Bouze-lès-Beaune
Tel: 03 80 26 01 37
Dine on the sunny terrace or beside the cosy fire according to the season. Regional cuisine with a range of menu options of varying prices. Closed Sun dinner, Mon, Tue and 20 Dec–mid-Jan. **€€–€€€**

Ma Cuisine
Passage Ste Hélène, 21200 Beaune
Tel: 03 80 24 70 72
The daily menu revolves around the wine list, which has over 800 different wines listed. Small and popular city-centre restaurant, so reservation advised. Closed Wed, Sat, Sun and Aug. **€€**

Besançon

Le Champagney
37 rue Battan, 25000 Besançon
Tel: 03 81 81 05 71
This 16th-century building is classified as one of the monuments of Besançon because it possesses the last four surviving gargoyles in the city. The cuisine is light and full of flavour, with the accent on presentation. **€–€€**

Cluny

Le Potin Gourmand
Place du Champ de Foire,
71250 Cluny
Tel: 03 85 59 02 06
A small restaurant and reasonably priced hotel in an old stone house formerly a ceramics workshop. The menu varies with the market, but one particularly tasty dish that's often on the menu is crab and courgette with sesame seeds in a shellfish sauce. **€€**

Dijon

Pré aux Clercs
13 place de la Libération,
21000 Dijon
Tel: 03 80 38 05 05
Rich traditional Burgundian cuisine cooked with panache by father-and-son team, Jean-Pierre and Alexis Billoux, and served with a delectable choice of highly prestigious wines. Closed Sun dinner, Mon and 10 days in Aug. **€€€€**

Les Villedieu

La Remise
25240 Les Villedieu
Tel: 03 81 69 25 57
Lively bar-restaurant serving fondues, light meals and home-made ice creams. A number of boats are for hire at nearby Malbuisson on Lac Saint Point. **€**

Tournus

Aux Terrasses
18 avenue 23 Janvie,
71700 Tournus
Tel: 03 85 51 01 74
Stylish restaurant with three dining rooms and a garden to choose from. The cuisine combines traditional dishes of Burgundy with influences from other parts of France. **€€**

Above: Le Potin Gourmand, Cluny.

Villers-le-Lac

Vedettes Panoramiques
2 place M Cupillard,
25130 Villers-le-Lac
Tel: 03 81 68 05 34
On Saturday evenings in July and August a cruise boat taking tourists to see the Saut du Doubs waterfall becomes a floating restaurant. The candlelit dinner trip through the gorge lasts 3 hours. Reservation essential. **€€**

Vézelay

L'Espérance
St-Père, 89450 Vézelay
Tel: 03 86 33 39 10
Booking is essential at chef Marc Meneau's celebrated hotel/restaurant, with its glass conservatory/dining room that feels like part of the garden. Exceptional cuisine by one of France's most innovative chefs, based on traditional Burgundy ingredients. Closed Mon lunch, Tue, Wed lunch, and Jan–Feb. **€€€€**

Villeneuve l'Archeveque

Auberge des Vieux Moulins Banaux
18 rte Moulins Banaux
89190 Villeneuve l'Archeveque
Tel: 03 86 86 72 55
Family-run restaurant between Sens and Troyes with 15 guest rooms attached. As the name suggests, it is in a 16th-century mill with millwheels and machinery intact. Booking advised. **€–€€**

LOIRE VALLEY

Angers

Une Ile
9 rue Max Richard,
49000 Angers
Tel: 02 41 19 14 48
The menu here follows the seasons and what's available in the market, but what you get depends on the whim of the chef. The seafood menu is especially good. You can't go wrong with the grilled foie gras either. Closed Sat and Sun. **€€**

Blois

Le Médicis
2 Allée François 1er, Route d'Angers, 41000 Blois
Tel: 02 54 43 94 04
A friendly restaurant and hotel near the Château de Blois where chef Grégory Boussard prepares his ingenious cuisine which is given exotic touches from the different countries where he has worked. Closed Sun eve and Mon from Nov–Mar. **€€**

Bouin

Domaine le Martinet
9 rue des Jardins,
85230 Bouin
Tel: 02 51 49 23 48
Restaurant and hotel in a peaceful spot near the coast, halfway between Nantes and Les Sables d'Olonne. Oysters are on the menu in season. Good choice of desserts. **€–€€**

Chartres

La Passacaille
30 rue Sainte Même,
28200 Chartres
Tel: 02 37 21 52 10
A cheerful Italian restaurant, located in the centre of Chartres, which serves up a good selection of pizzas and fresh pastas, as well as salads, carpaccios and grills. **€€**

Chinon

L'Ardoise
42 rue Rabelais, 37500 Chinon
Tel: 02 47 58 48 78
In his restaurant in the centre of Chinon, chef Stephane Perrot prepares high-quality cuisine including marinated salmon, carpaccio and sushi-style langoustines. **€€–€€€**

Au Chapeau Rouge
49 place du Général de Gaulle,
37500 Chinon
Tel: 02 47 98 08 08
This traditional restaurant, in the town centre at the foot of the château, serves gourmet cuisine using local and seasonal produce, including wild fish from the Loire, saffron and truffles. **€€–€€€**

Le Lude

L'Auberge Alsacienne
14 rue de la Boule d'Or
72800, Le Lude
Tel: 02 43 48 20 45
Restaurant and hotel in a small village near La Flèche in the Sarthe département. As the name suggests, the cuisine and the wine list are orientated towards Alsace. The menu includes a selection of home-made *flammenküchen*, thin-crust Alsatian-style pizza. **€**

Luché-Pringé

Auberge du Port des Roches
Le Port des Roches,
72800 Luché-Pringé
Tel: 02 43 45 44 48
Small family-run restaurant with rooms by the river Loir between Le Mans and Tours. Friendly service and fresh ingredients make for good value. **€€**

Maisonnais

Prieuré Notre-Dame d'Orsan
18170 Maisonnais
Tel: 02 48 56 27 50
A luxury restaurant and 7-room hotel in a former monastery with a re-created medieval garden, inspired by medieval tapestries and illustrations, attached to it. The kitchen is supplied with old fruit and vegetable varieties from the orchard and garden, and cheeses and wines from the surrounding Berry region. Vegetarians can be catered for. There are no phones or televisions in the hotel, to ensure absolute peace. Dinner only. **€€€**

Nantes

L'Atlantide
16 quai Ernest Renaud,
44100 Nantes
Tel: 02 40 73 23 23
A spacious and bright restaurant offering panoramic views of the Loire from its big bay windows. The specialities combine French cuisine with traditional Asian dishes. Closed Sun. **€€–€€€**

La Cigale
4 place Graslin, 44000 Nantes
Tel: 02 51 84 94 94
This historic Nantes café is decorated in exuberant Belle Epoque style and serves excellent fish and seafood. Open 7.30am–12.30am. **€€**

Le Un
1 rue Olympe de Gouges,
44000 Nantes
Tel: 02 40 08 28 00
An original restaurant near the town centre and not far from the Loire River, serving a good selection of tapas and main dishes at reasonable prices. On Saturday mornings there are cooking workshops given by the chefs and on this day it is closed at lunchtime. **€–€€**

Orléans

La Chancellerie
27 place du Matroi, 45000 Orléans
Tel: 02 38 53 57 54
Popular brasserie with outside tables in centre of Orléans, always full at lunchtime for good local dishes with Loire wines. Closed Sun dinner. **€€**

Le Lift
Place de la Loire, 45000 Orléans
Tel: 02 38 53 63 48
Refined, contemporary and creative cuisine is the hallmark of Philippe Bardau's restaurant. It's located in a modern building and is divided into different spaces. The tables on the terrace have great views of the city and of the Loire River. Brunch is served between 11am and 3pm on Sun. **€€–€€€**

Préban

La Cave Aux Moines
49350 Chenehutte-Treves-Cunault
Tel: 02 41 67 95 64
Subterranean restaurant occuping galleries dug out of the tufa rock in a village between Saumur and Angers. On the menu are cave-grown oyster, blue-stem and shitake mushrooms. Snails are another speciality. On the premises, there is also an underground nightclub. **€€**

Saumur

Auberge St-Pierre
6 place St-Pierre, 49400 Saumur
Tel: 02 41 51 26 25
This charming little restaurant is not far from the château in the old town; try the delicious pike or *coq au vin*. Closed Sun and Mon. **€€–€€€**

St-Benoît-sur-Loire

Grand Saint Benoît
7 place St-André,
45730 St-Benoît-sur-Loire
Tel: 02 38 35 11 92
The dining room of the Hôtel du Labrador has some good menus at reasonable prices. It stands opposite the 11th-century church on the main village square. Closed Sat lunch, Sun dinner and Mon. **€**

PRICE CATEGORIES

Price categories are per person for a three-course meal:
€ = under €20
€€ = €20–45
€€€ = €45–90
€€€€ = over €90

Above: the elegant Château de Noizay dining room.

Tours

Les Hautes Roches
86 Quai Loire, Rochecorbon, 37210 Tours
Tel: 02 47 52 88 88
The Loire's best-known troglodyte hotel has a gourmet restaurant on a terrace overlooking the Loire. Closed Sun dinner, Mon, Tue and Wed lunch. **€€€**

L'Odéon
10 place du Général Leclerc, 37000 Tours
Tel: 02 47 20 12 65
A creative and refined gourmet regional cuisine. Closed Sat lunch and Sun. **€€–€€€**

Le Petit Patrimoine
58 rue Colbert, 37000 Tours
Tel: 02 47 66 05 81
This tiny, bright bistro is popular for its fresh, market-inspired daily menu and regional favourites. Closed Sun and Mon. **€–€€**

Vouvray

Château de Noizay
Promenade de Waulsort, 37210 Noizay
Tel: 02 47 52 11 01
Superb hotel restaurant featuring a seasonal menu and fine local wines. Closed Tue–Thur lunch and mid-Jan–mid-Mar. **€ € €**

Normandy

Balleroy

Manoir de la Drôme
129 rue des Forges, 14490 Balleroy
Tel: 02 31 21 60 94
In an old mill outside the unusual village of Balleroy west of Bayeux, built around its 1630s château, this is one of Normandy's best gourmet restaurants, where chef Denis Leclerc creates delicate flavours using the finest fresh ingredients. Don't be afraid to drop the menu and follow his suggestions. Closed Sun eves, Mon, Tue midday and Wed. **€€€–€€€€**

Barfleur

Le Moderne
Place du Général de Gaulle, 50760 Barfleur
Tel: 02 33 23 12 44
Every kind of fresh fish and seafood, beautifully presented, whether in modest dishes or giant feasts to occupy a whole afternoon. Meats are not ignored either, with excellent duck and beef. Service is charming, the atmosphere relaxed. **€€–€€€**

Bayeux

La Table du Terroir
42 rue St-Jean, 14400 Bayeux
Tel: 02 31 92 05 53
The particular speciality of this informal restaurant in central Bayeux is the finest-quality meat, grilled over open fires. To follow that, try one of the scrumptious Norman apple-based desserts. **€€**

Cherbourg

Café de Paris
40 quai Caligny, 50100 Cherbourg
Tel: 02 33 43 12 36
Founded in 1803, this popular brasserie faces the old port of Cherbourg and the fishing harbour, and naturally specialises in fine fresh fish and seafood, with delicious salads of *Coquilles St-Jacques* (scallops) in the autumn–spring season. An enjoyable fixture in local life. Closed Sun. **€€**

Clécy

Le Moulin du Vey
Le Vey, 14570 Clécy
Tel: 02 31 69 71 08
One of the most exquisite of all Normandy's many ravishing hotel-restaurants, in a beautiful old mill with big windows opening onto the gorge of the River Orne, a summer terrace under the weeping willows, and a fireplace to keep everyone warm in winter. The seasonal menus feature refined variants on Norman and classic French cooking. **€€–€€€**

Cosqueville

Au Bouquet de Cosqueville
Hameau Remond, 50330 Cosqueville
Tel: 02 33 54 32 81
In a delightful location above a tiny beach along the coast east of Cherbourg, the "Bouquet" highlights fish and seafood in its menus – excellent lobster and platters of *fruits de mer* – but also has exquisite foie gras. Chef Stéphane Dieu prepares each dish with great attention to detail. Also a very pleasant hotel, with just seven rooms. Closed Mon and Tue. **€€–€€€**

Dieppe and Varengeville

À la Marmite Dieppoise
8 rue St-Jean, 76200 Dieppe
Tel: 02 35 84 24 26
A town with the character of Dieppe has to have its local culinary institutions, and this is one of them – renowned as the best place to try a *marmite dieppoise*, a rich seafood stew of sole, scallops and plenty of other things in a Norman cider and cream sauce, a dish to take your time over and really savour. There are other, less hefty, options on offer featuring fresh fish, and some meat dishes. Closed Sun eves and Mon. **€€–€€€**

La Buissonnière
Route du Phare d'Ailly, 76119 Varengeville-sur-Mer
Tel: 02 35 83 17 13
Eating on the garden terrace of this exquisite little restaurant, in the leafy lanes west of Varengeville, is a real pleasure. Inside, the dining rooms are stylish, with every detail taken care of; service is charming, and the cooking has a lighter style than traditional Norman cuisine, with original, fragrant seasonings. Closed Mon and Jan–Feb. **€€–€€€**

Café des Tribunaux
1 place du Puits-Salé, 76200 Dieppe
Tel: 02 35 14 44 65
Looking much grander than a simple café, this historic establishment where Oscar Wilde and many artists spent much of their time in Dieppe is still one of France's most characterful grand cafés. To eat, there is a choice of good-value snacks and brasserie dishes. **€–€€**

Gaillon–Vieux Villez

La Closerie, Château Corneille
17 rue de l'Église, 27600 Vieux Villez, near Gaillon
Tel: 02 32 77 44 77
In an 18th-century château smartly converted into a luxury hotel, La Closerie offers sumptuous cuisine that runs between traditional and creative. Sea bass with fennel is a speciality. It's in the countryside on the west bank of the Seine, just across the river from Les Andelys. **€€–€€€**

Giverny

Ancien Hôtel Baudy
81 rue Claude Monet, 27620 Giverny
Tel: 02 32 21 10 03
The hotel-bar-restaurant where Renoir, Cézanne and many others stayed when they came to visit Monet in Giverny is a delightful relic of Belle Epoque bohemia, which despite being carefully preserved never feels like a museum piece. There are no longer any guest rooms, but it's open all day in the Giverny season to serve a great-value mix of breakfasts, classic dishes and light modern options. Closed Nov–late Mar. **€–€€**

Honfleur

L'Absinthe
10 quai de la Quarantaine, 14600 Honfleur
Tel: 02 31 89 39 00
As well as having one of old Honfleur's most interesting luxury hotels *(see page 323)*, the owners of L'Absinthe also have this fine gourmet restaurant, in another historic building across the street. Service is impeccable, there's a neat terrace in summer, and the modern cuisine is subtly refined. **€€€–€€€€**

Le Bréard
7 rue du Puits, 14600 Honfleur
Tel: 02 31 89 53 40
Honfleur's scores of tempting restaurants can leave you paralysed with indecision, but in this tranquil modern restaurant young chef Fabrice Sebire has made a reputation as one of the town's finest, with a delicious blend of creativity and fine flavours. **€€€**

Sa.Qua.Na
22 place Hamelin, 14600 Honfleur
Tel: 02 31 89 40 80
The cutting edge of gourmet cuisine in Honfleur. Chef Alexandre Bourdas trained for several years in Japan, and brings a very eclectic approach to Honfleur's local seafood that has drawn huge acclaim. The decor, like the menu, is minimalist and chic. Closed Mon–Wed. **€€€–€€€€**

Lyons-la-Forêt

Hôtel La Licorne
7 rue de l'Hôtel de Ville, 27480 Lyons-la-Forêt
Tel: 02 32 49 18 90
The owners of this 19th-century house standing out in half-timbered Lyons began with an antiques shop, then added a restaurant, and then very charming hotel rooms. All are run with the same friendly attention to detail, and all are furnished with antiques. The menus run from crêpes, salads and snacks to generous grills and seafood combinations, and, unusually for Norman country restaurants, it's open on Sunday evenings. Restaurant closed Tue. **€–€€**

BELOW: gourmet dessert at Sa.Qua.Na.

Mont-St-Michel and its Bay

A l'Abris du Saunier
La Chaussée, Saint-Léonard, 50300 Vains
Tel: 02 33 70 88 60
In a pretty village on the north side of the bay, this bright modern restaurant-brasserie uses excellent fresh produce to create a menu with plenty of choice, from generous seafood and steaks to smaller options ideal for a lighter meal, and with plenty of child-friendly choices. There's an outdoor terrace in summer. Closed Tue and Wed except in July and Aug. **€€**

Au Marquis de Tombelaine
25 route des Falaises, 50530 Champeaux
Tel: 02 33 61 85 94
High on the cliffs at Champeaux, where the coast road south first enters the Bay of Mont-St-Michel, this popular, traditional restaurant has magical views of the Mount away across the sands. Its cooking combines traditional Norman tastes with creative touches. Closed Tue eve and Wed. **€€**

Chez François
2 rue Jérémie, 50530 Genêts
Tel: 02 33 70 83 98
In the middle of the old village of Genêts, from where guides depart on the across-the-sands walk to Mont-St-Michel, this cave-like granite bistro offers delicious local meats grilled over an open fire, a few non-meat options and scrumptious desserts, served at convivial long tables. Hugely popular at lunchtimes, so book. Closed Wed, Thur. **€€**

Pays d'Auge

Auberge des Deux Tonneaux
Le Bourg, 14130 Pierrefitte-en-Auge
Tel: 02 31 64 09 31
Dating from the 17th century, with black-and-white half-timbered walls, thatched roof and abundant flowers, this classic inn is one of the Norman buildings that looks like it could be a film set, but is certainly genuine. Inside it's all creaking beams and tiny wooden tables; outside in the garden, tables have superb views over the Touques valley, and it's an enjoyable place to try country classics like pork *grand-mère* washed down with local cider. **€–€€**

Restaurant Au P'tit Normand
Place de l'Eglise, 14340 Cambremer
Tel: 02 31 32 03 20
A friendly little restaurant on Cambremer's main square, with very good-value set menus as well as salads, omelettes and other lighter dishes, plus of course a good range of Norman cheeses. **€–€€**

Pont-Audemer

L'Andrien, Le Petit Coq aux Champs
Campigny, 27500 Pont-Audemer
Tel: 02 32 41 04 19
A Norman idyll, this thatch-roofed cottage in a tiny hamlet south of Pont Audemer contains a creative, modern gourmet

PRICE CATEGORIES

Price categories are per person for a three-course meal:
€ = under €20
€€ = €20–45
€€€ = €45–90
€€€€ = over €90

restaurant, presided over by chef Jean-Marie Huard. The garden is exquisite, and there are also 12 very chic guest rooms. **€€€**

Port-en-Bessin (D-Day Beaches)

Le Bistrot d'à Côté
12 rue Michel Lefournier,
14520 Port-en-Bessin
Tel: 02 31 51 79 12
On the quayside in the little harbour of Port-en-Bessin, in between the invasion beaches, this pleasant restaurant, with its maritime blue and white decor, serves delicious seafood favourites – brochettes of scallops are a menu regular. Naturally, everything is wonderfully fresh. Closed Tue and Wed except in July–Aug, and all Jan. **€€**

Rouen

Brasserie Paul
1 place de la Cathédrale,
76000 Rouen
Tel: 02 35 71 86 07
Simone de Beauvoir, Marcel Duchamp and many other Rouen residents have come in for their morning coffee at this classic brasserie, or stopped by for a late-night meal. Its location, opposite the cathedral, makes it an ideal spot for contemplating the architecture or the passing crowds. The menu is a traditional something-for-everyone brasserie list.
€–€€

La Couronne
31 place du Vieux Marché,
76000 Rouen
Tel: 02 35 71 40 90
Claiming to be the oldest *auberge* (inn) in France – founded in 1345 and so well before Joan of Arc was burned at the stake on the square outside –La Couronne is a tourist attraction in itself, with plush decor to add to its historic features. Despite its fame, the traditional Norman cooking generally keeps to a high standard.
€€–€€€

Les Nymphéas
7–9 rue de la Pie, 76000 Rouen,
Tel: 02 35 89 26 69
Chef Patrice Kukurudz has been one of France's foremost chefs for many years, and his Rouen restaurant, just off the place du Vieux Marché, continues to be a reference point. Signature dishes such as a *millefeuille* of red mullet are continually refined and reinvented. It's also ultra-comfortable, with a neat garden at the back, and the wine list is very grand. Closed Sun and Mon.
€€€–€€€€

Saint-Saëns

Le Relais Normand
21 place Maintenon,
76680 Saint-Saëns
Tel: 02 35 34 38 93
A typical village restaurant with tables on St-Saëns' charming main square when weather allows, with generous traditional fare such as beef fillet in a *girolles* mushroom sauce, or *côte de veau vallée d'auge* (veal with a cider and mushroom sauce), and lighter options, nicely prepared. **€**

Trouville

Les Vapeurs
160–162 quai Fernand Moureaux,
14360 Trouville-sur-Mer
Tel: 02 31 88 15 24
Les Vapeurs is perhaps the definitive French harbourside brasserie, and an unbeatable place to spend some time over a bowl of moules (maybe *marinière* or *à la crème normande*, with cider and cream) with frites and an ice-cold bottle of Muscadet. It's always bustling, and the clientele run from elderly regulars to actors and Parisian media types. Should you wish for a bit more tranquillity, the same owners' adjacent Les Voiles restaurant is more spacious. **€€**

BRITTANY

Brest

Ma Petite Folie
Port de Plaisance du Moulin-Blanc,
29200 Brest
Tel: 02 98 42 44 42
On a former lobster-fishing boat moored to the quay in Brest's marina, this restaurant offers copious seafood platters, and fresh grilled fish dishes. Closed Mon, Sun dinner. **€€€**

Carnac

L'Estaminet
73 rue St-Cornély, 56340 Carnac,
Tel: 02 97 52 19 41
Charming small restaurant with a garden terrace, and great-value menus offering a choice of seafood, meat and other dishes. Service is very attentive. **€–€€**

Concarneau

Crêperie Les Remparts
31 rue Théophile Louarn, Ville Close, 29900 Concarneau
Tel: 02 98 50 65 66
In the middle of the tourist-thronged walled town of Concarneau, this traditional crêperie has all the Breton sweet and savoury essentials. Closed Wed from Sept–May. **€–€€**

Dinan

La Fleur de Sel
7 rue Ste Claire, 22100 Dinan
Tel: 02 96 85 15 14
"Traditional and inventive cuisine" is promised by this enterprising little restaurant in old Dinan. Some of the flavour combinations can be a little surprising. Service is welcoming. Closed Sun eves and Mon. **€€**

Dinard–St-Lunaire

Restaurant du Décollé
1 pointe du Décollé,
53800 St-Lunaire
Tel: 02 99 46 01 70
A lovely airy restaurant with gorgeous views along the Emerald Coast from the cliffs of St-Lunaire, just west of Dinard. Creative menus are strong on fish and seafood, but there are fine salads too. Closed Mon and Tue (Apr–June, Sept–mid-Nov) and Wed–Thur (Feb–Mar only), and mid-Nov–Jan. **€€**

Douarnenez

Hôtel de la Plage
La Plage, 29550 Ste Anne-la-Palud
Tel: 02 98 92 50 12
Gourmet seafood and other succulent dishes in a magnificent location above the beach in a village just north of Douarnenez, with a view into infinity across the waves. Also a luxury hotel. **€€€**

Le Morpho Bleu
3 rue Anatole France,
29100 Douarnenez
Tel: 02 56 10 10 62
A laid-back spot that's Douarnenez's "literary café", hosting exhibitions, talks and various other events as well as selling fine local beers, ciders and other drinks. To eat, there are enjoyable platters of salads, cheeses, charcuterie and so on. **€**

Fougères

Crêperie du Théatre
3 place du Théatre,
35300 Fougères
Tel: 02 23 51 02 99
Like every Breton town, Fougères has a choice of crêperies to pick from, and this one has a nice location, with a terrace on a sloping square beside the grand theatre. Friendly service and low prices. **€**

Paimpol

La Vieille Tour
13 rue de l'Église, 22500 Paimpol

Tel: 02 96 20 83 18
This long-running restaurant doesn't try to follow trends, but it has many devoted fans due to its refined Breton and classic French cuisine and homely but professional service. Dishes such as a risotto of langoustines are prepared with flair. Closed Sun eves, Wed eves except in July–Aug, and Mon. **€€**

Perros-Guirec and Côte de Granit Rose

Le Mao
14 rue St-Guirec,
22700 Ploumanac'h
Tel: 02 96 91 40 92
A buzzy terrace restaurant just behind the lovely Ploumanac'h beach, with generous *plateaux de fruits de mer*, scallops sautéed in honey (in season), Breton sausages grilled over an open fire, and good salads. Closed Oct–Easter. **€€**

Les Triagoz
Forum de la Mer, place Coz Pors,
22730 Trégastel
Tel: 02 96 15 34 10
It's hard to be closer to the sea than at this fashionable modern beach bistro, with light, seafood-based dishes. Table space is at a premium around sunset. Closed Wed lunch and Oct–Easter. **€€**

Pont-Aven

Chez Jacky
Port de Belon,
29340 Riec-sur-Belon
Tel: 02 98 06 90 32
With a big terrace right on the banks of the Belon, one of Brittany's many small estuaries and just east of Pont-Aven, this is a wonderful place to eat exquisite local oysters and other seafood with a chilled glass of wine – they have their own boats and oysterbeds. You can also buy seafood to take away. Closed Oct–Easter. **€€**

Le Moulin de Rosmadec
Venelle de Rosmadec,
29930 Pont Aven
Tel: 02 98 06 00 22
There was nothing as sumptuous as this in Pont-Aven when Gauguin and his fellow artists made it famous. In one of the old stone mills along the shimmering River Aven, Frédéric Sébilleau's comfortable restaurant offers refined modern cuisine with, essential in Brittany, superb grilled lobster. Closed Sun eves and Thur except July–Aug. **€€€**

Sur Le Pont
11 place Paul Gauguin,
29930 Pont Aven
Tel: 02 98 06 16 16
www.surlepont-pontaven.fr
Franck Sébilleau, brother of Frédéric of the nearby Moulin de Rosmadec, has followed a different tack by opening this bright, fashionably minimalist bistro, with lighter but still sophisticated cooking at lower prices. Closed Tue eves, Wed and Sun eves. **€€**

Quimper

L'Ambroisie
49 rue Elie Fréron, 29000 Quimper
Tel: 02 98 95 00 02
An elegant modern option on one of the narrow streets of old Quimper, where chef Gilbert Guyon presents regional cuisine with a contemporary touch making fine use of Breton ingredients, served in a laid-back atmosphere. Closed Mon. **€€–€€€**

Rennes

Auberge St-Sauveur
6 rue St-Sauveur, 35000 Rennes,
Ile-et-Vilaine
Tel: 02 99 79 32 56
This charming restaurant is located in a fine half-timbered house that survived the fires of the 18th century, with intimate corners in which to enjoy traditional cuisine such as Breton lobster and an indulgent chocolate mousse. Closed Sun, Mon, Sat lunch and Aug. **€€**

Au Plaisir des Sens
54 rue d'Entrain, 35000 Rennes
Tel: 02 99 38 67 51
An inviting and inventive restaurant where staff and chef-owner Philippe Faget go the extra mile to produce original gourmet dishes with the very best market ingredients. The set lunchtime menu is an amazing bargain for this standard of cooking, with subtle options such as crayfish tails in *fines herbes* with cactus and other unusual accompaniments. Closed Sun eves, Mon and Sat midday. **€€–€€€**

Roscoff

Le Temps de Vivre
17 place Lacaze Duthiers,
29680 Roscoff
Tel: 02 98 61 27 28
Roscoff doesn't look the obvious place for a gourmet restaurant, but that's what Jean-Yves Crenn has created here, making spectacular use of the local lobster and other crustacea. The dining room's views are as beautiful as the food, and there's also a chic modern hotel. Restaurant closed Sun evenings, Mon, Tue midday. **€€€–€€€€**

Sables d'Or-Les Pins

La Voile d'Or
Sables d'Or-Les Pins,
22240 Plurien
Tel: 02 96 41 42 49
A prestigious hotel-restaurant with panoramic sea views above the beach just outside Sables d'Or, with refined menus using the best local produce. Particularly good are the lamb and monkfish. Closed Tue lunch, Mon. **€€€**

St-Malo

Le Corps de Garde
3 Montée de Notre Dame,
35400 St-Malo
Tel: 02 99 40 91 46
This easy-going budget crêperie is, in fact, the only restaurant on the walls of old St-Malo. Sitting snugly next to the Tour Notre Dame, so you can enjoy glorious views out to sea and across to Dinard while tucking into your crêpes or savoury galettes, maybe with a jug of local cider. **€–€€**

La Coquille d'Oeuf
20 rue de la Corne de Cerf,
35400 St-Malo
Tel: 02 99 40 92 62
A bright neighbourhood bistro on one of the most attractive streets of Intra-Muros St-Malo, with light, contemporary cuisine – there are fine salads, pasta dishes and vegetarian options as well meat, fish and seafood. Closed Mon. **€€**

Maison Tirel-Guérin
1 Le Limonay, La Gouesnière,
35350 St-Meloir des Ondes
Tel: 02 99 89 10 46
Both stylish and friendly, this original hotel-restaurant in a village between St-Malo and Cancale offers creative, enticing food, made using the best local produce: salt-marsh lamb from the Bay of Mont-St-Michel and Cancale oysters are among the highlights. The rooms adopt the same chic modern style. Closed Sun Oct–Feb. **€€–€€€**

Vannes

Restaurant de Roscanvec
17 rue des Halles, 56000 Vannes
Tel: 02 97 47 15 96
This restaurant in a venerable stone town house in old Vannes appears to be the essence of tradition from the outside, but the young team in charge runs it with a fresh, unfussy approach, and the cooking blends first-rate local ingredients with influences from around the world – Japanese ingredients, Thai and Indian-ocean seasonings – without sinking into faddishness. A place that's not afraid to be original. Closed Sun and Mon except July–Aug. **€€–€€€**

PRICE CATEGORIES

Price categories are per person for a three-course meal:
€ = under €20
€€ = €20–45
€€€ = €45–90
€€€€ = over €90

Activities

The Arts, Festivals and Events, Nightlife, Shopping, Outdoor and Children's Activities

The Arts

Live Entertainment

There is a huge variety of live entertainment on offer throughout France, much of it concentrated in Paris and other major cities. In the summer, many cities (and even small towns) present a programme of events, including music and drama festivals, featuring live bands, street theatre and other outdoor performances that are often free.

Summer is dominated by a wide range of arts festivals, while conventional theatre and opera seasons generally run from September to June, so that many theatres and music venues are closed in July and August.

Brittany is the best place to be for summer, as it hosts the largest number of festivals in northern France, presenting its own distinctive music, dance and Celtic culture events each year *(see page 281)*.

Son et lumière displays are the highlights of some sites, notably Amiens Cathedral, Chartres and Mont-St-Michel. Performances normally begin at dusk.

A programme listing all major festivals and *fêtes* throughout the country is published annually and is available from French Government Tourist Offices around the world. Guides to events in France can also be found on the national tourist office website. For more detailed local information and reservations contact the local tourist office *(see page 352)*. A national guide of historical shows (in French) can be found on www.fffsh.eu.

Theatre, Dance, Opera and Classical music

In Paris

The theatre and opera companies of the Comédie Française and Opéra National de Paris are most famous for their classical productions, while the Théâtre de la Ville, Théâtre National de la Colline and Théâtre National de Chaillot cater for more modern tastes in theatre and dance. The recently expanded Centre National de la Danse, in the suburbs but a short train ride from the centre, stages mainly contemporary dance performances.

Look out also for adventurous contemporary dance companies, concerts and performances at the Pompidou Centre, the excellent classical music seasons at the Musée d'Orsay and Musée du Louvre, and the many music recitals in churches, especially during the Festival d'Art Sacré each December. The following is a list of the city's major venues:

Centre National de Danse
1 rue Victor Hugo, 93500 Pantin
Tel: 01 48 40 95 68
www.cnd.fr

Cité de la Musique
221 avenue Jean-Jaurès, 75009 Paris
Tel: 01 44 84 45 00
www.cite-musique.fr

Comédie Française
2 rue de Richelieu, 75001 Paris
Tel: 08 25 10 16 80
www.comedie-francaise.fr

Opéra National de Paris
Opéra Bastille, 2bis place de la Bastille, 75012 Paris
Palais Garnier, place de l'Opéra, 75009 Paris
Tel: 08 92 89 90 90
www.operadeparis.fr

Théâtre du Châtelet
1 place du Châtelet, 75001 Paris
Tel: 01 40 28 28 00
www.chatelet-theatre.com

Théâtre National de Chaillot
1 place du Trocadéro, 75116 Paris
Tel: 01 53 65 30 00
www.theatre-chaillot.fr

Théâtre National de la Colline
15 rue Malte-Brun, 75020 Paris
Tel: 01 44 62 52 52
www.colline.fr

Théâtre Palais Royal
38 rue de Montpensier, 75001 Paris
Tel: 01 42 97 40 00
www.theatrepalaisroyal.com

Théâtre de la Ville
2 place du Châtelet, 75004 Paris
Tel: 01 42 74 22 77
www.theatredelaville-paris.com

Booking Tickets

You can also usually book with venues directly, and the FNAC stores, found in most French cities, have desks selling tickets for concerts, theatre, festivals and other events in their area. See www.fnac.com.

Hello Paris!
Tel: 01256 374280
www.helloparis.co.uk
Helpful UK agency that can smooth your way ahead of travelling with transport tickets, cabaret shows, sightseeing tours, museum cards, Paris Visite travel cards and other Paris tickets.

Check-Théâtre
33 rue le Peletier, 75009 Paris
Tel: 08 25 05 44 05; www.check-theatre.com
Tickets for all kinds of Paris events.

Other Cities

Below are some of the main regional venues, which present varied programmes of opera, ballet and classical music.

Grand Théâtre
Place du Ralliement, 49000 Angers
Tel: 02 41 24 16 40
www.nta-angers.fr

Opéra de Lille
2 rue des Bons Enfants, 59800 Lille
Tel: 03 20 42 23 65
www.opera-lille.fr

Opéra du Rhin
19 place de Broglie, 67000 Strasbourg
Tel: 03 88 35 77 26
www.operantionaldurhin.eu

Opéra de Rouen Haute-Normandie
7 rue du Docteur Rambert, 76000 Rouen
Tel: 0810 811 116
www.operaderouen.fr

Grand Opéra de Tours
34 rue de la Scellerie, 37000 Tours
Tel: 02 47 60 20 00
www.operadetours.fr

Théâtre Graslin
1 rue Molière, 44000 Nantes
Tel: 02 40 69 77 18
www.angers-nantes-opera.com

ABOVE: dancing in the street at the annual Strasbourg Fête de la Musique.

Live Music

The French music scene is very diverse, ranging from rock, acoustic music and Breton folk through world music to jazz and techno. The best occasion to discover all the different genres of music being performed in France (including classical music) is the national music festival the **Fête de la Musique**, held every year on 21 June. Inaugurated in 1982, this has become a hugely popular event, with free concerts by professionals and amateurs in streets and squares all over France, all night long.

Pop music in France reflects the international scene, and much of what you hear will be the same as anywhere else. Brittany stands out for the individuality of its music scene, based in Breton Celtic music. From its folk roots, strongly influenced by Irish musicians, Breton music has now become very eclectic, incorporating all kinds of global influences.

Jazz, popular in Paris since the 1920s, is still strongly represented. There is a choice of jazz clubs in main towns, and several major jazz festivals throughout the year.

Music venues range from sport arenas and modern concert halls to ancient *théâtres* and open-air arenas. In Paris the main venues include Bercy, a glass-covered pyramid hosting sporting events, music concerts and shows; Le Zénith, a modern concert hall considered to be the best Paris venue by top artists; Le Bataclan, a concert hall hosting international musicians from rock, to jazz to world music; and the recently restored Salle Pleyel, popular for jazz. There are also purpose-built Le Zénith venues throughout France in major towns such as Dijon and Nantes.

Paris Music Venues

Le Bilboquet
13 rue Saint-Benôit, 75006
Tel: 01 45 48 81 84
Historic jazz spot where jazz and dinner can be enjoyed at the same time.

Caveau de la Huchette
5 rue de la Huchette, 75005 Paris
Tel: 01 43 26 65 05
www.caveaudelahuchette.fr
Famous jazz club with a funky contemporary programme that attracts big crowds.

La Chapelle des Lombards
19 rue de Lappe, 75011 Paris
Tel: 01 43 57 24 24
www.la-chapelle-des-lombards.com
Lively music in a popular club.

New Morning
7–9 rue des Petites Ecuries, 75010 Paris
Tel: 01 45 23 51 41
www.newmorning.com
One of the world's foremost jazz venues, where all the greats have played since the 1940s.

Le Petit Journal Montparnasse
13 rue du Commandant Mouchotte, 75014 Paris
Tel: 01 43 21 56 70
www.petitjournal-montparnasse.com
Small, intimate club with performances from top jazz musicians.

Sunset/Sunside
60 rue des Lombards, 75001 Paris
Tel: 01 40 26 46 60
www.sunset-sunside.com
Two clubs in one: electric jazz and world music on the ground floor and acoustic jazz in the more intimate cellar.

Other Cities

A selection of music venues in other cities:

Lille

WildScat Jazz Club
19 rue Colbert, 59000 Lille
Tel: 06 77 99 92 37
Recently opened eclectic music venue and club.

Rennes

Ubu Rennes
1 rue St-Hélier, 35000 Rennes
Tel: 02 99 30 31 68
www.ubu-rennes.com
A cutting-edge range of music running from classic jazz and Latin to electronica and DJ nights.

Rouen

Hangar 23
16 place St-Sever, 76100 Rouen
Tel: 02 32 18 28 10
www.hangar23.fr
"Music and dance cultures of the world" is this hip centre's motto, and its programmes cover an inspiringly huge range.

Cinema

Cinema programmes in France change every Wednesday. Films marked VO *(version originale)* are screened in the original language, not dubbed into French. Look out for listings of VO films at mainstream cinemas in major cities. In smaller towns, cinemas occasionally offer films in VO, usually in late-night screenings. During the summer months open-air screenings are a regular happening.

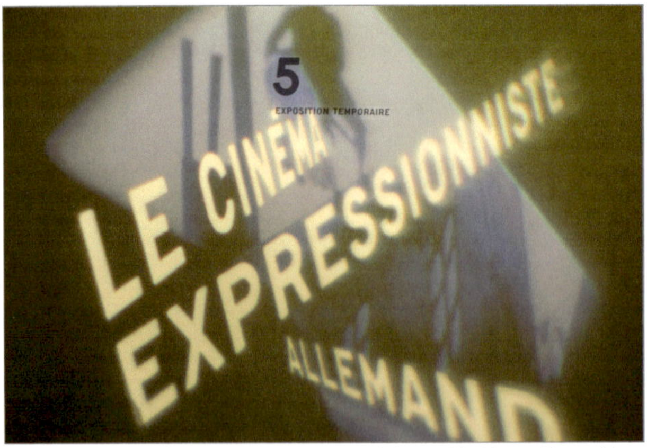

Above: the Cinemathèque Française holds one of the world's biggest film archives

Among the more noteworthy annual film festivals for English-speaking visitors are the American Film Festival at Deauville held in September, and the Festival of British film at Dinard in October.

In Paris, cinemas along the Champs-Élysées and around Odéon in St-Germain-des-Prés often show recent releases in their original language, as do the Latin Quarter arts cinemas for old films.

Listed below are some repertory cinemas that present interesting themed seasons, nearly always in VO:

Paris
Cinémathèque Française
51 rue de Bercy, 75012 Paris
Tel: 01 71 19 33 33
www.cinemathequefrancaise.com
Forum des Images
Max-Linder Panorama, 24 boulevard Poissonnière, 75009 Paris
Tel: 0892 68 00 31
www.forumdesimages.fr
Dijon
Cinéma ABC
7 rue Chapeau Rouge,21000 Dijon
Tel: 03 80 30 55 66
www.cinemaolympia.com
Lille
Le Métropole
26 rue des Ponts de Comines, 59000 Lille
Tel: 0892 680 073
www.lemetropole.com
Nantes
Le Cinématographe
12 bis, rue des Carmélites, 44000 Nantes
Tel: 02 40 47 94 80
www.lecinematographe.com
Quimper
Le Chapeau Rouge
1 rue Paradis, 29000 Quimper
Tel: 02 98 53 88 50
Strasbourg
Le Star
16 rue du Jeu des Enfants, 67000 Strasbourg
Tel: 03 88 32 44 97
www.cinema-star.com

Festivals and Events

Listed below are some of the main annual events; there are hundreds more in smaller towns and villages. For more specific information, contact local tourist offices or visit www.culture.fr and www.viafrance.com, where you can search events in France by month, location and category.

January: La Folle Journée classical music festival, Nantes; St-Vincent Tournante wine fête, Beaune.
February: Carnival in Dunkerque and the rest of Flanders
April: Independent Film Festival, Lille.
May: Mâcon wine fair; French Tennis Open, Paris.
June: Strasbourg Music Festival; Touraine Music Festival and Tours International Choral Music Competition; Chartres International Organ Festival; Fête de la Musique (France-wide, 21 June); Festival d'Anjou theatre festival; Festival de St-Denis (Paris) classical music and dance; Les 24 heures du Mans car race; Paris Jazz Festival; Gay Pride, Paris street parade, performances and parties.
July: Tour de France cycle race (France-wide); Francofolies de La Rochelle popular music festival; Lorraine Air Ballons hot-air balloon festival (2011, 2013); Anjou Festival; Bastille Day – celebrated throughout France on the 14th; Kann ar Loar Breton festival, Landerneau; Festival de Cornouaille – Breton culture festival, Quimper; St-Malo Route du Rock.
August: Lorient Interceltic Festival; Fêtes d'Arvor Breton festival, Vannes; Paris Quartier d'Été.
September: Dijon Music, Grape Harvest and Folk Fair; Chartres Cathedral Music Festival; Journées du Patrimoine (France-wide, third weekend in Sept); American Film Festival, Deauville; Grande Braderie de Lille; Festival d'Automne, Paris.
October: Planètes Jazz Tourcoing (Lille); Paris Motor Show (biennial, next in 2008); Montmartre Wine Harvest, Paris; FIAC Paris contemporary art fair; Nuit Blanche in Paris; Nancy Jazz Pulsations; Festival d'Art Sacré religious music festival, Paris.
November: Dijon International Gastronomy Fair; Paris-Photo, Paris; Beaujolais Nouveau celebrations; Beaune Wine Auction; Dijon Gastronomic Fair.
December: Transmusicales de Rennes rock festival; Paris Boat Show; Christmas markets, in Arras, Lille, all over Flanders and in Alsatian towns Strasbourg, Colmar and Kaysersberg.

Nightlife

Where to Go

Paris offers excellent nightlife, with a huge choice of venues and entertainment; in the provinces you need to be in major towns to find a similar standard. Many towns now organise festivals which run through the summer, and almost every town and village has its own *fête* at some point in summer, ranging from simple *boules* competitions with a dance, hosted by an enthusiastic (sometimes excruciating) band, playing traditional music (or, if you're unlucky, ancient pop songs), to a full-blown carnival with street theatre, fireworks and sophisticated entertainment.

Information about clubs, cinemas and other entertainment is readily available from local tourist offices or hotels.

Nightlife in Paris

Paris nightlife offers something for everyone, from elitist bars and clubs where you can do a bit of celebrity-spotting to underground cafés run by squatters. You can find jazz, salsa, tango, Congolese storytelling, and of course, traditional French *chansons*. Events are listed in the weekly magazine *Pariscope*, or to find out what's on online go to www.lemonsound.com and www.novaplanet.com.

Cabaret

Chez Michou
80 rue des Martyrs, 75018
Tel: 01 46 06 16 04
www.michou.fr
Shows by drag artists every night.

The Crazy Horse Saloon
12 avenue George V, 75008
Tel: 01 47 23 32 32
www.lecrazyhorseparis.com
Sexiest and most skimpily dressed of the big cabarets.

Le Lido
116 bis avenue des Champs-Élysées, 75008
Tel: 01 40 76 56 10
www.lido.fr
Traiditional cabaret glamour with countless costume changes, and three shows daily.

La Nouvelle Eve
25 rue Pierre Fontaine, 75009
Tel: 01 48 74 69 25
www.lanouvelleeveparis.com
A genuine Pigalle music hall, but without the vulgarity.

Nightclubs

Les Bains Douches
7 rue du Bourg-l'Abbé, 75003
Tel: 01 53 01 40 60
www.lesbainsdouches.net
Trendy venue, converted from an old public baths.

Batofar
11 Quai François-Mauriac, 75013
Tel: 09 71 25 50 61
www.batofar.org
Interesting live music and clubbing events on a renovated lighthouse ship on the Seine.

Cabaret
2 place du Palais-Royal, 75001
Tel: 01 58 62 56 25
www.cabaret.fr
Trendily designed basement club and lounge drawing showbiz and beautiful people. Strict door policy, so dress up.

La Loco
90 boulevard de Clichy
Tel: 01 53 41 88 89
Huge, popular nightclub with three dance floors.

Le Divan du Monde
75 rue des Martyrs, 75018
Tel: 01 42 52 02 46
www.divandumonde.fr
Throbbing, eclectic club (R&B, jazz, trance, etc.); no elitist door policy or dress code.

Rex Club
5 boulevard Poissonnière, 75002
Tel: 01 42 36 10 96
www.rexclub.com
A techno and house stalwart with big-name DJs.

Red Light
34 rue du Départ, 75014
Tel: 06 98 75 18 03
www.leredlight.com
House music with a mixed clientele.

BELOW: street performance.

Nightlife in Other Cities

See also live music *(page 339)* for multi-purpose venues in different cities. For information on nightlife all over France, try www.cityvox.com; www.citegay.fr or www.flyersweb.com.

Lille

Network Café
12 rue Faisan, 59800 Lille
Tel: 03 20 40 04 91
www.networkcafe.fr
Electronica, salsa and R&B all feature at this stylish club.

Rennes

El Teatro
3 rue St-Guillaume, 35000 Rennes
Tel: 09 50 32 15 25
www.elteatro.fr
Chic multi-space bar-club in one of Rennes' most historic 16th-century houses.

Rouen

Ibiza Club
29 blvd des Belges, 76000 Rouen
Tel: 02 35 07 76 20
www.discotheque-club.ibiza-club76.com
Classic big dance club loved by locals.

Tours

Le Louis XIV
37 rue Briconnet, 37000 Tours
Tel: 02 47 05 77 17
Popular bar that's a good place to meet up for a drink before wandering around town.

SHOPPING

Where to Shop

Since the 1980s most major towns in France have made the sensible decision to keep town centres for small boutiques and individual shops. Many of these areas are pedestrianised and very attractive, although beware – some cars ignore the *voie piétonnée* (pedestrianised road) signs. The supermarkets, hypermarkets, furniture stores and do-it-yourself outlets congregate on the outskirts of town, mostly designated as *Centres Commerciales*.

These centres, although aesthetically unappealing, are fine for bulk shopping for self-catering or for finding a selection of reasonably priced drinks to take home, but for gifts and window-shopping the town centres are far more interesting. It is here that you will find souvenirs with a particularly local flavour, alongside the beautifully dressed windows of delicatessens and patisseries. Markets are also a good source of handmade regional goods.

Clothing Sizes

Most shops are happy to let you try clothes on *(essayer)* before buying. Children's sizes, in particular, tend to be small compared with British and US age ranges. Hypermarkets are very good for inexpensive children's clothes, especially winter sports clothing.

Opening Hours

Food shops, especially bakers, tend to open early; small shops and department stores open from 9am, but sometimes not until 10am. In most town centres, just about everything closes from noon until 2.30pm or 3pm, but in Paris and other major tourist areas, some shops stay open all day. Most shops close in the evening at 7pm. City hypermarkets are usually open all day until 8pm or 9pm, but in more remote areas they may also close for lunch, and often shut at 7pm.

Shop for Lunch

If you want to buy a picnic lunch, remember to buy everything you need before midday, when most local shops shut for lunch. Good delicatessens *(charcuterie)* have delicious ready-prepared dishes, which make picnicking a delight.

Traditionally, bread shops and patisseries are the only shops open on Sundays (mornings only), but again, in tourist areas some hypermarkets now open on Sundays in the summer season. Many shops are closed Monday mornings and a considerable number close all day Monday.

Market Shopping

The heart of every French town is its market, and shopping for fresh produce there is one of the real pleasures of holidaying in France. Markets usually start early in the morning and close at midday, although some bigger ones are open in the afternoon too. French people usually visit early to get the best of the produce. Markets are a riot of colour and bustle; the most traditional have all kinds of stalls from flowers to domestic animals (do not be deceived – these are for the pot). Local cheeses, honey, wine, pâté and other specialities are often offered for tasting to encourage browsers to buy.

Small town markets are usually held only on one day each week, the same day since time immemorial; in country districts, towns near each other do not usually have markets on the same days. In cities, markets may be open every day during the week. The free *département* guides provided by local tourist offices always list market days in their areas, and it's very handy to get one if you want to make the best of local markets. At Easter and during the summer there are also extra *marches à l'ancienne* ("old-fashioned markets") in many areas that are known for the quality of their produce, opportunities for farmers to showcase their best products, often combined with demonstrations of traditional crafts. They are particularly popular in Normandy. Again, tourist offices have details.

Antique or second-hand *(brocante)* markets are found all around the provinces, as well as flea markets *(marchés aux puces)*, which are fun to look around – you may even find a genuine bargain antique amongst all the old junk. The most famous of these is **Les Puces de St-Ouen** at Porte de Clignancourt in Paris, open Saturday to Monday 6am–7.30pm. There are also *vide greniers*, which are the equivalent of car-boot sales.

ABOVE: Parisian street market.

Market Etiquette

Prices are usually by the kilo or by the *pièce*, that is, each item priced individually. Usually the stallholder *(marchand)* will select the goods for you. Sometimes there is a serve-yourself system – just observe everyone else. If you are choosing cheese, for example, you will often be offered a taste to try first, *pour goûter*. Here are a few useful words:

bag *le sac*
basket *le panier*
flavour *le parfum*
organic *biologique*
ripe *mûr*
tasting *la dégustation*
on peut goûter? *can I try it?*

"Vente Directe"

All around France you will be tempted by signs along the road offering *dégustations* (tastings) and *vente directe* (direct sales). Many wine and cider producers and farmers will invite you to try their drinks or other produce with an eye to selling you a case, or maybe a few jars of pâté. This is a good way to try before you buy and often includes a visit to the cider shed or wine cellar, and you have the added enjoyment of personal contact with the people who made what you take home, in their *terroir*.

When buying wine direct from a small vineyard or cooperative expect to pass a convivial moment tasting before you choose a bottle or two to take home. Champagne houses and grand vineyards, on the other hand, have smart estate shops and organised tours, for which you pay.

In towns in the main wine regions you will often find a *Maison des Vins*, a wine shop with a selection from all the neighbouring producers, which gives a good opportunity to try a range of regional wines.

Cider is produced on a much smaller, farm scale than wines, so cider-tasting in Normandy and Brittany is much more a matter of visiting farms, and often locating the farmer's family before they open up their shed. This, though, adds to the charm, and the farms, especially those of fine Calvados makers, are often imposing pieces of Norman architecture.

Tourist offices provide lists of wine producers or cider farms in their areas, often marked as a *Route des Vins* or *Route du Cidre*, which can be a great help in avoiding endless searches along impenetrable winding lanes.

Tax Refunds

On most purchases, the price includes TVA (VAT or value added tax). The base rate is currently 19.6 percent, but can be as high as 35 percent on luxury items. Non-EU residents can claim back TVA on certain products – called *détaxe* – if they spend more than €175 in the same shop. Ask the store for a *bordereau* (export sales invoice). This must be completed and shown, together with the goods, to customs officers on leaving the country. Follow the instructions on the form, and a refund will be sent to you in a month or two. Certain items purchased (e.g. antiques) may need special customs clearance.

OUTDOOR ACTIVITIES

There is a huge range of activities on offer, though cycling and walking are particularly popular ways for British visitors to enjoy the sights and surroundings of northern France.

Sports facilities are generally first-rate throughout France. Most towns have swimming pools and even small villages often have a tennis court, but you may have to become a temporary member to use it – enquire at the local tourist office. Male swimmers should be aware that in most French public swimming pools due to a health regulation men must wear trunks, not boxer shorts or anything that could possibly be worn in the street.

Many companies offer sporting and activity holidays in France, and local companies are listed in the guides provided by individual *départements* *(see page 352)*.

Water Sports

Water sports centres (often called a *base de loisirs*) are found in nearly all coastal towns and on many lakes and quiet stretches of river. They offer a range of leisure activities, and may have a café or bar, a restaurant, and picnic areas.

Many offer tuition in the various sports available – sailing, kayaking, windsurfing, and so on; fees are usually by the hour or half-hour. Where boating and windsurfing are permitted, equipment is often available for hire, or you can bring your own.

The central offices of the various water sports organisations in France provide lists of regional clubs.

Canoeing

Fédération Française de Canoe-Kayak
87 Quai de la Marne, 94340 Joinville-le-Pont
Tel: 01 45 11 08 50
www.ffck.org

Sailing

Fédération Française de Voile
17 rue Henri Bocquillon, 75015 Paris Cedex 16
Tel: 01 40 60 37 00
www.ffvoile.fr

Rafting

Société AN Rafting
Les Iles de Macot, 73210 Aime La Plagne
Tel: 04 79 09 72 79
www.an-rafting.com

Surfing

Fédération Française de Surf
Plage Nord, 40150 Hossegor
Tel: 05 58 43 55 88
www.surfingfrance.com

Kitesurfing

Fédération Française de Vol Libre
7 rue de Suisse, 06000 Nice
Tel: 04 97 03 82 82
http://federation.ffvl.fr

Fishing

With its wealth of waterways and lakes, France is ideal fishing country. To book fishing holidays (a weekend or longer) with accommodation, try *département* tourist offices *(see page 352)*. A permit *(permis)* is usually required for coarse fishing; enquire at tourist offices. Sea fishing trips are widely available – look out for sign boards on quaysides advertising trips.

For regional fishing information contact the Fédération Française de Pêche Sportif au Coup, tel: 02 32 53 03 35, www.ffpsc.fr; and for fly-fishing the Fédération Française de la Pêche à la Mouche et au Lancer, tel: 01 45 21 01 69, www.ffpml.com.

For deep-sea fishing the central association is the Fédération Française des Pêcheurs en Mer, tel: 05 59 31 00 73, www.ffpm-national.com. All these organisations essentially operate in French only, but a useful guide to inland fishing in English can be found on www.fishingfrance.net.

Air Sports

There are many small airfields that offer flying, gliding or parachuting. Paragliding *(parapente)* is also very popular. Beginners' flights can usually be booked at a reasonable fee; these organisations will have further information:

Fédération Française de Vol à Voile
29 rue de Sèvres, 75006 Paris
Tel: 01 45 44 04 78
www.ffvv.org
For fixed-wing gliding.

Cycling

Taking your own bicycle *(vélo)* to France is easy from the UK – they are carried free on most ferries and trains – or you can rent cycles for a reasonable cost; main railway stations usually have them for hire and you can often arrange to pick up at one station and leave it at another. Alternatively, try bicycle retailers/repairers or ask at the local tourist office.

An extensive network of *Voie Vertes* or "Green Ways", cycle routes, has been created around France that allow you to cover long distances by bike with only a few stretches on conventional road. They are mainly run on a regional basis, and so vary from one area to the other; in Brittany and western Normandy they are particularly well-established. Regional tourist offices provide handy guides on paper and on their websites.

Some youth hostels rent cycles and also arrange tours with accommodation in hostels or under canvas.

Cycling Holidays

Some specialist operators are listed here:

Fédération Française de Cyclotourisme
12 rue Louis-Bertrand, 94207 Ivry-sur-Seine
Tel: 01 56 20 88 88
www.ffct.org
This official federation organises over 60 guided tours each year, all over

Health and Beauty

Thalassotherapy – seawater-based therapy – was invented by the French, and centres are dotted all along the French coastline and especially around the Atlantic coast. Thalassotherapy and spa treatments are a great way to pamper yourself, and the centres are often linked to luxurious hotels. The Algotherm company (www.algotherm.fr) specialises in chic up-market establishments such as the very luxurious centre spas at Deauville. More Thalasso centres can be found in Granville, Dinard, Perros-Guirec, Carnac and Quiberon, among other resorts.

BELOW: sand yachting on a Normandy beach.

France. You must have your own bike.
Cyclists Touring Club
Tel: 0844 736 8451; www.ctc.org.uk
Headwater Holidays
Tel: 01606-720 199; www.headwater.com
Hotel accommodation, and your luggage transported.
Susi Madron's Cycling for Softies
Tel: 0161-248 8282; www.cycling-for-softies.co.uk
Cycling holidays in many regions, with comfortable accommodation.

Information and Tips

It is advisable to take out insurance before you go. The normal rules of the road apply to cyclists *(see Getting Around, page 309)*. Advice and information can be obtained from the Cyclists Touring Club in the UK *(see above)*. Their service to members includes competitive cycle and travel insurance, free touring itineraries and general information sheets about France. The club's French counterpart, Fédération Française de Cyclotourisme *(see page 343)* offers a similar service. Cycle Map Europe: France, Spain and Portugal by Richard Peace (2002) is a useful companion, and the IGN Cyclists' Map No. 906 *France Vélo* carries a mass of information.

Such is the French passion for cycling that local clubs organise many trips lasting a day or more and visitors are often welcome to join in. Weekend or longer tours are organised by the national Bicyclub. Lists of clubs and events are available from local branches of the Fédération Française de Cyclotourisme *(see page 343)*. They also produce leaflets giving suggested cycle tours for independent travellers, ranging from easy terrain to very hard going for the more experienced cyclist, with details of accommodation, cycle repairers and other facilities en route.

Mountain Biking

This sport is extremely popular in France. Many of the organisations listed under Cycling Holidays offer mountain bike holidays. Mountain bikes (in French VTT – *Vélo Tout Terrain*) and protective gear can all be hired locally. Ask at the local tourist office for rental outlets, or cycle shops/repairers.

Horse Riding

The official federation in charge of riding activities in France is the **Fédération Française d'Equitation**, tel: 01 58 17 58 17, www.ffe.com, which provides information on marked bridleways, maps, riding centres and insurance. Treks lasting a day or more and longer holidays on horseback can be organised locally, and in all forest areas – notably around Chantilly and in the Orne in Normandy – there are local riding centres offering trips of different levels of difficulty. Addresses can be obtained, as usual, from tourist offices *(see page 352)*.

A high-quality English-speaking private agency that provides riding trips throughout the country is **Riding in France**, tel: 04 37 02 25 00, www.rideinfrance.com.

Golf

Northern France has several celebrated courses including Le Touquet, Hardelot (near Calais), La Vallée (near Arras) and Deauville-St-Gatien, one of the most opulent courses in Europe. Tourist offices have details of all the courses in their area, or you can get comprehensive information (in French) from the **Fédération Française de Golfe**, tel: 01 41 49 77 00; www.ffgolf.org.

A British company that provides packages combining golfing on renowned courses with luxury hotel accommodation is **Golf in France**, tel: (UK) 0121 713 2277, www.golfinfrance.com.

BELOW: canoeing off the beach at Etretat.

Walking

France has more than 60,000km (38,000 miles) of long-distance walkways – *Grandes Randonnées* (GR) – and also many *Petite Randonnées* (PR). One of the most memorable in the north is the GR34, all the way around the coast of Brittany. Topo Guides (guides books with IGN 1:50,000-scale maps), published by the Fédération Française de Randonnée Pédestre (www.ffrandonnee.fr), provide details of footpaths, places to stay and transport. There is also a series of guidebooks in English published by Robertson-McCarta called *Footpaths of Europe* which includes the IGN maps. As well as this, most rural communes have signposted walks. Always wear appropriate footwear, a hat in hot weather, and take plenty of water too.

Spectator Sports

France has a notoriously ambiguous relationship with **football** (soccer), but in the north it is by a long way the most popular spectator sport. Lens, Valenciennes, Lille, Nancy, Strasbourg and Stade Rennais (from Rennes) are among the best-supported teams in France, and Paris-St-Germain gains a certain prestige simply from being in the capital. The season normally runs from August to May. Comprehensive information including results and forthcoming fixtures is provided in English on the official French football website, www.ligue1.com.

Rugby is in general much more popular in the south of France but there are two big clubs in the Paris area, Stade Français and Racing Métro 92, and all rugby (and most football) internationals are played at the **Stade de France** in St-Denis north of Paris. Information on French rugby and ticket sales for domestic and international games are provided (in French only) on the Fédération Française de Rugby website, www.ffr.fr.

Other big events in the French sporting calendar are the **Tour de**

Above: horse riding in Brittany

France cycle race, which runs around the country on a different course each year and focuses attention throughout July and August, the French open **golf** tournament, held on different courses and also in July, and the French open **tennis** championships (officially called Roland Garros), in Paris in late May–early June. Tickets for the latter are available directly from the championships website (in English), www.rolandgarros.com. Finals tickets are in great demand.

Tickets for other events can be bought directly from each venue, but the most convenient way to pre-book tickets for all sports in France (football, rugby, tennis tournaments other than Roland Garros) is through the ticket desks of FNAC stores in main cities, or through the English-language website, www.fnactickets.com.

Horse racing is very popular in France, with the very grand flat-racing courses of Longchamp in Paris, Chantilly and Le Touques, Deauville. The elite courses are regulated by France-Galop, which provides comprehensive information in English on www.france-galop.com. Trotting or harness racing, *le trot*, with horses pulling a small cart, is also popular, and usually has a more downmarket style than flat-racing. Main tracks are at Vincennes (Paris), Clairefontaine in Deauville (not the same as the flat track), Enghien and Caen. Some tracks also host flat races. For information (in French) see www.lescourseshippiques.com.

Children's Activities

Northern France offers a wide range of activities for families travelling with children. Rural France is a great place for children to explore and offers outdoor activities all year round, the coast has wonderful beaches, and cities are packed with places that provide amusement for the whole family. City parks and gardens can be a great source of inexpensive entertainment.

In Paris the **Jardin d'Acclimatation**, open all year round, at the Bois de Boulogne is an extensive amusement park featuring a menagerie, Explorodome museum, a mini-golf course, pony rides, a house of mirrors and a puppet theatre. The Cité des Sciences at the **Parc de la Villette** is another super place in Paris for children to discover science through play, and for those more artistically inclined the **Centre Pompidou** offers interactive expositions and workshops for children.

Disneyland Paris Resort (open all year) east of the city is the region's best-known children's attraction, attracting millions of visitors each year, but there are other fun theme amusement parks nearby such as **Parc Astérix** at Plailly (closed winter) which has stomach-churning rollercoaster and water rides, and live shows.

Aquariums are fun all year round, whatever the weather, and France boasts several ultra-modern aquariums. The **Aquarium de Paris** has recently been restored and now houses 15,000 fish, and 4 cinemas; **Océanopolis** at **Brest** and the **Grand Aquarium** in **St-Malo** take you on a voyage through the oceans from warm climate to icy waters, and at **Boulogne sur Mer** you can discover the many facets of marine life at the impressive **Nausicaá** sea life centre.

Zoos, themed animal parks, ornithological parks and botanical gardens are plentiful, and addresses can be obtained from local tourist offices. Some exceptional sites are listed below:

Château de la Bourbansais, 35720 Pleugueneuc, Ile-et-Vilaine. A delightful château just south of St-Malo, with fascinating historic relics, that is also an unusual private zoo and park, with plenty of family activities. Tel: 02 99 69 40 48; www.labourbansais.com.

Terra Botanica, Route de Cantenay Epinard, 49000 Angers. Ultra-modern botanical gardens in the Loire Valley (open Apr–Oct). Tel : 02 41 25 00 00; www.terrabotanica.fr.

Circus entertainment is popular in France and ranges from the small, family-run circuses that still travel around rural France to the grand traditional companies such as Arlette Gruss, Pinder, Bouglione, Franconi and Fratelli, and contemporary circuses like Plume and Eloïse. Circus art is developing, and to reflect this a festival of "new circus", **La Brèche**, is held each spring in Cherbourg and various other locations around western Normandy.

Beaches

There are many fine, sandy beaches on the northern coast of Normandy and Brittany, but don't expect the water temperatures to get very balmy, even in summer. Some of the best beaches include Le Touquet, Dinard, Perros-Guirec, Sables d'Or les Pins, St-Michel en Grève and Brignogan Plage. In southern Brittany Bénodet, Quiberon and Carnac have the best beaches, but often get packed. Explore a little along the coast and you can have much more room to yourself.

A – Z

A Handy Summary of Practical Information, Arranged Alphabetically

Admission Charges

The admission fees for visiting museums, galleries and monuments are generally €4–9 per adult, with free admission for children – check on the qualifying age: for some places it is under 18 and others 12 or 7 years old. Access to the permanent exhibitions of any state-owned museum or monument is free for all EU residents aged under 26 or over 60, and there are also special rates for students. Private attractions are generally a bit more expensive than public ones, and do not have such generous concessions.

Major towns often have special **city passes** that can be bought at the local tourist office or participating venues, which provide free admission for a range of attractions, which can be a great money-saver. In Paris, the **Paris Museum Pass** gives access to around 60 museums and monuments over a 2-, 4- or 6-day period, for an adult price of €32–64; it can be bought in advance through www.parismuseumpass.com, which also gives full details. The **Paris Visite** travel card also gives discounts to various attractions. In other cities, a local museum pass is usually combined with unlimited use of public transport, as in **Lille's City Pass Lille-Métropole**, which gives entry to all the main attractions in the Lille conurbation and the Musée Matisse in Le Cateau-Cambrésis plus local train travel for €20–45. Details of local schemes are provided by each tourist office.

Budgeting for Your Trip

Low-cost budget chain hotels start from around €35 for a room, mid-range hotels range from around €70 for a double in mid-season to €150 for more up-market lodgings in busier periods. Simple *chambres d'hôtes* (B&B) double rooms can still be found in most areas for about €40–50, but more charming ones will usually be over €60. Note that this includes breakfast, which in hotels is usually charged for separately (and is rarely as good). Prices for all accommodation in France vary by season, and can go up a great deal during peak seasons, typically July to August, especially anywhere around the coast.

Eating out at a crêperie or pizzeria will cost around €15–20 per person, while a three-course meal in a mid-range restaurant costs around €20–30, or €40–50 for a fixed-price menu somewhere a bit more stylish. If you opt for luxury, the sky is the limit, with gourmet restaurants easily costing over €100. Beyond food, the cost of going out varies a great deal by venue: the price of drinks in fashionable Paris cafés can be enormous, but in smaller places it's much more reasonable.

Transport costs can be reduced by making the most of the various discounts available for train travel, and multi-journey tickets and passes in cities *(see above and page 309)*. Car rental for a small car will be around €30 per day or less with prebooked deals.

Children

In France generally, children are treated as individuals not nuisances. It is pleasant to be able to take them out for a meal (even in the evening) without heads being turned in horror. French children, though, accustomed to eating out from an early age, are on the whole well behaved in restaurants, so it helps if one's own offspring understand that they can't run wild.

Many restaurants offer a children's menu; if not, they will often split a *prix-fixe* menu between two children. If travelling with very young children, you may find it practical to order nothing specific at all for them but just request an extra plate and give them something tasty to try from your own dish. French meals are usually generous enough to allow you to do this without going hungry.

Another option is to order a single simple, inexpensive dish such as an omelette, which most children will happily eat, and crêperies – universal in Brittany, not hard to find elsewhere – are another great standby for child-friendly food. As a last resort, in cities there are plenty of fast-food outlets, and the Hippopotâme chain is an enjoyable variation especially aimed at families.

Most hotels have family rooms so children do not have to be separated from parents, and another bed or cot *(lit bébé)* can often be provided for a small charge, but check availability when booking.

Climate

The French climate is varied and seasonal, and in most of the north it is typically temperate and pretty similar to that of southern England, that is, with moderate summer temperatures, damp autumns and early springs and chilly, unpredictable winters. Springtime is often suggested as the best time to see Paris, but be prepared for showers. In the autumn, mornings can be quite sharp, but by midday the skies are usually clear and bright.

Around the Atlantic coasts, above all in the Cotentin peninsula of Normandy and in northern Brittany, the ocean weather is especially variable, and can change from blasting winds and grey skies in the early morning to golden sunshine by lunchtime. In southern Brittany and especially along the Loire valley the climate is noticeably milder and often much warmer, with summer temperatures along the Loire often over 28°C (82°F). There can also be occasional heavy storms.

Given the variations of the weather, it's best to have some rainwear and at least a sweater at any time, although in summer you may well not need them.

CLIMATE CHART

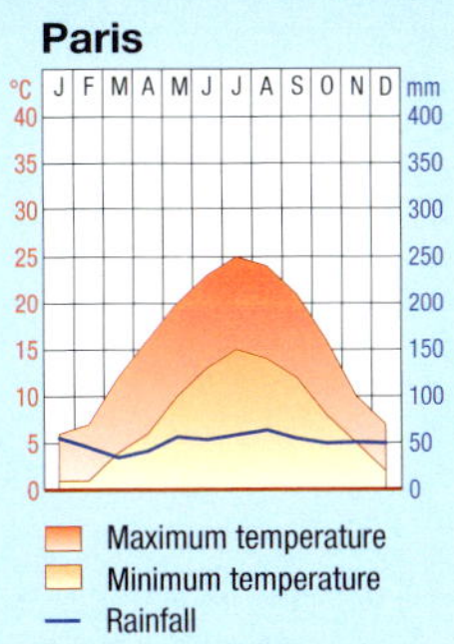

Crime and Security

Theft and crime exist here as anywhere else, but violent crime is not a serious problem, and sensible precautions with personal possessions are all that should really be necessary when visiting France. You should have comprehensive travel insurance covering all your possessions against loss or theft before arrival. In cities, avoid areas that look risky, and be particularly vigilant on the Paris Métro, where pickpocketing is most common, especially at peak times. At café and restaurant tables, especially outdoors, always keep your bag in sight and in front of you, never on the ground or hanging on the back of a chair, and always stay with your bags at train stations. Naturally, you need to be extra careful at night, and avoid using ATMs in city centres after dark.

If you do have anything stolen or are the victim of any other crime, report this immediately to the nearest police station *(commissariat de police)* or in small towns the *Gendarmerie*, the force in charge of rural policing. To phone for the police call **17**. If you have been robbed you will need to go to a police station to make a statement, which you will need to make an insurance claim. If your passport has been lost or stolen, notify your consulate immediately and follow their instructions *(see page 348)*.

Customs Regulations

Residents of EU countries can carry any amount of goods into and out of France without extra duty so long as they are for their personal use. Examples of amounts normally accepted to fit this criteria are 10 litres of spirits or strong liqueurs, 90 litres of wine, 3,200 cigarettes and 110 litres of beer.

For non-EU residents, duty-free allowances include: 200 cigarettes, 50 cigars or 250 grams tobacco, 1 litre of spirits and gifts worth up to €175. Any amount of currency exceeding €10,000 or equivalent must be declared on entry, and when leaving France. Value-Added Tax (sales tax) can be reclaimed by non-EU residents when they leave France on some more expensive items *(see Shopping, page 342)*.

Disabled Travellers

Major initiatives have been undertaken in France to improve provision for people with special needs, including a series of special signs for specific disabilities, such as impaired mobility, blindness or deafness, which direct people and carers to help points. Access has been improved to museums and major monuments, although this may still be limited at smaller historic châteaux.

The **Tourisme & Handicap** label is used to indicate museums, attractions, hotels and other facilities with full access and which meet other criteria. Accessible attractions and other facilities in Paris are listed on www.parisinfo.com, and the French Tourist Office (Maison de France) sites provide a great deal of other helpful information under What to Do/Special Needs Travellers.

Driving: The European blue-badge scheme applies, and there are free disabled parking spaces in all car parks and many streets. Ensure you have all the documentation with you. Adapted vehicles also pay reduced tolls on motorways.

Accommodation: Thanks to recent legislation, more and more French hotels have adapted rooms (many more than in the UK), and they can also be found in many attractive *chambres d'hôtes* (B&Bs). Local tourist offices and booking organisations such as those of the Logis de France hotel association or Gîtes de France indicate disabled facilities on their leaflets and websites. However, it's always advisable to check directly for specific facilities.

Transport: The SNCF, French railways, has an extensive scheme to provide full access for all to all its trains, called Accès Plus, with which anyone with mobility problems can reserve a guaranteed space and if necessary obtain assistance on and off the train for no extra charge. Some information is provided on the main SNCF English

website (www.sncf.com, under Everyday Life – Services +), but the full Accessibility site is still French-only. Work is also being done to provide disabled access at all stations. Many buses in Paris and other cities are wheelchair-accessible, but on the Paris underground networks there is full access only on some RER and one Métro line (no. 14). All taxis must carry wheelchair-users for no extra charge, and radio-taxi firms in Paris and other cities often have specially adapted taxis *(taxis aménagés)*.
SNCF Accès Plus: tel: 0890 640 650, www.accessibilite.sncf.com.
Info Mobi: tel: 0810 646 464, www.infomobi.com. Information (in French only) on disabled transport facilities in Paris and the Ile-de-France.

Other Information Sources

Access in Paris, published by the Access Project, 39 Bradley Gardens, West Ealing, London W13 8HE, www.accessinparis.org. An invaluable, wonderfully detailed guide to enjoying Paris for disabled travellers, available as a book or on the website.
Association des Paralysés de France: tel: 01 53 80 92 97, www.apf.asso.fr. Official body that publishes *Où Ferons-Nous Etapes?*, listing accommodation, and a great deal of other information for disabled travellers, in French only.
Society for Accessible Travel and Hospitality, www.sath.org, offers information and resources related to travel in the US and overseas.
Tourisme & Handicaps: tel: 01 44 11 10 41, www.tourisme-handicaps.org. A national labelling scheme for disabled facilities (French only).
Travel For All UK: tel: 0845 124 9971, www.tourismforall.org.uk. Travel information and support of all kinds for anyone with special needs.

Electricity

220 volts, with the standard European two-round-pin plugs. You will need adaptors to operate British three-pin equipment, and with older North American-110 volt flat-pin appliances, you may need a transformer as well as a plug adaptor.

Embassies and Consulates

In France

Australia: 4 rue Jean-Rey, 75015 Paris, tel: 01 40 59 33 06, www.france.embassy.gov.au
Canada: 35 avenue Montaigne, 75008 Paris, tel: 01 44 43 29 00, www.canadainternational.gc.ca
Irish Republic: 4 rue Rude, 75016 Paris, tel: 01 44 17 67 00, www.embassyofireland.fr
UK: 18 bis rue d'Anjou, 75008 Paris, tel: 01 44 51 31 00, http://ukinfrance.fco.gov.uk
US: 2 avenue Gabriel, 75008 Paris, tel: 01 43 12 22 22, http://france.usembassy.gov

Outside France

French Consulate, 21 Cromwell Road, London SW7 2EN, tel: 020-7073 1200, fax: 020-7073 1218, www.ambafrance-uk.org
Visa section: 6a Cromwell Place, PO Box 57, London SW7 2EW, tel: 020-7073 1250.
French Embassy, 58 Knightsbridge, London SW1X 7JT, tel: 020-7073 1000, fax: 020-7201 1004, www.ambafrance-uk.org
Cultural department: 23 Cromwell Road, London SW7 2EL, tel: 020-7073 1300.

Emergencies

All emergency services 112
Ambulance (SAMU) – dial 15
Police – dial 17
Fire *(sapeurs-pompiers)* – dial 18
In case of a serious accident or medical emergency call the *Service d'Aide Médicale d'Urgence* (SAMU, ambulance service), or the police or fire department. The *sapeurs-pompiers* are also trained paramedics, and they and the police work in close contact with the SAMU.

Etiquette

When greeting people shake the hand of every person present; friends and family kiss lightly on the cheek. When entering a shop, or walking up to a market stall, always say *"bonjour"* or *"bonsoir"* depending on the time of day, and *"au revoir"* when you leave. Failure to acknowledge the existence of shop staff with basic courtesy establishes a frosty atmosphere from the outset and will guarantee bad service. Always address people using *"Monsieur"* or *"Madame"*, and use the more formal *"vous"*, as *"tu"* among family and friends.

When invited to eat at a French person's home it is customary to arrive with a gift – usually flowers, rather than wine.

Gay & Lesbian Travellers

General information is available from Radio FG (98.2 MHz), www.radiofg.com and national magazines Têtu and Lesbia. A good source of listings of bars, clubs and associations is the Queer Resource Directory, www.france.qrd.org; Gay-séjour.com is also useful for listings of bars, clubs and beaches. For further information contact Centre Gai et Lesbian, 63 rue Beaubourg, 75003 Paris; tel: 01 43 57 21 47; http://cglparis.org.

Health & Medical Care

EU Citizens

All EU nationals can obtain free treatment from the French health service provided they have a European Health Insurance Card (EHIC), available through post offices and health centres. With the EHIC card you will also get a booklet outlining the procedures to be followed in each country. The EHIC will be fine for most situations and initial emergency care, but be aware that it does not cover you against all eventualities, notably the cost of repatriation in the event of a serious injury. Hence it's a good idea to take out private travel-medical insurance as well. If you expect to try any adventure sports you may also need extra cover.

There are also certain peculiarities to the French system that apply to all its users, French and foreign. Patients normally have to pay for treatments and drugs upfront, and then reclaim the cost from a health service office. Non-French EU nationals with an EHIC must also pay, and be careful to retain the *fiche* or bill from the doctor, and stickers from the packets of prescription drugs (pharmacists will attach them to the *fiche*). Follow the instructions given with your EHIC to reclaim about 80 percent of the costs. This can take time. If you see a doctor, expect to pay around €22 for a simple consultation, plus charges for any medicines.

If you have a medical emergency, in all cities and towns there are hospitals with general casualty/emergency departments *(urgences or service des urgences)* that are the best places to go to for immediate treatment. If you cannot get to one, call the SAMU ambulance service *(see above)*. The standard of treatment in French hospitals is generally high, and you should be able to find someone who speaks English to help you. Consulates (and often hotels) can advise on English-speaking doctors in each area, and in the Paris area there are two fully equipped

English-speaking private hospitals, the **American Hospital of Paris**, 63 boulevard Victor-Hugo, 92292 Neuilly, tel: 01 46 41 25 25, www.american-hospital.org, and the Hertford British Hospital, 3 rue Barbès, 92300 Levallois, tel: 01 46 39 22 22, www.british-hospital.org. Costs will be higher than at public hospitals.

Non EU-Citizens

Visitors from outside the European Union should have full private travel and medical insurance when visiting France, and if they have a medical emergency can use either private or public facilities, keep the same documentation as EU citizens *(see above)*, and then claim back on their insurance.

IAMAT is a specialised travel health service that provides insurance and a directory of English-speaking doctors in countries all around the world. **IAMAT:** tel: (USA) 1-716-754 4883; (Canada) tel: 1-416-652 0137; www.iamat.org.

Pharmacies

Pharmacies are plentiful in French towns, and identified by a green cross sign that is lit up at night. French pharmacists have extensive training, and for minor ailments, bites, scratches and so on it will often be easier to consult a pharmacist first before looking for a doctor. Outside of normal shop hours and on Sundays, a card in the window of each pharmacy will give the address of the nearest duty pharmacy *(pharmacie de garde)* that is still open.

Internet

The Internet is as widely used in France as anywhere else nowadays, but public access to the Net is often peculiarly hard to find. Internet cafés are quite common in Paris, but even in provincial cities there are only a few, and in small towns often none at all, so don't rely on checking the Net easily. Internet access points are provided in main post offices, tourist offices and sometimes rail stations, but you often have to wait in line and they can be expensive. If you travel with a laptop there are more options, as there are Wi-fi hotspots in many cafés and train stations, and many hotels and even *chambres d'hôtes* now offer Wi-fi connections. You will usually have to pay, in cafés and hotels, often by joining a subscription service such as Orange France. You pay for a certain amount of time, and if you have any left you can use it up at another hotel with the same service.

Note that French Wi-fi servers often use unusual frequencies, so you may need to reconfigure your system to get a signal.

Lost Property

If you lose something on a bus or the Métro, first try the terminus to see if it has been handed in. In Paris, after 48 hours, you can go to the *Bureau des Objets Trouvés*, 36 rue des Morillons, 75015 Paris, tel: 08 21 00 25 25 (calls can be answered in English). You must pay a small percentage of the value of any item reclaimed.

In small towns, the local Mairie will normally have its own *Bureau des Objets Trouvés*, where things may turn up, and it's also worth asking in police or *gendarmerie* stations.

Maps

A first essential in touring France is a good map. The Institut Géographique National (IGN) is the French equivalent of the British Ordnance Survey and its maps are excellent. For route planning, **IGN 901** is an ideal large-scale map, while the **Michelin M911** at the same scale shows just motorways and main roads, with good clear presentation if you do not intend to stray far off the beaten track.

For more detailed maps, the **IGN Red Series** (1:250,000) covers the country region by region at a good scale for touring. Michelin also produces regional maps at a similar scale (1:200,000). Both sets of maps are available as road atlases with different publishers.

The **IGN Top 100** (1:100,000, 1cm:1km (or 1inch:1.6 miles) are more detailed local maps that are very useful for travellers heading for a single main destination, and also quite good for walking. The essential maps for walkers, though, are the IGN Blue Series (Top 25), at 1:25,000 scale. Other specialist maps for walkers and climbers are produced by **Didier Richard** (Alpine maps), while the IGN also produces detailed maps of the Pyrenees and the national parks and many other special-interest maps.

Local tourist offices also provide town plans, *département* maps and a variety of other maps for free.

Shopping for Maps and Books

In France, most good bookshops and Maisons de la Presse should have a range of maps, and they can also be bought cheaply in supermarkets and service stations.

Stockists in the UK are:

- **Stanfords International Map Centre**, 12–14 Long Acre, Covent Garden, London WC2E 9LP, tel: 020-7836 1321, www.stanfords.co.uk
- **The Travel Bookshop**, 13 Blenheim Crescent, London W11 2EE, tel: 020-7229 5260, www.thetravelbookshop.co.uk
- **Nicolson Maps**, 3 Frazer Street, Largs, Ayrshire KA30 9HP, tel/fax: 01475-689242, www.nicolsonmaps.com

Media

Newspapers

Regional newspapers contain national and international as well as local news, and are often read in preference to the national press. The main national dailies are *Le Monde* (for a liberal overview of political and economic news), the more conservative *Le Figaro* and the left-wing papers, *Libération* and *L'Humanité*. *Le Point*, *Le Nouvel Observateur* and *L'Express* are the major weekly news publications. British and American papers, including *USA Today* and the

BELOW: *Libération*, France's left-wing daily, was founded by Jean-Paul Sartre.

International Herald Tribune, are widely available in major towns.

Television

By the end of 2011 all of France will be converted to Digital Video Broadcasting (DVB), which is called *'la television numérique terrestre'* (TNT) in France.) There are 18 free-to-air channels including the main national channels: TF1 (commercial) and France 2 (state-owned but largely financed by advertising); as well as France 3, which offers regional programmes, and France 4 covering mainly music, sport and films. 5-Arté is a Franco-German channel showing cartoons during the day and arts programmes and documentaries in the evening. M6 shows mainly American films and serials (dubbed into French). France 2 in particular sometimes shows films in English with French subtitles.

Radio

France Inter is the main national radio station (87.8 MHz); it broadcasts English-language news twice a day in summer (usually 9am and 4pm). In some areas the BBC's Radio 4 can be received on longwave (198 kHz), and the BBC World Service broadcasts on shortwave on various wavelengths during the day and evening. Radio Traffic (107.7 FM) is useful when driving and gives regular bulletins of traffic situations in English.

Money

France's currency is the euro (€), which is available in 500, 200, 100, 50, 20, 10 and 5 euro notes, and 2 euro, 1 euro, 50 cent, 20 cent, 10 cent, 5 cent, 2 cent and 1 cent coins. There are 100 cents to one euro.

Banks displaying a *Change* sign will exchange foreign currency and, in general, give reasonable rates; you will need to produce your passport when changing money. There are a lot of variations in opening times, but bank branches in cities are usually open Monday to Friday 9/10am–5pm, and some also open on Sundays. Small town and suburban banks may be closed on Mondays, and often close for lunch from 12.30–2pm. All banks are closed on Sundays and public holidays. At other times, the private *bureaux de change* found in Paris and some tourist areas generally give rates that are not too excessive, but avoid changing money in hotels, which always charge high commissions.

Travellers' cheques are less and less common now that ATMs are so widespread. A few hotels will accept them as payment, but not all banks will cash them. In remote rural areas you may have difficulty finding anywhere to cash travellers' cheques.

Credit and Debit Cards

Major credit and debit cards such as Visa, MasterCard, Switch and Delta are very widely used in France and effectively indispensable for many transactions such as train bookings or renting a car. American Express is much less popular and not accepted by many French businesses.

Cards in France use a chip-and-pin system exactly like that in the UK (the French for PIN is *code personnel*). When paying by card you may also be asked to show additional ID. If you have a US or Canadian card that is still not chip-and-pin coded you will have to ask that your card is swiped. Most waiters and shop staff, especially in Paris, are used to this.

All French bank branches have ATMs from which you can withdraw cash with a credit or debit card. However, remember that you now need to notify your bank or other card issuer before you use a card abroad (or it may be blocked), and check before travelling on the charges made for foreign cash withdrawals, which have been increasing.

Lost Credit Cards

It is also worth noting down the specific international emergency number given by your card provider:

Visa/Carte Bleue
Tel: 08 00 90 11 79
American Express
Tel: 08 00 83 28 20
MasterCard
Tel: 08 00 90 13 87

Opening Hours

Office workers normally start early – 8am is not uncommon – and often stay at their desks until 6pm or later. This is partly to make up for the long lunch hours (from noon or 12.30pm for two hours) which are still traditional in banks, shops and other public offices. Larger companies are increasingly changing to shorter lunch breaks as employees appreciate the advantages of getting home earlier to families in the evening.

Outside the major towns, even supermarkets and petrol stations often shut for a couple of hours over lunch and may close on Sundays and public holidays. Many shops in smaller towns and villages close on one day in the week, although you can usually find a bakery open in the morning. Plan your shopping to avoid being caught without food or fuel.

Pets

It is possible to take your pet to France and re-enter Britain with your pet without quarantine. You will need an EU pet passport (or a valid PETS certificate). For further information on requirements for issuing the pet passport you are advised to contact DEFRA in the UK (tel: 0845-933 5577, www.defra.gov.uk), or the French embassy in London (tel: 020-7073 1000, www.ambafrance-uk.org). Once in Europe, travelling between countries requires only a valid PETS certificate or pet passport.

BELOW: tourist office, Angers.

Public Holidays

It is common practice, if a public holiday falls on a Thursday or Tuesday, for offices to *faire le pont* (bridge the gap) and take the Friday or Monday as a holiday too. Major public holidays are:

1 January (New Year's Day)
Easter Monday (but not Good Friday); March/April
Whit Monday (Pentecost)
Labour Day (Monday closest to 1 May)
Ascension Day (May/June)
8 May (the end of World War I)
14 July (Bastille Day)
15 August (Assumption Day)
1 November (All Saints' Day)
11 November (Armistice Day)
25 December (Christmas Day, but not Boxing Day)

Postal Services

Provincial post offices – *postes* or PTTs (pronounced pay-tay-tay) – are generally open Monday–Friday 9am–noon and 2–5pm, Saturday 9am–noon (opening hours are posted outside); in Paris and other large cities they are generally open continuously from 8am–7pm. The main post office in Paris is open 24 hours every day, at 52 rue du Louvre, 75001 Paris.

Inside major post offices, individual counters may be marked for different requirements. If you just need stamps, go to the window marked *Timbres*. To send an urgent letter overseas, ask for it to be sent *priorité* or by *Chronopost*, which is faster, but expensive.

The easiest way to buy stamps *(timbres)*, however, is from tobacco shops *(bureaux de tabacs)* and sometimes from other shops selling postcards and greetings cards.

For a minimal fee you can arrange for mail to be held at any post office, addressed to *Poste Restante, Poste Centrale* (main post office), then the town's post code and name, e.g. 59000 Lille. A passport is required as proof of identity when collecting mail.

Religious Services

Some of the most impressive buildings in France are its cathedrals, churches and chapels, but because of their popularity as tourist attractions it can be easy to forget that they are places of worship. France is traditionally a Catholic country and main religious services are held on Sunday mornings; in small villages the services will be less frequent. Times of the Masses are usually posted at the church.

In Paris, Dinard and some other towns with long-standing English-speaking communities there are both Catholic and Protestant churches with services in English, and the Kehilat-Gesher synagogue (www.kehilatgesher.org) caters to a mixed Anglophone Jewish community in Paris. Details of local services in English are usually available from tourist offices.

Student Travellers

Students and young people under the age of 26 can benefit from cut-price travel to France and rail cards for getting around the country. If you wish to spend a prolonged stay in the region, it may be worth finding out about an exchange visit or study holiday. Several organisations provide information or arrange such visits. Volunteers are welcome at the camps organised on several of the archaeological sites in Burgundy (mainly in summer). Although unpaid, this is a good way to meet other young people of all nationalities and to learn French.

Once in France, students will find that a valid student ID card is useful in obtaining discounts on all sorts of activities, including admission to museums, cinemas, etc. If you do not have your ID card with you, reductions may be allowed by proving your age with a passport.

The **Centre d'Information et Documentation de Jeunesse** (CIDJ) 101 Quai Branly, 75740 Paris, Cedex 15, tel: 01 44 49 12 00, www.cidj.com, is a national organisation which provides information about youth and student activities.

Organisations in the US include:

- **American Council for International Studies Inc.**, 343 Congress Street, Suite 3100, Boston MA 02210, tel: 1-800-888 2247, www.acis.com.
- **Youth for Understanding International Exchange**, 6400 Goldsboro Road, Suite 100, Bethesda MD 20817, tel: 1-866-493 8872, www.yfu.org.

Telephones

The French telephone system is highly efficient, overseen by France Télécom, which also owns the Orange mobile phone company. Landline phone numbers all have ten figures, given in sets of two, e.g.: 01 23 45 67 89. The first two numbers are a regional code (01 is for Paris and area), but you must always dial the whole number, even in the same area. Note that numbers will be given in pairs of figures, unless you ask for them to be given *chiffre par chiffre* (singly). The only additional codes necessary are for dialling overseas. French mobile (cell) phone numbers also have ten figures, starting with either 06 or 07. Numbers that begin 08 are special-rate numbers: 0800 numbers are free, 0891 and 0892 can be quite expensive.

On France Télécom lines the cheapest times to call are weekdays 7pm–8am and at weekends after noon on Saturday. Mobile companies have their own charging structures.

For directory enquiry services, there is now a score of private operators, whose charges vary widely. They all have six-figure numbers starting with 118. For example France Télécom 118 712; Pages Jaunes 118 008.

Public Telephones

Nearly all public telephones in France operate with credit or debit cards or a phone card *(une télécarte)*. Charged with a certain amount of credit, they are simple to use and instructions are given in different languages on the phone. If you expect to use a public call box several times, they are worth getting, and can be bought from post offices, newsstands, railway stations and tobacco shops.

Mobile (Cell) Phones

Mobile (cell) phone coverage is good across nearly the whole of northern France, except perhaps in some remote parts of Brittany. French mobiles use the European-standard frequencies, so North American cell phones must have a tri- or quad-band facility (now pretty standard) to be usable here. Before using your mobile abroad you must notify your service provider so that they can enable the phone's roaming facility, and always check on current charges for using your phone in France. "Packages" of foreign calls can be a good way to cut costs.

Alternatively, cheap pay-as-you-go phones can be bought from any of the local providers such as Bouygues Télécom, Orange France or SFR, which have shops in most towns.

Telephoning Abroad

To make an international call, dial 00, then the country code, followed by the area code (omitting the initial 0 in the UK and some other numbers), and then the full number.

International dialling codes

France 33
UK 44
US 1
Canada 1
Ireland 353
Australia 61
New Zealand 64

Time Zone

GMT +1 (GMT +2 Apr–Oct). When it is noon in France, it is 6am in New York. Note that France generally uses the 24-hour clock.

Tourist Information

France provides an exceptional range of tourist information, through a variety of sources at different levels, which work together. To get an overview of the options in any region there is a *Comité Régional de Tourisme* (CRT), below which each *département* has a *Comité Départemental de Tourisme* (CDT), and each city, town and many smaller localities has its own *Office de Tourisme*. Many have accommodation booking and finding services, and all provide an invaluable range of free maps, guides to attractions in their area of all kinds, guides to local produce and farm producers and so on. CRTs and CDTs especially produce very useful guides to walking, cycling, riding and other routes, areas of natural beauty and local foods, and many offer well-planned hotel and tour packages and, in cities, interesting themed tours.

Listed below are the regional offices (CRTs) for the areas covered by this guide. Extensive information is also provided outside France by the Maisons de France or French Government Tourist Offices in various countries *(see below)*, and for in-depth planning in any specific area you can go directly to the tourism websites of the various *département* CDTs, which are all in English and other languages as well as French.

Alsace
tel: 03 89 24 73 50;
www.tourisme-alsace.com
Départements of the Bas-Rhin and Haut-Rhin.
Brittany (Bretagne)
tel: 02 99 36 15 15;
www.tourismebretagne.com
For Côtes d'Armor, Finistère, Ile-et-Vilaine and Morbihan.
Burgundy (Bourgogne)
tel: 03 80 28 02 80;
www.bourgogne-tourisme.com
For Côte-d'Or, Nièvre, Saône-et-Loire and Yonne.
Champagne-Ardennes
tel: 03 26 21 85 80;
www.tourisme-champagne-ardenne.com
For Ardennes, Aube, Marne and Haute-Marne.
Loire Valley
Centre-Val de Loire: Orléans, tel: 02 38 79 95 00;
www.visaloire.com
For Cher, Eure-et-Loir, Indre, Indre-et-Loire, Loir-et-Cher and Loiret.
Pays de la Loire: Nantes, tel: 02 40 48 24 20; www.enpaysdelaloire.com
For Loire-Atlantique, Maine-et-Loire, Mayenne, Sarthe and Vendée.
Lorraine
tel: 03 83 80 01 80;
www.crt-lorraine.fr
For Meurthe-et-Moselle, Moselle, Meuse and Vosges.
Nord/Pas-de-Calais
tel: 03 20 14 57 57;
www.tourisme-nordpasdecalais.fr
For the Nord and Pas-de-Calais.
Normandy
tel: 02 32 33 79 00;
www.normandy-tourism.org
For Calvados, Eure, Manche, Orne and Seine-Maritime.
Paris-Ile-de-France
tel: 01 73 00 77 00; www.pidf.com
For Seine-et-Marne, Yvelines, Hauts-de-Seine, Seine-St-Denis, Val-de-Marne and Val-d'Oise.
Paris
www.parisinfo.com
Picardie
tel: 03 22 22 33 66;
www.picardietourisme.com
For Somme, Aisne and Oise.

United Kingdom

Maison de la France/French Tourist Board
Lincoln House, 300 High Holborn, London WC1V 7JH; tel: 090 6824 4123; http://uk.franceguide.com

United States and Canada

Maisons de la France/French Tourist Board
New York: 25 Third Avenue, NY 10022, tel: 1-514-288 1904; http://us.franceguide.com
Los Angeles: 9454 Wilshire Boulevard, Beverly Hills, CA 90212, tel: 1-514-288 1904
Montreal: 1800 Avenue McGill Collège, Suite 1010, Montreal, Québec, H3A 3J6, tel: 1-866 313 7262; http://ca-en.franceguide.com

Selected Tour Operators

For specialist tours of World War I and World War II battlefields, *see page 88*, and canal and river trips, *see page 311*.

www.enfrancetours.com US based company organising tours of France in small groups.
www.frenchentree.com A guide to living and buying property in France, which also features a range of activities.
www.allezfrance.com Organises short breaks, self-catering and theme park holidays.
www.holidayfrance.org.uk Information on French holidays for every interest – art, golf, boat trips and various other activities.
www.arblasterandclarke.com Champagne weekends and other wine tours with excellent guides.

Tipping

Most restaurant bills include a service charge *(service compris)*, and this is generally indicated at the foot of the menu. If in doubt, ask: *Est-ce que le service est compris?* It is common to leave a small additional tip for the waiter if the service has been particularly good, since they actually get it, whereas service charges are administered by management.
It is customary to tip taxi drivers 10 percent, though this is not obligatory.

Visas and Passports

European Union citizens only need a national identity card to enter France, but those without them, such as UK and Irish citizens, must have full passports. Visitors from Australia, Canada, Japan, New Zealand, the United States and several other countries must have full passports but do not require visas for stays of no more than three months. Once they have entered France, they can enter any of the Schengen-area European Countries (most of the EU except Britain and Ireland) during the same three-month period with no extra formalities.

If you intend to stay in France for more than 90 days, then you should apply for a visa before you arrive; check with French consulates in your home country before travelling.

Weights and Measures

France uses the metric system for all weights and measures, although old-fashioned terms such as *livre* (about 1lb or 500g) are still used by some shopkeepers.

Language

Understanding the Language

French is the native language of more than 90 million people and the acquired language of 180 million. It is a Romance language descended from the Vulgar Latin spoken by the Roman conquerors of Gaul. People often tell stories about the impatience of the French towards foreigners not blessed with fluency in their language. In general, however, if you try your best to communicate in French, no matter how badly, people will be helpful. Moreover, many French people enjoy practising their English on visitors. Since so much English vocabulary is related to French, thanks to the Norman Conquest of 1066, travellers recognise many words, such as *hôtel*, *café* and *bagages*. You should be aware, however, of some misleading "false friends".

Words and Phrases

What is your name? *Comment vous appelez-vous?*
My name is... *Je m'appelle...*
Do you speak English? *Parlez-vous anglais?*
I am English/American *Je suis anglais(e)/américain(e)*
I don't understand *Je ne comprends pas*
Please speak more slowly *Parlez plus lentement, s'il vous plaît*
Can you help me? *Pouvez-vous m'aider?*
I'm looking for... *Je cherche*
Where is...? *Où est...?*
I'm sorry *Excusez-moi/Pardon*
I don't know *Je ne sais pas*
Have a good day! *Bonne journée!*
That's it *C'est ça*
Here it is *Voici*
There it is *Voilà*
Let's go *On y va. Allons-y*

Basic Rules

Even if you speak no French at all, it is worth trying to master a few simple phrases.

Pronunciation is the key; people really will not understand if you get it very wrong. Remember to **emphasise each syllable**, but not to pronounce the last consonant of a word as a rule (this includes the plural "s"), and always drop your "h"s.

Whether to use **"vous"** or **"tu"** is a vexed question; as society becomes less formal the familiar form of "tu" is used more and more. However, always use "vous" when speaking to adults you don't know; "tu" is acceptable when talking to children. It is better to use "vous" if in doubt. It is very important to be polite; always address people as **Madame** or **Monsieur**, and address them by their surnames until you are confident first names are acceptable. When entering a shop always say, *"Bonjour Monsieur/ Madame"*, and *"Merci, au revoir"*, when leaving.

See you tomorrow *A demain*
See you soon *A bientôt*
yes *oui*
no *non*
please *s'il vous plaît*
thank you *merci*
(very much) *(beaucoup)*
you're welcome *de rien*
excuse me *excusez-moi*
hello *bonjour*
OK *d'accord*
goodbye *au revoir*
good evening *bonsoir*
here *ici*
there *là*
today *aujourd'hui*
yesterday *hier*
tomorrow *demain*
now *maintenant*
later *plus tard*
this morning *ce matin*
this afternoon *cet après-midi*
this evening *ce soir*

Emergencies

Help! *Au secours!*
Stop! *Arrêtez!*
Can you help me? *Pouvez-vous m'aider?*
Call a doctor *Appelez un médecin*
Call an ambulance *Appelez une ambulance*
Call the police *Appelez la police*
Call the fire brigade *Appelez les pompiers*
Where is the nearest telephone? *Où est le téléphone le plus proche?*
Where is the nearest hospital? *Où est l'hôpital le plus proche?*
I am sick *Je suis malade*
I have lost my passport/purse *J'ai perdu mon passeport/porte-monnaie*

On Arrival

I want to get off at... *Je voudrais descendre à...*
What street is this? *A quelle rue sommes-nous?*
Which line do I take for...? *Quelle ligne dois-je prendre pour...?*
How far is...? *A quelle distance se trouve...?*
Validate your ticket *Compostez votre billet*
airport *l'aéroport*
train station *la gare*
bus station *la gare routière*
Métro stop *la station de Métro*

bus *l'autobus, le car*
bus stop *l'arrêt*
platform *le quai*
ticket *le billet*
return ticket *aller-retour*
hitchhiking *l'autostop*
toilets *les toilettes*
This is the hotel address *C'est l'adresse de l'hôtel*
I'd like a (single/double) room... *Je voudrais une chambre (pour une/deux personnes)...*
....with shower *avec douche*
....with a bath *avec salle de bain*
....with a view *avec vue*
Does that include breakfast? *Le petit déjeuner est-il compris?*
May I see the room? *Je peux voir la chambre?*
washbasin *le lavabo*
bed *le lit*
key *la clé*
lift/elevator *l'ascenseur*
air conditioned *climatisé*
swimming pool *la piscine*
to book *réserver*

On the Road

Where is the nearest garage? *Où est le garage le plus proche?*
Our car has broken down *Notre voiture est en panne*
I want to have my car repaired *Je veux faire réparer ma voiture*
the road to... *la route pour...*
left *gauche*
right *droite*
straight on *tout droit*
far *loin*
near *près d'ici*
opposite *en face*
beside *à côté de*
car park *parking*
over there *là-bas*
at the end *au bout*
on foot *à pied*
by car *en voiture*
town map *le plan*
regional or road map *la carte*
street *la rue*
square *la place*
give way *céder le passage*
dead end *impasse*
no parking *stationnement interdit*
motorway *l'autoroute*
toll *le péage*
speed limit *la limitation de vitesse*
petrol *l'essence*
unleaded *sans plomb*
diesel *le gasoil, gazole*
water/oil *l'eau/l'huile*
puncture *un pneu crevé*
wipers *les essuies-glace*
Sat-Nav GPS *(Ge- Pe-Es)*

Numbers

0	zéro
1	un, une
2	deux
3	trois
4	quatre
5	cinq
6	six
7	sept
8	huit
9	neuf
10	dix
11	onze
12	douze
13	treize
14	quatorze
15	quinze
16	seize
17	dix-sept
18	dix-huit
19	dix-neuf
20	vingt
21	vingt-et-un
30	trente
40	quarante
50	cinquante
60	soixante
70	soixante-dix
80	quatre-vingts
90	quatre-vingt-dix
100	cent
1,000	mille
1,000,000	un million

Shopping

Where is the nearest bank (post office)? *Où est la banque/Poste/ ptt la plus proche?*
I'd like to buy *Je voudrais acheter*
How much is it? *C'est combien?*
Do you take credit cards? *Est-ce que vous acceptez les cartes de crédit?*
I'm just looking *Je regarde seulement*
Have you got...? *Avez-vous...?*
I'll take it *Je le prends*
I'll take this one/that one *Je prends celui-ci/celui-là*
What size is it? *C'est de quelle taille?*
size (clothes) *la taille*
size (shoes) *la pointure*
cheap *bon marché*
expensive *cher*
enough *assez*
too much *trop*
each *la pièce (eg ananas, €2 la pièce)*
chemist/pharmacy *la pharmacie*
bakery *la boulangerie*
bookshop *la librairie*
library *la bibliothèque*
department store *le grand magasin*
butcher's *la charcuterie*
fishmonger's *la poissonerie*
delicatessen *le traiteur*
grocery *l'épicerie*
tobacconist *le tabac*
market *le marché*
supermarket *le supermarché*

Sightseeing

town *la ville*
old town *la vieille ville*
walled town *la ville close*
abbey *l'abbaye*
cathedral *la cathédrale*
church *l'église*
hospital *l'hôpital*
town hall *l'hôtel de ville/la mairie*
nave *la nef*
stained glass *le vitrail*
staircase *l'escalier*
tower *la tour (La Tour Eiffel)*
walk *le tour*
country house/castle *le château*
Gothic *gothique*
Roman *romain*
Romanesque *roman*
museum *le musée*
tourist information office *l'office de tourisme/le syndicat d'initiative*
free *gratuit*
open *ouvert*
closed *fermé*
every day *tous les jours*
all day *toute la journée*
all year *toute l'année*

Dining Out

Table d'hôte (the "host's table") is set menu that may be served in some *chambres d'hôtes* on request. **Prix fixe** or *Formule* indicates fixed-price menus in restaurants and brasseries. **Á la carte** means dishes from the menu are charged separately.
breakfast *le petit déjeuner*
lunch *le déjeuner*
dinner *le dîner*
meal *le repas*
first course *l'entrée/les hors d'oeuvre*
main course *le plat principal*
made to order *sur commande*
drink included *boisson comprise*
wine list *la carte des vins*
fork *la fourchette*
knife *le couteau*
spoon *la cuillère*
plate *l'assiette*
glass *le verre*
napkin *la serviette*
ashtray *le cendrier*
bill *l'addition*
I am a vegetarian *Je suis végétarien(ne)*
I am on a diet *Je suis au régime*
What do you recommend? *Que'est-ce que vous recommandez?*
Do you have local specialities? *Avez-vous des spécialités locales?*
I'd like to order *Je voudrais commander*

Non, Non, Garçon

Never use the word *garçon* (boy) for waiter, as this is highly insulting; say *Monsieur* or *Madame/Madamoiselle* to attract the waiter or waitress's attention.

That is not what I ordered *Ce n'est pas ce que j'ai commandé*
Is service included? *Est-ce que le service est compris?*
Enjoy your meal *Bon appétit!*

Breakfast and Snacks

baguette *long thin loaf*
pain *bread*
petits pains *rolls*
beurre *butter*
poivre *pepper*
sel *salt*
sucre *sugar*
confiture *jam*
oeufs *eggs*
...à la coque *boiled eggs*
...au bacon *bacon and eggs*
...sur le plat *fried eggs*
...brouillés *scrambled eggs*
tartine *bread with butter*
yaourt *yoghurt*
crêpe *pancake*
croque-monsieur *ham and cheese on toast*
croque-madame *...with a fried egg on top*
galette *buckwheat pancake*

First Course

An *amuse-bouche, amuse-gueule* or appetiser is something to "amuse the mouth", served before the first course.
anchoiade *sauce of olive oil, anchovies and garlic, served with raw vegetables*
assiette anglaise *cold meats*
potage *soup*
rillettes *rich terrine of shredded duck, rabbit or pork*
tapenade *spread of olives and anchovies*
pissaladière *Provençal pizza with onions, olives and anchovies*

La Viande – Meat

bleu *very rare*
saignant *rare*
à point *medium*
bien cuit *well done*
grillé *grilled*
agneau *lamb*
andouille/andouillette *tripe sausage*
bifteck *steak*
boeuf en daube *beef stew with red wine, onions and tomatoes*
boudin *sausage*
boudin noir *black pudding*
boudin blanc *white pudding (chicken or veal)*
blanquette *stew of veal, lamb or chicken with a creamy egg sauce*
boeuf à la mode *beef in red wine with carrots, mushroom and onions*
à la bordelaise *beef with red wine and shallots*
à la Bourguignonne *cooked in red wine, onions and mushrooms*
brochette *kebab*
canard *duck*
carbonnade *casserole of beef, beer and onions*
carré d'agneau *rack of lamb*
cassoulet *stew of beans, sausages, pork and duck, from southwest France*
cervelle *brains (food)*
chateaubriand *thick steak*
choucroute *Alsace dish of sauerkraut, bacon and sausages*
confit *duck or goose preserved in its own fat*
contre-filet *cut of sirloin steak*
coq au vin *chicken in red wine*
côte d'agneau *lamb chop*
dinde *turkey*
entrecôte *beef rib steak*
escargot *snail*
faisan *pheasant*
farci *stuffed*
faux-filet *sirloin*
feuilleté *puff pastry*
foie *liver*
foie gras *goose or duck liver pâté*
cuisses de grenouille *frog's legs*
grillade *grilled meat*
hachis *minced meat*
jambon *ham*
lapin *rabbit*
lardon *small pieces of bacon, often added to salads*
magret de canard *breast of duck*
moelle *beef bone marrow*
oie *goose*
pieds de cochon *pig's trotters*
pintade *guinea fowl*
porc *pork*
pot-au-feu *casserole of beef and vegetables*
Potjev'leesch *Flemish dish of a variety of pork meats, served cold*
poulet *chicken*
poussin *young chicken*
rognons *kidneys*
rôti *roast*
sanglier *wild boar*
saucisse *fresh sausage*
saucisson *salami*
veau *veal*

Poissons – Fish

Armoricaine *cooked with white wine, tomatoes, butter and cognac*
anchois *anchovies*
anguille *eel*
bar (or loup) *sea bass*
barbue *brill*
Bercy *sauce of fish stock, butter, white wine and shallots*
bouillabaisse *fish soup, served with grated cheese, garlic croutons and rouille, a spicy sauce*
cabillaud *cod*
calmars *squid*
coquillage *shellfish*
coquilles Saint-Jacques *scallops*
crevette *shrimp*
daurade *sea bream*
flétan *halibut*
fruits de mer *seafood*
hareng *herring*
homard *lobster*
huître *oyster*
langoustine *large prawn*
limande *lemon sole*
lotte *monkfish*
moules marinières *mussels in white wine sauce*
raie *skate*
saumon *salmon*
thon *tuna*
truite *trout*

Légumes – Vegetables

aïl *garlic*
artichaut *artichoke*
asperge *asparagus*
aubergine *aubergine/eggplant*
avocat *avocado*
céleri rémoulade *grated celeriac served with mayonnaise*
champignon *mushroom*
cèpes *ceps*
chanterelle *wild mushroom*
cornichon *gherkin*
courgette *courgette/zucchini*
chips *potato crisps*
chou *cabbage*
chou-fleur *cauliflower*
concombre *cucumber*
cru *raw*
crudités *raw vegetables*
épinard *spinach*
frites *chips/French fries*
gratin dauphinois *sliced potatoes baked with cream*
haricots *dried beans*
haricots verts *green beans*
lentilles *lentils*
maïs (doux) *(sweet) corn*
mange-tout *snow pea/mangetout*
noix *nut, walnut*
noisette *hazelnut*
oignon *onion*
persil *parsley*
pignon *pine nut*
poireau *leek*
(petit) pois *pea*
poivron *bell pepper*
pomme de terre *potato*
radis *radish*
ratatouille *Provençal vegetable stew of aubergines, courgettes, tomatoes, peppers and olive oil*

riz *rice*
salade Niçoise *egg, tuna, olive, onion and tomato salad*
salade verte *green salad*
truffe *truffle*

Fruits – Fruit

ananas *pineapple*
cerise *cherry*
citron *lemon*
citron vert *lime*
figue *fig*
fraise *strawberry*
framboise *raspberry*
mangue *mango*
pamplemousse *grapefruit*
pêche *peach*
poire *pear*
pomme *apple*
prune *plum*
pruneau *prune*
raisin *grape*

Sauces – Sauces

aioli *garlic mayonnaise*
béarnaise *sauce of egg, butter, wine and herbs*
à la crème normande *in a sauce of cream and cider*
forestière *with mushrooms and bacon*
lyonnaise *with onions*
meunière *fried fish with butter, lemon and parsley sauce*
meurette *red wine sauce*
Mornay *sauce of cream, egg and cheese*
Parmentier *served with potatoes*
paysan *rustic style, ingredients depend on the region*
pistou *Provençal sauce of basil, garlic and olive oil*
provençale *sauce of tomatoes, garlic and olive oil*

Puddings – Dessert

Belle Hélène *fruit with ice cream and chocolate sauce*
clafoutis *baked pudding of batter and cherries*
coulis *purée of fruit or vegetables*
gâteau *cake*
île flottante *meringues on custard*
crème anglaise *custard*
tarte tatin *upside-down tart of caramelised apples*
fromage *cheese*
chèvre *goat's cheese*

In the Café

drinks *les boissons*
coffee *café*
...with milk/cream *au lait/café crème*
...decaffeinated *déca/décaféiné*
...black/espresso *noir/express*
...American filtered coffee *filtre*
tea *thé*
...herbal infusion *tisane*
...camomile *verveine*
hot chocolate *chocolat chaud*
milk *lait*
... full cream *entier*
... semi-skimmed *demi-écrémé*
... skimmed *écrémé*
mineral water *eau minérale*
sparkling/still *gazeuse/non-gazeuse*
fresh lemon juice served with sugar *citron pressé*
freshly squeezed orange juice *orange pressée*
fresh or cold *frais, fraîche*
beer *bière*
...bottled *en bouteille*
...on tap *à la pression*
cider *cidre*
white wine with cassis (blackcurrant liqueur) *kir*
kir with champagne *kir royale*
with ice *avec des glaçons*
neat *sec*
red *rouge*
white *blanc*
rosé *rosé*
dry *brut*
sweet *doux*
sparkling wine *crémant/vin mousseux*
house wine *vin de maison*
local wine *vin de pays*
pitcher *carafe/pichet*
...of water/wine *d'eau/de vin*
cheers! *santé!*
hangover *gueule de bois*

Slang

McDo *McDonald's*
branché *trendy*
une copine/un copain *friend/mate*
un ami *friend, but* **petit(e) ami(e),** *boyfriend (girlfriend)*
un truc *thing, "whatsit"*
pas mal *not bad, good-looking*
La frangine *sister*
Le frangin *brother*
Le fiston *son*
Un pot/une pote *friend*
Un mec/un gar *bloke, guy*
Une gonzesse/une meuf *woman*
Un gamin/môme *kid*
Une bagnole *car*
Un bled *village*
Bosser *to work*
Le boulot *work*
Un bouquin *book*
Bourré *drunk*
Chouette *nice*
Un flic *policeman*
Le fric *money*
Piger *to get it*
Le Pinard *cheap wine*
Un plouc *hick*

Time

At what time? *A quelle heure?*
When? *Quand?*
What time is it? *Quelle heure est-il?*
• Note that the French generally use the 24-hour clock.

Days and Months

Days of the week, seasons and months are not capitalised in French.

Days of the Week

Monday *lundi*
Tuesday *mardi*
Wednesday *mercredi*
Thursday *jeudi*
Friday *vendredi*
Saturday *samedi*
Sunday *dimanche*

Seasons

spring *le printemps*
summer *l'été*
autumn *l'automne*
winter *l'hiver*

Months

January *janvier*
February *février*
March *mars*
April *avril*
May *mai*
June *juin*
July *juillet*
August *août*
September *septembre*
October *octobre*
November *novembre*
December *décembre*

Saying the Date

12 August 2011 *le douze août, deux mille onze*

On the Telephone

How do I make an outside call? *Comment appelle-t-on à l'extérieur?*
I want to make an international (local) call *Je voudrais une communication à l'étranger*
What is the dialling code? *Quel est l'indicatif?*
I'd like an alarm call for 8 tomorrow morning *Je voudrais être réveillé à huit heures demain matin*
Who's calling? *C'est qui à l'appareil?*
Hold on, please *Ne quittez pas s'il vous plaît*
The line is busy *La ligne est occupée*
I must have dialled the wrong number *J'ai dû faire un faux numéro*
Please speak more slowly *Parlez plus lentement, s'il vous plaît*

FURTHER READING

Arts and Architecture

Art and Architecture in Medieval France, by Whitney Stoddard. Harper & Row, 1972. Venerable book that remains an excellent introduction.

Art for Travelers: France, by Bill and Lorna Hannan. Arris Books, 2005. Helpful practical guide.

Châteaux of the Loire Valley, by Jean-Marie Perouse De Montclos. Konemann, 2007. Lavishly illustrated coffee-table book.

France: A History in Art, by Bradley Smith. Doubleday/Weidenfeld, 1984. The history of France through the eyes of artists.

The Gothic Enterprise: A Guide to Understanding the Medieval Cathedral, by Robert A. Scott. University of California, 2006. Fascinating analysis of the aims and techniques of medieval builders.

The Cathedral Builders, by Jean Gimpel. Pimlico 1993. A short, readable account of the creation of northern France's greatest buildings

Hip Hotels: France, by Herbert Ypma. Thames & Hudson, 2001.

Toulouse-Lautrec and the Fin-de-Siècle, by David Sweetman. Hodder & Stoughton, 2000. Deals not just with Toulouse-Lautrec himself but with all of decadent Paris in one of its most luminous eras.

Traditional Houses of Rural France, by Bill Laws. Collins and Brown 1991. An introduction to the country's vernacular architecture.

History

Athénais, the Real Queen of France: A Biography of Madame de Montespan, by Lisa Hilton. Little, Brown, 2002. Courtly shenanigans at Versailles.

Citizens, by Simon Schama. Penguin, 2004. Provocative, vivid one-volume account of France's great upheaval.

The Discovery of France, 2007, and ***Parisians: An Adventure History of Paris***, 2010, both by Graham Robb. Quirky, sometimes rambling but always surprising and engaging explorations of the lesser-known histories of France and its capital.

A Distant Mirror: The Calamitous 14th Century, by Barbara Wertheim Tuchman. Knopf, 1978. A classic journey through the France of the era of the Hundred Years War.

The Fall of Paris: The Siege and the Commune 1870–71, Penguin, 2007; ***The Price of Glory: Verdun 1916***, Penguin, 2007; ***To Lose a Battle: France 1940***, Penguin, 2007, and ***A Savage War of Peace: Algeria 1954–1962***, New York Review of Books, 2006, all by Alistair Horne. Classic, penetrating accounts of turning points in modern French history.

Fatal Avenue, by Richard Holmes. Pimlico, 2008. A thoughtful traveller's guide to all the often-overlapping battlefields of northern France, from the Middle Ages to 1945.

France Since 1945, and ***Children of the Revolution, France 1799–1914***, by Robert Gildea. Oxford Paperbacks, 2002 and 2009. Excellent contemporary histories.

The Golden Age of Burgundy: The Magnificent Dukes and their Courts, by Joseph Calmette. Weidenfeld & Nicholson, 2001. When Dijon eclipsed Paris.

Love and Louis XIV, and ***Marie-Antoinette***, both by Antonia Fraser. Phoenix, 2007. A guide to the Sun King's affairs, and one of Versailles' saddest tenants.

Madame de Pompadour, by Christine Pevitt Algrant. Grove Press, 2002.

Napoleon, by Vincent Cronin, Harper Collins, 2009. Blow-by-blow biography.

Normans: The History of a Dynasty, by David Crouch. Hambledon, 2006. William and his clan.

Paris: After the Liberation, by Antony Beevor and Artemis Cooper. Penguin, 1995. Excellent account of France in recovery.

Paris: The Secret History, by Andrew Hussey, 2006. Sometimes shocking and very readable history of Paris's underbelly.

A Race for Madmen: The Extra-ordinary History of the Tour de France, by Chris Sidwells. Collins, 2010. Richly coloured account of one of France's modern obsessions.

The General: Charles De Gaulle and the France He Saved, by Jonathan Fenby. Simon & Schuster, 2010. Considered judgement on the man who dominated postwar French politics.

Contemporary France and French Society

Sixty Million Frenchmen Can't be wrong: What makes the French so French by Jean Benoit Nadeau and Julie Barlow. Sourcebooks/Robson Books 2003. Highly readable overview of modern France by two Canadian journalists.

The End of the French Exception?: Decline and Revival of the 'French Model' edited by Professor Tony Chafer and Emmanuel Godin. Palgrave Macmillan, 2010. Thought-provoking study of how France is faring in an increasingly globalised world.

Travel Writing

Home and Dry in Normandy: A Memoir of Eternal Optimism in Rural France, by George East. Orion, 2005. Amiable and not overly stereotypical tales of expat life.

A Little Tour in France, by Henry James. New York: Farrar, Straus and Giroux, 1983. Originally published in 1885.

Megalithic Brittany: A Guide, by Aubrey Burl. Thames and Hudson, 1985. A good introduction to prehistoric monuments by a British archaeologist.

The Secret Life of France, by Lucy Wadham. Faber & Faber, 2009. Observant and much more informative than most expat-in-France books.

Literature

A Moveable Feast, by Ernest Hemingway. Scribner, 1964. The life of the artist in Paris.

The New Oxford Companion to Literature in French, by Peter France (ed.). Oxford University Press, 1995. Very comprehensive.

Oysters of Locmariaquer, by Eleanor Clark, 1964. Engaging account about oyster gathering in Brittany and the traditional life based around it.

Satori in Paris, by Jack Kerouac. Grove Press, 1966. Satori is Japanese for "sudden illumination". Ten days of travel as the author searches for Jean Louis Lebris de Kérouac in France.

French Literature

Alain-Fournier, *The Magnificent Meaulnes*, 1913. The only novel by a writer who died in the first days of World War I. Its action is set in the melancholy countryside of the Sologne region south of Orleans.
Barres, Maurice, *The Sacred Hill, 1913.* Celebration of Lorraine by a writer controversial for his political views.
Balzac, Honoré de, *The Chouans*, 1829, for the Revolutionary era, *Eugénie Grandet*, 1833, on provincial life, and any other of his prodigious output.
Chrétien de Troyes, Arthurian Romances (the modern title of his collected poems). A classic of medieval literature by a man about whom few biographical details are known.
Collette, *Claudine at School*, 1900. A tale about a young woman's awakening set in the writer's home region of Burgundy.
Darrieussecq, Marie, *Breathing Underwater*, 2002. One of the sharpest and most original of contemporary French writers, who has also produced several other short novels.
Flaubert, Gustave, *Madame Bovary*, 1857, *A Sentimental Education*, 1869 ; among the greatest of French novels, and also vivid images of Normandy and Paris.
Gracq, Julien, *A Balcony in the Forest*, 1958. A novel set in the Ardennes just before and during the German invasion of France of 1940.
Maupassant, Guy de, *Bel-Ami*, 1885, *Pierre and Jean*, 1888, and any of the short stories by an author very rooted in Normandy.
Proust, Marcel, *Remembrance of Things Past*, 1913–1927. Cabourg and the Côte Fleurie feature especially in the first two books, normally translated as *Swann's Way* and *Within a Budding Grove*.
Queneau, Raymond, *Zazie in the Métro*, 1959. Delightful ride through 1950s Paris.
Rabelais, *Gargantua and Pantagruel, 1532–64*. The spirit of the Loire.
Sand, George, *The Devil's Pool*, 1846 Perhaps the best known of her pastoral novels evoking her native Berry region.
Sartre, Jean-Paul, *Nausea*, 1938. The starting point for many modern French ideas.
Stendhal, *The Red and the Black*, 1830. A novel set in a fictional village in the Franche-Comté and the city of Besançon.
Vian, Boris, *Froth on the Daydream*, 1946. The best translation (others have different titles) of *L'Ecume des Jours*, a wonderfully surreal, amusing, romantic story of post-war Paris.
Hugo, Victor, *Nôtre-Dame de Paris*, 1831, and *Les Misérables*, 1862. Heavy going, but two central works of 19th-century France.
Zola, Emile, *Thérèse Raquin*, 1867, *Nana*, 1880, both on Paris, and *Germinal*, 1885, on the northern mining region, are just some of the powerful novels of the great chronicler of late 19th-century France.

Food and Wine

Culinaria France edited by André Dominé. Könemann, 1998. Large and detailed book looking at food and drink region by region.
French Country Cooking, by Elizabeth David. Penguin, 2001.
The French Kitchen: A Cookbook, by Joanne Harris and Fran Warde. Doubleday, 2002.
Raymond Blanc's Simple French Cookery, by Raymond Blanc. BBC Consumer Publishing, 2005.
Wine Atlas of France, by Hugh Johnson and Jancis Robinson. Mitchell Beazley, 2001. Well-illustrated atlas, concentrating on wine and vineyards, but also supplementary information on history, architecture and culture.

Send Us Your Thoughts

We do our best to ensure the information in our books is as accurate and up to date as possible. The books are updated on a regular basis using local contacts, who painstakingly add, amend and correct as required. However, some details (such as telephone numbers and opening times) are liable to change, and we are ultimately reliant on our readers to put us in the picture.

We welcome your feedback, especially your experience of using the book "on the road". Maybe we recommended a hotel that you liked (or another that you didn't), or you came across a great bar or new attraction we missed.

We will acknowledge all contributions, and we'll offer an Insight Guide to the best letters received.

Please write to us at:
Insight Guides
PO Box 7910
London SE1 1WE
Or email us at:
insight@apaguide.co.uk

Living in France

Buying a Home in France, by David Hampshire. Survival Books, 2006.
Buying a Property: France by Mark Igoe and John Howell. Cadogan Guides, 2008.
Living and Working in France, by David Hampshire. Survival Books, 2006.
Working and Living: France by Monica Larner. Cadogan Guides, 2007.

Natural History

Wild France by Bob Gibbons. New Holland 2009. A useful guide to the country's nature reserves and the species to look out for.
Where to Watch Birds in France by Phillippe Dubois. Helm 2006. A guide to the best birdwatching sites across a range of habitats.

Other Insight Guides

Insight Guide: France is the major book in the French series covering the whole country, with features on food and drink, culture and the arts. Other titles are *Southwest France* and *The French Riviera.*

Insight Step by Step

Insight's Step by Step guides provide a series of timed itineraries, with recommended stops for lunch. The itineraries are plotted on an accompanying pull-out map. Titles include *Paris* and *Nice & the French Riviera*.

Insight Smart Guides

Smart Guide: Paris puts the city at your fingertips. The best of Paris is listed by district, with detailed maps to provide orientation. The Paris A–Z lists over 400 amazing thigs to see and do, from architecture and bars to restaurants and shopping, and much more.

Insight Fleximaps

Insight Fleximaps have a tough, laminated rainproof finish and feature a list of the top 10 sites in a city or area, and an in-depth index. Fleximaps in the French series include *Paris* and *Nice, Cannes & Monaco.*

Art and Photo Credits

AKG London 50
Alamy 10BR
Art Archive 31, 34, 35, 39, 40, 42T, 43
AWL Images 148/149, 209T
carendt242 on flickr 335
Château de Noizay 334
Corbis 10BL/T, 51, 52R, 53, 81, 82, 120, 142T, 164, 229, 267
Kevin Cummins/APA 3, 5TR, 22R, 25, 64, 65L, 94/95, 102, 103B/M, 112, 114R/T, 115L/R, 117T, 118L, 121, 122L, 123, 124, 126, 128L, 129, 130, 131, 137, 138L/R, 306, 326T, 338, 349
Courtesy Disney 135, 142, 143
Dynamosquito on flickr 197
Fotolia 42, 60, 74, 136, 139,/T, 140/T, 143T, 160, 163, 215T, 216, 217, 218, 219/T, 220T, 224T, 227, 231, 233, 234T, 244T, 261/T, 266, 267T, 272, 277/T, 288, 289, 290/T, 293T, 296/T, 297, 298, 299/T
Fotolibra 164T, 166, 253L
Getty Images 83, 200/T
Grandes Etapes Françaises 321
Grand Hôtel des Bains 325
iStockphoto 6BL, 6ML, 7TR, 28T, 141, 144/T, 163T, 189, 224, 232T, 234, 239, 257M, 268T, 298T, 291, 292, 294, 295, 299L
Courtesy Le Bas Rupts 319
courtesy Les Crayeres Parc Restaurant 330
Christophe Marcheux 293
Courtesy Mercure Dieppe La Présidence 322
Ilpo Musto/APA 2, 4T, 5B, 6BR/T, 12/13, 76, 103T, 106, 107, 108, 109, 110, 111/T, 113/T, 114L, 116, 117, 118R, 119, 122R, 125, 127, 128R/T, 133L/T, 134, 168, 340, 342, 346
Courtesy Parc Asterix 169
Photolibrary 209ML
Pictures Colour Library 263
Sylvaine Poitau/APA 1, 4B, 5TL, 7BL/BR/ML/MR, 8B/T, 9BL/BR/T, 10M,11R, 14/15, 16/17, 18, 19B/M,T, 20, 21, 22L, 23, 24, 26/27, 38, 52L, 54/55, 56, 57, 58, 59L/R, 61, 62, 63, 65R, 66, 67, 68L/R, 69, 72, 73, 74T, 75, 77, 84, 88, 89, 90, 91/T, 92/93, 92B, 96/97, 98, 99T/B, 133R, 150, 151B/M/T, 152, 155/T, 156/T, 157, 158, 159BL/M/T, 161/T, 167/T, 170/171, 172, 173B/M/T, 174, 175L/R, 176, 177/T, 178L/R/T, 179/T, 180/T, 184, 185, 186T, 187, 188/T, 190/T, 191, 192, 193L/R, 194L/R, 197T, 198/T, 199/T, 201/T, 202L/R, 203L/R, 204, 205, 208/209, 210, 211B/M/T, 121, 213, 215, 220, 221, 222, 223/T, 228, 235T, 236, 237/T, 238/T, 243T, 244, 245/T, 246, 247/T, 248T, 250/T, 251/T, 254/255, 256, 257T, 258, 259, 262, 263T, 264, 265, 268, 269/T, 270, 271, 274/275, 276, 282, 283, 285, 286, 300, 301/T, 302/T, 303, 304, 307, 311, 312, 326, 327, 329, 332, 339, 341, 343, 344, 345,
Rex Features 29B, 85, 165, 181
Bartosch Salmanski 253BR
Scala Images 30, 32T, 33, 36, 37, 41, 44, 45, 78, 79, 80, 242
Small Luxury Hotels of the World 241
Still Pictures 11L, 225, 226, 232
Superstock 147, 235, 240, 252, 257B, 273/T, 287
Terra Botanica 248
Tips Images 195
Topfoto 29T
US Library of Congress 86, 87L/R

Photo Features

70/71: **Alamy** 70/71, 70BL, **APA/ Sylvaine Poitau** 70BM, 71M, **Istockphoto** 70BR, **Fotolia** 71BL/BR/TR

182/183: all images **Comité Interprofessionnel du Vin de Champagne (CIVC)** except 183TR **Getty Images** and 182BR **APA/ Sylvaine Poitau**

206/207: **Istockphoto** 206/207, 206BL, **Fotolia** 206BR, **Superstock** 207BL

280/281: **APA/Sylvaine Poitau** 280/281, 281M, **Fotolia** 280BM/BR, **Getty Images** 280L, 281BM/BR, **Werner Forman Archive** 281BL, **Corbis** 281TR

Map Production: Stephen Ramsay and APA Cartography department

© 2011 Apa Publications GmbH & Co. Verlag KG (Singapore branch)

Production: Tynan Dean, Linton Donaldson and Rebeka Ellam

INDEX

Main references are in bold type

D

E

N

M RER T
Paris
RATP
32 46 • wap.ratp.fr
www.ratp.fr
Propriété de la RATP - Agence Cartographique - PMI 07-2009- CC Design: bdcconseil - Reproduction interdite
A
Asnières–Gennevilliers
Les Courtilles
13
Les Agnettes
Gabriel Péri
Saint-Ouen
C
Mairie de Clichy
Porte de Clichy
Brochant
Garibaldi
Mairie de St-Ouen
Carrefour Pleyel
Porte de St-Ouen
Guy Môquet
La Fourche
de Clign
Lama Caulainco
Abbes
Blanche
Pig
Place de Clichy
Pont de Levallois Bécon
3
Anatole France
Louise Michel
Porte de Champerret
Pereire–Levallois
Pereire
Wagram
Malesherbes
Villiers
Rome
Liège
Trinité d'Estienne d'Orves
St-Geor
Notre-Dar de-Lore
T 2
1
La Défense
Grande Arche
Esplanade de La Défense
Pont de Neuilly
Les Sablons
Porte Maillot
Neuilly–Porte Maillot
Argentine
2
Porte Dauphine
6
Charles de Gaulle Étoile
Avenue Foch
Victor Hugo
Kléber
George V
Franklin D. Roosevelt
Monceau
Courcelles
Ternes
Europe
Gare St-Lazare
St-Lazare
14
St-Augustin
Miromesnil
St-Philippe du-Roule
E
Haussmann St-Lazare
Chaussée d'Antin La Fayette
Havre Caumartin
Opéra
RoissyBus
Auber
Quatre
Madeleine
Pyramides
Palais Royal Musée du Louvre
Louvre Rivoli
Boissière
Alma Marceau
Champs Élysées Clemenceau
Concorde
Tuileries
Musée d'Orsay
Pont N
Avenue Henri Martin
Rue de la Pompe
Iéna
Trocadéro
Pont de l'Alma
Invalides
Assemblée Nationale
Boulainvilliers
La Muette
Passy
La Tour Maubourg
Champ de Mars Tour Eiffel
Bir-Hakeim
Varenne
Solférino
Rue du Bac
St-Germain des-Prés
St-M
Ranelagh
Avenue du Pdt Kennedy
Dupleix
École Militaire
La Motte Picquet Grenelle
Saint François Xavier
Sèvres Babylone
Vaneau
Mabillon
St-Sulpice
Lu
Jasmin
Avenue Émile Zola
Duroc
Rennes
St-Placide
Notre des-C
Michel-Ange Auteuil
Porte d'Auteuil
Église d'Auteuil
Javel
Charles Michels
Cambronne
Ségur
Montparnasse Bienvenüe
Vavi
Mirabeau
Javel André Citroën
Commerce
Falguière
Sèvres Lecourbe
Pasteur
Gare Montparnasse
Edgar Quinet
Ra
Michel-Ange Molitor
Chardon Lagache
Félix Faure
Gaîté
Boulogne Jean Jaurès
Exelmans
Pont du Garigliano
Boucicaut
Volontaires
Bd Victor
T 3
Pernety
D
10
Marcel Sembat
Porte de St-Cloud
Lourmel
Vaugirard
Boulogne Pont de St-Cloud
8
Balard
Convention
Plaisance
T 2
Porte de Versailles
Pte de Vanves
Billancourt
Issy Val de Seine
9
Pont de Sèvres
Corentin Celton
Malakoff Plateau de Vanves
Porte d'Orléans
Issy
12
Mairie d'Issy
Malakoff Rue Étienne Dolet
Anton
C
Châtillon–Montrouge
13
B